The Modern Economy and Values

The Modern Economy and Values

By

Gia Zoidze and Shota Veshapidze

Cambridge
Scholars
Publishing

The Modern Economy and Values

By Gia Zoidze and Shota Veshapidze

This book first published 2022

Cambridge Scholars Publishing

Lady Stephenson Library, Newcastle upon Tyne, NE6 2PA, UK

British Library Cataloguing in Publication Data
A catalogue record for this book is available from the British Library

ISBN (10): 1-5275-8915-3
ISBN (13): 978-1-5275-8915-5

TABLE OF CONTENTS

INTRODUCTION

The post-bipolar world, a complex of political and economic alliances that no longer orientate toward either the US or the former Soviet Union, is characterized by aggravated social problems (ecological, demographic, economic, energy or trade crises), the growing negative social consequences that accompany scientific and technological progress.

Humanity is facing the challenges of human destiny, its presence, culture and values. The problems of man, culture, economy and values are now universally relevant.

The value system that society uses as a guide has become the norm in the behavior of a large portion of people. These values are not equally acceptable to all, some even violate them, but society has developed formal (laws) and informal (customs) institutions to uphold them.

Any normal state promotes the realization of interests that, under normal circumstances, are based on these values. Values do not form a frozen system. This system is constantly updated and progressive people play a big role in updating it.

In democratic governance, it depends on the principles and efforts of society and individuals, themselves, how they will have to live in the environment. A liberal, democratic society is based on values such as the rule of law, free political and personal choice, freedom of speech, freedom of religion, and equality of the sexes.

Along with the true values that are acceptable to society, which strengthen the foundations of socioeconomic progress, there are also falsehoods, negative values, or pseudo-values that lead to the opposite results. For example, liberalism is a value in itself, but its extreme forms, pseudo-liberalism or ultraliberalism, often have disastrous consequences, especially in the case of international (transnational corporate) politics.

In the conditions of modern globalization, the cognition of the values that define the culture of a society, its social, political, and economic thinking, acquires priority importance.

We call value a common sign of the abundance of social events that is especially important and desirable to people. In this general sociological (non-economic) view, value is an ideal phenomenon because people attach importance to desirable (or undesirable) social events—they consider them important and desirable (necessary).

Clearly, not every wish is worth it. Value is what is acceptable, that is, universally acceptable (at least, it must be acceptable based on its results). This or that thing is not a value because many or a few (even one) like it, but because, despite the approval/disapproval, it can bring positive results. However, values (value orientations) can become obsolete, turn from positive to negative, and push society backwards.

Value is something that has no independent existence (ideally) and is the determinant of every reality. It can be said that values are the ideal to which we must constantly strive; which society does not want, but what society should want; and which we can never achieve, because the pursuit of values means the constant pursuit of perfection. It also means that we should not be satisfied with the current environment, we should always want better, we should be driven by a better eternal urge, which we should constantly experience and should constantly feel, to which we should constantly strive.

Umberto Eco said: "I write not what people want, I write what I want people to want." People are human beings everywhere, they should be driven by the same values; that which is sin and evil for one should be sin and evil for another.

In our reality, there are events for which it is relatively easy to quantify and determine the "price." The concept of "value" refers to events for which quantification, pricing, is the most difficult problem, if at all possible. Take, for example, the modern values that are increasingly accepted (recognized) in Western civilizations: human rights, freedom, equality, justice, universal well-being, tolerance, patriotism, and so on.

Can these values be quantified? It is also impossible to quantify a democratic value such as, for example, "civil society," which is a concept of collective importance (value).

Let us now touch on economic values. Here, we face the same problem: their exact definition (measurement) is impossible. However, the economic goods or commodities exchanged reflect their value, thus, giving an accurate quantitative dimension to each individual moment and place.

However, this is constantly changing in time and space, making it impossible to measure. The public gets information about an item's value only through the price that expresses it, but it never matches—it always deviates from it.

The public value of a product is expressed in the quantity of other goods, and, if we use the terms accepted, the alternative value of the goods is the definite quantity of the goods that we can receive in exchange for the given goods (or those which we have refused). The monetary expression of value is a quantified quantity—a price which, as we have said, is always deviated from. The price may remain the same, but the value of the goods is constantly changing.

There is no sharp line between economic and non-economic values. Directly or indirectly, they are subject to choice. According to our traditional notion, you are worthy when you defend the truth; when you defend freedom; when you defend the right to speak; when you protect the dignity of others; when you defend the right to life; when you defend the homeland; when you defend the right to love; when you just defend; when you follow the customs of your ancestors; when you protect the future of your children; and many others. In a sense, it can be said that the classification of values should be based on what makes a person worthy.

It is recognized that man has studied many scientific disciplines, but none of them, or all together, can answer the question: "What is humanity?" These sciences will study man in different ways, but the latter is more than the sum of his qualitative characteristics. Therefore, the combination of this knowledge cannot reveal the secret of man.

This requires access to the essence of humanity. The anthropology of philosophy is the science that studies the essence of man, his special place in his world: "The philosophical doctrine of man, which has been widely developed in recent years, is considered as a philosophical discipline that answers the question: 'What is a man?'"

The peculiarity of this philosophical approach is that it seeks to relate closely, organically, to the problems of culture and values and, through them, to the real, social and ideological processes taking place at the global level. The expression of the inner connection of these problems is, first of all, that man should be perceived according to the culture he has created, because the latter reveals the values formed and implemented in him.

Values are the expression of the purpose and means of human cultural-creative activity, and culture—the transformation of man and the world by him, the cognition of certain values.

Value is in the field of cultural and economic activity in the human world. Creating yourself and a new "second nature" is the same as creating yourself and the world. That is when human values are created (something is considered the purpose of an action only if it is perceived as valuable, to satisfy this or that human need, or if it can make human life meaningful, valuable).

Subjectivism is excluded in understanding the relativity of values. Value is determined by human (subjects) needs and interests. However, these needs/interests (and the hierarchy of values associated with them) vary from person to person and group to group: one may not even agree with what the other values. Finding out who is right and who is wrong would take us far.

Another concept is where everything is valuable, there is nothing valuable. However, this relativity either means that only those goods that respond to the needs and interests of specific historical social groups of people are valuable or it means that there is no unconditional super-value—for goals that a person faces that, as a categorical need, are the measure of all other values.

It may also be important to note that human development is not far removed from its animal instincts. He may also be outraged that he still has an animal origin that is critical of some aspects of human culture. However, it is impossible not to see true, ideal values in the history and culture of humankind on our planet—high cultural achievements, inspired by natural matter. It is also noteworthy that humanity has fought and will fight for the realization of even the grains of these absolute, unconditional values.

Culture is the product of the realization of creative, transformative or self-transforming human activity and values (the means of human material/spiritual activity).

Connecting areas of culture and values is not entirely easy because they have not yet developed into an independent philosophical discipline, and the regularities of their existence in the field of philosophy are often the subject of debate.

It is the fault of the fragility of the above connection that the problems of value theory and philosophy of culture are insufficiently developed/studied.

However, the connection between these disciplines is so close that resolving them separately is doomed to failure.

Culture is the unity of all that realizes the values that people recognize (one group, class, nation…), and value is everything that people aspire to as a goal, or view as a means to an end. As for the understanding of values: the special specificity of mastering the world through thinking (such as it is in its objective existence, independent of our feelings, needs and interests) is that the object of judgment exists as something independent (this happens until we perceive it only theoretically).

This way of perceiving the world is characteristic of science—the discussion of the world as a law-related fact, object, and event in one time and space.

In a similar way, one cannot know only the external world, but also man himself, his connection with this world, because man is also one of the facts. However, since he is not just one grain in the chain of facts, but also the creator of the new—social and cultural—he is dealing not only with facts, but also with qualities completely different from them.

Man is not only objectively connected with external events, he is also a subject, transforming according to their goals and needs. This is a completely different way of grasping the universe. At this time, the world is perceived not as a neutral, objective reality, but, precisely, in relation to its subjective aspirations.

In this context, external events are already considered as necessary and unmet needs, or either valuable or unrecognized goals. It is already an evaluative, value cognition, and the latter is related to the subjective/creative approach to the world, to its practical transformation.

Value is always important to someone or something, and it is obvious that this is not a natural/real property of things. This can be seen from the fact that if the existence of a property depends on the existence of an object containing it, the existence of a value is not determined by the actual existence, or absence, of its train. For example, the idea of absolute justice as a value is not at all diminished by the fact that it has not yet been realized in the world.

Cost requires its full realization. This is a self-inflicted task, the solution to which is vital for us.

There is no nation or people in the history of the world, and there is not even a community, that has survived to the present day, created anything big or small, and has had its own genius, its own values. Without values, nothing important is done and nothing is created.

The identity of each nation is based on its values, achieved by it and reflected in it. Each person will be identified according to what dignity and what values he carries.

In addition, at the modern stage, humanity increasingly perceives itself as a single organism. Europe, America and Asia are getting closer and closer to each other, gradually forming a common culture, common business rules, standards of conduct and education. The peoples of these countries, in unity, preserve the traditions of their own culture and, at the same time, increasingly identify with some new civilizational unity established, and "rules of the game" developed that allow them to operate freely and confidently in almost any major city on the planet.

Such a unique situation, based on a defined ideological provision, will undoubtedly bring success to a country and ensure its security.

The book we present to the public is based on our published articles on the issues discussed. In addition, the monograph provides the results of a desk survey on the latest reality.

CHAPTER 1

ECONOMY, CULTURE, VALUES

1.1. Values and Economic Models

To establish what can and cannot be done in the economy, a general grasp of economic science teaching methods is required, as well as a focus on the topic of economics and functions, as well as reporting levels. The basic functions, levels of economic analysis, the relationship between economic laws and principles, the role of assumptions, positive and normative analysis, in the main role of economic activity, the main economic problems, the limitations of unlimited desires and their satisfaction are all discussed in the economic theory of the system.

Economic approaches are also crucial. The economic analysis will assist us in determining the value of government action in the economy. Although separating "efficiency" and "fairness" is an illusion, to attain the most significant participants in economic independence, it is necessary. To accomplish this, we'd need to have something like a "quota" that opposes government intervention in the economy, yet advocates for equality. We must support "quotas," or economic meddling, if we believe that equality cannot be accomplished without them (Veshapidze 2015).

Like the neoliberal argument, that "competition everywhere feasible, regulation anywhere required," the basic operational principle should be "quotas everywhere where they are essential, and avoided wherever possible."

The economy is called the activity of society, as well as the set of relationships that are formed in the system of production, distribution, exchange and consumption. These two concepts are similar and partly different. The basis of farming is the resources that people use to achieve their goals. In this process, people follow different rules, the combination of which is the economy. Man will turn the various resources he uses in the production process into wealth using different rules.

Without each other, these two terms do not exist. The difference between them is so insignificant that they can even be considered synonymous. Theoretical and applied economics is not a peculiar synthesis of all economic sciences, but of its directions, which are especially relevant for the study and regulation of current processes in economic life.

The word "economy" comes from the Greek language and means "a person who runs a household." Economics is about understanding how individuals make decisions and how people interact with each other. All these decisions and interactions, together, make up the "economy" (Mankiw 2014).

Modern economic theory studies the behavior of people as economic entities, at all levels of the economic system, in the process of producing material wealth and services, exchanging, distributing and consuming them, to meet human needs, under limited resources, by the family, the firm and society as a whole. There are five main functions of economic science that economic science performs in the life of human society (Kozyrev 2000).

1. Scientific-cognitive function. By studying economic science, a person will become acquainted with an important part of human society, the processes of production, distribution, exchange and consumption of material wealth and services, without which human society cannot exist.

2. Critical function. In real life, we are dealing with many different forms of farming, some of which are more efficient, while others are less efficient. Consequently, there are different views, and heterogeneous approaches and decisions on the same issue in science. Under these conditions, economic science must give us an objective critical or positive assessment of both economic life and the theoretical concept.

3. Practical (pragmatic) function. The practicality of economic science is manifested in the fact that every head of state, firm, any other economic entity, consciously or without their activity, is guided by its principles and laws. Of course, the practical aspects of economics should not be understood in a primitive way, given that science cannot teach us how to run a household, or horticulture or farming, it does not give us a recipe for how to extract oil and gas, or how to manage the firm and its staff. To achieve these goals, we need knowledge of other special sciences.

Economic science is the driver of successful economic development, at both the micro and macro levels, and no more.

4. Prognostic function. An in-depth study of all aspects of economic life enables individual, firm and society, as a whole, to anticipate events, to make scientific predictions of the future economic situation at both the micro and macro levels. Any completed economic activity of economic life often leads to unforeseen or unexpected, or preconceived, consequences. It is fair to say that knowledge leads to foresight, and foresight leads to positive activity.

5. Methodological function. In the literature, we can often meet fair assertions that economic theory is not only a theory but also a method, a kind of intellectual tool, a technique of thinking. Well-known American economist Paul Heine rightly remarks: "The economist knows the real world no better, in most cases worse than managers, mechanics, business people in general. However, economists know how different things are interrelated."

Economic science methodologically teaches us not only what we should do, but also what we cannot do. The latter is no less important than the former. A characteristic feature of economics, which discusses how to achieve "efficiency" and "equality," is that it addresses real-life issues that affect everyone and everyone individually. There are no exceptions here.

No one in the world can abstract the problems of running a household, or escape them, no society cannot solve the most difficult problems of the organization of economic life. The sounds of economic calls concern everyone.

Thus, economic science helps us to understand the surrounding agricultural life, to assess the benefits and harms of events; it teaches us new rules of cognition of economic events; and finally, it allows us to anticipate some of the consequences of our practical activities, while foresight leads to reasonable action.

It gives us the key to solving many socioeconomic and political problems, the key but not the recipe. Nowadays, there are three levels of economic analysis:

- Microeconomics,

- Macroeconomics,
- International Economy.

We can also imagine a division, according to which there are five levels of economic analysis:

1. **Microeconomics,**
2. **Mesoeconomics (National Economy),**
3. **Macroeconomics,**
4. **Mega Economy (World Economy),**
5. **Hypereconomics.**

I. Microeconomics—the basis of the analysis is a small economic unit, a separate firm, a union.

II. Mesoeconomics—studies the laws and behavior of the national economy or fields of the national economy, defined subsystems (agro-industrial complex, regional economy...).

III. Macroeconomics—studies the country's economy as a whole. Macroeconomic objects are society income and wealth, and economic growth rates and factors. Macroanalysis is aimed at solving the following economic problems: fighting inflation, unemployment, stimulating business activity, and more.

IV. Megaeconomics—will study the laws and behavior of the world economy as a whole.

V. Hypereconomics—also called the latest economic theory, will study the concepts of philosophy and natural sciences in economics (synergistic economics, physical economics...).

We note that practice, real economic life, plays an active role in the cognition process. Its role is threefold: first, it is the basic starting point of the cognitive process; second, economic reality is the goal of the cognitive process, since we study economic science not as an end in itself, but as a means of improving real life; third, economic practice is the criterion of truth and error of the economic life around us.

This is confirmed by the expression: theory is formed by practice, inspired by practice, and verified by practice. Despite its great importance, and the enormous role of practice, the mainstay of scientific cognition is the second stage, abstract scientific thinking, which involves the use of defined methods of cognition. Cognitive methods, in turn, are needed to understand economic categories, to discover economic laws.

The study of any science should begin with the study of its principles and methods. The basic economic principles used by theoretical and applied economics are the following: the principles of the interaction of theory and practice, the unity of micro and macro-analysis, and real historicism (the laws of economics operate differently in different historical contexts).

The principle of interaction between theory and practice is one of the main principles of economics. Theory is the result of rational thinking, the regularity of economic development, and the cognition of laws. It is a necessary condition for making the right decisions regarding the use of material resources, and the sale of goods and services in the domestic and foreign markets.

Knowledge of economic theory enhances education, develops economic thinking, and facilitates success. However, without a close connection with practice, theory loses its significance. It is practice that gives theory a social order for research, gives material for scientific analysis, and, finally, makes an unbroken and fair "judgment" for any theory.

J.M. Keynes, in order to overcome the worst crisis in the history of capitalism, developed the theory of deep intervention of the levers of state regulation in the market economy. It was necessary to replace the war-torn economy with something new. This is what prompted the development of the "social market economy" model (Keynes 2018).

In Georgia, too, the real reality has shown that the administrative-command system has exhausted itself. In this regard, there was a need to address the problems of transition from the administrative-command system to the market economy.

This task, the solution of which has not yet been completed, is the greatest stimulus for the development of theoretical thought. The second important principle of theoretical and applied economics is the unity of micro and macroanalysis.

A simple analogy can be used to prove the great importance of the application of this principle. When we look at the forest from a distance, we can see only its outline, size, but not individual trees, shrubs, land cover. All this can only be seen up close. In this case, you cannot look at the overall outline of the forest.

When studying economics, we see exactly this analogy. Only a consistent analysis of microeconomics and macroeconomics allows us to get a more or less complete impression of the economic life of a society. It seems clear that the practical function of the economy is to make recommendations for engaging in a market economy on the right, on favorable terms, to achieve high results in business.

Nobel laureate **Paul Samuelson** identifies three central problems common to all farms:

1. What should we produce and in what quantities?
2. How should the goods be produced, i.e., should it work, with what resources, and with what technology?
3. For whom are the manufactured goods intended?

Does microeconomics answer these questions? At first glance, it answers, because it is precisely microeconomics that develops recommendations in the field of practical activities of enterprises and firms (Samuelson 1954).

However, a deeper approach to the analysis of economic activity found that a comprehensive answer to the questions posed by Samuelson was impossible without macroeconomic information.

Determining what, and in what quantities, should be produced can only be done if the needs of the whole society are known, taking into account the established dynamics and perspectives of public production.

No less important are the data on the growth factors in society, their combinations, the social, sectoral and reproductive structure of the economy, the level of balancing of the national economy, the number of incomes and expenditures of the population, etc.

Finally, another principle—real historicism. Its essence lies in the fact that the laws of economics operate differently in different historical contexts. Market laws apply where the exchange of goods takes place. However, it is impossible to approach the same market relations that existed a thousand years ago with those that were formed in the modern market economy.

It is especially important to take into account the real economic situation that characterizes the countries that are moving from the administrative-command system to the market system. For example, we need to distinguish how economic systems operate in conditions of assembled competition and still insurmountable monopolies.

Modeling of economic processes has been widely used in economic analysis. Modeling itself is a method of studying real events and processes through the analysis of artificially created theoretical constructions. It gives us a simplified reflection of reality. The task of modeling is to investigate the impact of changing factors and economic conditions (assumptions), to anticipate the consequences of this change, and to theoretically substantiate observational (study) relationships. The theoretical structure is used in the form of object analysis—these are models that are, in themselves, simplified constructions of real events.

The schematic model of reality is based on simplifying reality, but does not distort it. The components used in building the model should be simple to use, but, at the same time, quite real. In other words, a model is a theoretical construct that is a simplified, empirically explicit description of a real relationship. For example, a geographic map is a relief model of a given area.

Modeling as an economic analysis involves clear formulation of the problem, simplicity and operability (the ability to present the relationship in a formalized form). When pointing out the strengths of the method, we need to pay attention to its limitations.

First, the construction of any model is based on the introduced assumptions and selected variables, which, already, in themselves, introduce an element of subjectivity.

Second, based on one of the assumptions, the model denies all the rest, which is a significant distortion of reality.

Third, since the analysis of the model is carried out in accordance with the principle of "other equal conditions," the hypotheses expressed in the form of a hypothesis are the result of observations of the influence of a particular factor, and, therefore, will have limited significance. All this makes it difficult to prove the hypotheses based on modeling without the use of assumptions in economic theory.

Economic theory, like any theory, does not have the ability to reflect all the richness of life and is, therefore, built on assumptions. These assumptions simplify the notions of real farm life. However, they also help us to better understand many of the theoretical provisions of economic life as a whole. So, economists usually assume that consumers are striving to maximize the satisfaction of needs within their revenues (so-called consumer budgets). In fact, such behavior is typical for most consumers.

One of the most common is the assumption of "other equal conditions" (Latin—Ceterius paribus). It implies that, when the variables under consideration change, the other variables remain unchanged. Thus, if the impact of price changes on the volume of goods sold is considered, then it is implied that the quality of the goods, the requirements of the buyers and the rest remain unchanged.

Assumption often allows us to better delineate, or characterize, the boundaries of an event. In the same way, assumptions are made in the economy in the short-term and long-term, which allow us to look at economic events differently and make decisions based on which period of time is considered. Thus, in the short term, the firm may suffer losses and not be reimbursed, as the reasons for its loss may be temporary, or short-term in nature. The existence of a loss in the long run will lead to the closure of the firm before bankruptcy...

Economic analysis can be carried out from the position of describing the economic reality and its characteristic regularities, but it can also be done from the position of making recommendations on the decision from the choice of options.

There are, therefore, two types of economic analysis: positive and normative. Positive analysis is aimed at determining the relationship between variables and aims to predict the outcome of a change in a particular variable. It is about finding answers to the questions: "What kind of attitude do we have in a given case?" and "What will be the result of changing one variable?"

If we are talking about the behavior of producers, then a positive analysis is limited to determining the relationship between the market price of a product and the choice of output volume, as well as predictive evidence of the firm's response (change in output volume) to price change.

Positive analysis related to the description of reality and the prediction of the outcome of any variable change has no evaluative reasoning about the outcome obtained. Positive analysis only shapes perceptions of economic behavior, it does not evaluate it.

Normative analysis is related to the development of targeted guidelines and evidence of an evaluative nature. Its essence is to determine the best alternative and it manifests itself in the answer to the questions: "How should it be?" or "What is better?" The assertion that progressive taxation of citizens' incomes is fairer than the use of the same tax rate, as well as the pirouette assertion, are clear examples of normative analysis.

What is evaluative in content, normative evidence reflects subjective thought, but it is based not on economic regularities but on the value norms that guide people in the process of normative analysis. For example, the content of the above normative reasoning will depend on how the notion of "justice" is interpreted. In addition, normative proof has the character of a rule (reference) and not of prophecy as positive.

Therefore, it cannot be confirmed or refuted by the facts of real reality. However, normative analysis is quite useful as an economic policy tool in which the task walks according to the criteria adopted before choosing the best way to achieve the goal.

There is a close connection between positive and normative analysis. Positive analysis reveals the patterns that help us determine the optimal choice of means to achieve the normative goals. Normative analysis, which is related to the development of recommendations, often becomes the reason for choosing a subject for positive analysis.

History teaches us that our very distant ancestors did not run any farms. To feed themselves, they engaged in collecting, hunting, and fishing. But such a rule of being did not provide the necessary number of means of subsistence. Primitive man was doomed to starvation and low life expectancy (forty years).

A solution to this impasse was found ten thousand years ago. If animals are satisfied with what they find in nature, humans, themselves, have learned to produce all the things they need and use. When they started farming, they created a high material and spiritual culture. One hundred centuries ago, people started farming to provide for themselves with the necessary vital wealth.

Why is a person engaged in agricultural activities? Why are people interested in the economy? Why does the economy determine the irreplaceable interest of people? Everyone expects him to solve the tasks on which his life and well-being depend because “economic interest” is a vital reason that pushes people to engage in agricultural activities and get the means for all-round development and because the main purpose of the economy is to increase human vitality and well-being.

The above goal is hindered by an economic problem, which is expressed as follows: desires and limitations of means (Figure 1).

Figure 1. The Main Problem of the Economy

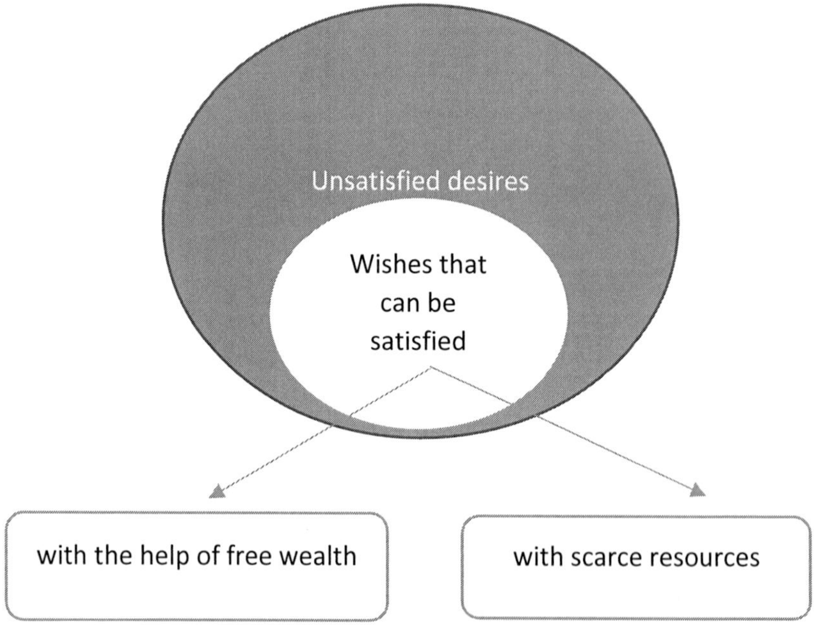

Source: Harvey, J., and E. Jowsey. 2007. *Modern Economics: An Introduction.* London: Macmillan International Higher Education.

This is the economic problem of unlimited or indefinite desires and limited or definite means. We can never overcome this difficulty, but we can try to get as much as possible out of what we own, what we have at our disposal, and what is at our disposal. That's it, we always have savings or frugality. Housewives, pupils, students, entrepreneurs, and government face the problem of economy (savings).

1.2. Values: Boundaries and Obstacles

Values are diverse and innumerable, and their distribution/restriction mechanisms are diverse. In this case, we mean the mechanisms of government, but the subjects of values are not only the authorities, but also individual people, units of people and whole people. They are the main actors in the creation and implementation of such values as love, trust, friendship, support, devotion, etc.

We will not touch on the classification of values, we will only mention that it is complicated by various factors, especially the fact that it is essentially impossible to define the scope of values, because they even overlap, which is easily noticeable in the example of values populated above. We will only touch on the social values—the boundaries of the subject of our conversation—to distinguish them from economic values. By doing so, we are essentially defining their essence (Gvelesiani and Veshapidze 2016).

The values we are talking about are the social orientations of people and societies. The term "social" is used, here, in its narrow sense to oppose economic values, and in its broadest sense it encompasses everything that belongs to public life. Take a life example, some prefer opera to attending a concert of pop singers, and some vice versa; among foods, some prefer vegetables and some meat, and so on. These landmarks are not valuable.

Value in the social sense is a common sign of the abundance of social events that is particularly important and desirable to individuals and societies. It is also possible to find such signs in our example.

The general sign (value) is prosperity, to which the whole society and each of its members aspire. However, how do some people imagine it? Let us turn to our example again: there are people who are slaves to the stomach, while a fan of this or that singer will go hungry to listen to him. Here, we are dealing with extreme value orientations.

The law is that, in the wake of the growth of prosperity, people spend more and more of their income on services, including those who spend more and more on spiritual needs. But these parts have different customers, i.e., their individual value orientations are different.

The society, through its institutions, has a duty to study the consumption structure of households and to adjust this orientation for itself and in favor of each member. The means of achieving this goal are the investment-sectoral and tax policies by which the society, in the form of state and self-governing bodies, influences the supply; a pricing policy that targets both supply and demand, and so on.

The social sign is associated not only with the choice between material and spiritual goods. It also seems to be a choice between those great blocks of spiritual goodness, some of which cause more benefit to society, some less, and some of which degrade spirituality, that is, not goodness but evil; it is not a value, but its antipode, which, in scientific language, can be entered as a negative value.

If the government is concerned with the spiritual development of the people, in particular with the development of high taste and high value orientation in them, it should stimulate the supply and consumption of spiritual products (literature and art) that meet these requirements by winning the aforementioned or other tools. To do this, we need to look for relevant experience both in the present and in the past (including the Soviet experience with the note that pieces in the field of literature and art, at that time, were considered high-value products that served the communist ideology).

Good and evil, which we have mentioned here, are general concepts that fit into the whole system of values and extend to each of them, so discussing values in terms of these two concepts tells us a lot about their identity and peculiarities. Values in themselves must represent goodness, and true values represent them.

However, goodness is always seen in opposition to evil, and orienting oneself by the value of the behavior of individuals or their unity against goodness does, indeed, bring harm or evil to society.

Here is a guide for us: **Ilia Chavchavadze's** surprisingly deep and simple words, "Good and evil, sin and grace alone are the work of human understanding .... and since man is human everywhere, therefore, which in one case and for one is sin and evil, it must be sin and evil for another man everywhere, always and in all cases. We see and are convinced by examples day by day that this is not the case. Why? ... e.g. 'Why' until now man has not found a convincing answer." (Chavchavadze 1955).

We do not have a "confident answer" to the "why," today, and maybe we will never have one. But, based on the quote, we can talk about many things: ideal and real, objective (true) and subjective values, society and individual values, the relativity of the measurement of values, the contradictions and struggles of values, and so on.

We do not have the answer, primarily because social values are precisely the manifestation of the voice of the human heart, and that, in absolute form, they can only be imagined in the world of Platonic ideas, where the highest value is goodness. The word "kindness" is said about many things in Georgian and other languages—it is also said about a person, useful human behavior, etc. And it speaks to every true value that should be the guiding principle of human behavior.

In this sense, value is not even what people like and want, but what they should want and what they should strive for as perfection in personal and public life. But life has its contradictions, at any stage of society's development, and people are only able to fully or incompletely realize the values that are useful to society at this stage.

Values are useful for the whole society; values can move all of humanity forward. They carry a universal character, regardless of whether they deserve universal approval or not and regardless of how many people will be liked and recognized (whether it will be many or few people, it does not mean anything here).

Replacing values may seem immature, premature. In this case, the victory of conservative thought is useful. Ilias's assessment of such situations is correct: "True conservatism sues and protects only the old, which, in his sincere opinion, is still useful and necessary for life." The word "sincere" is also included in the sentence, because a sincere opinion is not always correct.

Thus, every human being has his own measure of every value, starting with good and evil, and this individual measurement is also constantly changing. Measurement and its variability also depend on many things, first of all, on the nature and mood of a person, his physiological and social condition and the variability of this condition.

Now, let us ask, will conflicts be considered abusive between family members, employees of the organization, friends, or between others and others? The correct answer is—there comes a case.

Science has found that a conflict-free society loses its drive for development, while philosophy has found, even earlier, that development is governed by the law of unity and struggle. In value conflicts, several major blocks can be distinguished:

- ❖ **First**: Contradictions in the "self" of a group of separate or homogeneous, overlapping values (such as love and friendship and the like). Democracy, for example, means the power of the majority (people) and leaves minorities and units vulnerable, no matter how important their needs and opinions are. That is why democracy is being replenished with minority protection mechanisms that are associated with democracy as part of our imagination. In fact, it is a foreign element added to it from the outside. Also, the market economy has many shortcomings, due to which it is filled, more or less successfully, with components such as social policy, antitrust and anticyclical regulation of the economy, etc. The complementary mechanisms of both are introduced by the state based on its governing experience and the research and conclusions of scholars, which are also based on value orientations, but this does not mean that the state instills objective (even more—flawless) values in society.
- ❖ **Second**: Contradictions between separate values. Take high macroeconomic values such as full employment and stability: when we approach full employment, prices accelerate growth and the likelihood of an economic crisis increases. There are no less sharp contradictions between the orientations of individual values when we make choices. Suppose we make sacrifices for the welfare of our fellow man if we choose our own needs. When Demetrius II, the

Self-Sacrificer or the Devoted (Georgian: დემეტრე II თავდადებული), sacrificed his life for the safety (and therefore wellbeing) of his people, it showed how he compared these two values and to which side he pushed the scales. Many other kings would have behaved differently. The diversity of such decisions reflects both the differences in individual assessments of values and their contradictions.

- **Third**: Contradictions between individual and societal values. These contradictions are, for the most part, a special kind of inter-value contradiction. Extend the processes already mentioned above: labor-skilled people aspire to find favorable employment. With full-time employment, their choices increase, resulting in higher wages, prices, and the likelihood of a crisis. As for the case of individual values, a clear example of this is the public values reflected in state law and their violation by people.
- **Fourth**: Contradictions at the crossroads of time (epochs) or between traditional and new values. What we call values are formed, at least initially, by the agreement of people, by reconciling their thoughts and spreading these values to other people (or by sharing these thoughts), but their primary source is the attitude of individual people towards a particular social event. The new attitude paves the way by fighting the old attitude, and if it is immature or totally unacceptable it sooner or later fails, and the mature—also sooner or later—narrows down, or even replaces, the old. It is not easy to harass and change an attitude rooted in public opinion.
- And, finally, the **fifth**, especially important for us, are the contradictions between the values of space and the great territorial units of people—peoples (nations). This class of contradictions inherently repeats the previous four (and that was the purpose of reviewing those four), but is still a separate class because we are dealing with a higher level of contradictions. At this level, either one person (or perhaps his government) seeks to share the values of other peoples and confronts the conservative sentiments of his countrymen—perhaps also his own government—or these other peoples seek to spread their own

> values over him. In this case, he may encounter obstacles due to the immaturity or, in general, the absence of pre-objective and subjective conditions. Expansion has historically taken place in order to subdue the conqueror by the conqueror, because when the conqueror is deprived of his faith and language, he becomes more manageable.

In modern civilization, the extension of one's own national values to others can be done for good purposes—when one person sincerely considers their values to be true (or more advanced). But, it can also happen with the natural urge of people and entire nations to establish their own values in different nations. In both cases, great care is needed because the spatial distribution of values may encounter a totally different national soil on which a foreign seedling cannot rejoice and, for a good, long time, cannot give us the desired fruit.

The problem is complex and requires a lot of thinking. Bitter experience also dictates caution: the most valuable product of a society's economic development is a competitive market mechanism, not private property. The institution of private property needs a reasonable establishment in order to create a precondition for the development of a market mechanism.

Our reasoning, above, has mainly concerned the criteria by which the essence of values, their boundaries, and the classification of contradictions significant to them are established. They have led us to the contradictions that accompany the spread of values between different peoples; how to overcome obstacles on the way to sharing and implementing progressive values is the subject of a separate discussion.

1.3. Modern Economic Achievements and Peculiarities

The famous English professor **Jack Harvey**, in his general course on "Modern Economic Theory," states the following: The science of economics deals with the problem of choice. Due to the lack of resources at our disposal, we cannot meet all our desires and needs at once, and, therefore, we are forced to choose (Figure 1).

If we choose something, then we have to give up something. If a newspaper carrier spends his Christmas tips on a bicycle, then he will probably not have enough a pneumatic gun, but he should have one too. A worker who agrees to do overtime work after dinner on Saturday, in his spare time, refuses the opportunity to watch a football match (Harvey and Jowsey 2007).

When a farmer sows wheat all over the field, he refuses to plant rye there. Countries have to solve the same problems as a whole. If additional materials and capital are needed for the construction of houses, roads and hospitals, then less resources will be left for the construction of new offices, power plants, sports centers and so on.

Accepting something in any field means giving up something else. So, we're talking about an alternative cost (opportunity cost), that is, the value of something else that we have to give up (more precisely, another better option).

In practice, an economic problem means not so much a complete rejection of one commodity in favor of another, but a decision to choose a slightly larger quantity of one commodity and a lesser quantity of another commodity. Only a small amount of wealth is so large that no one will pay for it. One such wealth is air (Veshapidze 2015).

Another example, in some years, the grape or apple crop is so large that gardeners offer everyone: "Take as much as you can." Such wealth is called free. But most wealth belongs to the rare wealth, that is, it can be obtained only by giving up something.

If we want to master it, we will have to save it, so it is also called economic wealth. However, once and for all, there is no boundary between economic and non-economic wealth. Rarity mostly depends on demand.

Thus, wealth is called economic if its possession is the result of a subject's refusal to acquire other wealth. For example, ambient air is not an economic asset, and air in a building equipped with air conditioning and air purifiers is an economic asset—we have to pay for it.

The same can be said for comparing flow water in a pipeline with water. As long as the pipeline water is not worse in quality than the flow, it is an economic asset.

Its delivery at the required time and place is the result of the cost of laying the pipeline, building water pumping stations, water treatment facilities, sewerage systems.

The following methods of economics are distinguished:

- **Comparative analysis method**
- **Method of scientific abstraction**
- **Graphic representation method**
- **Economic-mathematical modeling method**

The method of **comparative analysis** means comparing private and general economic indicators, combining them to get the best results. Any entrepreneur is obliged to compare the costs of his firm with the costs of a competitor, to consider different alternatives to his activity. What is more favorable for the formation of a centralized investment fund is the establishment of a high rate of profit taxation of the enterprise or its reduction, thereby expanding the scope of investment activity, the well-known approach "costs—results" is mainly based on comparative analysis.

The method of scientific abstraction involves the separation of less important events in the process of cognition of economic events and the separation of the main group of the subject or event. For example, when explaining the law of demand, only the relationship between demand and price is analyzed, and the rest of the conditions (state pricing policy, market filling level, internal and external competition, development of market infrastructure, etc.) are not taken into account. Once the main factor has been identified, the abstraction is filled with a relevant perspective study of temporarily unforeseen factors.

The method of graphic representation is widely used in economics. It helps us to understand the ratio of different economic indicators, to assess their "behavior" as a result of changes in the economic situation. For example, we can take the Laffer curve, which expresses the relationship between budget revenues and taxes. Graphic representation is very convenient for microanalysis. It has one feature: economists often change the location of variables and place the dependent variable on the abscissa axis, while the independent variable is placed on the ordinate axis, such as the Laffer curve. Thus, the graphical representation method helps us to clearly imagine the development of economic situations, in many cases allowing us to express, with final accuracy, the relationship between economic parameters.

A powerful, modern method of studying and solving economic problems is **the method of mathematical modeling**, that is, the description of an economic event in a formalized language with the help of mathematical symbols and algorithms. First, such a compact view enhances the visibility of complex economic problems, expands the field of cognition, and often gives us a new view of the objective regularity of economics. Second, the mathematical model is understood by the electronic computing machine (ECM), which collects innumerable data based on the laws of formal logic, giving economists unparalleled analytical capabilities using statistics and mathematical methods. In addition, by compiling solutions and comparing them with practical results, the computer can detect patterns in errors in mathematical rules and make corrections to the recommendations provided.

But, the reliability of the obtained results depends, first of all, on the adequacy of the mathematical model for the real economic processes. Although each conditional notation of the economic-mathematical model is used for the simplicity of describing and calculating events, it should reflect the most important factors and laws of the development of economic processes for the researcher.

If we achieve this, then, the resulting model will be homomorphic, that is, one that gives a picture as close as possible to the reality of the described events and processes. The homomorphism of the model (in Greek, homos—equal, homogeneous—and morphe—face, origin) is achieved by the method of systematic analysis of the economic object, which determines the boundaries of its integrity, essential (most influential) characteristics and the ranges of their change.

The modern economist cannot bypass systemic analysis in mathematical modeling when an object or event is considered separate from the outside circle. There is a total unity of the elements. Removing an element from the system, according to the researcher, changes its important properties in such a way that it loses its originality and turns into another system.

The integrity of the system is ensured for the purpose of its development and solid interactions (connections) between the elements. Thus, the subjective view of the researcher separates the system from the environment, by separating the elements in it, without which it cannot exist, and establishes the connections between them: that is, the real object is purified from all non-essentials.

If an economic factor is chosen as an element, then a change in its magnitude should affect the change in the overall characteristics of the system; that is taken as an argument. The range of changes of elements and argument parameters is bounded by the sphere of existence (environment).

Connections are expressed in the form of functional relationships; their mathematical representation gives us a set (system) of equations, which is a mathematical model of its own economic connections.

Based on the teachings of English scholar John Stuart Mill, a great political economist, R. Edward Freeman, a professor at the University of Cambridge, and others, Ilia Chavchavadze arranged the methods of economic research as follows:

- "Comparative method"
- Easy transfer of opinion and "documentation"
- Quoting what the authorities say
- Step-by-step research
- Study of the "internal well-being" of the case
- Systematic research method
- Approach to statistical materials
- Rely on the truth and not on the majority or the minority
- The importance of abstract thinking
- Applied purpose of economic research (Veshapidze, Mchedlishvili 2020)

Today, scholars consider methodological pluralism to be the most acceptable. It is, therefore, not possible to give preference to any one-handed method. We must use all the methods that will facilitate the analysis of the extracted materials.

The method of comparative analysis, the method of scientific abstraction, the method of graphic representation, the method of economic-mathematical modeling and others deserve special mention. As they say, you have to saturate your memory with dates and facts and then you will be able to re-evaluate your previous history or, more precisely, re-evaluate it.

In his glorious book, *History of the Georgian State and Law*, the famous Georgian professor **Giorgi Nadareishvili** noted, "If we obscure the material of historical-legal nature with the fog of theory, we will not get the desired result. As J.W. Goethe would say, the theory is colorless here, but the golden tree of life is evergreen. The theory should not contradict the facts." (Nadareishvili 2005)

Of particular importance to the subject of economics is the systematic approach to world economic events and processes. Academician Iveri Prangishvili's article, "Systemic Approach, Systemic Thinking and Management Issues," is dedicated to understanding this method in modern language and approaches. A systematic, holistic approach to different problems allows us to study the problem in a complex and comprehensive way, to prioritize and to optimize the basic parameters of the system. For example, the national security system of the country is evolving at the intersection of such sciences as political science, military science, sociology, informatics, ecology, economics.

Today, in an age of ongoing systemic crises in public life, the importance of a systemic approach is growing, as these crises can only be countered by systemic methods of combating them.

A systemic approach to the national interests of the country is a key condition for the revival of the country and its economic and military security. The application of this approach is of particular importance in the study of global problems. These problems (environmental, social, economic, military, techno-genetic, security) and their systematic understanding are of universal importance. They are so complex that trying to solve them will not give us a positive result if we do not simultaneously affect many parameters of this system.

If we are exploring a new object and do not have existing models for it, then systemic thinking, holistic approach, intuition, and hidden knowledge help us to develop new, more effective models. Science does not have the measure to measure the level of systemic thinking, but it can be argued that systemic thinking has already reached the stage of development where a person, using his cognitive models, is able to understand the essence of complex technical, socioeconomic, mental or other problems.

In order to focus properly on when to intervene in the economy and when not to intervene, we need to rely on the core values of society. Any law intervening in this is a new mechanism of restriction of liberty, we know it.

But, in the meantime, we know very well that if we do not restrict something by law, then our long-awaited freedom can never be achieved... It is this interference in life that we must consider as the true direction.

CHAPTER 2

VALUE DETERMINISM OF ECONOMICS

2.1. The Phenomenon of Value

The phenomenon of value is not even what people want, but it is what people undoubtedly want. Values are the eternal guide of our lives and the source of its perfection.

Any society is based on a certain value system, on which a large part of it agrees, it is a part of the state society and, for it, these values are the starting point. It more or less comprehends them, completes them and, thus, raises them to the level of common national consciousness, but it also has its own value orientations that correspond and complement, differ and, in many cases, even oppose the orientations to the value of society.

Consensus is greater in a liberal, democratic society. Its value system has grown from the core of traditional and modern values and is, today, filled with post-modern content.

The value system that society uses as a guide has become the norm in the behavior of a large proportion of people. These values are not equally acceptable to everyone. Some even violate them, but society has developed formal (laws) and informal (customs) institutions to protect them (Veshapidze 2018).

Any normal state promotes the realization of interests that, under normal circumstances, are based on these values. Values do not form a frozen system. This system is constantly updated and progressive people play a big role in updating it.

Democratic governance itself depends on the principles and efforts of society and individuals, how they will have to live in the environment. A liberal, democratic society is based on values such as the rule of law, free political and personal choice, freedom of speech, freedom of religion (belief), and gender equality.

In addition to the true values that are acceptable to society, which strengthen the foundations of socioeconomic progress, there are also falsehoods, negative values, or pseudo-values that have the opposite effect. For example, liberalism is a value in itself, but its extreme forms, pseudo-liberalism or ultraliberalism, often have disastrous consequences, especially in the case of international (transnational corporate) politics.

Knowledge of the values that define a society's culture, its social, political, and economic thinking, is of paramount importance. To do this, we must first define the concept itself.

We call value the common sign of the abundance of social events that is especially important and desirable to people. In this general sociological (non-economic) view, value is an ideal phenomenon because people attach importance to social events that are desirable (or undesirable) to them—they consider them important and desirable (necessary).

Without value orientation, every human behavior and every reasoning would lose its meaning, however, the values themselves are rarely named. There are many sources and means to find and read about values.

Values can be found in historical chronicles, philosophical treatises, hymns, poems and even personal letters, in ancient or modern laws or concepts, in the press, in encyclopedias, in books, on the Internet and so on.

The highest values—love, friendship, virtue, etc.—are in the person himself and are manifested in relationships with other people. Therefore, it is possible to find them in these relationships, even in ordinary conversations. People often talk about the lives of prominent or ordinary people precisely because of this, and it is important to use examples to illustrate our different values (society, nation, individuals).

Today, scholars consider methodological pluralism to be the most acceptable. Therefore, it is not possible to give preference to any method by hand. We must use all the methods that will facilitate the analysis of the extracted materials.

A systematic approach to world economic events and processes is of particular importance for the study of large systems, including society as a whole, economics, macroeconomics, and the world economy.

A systematic, holistic approach to different problems is based on understanding the nature, role, importance and interdependence of factors in their unity, or complex. This gives us the opportunity to study the problem in a complex and comprehensive way, to set priorities and to optimize the basic parameters of the system.

Today, in an age of ongoing systemic crises in public life, the importance of a systemic approach is growing, as these crises can only be countered by systemic methods of combating them. This approach is an opportunity to identify the nature of systemic contradictions, identify the complexity of interrelationships, and develop a problem-solving strategy.

A systemic approach to the national interests of the country is the main condition for the revival of the country, ensuring its economic and military security. The application of this approach is of particular importance in the study of global problems. These problems (environmental, social, economic, military, technogenetic, security) and their systematic understanding are of universal importance. They are so complex that trying to solve them will not give us a positive result if we do not simultaneously affect many parameters of this system.

The goal of systemic thinking is to perceive the environment correctly and as a whole (systematically): to understand the information obtained by observation as a whole, to get acquainted with the laws and regularities of the material and intangible world, and to learn to apply these laws and regularities in human activities (primarily, the creation and management of complex systems).

If we are exploring a new object and do not have existing models for it, then systemic thinking, a holistic approach, intuition, and hidden knowledge help us to develop new, more effective models (Shengelia 2016).

Science does not have the means to measure the level of systemic thinking, but it can be argued that systemic thinking has already reached the stage of development where a person uses the cognitive models at his disposal to understand the essence (complexity) of complex technical, socioeconomic, mental or other problems.

Typically, a culture includes the following subsystems and components (Table 1):

Table 1. Culture Subsystems and Components

1. **Material Culture:**	▪ Production forces (production tools, technologies, communications, personnel qualification, science, etc.); ▪ Productive relations; ▪ Consumer items (housing, clothing, food, etc.); ▪ Human-transformed (cultural) landscape.
2. **Spiritual Culture:**	▪ Language, script, literature; ▪ Character, morality, ethics; ▪ Religion; ▪ Ideology, philosophy, law; ▪ Art; ▪ Education.
3. **Public Institutions:**	▪ Health, social security; ▪ Political groups, parties; ▪ Public organizations; ▪ Government management system.

Finally, culture is the learned behavior of a person in a society, on which the material and spiritual development of that society depends (Shengelia 2018).

In modern society, culture begins with education and progresses in the footsteps of science, technology, literature and art development. One of the main reasons for the development of culture is the constant renewal of the productive forces to a higher level, generation and introduction of technical and technological innovations.

2.2. Civilization Resources and Society

Development of a society, ensuring its well-being, is impossible without proper resources.

Examples of quantitative resources are

- time,
- people,

- material resources.

While, qualitative resources are

- country history,
- traditions,
- social achievements,
- public values.

One of the key conditions for progress is that society must have a system of values, goals, that will stimulate the development of the economy and society as a whole.

It is the prevailing civilizational ideology, viewed as a system of values, norms of behavior, and means of world perception, that distinguishes one civilization from another. Historically, the newly created modern European civilization is quite unique.

If our contemporaries met a representative of the ancient Egyptian, ancient Roman or ancient Chinese civilizations, they could not understand each other because of the different levels of development of science, technology and economics. This could have been overcome quickly, but a complete misunderstanding would have arisen when discussing the development goals of society and the system of human values.

Civilization is not a petrified construction and it has the ability to borrow, from other civilization systems, the institutions and elements of ideology that give them a competitive advantage in the evolutionary struggle. By introducing these elements and finding them reasonably compatible with their own culture and customs, a civilization can increase their own competitiveness and try to win the battle for economic leadership.

There is another, no less important, circumstance that prepares us to study the cultural and ideological foundations of various existing civilizations. The world economy today is no longer just a theory, many people are in direct contact with representatives of other countries and civilizations.

In a mega-economic environment, people are approaching. They do joint business, do joint research, travel to different countries, and, finally, communicate online. All you need to do is get to know your partner, and, in order to better understand and predict his or her behavior, you need to know his or her value system and worldview, which are rooted in the national culture, ideological civilization, and religion to which he or she belongs.

In modern economic life, this knowledge can be used in business negotiations, in the early stages of marketing research, in moving goods to overseas markets, and in solving many other tasks.

Values are not a fossilized phenomenon in one place. They experience life changes. Sometimes they even lose their true face and are even devalued.

Depreciation of values, of course, takes place everywhere, including in the field of economics. American consumer behavior, shaped by the global financial crisis, was driven by the fact that it was spending more than it was generating. On the one hand, it facilitated the development of business as it created the proper demand.

Now is another time. The behavior that has developed to date has undergone a drastic change. As a result of the change in values, Americans suddenly became wiser in financial matters, or learned from the mistakes of the past (the mistake of spending money generously). This is what life itself demanded. Americans have had no choice but to save money. Spending diligently made them think about what is important in this life and what makes them happy.

One of the main signs of value is that it is an aspiration to a great goal, embedded in its bed. As soon as it falls out of the bed, it depreciates, and the society moves into falsified conditions. In our time, impairment of values is not specifically anyone's fault. It is conditioned by our place of living, environmental conditions and time (Bogdanowicz and Bailey 2002).

One of the most difficult problems in the process of the modern transformation of society is how to maintain, how to save it from devaluation its values, without which we cannot reach the desired results, or how to define the fundamental values, without which human development and growth of goodness in society are impossible.

Today, the transformation is taking place all over the world, especially, because of the many contradictions, between the new civilizational tendencies and the old ones, as well as the conservative relations and lifestyles of the leading capitalists.

The transformation of socioeconomic systems in individual countries can be caused not only by internal factors, but also by the inconsistency of the realities of life in these countries with the general requirements of global laws of civilization, as well as the level of intellectual and cultural development of the advanced part of humankind.

An acute crisis, which particularly strongly affects people's interests, can arise in certain areas of life. So, for example, the reason for the transformation is the restriction of democracy, civil liberties, and so on.

The criterion for the current transformation and the evaluation of its consequences is human development—the increase of goodness in society. That is, how life and its changes are in line with universal values—morality, justice, freedom, truth, etc.

The conclusions and lessons of the history of humankind are of great importance. They are the focus of our correct, rapid and error-free development. The findings are a systematic statement of historical experience of economic development.

There should be a sufficient number of people in society who will be engaged in processing information, gaining new knowledge and leading it to technological innovations. To do this, the economy must create enough products to free part of its members from the routine labor of earning a daily living.

The production of knowledge and technological innovations will be carried out automatically if people prone to scientific and inventive activities have the opportunity for creative work, where they will be able to access the equipment necessary for research.

Hence, the need to meet the second condition—the economy must be organized in such a way that people who are naturally endowed with a talent for science or as an inventor could work hard to develop science and technological innovations. For this, it is necessary to have economic institutions that redistribute public wealth in such a way as to provide work in the field of science.

Science has always been closely linked to education, in the language of the market, to the field of knowledge acquisition. It was educational institutions and organizations that enabled the development of science. From the Middle Ages, science schools developed alongside universities.

Scientific knowledge has only recently come out directly onto the technological innovation market. For successful development, it is necessary to create economic institutions that provide production with technological innovations.

We have seen many times in history when technological innovations were carried out properly and had sufficient institutional support, but economic development was practically non-existent. As it has turned out, it is necessary to fulfill another condition: the society must have a system of values, those goals that will stimulate the development of the economy (Zoidze 2021).

It is the prevailing civilizational ideology, viewed as a system of values, norms of behavior, and means of world perception, that distinguishes one civilization from another.

At the modern stage, humanity increasingly perceives itself as a single organism. Europe, America and Asia are getting closer and closer to each other, gradually forming a unified culture, common business rules, and standards of conduct and education.

The peoples of these countries work together to preserve the traditions of their own culture and, at the same time, to identify more with the "rules of the game," established and developed at the level of a new civilizational unity, which allows them to operate freely and confidently in almost any major city.

CHAPTER 3

THE CORRELATION BETWEEN VALUES, EDUCATION AND ECONOMIC SECURITY

3.1. Sustainable Development and Security of the Economy

Education, in the context of modern globalization, lays the most solid foundations for individual and national economic security, making it a crucial political, economic, social, and environmental prerequisite. Universal competition improves the performance of a market economy. In addition, economic threats related to other security sectors should be considered. It is critical that the educational system develops a strategy for equipping future generations with the information and skills required to effectively realize a country's competitive advantage and build the economy.

On the one hand, a strong sense of personal security sets the groundwork for the efficient functioning of political and socioeconomic institutions, promoting long-term economic growth and national security; on the other hand, a high degree of national security ensures long-term personal security. States and education authorities should be able to quantify the plans and processes that ensure that relevant initiatives are implemented successfully.

Economic security may be viewed as a leading predictor of a country's overall security. Other degrees of security become simpler to obtain as a result of achieving economic security. The country's environmental security is heavily dependent on its economic and political stability. For regional and international security, security analysis in all sectors and their value for the overall security of the country is critical (Veshapidze *et al.* 2021).

For a long time, a crucial aspect of security - the economy -has had insufficient attention. Economic security is being given precedence in boosting the country's defense capabilities and physical security. The interrelationships between distinct components of general security need to be researched and studied more thoroughly.

Education goals, implementation methods, and outcomes, in turn, are a key predictor of economic security. The important priorities of the mandate will be adequately recognized, a plan will be established, and existing resources will be appropriately mobilized and managed to offer excellent education if the education system has a suitable political mandate, internal resources, and external support for education reform.

Quality education is an unquestionable requirement for a stable and sustained political, economic, and social environment because it establishes the strongest foundations for individual (micro-level) and national (macro-level) economic security.

We won't offer anything new if we suggest that the power of a strong military isn't the sole factor that determines long-term peace and growth.

Military security has been studied for the longest, but economic security is a newer, but largely acknowledged, approach to general security. The oil-related shocks of the 1970s spurred security specialists to recognize the importance of economics for nation's governments and their inhabitants' well-being. The fall of Soviet-style communism and the rise of a market-based economic system highlighted the need for paying attention to this aspect of public life.

Buzan shifted the direction of comprehending security levels and sectors with his 2008 work, *People, States, and Fear*. At three levels, he identified people, governments, and international systems. "New Patterns of Global Security in the Twenty-First Century," a separate study, examined security issues in the political, military, economic, social, and environmental realms (Buzan 1991).

Buzan observed that defining economic security is difficult, since the market economic system's key feature is the so-called "perpetual threat," a competitive and unpredictable system, i.e., if there is global competition and a continual danger of failure, a market economy will work better.

As a result, economic security appears to be incompatible with global market processes, such as expanding free trade and increased competition, at first appearance. In addition, economic vulnerabilities relating to other security areas should be considered. The many aspects of security are intertwined and condition one another. Economic threats, for example, might undermine a country's internal political stability. In terms of fiscal limits, it is apparent that military security is dependent on economic security.

Economic security should be studied in terms of how a state utilizes economic processes to protect territorial integrity, how well it satisfies the needs of its population, how it maintains political and cultural independence, and how it avoids foreign military attack (Horrigan *et al.* 2008).

Economic and financial security are assumed to be evaluated and assessed in the same place. Economic and financial security, for example, is defined as the continuation of a stable income or other resources to ensure living standards now and in the foreseeable future, which includes probable continuing solvency; forecasting the future income of an individual or other economic entity (e.g., the country as a whole); and employment or job security.

Financial security refers to an individual's, or family's, ability to manage their money and savings. Economic security also takes into account society's productivity levels, jobless citizens' monetary allowances, and the implications of all of this.

3.2. The Impact of Education on Economic Security and Development

Lucien B. Keane attempted to relate the education sector's failings to economic instability and insecurity as early as 1935, following the Great Depression. This was one of the early tries. A peaceful society is essential for building a sustainable future. Education becomes the primary catalyst for accomplishing interconnected objectives.

Improving education for peace and sustainable development will have a long-term influence on not just teaching outcomes and educational quality, but also on the establishment of a more inclusive, equitable, and fair society.

This will promote a positive school culture and increased student engagement, as well as the implementation of practices that are consistent with the values of equality and mutual respect, as well as the development of skills and attitudes that will enable citizens to create healthy and fulfilling living conditions. This comprises the willingness to work together to achieve common goals, problem-solving abilities, information and communication technology education, as well as social and cultural competences (UNESCO

2019).

It is important to highlight that education does not include fact interpretation. It entails much more than simply recalling data and grasping basic phrases and concepts. A successful education should enable the learner, and, later, the student, to convert remembered and understood knowledge, apply it, and reflect on it in order to meet real-world obstacles and attain the core goals of personal and national economic security.

These two levels result in reciprocal gains. On the one hand, a strong sense of personal security sets the groundwork for the efficient functioning of political and socioeconomic institutions, promoting long-term economic growth and national security; on the other hand, a high degree of national security ensures long-term personal security.

The Anglo-Saxon and Asian methods will be discussed here. Education, according to the Anglo-Saxon perspective, is considered at the individual level and is a determinant of each individual's economic security. The Asian strategy focuses on national education and the development of a skilled workforce.

Economic security is thought of on two levels. One is at the individual level, where education is seen as a determinant of one's economic security, whereas education at the national level must assure the training of a quality and competitive workforce. The educational system must design a strategy to equip future generations with the information and skills required for a country's competitive advantage to be effectively realized. Clearly, the purpose is to expand the economy of the country.

Economic dangers are exacerbated by unstable governments, inequality, and a scarcity of trained workers. National security would be threatened if the education system fails to handle these issues. A successful economy relies heavily on education (Brown 2010).

Education's productivity is a potent weapon for economic development and social transformation, and it promotes individual and national freedom and self-confidence.

America's prosperity rests on the success of individual people simply because the growth of humankind depends directly on the progress of the nation, said Arne Duncan, the US Secretary of Education, in a speech to the Council of Foreign Affairs, in 2010. He added that, in the twenty-first century, he felt that education has enormous potential for growth and improvement. (Shiplett *et al.* 2011).

Politics should, ideally, affect education strategy and values, but education must always be placed above politics.

Is that what's going on? Government support is always necessary for public education institutions. As a result, they are frequently constrained and even directly impacted by political ideas. One of the distinctions between public and private sector enterprises is that they are held to various levels of public accountability.

The education sector bears a special responsibility to the public and the outside world. Political and regulatory restrictions regulate public sector organizations. If political reform choices are hindered and postponed, creative and talented teaching concepts will fade as well. In other circumstances, schools and universities are rigid and reluctant to adapt to planned policy changes, owing to the fact that most instructors take an overly conservative attitude to their responsibilities.

Schools and institutions face similar challenges in adjusting to their surroundings. A hybrid government system is exemplified by the Ministry of Education. It is a challenging effort to respond appropriately to public expectations, reflect on national policy development goals, and adhere to development trajectories. Because education is a complex and rigid system, reaching consensus on growth directions is challenging. This is due, in part, to a shortage of instructors with the requisite abilities, as well as the fast-changing political, economic, and financial climate.

Strategy and its directions are rarely defined consistently, and they do not always represent the pre-determined and agreed-upon aims and objectives of excellent education. As a result, seeing the difference between 0.5 % and 5 % of GDP spent on education is nearly impossible or irrelevant. Large spending alone will not be enough to solve educational challenges, especially if it is difficult to compare the qualitative results gained with these prices.

As a result, graduates from various levels of educational institutions, as well as standardized exam results, are frequently insufficient to assess strategic success and prepare for future reforms. Governments lack the experience and political will to require realistic reports that clearly demonstrate the relationship between the system's aims and the outcomes accomplished. In order to prevent stagnation in the reform process, a consensus on the system's direction must be obtained. As a result, graduates of educational institutions will be able to contribute to long-term economic growth by utilizing the full extent of their abilities.

If the government gives the system a clear mandate, it will be easier to fulfill this aim. The mandate will provide a firm foundation on which to build realistic plans for the system's future. Some instances demonstrate how governments issue directives to strengthen economic education while also providing guidance to the educational sector. For example, the mandate states: "...to revamp the curriculum and assessment processes for teaching such global capabilities as are important for the present and future economy."

Critical thinking, problem-solving abilities, innovation, creativity, entrepreneurship, self-organization, teamwork, communication, global citizenship, and sustainability are among these competences. Further, schools and universities can divide this mandate into sections, develop learning themes and directions specific to each section, improve curricula and syllabi, and train teachers and instructors. As a result, a strong circle will guide the country toward long-term growth.

International organizations seek to establish a broad foundation for high-quality education. "By 2030, all students must acquire the knowledge and skills that will contribute to sustainable development," says the UN Sustainable Development Goal for Education. "This will be accomplished through education in areas such as self-sustaining development and sustainable lifestyles, human rights, gender equality, the establishment and strengthening of a culture of peace and nonviolence, world citizenship, cultural diversity, and the contribution of cultures to sustainable development."

States and education organizations should be able to measure the strategies and processes that guarantee that mandates and related projects are implemented successfully.

Education is a complex system to assess. Supportive education finance, in theory, should represent meaningful and effective connections between plans and resource restrictions. Due to financial restrictions, educational institutions are sometimes forced to expand class sizes without making other required reforms.

"It is apparent that we should apply the notion of economy in the examination of education as a public product," according to certain academics. "Measures that serve to optimize outcomes should be examined," says the evaluation, which should differentiate priorities, rational decision, and allocation of available resources to fulfill the goals as much as feasible (Siwińska 2003).

The relationships between educational resources and system results are depicted in Figure 2.

There are some sectors of economic activity where measuring the degree of outcomes or successes on the path to the targeted goals is nearly difficult. In this way, defense and education are related. The ultimate test of the military's effectiveness is war, but this is, of course, an "unacceptable prospect." For example, the effectiveness of defense, as a public product, can only be measured by the outcome of war—the armed forces either win or lose the war.

Similarly, the outcome of education, as a second public product, may be assessed according to any country's and society's ultimate desired goal—the capacity to endure under extraordinarily challenging political, economic, social, and environmental circumstances. Quantitative measures, such as the number of high school and college graduates, the number of educated and retrained instructors, and even curricular modifications, do not completely represent the efficient use and management of budget dollars for education reform.

Economic security may be viewed as a leading predictor of a country's overall security. Other kinds of security can be attained more readily by obtaining economic security, according to studies. The country's environmental security is heavily dependent on its economic and political stability. Security analysis of each sector and their relevance for the country's overall security is also critical for regional and worldwide security.

The fact that there is a substantial correlation between education and economic security is no longer debatable. The effects of the educational system can have two outcomes: they can improve a country's economic security or, conversely, they might make it more susceptible.

Figure 2. Sustainable Education Structure of System Efficiency for Sustainable Economic Development

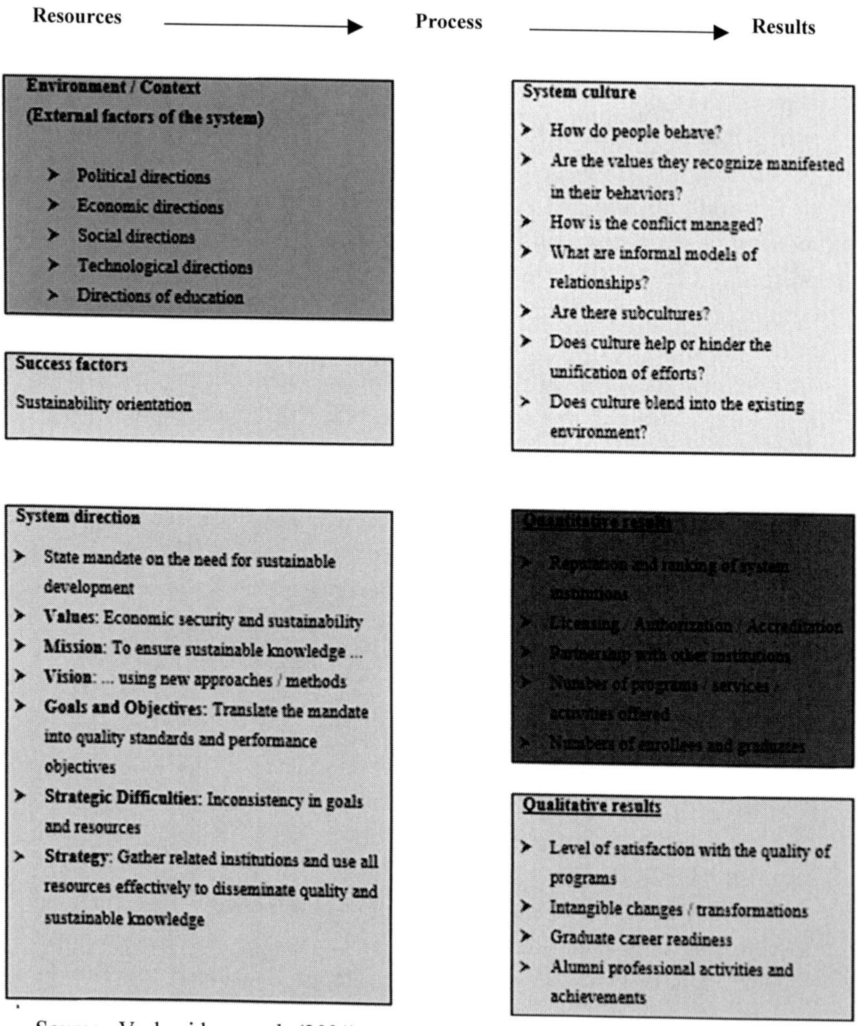

Source: Veshapidze *et al.* (2021). "On the Relationship between Education and Economic Security." *Ecoforum Journal* 10(3).

To keep up with today's quickly changing needs, the education system should ensure the growth of the system's internal competencies. Competitive education is a major driver of the country's economic development. Education management will not be able to safeguard itself against compromise and dysfunction if governments' efforts in this regard fail.

To reflect and satisfy the evaluation system's purpose of establishing sustained economic security and peace, new measures of educational system results must be devised and deployed.

CHAPTER 4

ON BUDGETARY INTERVENTION BY THE STATE IN THE ECONOMY

In the face of increased competition in modern international marketplaces, the execution of a successful budget strategy is becoming increasingly important for a country's growth. It is especially critical for nations in transition or rising economies. State budget policy is a complicated and vast issue at its heart. As a result, the research naturally takes a certain course, which entails evaluating the state budget's expenditure component and its purpose. The primary focus of the neoliberal-classical debate is on determining the best way to intervene in the state economy. The state budget plays a significant role as one of the instruments of economic policy (Veshapidze and Zoidze 2022).

State economic programming and regulation should be viewed as a collection of economic policies that supplement the free market, are connected to problems that the supply-demand mechanism does not handle, or are related to adverse reactions.

The state's role in the modern economy includes more than only economic policies, which are often conveyed solely through monetary, fiscal, and other activities. It involves legislative tasks such as ensuring that workers are safe at work, regulating the minimum wage, resolving social issues, and more.

It is critical that the state and the market maintain regular, active dialogue in order to increase well-being and living standards through mutual agreement. Georgia is expected to reach double-digit GDP growth rates in the next years as a consequence of sound government policy and market regulation.

Overregulation and self-regulation of the economy are, of course, unproductive. In the first scenario, there is a "slowdown" in economic progress and a rise in regulatory body corruption; in the second situation, there is full chaos and serious violations of consumer and investor rights. The "golden interval" is the more beneficial of these two techniques, according to world economic reform experience.

From the aforementioned perspective, it is extremely difficult and crucial to define property rights, which is impossible without the assistance of the state. Another sector of the economy where a particularly tough challenge occurs is the monetary system, for which the government has traditionally been held responsible.

It is true that the market's role in the evolution of civilization is widely acknowledged, but it is neither an all-powerful phenomenon nor a solution for all problems. There are several "typical" scenarios in which the market makes mistakes, which are referred to as "market failures" or "market fiasco" in economic theory. Normal societal functions, such as research, education, culture, and social security, are frequently involved in such failure zones.

The contemporary state is not outside of the market and does not "look down" on it; rather, it is organically entrenched in it—the state is an active market actor, accountable for the achievement of the interests of the entire society. At the same time, it varies significantly from other market participants in that it focuses on maximizing the socioeconomic utility of society as a whole rather than individual utility (profit).

The state's economic role in a post-industrial society is achieved in the following functions:

- Regulation of production in sectors where natural monopoly circumstances exist (electricity generation and distribution, telecommunications, transportation, communications, water supply, and so on);
- Correcting the undesirable social effects of a market economy, which should prevent social inequality, unemployment, and poverty from worsening;
- Using macroeconomic policy instruments to safeguard the economy from crisis declines and increasing inflation, the economy may be stabilized.

It's worth noting that, although the state's role and functions were once confined to financial-budgetary policy, today, this role is mostly seen as one of the technological tools for influencing the economy. However, no government, regardless of its political goals and ambitions, can avoid participating in the economy and being concerned about the country's high business efficiency in any way. As a result, the state's economic mission is to promote and preserve the market economy's proper functioning, which it cannot do without meddling in the economy (Shengelia 2017).

The EU's present reality indicates that parts of the nation-sovereign state's tasks are being moved to this major regional union's level: the European Central Bank, for example, determines the most significant monetary policy parameter. At the same time, despite the current terrible position in the EU, national governments remain adamantly opposed to the transfer of budgetary powers to supranational bodies.

It should also be emphasized that globalization itself poses a number of problems that are virtually impossible to solve without state participation (for example, regulating migration, drug trafficking, the spread of terrorism, money laundering, control of transnational corporations, etc.). At the same time, it is self-evident that no government, today, can create and implement economic policies without taking into account the standards of conduct of other nations, particularly the leading globalization subjects.

The contemporary state has a critical function to play. Only it can meet the demands of the global market and build a national economy structure that is appropriate for the circumstances, in which it plays a critical role: accelerating scientific and technological progress, and generating an information economy based on the creation of new knowledge and the dissemination of old knowledge. Furthermore, the degree of income distribution equality attained in post-industrial states is relatively high, which is highly essential since it guarantees social stability and shields society from major oscillations and revolutions. The state encourages the population's individual earnings to be equalized.

Given the present difficulties of globalization, it is impossible to picture a country achieving a high level of economic development and, as a result, national market competitiveness without a strong budget strategy. The budget is the primary financial entity through which the government intervenes in the country's economic life. It is the state's major financial plan. It is presented in the form of a balance sheet and is divided into two sections: income and spending.

The revenue section contains the articles under which the state must obtain income, i.e., where monies must be raised. These revenues are totally collected in the treasury, i.e., at the state's cost. The state subsequently uses or spends these revenues for state and public purposes, as shown in the budget items.

The state budget also considers the scope and magnitude of government intervention in the economy. Because the process of mobilizing financial resources through the state budget system and subsequently spending them has the largest influence on the whole course of society's economic life, the budget system is one of the most important aspects of state economic policy execution. Taxes and costs are utilized to influence agricultural activity. In this situation, we're discussing the budget system's role in economic regulation (Veshapidze and Zoidze 2022).

Anti-cyclical and anti-inflation policies, as well as measures to accelerate or restrain economic development, are frequently implemented through the budget. The experience of developed nations demonstrates that keeping government expenditure (total budget) between one quarter and one third of GDP creates a stabilizing force that protects the developed market economy from excessive economic downturns and dangerously low private investment activity.

Furthermore, the budget system is a key instrument for allocating income created in society via taxes, social payments, and aid systems. The state risks exceeding the sensible bounds of GDP distribution through the budget as it performs the tasks of the budget system, therefore, the overall level of taxes, their structure, as well as the volume and structure of expenditures should not slow down. If the budget surpasses two thirds of GDP, the country's economy cannot flourish.

Sweden's development experience shows that the "inflation" of the GDP share in the budget was followed by the suppression of the economic stimulus, the depressive economy, which forced the government to implement reforms aimed at further liberalization of the economy, i.e., "excessive" interference in economic life.

The optimum redistribution of financial resources between individual sectors and sectors of the economy, which attempts to use the limited resources as rationally and effectively as possible, occupies one of the most significant places in the state's economic functions. It should be highlighted that the state's economic and political strength is inextricably tied to the budget system's long-term growth, as the budget system's strength contributes to the country's economic independence and stability.

The level of mobilization of Georgia's state budget revenues has significantly changed as a result of the gradual transition to a market economy, as evidenced by the following developments in the analytical years: increased state budget revenues, improved tax administration, improved legal framework, reduced scale of mass corruption, streamlined accounting system, and reduced scale of the shadow economy, which in turn provided the stats.

Modern reality necessitates a greater focus on the social realm in order to maximize the utilization of the state budget's money to enhance the country's social position. Today, the most important aim of Georgia's state budget is to ensure the population's health and social security. Of course, state policy could be improved in this regard, but the focus should also be on lowering the number of vulnerable individuals, which includes reducing poverty. This is one of the elements of a successful budget strategy.

The state budget of Georgia has been increasing in recent years, leading us to believe that the standard of living for Georgian households should be improved. It should also be emphasized that the health and social guarantees program was greatly needed and timely during this critical period (Veshapidze and Zoidze 2022).

In Georgia, reducing inequality, poverty, and unemployment, as well as generating new jobs in the private sector, are critical to achieving social cohesion and economic progress. It is vital to acquire a high level of production in order to overcome these issues. This may be accomplished through successful reorganization and the creation of policies aimed at the development of human capital through the provision of high-paying jobs.

The necessity to increase workforce expertise and experience, technology, infrastructure, and logistics has been demonstrated by the diversification of Georgian export rates. Budget expenditures must be examined in order to assess budget policies; Table 2 shows important statistics on state budget expenditures and non-financial assets. The study spans the years 2004 to 2019.

Table 2. Budget Expenditures and Non-Financial Asset Growth in a Functional Context, 2004–2019 (in %)

%	Health and social protection	Defense, order, security	General purpose public service	Education	Transport	Agriculture	Fuel and energy
2004	24	20	10	3.3	3.5	2.6	7
2005	23	23	12.6	3.1	4.4	2	10.2
2006	20	27.5	11.3	8.8	5.2	2	6.1
2007	21	52.1	12.3	7.8	5.1	1.2	0.7
2008	21	39.2	21	6.4	4.2	0.7	1.5
2009	26.4	27.4	23.7	7.3	8	1	0.4
2010	26.2	23	26.7	8.3	8.2	0.5	0.3
2011	26.3	22.7	26.4	8.2	8.6	0.5	0.7
2012	27.2	21.6	25.3	8.8	5.3	2.9	1.5
2013	31.4	18.8	25.8	8.6	7	2.1	0.5
2014	34	19	21.3	9.8	7.1	2.7	1
2015	34.6	18.2	22.7	10	6.4	2.3	0.3
2016	36.5	18	18.6	10.9	7	2.5	0.2
2017	35	17	18.1	11.3	9.2	2	0.12
2018	33.2	16.3	18.6	11	11.5	1.6	0.15
2019	35.5	17.2	12.8	11.7	11.1	2.4	0.7

Source: The Ministry of Finance of Georgia.

NOTE: Apart from this, other areas were financed from the state budget, however, due to their small share and lower interest, in economic terms, this table is not discussed (for example, culture, sports, etc.).

As can be seen, the state's priorities in 2004 were health and social security; defense, order and security; general purpose public services; and energy projects. The costs of health and social protection, education, and agriculture, as well as public services, defense, order and security, transportation (road infrastructure), and fuel and energy will all decline modestly the next year.

In 2004, 2005, and 2006, significant investment for energy initiatives lasted barely three years. From 2004 to 2019, the prices of education and transportation infrastructure increased substantially year after year, with annual increases of around 10 % in both directions.

Based on these facts, the budget strategy is competent in responding to the major improvement in the investment climate and is truly relevant, as seen by the increasing trend of foreign direct investment since 2004.

The problem of the international trade imbalance, on the other hand, remained unsolved. From 2004 to 2013, health and social care spending fluctuated from 20 % to 27 %, on average, but, since 2013, it has risen to over 30 % and is now at 35.5 %. All of this is due to Georgia's unfavorable socioeconomic status.

The macroeconomic statistics for Georgia show that the Georgian economy has been confronted with significant obstacles. The country's unfavorable interest rates could not be lifted due to low economic development. The country's GDP per capita is extremely low, and it is expanding at an unfavorable, near-zero pace each year. According to preliminary predictions, the already dismal economic growth rates in the country have been lowered to around -6 % as a result of the Covid pandemic.

The goal of budget policy should be to ameliorate this situation, which entails lowering the number of people receiving social assistance while also enhancing the quality of the support that remains.The health-care system in wealthy European nations is flawless, thanks to years of enormous public investment (on average, 50 % of the budget). As a result, the rising trend in Georgia's health and social care expenditures is perfectly reasonable in terms of quantity, and the refinement and enhancement of this area's quality is the key problem (Veshapidze and Zoidze 2022).

To avoid a major economic catastrophe in Georgia and to expand economic sovereignty, it is necessary to fundamentally change the current economic course and develop a new political platform, which the government is pursuing. This course will be centered on the government's optimal intervention in the economy, resulting in the highest priority protection of human rights.

The country must develop a "Georgian model" of economics that takes into account local values without debate, since this will be the "core" of the new economic system. It will deliver genuine wealth to up to four million people by attracting investment, creating employment, and boosting exports.

Budget policy has a big impact on the efficacy of government intervention in the economy. Priority expenditure by the government has a direct impact on the economic progress of emerging nations. Disorganized infrastructure, a non-competitive and non-legal/unfair environment, insecurity of private property, and other factors stymie commercial development in the country.

As a result, the state should allocate the necessary funding in this direction. The state's budget policy is incorrect if it fails to respond properly to contemporary difficulties while having ample financial resources. Along with successful initiatives to interfere in the state economy, there have been instances when the market might have handled the problem more effectively, despite the fact that state economic regulation has always been strategic and tactical in nature. State economic programming and regulation should be viewed as a collection of economic policies that supplement the free market, are connected to problems that the supply-demand mechanism does not handle, or are related to unwanted side effects. The goal of government involvement in the economy is to achieve as many of the market economy's finest attributes as feasible.

The increasing rate of public debt in Georgia's consumer sector is noteworthy, and it requires a more thorough examination of economic policies. The current economic advantages of public debt are relatively modest (e.g., underdevelopment of the real sector), but they do provide some long-term prospects (e.g., improved infrastructure). Health and social care expenditures in the state budget are substantially larger and are acknowledged as a priority in a developed country, compared to a developing country.

The rising trend in Georgia's health and social protection spending is perfectly predictable from a quantitative standpoint, and the primary task is to refine and enhance the quality of this direction. The appropriate budget policy will greatly contribute to Georgia's double-digit GDP growth rates over the next five years.

CHAPTER 5

VALUE-BASED EDUCATION IN THE GLOBAL ECONOMY

5.1. Education: A Prerequisite for Georgia's Economic Prosperity

The country's economic prosperity is primarily dependent on achieving a high level of education. The association between its outcomes and the country's GDP is fairly high, according to worldwide rankings that examine students' talents. Investing in education is several times more rewarding than investing in other areas.

In Georgia, attaining the appropriate degree of education, especially higher education, is highly responsible for the growth of the country's gross domestic product and, as a result, education financing. As a result, it is critical to improve the population's abilities (invest in education) in order to boost the country's GDP.

Even in the face of poor economic performance, experience has demonstrated that a progressive educational system may accomplish great improvement in a short period of time. It is critical for Georgia to concentrate on system principles such as interdisciplinary and multidisciplinary approaches, individual student orientation, development of thinking skills, improving social security and labor relations, efficiency and equality protection, innovation orientation, and inclusive and quality education.

The country's economic prosperity is primarily responsible for achieving a high level of education. A country's prosperity is determined by its productivity, which is determined by elements such as physical capital, natural resources, human capital, and technology. Georgia does not have a lot of physical capital; nevertheless, it does have certain natural resources (their appropriate use necessitates knowledge), knowledge necessitates technical growth, and human capital indicates the presence of knowledge and experience. As a result, Georgia places a high focus on the quick development and improvement of the educational system (Veshapidze *et al.* 2021).

Education is a high-priority sector of economic policy in Georgia. The trend in education spending in the country is rising. In absolute terms, the funding of education through the state budget emphasizes the necessity for continued rapid expansion. Raising the educational system's overall level, especially that of higher education, is contingent on the country's economic development and rapid expansion.

5.2. Importance of Educational Ratings

Various worldwide rankings give useful information on the status and quality of a country's education system. Georgia is ranked outside of the top one hundred states in terms of educational quality, according to recognized rankings. In most of the rankings, Switzerland, Singapore, and Finland are tied for the top position in terms of educational quality.

However, there is no one-size-fits-all method for categorizing the greatest and worst educational systems. The Organization for Economic Co-operation and Development (OECD) compiled one such list by surveying adults aged twenty-five to sixty-four who had finished a vocational training program or earned a two- or four-year graduate degree (Veshapidze *et al.* 2021).

According to these figures, Canada is the most educated country in the world, according to an OECD survey published in 2021. More than 56 % of individuals in the United States have continued their education after graduating from high school. Japan is in second position. In this country, more than half of the people have finished high school. Israel trails behind Japan, where 49.9 % of individuals have completed a post-secondary degree. According to these figures, South Korea, the United Kingdom, the United States, Australia, Finland, Norway, and Luxembourg have the highest levels of education.

The US News and World Report Rankings provide another perspective on the best-educated countries. This assessment was based on three factors:

1. A well-developed system of public education,
2. Rank of higher quality education,
3. How do people in this nation feel about university education?

The United Kingdom is in first place according to this rating. The United States comes in second, with around 70 % of graduates going on to further study. Canada is ranked third, ahead of Germany and France (Galt and Taggart 2020).

The association between the outcomes of these evaluations and the country's GDP is fairly high, according to international ratings. High GDP levels define countries that perform highly in international rankings. Investing in education is four times more rewarding than investing in other areas, according to much fundamental research. As a result, it is critical to improve the population's abilities (invest in education) in order to boost the country's GDP. Otherwise, it will continue to expand at a low rate, one that is commensurate with its human capital resources.

Countries with inadequate education systems include those with internal strife, economic challenges, or a lack of financial assistance.

However, with acceptable changes, even at a low economic rate, it is feasible to considerably boost educational attainment. There are several examples around the world that support this claim. The Republic of Korea was a war-torn country in the 1950s, with few people knowing how to read or write. Nonetheless, the country delivered high-quality universal secondary education in 1995. South Korean pupils, in fact, achieved the greatest marks in worldwide knowledge examinations.

Even though Vietnam is a far lower-income country, fifteen-year-old Vietnamese pupils exhibited the same level of knowledge as German students in 2012, according to the OECD's Program for International Student Assessment (PISA) (Tsiklauri 2016).

Peru achieved one of the most obvious increases in education, between 2009 and 2015, while the reading rate in primary schools in Liberia, Papua New Guinea, and Tongo increased dramatically in a short period of time as a response to results-based policies.

In Georgia, achieving the necessary level of education, especially higher education, is heavily dependent on the country's GDP and, as a result, education spending growth. Table 3 and Figure 3 depict these figures.

Table 3. GDP of Georgia, Funding of the Ministry of Education in the State Budget and Share of the Education Budget in Relation to GDP, 2012–2021*

Year	GDP (in current prices, mln)	GDP growth in % (base year 2012)	Education funding in the state budget	Increase in the share of education funding in % (base year 2012)
2012	27 227	100 %	1,092.30	100 %
2013	28 593	105 %	1,202.50	110.10 %
2014	31 124	114.31 %	1,276.10	116.80 %
2015	33 935	124.64 %	1,338.60	122.50 %
2016	35 836	131.62 %	1,428.00	130.70 %
2017	40 762	149.71 %	1,528.80	140 %
2018	44 599	163.80 %	1, 570	143.70 %
2019	49 253	180.90 %	1,644.70	150.60 %
2020	49 407	181.50 %	1,538.80	140.90 %
2021*	53 443	196.30 %	1,802.60	165 %

Source: Ministry of Finance of Georgia State Treasury; National Statistics Office of Georgia.

Education is definitely a priority area of economic policy in Georgia, according to data research. In absolute terms, the funding of education through the state budget emphasizes the necessity for continued rapid expansion. The trend in education spending is rising. It has an increasing curve. As a result, boosting the overall level of education (especially higher education) will be heavily reliant on the country's economic strength and quick expansion.

Figure 3. Increase in the Share of GDP and Education Funding in Georgia (base year: 2012)

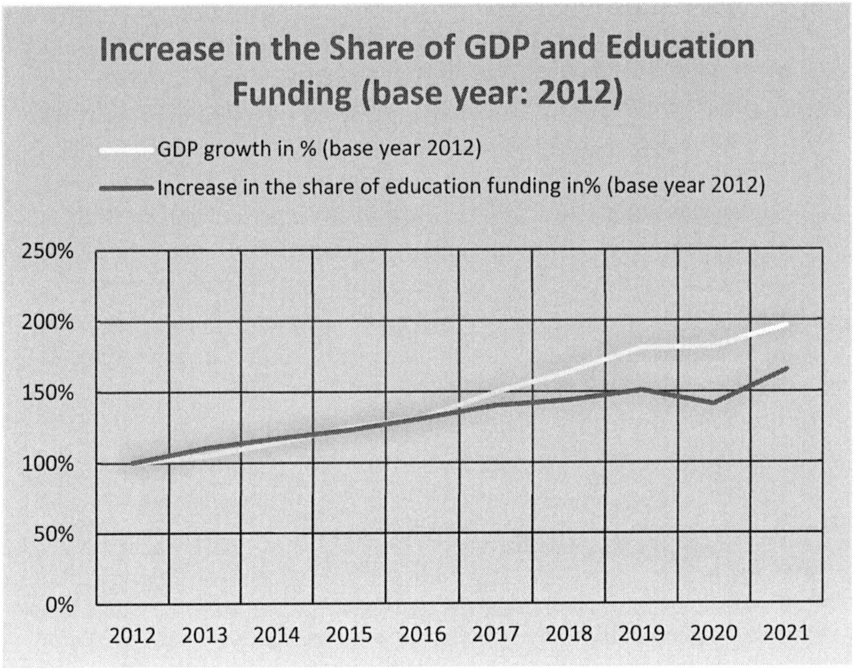

Source: National Statistics Office of Georgia, 2021

The quantity of money invested has a considerable impact on the country's educational system. However, there is no one-size-fits-all formula for allocating a portion of GDP to this purpose. It's also worth noting that there is, presently, no global research or ranking that examines and compares countries' educational systems. Only a few elements of the educational system may be compared by nation (Zoidze and Veshapidze 2021).

There is potential to increase the level of higher education in Georgia with the support of Georgia's key allies—the United States, NATO, the European Union, and the United Kingdom. The real possibility of this is conditioned:

- Visa-free travel to the EU,
- dual citizenship established by Georgian legislation,
- numerous opportunities for sending students abroad through exchange programs,
- favorable conditions for students leaving Georgia,
- the establishment of a world-class international university in Georgia, etc.

Higher education, nowadays, only marginally enhances the prospects of finding work in Georgia and only slightly improves the income supplement. Georgia's educational system does not satisfy labor market criteria. This indicates that the number of Georgian students seeking quality education overseas is growing. According to Eurostat, 11,300 Georgian students studied abroad in 2019, up from 7,100 in 2013. In 2019, more than half of the international students studied in Central and Eastern Europe, 35 % in North America and Western Europe, and the remaining 13 % in Asia.

Despite substantial advances, Georgia has to continue to establish institutions that will allow us to fully fulfill the higher education system's potential. Long-term educational reform is the only way to achieve this. The World Bank supports such programs in Georgia. It's important to note that over four billion dollars have been spent in more than one hundred World Bank projects in our nation during the course of our twenty-five-year partnership.

Self-discipline, hard work, and picking the correct approach are all considered prerequisites for a competitive, successful career in American and European schooling. It is critical to encourage students and learners to grasp knowledge on their own. They must be able to solve difficulties rather than rely on tools. When people realize why they need the tools, it will be much more effective.

One of the primary drawbacks of current programs is that they frequently dive further into a topic without fully presenting the fundamentals, crucial concepts, and disputed problems. It is critical to consider knowledge as a semantic tree. First of all, let us grasp the essential concepts: a tree stem and huge branches. After that, we should move on to the leaves (details). They won't have anything to "cling to" if we don't (Rodrik 2021).

Testing knowledge using present exams not only fails to provide results, but also has a negative impact on learning. Knowledge testing is necessary in and of itself, but not in the form of excessive test assignments. Prestigious courses can be regarded when they educate thinking and build the abilities needed for feedback when students are able to objectively examine their own errors (Veshapidze *et al.* 2016).

The example of Finland, one of the countries with a good education system, is informative in this regard (Figure 4).

Figure 4. Education Management System, Finland

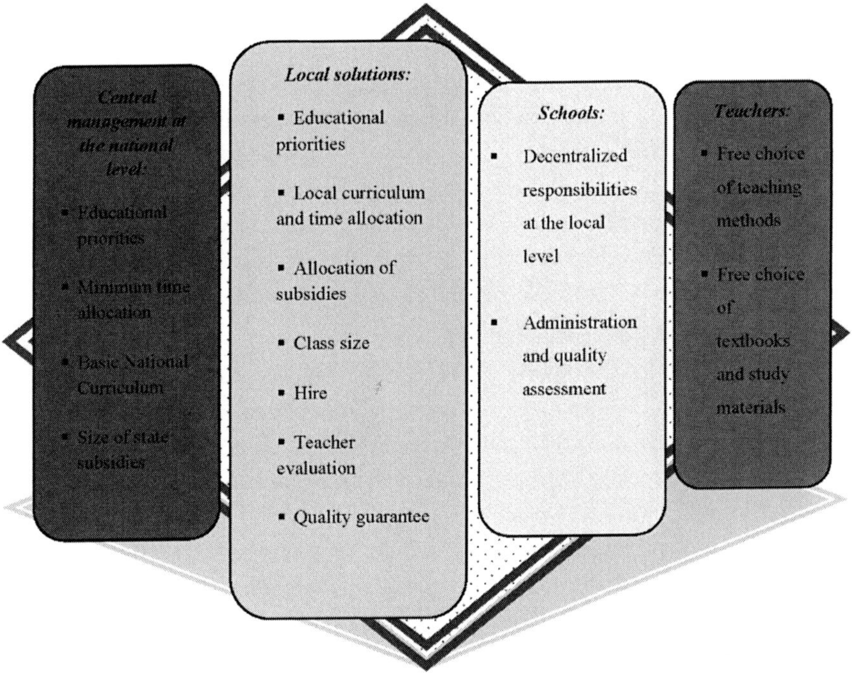

Source: Compiled by the authors, based on materials from the Finnish National Education Agency and the Finnish Ministry of Education and Culture.

In worldwide comparisons, Finland's educational system is one of the best. As a result, other nations, like Georgia, may be interested in focusing on key aspects of this system that have allowed the country to achieve great development in a short period of time. Its basic tenet is

- an interdisciplinary and multidisciplinary approach,
- a student-centered, individual approach,
- development of cognitive abilities, particularly at the primary level.

This entails implementing this interdisciplinary approach in such a manner that various disciplines consider and study the same topic. It is more vital to develop a mentality than it is to memorize facts (understanding the information provided).

The Georgian education system's national model focuses on the transmission of these aspects, which must be modified to Georgia's strengths (Zoidze 2021).

On May 29, 2019, the World Bank Executive Board authorized the Education Reform Project in Georgia, and, on June 18, a finance agreement was signed. The project complies with the World Bank's Partnership Strategy for 2019–2022 and aids the Georgian government in executing the Education Reform Agenda for 2018–2023.

According to the World Bank Group, education reform in Georgia should promote inclusive growth, boost competitiveness, invest in human capital, and strengthen the country's resilience. In terms of staff credentials, it is critical to close the gap between learning results and labor market expectations.

This project's main objectives include promoting preschool education and increasing access to it; improving teaching quality; improving the higher education funding model and bringing it up to international standards; strengthening the system and improving stakeholder communication; and improving project management, monitoring, and evaluation.

The project's infrastructure component will include the building of five new schools, the restoration of around sixty existing schools, and the introduction of more than one hundred and fifty child-centered and modern preschool education programs for school readiness over the course of six years. In total, approximately 116,000 preschool and secondary school pupils will benefit from the programme (Galt and Taggart 2020).

The initiative also gives assistance to disadvantaged sections of the community based on the principles of human equality (students with low socioeconomic status in rural and mountainous regions, ethnic minorities and students with different educational needs). The initiative will also aid students in higher education institutions through up to forty-five grants offered to updated academic programs, in line with job market requirements.

Furthermore, in Georgia, there are varying prospects for adequate education, depending on the location, outside of Tbilisi. As a result, the level of education in the districts is insufficient and must be improved.

Countries with internal strife and/or economic challenges, on the other hand, are among those with bad educational institutions.

Georgia's educational system, on the other hand, needs structural improvements. It is critical to implement long-term reforms based on innovation, inclusive and quality education, adherence to the principle of efficiency and equality, regulation of social issues in accordance with European standards, increased access to pre-school education, provision of a conducive learning environment, and human development in order to improve Georgia's educational system.

It's also critical to enhance the higher education financing model and align it with worldwide standards, as well as to strengthen the system and increase stakeholder communication, as well as to improve project management, monitoring, and evaluation.

The most important thing is to have a sophisticated education system in Georgia. This entails ongoing and persistent education, as well as quick and long-term development possibilities in all sectors of the economy, business, science, and public life.

CHAPTER 6

THE MAIN CHALLENGES OF HIGHER EDUCATION IN GEORGIA

6.1. Directions of Georgia's Security Policy

Georgia's security strategy is an essential component of education policy, which includes higher education. Institutions play a crucial role in its growth. Regulatory norms, institutions, values, cultural patterns, and forms of ownership are all acknowledged paths for advancing the education system, its organization, and institutionalization.

All types of discrimination in the labor system and the educational system are prohibited under Georgian law, though there are no ordered, social protection-oriented structures or any clearly established priorities. In Georgia's public and private higher education institutions, considerable experience has been collected on this subject. The enactment of Georgia's Organic Law on the Labor Code paved the way for this strategy.

Georgia requires the establishment of institutions that will enable us to fully fulfill the higher education system's potential. Long-term education reform, which is publicly supported by the World Bank, is also essential (Veshapidze and Zoidze 2021).

Achieving a high level of education is largely due to the country's economic development. This leads to an increase in investment in education. It is also important to develop the skills of the population in order to increase the country's GDP. World experience shows that it is possible to significantly increase achievements in the field of education, even at a low economic rate.

The main thing is to create a European standard education system in Georgia. Its principles were thoroughly elaborated by Ilia Chavchavadze and Niko Nikoladze, in the nineteenth century. For this, it is crucial to harmonize the Georgian education system with European education, science, its governance rules, institutions and principles.

Every person has a certain relationship with an object that is important to him, which is related to the satisfaction and use of his needs. Such a goal, an aspiration, a demand, is his interest. Interest can be political, economic, spiritual, aesthetic, ethical, etc.

In addition to individual interests, there is a common interest of members of any group, which is often completely different from the unity of individual interests, that exists in any one social sphere.

There are even national, or state, interests. This term is the main defining concept of foreign policy, which is based on the principles of national security and survival, and is applied only to states.

The state, in pursuit of the interests of the country, determines the areas of national security policy, plans it and coordinates it. National security policy is an activity carried out to ensure the interests of the state. It means overcoming threats inside and outside the country. To do this, the state identifies risks and challenges, and assesses, avoids and prevents them.

The main directions of Georgia's security policy are

- de-occupation of the occupied territories of Georgia,
- development of state institutions and strengthening of democracy,
- development of the defense and security system of Georgia,
- economic security policy,
- education policy, and more.

Education policy includes ensuring inclusive and equal education, and creating opportunities for continuous learning for all. Its integral part is higher education.

The leading role in the development of higher education in Georgia is played by the combination of institutions, i.e., norms of regulatory law, institutions, values, cultural samples, and forms of ownership. Institutions are a recognized area of progress in the system and its arrangement, institutionalization, and institutionalism.

Georgia joined the Bologna Process, which aims to bring European education systems closer together and harmonize them, creating a common European space for higher education, in May 2005. The main goal of the process is to make people and states especially aware of the role of universities in an ever-changing and growing international community (Veshapidze and Zoidze 2021).

The results of sharing this document were reflected in the new institutions of higher education in Georgia:

- Property institutions have changed, universities have become autonomous institutions, and university teaching and research have become inseparable, developing research and innovation and constantly striving for universal knowledge.
- The freedom of teachers and students in research and teaching is ensured, they enjoy the use of an environment in which it is possible to acquire culture and knowledge.

Universities promote student and teacher mobility. At the same time, universities consider the general policy of equivalent status, ranks, exams (without distrust of national diplomas) and scholarships to be an important factor in carrying out their mission in the current conditions.

The goals of higher education in Georgia are to promote the values of Georgian and world culture, to provide higher education in accordance with the interests and opportunities of the individual, to realize personal potential, to ensure the competitiveness of higher education in the domestic and foreign labor market, and to create scientific research encouragement.

To achieve these goals, the state will take appropriate measures. In particular, in order to achieve the set goals, the higher education institution (which is important together with others) provides

- ➢ access to and openness to higher education;
- ➢ academic freedom;
- ➢ access to higher education throughout life;
- ➢ involvement of academic staff, research staff and students in the decision-making process and control over its implementation;
- ➢ publicity and transparency of the management of the higher education institution and the competitions in this institution,

- prohibition of any discrimination in the field of higher education, including on grounds of academic, ethnic, social or religious affiliation and/or opinion, sex and other grounds.

The reformed education system, undergraduate, graduate and doctoral, should enable Georgian citizens in universities, training universities and colleges to make the most of their opportunities and be competitive in the Georgian and world labor markets.

To this end, the refinement and development of the higher education system is of great importance. Promoting quality higher education is one of the preconditions for increasing Georgia's scientific potential and advancing the economy. It is also important to enhance international cooperation in the field of scientific research and modern technologies.

Initially, the Law of Georgia on Higher Education contained a rigid, threatening record of the employment of academic staff at a higher education institution. In this case, we mean that a person who has reached the age of sixty-five may not have been elected to the academic position of a state-established higher education institution, and a person who has reached the age of sixty-five may have been dismissed after the expiration of his/her term.

The above entry of the law posed a threat that personnel who had reached the age of sixty-five, who had acquired the proper knowledge and accumulated extensive experience, would no longer be able to take part in the competition and hold a competitive academic position. This norm later evolved. Currently, exceptions can be established, by law, in the charter of a higher education institution.

Now, as a rule, the admission of personnel of the mentioned age to the competition is decided by the Academic Council of the higher education institution. Such a change was timely and justified. In a situation where there was no orderly, social security-oriented system, or any clearly defined priorities, this was a significant challenge.

It should be noted that such age restrictions are not imposed in Estonia, Latvia, Lithuania, or any other EU and post-Soviet countries. In EU countries, academic staff themselves decide whether to retire after reaching retirement age, where they will receive almost no less than they were paid as a result of working in an academic position.

The main thing is to select a competition commission that will ensure the holding of an academic position only through open competition, which must comply with the principles of transparency, equality and fair competition. Sufficient experience has been gained in this field in public and private higher education institutions of Georgia. This approach was developed by the adoption of the Labor Code of Georgia in the Organic Law of Georgia.

According to the new norm, the code stipulates that labor relations arise on the basis of equality of the parties, by agreement reached as a result of free expression of will.

This is also very important in labor and pre-contractual relationships, including when posting a job vacancy and at the selection stage. The code prohibits discrimination against any race, skin color, language, ethnic or social background, nationality, origin, property or rank, place of residence, age, sex, sexual orientation, disability, religious, social, political or other affiliation (including trade union affiliation), marital status, political or other views, or on any other grounds.

This law clarifies what is meant by this discrimination. According to this law, labor discrimination is the intentional or negligent discrimination or exclusion of a person based on his/her race, skin color, language, ethnic or social background, nationality, origin, property or rank, employment status, place of residence, age, sex, sexual orientation, disability, state of health, religious, social, political or other affiliation (including trade union affiliation), marital status, political or other views, or any other objective that leads to denial or encroachment of equal opportunities or treatment in employment or occupation.

6.2. The Quality of Higher Education in Georgia

The quality of higher education in Georgia is regulated by the relevant norms of quality assurance. There is a quality assurance mechanism for the systematic evaluation of the quality of teaching and research work in the higher education institution, as well as the professional development of its staff, including in the basic educational unit, which operates in accordance with the charter of the higher education institution.

Based on the connection of foreign countries and their higher education institutions with the relevant services, the quality control transparency and the methodology of their provision are formed.

Ivane Javakhishvili Tbilisi State University, Ilia State University and Georgian Technical University are mostly included in various world rankings of universities from Georgia. One of the most important world rankings is the QS World University Rankings, which uses the following indicators to compile university rankings: academic reputation, employer reputation, student-to-staff ratio, staff citation rate, foreign staff, foreign students.

Accordingly, the ranking covers the evaluation of the university teaching-learning, research and internationalization, and the reputation of the university.

Ivane Javakhishvili Tbilisi State University was ranked 601–650 in the QS World University Rankings, in 2021, and was promoted by thirty places in the 2022 rankings, being ranked 571–580. Ivane Javakhishvili Tbilisi State University is still the only university in the South Caucasus to be represented in the QS World University Rankings for the second year in a row. The Massachusetts Institute of Technology (MIT) tops the 2022 QS World University Rankings (Veshapidze and Zoidze 2021).

Achieving the desired level of education in Georgia, including higher education, is largely due to the increase in the country's GDP and, consequently, education funding. Therefore, the economic strengthening of the country, its rapid growth, will depend significantly on the education sector as a whole, including raising the level of higher education.

With the help of Georgia's strategic partners—the United States, NATO, the European Union, and the United Kingdom—there are opportunities to raise the level of higher education in the country. The real possibility of this is due to

- visa-free travel within the EU;
- dual citizenship introduced by the legislation of Georgia;
- extensive opportunities for sending students through exchange programs in Europe, setting the same tariffs for students leaving Georgia while studying there as for EU citizens;

- the Erasmus program, which is noteworthy and gives our citizens unprecedented opportunities to get an education in Europe, just like Europeans;
- add to all this the fact that Georgia was able to establish the Kutaisi International University under the conditions of the Covid pandemic.

It should be noted that, during the twenty-five-year cooperation with the World Bank, approximately $ 4.3 billion has been invested in more than one hundred projects by the bank in Georgia (Zoidze 2021).

Today, higher education slightly increases the chances of employment in Georgia and slightly improves the salary supplement. Georgia's education system does not meet the requirements of the labor market. This means that the number of Georgian students who have gone abroad to receive quality education is increasing.

International ratings show that the main challenge for Georgia's education system is internal conflict, as well as economic problems in funding educational programs. Issues related to students' socioeconomic status, living conditions, study and international mobility are important.

Despite significant progress, Georgia needs further development of institutions that will enable us to realize the potential of the higher education system effectively. This is possible through long-term education reform. Such projects are supported by the World Bank in Georgia.

Experience in American and European education is a prerequisite for a competitive, successful career—self-discipline, hard work and choosing the right strategy. Obviously, you cannot achieve anything without hard work.

Therefore, it is important to practice, work on yourself, because any person, in any position, is required to do the maximum. A person should also be able to move strategically, purposefully towards the set goal and correctly determine at each stage what is needed. It is important to motivate pupils and students so that they can learn and master knowledge independently. They need to be able to solve problems and not use tools. It will be much more effective when they themselves understand why they need the tools.

Testing knowledge in the form of current tests not only does not yield results, but also has a detrimental effect on learning. By itself, knowledge testing is needed, but not in the form of excessive test assignments.

Prestigious courses can be considered so when they teach thinking and develop the skills needed for feedback, when students can analyze their own mistakes impartially.

The World Bank Executive Board approved a financing agreement, on May 29, 2019, which was signed on June 18, within the framework of the Education Reform Project in Georgia. The project is fully in line with the World Bank's 2019–2022 Partnership Strategy and assists the Government of Georgia in implementing the Education Reform Agenda for 2018–2023.

It is important to reduce the gap between learning outcomes and labor market expectations in terms of staff qualifications.

CHAPTER 7

THE IMPACT OF EURO-ATLANTIC VALUES ON THE MODERN ECONOMY

7.1. Transformation and Priorities of Values in the Context of the Global Economy

During the last thirty years, Georgia has recognized the fundamental values that are generally accepted in many European countries. These are democracy, freedom of speech, freedom of the media, independence of the judiciary and protection of minorities.

The Georgian people have chosen Euro-Atlantic integration as the only foreign policy vision that fully aligns with our values and aspirations on the path to security, democracy, peace and prosperity. European values are natural for Georgia. Europe has concrete examples of how a small country can survive and maintain its independence on its territory (Veshapidze *et al.* 2016).

Various studies have shown that, for the average citizen, Europe is a union of rich countries where different values are adopted before they become dangerous to society. To achieve this goal, government agencies, non-governmental organizations, educational institutions and the media must work to provide relevant education and information.

Values are the eternal guide of our lives and the source of their perfection. Therefore, focusing on them is crucial. Naturally, we have questions: What benefits can the implementation of foreign values bring to the national economy? Is it possible to introduce them in other countries, for example, in Georgia?

Simply put, “value is what fits a person’s place in the world,” is something that has no independent existence (ideally), and is the determinant of every reality.

Values are the ideal we must constantly strive for, which is what society wants, which we can never achieve because the pursuit of values means the constant pursuit of perfection, which means that the existing environment should not satisfy us. We must always want better, we must be driven by the eternal urge for better, which we must constantly experience, we must constantly feel, to which we must constantly strive. Umberto Eco stated it perfectly: "I write not what people want, I write what I want people to want."

"Value" can be imagined in two ways. One part of it that is acceptable, which has passed the test in the process of its implementation and proves that we are going in the right direction or if we have chosen the wrong orientation, i.e., what we have already achieved and implemented, what is already experienced, is old and proven, sometimes called conservative. (Veshapidze 2012)

The English statesman of the eighteenth century, Edmund Burke, called the life experience that humanity had accumulated over many centuries the "mind" of humanity (Shakarishvili 2008), which is what we should want.

In addition, value has another side - a new, changeable, unproven, inexperienced, unrealized part, that is, what we also want. Values are what we can never adequately, ideally achieve. Values do not stop at one point. So be it, I would have rushed towards it and, someday, I would have achieved it but, today, whatever we want, or what we are going for, before we implement it, its "coordinates" have already changed, and, therefore, we must want it in a changed form.

In general, it should be said that there are no values in the pure form, but in the values of any of the countries there is something so eternal, traditional, which is why they are called "European," "Euro-Atlantic," "Asian," "Russian," or "Georgian" values. Take, for example, values such as personal conscience, freedom, unity, equality, justice. It is with these values that we realize what Europe is to us.

European values are universal in nature and are more or less the same for all eras, societies or states, due to the universality of eternal values such as freedom of the individual, human dignity, the rule of law, national and cultural identity, etc. (Zoidze 2021)

The value system that should contribute to the creation of a new society does not yet exist in a fully established form in Georgia.

European countries, having gone through a rather long and controversial path to establish a value system based on Christianity, have been able to set its high standards. In this way, they were able to cope relatively painlessly with all the difficulties and, at the beginning of the twenty-first century and earlier, established themselves in the first and foremost positions.

This was brought to them, first of all, by the establishment of an orderly system of values. Since these countries were the first to be able to establish the most dignified, humane and just system of values, these values can be called European or Euro-Atlantic values. It is the common values that underpin the world's most unique integration union - the European Union. It is these common values that laid the foundation for a united Europe, which was signed on March 25, 1952, with the Declaration of Rome.

European values have little to do with cultural heritage (do not neglect it in the slightest, do not violate it), and are the most effective model of life and work. First and foremost, European values are security, prosperity, peace, democracy, the rule of law and freedom of speech (Shengelia 2018).

Systematically, Georgia is still quite far from well-established values. In a sense, we can ask such a question: Europe has established a system of values based on Christianity, but isn't Georgia also based on these values? So what is the point? How is the Georgian value system different from the European one, which we aspire to?

This is related to the implementation of the value system, the maturity of approaching it, reaching its perfection, raising it to modern standards, which is faced by many circumstances in Georgia. Therefore, we need, first of all, to overcome these obstacles.

In order to improve the lives of the people, we need to put every citizen in the service of the country and work selflessly. The highest priority is to serve the most important, unique value in the world - each person.

The main focus of achieving this goal should be the solution of such priority tasks:

- Escape from the extreme hardships of most people;
- We need to develop democratic institutions, and establish justice and the rule of law;
- The country must implement large-scale reforms in all strategic directions and the government's policy must be based on the clearly

expressed interests of the Georgian people.

Until the twenty-first century, Georgia had gone through the most difficult way. The country has miraculously survived many times. In the struggle for self-determination throughout this long history, the nation has established its eternal values of survival. Consequently, the only right way to save a nation, as evidenced by long historical experience, is to strengthen national, traditional values.

At the same time, we should not forget to take into account the global factor. Full integration with the outside world has become a necessary condition for the development of the Georgian nation and, in general, everyone. That is why society needs a moderate change in values (Zoidze 2021).

This, on the one hand, is impossible without relying on a proper national foundation and, on the other hand, the foundation cannot always be solid without the necessary change due to globalization. Society needs the homogenization of national values.

Giorgi Shakarishvili, PhD in social policy, rightly stated in a letter sent from Geneva: "One glance at the history of Georgia is enough to see how diverse the influence of different ideologies, civilizations and cultures on Georgian society is." The orthodox Christian base, which originated in Byzantium, was influenced, for centuries, by the Arabs and Mongols, then by Islamic influences, followed by a communion with European culture through Tsarist Russia, which was later replaced by a historically short but strongly entrenched Soviet ideology (Shakarishvili 2008).

Naturally, such dynamism of influences could not but cause the heterogeneity of public values, as a result of which today's ordinary Georgian, according to their cultural, traditional or moral values, is a kind of hybrid in which traditional Georgian moral/natural qualities are mixed in different doses with Eastern conservatism, European liberalism and Soviet verticalism.

Each of these values is characterized by appropriate public behavioral expression. In many cases, different types of public values are inversely related to each other, which makes the solution to social behavior unpredictable and difficult/interesting.

Against the background of all this, it is probably desirable to, more or less, harmonize these values, the only right way of doing which would be to strengthen national, traditional values.

At the same time, being an integral part of today's modern world, it is also important to moderate the romantic/emotional dominance of the traditional social values in the Georgian society with the modern globalist/pragmatic component, which will help the society to fully integrate and cooperate with the outside world. This is one of the crucial factors for the development and success of the country (Ghoghoberidze 2005).

In order for this society to successfully cope with this task, it is necessary to develop such forms of relations between individuals and individuals, as well as individuals and society, society and government, such as solidarity, tolerance, trust, mutual support, and cooperation. Consequently, the society needs the development of social capital, which is, first of all, the prerogative of the educational system.

At the same time, society must overcome a kind of "thinking deficit," overcome spontaneity, emotionality, short-sightedness in making public decisions, and establish analysis and foresight. Society needs to become focused on long-term results instead of instant effects.

In addition, the society must achieve the true democracy of the country, which is determined not by how free the means of protest are, but by how active the participation of the population in the governing process is. The society needs to create a springboard for an active dialogue between the population and the government.

Giorgi Kavkasidze, chairman of the Georgian community in Switzerland, notes that there is a big difference between Western and Georgian values and thinking. The difference is that in the West, every action is result-oriented, while in Georgia it is principle-oriented. In Georgian society, relatively, Westerners are more direct and honest; there is disrespect and disobedience of the law in the Georgian society, while in the West there is a deep obedience to the law. Since the main reason for this is the difference in values, Western values must be synthesized within Georgian culture, way of life and lifestyle (Kavkasidze 2009).

Georgia is a country focused on Euro-Atlantic values. A significant part of Georgian society unanimously agrees with the country's Western course.

Therefore, at the same time, naturally, the question arises: will we lose our national values?

As Ia Antadze notes, "The most common doubts in the public consciousness are about national identity: Are Georgian traditions endangered? Will the values recognized by many generations be eroded? Protests against TV productions are especially common: 'It is impossible to show so much blood!' 'The moral of the TV series kills young people!' 'Hollywood movies instill a cult of violence!'"

The reasonable answer to these questions is that "if values change in Georgia, the level of aggression increases, or traditions are lost, we must find the reason in our own families and environments; if the role of culture is diminished or scientists feel overwhelmed, we should ask the answer to our own society and government. European integration does not endanger the country's identity, as evidenced by the experience of old or new EU member states. If the fear of losing national identity has any basis, this basis is to be found in itself and not in Europe." (Antadze 2007)

This fair reference requires that if you have ambitions to join the EU and NATO, you should also buy the right ammunition, that is, change your values in the same way that EU countries have changed. They have risen to common European values in such a way that they have integrated with each other in such a way that they have not lost their identity, eternal values and traditions, but have preserved and strengthened them on the basis of this integration.

In order for Georgian society to absorb European values, to become an organic part of it, the society will not be able to achieve this by becoming a legal entity in the European Union or NATO, it will not be able to become a real part of it. As they say: "Starting with the current culture—which should at least be reflected in the care of one's own garbage—and ending with the political culture—which should be confirmed by even one precedent of a peaceful change of government—the country seems to have a difficult path to Europe ..." (Antadze 2007)

Therefore, the main task is for Georgia to adapt its current and political culture and, in general, all its aspects to the standards of the modern civilized world as soon as possible. This is the main task of Georgia's rapid development at the stage of modern globalization. For this, it is necessary to establish the right value system in Georgia. To do this, you need to precisely define the priorities, what is important, what way to go, to plan purposeful activities. In this regard, the main role belongs to the state.

The history of Georgian culture, even its superficial review, clearly shows that Western values, including fundamental human rights, were not foreign to the Georgian world, and in this respect there was never a conflict between them. The main thing is that the Georgian society does not lose its national identity and, thus, rises to the standards of Euro-Atlantic fundamental values.

To achieve this goal, Georgia must unwaveringly strive to establish a tradition of democratic governance, strengthen state institutions, and ensure citizen participation in governing the country.

Particular attention should be paid to economic progress, to create conditions for the well-being and dignified living of each person; the democratic and peaceful development of Georgia; guarantees of the well-being, preservation of ethnic, cultural identity and inviolability of political rights for all citizens; and the unconditional, safe and dignified return of IDPs and refugees to their homes, the provision of decent living conditions for them and the protection of their rights.

7.2. European Values: What Should Be and How Should They Be Implemented in Georgia?

The identity of each nation is based on its values - their realization is achieved and reflected in them, as values are a concentrated expression of the nation's culture. If a nation loses its orientation with a different value from other nations, then it loses its face. The era of globalization is increasingly showing the attractiveness of the values of the "golden billion" countries. Does this pose a threat to the identity of the nations that share and implement their values?

Culturally backward nations will sooner or later face this threat. For a cultural nation like Georgia, it would be natural for its national culture to absorb progressive foreign values and, thus, further elevate and enrich itself.

Historical experience also shows that, even from the relatively low culture of the conquerors, the Georgian nation was able to obtain rational grains, although, on the whole, hardship caused great damage to its spirituality (Gvelesiani and Veshapidze 2016).

The pursuit of the values of the "golden billion" is natural, today, and brings more goodness than sharing foreign values in the past brought us. But it comes down to the reasons and forms in which it arises: the reasons for perfecting our own values and ourselves, whether by mere obsession and turning a blind eye to life there or by blindness. How do we imagine sharing them - are we going to blindly copy them or adapt them to the values at our roots?

Thus, the principle of which foreign values to pursue is the following: we should try to implement any progressive values that are compatible with our culture no matter what country or people they come from. Here, we will specify the task according to our topic: to find out why the spirit of Georgian culture is relatively closer to European values than to other regions and countries, including the richest, the USA.

A general comparison also shows that Western European values have deeper traditional roots, are more humane and tolerant than American values. Thus, they are more compatible with the nature of Georgia. Man himself stands on the peak of true values. He is his life, his freedom, his prosperity and his highest value. In the US, he also stands on this peak, but state policy still makes choices in favor of predominantly strong, "sluggish" people, because the country expects more benefits from them. This suggests that, in reality, their very existence is regarded as of higher value than that of the rest.

This principle has its positive side, it gives an impressive economic result for the country and, thus, an impressive example to the whole world. The principle of Western European politics is not the opposite, but it is not so linear. It is more capacious and in-depth. It strives to create a relatively equal starting position for every human being, to ensure not only their existence, but also the free development and manifestation of their talents and skills. Social policy in the US is no less effective than in Western European countries. Only its scale is relatively narrow, because this country is not building a social market economy, and the EU is exactly such an economy, "written on the flag."

Democratic values and their strengthening institutions are also stronger in Western Europe. Suffice to say that in the United States, which is called the Pillar of Democracy, local government enjoys broad legitimacy, but it is still a state structure and not a territorial (local) self-government body.

Europe is on a course of self-development. It may be thought that Western Europeans are very different in character, and that, for example, the German character may be closer to the American than to the French or Spanish. But it was German scientific thought that prepared the concept of a social market economy (which began to take shape in the era of fascism) and was first implemented by the West German government (Georgia also aimed to build a socially oriented market economy in the early years, but unfortunately this goal failed).

Let us also cite the example of antitrust legislation. This legislation is of two kinds: one prohibits monopoly, the other is more "soft," does not prohibit it but restricts it in decisions that harm society. The first, more rigid, is carried out by the US and it also extended to Japan after their defeat in World War II. But this legislation is valid within the country, otherwise most of the largest corporations represented in the world markets would be American and Japanese. Quite rightly, Georgia has taken the example of German legislation. However, here, it fails to work effectively due to the weakness of matching institutions.

Western European values are not homogeneous and many of them can be considered incompatible not only with Georgian culture, but also with each other. The benefits of globalization and economic integration, and the soft nature of Europeans, have their desired results: the European Union, which currently consists of twenty-seven sovereign states, sees diversity of values as its wealth. Diversity is also the most characteristic general sign of our era in all spheres of public life, and the Georgian nation did not even start striving for diversity today, it has been striving for it for a long time. The product of this aspiration is a unique and, at the same time, highly diverse Georgian culture, but imbued with a common national spirit. This is also one of the factors that speaks of the closeness of the soul of Georgian and Western European values.

A century and a half ago, Ilia Chavchavadze praised the relationship between Georgian and European spirituality and the kindness that the Georgian nation, and not only them but other nations, could receive by sharing advanced European values.

Ilia Chavchavadze believed that these values were universal and acceptable to everyone. To clarify this, he published letters in his "Iveria" with rubrics such as "Domestic Review," "Political Review" and others. He analyzed the content of values, such as freedom, women's rights, and moral purity (its importance for the future of the nation), discussed the goodness of the founding societies created in England, and pointed to the need to introduce an international tribunal. It is noteworthy for Georgia that "France's moral strength is in the love of the homeland."

Chavchavadze especially emphasized that "equality before the law is the cornerstone of the foundation of a decent society," that "the nation's health is one of the biggest concerns of the state," and that "there is a need for an institution where fun, interviews, leisure can be provided," etc. He saw the implementation of European values as a means of protecting the whole nation and each individual, of translating their well-being into the primary concern of the state, of achieving human rights, their life, liberty, protection of property, equality and harmony. He spoke about the need for "europeanization" of Georgian literature (i.e., its orientation towards European values).

Chavchavadze praised the example of Japan: "Japan is more courageous in this regard," he wrote. Their new ruler was a staunch supporter of European education and unwavering commitment to adapting everything to increasingly governing the country, the rule and order of Europe. "Japan today has a lot of European education ... youth ... literature, more or less winged and widespread, and who knows, Japan will be the first to rule Asia under the influence of European civilization and education will shed its radiant light from there to the whole of Asia."

The quotations refer to the category of values, the implementation or restriction of which is played by the political will and the efforts of the authorities. Ilia Chavchavadze's many other remarks, including the statement that, in order to share European experience in Georgia, order of state governance and self-government should be given priority and that legislative and economic reforms are required to do so. Values such as human rights, the rule of law and equality before it, market economy, democracy, security, etc., which do not come down from the pages and screens of the media today, belong to this category of values.

The subject of this section - which European values should be implemented and how should they be implemented in Georgia -requires the political will of the government, and its efforts. However, the sharp experience and contradictions of values accumulated in this field dictate that each such step requires "measurement a hundred times." The clause in the EU-Lisbon Treaty, according to which the EU should promote its values around the world, is also thought-provoking.

Therefore, the general conclusion of this subsection is as follows: it is better to do a scrupulous study with our European benefactors about which European values can be "planted on Georgian soil" and what is needed for them to "flourish."

We cannot say that such provisions include respect for human dignity, pluralism (diversity), inadmissibility of discrimination, tolerance, equality between women and men and those with them in the foreground in EU documents—we cannot talk about how to raise them on Georgian soil, because they are born on this soil. From the very beginning, the values of the Georgian people were such values as freedom, protection of human rights, including minority rights, and some other values mentioned in the same documents.

Georgians can be proud of all this and that is why we consider European culture close to the Georgian people. What is to be found out is under what conditions, in what form and by what means (by what institutions) they are carried out, here and there, today. Institutions were formed, there, during a long historical period, and this was done in the wake of the change/development of socioeconomic structures and the adaptation to them.

At first, the Georgians only started moving towards modern structures with zigzags, delays, paired with backwards movement. The result was various deformations of the named values and their inconsistent implementation.

The result is a sharp representation of Georgia in upholding values such as the rule of law and justice, which are also named alongside the values listed above in EU documents. Disobedience to the law began in the Soviet era, when the government could no longer restrain the growth of the shadow economy and when counterfeiting became the main source of a luxurious, or even normal, life.

The law demanded order and regulation but illegal actions prevailed in society and this controversy gave birth to a powerful corruption machine. The initial chaos of the post-Soviet period further intensified these processes. Privatization among them was carried out on an elite-kidnapping basis. If the law had long been a symbol of justice, it was paradoxical—forgiving of petty offenders, most of whom had no other means of subsistence. And the forgiveness of lawlessness, whether at the head or not, then, at least, becomes a tributary of corruption.

Time only changed the face of the corruption machine, otherwise, after small pauses, it continued to develop, and, even now, the conditions have not been created for the harmful practice mentioned to be completely eliminated from society. Social differentiation, naturally, did not deepen as a result of the market mechanism in Georgia, but as a result of injustice and, above all, this led to a systemic deformation of value orientation.

To improve the situation, the Georgian society will undoubtedly need to study and share European experience, but moving "on foot" with Europe is still a difficult mission. Neither the insufficient growth rates of the country, today, nor the level of development of the socio-economic structures established in the country will allow us to do this.

The administrative "strengthening" of legal institutions will only lead to the fact that some of the corrupt people in Georgia, who, today, are using even the most rigid methods, will "set foot" on the "civil" methods used in the West. There is corruption in the West too!

Claims that the virus of corruption can never rejoice in Finland are explained by the following valuable orientations of the Finns: Finns do not aspire to luxury - luxury is considered to be the oriental entertainment of medieval times; they view the embezzlement of budget funds as hatred of future generations; they believe that it is better for their children and grandchildren to find a way of life for themselves; and they believe that the thief will never be free because he cannot be freed from the fear of imprisonment.

It is worth spreading information about these high and beautiful values, but it would be utopian to dream that, in this way, other nations (including Georgia) will be able to "copy" them. They would not only face the current structures, but also the Georgians themselves, with their different characters to the Finns, which are suitable for these structures today.

Otherwise, we do not think that the Georgian society will fall short of any developed society in worshiping love and condemning hatred. The Georgian only prefers to donate to charity and not become its petitioner.

There is another way between these two options: a boring and, in many cases, unbearable poor life. Many traded poverty for luxury, even at the cost of great risk. This is a dangerous reserve of corruption.

We do not compare the bad and the good of the values of these two nations mentioned here. We judge only because maximalism is not a natural shortcoming of Georgians—that its ugly manifestation is due to the existing structures and conditions. Until they are changed, propaganda and tightening the law will not give us the desired result.

The solution is not to try to suppress Georgian maximalism, but to change the structures that encourage its manifestation. It seems that the case concerns extreme systemic/structural changes, but, in our opinion, we should look for the key to its solution in the development of a single democratic institution. This institution is territorial (local) self-government.

In Western Europe, it received special attention in the 1980s. Why not earlier? Earlier, in the 1930s and 1950s, the Keynesian revolution in macroeconomic theory and practice enhanced the regulatory functions of the state, leading to success before the 1970s.

The state was "aggravated" and afflicted with a disease similar to that of the Soviet state: corruption and inflexibility. At the turn of the seventies and eighties of the twentieth century, new forces came to the helm of government, and the reforms carried out by them, in particular, the statehood, also brought local self-government to the fore: the state extended its rights and delegated part of its functions to it. This undoubtedly contributed to the development of democracy, but the local apparatus became an appendage of the state apparatus: it was tasked with delivering public goods of local importance that the state could not afford.

The same model has been introduced in Georgia, since 1997, and it has become part of the corruption machine. Europe is still trying to involve the general public in self-government activities. A similar attempt has been formally made in Georgia. To be real, who would bother unselfishly, on a public basis, to take part, for example, in the networking of libraries, landscaping, cleaning, public transport or other common affairs? Such is the nature of public good: everyone wants to do their duty by someone else.

The vertical of true self-government must be directed opposite to the state vertical, from the bottom up (from the "ordinary" to the self-governing body as the executor), and is even directed where true self-government exists. This is not the case in local self-government and it cannot be (as we know from personal contacts, it is difficult in Europe as well).

It cannot be because it is state-initiated and is not "built" from below or created by the people themselves to pursue their diverse interests. For these purposes, the population forms a thousand (literally) unions, and no one thinks of synthesizing the functions of consumer-type societies and the delivery of public goods into one structure.

True self-government exists and develops beyond local government (in both consumer and other equity, partnership) societies. It was not the foundation of its existence, nor is it, today, the supply of public goods. The condition of self-government is twofold: equality of participants and their participation in common property.

The historical community was also built on this principle: whether it was free or a unit of the feudal structure, it was a territorial-economic whole with a combination of personal (private) and community property.

It is the Georgian community that has laid the foundation for most of the common Georgian national values, among which we especially mention the support in times of trouble or misery. The village cared for the widow and/or orphan and also helped run the farm.

That is, along with the economy, the community also performed a social function. The notions of democracy and self-government are closely related to each other in terms of historical community, including those of ancient or medieval cities, where the privileged strata were the subjects of self-government—patricians, guilds of merchants, and craftsmen.

The development of a market economy, the disintegration of natural resources, and the severance of much of the local economic ties have lost many functions of local self-government and weakened it. This was reflected, for example, in the fact that Napoleon replaced large historical provinces with smaller departments and, thus, strengthened his oversight of the communes.

Processes in the same direction have further developed since the middle of the twentieth century, as mentioned above. This may explain why, in the 1980s, during self-government reform, no one in Europe remembered its traditions. They were already forgotten.

The Georgian people have preserved the values that have been established in the historical community. Unfortunately, in the light of the hardships of recent decades, old neighborly and kinship relations are gradually losing their strength, but they are not yet forgotten and give rise to true self-government in small territorial units from which territorial self-government can grow in the future.

In our opinion, it is possible to implement European values related to the Georgian society in Georgia through these and similar ways and methods.

Chapter 8

Economic Policy Priorities under the COVID-19 Pandemic

8.1. New Economic Paradigm in the Context of Covid-19

The purpose of this chapter is to examine the key problems of the new economic paradigm in the context of Covid 19, as well as the state's economic function and size of intervention in the economy.

Globalization is one of the most important factors influencing a country's economic situation in the modern world (Veshapidze *et al.* 2020).

In the context of globalization, the state's most important function is not only to protect the national economy from external influences (so-called "external shocks"), which is nearly impossible today, but also to effectively participate in international economic ties and boost the country's global competitiveness. The modern state plays a crucial role in this regard. Georgia, on the other hand, must build a "Georgian model" of economy that will serve as the "core" of an economic model that will attract investment (in the real economy), create jobs, grow exports, and bring true prosperity to all Georgians (Zoidze 2021).

Today is the day when the country's economic priorities are set and the country's unique economic potential is realized, thanks to the initiative of the government. The modern economic crisis, which was sparked by the Covid pandemic, has proved that there is a way out of the current situation when the anti-crisis policy is built on increasing government intervention in the economy. In order to do this, the government and the public sector must play a greater role in crisis management.

Countries all around the world have faced several obstacles as a result of the pandemic crisis. Georgia (together with practically every other country on the planet) was severely harmed by these issues, which resulted in an economic catastrophe in 2020–2021. Excessive control of the economy, as well as its self-flow, will be ineffective in such circumstances. In the first scenario, there is a "slowdown" in economic development and a rise in regulatory body corruption, while in the second situation, there is full chaos and serious violations of consumer and investor rights. Economic changes throughout the world have proven that using the "golden interval" between these two techniques is the most beneficial.

The fact that total freedom is unachievable determines the need for government involvement. As a philosophical paradigm of social order, anarchy is practically unattainable. One person's freedom comes to an end when it threatens the freedom of another.

Determining property rights, which is impossible without the intervention of the state, is likewise difficult and vital in the above sense.

Another sector of the economy where a particularly tough challenge occurs is the monetary system, for which the government has traditionally been held responsible. In every country, the necessity for government engagement in this area is undeniable.

At this time, two major factors are influencing the state's economic role: globalization and the emergence of a post-industrial society. Globalization has increased the interdependence of a country's government in the formation and execution of its national economic policy, as well as its reliance on international (supranational) institutions. All of this, of course, reduces national governments' independence and emphasizes the necessity for standard, unified regulatory systems and agreements in one country or another (Zoidze 2021).

As a result, the question may arise: Is the function of the state weakened in the formation of economic policy in the global globe, or is the state dead?! The scientific community is mostly supportive of this viewpoint. The question is how accurate these theses are in terms of reality.

From the beginnings of ancient states, economic philosophy, mass-conscious conceptions, theological judgments, allusions to economic connections and governance, and, subsequently, political party plans arose (Veshapidze 2015).

Economic doctrine - a theoretical idea that represents the underlying rules of economic activity, depicts the interaction between its topics, and discloses the driving forces and essential variables in the formation, distribution, and exchange of wealth—can be conditionally distinguished from them. The emergence of the capitalist commodities economy is linked to economic ideology, which stretches back to the sixteenth century.

For a deeper comprehension of the new, it is necessary to revisit old notions. Modern theories cannot be fully comprehended unless they are viewed as a legacy of the past. New economic theories, on the other hand, cannot simply be refinements of previous ones. Good new theories incorporate just a portion of previous theories, with certain bits remaining unread for the time being (North 1993).

The widely recognized classification of economic theory into ancient Greek, mercantilist, physiocratic, classical, Marxist, neoclassical, institutional, Keynesian, monetary economic thought, and neoclassical synthesis is contingent on the methodological character of several schools.

A lot of well-known scientists' work has a synthesis quality to it that cannot be assigned to any of the scientific paths listed above. As a result, today's economists are attempting to establish a healthy balance of everything in their approach, a synthesis that has lasted the test of time and is still true and relevant today. It is a mix of contemporary, neo-Keynesian, and neoliberal provisions, as well as certain classical political economics postulates, with their older neoclassicists (Veshapidze 2015).

The new paradigm of economics and its teachings are founded on these postulates. This is a CORE program whose key benefit is that it replaces the economy's typical orientations with more realistic and beneficial alternative orientations. Mercantilist, classical liberal, Keynesian, social democratic, ordoliberal (West German), and neoliberal political paradigms are no longer considered as universal policies that can be applied anywhere, at any time.

Any query on this or that economic policy will be addressed accurately, according to this program, "depending on the circumstances." To gain the specifics on which the intended result is based, we need economic information and analysis. Not preconceived assumptions, contextuality, and not universality are truly helpful concepts in economic science.

There is a time for budget expansion and a time for budget limits, according to economic theory. There are moments when the government must intervene in the value chain, and other times when the government must leave the markets alone. The tax must be high at times and low at other times. In certain regions, trade should be more open, while in others, it should be more restricted. Relationships between real-world situations and the propriety of specific sorts of government involvement must be demonstrated (Zoidze and Abuselidze 2021).

Most economists in the West have recently been attempting to combine classic Smith and Marshall microeconomics with modern income-level macroeconomics in order to achieve a "neoclassical synthesis" through effective credit and monetary policies, ensuring that both approaches are still relevant today.

According to Nobel Laureate in Economics **Paul Samuelson**, **Adam Smith**'s *The Wealth of Nations* is the "birthday of political economy," and what came before it is the "prehistory of economics," a memory from the dawn of time when borrowing and lending were forbidden in state policy, and mercantilists advocated protectionist tariffs as "prince's advisers" for the sake of national prosperity, and when the physiocrats, who "believed in the cycle of economic life," hoped for "the renovation of pre-revolutionary France's old government."

Adam Smith has been hailed as a "forerunner of free competition" and a preacher of the "growing bourgeois class" by this author, and his work has been hailed as a "masterpiece" that "had a significant influence on the following century." Then, there's **T. R. Malthus's** ideas, as well as **D. Ricardo**, the "key figure of this century." That is, T. R. Malthus impacted D. Ricardo, as the population rose, by advancing the hypothesis of a drop in workers' pay.

Modern post-Keynesian economics is one of the branches of neoclassical economics. The latter was, in turn, founded on **Karl Marx**'s *Das Capital*, which was derived from earlier writings. The so-called neoclassical revolution, which established mathematical methods for assessing demand, utility, and universal economic equilibrium, as well as making political economics more "scientific," has given them due credit.

The fact that the Englishman **A. Marshall** and the American **J. B. Clark,** who contributed the most to the neoclassical revolution, grew increasingly obsessed with the glory they had attained and the high position they held in society is significant. **L. Walras** and **W. Pareto** introduced mathematics into economics, resulting in the development of fundamental economic analytical tools (Veshapidze 2015).

Political economy, on the one hand, went too far in describing the economic situation and business cycles in the years following World War II as a result of the Keynesian Revolution. The neoclassical economy of the period, on the other hand, "failed to produce sophisticated macroeconomic models suited for its highly developed microeconomics."

Only **J. M. Keynes'** fundamental *General Theory of Employment, Interest and Money*, published in 1936, prevented economic research from becoming "out of date," and Sey's legal confidence in a crisis-free society vanished (Keynes 2018).

The views of post-Keynesians produced results, which revealed themselves in the better functioning of a mixed economy during the post-Keynesian political economic period. Since World War II, there has been an enormous growth in productivity and living conditions. However, this did not address the difficulty of identifying the one and only optimal economic policy model. The necessity to choose between full employment and price stability could never be removed from society.

The Chicago School, proponents of free competition, notably **M. Friedman**, and other really "market priced" campaigners have all attempted to achieve this. After that**, J.K. Galbraith** chastised the economic orthodoxy. This was followed by the formation of the New Left school, which was critical of economic science's mainstream path. It contains so-called "radical economists" from the United States.

Over the last century, the struggle against calamities like mass unemployment and inflation has been and continues to be the most serious concern in the socioeconomic development of market economies, as well as in economic science. How can we attain full employment and consistent rise in the population's real incomes? What are the "secrets" of an economic cycle that is devoid of crises? As a result, economists developed the neoclassical synthesis.

The "neoclassical synthesis," according to Paul Samuelson, is a blend of modern, neo-Keynesian, and neoliberal premises and "truths" with its older neoclassicists, as well as certain classical political economics postulates, particularly the modern theory of income production.

8.2. Values, Education and Security under Covid-19

Given recent events, it is safe to conclude that something new in the field of economic policy has evolved.

Joe Biden, the President of the United States of America, has advocated for a significant increase in government spending on social programs, infrastructure, and the transition to a green economy. He wants to use government procurement to re-establish domestic production chains and restore manufacturing jobs in the United States. The country's finance minister, Janet Yellen, is calling for a global coordinated increase in corporate taxation. Chairman of the Federal Reserve, **Jerome Powell**, who has generally been the government's major "hawkish" on price stability, is attempting to calm inflation worries and has shown support for more budget growth (Rodrik 2021).

All of these political shifts mark a significant departure from Washington's previous position. Is all of this pointing to the birth of a new economic policy paradigm?

Economic policy in the United States and the West as a whole has been in need of reform for a long time. Since Keynesianism was seen as both erroneous and excessive state regulation, the concepts that have ruled since the 1980s (also known as the Washington Consensus, Market Fundamentalism, and Neoliberalism) first gained popularity. However, these ideals took on life of their own, resulting in a highly financialized, unequal, and unstable economy that is ill-equipped to deal with the most pressing issues of our time: climate change, social inclusion, and innovative new technology (Rodrik 2021).

Starting the essential paradigm change in terms of how we teach economics would be beneficial. Market power is regarded as important for overall economic growth by economists. One of economics' crown jewels is Adam Smith's "invisible hand" (the theory that selfish people seeking personal riches may promote communal prosperity rather than societal disaster). It is, however, profoundly irrational, which may explain why economists spend so much time lecturing about the magical power of markets.

The economy, on the other hand, is hardly a chant of praise for free markets. Furthermore, the majority of economic education emphasizes (concentrates) on how markets can lead to excessive inequality and ineffective resource allocation.

One of many possibilities is to construct ideal competitive marketplaces that harmoniously generate a stable equilibrium. Smith's model isn't the only one that exists. Nonetheless, many economists have an article-posing reflex: while contemplating any suggestion for a possible rejection of laissez-faire principles, they always regard well-functioning, competitive markets as the primary priority (non-interference in the state economy).

The new economics teaching paradigm, as well as economics itself, leads to a deeper understanding of its social implications. However, we must keep in mind that this does not constitute a new economic policy paradigm. That is exactly as it should be.

Mercantilist, classical liberal, Keynesian, social democratic, ordoliberal (West German), and neoliberal political paradigms have all had severe problems since they were considered as universal plans that could be adopted anywhere, at any time. However, the shortcomings in each of these paradigms have largely overshadowed their seminal contributions to our understanding of economic governance. As a result, opinions on the government's role in the economy fluctuated wildly between extreme optimism and pessimism (Rodrik 2021).

Making links between real-world situations and the appropriateness of various forms of government involvement is one of the reasons why the economy is doing so well. Existential challenges face our civilizations, needing new economic strategies and significant political change. The Biden administration ushered forth sweeping and long-overdue economic reforms. Those seeking a new economic paradigm, on the other hand, should exercise caution in their pursuits. We should learn to adjust our policies and institutions to changing requirements, not to develop a new frozen dogma.

Although the market's importance in the evolution of civilization is unanimously acknowledged, it is not an all-powerful phenomenon or a reliable method for solving all issues. In real life, there are many instances where the market makes errors. Zones of such market failure frequently include areas critical to society's long-term stability and development: research, education, culture, and social security (Figure 5).

Figure 5. Positive and Negative Effects of State Intervention

Positive side	Negative side
• Provide public goods that aren't available on the free market, such as law and order. • Provide vital goods and services that are underserved in the free market (e.g., education and health). • Minimize unfairness and poverty by utilizing the tax and welfare systems. • Government regulations can safeguard the environment, employees, and customers. • Ensure the long-term interests of the environment • Monopolistic power should be kept to a minimum.	• Government failures include insufficient information and time gaps. • There are little incentives in the public sector to be efficient. • Influence of major lobbying organizations on government. • Higher taxes deter people from doing what they want to do. • Welfare programs have unfavorable outcomes. • If the government owns the enterprise, there may be fewer possibilities.

Source: T. Pettinger. 2019. "Pros and Cons of Government Intervention." *Economics Help.*

The state's economic involvement in the post-industrial period is manifested in the following functions:

- regulation of natural monopoly circumstances (electricity production and distribution, telecommunications, transportation, communications, water supply, and so on);
- correcting undesirable social repercussions in the state, which should diminish social inequality, unemployment, and poverty;
- long-term economic development utilizing macroeconomic policy tools, which should be aimed at preserving the economy from crises and increasing prices.

The current situation in the EU demonstrates that various national tasks are being delegated to this greatest regional entity (for example, the development of a common monetary policy for EU countries is carried out by the European Central Bank). However, it should be highlighted that globalization causes a slew of issues, many of which are essentially unsolvable without government action (for example, regulating migration, combating the spread of drug trafficking and terrorism, controlling transnational corporations, etc.).

Striking for a high degree of income distribution equality at the state level is critical because it contributes to social stability and protects society from severe volatility and civil turmoil.

Many scholars regard achieving a specific degree of income distribution equality as increasing general public access to education, resulting in the accumulation of human capital and the creation of small businesses, which, as we have seen, play a critical role in contemporary society.

There are other equally essential facets to this problem. Expenditures on education and health care, in particular, are crucial not just in terms of the individual's growth as an independent value and the most important productive element. Emission also implies that it helps to balance the population's individual earnings.

Today, no country's government can formulate and implement economic policies without taking into account the rules of behavior of other countries and, in particular, international organizations.

Globalization is one of the primary variables impacting the state's economic position in the modern world. The most important function of the state in the context of globalization is not only to protect the national economy from external influences (so-called "external shocks"), which is virtually impossible today, but also to effectively participate in international economic ties and increase the country's global competitiveness. In this aspect, the contemporary state plays a critical role (Zoidze 2021).

Given that international economic research has yet to develop a model of budget system that is acceptable to all countries and operates with comparable efficiency, it is unsurprising that Georgia's budget system requires major modification and change, at this time. In order to find a way out of the current predicament, the government began to "copy" foreign nations' "ready-made" economic models, which is yet another conceptual blunder.

Georgia must construct a "Georgian model" of economy that will serve as the "heart" of a new economic system that would attract investment (in the real economy), generate employment, expand exports, and deliver true prosperity to all Georgians. Today is the precise time when, at the state's initiative, the country's economic priorities are created and the country's distinctive economic potential is fulfilled (Zoidze 2020).

For example, the president of the European Bank for Reconstruction and Development (EBRD) and the Government of Georgia have a goal for building and promoting Georgia as a regional transportation and freight "center" (due to the unique location of Georgia—in terms of trade and transport routes).

To make this vision a reality for Georgia, it will be necessary to establish a non-commercial "hub" with state participation—in the form of a commodity exchange—that will promote

- the demonopolization of the economy,
- the increase and activation of commodity and foreign exchange flows,
- the development of the logistics network, the optimal loading of seaports,
- and the establishment of Georgia's economic model's uniqueness.

In summary, the state's constructive "intervention" in economic processes is required, but only on one condition: that it is effective.

It's worth noting that, while the state's role and functions were formerly confined to fiscal policy, today, they're mostly viewed as one of the technological tools for affecting the economy. However, no government, regardless of its political goals and ambitions, can avoid participating in the economy and being concerned about the country's high business efficiency in any way. As a result, the state's economic mission is to promote and preserve the market economy's proper functioning, which it cannot do without meddling in the economy (Zoidze 2021).

In the face of increased competition in modern worldwide markets, the execution of a successful fiscal strategy is becoming increasingly important for the country's prosperity.

Today, the most important aim of Georgia's state budget is to protect the population's health and social security. Of course, state policy could be improved in this direction, but the focus should also be on lowering the number of socially vulnerable individuals, which implies reducing poverty. This is one of the elements of a successful budget strategy.

The state's hopeful future aspirations might be regarded as a stimulant for the economy's reproductive process. These are the key public goods that are critical for economic growth in industrialized nations, but they are insufficient in emerging countries, necessitating an active state investment strategy (e.g., investments in infrastructure, education, etc.) (Veshapidze *et al.* 2021).

According to several surveys, the most pressing concerns in Georgia are the decrease of inequality, poverty, and unemployment, as well as the creation of new private-sector jobs, without which social bonds and economic progress will be impossible to achieve. It is vital to acquire a high level of production in order to overcome these issues. It may be accomplished through successful reorganization and the creation of policies aimed at the development of human capital through the provision of high-paying jobs.

Fiscal policy has a substantial impact on the efficacy of government involvement in the economy. Prioritization of public finances has a direct impact on emerging nations' economic progress. For example, if a country's economic development is hampered by unorganized infrastructure, a non-competitive environment, private property insecurity, and so on, the government should allocate sufficient financing in this area. The budget policy is incorrect if the state does not respond properly to contemporary difficulties while having enough financial resources.

The modern, crisis-driven economic crisis has demonstrated that a route out of the current predicament is conceivable if the anti-crisis strategy is based on increased government intervention in the economy. To accomplish this, the government and the public sector must play a larger role in crisis management.

Within the country, Covid-19, like many other catastrophes, has generated fresh data and demonstrated the necessity for a development strategy with defined goals. The pandemic has demonstrated that an economy based only on market principles is unable to meet global concerns. The state continues to have the primary duty for delivering health, education, and social services. In fact, you should be in debt (Zoidze and Abuselidze 2021).

However, a new equilibrium must be found in which the private sector's freedom of action is not curtailed—rather, it is safeguarded—and the public sector's role is maintained. The goal to eliminate the public sector has proven to be foolish, as we have witnessed. But, for every dollar invested, the efficiency, flexibility, and accountability inherent in the private sector must be developed.

Based on the examination of the macroeconomic indicators in Table 4, below, it can be concluded that the Georgian economy faces a serious challenge in the form of low economic growth rates, which are unfavorable to the country. The country's GDP per capita growth is still negligible. The country's GDP has dropped by nearly 7 %, according to preliminary figures. Approaches to government intervention in the economy inevitably vary under such circumstances (Veshapidze and Zoidze 2021).

We might presume that there is a risk of a major economic catastrophe in Georgia, based on the examination of the stated macroeconomic data. It is critical to radically reassess the state's current political direction and build a new political platform in order to prevent this catastrophe and promote economic autonomy.

Table 4. Annual Data of Georgia's GDP Indicators and the Ratio of the State Budget Payments to GDP, 2015–2021*

	2015	2016	2017	2018	2019	2020	I 21*	II 21*
GDP at current prices, billion GEL	33.9	35.8	40.8	44.6	49.3	49.3	11.5	15.5
GDP at constant 2015 prices, billion GEL	33.9	34.9	36.6	38.4	40.3	37.6	8.8	11.2
Real GDP growth, %	3.0	2.9	4.8	4.8	5.0	-6.8	-4.1	28.9
GDP deflator change, %	5.8	2.6	8.5	4.4	5.2	7.3	7.9	11.6
GDP per capita (at current prices), GEL	9,109.4	9,613.9	10,933.9	11,968.0	13,239.4	13,234.1	3,081.3	4,161.4
GDP per capita (at current prices), USD	4,012.6	4,062.1	4,358.5	4,722.0	4,696.2	4,255.7	929.7	1,250.7
GDP at current prices, billion USD	14.9	15.1	16.2	17.6	17.5	15.8	3.5	4.7
State budget payments, billion GEL	9.70	10.29	11.76	12.59	13.09	14.85	-	-
Ratio of state budget payments to GDP, %	28.61	28.74	28.82	28.22	26,55	30.12	-	-

Source: Compiled according to the official data of the Ministry of Finance of Georgia and the National Statistics Office of Georgia.
Note: 2021 data are taken for I and II quarters.

Based on the aforementioned Georgian economic situation, the following practical initiatives will be tremendously successful for Georgia's long-term and steady economic development:

- Using legislative and normative actions to improve administrative control. Furthermore, it is critical to completely rewrite the Labor Code in order to preserve employees' rights to the greatest extent feasible.
- Reforming the taxation system (e.g., introducing a progressive income tax). Progressive income tax is used in a number of nations across the world, and it helps to equalize public earnings greatly. In this situation, the taxable interest rate might be anything from 15 % to 50 %.
- The exact priority areas of the economy that will be covered by state property and governance must be determined. The government's active participation in economic operations will help the country gain economic independence. All of this will, in turn, result in the development of new employment.
- It is critical to establish a variety of economic regulations (e.g., subsidies). Direct and indirect export subsidy programs that are well-targeted can have a significant influence on a country's long-term strategic growth. The appropriate creation and execution of subsidy programs, on the other hand, can solve the state's fundamental socioeconomic issues.
- The utilization of offshore zones as a tool for Georgia's economic growth is critical. As is well known, this method envisions a tax structure that is either zero or symbolic, which is one of the primary attractions for foreign investment. For this, we must set up offshore zones in Georgia, which will necessitate as much varied infrastructure development as feasible. The successful execution of this project in these offshore zones will help the strengthening of the region's infrastructure, as well as the quick influx of foreign direct investment into the nation and the creation of new employment.

The major purpose of government involvement in the economy is to properly display the best aspects of the market economy. However, there are many examples of disastrous failures when the market itself might have better addressed the problems that developed, in addition to effective initiatives that interfere in the state economy.

Regardless of these examples, the state's economic control has always been strategic and tactical. There are and will always be state problems in any country that are either not handled by the supply-demand mechanism or have undesirable side consequences. On the basis of the occurrence of such circumstances, a set of free market economic measures is being constructed through state economic programming and regulatory mechanisms (Veshapidze and Zoidze 2021).

Economics is a science that is notoriously wrong. As a result, rather than reliable forecasting or correct information, the reproduction process is heavily reliant on product sales projections. In reality, this helps to explain why there are so many crisis times. That is why the state supports economic growth by producing the major public goods (future optimism), and why the state's economic capacity may be linked to the factors of production.

Furthermore, the population must have access to the following essential social rights: social protection, employment, housing, health care, and education. These rights are frequently inaccessible to those who need them the most.

Employment is a crucial part of exercising fundamental human rights and participating in civic life. At the same time, the most significant aspects in the battle against poverty are universal access to employment and the provision of appropriate working conditions for society. As a result, each state attempts to assist as many people as possible in moving from a passive to an active position in the economic process through social safety programs and the development of economic ties. This is where the need to invest in everyone's education comes into play, because a knowledge-based economy will be the most crucial component in future economic growth.

In light of the foregoing, it is vital to rethink and modify the state's position and rights in modern economic interactions. During the reform, the need to establish the state as a driver of economic prosperity should be underlined. It should also involve legislative efforts such as worker safety compliance, minimum wage regulation, and social dispute resolution, among others.

BIBLIOGRAPHY

1. Abesadze, Ramaz. 2018. "Modern Trend of Economic Development." *Modern Tendencies of Development of Economy and Economic Science*: 11.
2. Abesadze, Ramaz, and Vakhtang Burduli. 2018. "Modern Global Trends and Sustainable Development Problems." *Transformacje*.
3. Abuselidze, George, and Gia Zoidze. 2022. "Tomorrow's Economic Wealth: Dilemmas of Education System."
4. Abuselidze, George, and Gia Zoidze. 2021. "The Gravity of Cryptocurrency and Prospects in a Post-Pandemic Economy." In *SHS Web of Conferences*, vol. 126. France: EDP Sciences. https://doi.org/10.1051/shsconf/202112604001.
5. Abuselidze, George, and Lela Mamaladze. 2020. "The Impact of the COVID-19 Outbreak on the Socio-Economic Issues of the Black Sea Region Countries." In *International Conference on Computational Science and Its Applications*, 453–67. New York: Springer Cham.
6. Abuselidze, George. 2014. "Global Competitiveness and Economic Sovereignty of Some Compatibility Issues with Modern Conditions." *International Conference on Critical Issues in Business and Economics (ICIBE 2014)*.
7. Aleksandrova, E., and S. Barbasheva. 2020. "Modern Educational Technologies in the Teaching Foreign Languages to Postgraduate Students." *Sciences of Europe* 60 (4): 48–51.
8. Antadze, Ia. 2007. "What is the distance to Europe? *Radio Liberty*.
9. Asatiani, Rozeta. 2014. *Where Does Georgia Go? The Conceptual Analyses of Social-Economic Development*. Siakhle: Publishing House.
10. Asatiani, Rozeta. 1993. *Services and Market System*. Tbilisi: TSU.
11. Barak, Moshe, and Givi Bedianashvili. 2021. "Systematic Inventive Thinking (SIT): A Method for Innovative Problem Solving and New Product Development." *Proceedings on Engineering* 3 (1): 111–22.

12. Başar, S., A. A. Çelik and T. Bayramoğlu. 2018. *Selected Studies on Economics and Finance*. Newcastle, UK: Cambridge Scholars Publishing.
13. Bedianashvili, Givi. 2018. "Knowledge Economy, Entrepreneurial Activity and Culture Factor in Modern Conditions of Globalization: Challenges for Georgia." *Globalization and Business* 5: 32–37.
14. Bedianashvili, Givi. 2017. "Formation of Knowledge Economy and Innovative Entrepreneurial Policy: Institutional Aspects." *Globalization and Business*.
15. Bedianashvili, Givi. 2016. "The Global Business Environment, European Integration and the Cultural Potential of Social-Economic Development of Georgia." *Globalization and Business*.
16. Berishvili, Khatuna. 2017. "Identification of Integration Processes in Conditions Economic Turbulence and their Use in Development of the Countries with Small Economy." *EcoForum* 6 (2): 0–0.
17. Berishvili Khatuna. 2016. "Formalized Cross-Cultural Analysis of Mental Determinants and Their Influence on International Business." *International Journal of Management and Applied Science* 2 (5).
18. Blaug, Mark. 1997. *Economic Theory in Retrospect*. Cambridge: Cambridge University Press.
19. Bogdanowicz, Maureen S., and Elaine K. Bailey. 2002. "The Value of Knowledge and the Values of the New Knowledge Worker: Generation X in the New Economy." *Journal of European industrial training*.
20. Bond, Michael H. 1988. "Finding Universal Dimensions of Individual Variation in Multicultural Studies of Values: The Rokeach and Chinese Value Surveys." *Journal of Personality and Social Psychology* 55 (6): 1009.
21. Borisov, E. F. 2017. *Fundamentals of Economics: A Textbook and a Practical Course for SPO*. Reprint and Additional. Moscow: Yurayt Publ.
22. Boswell, Jonathan. 2013. *Community and the Economy: The Theory of Public Co-operation*. Abingdon, Oxfordshire: Routledge.
23. Bozeman, Barry, and Japera Johnson. 2015. "The Political Economy of Public Values: A Case for the Public Sphere and Progressive

Opportunity." *The American Review of Public Administration* 45 (1): 61–85.

24. Brown, S. 2010. "Education and Economic Security." In *Ohio: College Presidents Conference.*
25. Brownell, Philip, ed. 2019. *Handbook for Theory, Research, and Practice in Gestalt Therapy.* Newcastle, UK: Cambridge Scholars Publishing.
26. Buzan, Barry. 1991. "New Patterns of Global Security in the Twenty-First Century." *International Affairs* 67 (3): 431–51.
27. Buzan, Barry. 2008. *People, States and Fear: An Agenda for International Security Studies in the Post-Cold War Era.* Colchester, UK: ECPR Press.
28. Chang, Seohee. 2018. "Experience Economy in Hospitality and Tourism: Gain and Loss Values for Service and Experience." *Tourism Management* 64: 55–63.
29. Chavchavadze, Ilia. 1955. *Complete Collection of Essays in 10 Volumes. Volume V.* Tbilisi: State Publishing.
30. Fedoryshyna, Lidiia. 2020. "The Mechanism of Fiscal Policy." *Three Seas Economic Journal* 1 (1): 28–32.
31. Fisher, E., and Fernando Vega-Redondo. 2006. "The Linchpins of a Modern Economy." In *AEA Annual Meeting, Chicago, IL.*
32. Frangishvili, Iago. 2004. "Systems Approach, System Thinking and Management Issues." "Comment" no 1 (Winter).
33. Franke, George R., and S. Scott Nadler. 2008. "Culture, Economic Development, and National Ethical Attitudes." *Journal of Business Research* 61 (3): 254–64.
34. Gechbaia, B., and V. Koval. 2021. "Entrepreneurial Activity in the Conditions of Implementation of the Public-Private Partnership." *The authors are responsible for the content and language of their papers*: 91.
35. Gechbaia, Badri. 2015. "Teamwork, Some of the Issues in Modern Management." *Глобальне управління та економіка* 1: 191–93.
36. Ghoghoberidze, Lana. 2005. "Europe of 800 Million Europeans." *24 Hours* 97.
37. Grobnev, L., and R. Nureyev. 2000. *Economy. Basics Course: Textbook.* Moscow, Russia: Vita-Press.

38. Gvelesiani, Merab, and Shota Veshapidze. 2016. "European Values: What Can We Implement from Them and How Can We Implement Them in Georgia." *Globalization and Business*.
39. Gvishiani, Zurab. 2014. *Economics: Structural-Logical Schemes. Auxiliary Guide*. Tbilisi: Meridian.
40. Hall, Stephen, and Timothy J. Foxon. 2014. "Values in the Smart Grid: The Co-Evolving Political Economy of Smart Distribution." *Energy Policy* 74: 600–09.
41. Harrison, Lawrence E. 1992. *Who Prospers: How Cultural Values Shape Economic and Political Success*. New York: Basic Books.
42. Harvey, Jack, and Ernie Jowsey. 2007. *Modern Economics: An Introduction*. London, UK: Macmillan International Higher Education.
43. Hellevik, Ottar. 2003. "Economy, Values and Happiness in Norway." *Journal of Happiness Studies* 4 (3): 243–83.
44. Hofstede, Geert, and Michael Harris Bond. 1988. "The Confucius Connection: From Cultural Roots to Economic Growth." *Organizational Dynamics* 16 (4): 5–21.
45. Hofstede, Geert. 1984. *Culture's Consequences: International Differences in Work-Related Values*. Vol. 5. Thousand Oaks, California: Sage.
46. Horrigan, Brenda L., Theodore Karasik and Rennison Lalgee. 2008. "Security Studies:" 1892–900.
47. Huntington, Samuel P. 2000. "The Clash of Civilizations?" In *Culture and Politics*, 99–118. New York: Palgrave Macmillan.
48. Huntington, Samuel P., and Robert Jervis. 1997. "The Clash of Civilizations and the Remaking of World Order." *Finance and Development-English Edition* 34 (2): 51–51.
49. Iastremska, Olesia, and Oleksandra Kononova. 2021. "Forecasting of the Tourism Industry Development and the COVID-19 Pandemic Consequences: Geographical and International Orientation." *Three Seas Economic Journal* 2 (2): 54–61.
50. Inglehart, Ronald. 2000. "Culture and Democracy. Culture Matters: How Values Shape the Human Progress. L. Harrison y S."
51. Inglehart, Ronald, and Wayne E. Baker. 2000. "Modernization, Cultural Change, and the Persistence of Traditional Values." *American Sociological Review*: 19–51.

52. Inglehart, Ronald. 1997. *Modernization and Postmodernization: Cultural, Economic, and Political Change in 43 Societies*. New Jersey, US: Princeton University Press.
53. Kavkasidze, Giorgi. 2009. "What Needs to Change in Georgia?" *24 Hours* 83: 2121.
54. Keynes, J. M. 2018. "The General Theory of Employment, Interest, and Money." New York: Springer.
55. Kharitonashvili, Jemal. 2019. "History of Economic Thought." Tbilisi: Ivane Javakhishvili Tbilisi State University Publishing House.
56. Khoshtaria, Tornike, Davit Datuashvili and Arian Matin. 2020. "The Impact of Brand Equity Dimensions on University Reputation: An Empirical Study of Georgian Higher Education." *Journal of Marketing for Higher Education* 30 (2): 239–55.
57. Kostyukov, V.N. 1976. *Scientific Research Methodology*. Kiev.
58. Kozyrev, Vitaly. 2000. *Fundamentals of Modern Economics: Textbook*. 2nd ed. Revised. Moscow: Finance and Statistics.
59. Lee, Roger. 2006. "The Ordinary Economy: Tangled Up in Values and Geography." *Transactions of the Institute of British Geographers* 31 (4): 413–32.
60. Liñán, Francisco, and José Fernandez-Serrano. 2014. "National Culture, Entrepreneurship and Economic Development: Different Patterns across the European Union." *Small Business Economics* 42 (4): 685–701.
61. Lordkipanidze, Revaz. 2019. "Confirmations about Need of Real World Market." *International Charity Scientific-Research Partnership of Physical Persons* 16.
62. Lordkipanidze, Revaz. 2019. "I See Future Unprecedented Scientific Jump of World Economy." *Tbilisi, General Coordinator of International Charity Scientific-Research Partnership, As E-Book,* 11.
63. Lordkipanidze, Revaz. 2019. "Usefulness and Harms of Economic Unions on Examples of the European Union (Historically Needed) and the Former USSR ('Sweet' Horror)." *Tbilisi, General Coordinator of International Charity Scientific-Research Partnership, As E-Article,* 9.

64. Makalatia, Givi. 2020. “The Role of Budget Policy in Economic Growth on the Example of Georgia.” Tbilisi: TSU.
65. Mankiw, N. Gregory. 2014. *Principles of Economics*. Boston, MA: Cengage Learning.
66. Mekvabishvili, Elguja. 2016. “Unity of Globalization and Modernization–The Modern Economic Development Paradigm.” *Globalization & Business*.
67. Movsesian, A. G., and S. B. Ognivtsev. 2001. *World Economy: A Textbook*. Moscow: Finances and Statistics.
68. Nadareishvili, Giorgi. 2005. *History of the Georgian State and Law*. Tbilisi: Bona Causa.
69. North, Douglas. 1991. “On the Costs of SME Entities to Submit Statistical Reports.” *Institutions. Journal of economic perspectives* 5: 97–112.
70. North, Douglass C. 1993. “Institutions and Economic Performance.” In *Rationality, Institutions and Economic Methodology*, 253–73. Abingdon, Oxfordshire: Routledge.
71. O’Brien, Martin. 1999. “Rubbish Values: Reflections on the Political Economy of Waste.” *Science as Culture* 8 (3): 269–95.
72. Panaskertel-Tsitsishvili, O. 2010. “Liberalism—the Savior of the World, if—Vice Versa.” *Republic of Georgia* 130.
73. Papava, Vladimer. 2020. “Coronomic Crisis: When the Economy is a Hostage to Medicine.” *Eurasia Review*.
74. Papava, Vladimer. 2020. “On the COVID-19 Pandemic Economic Crisis and the Reorientation of the Georgian Economy.” *Reflecting on a Changed World*.
75. Papava, Vladimer. 2017. “Primitivism as a Trait of Georgia’s Modern Economic Policy.” *Central Asia-Caucasus Analyst*.
76. Papava, Vladimer. 1994. “The Role of the State in the Modern Economic System.” *Problems of Economic Transition* 37 (5): 35–48.
77. Pavlovych, L., I. Kamyshna and T. Bakaliuk. 2021. “Improvement of Organization of Independent Work of Students.” *Sciences of Europe* 79 (3): 18–19.
78. Pettinger, Tejvan. 2019. “Pros and Cons of Government Intervention.” *Economics Help*.

79. Phelps, Edmund S. 2007. "Macroeconomics for a Modern Economy." *American Economic Review* 97 (3): 543–61.
80. Popova, Irina, and Nataliya Demchenko. 2020. "Territorial Societies Features: European Experience." *Three Seas Economic Journal* 1 (1): 20–27.
81. Qoqiauri, Lamara, Badri Gechbaia and Nino Qoqiauri. 2021. "Theoretical Aspects of the Innovation Ecosystem."
82. Reed, Darryl, and John Justin McMurtry, eds. 2008. *Co-operatives in a Global Economy: the Challenges of Co-operation across Borders*. Newcastle, UK: Cambridge Scholars Publishing.
83. Rodrik, Dani. 2021. "Beware Economists Bearing Policy Paradigms." *The World's Opinion Page: Project Syndicate.*
84. Samuelson, Paul A., and William D. Nordhaus. 2010. "Economics (19. Aufl.)."
85. Samuelson, Paul Anthony. 1966. *The Collected Scientific Papers of Paul A. Samuelson*. Vol. 2. Cambridge, Massachusetts: MIT Press.
86. Samuelson, P. A. 1954. "The Pure Theory of Public Expenditure." *The review of economics and statistics* 36 (4): 387–89.
87. Schwartz, Shalom H., and Wolfgang Bilsky. 1987. "Toward a Universal Psychological Structure of Human Values." *Journal of Personality and Social Psychology* 53 (3): 550.
88. Schwartz, S. H., and W. Bilsky. 1987. "Toward a Theory of the Universal Structure and Content of Values." *Journal of Personality and Social Psychology* 5.
89. Schwartz, Shalom H., and Maria Ros. 1995. "Values in the West: A Theoretical and Empirical Challenge to the Individualism-Collectivism Cultural Dimension." *World Psychology* 1 (2): 91–122.
90. Schwartz, Shalom H., and Anat Bardi. 1997. "Influences of Adaptation to Communist Rule on Value Priorities in Eastern Europe." *Political psychology* 18 (2): 385–410.
91. Shakarishvili, G. 2008. "Public Broadcaster Reform: The Role of the Mass Media in National Construction." *24 hours* 31.
92. Shengelia, T., K. Berishvili and K. Jganjgava. 2021. "Anti-Crisis Strategy Caused by Uncertainty of the Small Businesses under the Covid-19 Pandemic." *Sciences of Europe* 81–82: 3–6.

93. Shengelia, Temur. 2018. "Influence of Cultural Determinants on the Process of Business Innovations Management." *Ecoforum Journal* 7 (1).

94. Shengelia, Temur. 2017. "Interpersonal and Organizational Trust, as Factor of Social Capital, and its Influence on the Motivation of International Company Employees." *Ecoforum* 6 (2): 0–0.

95. Shengelia, Teimurz. 2016. "Generation of Knowledge Into Conception of Cultural Pragmatizm and its Influence on International Business." *Ecoforum Journal* 5 (2).

96. Shengelia, Teimuraz. 2013. "Metamorphoses and Results of Business Development in Georgia." In Materials of reports made at the International Scientific-Practical Conference held at Paata Gugushvili institute of Economics of Ivane Javakhishvili Tbilisi State University in, 74–78.

97. Shengelia, Teimuraz. 2012. "Globalization and International Business Environment in Georgia." In TSU, Collection of International Scientific-Practical Conference.

98. Shiplett, Myra Howze, Wendy Russell, Anne M. Khademian and L. Peters Gant. 2011. "A Well-Educated Workforce: Vital Component of National and Economic Security." *Economic Security: Neglected Dimension of National Security*: 83-97.

99. Sichinava, Alexander, Medea Chikava, Shota Veshapidze, Dali Sekhniashvili and Nino Pailodze. 2013. "Realities of Internationalization of Higher Education in Georgia."

100. Silagadze, A. 2008. *Origin of Liberal Economic Doctrines*. Tbilisi: Innovation.

101. Silagadze, Avtandil, and Tamaz Zubiashvili. 2016. "Georgia's Economy against the Background of the Associate Agreement with the European Union." *International Journal of Business and Management Studies* 5 (2): 533–40.

102. Siwińska, J. 2007. "Sektor Publiczny w Gospodarce." *Ekonomia dla prawników i nie tylko.* Warszawa: Wydawnictwo Prawnicze LexisNexis.

103. Sjöblom, Paula, Ulla Hakala and Terhi Ainiala, eds. 2014. *Names in the Economy: Cultural Prospects*. Newcastle, UK: Cambridge Scholars Publishing.

104. Steiner, Philippe. 2009. "Who Is Right about the Modern Economy: Polanyi, Zelizer, or Both?" *Theory and Society* 38 (1): 97–110.
105. Stratton, Jon. 2011. *Uncertain Lives: Culture, Race and Neoliberalism in Australia*. Newcastle, UK: Cambridge Scholars Publishing.
106. Tabatadze, Shalva. 2015. "Teachers' Approaches to Multicultural Education in Georgian Classrooms." *Journal for Multicultural Education*.
107. Tabellini, Guido. 2010. "Culture and Institutions: Economic Development in the Regions of Europe." *Journal of the European Economic association* 8 (4): 677–716.
108. Taylor, Steven. 2019. *The Psychology of Pandemics: Preparing for the Next Global Outbreak of Infectious Disease*. Newcastle, UK: Cambridge Scholars Publishing.
109. Tchania, Maia. 2017. "Modification of the State Role in the Conditions of Economic Globalization." Ivane Javakhishvili Tbilisi State University, Faculty of Economics and Business, Proceedings of the II International Scientific Conference—"Challenges of Globalization in Economics and Business," Tbilisi.
110. Tchania, Maia. 2016. *Entrepreneurship—As a Starting Point for Economic Development of the Country*. Tbilisi: Universal.
111. Toynbee, Arnold J. 1987. *A Study of History: Volume I: Abridgement of Volumes I–VI*. Vol. 1. Oxford, UK: Oxford Paperbacks.
112. Tsiklauri, M. 2016. "PISA Tests and their Impact on Georgian Education System."
113. Tukhashvili, Mirian. 2018. "Retrospective Comprehension of Post-Soviet Georgia's Population Migration." *Bull. Georg. Natl. Acad. Sci* 6 (2): 175–82.
114. Tvalchrelidze, Alexander, and Avtandil Silagadze. 2013. "Macroeconomic Model for Oil-Exporting Countries." *Central Asia and the Caucasus (14046091)* 14 (4).
115. Uplisashvili G. 2012. "Fixed Taxation Regime in Georgia." In Proceedings of the International Scientific-Practical Conference: "Problems of Sustainable Economic Development: Reality and Perspectives," Kutaisi University, Kutaisi.

116. Vermeij, Geerat J. 2009. "Comparative Economics: Evolution and the Modern Economy." *Journal of Bioeconomics* 11 (2): 105–34.
117. Veshapidze, Paata. 2004. "The Absence of a Free Press is Tyranny." *24 Hours* 121: 670.
118. Veshapidze, Shota. 2020. "Religion and National Values in Georgia." In *World Economy and International Economic Relations*, vol. 3, 33–36.
119. Veshapidze, Shota. 2018. "Economic Vision of the Human Values." *Smarty*.
120. Veshapidze, Shota. 2017. "The Traditions Orientated on European Values in Georgia." *Sciences of Europe* 13, 4 (13): 14–18.
121. Veshapidze, Shota. 2015. "Economic Science Teaching Methodology: What Should Be Considered as the Right Direction of Interference in Life, or What Can and What Cannot Be Done." *The New Economist* (2).
122. Veshapidze, Shota. 2012. "Human Values and Value Orientations of the Economy." Digital Library "Iveriel."
123. Veshapidze, Shota, and Nugzar Babuadze. 2010. "The Role of Value in the Modernization of Economy." Materials of reports made at the International Scientific-Practical Conference held at Paata Gugushvili Institute of Economics.
124. Veshapidze, Shota, Nugzar Babuadze, and Tamari Beridze. 2015. "Nobel Prize Laureate in Economy Simon S. Kuznets about Actual Problems of a Sustainable Development of National Economy." In Materials of reports made at the International Scientific-Practical Conference held at Paata Gugushvili Institute of Economics of Ivane Javakhishvili Tbilisi State University, 79.
125. Veshapidze, Shota, Ketevan Chiabrishvili, Tamaz Zubiashvili and Gia Zoidze. 2021. "On the Relationship between Education and Economic Security." *Ecoforum Journal* 10 (3).
126. Veshapidze, Shota, Mariam Darbaidze and Tamar Beridze. 2016. "Euro-Atlantic Values: What Tie up Us:" 230–35.
127. Veshapidze, Shota, and Shota Karalashvili. 2018. "Pension Reform in Georgia." *Ecoforum Journal* 7, no. 2.
128. Veshapidze, Shota, and Zurabi Mchedlishvili. 2020. "From Ilia Chavchavadze's Economic Views: Competition, Private Property

and International Trade." *Ecoforum Journal* 9, no. 2.

129. Veshapidze, Shota, and Dali Sekhniashvili. 2021. "The Importance of Capital Market Development for Improving the Investment Ecosystem in Georgia." *World Economy and International Economic Relations.*
130. Veshapidze, Shota, and Gia Zoidze. 2022. "On State Intervention in the Economy through the Budget in Georgia." In *World Economy and International Economic Relations. International Scientific Collection* Vol. 5. Kyiv: CUL.
131. Veshapidze, Shota, and Gia Zoidze. 2021. "Institutional Evolution of Higher Education in Georgia." *The New Economist* 16 (2): 1–1. DOI: 10.36962/NEC6102202133.
132. Veshapidze, Shota, Gia Zoidze and Khatuna Berishvili. 2021. "The Economic Determinant of the Education System." *Sciences of Europe* 81–82: 6–12. DOI: 10.24412/3162-2364-2021-81-2-6-12.
133. Veshapidze, Shota, Gia Zoidze and Elza Vekua. 2020. "The Challenges of COVID-19 and the Economic Role of the State in the Context of Globalization." *Social Economics: XXI Century's Actual Problems.*
134. Veshapidze, Shota, and Tamaz Zubiashvili. 2020. "About the Origins of Modern Geoeconomic Foundations of Georgia." *Ecoforum Journal* 9, no. 2.
135. Weber, Max, and Stephen Kalberg. 2013. *The Protestant ethic and the spirit of capitalism*. Abingdon, Oxfordshire: Routledge.
136. Winck, Ben. 2021. "Nobel Prize-Winning Economist Paul Krugman Explains Why He's More Left-Wing than the Modern Monetary Theory Crowd." *Business Insider*.
137. Yadgarov I. S. 2014. "History of Economic Doctrines." In *textbook, edited by Academician A. Silagadze.* Tbilisi.
138. Yasin, Evgeny. 2003. "Economy Modernization and the System of Values." *VOPROSY ECONOMIKI* 4.
139. Zak, Paul J., and Michael C. Jensen. 2010. "Moral Markets: The Critical Role of Values in the Economy."
140. Zoidze, Gia. 2021. "Importance of Euro-Atlantic Integration: Democracy, Security and Economic Development." *Three Seas Economic Journal* 2 (3): 1–7.

https://doi.org/10.30525/2661-5150/2021-3-1.

141. Zoidze, G. 2021. *Basic Paradigms of Institutional Economics*. Tbilisi: Universal, 202
DOI: 10.5281/zenodo.5544934.

142. Zoidze, Gia, and George Abuselidze. 2021. "Covid-19 Pandemic And Currency Risk Analysis In Georgia." *Entrepreneurship* 9 (2): 33–46. DOI:10.37708/ep.swu.v9i2.3.

143. Zoidze, Gia, and Shota Veshapidze. 2022. "Transformation of Economic Policy Priorities Under Covid-19." *Three Seas Economic Journal* 3(2), 35-43.

144. Zoidze, Gia. 2020. "Georgian Agro-Sphere Development Priorities and Ways of Carrying Out Some Improvements." *Myśl Ekonomiczna i Polityczna* 2 (69): 55–71.
DOI: 10.26399/meip.2(69).2020.10/g.zoidze.

145. Zoidze, G. 2020. "Risks Caused by Pandemics and Anti-Crisis Management. Ivane Javakhishvili Tbilisi State University, Paata Gugushvili Institute of Economics." In *Proceedings of Materials of International Scientific Conference Dedicated to the 115th Birth Anniversary of Academician Paata Gugushvili*: 190–95.
DOI: 10.5281/zenodo.5544942.

146. Zubiashvili, Tamaz, and Shota Veshapidze. 2019. "Labour Emigration and Employment in Georgia." *Humanities and Social Sciences Review* 9 (1): 127–36.

147. Zubiashvili, Tamaz, and Tamar Atanelishvili. 2017. "Some Aspects of National Economic Doctrine." *Ecoforum Journal* 6 (1).

148. Zubiashvili, T. 2012. "Educational and Labor Emigration of Youth from Georgia." In *Youth Employment: Challenges and Opportunities*. The West University of Timisoara, Romania: Eurostampa, 317–27.

149. Galt & Taggart, Education Sector in Georgia. Georgia Education, Sector Review July 28, 2020. Bochorishvili E., Peranidze N. (In Georgian). Available at:
https://galtandtaggart.com/upload/reports/14673.pdf (Accessed: 15 December 2021).

150. Georgia is one of the countries with the worst education system - education system by country. (2021). Available at:

essentials

essentials liefern aktuelles Wissen in konzentrierter Form. Die Essenz dessen, worauf es als „State-of-the-Art" in der gegenwärtigen Fachdiskussion oder in der Praxis ankommt. *essentials* informieren schnell, unkompliziert und verständlich

- als Einführung in ein aktuelles Thema aus Ihrem Fachgebiet
- als Einstieg in ein für Sie noch unbekanntes Themenfeld
- als Einblick, um zum Thema mitreden zu können

Die Bücher in elektronischer und gedruckter Form bringen das Expertenwissen von Springer-Fachautoren kompakt zur Darstellung. Sie sind besonders für die Nutzung als eBook auf Tablet-PCs, eBook-Readern und Smartphones geeignet. *essentials:* Wissensbausteine aus den Wirtschafts-, Sozial- und Geisteswissenschaften, aus Technik und Naturwissenschaften sowie aus Medizin, Psychologie und Gesundheitsberufen. Von renommierten Autoren aller Springer-Verlagsmarken.

Weitere Bände in dieser Reihe http://www.springer.com/series/13088

Henning Fouckhardt

Lehren und Lernen

10 Tipps aus der Praxis

Springer Spektrum

Henning Fouckhardt
Technische Universität Kaiserslautern
Kaiserslautern, Deutschland

ISSN 2197-6708 ISSN 2197-6716 (electronic)
essentials
ISBN 978-3-658-18063-8 ISBN 978-3-658-18064-5 (eBook)
DOI 10.1007/978-3-658-18064-5

Die Deutsche Nationalbibliothek verzeichnet diese Publikation in der Deutschen Nationalbibliografie; detaillierte bibliografische Daten sind im Internet über http://dnb.d-nb.de abrufbar.

Springer Spektrum

Springer Spektrum ist Teil von Springer Nature
Die eingetragene Gesellschaft ist Springer Fachmedien Wiesbaden GmbH
Die Anschrift der Gesellschaft ist: Abraham-Lincoln-Str. 46, 65189 Wiesbaden, Germany

Denen gewidmet, die sich wirklich Mühe geben

Was Sie in diesem *essential* finden können

- Welche Details für die Lehre und das Lernen wichtig sind
- Welche Relevanz Üben und Konzentration für das Lernen hat
- Wieso der leichteste Weg der falsche sein kann

Vorwort und Überblick

Dieses Buch ist kein Fachbuch der Didaktik, sondern entstand aus dem Wunsch, Erfahrungen aus einer 25-jährigen Lehrtätigkeit in den Natur- und Ingenieurwissenschaften an zwei deutschen Universitäten wiederzugeben und Schlüsse zu ziehen.

Die Folgerungen widersprechen teilweise der heute weit verbreiteten Denkweise, Lernen müsse und könnte – wenn sich die Lehrenden nur richtig Mühe geben würden – in jeder Minute eine einzige Freude sein. Diese Vorstellung ist ein Irrglaube und seine Verbreitung erschwert die Lehre zunehmend, da sie bei Schülern/Studierenden und deren Eltern eine falsche Erwartungshaltung gegenüber den Lehrenden weckt. Lernen und Studieren hat immer viel mit (teilweise auch mühevoller) Eigenleistung der Lernenden zu tun: Lesen, Zuhören, Mitdenken, Fragenstellen, Diskutieren. Den Nürnberger Trichter, über den die Lernenden mühelos Wissen, Fertigkeiten und Kompetenzen in sich „einfüllen" lassen können, gibt es nicht.

Die zunehmende Demokratisierung der Gesellschaft hat zu der Forderung nach *Transparenz* aller Entscheidungen und Handlungen geführt – zumindest im öffentlichen Bereich. Und dies ist auch gut so. In den Schulen und Hochschulen führt diese Forderung nach Transparenz und – damit verbunden – auch nach Mitgestaltungsmöglichkeiten dazu, dass sich die Lehrenden Autorität und Respekt erst erwerben müssen. Lernmethoden & -inhalte werden ständig von verschiedenen Seiten (Schülern/innen, Studierenden, Eltern, Bildungspolitikern/innen, Journalisten/innen, ...) infrage gestellt.

Einerseits ist dies gut; denn es kann und sollte dazu führen, dass die Lehrenden immer wieder über diese Themen nachdenken, ihre eigenen Vorgehensweisen überdenken und neuen Gegebenheiten und Möglichkeiten anpassen. Andererseits bringt dies eine Unruhe in die Lehre, die auch der Sache abträgliche Aspekte beinhaltet. Vergessen wir nicht, dass ein 18-Jähriger nicht wissen kann, was er im

Alter von 35 Jahren im Beruf an Wissen, Fertigkeiten und Fähigkeiten brauchen wird, auch wenn ihm mit 18 ganz sicher erscheint, dass er diesen und jenen Stoff niemals in seinem Leben wird nutzen können!

Die Forderung nach Transparenz & Mitgestaltungsmöglichkeiten darf nicht dazu führen, dass Lernende jeden schwierigen Lerninhalt infrage stellen oder gar ablehnen dürfen, sodass sich Lehrende letztlich nicht mehr an die schwierigen Themen, aus denen die Schüler/innen und Studierenden sehr viel lernen könnten, herantrauen. Fordern heißt Fördern. Die Lehrenden dürfen von den Lernenden fordern, mitzudenken und mitzuarbeiten.

Ein zweiter ganz wichtiger Aspekt der veränderten Gesellschaft ist *Vielfalt.* Fast kann schon festgestellt werden, dass Vielfalt an sich einen neuen Wert darstellt. *Vielfalt ist Leben!*

Aus der Didaktik und Hirnforschung ist schon lange bekannt, dass unterschiedliche Menschen unterschiedliche bevorzugte Wege haben, sich ein Themenfeld zu erschließen: der erste muss es verbal erklärt bekommen, die zweite muss dazu eine Zeichnung sehen, der dritte muss eine Rechnung machen … Schon dadurch ist eine gewisse Vielfalt in der Lehre schon immer gerechtfertigt gewesen.

Aber durch die gesellschaftlichen Veränderungen hat die Vielfalt/Vielfältigkeit auch einen eigenen Wert bekommen. Die Schüler/innen und Studierenden erwarten heute quasi, dass ein Sachverhalt von verschiedenen Seiten mit verschiedenen Methoden beleuchtet wird. Es ist also nicht nur eine Frage des Angebots, sondern tatsächlich auch der Nachfrage.

Heute ist es in der Lehre sehr wichtig, den richtigen Zugang zu den Lernenden zu finden. Und dabei spielen sehr viele Aspekte eine Rolle. Gleichwohl sind Lehre und Lernen immer eng mit Kommunikation verbunden. Kommunikationspfade zu den Lernenden zu finden, ist eine der wichtigsten Aufgaben der Lehrenden. In diesem Zusammenhang sei auf das aus meiner Sicht sehr gute Buch „‘Spielend’ unterrichten und Kommunikation gestalten“ von Maike Plath, die 2. Aufl. erschienen 2015 im Beltz-Verlag, verwiesen. Nicht optimal ist an jenem Buch m. E. nur der Titel, da er missverstanden werden kann. Es geht nicht um spielerisches Lehren oder spielerisches Lernen. Besser wäre „‘Schauspielend’ unterrichten …“. Zum Beispiel könnte ein Dozent die Rolle dessen einnehmen, der gegen alles ist („Die Newtonschen Axiome stimmen doch gar nicht! Woran soll man das denn erkennen können?“), sodass die Studierenden ihn überzeugen müssen. (Gleichwohl muss er bei allen Rollen, in die er schlüpft, authentisch zu bleiben versuchen.) Menschen lieben Geschichten. Und daher sollten Lehrende versuchen, Geschichten zu erzählen, aber keine Märchen.

Um diesen sehr wichtigen Aspekt, nämlich dass Lehren und Lernen Kommunikation ist, geht es in meinem Buch nicht zentral. Er spielt zwar in fast alle Erläuterungen hinein, aber nicht auf einer psychologischen, sondern eher auf einer handwerklichen Ebene – wie z. B. können Kleinigkeiten eine inhaltsreiche Kommunikation erschweren oder verbessern.

Eine andere wichtige Erfahrung ist, dass es heute in der Informationsgesellschaft genau so schwierig ist, an wichtige und richtige Informationen zu kommen, wie vor 40 Jahren. Man sollte meinen, dass es mit dem „World Wide Web" (WWW) und Speichermedien, wie der „Digital Video/Versatile Disc" (DVD™), die so viel Informationen fassen, wie sie früher an Büchern nicht in eine Heimbibliothek passten, einfach sein müsste, an Informationen zu kommen. Wo früher der mühselige Weg in die Stadtbibliothek anstand und man, wieder zu Hause, feststellte, dass man sich doch nicht die zur Vorbereitung des Referats am besten geeigneten Bücher mitgebracht hatte, sind heute nur ein paar Schritte zum PC notwendig, um im WWW zu sein. Aber tatsächlich erfordert es auch Strategien, im WWW in akzeptabler Zeit an Informationen zu kommen. Und selbst dann kann man nicht sicher sein, fundierte Informationen gefunden zu haben.

Die „Älteren" wie ich hatten Gelegenheit zu lernen uns zu konzentrieren, weil es die Flut von medialen Ablenkungen früher nicht gab. Informationen zu sammeln, heißt heute aber als Kehrseite der Medaille Vielfalt, ständig aus einem riesigen Angebot etwas herausfiltern und hoffen zu müssen, dass man den Kern der Sache erwischt hat. Aber manchmal bleibt doch etwas vom Kern der Sache verborgen.

Ingenieure/innen und Physiker/innen nennen dieses Problem „undersampling". Aber dieses *zu seltene Hinsehen* an einer Stelle ermöglicht mehr Hinsehen links und rechts und oben und unten; vielleicht könnte man dies „broader sampling" *(breiteres Hinsehen)* nennen.

Mag sein, dass die heutigen Jugendlichen und jungen Menschen bisweilen den Wald vor lauter Bäumen übersehen; aber den See und das Feld und das Dorf nebenan erkennen sie. Mit dieser Technik erwischen die jungen Leute Verknüpfungen, die wir Älteren nicht gesehen haben, weil wir uns jeweils nur auf eine Sache konzentriert haben (im Wald geblieben sind).

Einerseits müssen Lehrende akzeptieren und berücksichtigen, dass Vielfalt in jeglicher Hinsicht Teil der neuen Gesellschaft ist und *an sich* einen Wert darstellt, eben auch Vielfalt in der Darstellung. Zum anderen ist „weniger oft mehr". Man sollte nicht krampfhaft nach der vierten, fünften, … Form der Darstellung suchen. Je mehr Medien ich in meiner Lehre einsetze, desto schlechter sind die Ergebnisse von Übungen und Klausuren. Konzentration auf einige wenige Methoden (aber eben nicht nur auf eine) ist wichtig. Und je nach Lehrstoff mögen andere Methoden sinnvoll sein.

In den Kap. 1–10 dieses Büchleins wird je ein Tipp für gute Lehre, gute Lehrvorträge und gutes Lernen gegeben. Die Kap. 1–4 und 10 sind eher auf die Lehre ausgerichtet, die Kap. 5–9 eher auf das Lernen. Das hier beide Seiten miteinander dargestellt werden, liegt daran, dass sie eng verwoben sind. Zum Beispiel kann es auch für Schüler/innen und Studierende hilfreich sein zu wissen, warum Lehrende so handeln, wie sie es tun.

Auf eines können die Lehrenden heute bei den Lernenden zählen und setzen: Lebensfreude. Die Null-Bock-Generation scheint aus Schule und Hochschule herausgewachsen zu sein. Wie kann man diese Lebensfreude nutzen und auch in Begeisterung für das Lernen ummünzen, für den Spaß an dicken Brettern statt am Dünnbrettbohren? Man sollte den Schülern und Studierenden etwas zutrauen/zumuten und ihnen zeigen, dass sie etwas können, … dass ihre Ideen gebraucht werden. Fordern heißt Fördern.

Kaiserslautern, Deutschland
Februar 2017

Henning Fouckhardt

Inhaltsverzeichnis

1 Details der Darstellung sind wichtig

▶ Verwirren ist einfach, Erklären ist schwierig!

1.1 Wer ist die Zuhörerschaft?

Gleichgültig ob es um Unterrichtsstunden oder Vorlesungsstunden oder auch nur um einen einzelnen Vortrag geht, die wichtigsten Fragen müssen für Vortragende, Lehrer/innen und Dozenten/innen immer lauten: „Vor wem trage ich vor? Wie viele Personen hören zu? Wie alt sind sie? Was ist ihr Vorwissen? Gibt es Wissen, das erst nachgeliefert und vorbereitet werden muss, bevor das Hauptthema angesprochen werden kann?" Die allermeisten schlechten Vorträge sind an der Nichtbeachtung dieser Fragen gescheitert.

Dabei ist auch wichtig, dass der Vortrag eine Dramaturgie hat: erst muss das thematische Umfeld abgesteckt, dann das Problem dargestellt werden, danach die Möglichkeiten, es zu lösen, aber auch Schwierigkeiten, die dem entgegenstehen, schließlich die erfolgreiche Lösung. Insofern ist ein guter Vortrag ähnlich wie jeder gute Roman oder Spielfilm aufgebaut. Dazu gehören auch Phasen mit größerer Spannung und Geschwindigkeit (in denen die Zuhörer/innen genau hinhören müssen, um die Zusammenhänge zu verstehen) und ruhigere Phasen, in denen sie durchschnaufen können.

Für die Dramaturgie ist das Betonen von wichtigen Wörtern unerlässlich, der Einsatz von Gesten und Grimassen, um eine Aussage zu unterstreichen, der gezielte Einsatz von kleinen Pausen nach wichtigen Aussagen. In einem Vortrag könnte jeder Satz inhaltlich korrekt sein und jeder zweite Satz eine Neuigkeit enthalten; wenn die Betonung fehlen sollte, werden die meisten Zuhörer/innen den Wert der Aussagen nicht erkennen.

H. Fouckhardt, *Lehren und Lernen*, essentials,
DOI 10.1007/978-3-658-18064-5_1

Wie schon ausgeführt, all dies gilt nicht nur für einzelne Vorträge, sondern im Prinzip für jede Unterrichts- oder Vorlesungsstunde. Setzt eine solche Forderung nicht alle Lehrenden unter Druck? Nicht wirklich; denn ihr kann mit relativ wenig Aufwand nachgekommen werden.

Vor Jahren fragte ich einen Physiker-Freund, wie es zu seiner schnellen Karriere im Mobilfunkbereich gekommen war. Abgesehen von einigen Randbedingungen, auf die er wohl kaum Einfluss gehabt haben konnte (wie den Boom der Mobilfunkbranche), führte er seinen Erfolg auf einen Umstand zurück: im Gegensatz zu den meisten Kollegen bereitete er sich auf jede Sitzung, an der er teilnahm, mindestens einige Minuten vor, selbst wenn seine eigene Arbeit bei dieser Sitzung nicht diskutiert werden sollte. Er fragte sich: was ist die Ausgangslage, was wollen wir bei dieser Sitzung erreichen, welche Möglichkeiten haben wir dazu wahrscheinlich, was sind die Probleme, wie könnte man sie eventuell lösen und wer könnte dies tun? Schon diese Vorbereitung führte dazu, dass er Lösungen schneller sah als andere. So bekam er die Aufgaben, die zwar schwierig waren, aber auch spannend (und mit denen er sich Lorbeeren verdienen konnte).

Man sollte sich vor jeder Vorlesungsdoppelstunde vergegenwärtigen, welche Themen in den kommenden 90 min anzusprechen sind, wie das nächste Thema aus dem davor hervorgeht, was das Problem dabei ist, wie dies thematisch eingebettet werden kann. Das klappt zwar nicht immer, aber doch häufiger und besser als man meinen könnte.

„Wir haben uns letztes Mal mit dem Begriff Kraft auseinandergesetzt. Wie messen wir Kräfte? Wie addieren wir Kräfte? Warum spüren wir Kräfte, die wir ausüben? Denken Sie an das 3. Newtonsche Axiom über Kraft und Gegenkraft! Aber dabei sind wir immer von Bewegungen auf einer geraden Linie (Translationen) ausgegangen. Heute werden wir merken, dass Kräfte alleine unter Umständen noch gar nichts ausrichten können, wenn es um Drehungen (Rotationen) geht. Es kommt auch auf den Hebelarm an, an dem die Kraft angreift, und darauf ob die Kraft in Richtung des Hebelarms oder schief oder senkrecht dazu angreift. Am Ende wird eine für uns neue Größe (das Drehmoment) stehen, die bei Drehungen die Kraft ersetzt.“

Für nicht physikalisch Interessierte mag dieses Beispiel – ob mit oder ohne Verpackung – wenig spannend sein. Für Interessierte erleichtert diese Verknüpfung den Zugang zur neuen Größe Drehmoment, deren Sinn man ansonsten vielleicht gar nicht einsehen mag. Studierende haben oft das irrige Gefühl, dass schwierige Begriffe und Gesetzmäßigkeiten nur als Schikane für sie eingeführt werden.

Ein großer Fehler, den man beim Lehren machen kann, ist das bloße Aneinanderreihen von Fakten. Dabei können die Einzelerklärungen noch so gut, die Beispiele noch so einleuchtend sein, ohne die Brücken *vom* vorhergehenden Thema und *zum* nachfolgenden, werden die Erklärungen verpuffen.

1.2 Wie sind die Räumlichkeiten?

Man mag es zunächst nicht glauben, aber der Unterrichtsraum oder Hörsaal oder Vortragsraum entscheidet über den Erfolg der Lehrbemühungen mit. Oder anders herum gesagt: die Möglichkeiten und Unmöglichkeiten des Raums müssen berücksichtigt werden, um optimale Wirkung zu erzielen.

Der schlimmste denkbare Vortragsraum enthält eine oder mehrere tragende Säulen – mehr oder weniger mittendrin. Gleichgültig wohin man projiziert, gleichgültig wohin man sich stellt, es gibt immer einige Zuhörer/innen, die nicht alles sehen können. Und wenn sie sich nicht umsetzen können, weil der Saal gefüllt ist, hat man keine Chance, das Problem zu umgehen.

In allen anderen Räumen hat man Möglichkeiten zur Optimierung bis hin dazu, bei Projektionen in einem schmalen Raum *hinter* dem Publikum zu stehen. Aber die Situation muss vorher durchdacht werden. Wenn man zu einem Vortrag eingeladen wird, sollte man sich, wenn die Chance besteht, bereits kurz nach der Ankunft den Vortragsraum zeigen lassen. Dann kann ein Teil des Gehirns schon darüber nachdenken, wie der Raum beim Vortrag am besten genutzt werden kann.

Und zu den Räumlichkeiten gehört die Technik des Raums: Ist ein Mikrofon vorhanden und funktionsfähig? Ist sein Einsatz notwendig oder störend? Funktioniert der Beamer auch mit diesem Rechner? Rechtzeitig ausprobieren! Welche Abhilfe gibt es? Wer könnte helfen?

Deswegen bitten Konferenzorganisatoren/innen darum, schon vor der Sitzung mit den eigenen Vortragsutensilien aufzutauchen und alles auszuprobieren. Und wer das nicht für nötig hält, bereut es immer.

1.3 Versetzen Sie sich in die Zuhörerschaft!

Jeder von uns kennt Lehrende, die zwar ganz offensichtlich ihren Stoff beherrschen, vielleicht geradezu in ihm aufgehen, aber es nicht schaffen, ihn klar herüber zu bringen.

Es ist überaus verblüffend, durch welche Kleinigkeiten man als Dozent/in die Zuhörerschaft unbeabsichtigt auf eine falsche Fährte schicken kann. Auf einer Folie die Kurve für den Strom gelb dargestellt und die für die Spannung blau (weil der Computer laut Voreinstellungen das automatisch so gemacht hat) und bei der nächsten Folie anders herum (weil ein anderer Computer anders eingestellt war), und die meisten Zuhörer sind vollkommen durcheinander. Und warum? Weil man selbst den Farben der Kurven keine Bedeutung beigemessen hat, die Unterschiede also selbst gar nicht bemerkt oder gar nicht für wichtig gehalten hat.

Der/die Vortragende muss sich in die Zuhörerschaft versetzen! Er/sie hatte vorher Gelegenheit, sich über jede Folie mindestens minutenlang Gedanken zu machen. Die Zuhörer/innen haben nur ein paar Sekunden Zeit zu erfassen, worum es geht; dann folgen schon weitere Informationen. Vielleicht steht auf der zweiten Folie sogar zusätzlich explizit in der Legende, dass die Stromkurve nun die blaue ist. Aber es strömt zu viel auf die Zuhörer/innen ein, um dies zu erkennen.

- Die Farben von Messkurven sind natürlich nur ein Beispiel.
- Genauso verwirrend sind nicht durchgängige Symbole für Messpunkte, …
- unterschiedliche Skalierungen für Diagramme,
- unterschiedliche Einheiten,
- ein Rahmen um ein Diagramm und kein Rahmen um ein anderes,
- Bullets bei einer Auflistung und Spiegelstriche bei einer anderen oder sogar innerhalb derselben,
- große Schriftfonts für die Überschrift einer Folie und kleine für die (gleichrangige) Überschrift einer anderen,
- grundlos unterschiedlich große Fotos auf einer Folie,
- Fotos die nicht auf derselben Höhe wie der Text stehen, der sie beschreibt;

die Liste ist schier endlos. Natürlich muss man immer abwägen, wie viel Zeit man zur Optimierung des Vortrags aufwenden möchte und kann.

Aber es ist wichtig, sich der vielen Stolpersteine bewusst zu sein. Leitlinie muss sein, sich in die Lage von Zuhörern/Lernenden zu versetzen, für die der Gegenstand des Vortrags unbekannt ist.

1.4 Vortragen kann man nicht lernen – oder doch?

Man kann nicht lernen, *brillante* Vorträge zu halten. Eloquenz ist nur bedingt erlernbar. Und Charisma hat man, oder man hat es nicht. Es gibt Vortragende und Lehrende, die den ersten Satz ihres Vortrags sprechen und schon damit den Saal in ihren Bann schlagen, Theoretiker/innen auf Experimentalphysik-Konferenzen, bei deren Vortrag man (außer ihrer Stimme) eine Stecknadel fallen hören könnte, Dozenten/innen bei denen aufgrund ihres Erscheinungsbilds die Zuhörer/innen an ihren Lippen kleben. (Nicht in jedem Fall mögen dabei die Worte bis in die Gehirne der Zuhörer/innen vordringen, wovon „Indiana Jones"™ ein Lied singen kann.)

Aber man kann erlernen, *sehr gute* Vorträge zu halten. Kleinigkeiten *in der Darstellung* zu berücksichtigen, wie im letzten Abschnitt ausgeführt, ist ein wichtiger Punkt. Umgekehrt sollten bei der Beschreibung eines Sachverhalts nicht sofort alle *inhaltlichen* Einzelheiten erwähnt werden, die in diesem Zusammenhang irgendwie wichtig sein könnten. Damit wäre die Zuhörerschaft überfordert. Unter Umständen sollte man bestimmte Einzelheiten überhaupt nicht erwähnen, bis in der Diskussion von selbst die Fragen darauf kommen. Weniger ist hier eindeutig mehr!

Nicht aufgeregt vor dem Auditorium herumzuspringen, ist ein anderer wichtiger Punkt. Gleichwohl kann es hilfreich sein, starke Gesten zu verwenden (geballte Fäuste, aufzeigende Zeigefinger, mit ausgestreckten Armen das Publikum scheinbar zu umarmen oder sogar ganz gezielt bei einem wichtigen Argument direkt auf das Publikum zuzugehen).

Aber es reicht nicht aus, von diesen Regeln zu wissen, man muss sie auch einstudieren, immer wieder. Alle Mitarbeiter/innen meines Lehrstuhls, die auf eine wissenschaftliche Konferenz fahren wollen und sollen, um dort einen Vortrag zu halten, müssen vor ihren Kollegen/innen Probevorträge halten. Manchen fällt es leichter und sie benötigen nur drei Probevorträge, bis das Resultat akzeptabel ist. Anderen fällt es schwerer und sie brauchen vielleicht acht Probevorträge. Aber es hilft und beim nächsten Konferenzbeitrag ist die Anzahl der notwendigen Probevorträge schon geringer.

Das mag manchem übertrieben erscheinen. Und sicher muss auch hier immer eine Kosten-Nutzen-Rechnung erfolgen. Aber meistens lohnt der Nutzen die Kosten. Ein Probevortrag hilft zu erkennen, ob Überleitungen flüssig sind, ob eine andere Folienreihenfolge sinnvoller wäre, ob vielleicht wichtige Puzzlesteine der Erklärung bisher ganz fehlen.

In den letzten Abschnitten war viel von Vorträgen die Rede. Gelten die Hinweise auch für Unterrichts- oder Vorlesungsstunden. Der Nutzen wäre sicher genauso hoch; aber natürlich fehlt die Zeit, diesen Aufwand jedes Mal zu treiben. Was kann man also tun?

Bei wichtigen Themen oder solchen, die schwer darzustellen oder zu verstehen sind (die spezielle Relativitätstheorie – selbst bei nur phänomenologischer Darstellung ohne viele Formeln – mag als Beispiel dienen) sollte der Aufwand fast so groß wie vor einem wichtigen Vortrag sein. Es kann auf einen bestimmten Satz ankommen. Ein falscher Satz schickt die Zuhörerschaft in die falsche Richtung, ein gezielter wohlüberlegter Satz oder eine gute Analogie oder ein gutes Beispiel (das man sich nicht erst im Hörsaal überlegt) kann die Tür zum Verständnis öffnen. Bei anderen Themen ist die Vorbereitung mit weniger Aufwand möglich. Niemals sollte sie fehlen.

Und genauso wichtig ist die Nachbereitung. Jedes Mal gibt es ein paar Punkte, bei denen man als Dozent/in merkt, dass die Erklärung noch Verbesserungen vertragen kann. Sie sollte man direkt nach der Stunde, solange die Erinnerung noch „warm“ ist, in die eigenen Unterlagen einbauen, um es beim nächsten Mal besser zu machen. Diese Nachbereitung erfordert meist wenig Zeit (vielleicht 5–15 min pro Doppelstunde), ist aber für die Zukunft unbedingt vorteilhaft.

Das bedeutet aber auch, dass keine einzige Darstellung eines Sachverhalts, die man zum ersten Mal gibt, perfekt sein kann. Wenn man bereit dazu ist, diesen (gar nicht so großen) Aufwand zu treiben, erfolgt die Optimierung von Mal zu Mal.

1.5 Nachsicht

Die obigen Ausführungen mögen manche/n Schüler/in oder Studierende/n oder gar Eltern bewegen, etwas gnädiger mit Dozenten/innen, zumindest mit jungen, zu sein. Wie schnell ist das Urteil gefällt: der/die kann nicht erklären. Und dabei vergisst man leicht, wie unklar man sich tagtäglich selbst ausdrückt, wenn man sich nicht in die Rolle des Gegenüber versetzt.

Ein Beispiel: Bei dem Tempo, das dem heutigen Profi-Fußball innewohnt, ist offenbar keine Zeit mehr für den Konjunktiv.

Manuel Neuer (den ich bewundere) nach dem Viertelfinal-Spiel gegen Frankreich bei der Herren-Fußball-WM 2014 in Brasilien in einem ARD-Interview über einen Angriff der Franzosen: „Ich muss die kurze Ecke zuhaben. Und wenn er dann ’reingeht, dann ist es ein Torwartfehler.“

Er meinte wohl: „Ich musste die kurze Ecke zumachen. Wenn der Ball trotzdem ’reingegangen wäre, wäre es mein Fehler gewesen.“

Oder Tom Bartels (den ich sehr schätze) (ARD) zu einem Kopfball von Benedikt Höwedes an den Pfosten im Endspiel:

„Wenn er den ’reinmacht, zählt das Tor. Nach dem Kopfball Abseits.“

Er meinte wohl: „Wenn er den ’reingemacht hätte, hätte das Tor gezählt. Erst nach dem Kopfball entstand die Abseitssituation.“

Für alle, die unmittelbar zugesehen haben, war deutlich, was Tom Bartels meinte, auch wenn er die Gegenwartsform und nicht den Konjunktiv verwendet hatte. Aber für jemanden, der gerade einmal nicht hingesehen hatte, waren die Sätze unverständlich.

Nun ist es natürlich klar, dass im Alltag in einer Ad-hoc-Situation nicht jeder Satz wohl durchdacht und ausgereift sein kann. Schließlich erhält Manuel Neuer seine Entlohnung auch nicht für das Reden. Und selbst bei einem Sportreporter

kann man in der Hitze des Gefechts nicht formvollendete Sätze erwarten. (Vielleicht würden die der spannungsgeladenen Situation auch gar nicht gerecht werden.) Aber es ist wichtig, sich klar zu machen, wie schnell man Zuhörer/innen verwirren kann. Und Dozenten/innen sollten zumindest an den wichtigsten Stellen Verwirrungen ausschließen.

Nun geht es nicht immer nur um sprachliche Unklarheiten, die verwirren können, sondern auch um inhaltliche. In den letzten Jahren ist in deutschen Nachrichtensendungen häufig von der „schwarzen Null" im Haushalt die Rede, die Finanzminister Schäuble anstrebe oder sogar erreicht hat. Gemeint ist aber, dass es keine Neuverschuldung gegeben hat. Mit anderen Worten: Der Gesamt-Bundeshaushalt ist in den roten Zahlen; aber die roten Zahlen werden nicht größer. Der Unterschied zwischen dem, was gesagt wird, und dem, was gemeint ist, ist in der Mathematik der Unterschied zwischen einer zeitabhängigen Funktion $y(t)$ und ihrer Ableitung dy/dt, ein wichtiger Unterschied. Ein über der Zeit konstanter negativer Wert zeigt eine Ableitung mit dem Wert 0, aber der Wert ist und bleibt negativ.

Oder der Chef einer Firma, die an der Börse gehandelt wird, kündigt einen Quantensprung in der Entwicklung des Unternehmens an. Ist es Wohlwollen oder gleiche Unkenntnis, die einen sofortigen Kurssturz verhindert? Denn ein Quantensprung ist ja der kleinstmögliche Sprung, der stattfinden kann. Das meinte der Firmenchef sicher nicht.

Kleine Unterschiede entscheiden darüber, ob etwas richtig oder falsch ist oder ob etwas verstanden wird oder nicht. Grundsätzlich ist eine genaue Ausdrucksweise unerlässlich.

2 Überleitungen liefern den roten Faden

▶ Scheinbar Selbstverständliches muss auch erwähnt werden!

2.1 Ein falsches Wort

Zu der Aussage „Details sind wichtig" aus Kap. 1 gehört auch die Feststellung, dass einzelne Wörter darüber entscheiden können, ob etwas Sinn macht und verstanden wird oder eben nicht. Im Zusammenhang mit Überleitungen sind dabei besonders die richtigen Adverbien und Pronomen wichtig.

Um wieder ein Beispiel aus dem Fußball zu nennen:

Mats Hummels (ebenfalls von mir sehr bewundert) in einem ZDF-Interview nach dem 7:1 gegen Brasilien auf die Frage, warum er sich denn gar nicht so richtig freue: „Ohne arrogant sein zu wollen, wissen wir das seit über einer Stunde, dass wir weiter sind. Also da ist es dann so, dass die ganz großen Emotionen nach dem Abpfiff dann *erst 'mal* noch nicht aufkommen. …"

Er meinte sicher, dass die Freude in so einem Fall beim Abpfiff *nicht mehr* richtig aufkommt. Der Unterschied zwischen „noch nicht" und „nicht mehr" macht den Unterschied zwischen Unverständnis und Verständnis.

Noch schlimmer ist das Unverständnis, wenn in naturwissenschaftlichen Darstellungen durch unklare Formulierungen (meist ungewollt) Ursache und Wirkung vertauscht werden: „Weil das Drehmoment groß ist, ist der Hebelarm lang" statt richtigerweise „weil der Hebelarm groß ist, ergibt sich ein großes Drehmoment". Drei solche Fehler kurz hintereinander in einer Vorlesung und 95 % der Zuhörer/innen melden sich geistig ab – mit Recht.

Die Vorstellung, dass ein einzelnes Wort oder eine einzelne Begründung darüber entscheiden kann, ob die Zuhörerschaft den Stoff versteht oder nicht, ist insbesondere für junge Dozenten/innen beunruhigend (falls diese Erkenntnis

H. Fouckhardt, *Lehren und Lernen*, essentials,
DOI 10.1007/978-3-658-18064-5_2

überhaupt schon herangereift ist). Erleichterung dazu kann aus der Überlegung gewonnen werden, dass man auch langsam sprechen darf und beim langsamen Sprechen an den wichtigsten Stellen der Erklärung mehr Zeit hat, seine Gedanken zu ordnen und die Formulierungen sorgfältig zu wählen. Dieses Vorgehen hat noch andere Vorteile. Durch den Wechsel zum langsamen Sprechen wird die Wichtigkeit der Stelle im Gedankengang betont. Und die Schüler/innen und Studierenden haben die Möglichkeit, den nun ganz sorgsam gewählten Worten auch sorgfältig zu lauschen – eine „double win"-Situation. Also keine Angst vor Pausen und langsamem Sprechen, zumindest wenn es ganz wichtig wird!

2.2 Triviales ist oft nicht trivial! Redundanz und klare Aussagen sind wichtig!

Als Student habe ich Bücher gehasst, in denen Formulierungen wie „Trivialerweise sieht man sofort ..." vorkamen. Trivial waren solche Passagen in den seltensten Fällen. Und heute muss ich annehmen, dass Autoren/innen, die so etwas schreiben, selbst den Zusammenhang nicht voll verstanden haben oder sich zumindest um eine schwierige Erklärung drücken wollen.

Und selbst wenn etwas zu einem bestimmten Zeitpunkt der Vorlesung trivial sein müsste, weil schon mehrfach darüber gesprochen wurde, ist es manchmal trotzdem ratsam, darauf hinzuweisen, ... dass gerade wieder eine Situation vorliegt, wie sie neulich besprochen wurde, sodass sich zwangsläufig dieselben Schlussfolgerungen wie neulich ergeben. Redundanz ist wichtig!

Dozenten/innen wissen, welchen Gedankengang sie in den nächsten 30, 45, 60 oder 90 min darlegen wollen, was die Voraussetzungen sind, von denen sie ausgehen, was die Phänomene sind, die sie erläutern wollen, und was die Schlussfolgerungen sind, die sie daraus ziehen wollen. Die Zuhörerschaft weiß dies nicht. Nicht nur, dass auf sie viele neue Informationen einströmen; darüber hinaus müssen die Zuhörer/innen in der Kürze der Zeit auch noch einordnen, welchen Stellenwert die gerade gesagte Information hat. Ist es eine Voraussetzung, von der ausgegangen wird? Ist es eine Nebenbedingung, die nur im Spezialfall zu berücksichtigen ist? Ist es die zentrale Aussage, um die sich die gesamte Erläuterung dreht?

Diese Fragen beziehen sich auf das „Metawissen". Dieser Begriff wird unterschiedlich verwendet. Hier soll darunter das Wissen über die Zusammenhänge und die Einordnung der bloßen Fakten verstanden werden, quasi ein Wissen einer höheren Qualität oder auf einer höheren gedanklichen Ebene. Es ist vielleicht die wichtigste und vornehmste Aufgabe eines/r Dozenten/in, dieses Metawissen zu liefern:

- „Das Wesentliche am hydrostatischen Auftrieb sind die unterschiedlichen Massedichten von Flüssigkeit und schwimmendem Körper. Alles andere folgt daraus."
- „Die Gravitationskraft ist um 43 Größenordnungen/Zehnerpotenzen schwächer als die Coulomb-Kraft. Deswegen ist die Massenanziehung irrelevant, wenn es um die elektrische Wechselwirkung geladener Teilchen geht."

Es ist erstaunlich, dass man ähnlich klare Aussagen in Lehrbüchern kaum findet. Vielleicht haben die Autoren/innen manchmal Sonderfälle im Kopf, die die Aussage nicht ganz so klar und sicher sein lassen. Nach meiner Erfahrung sind solche klaren Aussagen für die Lernenden aber sehr wichtig. Lieber die Sonderfälle erst dort, wo sie auftreten, erläutern und auch auf die frühere (allzu klare) Aussage verweisen, sie explizit korrigieren, als niemals eine klare Aussage zu machen! Denn die klaren Aussagen helfen den Lernenden, die richtige Richtung zu finden.

Als junger Dozent versuchte ich, nur absolut richtige Aussagen zu machen. Wenn es viele Nebenbedingungen für eine Aussage gab, nannte ich alle diese Nebenbedingungen gleich mit – in demselben Satz – mit dem Erfolg, dass alle Aussagen so verklausuliert waren, dass gar nichts mehr bei den Studierenden ankam. Heute mache ich einfachere Aussagen, wie: „In den meisten Fällen gilt … Aber es gibt auch Ausnahmen, die wir später behandeln werden." Ich habe den Eindruck, dass nun bei den Studierenden mehr ankommt.

2.3 Metawissen

Dieser Ausdruck wurde eben schon erwähnt. Metawissen sollte der Kern jeder Überleitung von einem Thema zum nächsten sein, von einer Folie eines Vortrags zur nächsten, von einer mathematischen Herleitung zur nächsten:

- „Auf dieser Folie war *gerade* von drei Möglichkeiten die Rede, das Problem der Wärmeabfuhr zu lösen. *Jetzt* sollen diese drei Methoden näher betrachtet werden. (Folienwechsel) Auf dieser Folie geht es um den ersten der drei Ansätze, eine bessere Wärmeabfuhr zu erzielen. Er zeichnet sich dadurch aus, dass Substrate verwendet werden, die eine besonders große Wärmeleitfähigkeit zeigen. …"
- „*Eben* wurde eine neue Messtechnik erläutert, mit der während der Herstellung einkristalliner Schichten Aussagen über die Qualität der Kristalloberfläche gewonnen werden können. *Nun* sehen wir uns einige Messergebnisse

dieser Technik an und versuchen, aus den Ergebnissen, Rückschlüsse auf die Oberfläche zu ziehen. …"

- „Sie haben *eben* in einer Graphik ein Messergebnis der Größe y in Abhängigkeit der Größe x (also $y(x)$) gesehen. Erwartet hatten wir, wie *anfangs* im Vortrag erläutert, eine exponentielle Abhängigkeit. Für große Werte von x ergab sich aber eine Abweichung von der Erwartung. Um diese Abweichung und den Grund dafür soll es auf dieser Folie gehen. …"

Wichtig an diesen Beispielen sind zum einen die *kursiv* gedruckten Wörter. Sie unterstreichen die Zusammenhänge und die Abfolge der Gedanken. Ohne sie wären die Aussagen nicht falsch, aber für die Zuhörer/innen schwerer bzw. nicht so schnell zu erfassen. Diese wenigen geeignet eingestreuten Wörter können die Zuhörerschaft extrem unterstützen.

Zum anderen soll mit den Beispielen erläutert werden, dass es – zumindest an wichtigen Stellen – nützlich ist, die Sätze aneinander anzuschließen, indem einzelne Ausdrücke wiederholt werden. Damit wird erreicht, dass der gedankliche Faden ganz offensichtlich nicht abreißt:

„… ergab sich *aber* eine Abweichung von der Erwartung. Um diese Abweichung und den Grund dafür soll es auf dieser Folie gehen. …"

Überleitungen sollten das Metawissen enthalten. Sie sollten den Zuhörern/innen erlauben, Zusammenhänge zu sehen und zu verstehen. Insofern sind gute Überleitungen eines der wichtigsten Instrumente für gute Lehre.

Selbst nach Projektarbeit von Schülern/innen oder Studierenden sind Zusammenfassungen des/der Lehrenden hilfreich. Er/sie kann in diesen Zusammenfassungen die Zusammenhänge durch Überleitungen zwischen verschiedenen Gedankengängen deutlich machen.

3 Für die Hilfsmittel gibt es kein Patentrezept

▶ Tafel, Folie oder Beamer sind alleine keine Allheilmittel.

3.1 Die eine Methode

Als ich 1991 als junger Professor anfing zu lehren und Kollegen fragte, hörte ich gebetsmühlenartig, dass ich doch alles an die Tafel schreiben und den Overhead-Projektor nur nutzen sollte, um wichtige Abbildungen zu präsentieren. (Beamer gab es damals noch nicht.) Ich selbst nahm diesen Ratschlag nur allzu gerne auf, weil ich es selbst nicht anders kannte und mir diese Form der Präsentation des Lehrstoffes daher als die natürlichste erschien. Im Laufe der Jahre kamen mir immer mehr Zweifel an dieser Methode, Zweifel, die von zwei Seiten genährt wurden.

Zum einen verleitet das Anschreiben an die Tafel die Studierenden dazu, alles mitzuschreiben – aber zunächst einmal ohne viel nachzudenken.

Steht man an der Tafel und malt (womöglich etwas gedankenverloren) einen Strich auf die Tafel, hört man 300 Leute einen Strich auf ihre Notizhefte kratzen. Steht man dann direkt vor der Zuhörerschaft (weit weg von der Tafel) und versucht einen wichtigen Sachverhalt eindringlich darzustellen, fängt die Hälfte der Leute an, mit dem Nachbarn zu reden, ein Butterbrot auszupacken, in ihrer Aktentasche zu kramen, …

Zum anderen hat der Tafelanschrieb viele Tücken. Am dramatischsten sind diese bei mathematischen Herleitungen, die in der Physik ja häufig vorkommen und auch relevant sind. Formeln anzuschreiben birgt die Gefahr, dass man Schreibfehler (quasi Tippfehler) in die Formeln einbaut, die im schlechtesten Fall weder vom Dozenten noch von den Studierenden erkannt werden, im besten Fall zu störenden Diskussionen führen, wo etwas falsch sei und wie dieser Fehler nun

H. Fouckhardt, *Lehren und Lernen*, essentials,
DOI 10.1007/978-3-658-18064-5_3

zu beheben sei. Hinzu kommt, dass übliche Tafeln so klein sind, dass man spätestens nach 20 min anfangen muss, Teile des Geschriebenen wieder wegzuwischen, um Platz für den weiteren Anschrieb zu haben. Und wenn man Teile des alten Geschriebenen retten möchte, beginnt ein heilloses Durcheinander darüber, wo man sinnvoll weiterschreiben kann und die Verwirrung der Zuhörer- bzw. Mitschreiberschaft ist vorprogrammiert. Aber der vielleicht in den Naturwissenschaften und speziell der Physik wichtigste Aspekt ist, dass sich lange Herleitungen auf diese Art und Weise durchaus über eine Doppelstunde erstrecken können. Dabei geht der rote Faden mit absoluter Sicherheit verloren und genau das sollte doch eigentlich nicht passieren.

Und in einer realen Vorlesungssituation gibt es viele Studierende, die – und das kann man leider nicht verhindern – stupide mitschreiben, ohne das Gehirn anzuwerfen, gerade wenn man den Tafelanschrieb bevorzugt und ein Mitschreiben erwartet. Diese Studierende haben vielleicht wirklich die Absicht, den Stoff später in Ruhe nachzuarbeiten. Aber das unterbleibt oft oder wird dadurch erschwert, dass das (Mit-) Geschriebene ohne weitere Hinweise zum Verständnis nicht ausreichend ist, wenn dem Stoff nicht schon während der Vorlesung konzentriert gefolgt wurde.

In 25 Lehrjahren (die des Lehrens und gleichzeitig die des eigenen Lernens als Dozent) bin ich zu dem Schluss gekommen, dass der Tafelanschrieb nur sehr gezielt und sporadisch erfolgen sollte, weil er die Aufmerksamkeit ansonsten geradezu vernichtet. Heute sage ich den Erstsemester-Studierenden explizit mehrfach, dass sie *nicht* mitschreiben, sondern lieber zuhören sollen, dass sie später anhand des Vorlesungsskriptes oder der empfohlenen Lehrbücher nacharbeiten sollen. Und ich habe den Eindruck, dass dieses Konzept größere Früchte trägt.

Früher erhielt ich typischerweise Zwischenfragen wie „Soll der Buchstabe da ganz links in der zweiten Zeile ein ‚f' oder ein ‚t' sein?" oder „Was soll ‚sin' bedeuten?" (der Sinus sollte seit der Mittelstufe bekannt sein), Fragen, die eher auf das vollständige Ausschalten des Gehirns bei den Studierenden schließen lassen.

Heute lassen die nun üblichen Fragen eher erkennen, dass jemand mitgedacht hat, aber einen Zusammenhang noch nicht ganz versteht. „Warum wird dort nicht nur von 0 an über die Zeit integriert, sondern von minus Unendlich, obwohl der Vorgang doch erst beim Zeitnullpunkt einsetzt?", „Warum wird der Apfel durch den hydrostatischen Auftrieb nicht vollständig aus dem Wasser gehoben?" Auf solche Fragen kann man aufbauen und versuchen, die Lernenden an den Punkt zu führen, sich selbst diese Frage zu beantworten.

Aber was mache ich als Dozent nun anders, während die Studierenden zuhören sollen (und natürlich auch Fragen stellen und mitdiskutieren können)?

Zunächst einmal bedeutete es für mich einen großen innerlichen Schritt, von dem Credo des immerwährenden Tafelanschriebs abzurücken. Und dabei half mir ein von mir sehr geschätzter, altgedienter Kollege, der mir eines Tages davon berichtete, dass er in den Vorlesungen eigentlich nur vorbereitete Overhead-Folien auflegen würde, die den Studierenden als File zur Verfügung gestellt wurden, und anhand dieser Folien Zeile für Zeile Zusammenhänge und auch mathematische Herleitungen erklären würde. Wichtig sei es, sich für jede Zeile Zeit zu lassen und nicht den Stoff herunterzurattern. (Der Tafelanschrieb hatte tatsächlich immer den Vorteil, dass ein Herunterrattern unmöglich war.)

Diese Erkenntnis aus erfahrenem und geschätztem Munde half mir, alte gedankliche Ketten zu lösen und neu nachzudenken. Natürlich war ich der Meinung, dass ich es noch besser machen könnte als der Kollege und dass seine Vorliebe für den Overhead-Projektor aus Gewohnheit und Unkenntnis über die Möglichkeiten des gerade neu aufkommenden Beamers resultierte. Also erstellte ich Skripte – angepasst an die Möglichkeiten im Umfeld des Beamers: mit wenig Text und wenigen wichtigen Aussagen pro Seite.

Aber ich musste sehr bald erkennen, dass das bloße Projizieren an die Wand, ggf. unterstützt durch Führung der Blicke mithilfe eines Laserpointer-Leuchtpunkts, nicht den gewünschten Erfolg hatte. Gerne hätte ich – während der Vorlesung – zusätzliche Markierungen unter den Augen der Studierenden ergänzt, was in den Anfangstagen des Beamers noch nicht möglich war. Hier hatte der erfahrende Kollege mit seinen Overhead-Folien echte Vorteile; denn er konnte diese Ergänzungen während der Vorlesung unter den Augen der Zuhörer-/-seherschaft direkt auf den Folien und an der richtigen Stelle vornehmen: Unterstreichungen, kleine Nebenrechnungen, kleine Zeichnungen, … das was man braucht, um über Verständnisklippen hinwegzuhelfen.

Deswegen wechselte ich an vielen Stellen von der Beamerprojektion zurück auf Folien und umgekehrt, was aber zu viel Unruhe führte. Die Studierenden wurden abgelenkt, weil ständig entweder der Beamer dunkelgetastet und der Overhead-Projektor angeschaltet werden musste oder umgekehrt und weil ich andauernd zwischen den Geräten oder ihren Schaltkästen umherlaufen musste. Den Teufel mit dem Beelzebub ausgetrieben!

Eine wirkliche Verbesserung durch den Beamer ergab sich erst mit neuer Software wie z. B. „Adobe Annotator“™, mit der in dem projizierten pdf (File) während des Vortragens Änderungen eingebracht werden können. Dazu werden diese Änderungen direkt auf das Display eines geeigneten Tablet-PCs geschrieben, der mit dem Beamer verbunden ist. Diese Konstellation hat letztlich die gewünschte Freiheit und die Möglichkeiten gebracht, die ich im Sinn hatte.

Dass dies den erwünschten Erfolg hatte, zeigten die regelmäßigen Vorlesungsumfragen am Ende der Vorlesungszeit. Zunächst hatte ich mit Beamer statt Tafelanschrieb die Studierenden nicht besser erreichen können, sodass der Beamer abgelehnt wurde und die Kritiken harsch ausfielen. Mit den gerade genannten Möglichkeiten hatten die Studierenden etwas davon und die Kritiken fielen überwiegend positiv aus.

3.2 Der Mittelweg

Nun könnte man aus den obigen Äußerungen schließen, dass man ab sofort immer die Variante ‚Beamer plus geeignete Software für „real time"-Notizen' wählen sollte. Aber dem ist nicht so. Schon die heute gewünschte Vielfalt, von der im Vorwort die Rede ist, erfordert einen gewissen Wechsel, dort wo es inhaltlich Sinn macht, z. B. …

- Overhead-Folien, wo Bemaßungen gebraucht werden (auf einem Overhead-Projektor kann man besser und genauer zeichnen als auf einem Tablet-PC),
- Zeichnungen und Schreiben an der Tafel, wenn z. B. eine Einordnung in Kategorien vorgenommen und dann mit Faust oder Zeigestock und Gesten der Betonung auf einen Zusammenhang hingewiesen werden soll – schon durch diese andere Art der Darstellung wird der Inhalt herausgehoben und betont,
- eine Animation, die nicht in das Beamer-projizierte Skript-File eingebunden ist, sondern extra projiziert wird.

Bisher war im Wesentlichen von Tafel, Overhead-Projektor und wohldosierter Beamer-Projektion eines Skript-Files die Rede. Natürlich gibt es weitere Möglichkeiten, wie die auch schon erwähnte Beamer-Projektion einer Animation oder einen Schauversuch im Hörsaal oder die Vorführung einer Filmsequenz. Wo sinnvoll, können selbstverständlich auch sie eingesetzt werden. Die Kriterien sollten sein:

- Vielfalt/Vielfältigkeit in der Darstellung ist hilfreich,
- zu viel Vielfalt ist schädlich, vielleicht sollte also statt von „Vielfalt" eher von „Mehrfalt" die Rede sein,
- die Methode sollte dem Zweck angepasst sein, der erreicht werden soll: eine Filmsequenz oder eine Animation kann z. B. sinnvoll sein, wenn es um Bewegungen oder Fahrten durch verschiedene Perspektiven geht, nicht aber wenn es um einen Versuch geht, den man „live" genauso und authentischer vorführen könnte.

3.3 (Neue) Medien

Der letzte Abschnitt endete u. a. mit den folgenden allgemeinen Regeln:

- Vielfalt in der Darstellung ist hilfreich,
- zu viel Vielfalt ist schädlich.

Ist dies nicht ein Widerspruch, zumindest eine Gratwanderung?

Ersteres nein, letzteres ja!

Leitlinie für die Nutzung neuer und alter Medien sollten immer folgende Fragen sein: Liefert das Medium in diesem inhaltlichen Zusammenhang einen Vorteil für die Darstellung? Gibt das (neue) Medium einen Mehrwert, der ohne es nicht erreicht werden könnte? Nur wenn diese Fragen positiv zu beantworten sind, sollte man das Medium einsetzen.

Zum Beispiel können zwar dreidimensionale Gebilde und Bewegungsabläufe im dreidimensionalen Raum in einer Vorlesungs- oder Unterrichtsstunde anschaulich gemacht werden, indem ein realer Versuch durchgeführt wird. Schwieriger ist dies aber selbstverständlich, wenn die Anordnung nur zweidimensional (auf einer Folie, der Tafel, mit einer Projektion auf die Wand) dargestellt werden kann (z. B. bei einem Aufbau zur Radioaktivität, wofür bei einem Vorlesungsversuch ein erheblicher Sicherheitsaufwand getrieben werden müsste). In dieser Situation helfen Animationen (kurze Videosequenzen), bei denen die Gebilde gedreht werden. Dann hat das Gehirn eine Chance, sich die Dreidimensionalität der Anordnung hinzurechnen.

Ein anderes Beispiel dafür, wo neue Medien helfen können, ist die Kommunikation zwischen dem/der Dozenten/in und der Zuhörerschaft. Man kann als Dozent ein Dutzend mal sagen, dass alles gefragt werden darf und keine Frage übel genommen wird, ein bis zwei Drittel der Studierenden oder Schüler/innen wird sich niemals trauen, während der Vorlesungs- oder Unterrichtsstunde eine Frage zu stellen oder sich auf eine Frage des/der Dozenten/in zu melden und zu antworten. Anonyme „voting tools[1]" (Systeme für anonyme Umfragen/Abstimmungen unter Studierenden) können hier helfen.

Zum Beispiel kann eine „multiple choice"-Frage gestellt werden, die dann von allen Zuhörern/innen per Knopfdruck beantwortet wird (wie beim Publikums-Joker im Fernsehen). Der/die Dozent/in erhält so eine Rückkopplung, wie viel schon angekommen ist und ob er/sie einen Zusammenhang besser noch

---

[1] http://www.uni-kl.de/eteaching/werkzeugkasten/voting-tool/

einmal erläutern sollte. Oder ein „Panik-Knopf“, der so eingestellt ist, dass der/die Dozent/in ein Signal erhält, wenn mehr als die Hälfte der Zuhörer/innen den Knopf drückt, weil sie gerade gar nichts versteht, ist hilfreich. Denn so kann man verhindern, dass sich zu viel Frustration über Unverstandenes ansammelt.

Aber der Aufwand, solche „voting tools“ zu betreiben, zu reparieren, geeignete „multiple choice“-Fragen vor der Stunde vorzubereiten, ist leider noch sehr hoch.

4 Projektarbeit und individuelles Lernen, das wär's ... in einer idealen Welt

> Projektarbeit wäre sinnvoll, ist aber oft nicht sinnvoll möglich.

4.1 Definition der Projektarbeit

Unter Projektarbeit sei hier die Arbeit zur Lösung einer mehr oder weniger isolierten, aber *nicht geringfügigen* Fragestellung verstanden: das Erkennen des Problems, Überlegungen zu Lösungsmöglichkeiten, die experimentelle und theoretische Untersuchung und Evaluation dieser Möglichkeiten, die Wahl einer bestimmten Methode oder einer Kombination, die Verifikation oder Falsifikation des Ansatzes, die Einordnung der Ergebnisse. In diesem Sinne ist die Lösung einer mathematischen Übungsaufgabe keine Projektarbeit, auch wenn sie Aspekte davon enthält.

Im Prinzip kann Projektarbeit im Schul- oder Hochschulumfeld auch von einer Einzelperson durchgeführt werden. Aus meiner Sicht wird Projektarbeit aber umso sinnvoller, wenn 2–4 Schüler/innen oder Studierende gemeinsam an der Aufgabe arbeiten. Dann können sie in der Diskussion miteinander Ideen generieren, ihre Ansätze untereinander infrage stellen, Korrekturen vornehmen und gemeinsam lernen. Voraussetzung dafür ist oft, dass die Beteiligten ähnlich in ihrem Vorwissen und ihrem Können liegen, sonst wird einer die Gruppe dominieren oder ein anderer sich nur anhängen. Die Teammitglieder sollten auch ähnlich engagiert und sich möglichst auch sympathisch sein[1].

[1]Die Variante Projektarbeit im Team mit einer Person, die man nicht mag, wird zwangsläufig später im Berufsleben häufiger werden.

H. Fouckhardt, *Lehren und Lernen*, essentials,
DOI 10.1007/978-3-658-18064-5_4

Im obigen Sinne gibt es viele Arten von Projektarbeit:

- Praktika, wenn die Praktikanten/innen eine eigene Aufgabe bekommen und nicht einfach „uralte Rezepte nachkochen“ müssen,
- Miniaturforschung („forschendes Lernen“)[2] – kleine Forschungsaufgaben, die an einigen wenigen Tagen abgewickelt werden können plus der dazu gehörigen Auswertung und Evaluation,
- eine Messreihe, selbstständig geplant, durchgeführt und ausgewertet, auch wenn die thematische Einbettung von anderen stammt,
- „Jugend forscht“™,
- die Erstellung einer Videoaufnahme von einem Versuch im Bereich Mechanik/Kinematik (z. B. zum schiefen Wurf) und die Auswertung der Abhängigkeiten bestimmter physikalischer Größen (z. B. der Höhe des geworfenen Körpers als Funktion der Zeit) aus diesen Videoaufnahmen.

Auch hier ist die Liste von Möglichkeiten schier endlos.

4.2 Der Wert von Projektarbeit

Einerseits ist es natürlich wichtig, schwierige Zusammenhänge in einer sinnvollen Reihenfolge darzustellen (wobei es dafür oft nicht nur eine einzige Möglichkeit gibt). Bevor man z. B. die schon erwähnte physikalische Größe „Drehmoment“ einführt, ist es nicht nur hilfreich, sondern unbedingt erforderlich, den Begriff der „Kraft“ schon behandelt zu haben. Andererseits führt eine bestimmte Reihenfolge – als lineare Abfolge von Gedanken und Begründungen – bei Detaildarstellungen auch leicht dazu, die Querverzweigungen und weitere Zusammenhänge zu übersehen.

Hiergegen kann Projektarbeit, wie im ersten Abschnitt definiert, helfen. Insbesondere ist dabei wichtig, dass ein gut definiertes Projekt noch genügend Möglichkeiten für falsche Ansätze, systematische Fehler und Irrwege enthalten muss. Die Aufgabe darf daher nicht zu eng gestellt werden. Die Schüler/innen und Studierenden sollen z. B. selbst herausfinden, dass der Luftzug der Klimaanlage die Schwingungsdauer eines Pendels, dass das Corpus Delicti darstellt, verändern kann. Sie sollen selbst erkennen, dass die wackelnde Aufhängung einen Einfluss hat, ohne dass ihnen vorher mitgeteilt wird, dass die Aufhängung wackelt.

---

[2]nach Ludwig Huber, emer. Prof. der Univ. Bielefeld: Ludwig Huber et al. (Hrsg.): Forschendes Lernen im Studium. UVW, Webler (2009). Ludwig Huber et al. (Hrsg.): Forschendes Lehren im eigenen Fach. wbv (2014).

Insofern geht Projektarbeit über typische Hausaufgaben/Übungsaufgaben weit hinaus. Lehrende legen Hausaufgaben sehr detailliert fest und schließen bestimmte Nebeneinflüsse explizit aus; Spielraum in den Eigenheiten des Problems gibt es nicht. Demgegenüber sollte es gerade ein Ziel der Projektarbeit sein, dass die Lernenden erkennen, wie zunächst für unwichtig gehaltene Randbedingungen doch einen Einfluss haben.

Und umgekehrt kann ein in der Aufgabenstellung explizit ausgeschlossener Lösungsweg die Schüler/innen und Studierenden zu neuen Wegen animieren. In diesem Zusammenhang erinnere ich mich noch gerne an eine Aufgabenstellung, die Mitstudenten und ich in einem physikalischen Praktikum erhielten: wir sollten einen Zusammenhang zwischen zwei physikalischen Größen experimentell ermitteln und zwei Integrale über die gefundene Funktion miteinander vergleichen – *ohne zu rechnen*! Die Aufgabe war überaus sinnvoll; denn häufig bekommt man experimentell eine Kurve heraus, die sich nicht als eine der üblichen Standardfunktionen darstellt, sodass man die Funktion gar nicht einfach angeben könnte, wenn man denn rechnen wollte. (Natürlich könnte man eine Potenzreihenentwicklung vornehmen und so einen Fit an die gemessene Funktion legen; aber diese Möglichkeit sei hier ausgeschlossen.) Einer von uns kam auf die Idee, die Flächen unter den auf Papier gezeichneten Messkurven mit einer Schere auszuschneiden und mit einer Mikrogrammwaage abzuwiegen. Wir mussten nur darauf achten, dass die Blätter, auf denen wir die Kurven zeichneten, aus gleich starkem/dickem/schwerem Papier gemacht waren und dass wir bei den Diagrammen dieselbe Skalierung verwendeten. Auch die Erkenntnis über diese Voraussetzungen war Teil des Lernerfolgs. In diesem Moment habe ich begriffen, was Integrieren *wirklich* bedeutet, … mehr als es die gut gemeinten Ansprachen des Dozenten oder Betreuers jemals hätten erreichen können. Das macht den Wert von Projektarbeit aus.

Sinnvolle Projektarbeit heißt Eigenverantwortung der Schüler/innen oder Studierenden. Eine sinnvolle Projektarbeitsaufgabe zu stellen ist schwierig, weil der für die Arbeit zur Verfügung stehende Zeitraum gegen die möglichen Irrwege und Lösungsmöglichkeiten abgewogen werden muss. Es sollen ja einerseits nicht zu wenige Möglichkeiten gegeben werden. Andererseits soll die Aufgabe in dem vorgegebenen Zeitraum durchaus lösbar sein, um den Lernerfolg und auch das Anhalten der Motivation zu gewährleisten.

4.3 Hindernisse für Projektarbeit

Projektarbeit setzt in hohem Maße voraus, dass die Schüler/innen oder Studierenden zu der betreffenden Thematik bereits ein erhebliches Maß an Vorwissen und auch an Fertigkeiten/Methodenkenntnissen haben. Zum Beispiel macht eine Projektarbeit zu dem Schwingungsverhalten eines Pendels keinen Sinn, wenn die Teilnehmer/innen noch nicht wissen, was eine Bewegungsgleichung ist und wozu sie gut ist, wie man aus der Ortsfunktion über der Zeit die Funktionen für die Geschwindigkeit und die Beschleunigung über der Zeit gewinnt.

Jürgen Klinsmann, der damalige Trainer der US-amerikanischen Herren-Fußball-Nationalmannschaft, wurde in den USA 2014 teilweise scharf kritisiert, weil er die Möglichkeit des Gewinns der Weltmeisterschaft durch die US-Mannschaft von vornherein ausschloss. Dieses Vorgehen widersprach dem amerikanischen Credo „We can do it!" Aber Klinsmann beharrte auf seiner Einstellung, weil unrealistische Ziele eine falsche Herangehensweise nach sich ziehen, die Verbesserung behindern sowie Frustration und Demotivation hervorrufen. Natürlich sollte man sich durchaus sehr hohe Ziele setzen, wenn man hohe Ziele erreichen will; aber zu hohe Ziele können auch das Gegenteil bewirken, wie Klinsmann wusste.

In einer Projektarbeit einen neuen physikalischen Effekt zu entdecken, ist ein zu hohes Ziel, das den Wert der Projektarbeit vernichtet. In einer Woche einen neuen Laser-Typ zu entwickeln, ist ein unrealistisches und daher kontraproduktives Ziel für eine Projektarbeit. Wohldosiert müssen Aufgabe und Lösungsmöglichkeiten sein, wenn die Projektarbeit erfolgreich sein soll. Und mit „erfolgreich" ist hier nicht die Erzielung eines bestimmten Ergebnisses gemeint, sondern der Lernerfolg.

Eine andere wichtige Voraussetzung für erfolgreiche Projektarbeit wird von geeigneten Arbeitsmöglichkeiten gebildet. Projektarbeit in Dreiergruppen in einem vollen Hörsaal mit 300 Leuten wäre selbst dann nicht sinnvoll, wenn die „Projektarbeit" nur darin bestünde, einen Kurvenverlauf durch eine Potenzreihe zu nähern. Die Ruhe fehlt; die Möglichkeit, einige Bücher zu konsultieren, ist wahrscheinlich nicht gegeben. Für eine Projektarbeit im Labor müssen die Probanden die wichtigsten Gerätschaften schon kennen, um damit sinnvoll arbeiten zu können. Die Gerätschaften müssen zugänglich und verfügbar sein. Der/die Dozent/in kann z. B. nicht erwarten, dass sich die Studenten selbstständig eine teure Hochgeschwindigkeitskamera beschaffen oder auch nur ausleihen.

Ich erinnere mich ungern an einen Vorgesetzten (er hielt sich für einen großen Motivator), der immer wieder betonte, es sei ihm völlig egal, wie wir etwas machten, wenn wir es nur machten, und er gäbe uns jede Freiheit dazu. Und die

Ziele, die er setzte, erinnerten mich an Aufgaben wie „Springen Sie sechs Meter hoch, aber ohne Stab!“, also weit weg von jedem Realismus. Und solche Form der Motivation verfehlt ihr Ziel und verkehrt sich ins Gegenteil. Vorgesetzte haben nicht nur die Aufgabe, geeignete Arbeitsbedingungen zu schaffen, sondern auch sinnvolle Aufgaben zu stellen. Dasselbe gilt für Dozenten/innen an Schulen und Hochschulen.

4.4 Kompetenz oder Wissen?

Mit Recht wird von vielen Didaktikern/innen mindestens in den letzten 10 Jahren immer mehr gefordert, Lehre auf sinnvolle Kompetenzen auszurichten. Denn die Lösung einer schwierigen Aufgabe hat mit vielen Fähigkeiten zu tun: Teamfähigkeit, Aufgabenteilung, Fähigkeit schnell an richtige Informationen zu kommen, Abstraktionsvermögen und Analyse des Problems, Lösungsplan inkl. Auswahl geeigneter Methoden und vieles mehr.

Das bloße Einsetzen von Zahlen in Formeln und vielleicht noch das Umstellen der Formel kann nicht genug sein, um Kompetenzen zu erlangen. Insofern haben Dozenten/innen und ihre Mitarbeiter/innen eine große Verantwortung bei der Auswahl von Übungsaufgaben. Mindestens sollten letztere oft in einen Alltags-Kontext eingebettet sein, um die Motivation zu wecken und um die Fähigkeit zur Analyse der Situation zu fördern.

Aus dieser Sicht wäre Projektarbeit das Mittel der Wahl – eine große Aufgabe in einem Team von 2–4 Leuten lösen, mit experimentellen und theoretischen Anteilen, mit Aufarbeitung und klarer Darstellung der Ergebnisse mit heute üblichen Methoden. Bei typischen Anfängerzahlen von 50–450 Studierenden bei 3–5 Betreuern/innen ist dies aber ein Wunschdenken und im besten Fall höchstens einmal exemplarisch durchführbar. Ich habe zwar schon häufig eine gegenteilige Meinung gehört, aber ausschließlich von Leuten, die ihre gut gemeinten Methoden noch niemals bei mehr als 30 Studierenden ausprobiert haben (wie sie ehrlicherweise auf Nachfrage zugaben).

Ein aus meiner Sicht sehr wichtiger Aspekt soll hier aber auch erwähnt werden. Kompetenzförderung ist nicht das alleinige Allheilmittel. Kompetenz setzt auch immer Wissen über Fakten und Methoden voraus. Die prinzipielle Kompetenz, etwas klar und schlüssig darzustellen, läuft ins Leere, wenn die Zusammenhänge bisher nicht erkannt worden sind. Insofern ist auch und vorab die Aneignung von Faktenwissen und Methodenkenntnis unerlässlich. Und das macht nicht immer nur Spaß. Das ist harte Arbeit; da muss man durch. Und Lehrende sollten sich nicht scheuen, das von Lernenden einzufordern.

4.5 Beaufsichtigtes Selbstlernen

(der kleine Bruder der Projektarbeit, in Maßen einzusetzen)

„Peer-reviewed learning“ (die Studierenden untereinander sowie der Dozent als „peers“/Gleichrangige) ist u. a. ein Kind des kanadischen Professors Eric Mazur (E. Mazur: Peer instruction – a user's manual. Prentice Hall Series in educational innovation [1997]). Er führt in seinem Buch sehr schön aus, was er darunter versteht, wie vorzugehen ist, welche Vorarbeiten zu leisten und wie Lerneinheiten durchzuführen sind.

In Kurzfassung formuliert, geht es darum, dass schon in einer Vorlesung kleine Diskussionsgruppen zu einer Fragestellung gebildet werden. Vertreter/innen der Gruppen tragen dann das Ergebnis einiger Gruppen vor. Der/die Dozent/in kann korrigieren oder Ergebnisse hervorheben. Die Idee, die dahinter steckt, ist die Idee der Projektarbeit – übertragen auf eine Vorlesungssituation.

Ich habe diese Technik zunächst als vielversprechend empfunden – gerade vor dem Hintergrund von Anfängervorlesungen mit vielen Zuhörern (50–450). Die (vielleicht nicht ausreichend systematisch angelegten) Versuche von mir, diese Technik anzuwenden, waren dann aber sehr ernüchternd. Bei deutlich mehr als 50 Zuhörern/innen kommt sofort eine erhebliche, unkonzentrierte Unruhe auf, die der Sache abträglich ist. Und nicht wenige der Zuhörer/innen nehmen solche Fragestellungen sofort zum Anlass, sich mental erst einmal auszuklinken, was man an der Körperhaltung sofort erkennt. Es existieren sehr positiv zu bewertende Aktivitäten, die als „peer reviewed learning“ firmieren. Letztlich handelt es sich bei einem Teil davon aber um die Anwendung von „voting tools“.

Aber der vielleicht wichtigste Einwand ist, dass die Leute sich inhaltlich auf die Vorlesung vorbereitet oder in der aktuellen Doppelstunde bis dahin das meiste aufmerksam verfolgt und verstanden haben müssen, um mit so einer Fragestellung sinnvoll und gewinnbringend für sich umgehen zu können. Diese freiwillige Vorbereitung auf eine Vorlesung habe ich in 25 Dienstjahren nur im Einzelfall erlebt.

„Peer-reviewed learning“ könnte im Prinzip in fortgeschrittenen Vorlesungen mit Zuhörerzahlen zwischen 10 und 30 etwas bringen. Aber hier ist es nicht unbedingt notwendig, weil der/die Dozent/in andere Möglichkeiten hat, mit den Zuhörern/innen in Kontakt zu treten, mit ihnen in eine Diskussion einzutreten und sie zum Mitmachen zu animieren.

5 Eine Vorlesung liefert Unbe-schreib-liches

- Achten Sie auf Bemerkungen, die nicht in Büchern stehen!

5.1 Ein Buch

In zunehmendem Maße erwarten Studierende, dass ihnen in den Vorlesungen alles bereitgestellt und nahegebracht wird, was sie zum Verständnis und zur Verinnerlichung des Stoffes brauchen – „full service“. Bis vor ca. 10 Jahren noch war es fast selbstverständlich, dass sich die Studierenden die in den Vorlesungen empfohlenen Bücher kauften, um damit zu arbeiten und zu „studieren“. Heute – so sagt man mir in der Buchhandlung auf dem Uni-Campus – kaufen nur noch ca. 20 % der Studierenden diese Bücher.

Das liegt an zwei Gründen: Zum einen ermöglichen einige Verlage den kostenlosen, legalen Download von Lehrbüchern (auch neuerer Auflagen), die schon länger auf dem Markt sind. Zum anderen hat ein Teil der verbliebenen Studierenden gar nicht mehr vor, die Bücher zu lesen und mit ihnen zu arbeiten.

Von diesen gar nicht wenigen Studierenden wird der Sinn und Wert, sich den Stoff eine Buches zu erarbeiten, nicht erkannt, der Zeitaufwand dafür als zu groß, die Arbeit damit als zu mühselig erachtet. Der in den Vorlesungen dargebrachte Stoff soll so „handlich“ sein oder zumindest herübergebracht werden, dass ein Nacharbeiten gar nicht notwendig ist. Dabei wird nicht gesehen, dass erst durch das eigenständige „Erarbeiten“ des Stoffes z. B. anhand eines Buches ein Verständnis ermöglicht wird, das über bloßes Auswendiglernen hinausgeht.

H. Fouckhardt, *Lehren und Lernen*, essentials,
DOI 10.1007/978-3-658-18064-5_5

5.2 Eine Vorlesung

Wenn für eine Vorlesung ein bestimmtes Buch und eventuell auch noch weitere Bücher empfohlen werden und wenn vielleicht sogar noch ein Skript existiert, könnte man auf die Frage kommen, wozu eine Vorlesung dann überhaupt noch notwendig ist.

Die Antwort ist:

Es geht darum, eine konkrete Hilfestellung zur Erfassung des Stoffes und zur Verwendung und Interpretation der Buchtexte zu liefern. Zwar werden Lehrbücher heute so gestaltet, dass wichtige Sachverhalte oder Aussagen in Fettdruck oder vor farbigem Hintergrund gedruckt werden. Aber damit müssen die Studierenden erst einmal umzugehen lernen. Und anfangs begreift man vielleicht gar nicht, warum diese farbig hinterlegte Aussage so wichtig sein soll, … was an dem einen Gedanken so besonders ist.

„Warum weist das Buch so penetrant darauf hin, dass die Kraft F nicht einfach das Produkt aus Masse m und Beschleunigung $\ddot{x}$ [1] ist (also $F = m \cdot \ddot{x}$, wie man es $100\times$ in der Schule gesehen hat), sondern nach Newton die zeitliche Ableitung des Impulses p (also $F = \dot{p}$)?" Der Grund liegt darin, dass Newton ein sehr schlauer Wissenschaftler war und auf diese Art und Weise auch gleich die Fälle mit eingeschlossen hat, bei denen sich die Masse im Laufe der Zeit ändern kann (z. B. bei Raketenstarts durch Abbrand des Treibstoffs, bei Schüttvorgängen bei fahrenden Zügen etc. pp.); denn nach der Produktregel für Ableitungen ist:

$$F = \dot{p} = \frac{d(m \cdot \dot{x})}{dt} = m\ddot{x} + \dot{m}\dot{x}. \tag{5.1}$$

Es kommt also aufgrund der veränderlichen Masse ($\dot{m} \neq 0$) noch ein Term hinzu; ihn nicht zu vergessen, rechtfertigt den farbigen Hintergrund.

Ein Dozent ist somit quasi ein Conférencier, der das Publikum durch das Programm führt, und ich meine das überhaupt nicht abschätzig.

Ein wichtiger Aspekt kommt hinzu. Manchmal ist den Studierenden mit einem Vergleich oder einer Analogie oder einer extremen Vereinfachung geholfen, über die Schwelle zum Verständnis zu kommen. Aber dieser Vergleich, diese Analogie oder diese Vereinfachung ist vielleicht so grob, dass der/die Dozent/in sie niemals in ein Skript oder ein Lehrbuch schreiben würde, um nicht von Kollegen/innen deswegen kritisiert zu werden.

---

[1] Die Beschleunigung $a = \ddot{x}$ wird hier durch die zwei Punkte über dem x als zweifache zeitliche Ableitung des Weges geschrieben.

6 Probleme lösen lernen, Techniken erwerben, üben

> Die Suche nach dem Weg des geringsten Widerstands ist der schlechteste Ansatz zum Studieren.

6.1 Was macht Erfolg aus?

Abgesehen von vielen Zufällen, die darüber entscheiden, ob man mit der richtigen Idee am richtigen Ort im richtigen Zeitfenster ist, hat es meiner Meinung nach mit fünf Aspekten zu tun, ob ein Mensch großen Erfolg bei einer nicht zu banalen Tätigkeit erlangt – in folgender Reihung mit abnehmender Wichtigkeit:

1. Übung (Transpiration),
2. Talent und Begeisterungsfähigkeit für die bewusste Sache, damit der Fleiß und die Bereitschaft zum Üben bereitwillig aufgebracht werden (Inspiration Teil 1),
3. Kreativität und Mut, um Neues auszuprobieren und auch für sich selbst die Begeisterungsfähigkeit zu erhalten (Inspiration Teil 2),
4. praktische und emotionale Intelligenz, d. h. die Fähigkeit, die Erkenntnisse den Entscheidungsträgern in einem geeigneten Kontext auf einladende Art zu vermitteln, letztere von der eigenen Sache zu begeistern,
5. allgemeine Intelligenz.

Auffälliger- und verblüffenderweise ist die allgemeine Intelligenz ganz hinten angeordnet. Lewis M. Terman, ein Psychologieprofessor an der Stanford University hat ein mehrbändiges Werk (Band I von 1926) mit dem Titel „Genetische Studien der Genialität" verfasst. Basis der Ausführungen waren Untersuchungen, die Terman über viele Jahre gleichzeitig an über 1400 Personen, beginnend in deren Kindesalter, durchgeführt hatte. Diese über 1400 Personen waren nach

H. Foeckhardt, *Lehren und Lernen*, essentials,
DOI 10.1007/978-3-658-18064-5_6

einem mehrstufigen Intelligenz-Auswahltest identifiziert worden. Ihre Intelligenzquotienten (IQ) gehören zu den allerhöchsten bekannten und reichen bis hinauf zu etwa 200 (Einstein hatte einen IQ von 150). (Übliche IQ-Tests fragen aber nur die allgemeine Intelligenz ab.)

Termans Arbeitshypothese war, dass letztlich der Intelligenzquotient über den Erfolg in Beruf und Leben entscheidet. Doch nach langer Forschung musste er erkennen, dass dem nicht so ist. Einige seiner Probanden konnten als Totalausfall gewertet werden. Viele waren in ihrem Beruf erfolgreich; aber kein einziger hatte außergewöhnlichen Erfolg. Demgegenüber wurden zwei Personen in dem Auswahlverfahren von Terman zu Beginn aussortiert, die später sogar den Nobelpreis erhielten. Malcolm Gladwell beschreibt u. a. all dies sehr amüsant in seinem Buch „Überflieger", Piper-Verlag (2012).

Viel wichtiger als alle anderen Aspekte ist Übung sowie die Bereitschaft und die Gelegenheit dazu. Dies hat sicher mit Talent und Begeisterungsfähigkeit zu tun und auch mit Kreativität und dem damit verbundenen Wunsch, immer wieder neue Kombinationen des Bekannten auszuprobieren oder auch etwas ganz anderes zu versuchen. Und die Bereitschaft mag zunächst, solange der erste Erfolg noch ausbleibt und das Üben sehr mühselig und frustrierend ist, auch noch relativ klein sein. Aber Übung bleibt die wichtigste Zutat zum Erfolg. Sehr erfolgreiche Menschen üben nicht erst, seit sie erfolgreich sind. Sie sind so erfolgreich, weil sie schon sehr lange sehr viel geübt haben.

6.2 Die 10.000-Stunden-Regel

Die Psychologen K. Anders Ericsson, Ralf Th. Krampe und Clemens Tesch-Romer stellten Anfang der 90er Jahre des letzten Jahrhunderts in mehreren wissenschaftlichen Artikeln fest, dass hauptsächlich die Gelegenheit und Zeit zum Üben darüber entscheiden, ob jemand eine hohe Expertise bei bestimmten Tätig- oder Fertigkeiten erwirbt. Talent spielt nur eine untergeordnete Rolle.

Zwar ist es nicht möglich, ohne Talent Expertise zu erlangen; unmusikalische Menschen werden nicht Opernsänger/innen werden können. Aber wenn Talent vorhanden ist, ist Expertise noch überhaupt nicht garantiert. Auch dies wird sehr anschaulich in dem schon erwähnten Buch „Überflieger" von Malcolm Gladwell (Piper-Verlag [2012]) beschrieben.

Die genannten Autoren sprechen von der 10.000-Stunden-Regel. Erst ab 10.000 Stunden Übung kommt man in die Nähe von Expertise. Und um sie zu steigern, sogar nur um sie zu halten und um Virtuosität zu erlangen, muss ständig viel weiter geübt werden.

10.000 Stunden entsprechen ca. 5–10 Jahren, wenn man bedenkt, was an Zeit übrig bleibt, wenn man all die andere Zeit, die man zum Essen, Schlafen, für die Körperhygiene und eine typischerweise gegebene andere Standardtätigkeit, wie den Schulbesuch, abzieht.

Es braucht etwa 10.000 Stunden oder 5–10 Jahre, bis sich Gehirn, Nervensystem oder/und Muskulatur so extrem auf eine Tätigkeit oder Fertigkeit eingestellt haben, dass eine hohe Expertise möglich ist und bei der Ausübung dieser Tätigkeit oder Fertigkeit eine großer Erfolg zu erwarten ist. Das gilt übrigens genauso für eine Pianistin wie für einen Fliesenleger. Fliesenlegen kann sicher nicht als banale Tätigkeit angesehen werden, wie ich aus eigener Erfahrung weiß.

In meinen Erstsemester-Vorlesungen passiert es mir immer wieder, wenn ich mit einem neuen (schwierigen) Thema, z. B. Strömungsphysik, beginne, dass einzelne Studierende mehr oder weniger laut und demonstrativ die Beine hochlegen und beginnen, sich anderweitig zu beschäftigen. Mal abgesehen von der Unhöflichkeit, die das ihren Kommilitonen/innen und mir gegenüber, die wir uns konzentrieren wollen, bedeutet, hat dieses Verhalten noch einen ganz anderen Aspekt. Wenn ich diese Leute im Hörsaal vor den anderen Studierenden anspreche, erhalte ich meist die Antwort, sie wüssten schon, dass sie dieses Thema in ihrem Berufsleben niemals brauchen werden würden; sie würden in eine andere Richtung gehen wollen. Diese Einschätzung ist so falsch, wie man es nur einem 18-/19-Jährigen zubilligen sollte.

Zum einen gehen ca. 85 % unserer (naturwissenschaftlich-technischen) Absolventen/innen in die Industrie. Dort dauern Produktzyklen heute typischerweise zwischen drei Jahren und drei Monaten und der Weltmarkt zwingt die Firmen, sich ständig neu zu positionieren und zu definieren. Man kann also gar nicht wissen, ob man drei Jahre nach der Einstellung bei einer Firma nicht doch die zuvor abgelehnte Thematik bearbeiten muss, möchte man seine Stelle behalten.

Natürlich kann man auch dann noch den Stoff nacharbeiten. Aber es zeigt sich, dass die Hemmschwelle dafür groß ist, wenn man diesem Thema vorher nie ausgesetzt war. „Was Hänschen nicht lernt, lernt Hans nimmer mehr."

Zu ernst sollte diese Weisheit unserer Vorfahren natürlich nicht genommen werden. Denken wir zum Beispiel an viele ältere Mitbürger/innen, die sich noch den Umgang mit Computern und Smartphones erschließen, obwohl sie diesen technischen Geräten in ihrem Berufsleben kaum ausgesetzt waren. Aber ganz von der Hand zu weisen ist dieser Satz auch nicht – eben wegen der inneren Hemmschwelle und vielleicht sogar wegen der Angst, die viele Menschen vor ganz Neuem haben.

Zum anderen sollten weder Schul- noch Hochschulbildung das Ziel und die Aufgabe haben, den Schüler/innen und Studierenden nur exakt diejenigen Fähigkeiten, Fertigkeiten und Kenntnisse zu erschließen, die sie oberflächlich betrachtet in

ihrem Berufsleben brauchen – nicht mehr und nicht weniger. Leider wird dies von verschiedenen Seiten immer mehr von den Schulen und Hochschulen eingefordert. Meiner Ansicht nach sollten vielmehr Einblicke in Themenbereiche vermittelt und Techniken zum Umgang mit Problemen aus diesen Bereichen erschlossen werden.

Und zum dritten – und vielleicht ist das sogar der wichtigste Aspekt – muss man üben, üben, üben, *wobei es relativ egal ist, worum genau es in den Übungen geht.*

Die Einschätzung der oben erwähnten störenden Studierenden liefe darauf hinaus, dass ein angehender Instrumental-Musiker sagt: „Nein, Tonleitern übe ich nicht, weil ich später in Konzerten auch keine Tonleitern vortragen werde!" Aber die Tonleitern müssen geübt werden, um Fingerfertigkeit zu erlangen. Und mit den Fingern ist es dabei nicht getan. Die Bewegung der Finger beim Umschalten von einem auf einen anderen Ton, von einem auf einen anderen Griff muss für Gehirn, Nervensystem und Muskulatur zur Selbstverständlichkeit werden. Sie muss unterbewusst ablaufen können, um Schnelligkeit und Virtuosität zu ermöglichen.

Eine angehende Physikerin muss etliche Male Formeln nach bestimmten Größen aufgelöst haben um zu wissen, was dabei für Sonderfälle auftreten können und wie sie gemeistert werden können. Sie muss etliche Male Formeln umgestellt haben, um eine quadratische Gleichung oder eine Differenzialgleichung wiedererkennen zu können und sich an den Lösungsweg zu erinnern. Sie muss etliche Male Lösungen für die üblichen Differenzialgleichungen gefunden haben, um bei einer etwas anderen Differenzialgleichung ein Repertoire an Möglichkeiten zu haben, eine Lösung zu suchen.

Die Tonleitern sind Voraussetzungen für das virtuose Spiel von Sonaten. Der Vietarische Wurzelsatz (heute *pq*-Formel genannt) wird gebraucht, um auf den Mond zu fliegen.

Einer der erwähnten Studierenden sollte beim Thema Strömungsphysik eben nicht abschalten, weil er später vielleicht an der Flüssigkeitskühlung für einen Computerchip arbeiten wird. Und selbst wenn nicht: mit Aufgaben auch aus der Strömungsphysik kann er sein Gehirn trainieren.

6.3 Virtuosität nicht angestrebt?

Wenn ich bei Motivationsproblemen einiger Studierender in der Vorlesung Hinweise gebe, wie sie im letzten Abschnitt formuliert worden sind, erhalte ich von einigen meist die nur scheinbar „coole" Antwort, dass sie gar nicht virtuos werden wollen; ihnen reiche auch ein Job als …[1] Und leider schließen sie aus diesem

[1] Hier möchte ich extra keine Beispiele nennen, weil jedes Beispiel falsch wäre.

Gedanken fälschlich, dass sie sich so gut wie keine Mühe geben müssen, wenn sie nicht virtuos werden wollen.

Auch hierbei liegen diese Studierenden falsch. Man kann nicht die Rechnung aufmachen: oberhalb 10.000 Übungsstunden Expertise und angehende Virtuosität, alles darunter zwar keine Virtuosität, aber immer noch sehr gute Expertise. Natürlich gibt es eine Staffelung. Jede Stufe der Expertise setzt einen bestimmten Mindestaufwand voraus. Aber warum sollte man sich eine Erfolgsbegrenzung durch zu wenig Einsatz gleich zu Beginn der Ausbildung und Laufbahn selbst auferlegen. Das ist, als hörte man auf, mit einem Musikinstrument zu üben, bevor es jemals richtig Spaß gemacht hat, es zu spielen … bevor man so gut ist, dass man auch anspruchsvolle, aber besonders lohnenswerte Stücke spielen kann.

Noch relativ leicht kann ich nachvollziehen, warum man in der Schule – so jung wie man ist – noch nicht begreift, wozu man das alles braucht, und warum man versucht, mit möglichst wenig Aufwand die Schule hinter sich zu bringen. Aber bei einem Studium, das man sich selbst gewählt hat, ist es unverständlich, wenn man nicht versucht, so viel wie möglich daraus zu ziehen. Das bedeutet,

- möglichst mehr Übungsaufgaben zu lösen zu versuchen, als man braucht, um gerade eben die Zulassung zur Prüfungsklausur zu erhalten,
- möglichst mehr Vorlesungen als vorgeschrieben zu hören,
- möglichst sich als Zuhörer/in in wissenschaftliche Vorträge zu setzen, selbst wenn man anfangs nicht allzu viel verstehen wird,
- während des Studiums einen Job als Hilfswissenschaftler/in anzunehmen, um in verschiedene Probleme hineinzuschnuppern und von den Erfahrungen der anderen zu lernen, u. v. m.

„Lean study“ macht keinen Sinn. Ein „schlankes“ Studium kann ja nur bedeuten, nicht links und rechts zu gucken. Und das läuft dem Sinn und dem Ziel des Studiums entgegen. Man sollte sich dem Studium, dem Angebot der Fakultät, soweit es irgendwie zeitlich geht, so viel wie möglich „aussetzen“. Bill Gates hat jede Programmieraufgabe, die ihm über den Weg lief, genutzt, um seine Fähigkeiten und Kenntnisse zu erweitern. So geht Studieren, selbst wenn man am Ende damit zufrieden wäre, nicht der weltbeste Virtuose geworden zu sein.

Nun werden viele der heutigen Schüler/innen und Studierenden einräumen, dass die Curricula bei ggf. zwölf Schuljahren und einem Bachelor-/Master-Studium so „verschult“ sind, dass kein Spielraum mehr bleibt, um links und rechts zu sehen. Aber das stimmt nicht ganz. Zum einen bieten auch die heutigen Curricula noch gewisse Spielräume (mehr wären wünschenswert). Und zum anderen ist es auch die Frage, ob man bei den Pflichtveranstaltungen gerade so viel „übt“,

wie erforderlich ist, um mit möglichst wenig Zeitaufwand halbwegs durchzukommen, oder ob man sich mehr Mühe gibt.

Im englisch/amerikanischen Sprachraum wird letzteres „die extra Meile gehen“ genannt. Sollte man im Studium nicht versuchen, ein Fundament für den Beruf zu schaffen, auf das man dann so lange wie möglich aufbauen kann! Und darüber hinaus: wenn man nie gelernt hat, die extra Meile zu gehen, wie wird es dann im Beruf klappen. Und die Firmen leben heute – bei globaler Konkurrenz – davon, dass Mitarbeiter/innen bereit sind, die extra Meile zu gehen, egal ob wir das gut und richtig finden oder nicht.

6.4 Mensaessen

Immer wieder hört man von einigen Studierenden oder einigen jungen Berufsanfängern/innen, dass das einzige, was sie im Studium für ihre Berufstätigkeit gelernt hätten, die Gewöhnung an schlechtes Kantinenessen sei.

Man mag dies einfach nur als Witz auffassen und darüber schmunzeln. Vielleicht ist es auch nur Wichtigtuerei. Aber wer so etwas ernsthaft sagt, hat einen wichtigen Gedanken (der eben auch in diesem Kapitel ausgedrückt werden soll) nicht verstanden. Zum einen ist die Wahrscheinlichkeit, im Studium ganz konkrete Hilfen und Techniken für den Beruf zu erlernen, umso größer, je mehr man im Studium zu machen versucht – eigentlich ein ganz logischer Gedanke. Und zum anderen dient ein seriös betriebenes Studium, egal an welchen Problemen man sich müht, zum „Üben“.

Ich möchte meinen Gedanken sogar so weit treiben zu sagen, dass Frau Dr. Angela Merkel in ihrem Physikstudium (zumindest teilweise) genau das gelernt hat, was sie tagtäglich als Bundeskanzlerin braucht, nämlich

- Probleme in ihre Bestandteile zerlegen (analysieren),
- Gedankengänge logisch aufbauen,
- Lösungswege ergründen,
- sich unter den gegebenen Bedingungen für einen Lösungsweg entscheiden.

Also: setzen Sie sich dem Studium aus!

7 Prüfungen sind doch wichtig

> Nutzen Sie Prüfungsvorbereitungen, um Verknüpfungen herzustellen, die Ihnen sonst verborgen blieben!

7.1 Randbedingungen

Ideal wäre es, wenn die Dozenten/innen Zeit hätten, mit jedem/r einzelnen Studierenden häufig zu reden, ihn/sie von Anfang an unter Anleitung der Diplomanden/innen und Doktoranden/innen in ihre Forschung einzubinden und sie so direkt an schwierige Problemstellungen heranzuführen. Bis in das erste Drittel des 20. Jahrhunderts hinein war das Physik-Studium in Deutschland ähnlich organisiert. Es gab so wenige Studierende, dass jeder Anfänger quasi einem Professor zugeteilt und in dessen Gruppe aufgenommen wurde. Genau genommen bewarb man sich um einen Studienplatz direkt bei einem bestimmten Professor. Danach hörte man durchaus auch viele Vorlesungen bei anderen Professoren, aber man blieb der einen Gruppe zugeordnet und konnte dort natürlich auch Fragen zu anderen Lehrveranstaltungen stellen. Durch die Zuordnung zu einer Gruppe entstand ein extrem gutes Betreuungsverhältnis.

Dies ist bei jährlichen Anfängerzahlen von deutlich mehr als dem Dreifachen der Professorenzahl kaum machbar. In deutschen Fachbereichen der Naturwissenschaften sprechen wir heute grob von jeweils 20–30 Professoren/innen und Anfängerzahlen zwischen 80 und 450. Bei solchen Zahlen ist individuelles Beibringen des Stoffes im Normalfall nicht möglich.

Und es ist auch nicht möglich, in individuellen Gesprächen herauszufinden, inwieweit der Stoff verinnerlicht wurde. Daraus ergibt sich der Zwang zu formalisierten Prüfungen, typischerweise Klausuren oder einzelnen mündlichen Prüfungen.

H. Fouckhardt, *Lehren und Lernen*, essentials,
DOI 10.1007/978-3-658-18064-5_7

7.2 Vergleichbarkeit

Nach außen:

Hochschüler/innen möchten überwiegenderweise, aufbauend auf dem im Studium erworbenen Wissen und den Fähigkeiten und Fertigkeiten, einen Beruf ergreifen. Die Firmen verlassen sich darauf, dass hinter einem bestimmten Abschluss auch ein mehr oder weniger einheitliches Wissen & Können steht. Dies kann nur garantiert werden, wenn das Curriculum abgeprüft wird. Wir alle wissen aus unserer Vergangenheit, dass wir wahrscheinlich nicht so detailliert hingeschaut hätten, wenn wir uns keinen Prüfungen gegenüber gesehen hätten. Die PKW-Hauptuntersuchung ist für uns alle doch immer wieder ein Ansporn, kleinere Reparaturen am Auto vornehmen zu lassen, die wir ansonsten noch eine Weile vor uns herschieben würden.

Nach innen:

Prüfungen und Prüfungsergebnisse erlauben somit aber nicht nur einen Vergleich der Absolventen/innen aus Sicht der Firmen. Sie erlauben den Studierenden selbst ihre eigene Einordnung während des Studiums. Ein Student, der Prüfungen immer nur gerade so besteht, sollte sich selbst oder jemand anderen um Rat fragen, was er falsch macht, wie er das Studieren für sich anders organisieren könnte oder ob dieses Studium für ihn wirklich die geeignete Ausbildung darstellt.

7.3 Der noch wichtigere Grund

Der wichtigste Grund für Prüfungen sind aber die Prüfungsvorbereitungen. Zwar erinnern sich wahrscheinlich viele von uns daran, dass unsere Studentenbude nie sauberer war als unmittelbar vor wichtigen Prüfungen. Dann erschien uns sogar Saubermachen attraktiver als das Lernen für die Prüfungen. Aber wenn wir ehrlich sind, erinnern wir uns auch, dass wir beim konzentrierten und ausführlichen Wiederholen und Lernen Verknüpfungen des Gelernten erkannt haben, die uns vorher verschlossen geblieben waren, z. B. dass die Differenzialgleichung, die die zeitliche und räumliche Änderung der Temperatur in einer Materialprobe beschreibt, dieselbe Form wie die Differenzialgleichung zeigt, die die Diffusion von Teilchen beschreibt. Temperatur „diffundiert" also, wie erstaunlich.

Mit solchen und ähnlichen Erkenntnissen können verschiedene Gebiete der Physik, die zunächst disjunkt erscheinen, miteinander verknüpft werden. Erkenntnisse aus dem einen Gebiet können so auf ein anderes übertragen werden. Dieses Erkennen von Gemeinsamkeiten in verschiedenen Themenbereichen macht einen

wesentlichen Aspekt der Physik sowie aller Natur- und Ingenieurwissenschaften aus. Nicht umsonst versuchen die Physiker/innen u. a., mit einer einzigen Weltformel alle bekannten Wechselwirkungen zu beschreiben, also miteinander zu vereinigen.

Solche Erkenntnisse brechen sich ihre Bahn nur, wenn der Blick etwas erweitert wird, die Vogelperspektive eingenommen wird. Und das sollte für Studierende nun einmal dann der Fall sein, wenn sie in Prüfungsvorbereitungen stecken. Letztere machen also einen wesentlichen Teil dessen aus, was man „Studieren" nennt.

Prüfer/innen können diese Tendenz natürlich unterstützen, indem sie Verständnisfragen stellen und weniger solche, bei denen man viele Einzelheiten auswendig gelernt haben muss.

8 Setzen Sie sich dem Studium aus!

▶ Richten Sie Ihr Leben nach dem Studium – und nicht umgekehrt!

8.1 Konzentration und Umfeld

Bereits das Kap. 6 endete mit der Aufforderung „Setzen Sie sich dem Studium aus!“ Dort ging es um den Inhalt des Studiums und die Mühen, die damit verbunden sind, wenn es ernsthaft betrieben wird.

Nun soll auch das persönliche Umfeld der Studierenden angesprochen werden. Dabei bin ich mir als Verfasser dieser Zeilen sehr wohl bewusst, dass es heute sehr viele Lebensentwürfe gibt, die man sich selbst gewählt hat oder die durch äußere Umstände aufgezwungen wurden. Zum Beispiel hat heute eine nicht verschwindende Zahl von Studierenden ihren Lebensunterhalt selbst zu verdienen oder altersbedingt dauerhaft kranke Familienmitglieder zu pflegen. Für sie muss es wie ein Hohn erscheinen, wenn ich gleich Tipps für die Tageszeitplanung gebe. Wenn ich dies tue, dann nur gegenüber Studierenden, die tatsächlich die Möglichkeit haben, ihren Tagesablauf frei zu gestalten. Es geht um die Optimierung des Studienerfolgs (auch zeitlich).

Ein übliches naturwissenschaftlich-technisches Studium ist nach Umfang und Tiefgang (Quantität und Qualität) so aufwendig, dass es kaum im Alleingang zu bewältigen ist. Viele Dozenten/innen legen es darauf an, dass die Inhalte und Übungsaufgaben im Normalfall nicht alleine zu erschließen sind. Denn sie wissen, dass die Diskussion über Probleme unter den Studierenden und das Erklären eines schwierigen Sachverhalts gegenüber einem Freund einen wichtigen Teil des Studierens ausmachen.

In den ersten Semestern empfehlen viele Dozenten/innen, sich in Arbeitsgruppen von 2–4 Leuten zusammenzuschließen und gemeinsam zu arbeiten, weil

H. Fouckhardt, *Lehren und Lernen*, essentials,
DOI 10.1007/978-3-658-18064-5_8

dabei üblicherweise mehr herauskommt als bei einer Einsiedlertätigkeit. Jeder der Gruppe hat 'mal eine Idee, die eine Blockade aufhebt. Und selbst wenn die Idee nicht von den anderen in der Gruppe stammt, haben sie davon mehr, als wenn sie bei der ersten Blockade alleine sofort hätten aufgeben müssen. Hinzu kommt, dass die Studierenden auf diese Weise mitbekommen, dass nicht nur sie Schwierigkeiten haben. Das beruhigt und erlaubt, die Energie auf das Wesentliche zu richten.

Ich arbeite seit 20 Jahren an einer Regionaluniversität, will heißen an einer Universität, an der ein großer Teil der Studierenden aus der Umgebung kommt (aus dem sogenannten „Waschmaschinenradius"). In unregelmäßigen Abständen werden Umfragen gemacht und ergeben, dass bis zu etwa 50 % der Studienanfänger/innen noch bei ihren Eltern wohnen.

Ganz unabhängig von einer Ausbildung und speziell dem Studium halte ich es für einen jungen Menschen für seine persönliche Entwicklung für sehr wichtig, rechtzeitig das Nest zu verlassen. Wenn dieses Flüggewerden mit dem Beginn eines Studiums zusammenfällt, sind natürlich zwei Probleme gleichzeitig zu überwinden: den vielen Anforderungen des Studiums gerecht zu werden (inhaltlich und organisatorisch selbst Verantwortung für die Durchführung zu übernehmen) und sich gleichzeitig in einer neuen Umgebung zurecht zu finden, ein Konto einzurichten, rechtzeitig einzukaufen, bevor der Kühlschrank leer ist, die Bude sauber zu halten, herauszufinden wo man die Wäsche waschen kann und dies auch regelmäßig tun, einen Schreibwarenladen zu finden etc. pp.

Aber diese „Doppelbelastung" löst sich ganz schnell in eine Einfachbelastung auf. Man muss nur *einen* Waschsalon und *ein* Schreibwarengeschäft kennen. Ein Lebensmittelgeschäft in der Nähe wird sich auch schnell finden. Und sich als junger Mensch auf diese Art eine Stadt „zu erobern", ist auch ein erhebendes Gefühl, das Selbstvertrauen gibt.

Für das Studium ist es wichtig, dass man sich mehrfach in der Woche am späten Nachmittag oder Abend Zeit nehmen kann, sich mit der eigenen Arbeitsgruppe zu treffen, um Vorlesungen nachzubearbeiten und gemeinsam Übungszettel zu bearbeiten – am besten ohne Zeitbegrenzung nach hinten. Da sind die mit dem Abendbrot zu Hause wartenden Eltern das letzte, was dem Studium hilft.

Richten Sie Ihr Leben nach dem Studium – und nicht umgekehrt! Dem eigenen Beruf würde man auch so viel Stellenwert einräumen, dass man (im Normalfall) bereit ist, dafür umzuziehen und die Tages- und Wochenplanung danach zu richten. Diesen Stellenwert sollte auch schon das Studium haben, damit es optimal klappen kann. „Überstunden" (um sich durch ein schwieriges inhaltliches Problem durchzubeißen) sollten möglich sein und möglichst wenig durch äußere Umstände behindert werden.

8.2 Arbeitsmöglichkeiten

Zu einem geeigneten Umfeld zum Studieren gehört auch ein geeigneter Arbeitsplatz in der Studentenbude. Die Spüle neben dem Waschbecken ist dafür denkbar ungeeignet. Ein großer Schreibtisch wäre optimal, auf dem viele Bücher Platz haben, an denen man gerade gleichzeitig zur Lösung eines Problems arbeitet – mit entsprechend guter Beleuchtung.

Smartphone und E-Mail-Zugang häufiger einmal auszuschalten, wäre sinnvoll. Es ist neurologisch erwiesen, dass das Gehirn einige Minuten Zeit braucht, um sich voll auf eine bestimmte Aufgabe konzentrieren zu können. Wird man alle paar Minuten gestört – und sei es nur durch den Alarmton (ohne dass man tatsächlich ans Smartphone ginge) –, ist ein konzentriertes Arbeiten unmöglich. Man glaubt dann nur, gearbeitet zu haben. Aber an die wichtigen Zusammenhänge ist man nicht herangekommen.

Die wichtigsten Bücher sollte man in der Studentenbude griffbereit haben, auch um darin Notizen machen zu können. Man spart an der falschen Stelle, wenn man versucht, an Büchern zu sparen. Und wenn man sich doch nicht alle leisten kann, sollte man die Literaturarbeit in die Bereichsbibliothek an der Uni verlagern (natürlich ohne dort Markierungen in den Büchern zu hinterlassen). Ich erinnere mich gerne an mein Studium in Göttingen, wo man in der Mathematik-Bibliothek oft die Studierenden hinter Bergen von Büchern nicht erkennen konnte, durch die sie sich gerade durchkämpften, um einen Sachverhalt zu verstehen. Das ist „Studieren".

8.3 Der Ausgleich

Ein ernsthaft betriebenes Studium ist mit viel Arbeit verbunden. Das sollte aber nicht dazu führen, dass die Arbeit um der Arbeit willen erledigt wird. Eine Studentin, die zum zweiten Mal durch die Klausur gefallen war, fragte mich einmal ganz verzweifelt, was sie denn noch machen könnte, sie würde so viele Stunden arbeiten, aber offenbar ohne Erfolg. Ich fragte sie, was sie denn all die Stunden gemacht hätte. Und sie antwortete, dass sie die gelösten Übungsaufgaben viele Male abgeschrieben hätte. Das macht natürlich keinen Sinn. Besser wäre gewesen, sie hätte sich neue Aufgaben besorgt und versucht, nun diese zu lösen. Beschäftigungstherapie führt im Studium nicht zum Erfolg.

Aber das eigentliche Problem dieser Studentin war ein ganz anderes. Das wiederholte Aufschreiben der Aufgaben deutet auf einen Zustand hin, den man heute fast schon als Burn-out bezeichnen würde. Sie kam aus dem Hamsterrad nicht

mehr heraus. Wenn sie in derselben Zeit zur Entspannung geschlafen hätte, wäre der Wert für ihr Studium größer gewesen. Deswegen ist es wichtig, sich auch Auszeiten zu gönnen.

Ein paar Dinge kann man von Amerikanern lernen. Eine Weisheit drückt sich in folgender Formulierung aus: „Work hard and play hard!"

In diesem Zusammenhang frei übersetzt: „Wenn Du arbeitest, arbeite intensiv! Wenn Du frei hast, mach' richtig frei!"

Dazu gehört, dass der spannende Roman bis zum Abend warten muss, solange man die Übungsaufgaben noch lösen muss. Dazu gehört, dass man die üblichen Freizeitaktivitäten vor Prüfungen zurückstellt, um sich in Ruhe vorbereiten zu können. Dazu gehört aber auch, dass man bei der Heimfahrt zu den Eltern über Weihnachten keine Bücher aus dem Studium mitnimmt. Man möchte zwar immer noch arbeiten, aber kommt nicht dazu. Also hat man weder gelernt, noch sich richtig entspannt, weil man immer gedacht hat: „Ich müsste ja eigentlich noch lernen!"

Unverplante Freiräume muss man sich schaffen; das ist im Studium genauso wichtig. Auch dadurch wird das Studium unterstützt.

9 Fokussierung ist wichtig

▶ Bleiben Sie am Ball wie ein Terrier am Knochen!

9.1 Zuhörenkönnen

Eine der schwersten Regeln habe ich mir für dieses späte Kapitel aufgehoben. Auch sie ist mit dem Begriff der Konzentration verbunden. Es geht um Zuhörenkönnen und das Erlernen dieser Fähigkeit. Wer etwas lernen möchte, muss bereit sein zuzuhören, d. h. auf die Nebensätze der Dozenten/innen zu achten, die in keinem Buch stehen, … den manchmal mühseligen Gedankengängen zu folgen, mit denen ein schwieriger Sachverhalt zu erklären ist.

Die Menschen aus meiner Generation hatten es mindestens in diesem Punkt deutlich einfacher als die heutige Generation. Als wir in Schule, Ausbildung und Studium waren, gab es nicht mehr als 30 Fernseh- und 100 Rundfunkprogramme, Internet-Radio, E-Mails, Smartphones … Wir mussten quasi gar nicht viel tun, um konzentriert zu sein und zu bleiben. Heute muss man aktiv etwas dafür tun, sich konzentrieren zu können.

Nun ist nicht jeder Dozent ein begnadeter Lehrer. Und auch von mir möchte ich das nicht behaupten. Aber alle an den Studierenden interessierten Dozenten/innen geben sich von sich aus Mühe, das Umschiffen der schwierigen Klippen des Stoffes zu erleichtern. Sie finden Analogien oder anschauliche Beispiele, an denen ein Sachverhalt klarer wird. Sie streuen, um die Motivation zu steigern, Erkenntnisse ein, die man sich sonst erst nach vielen Jahren selbst aneignen kann. („In der Wellengleichung, die aus den Maxwellschen Gleichungen hervorgeht, taucht die Lichtgeschwindigkeit auf – unabhängig von jedem denkbaren Bezugssystem. Also schon hier ist die Universalität der Lichtgeschwindigkeit implizit enthalten.“)

H. Fouckhardt, *Lehren und Lernen*, essentials,
DOI 10.1007/978-3-658-18064-5_9

Die Studierenden sollten bereit sein, diese Hinweise aufzunehmen oder einen Querverweis zu verstehen, den sie vorher noch nie gehört haben. Genau das sind Stellen, wo das Verständnis wachsen kann – sinnvollerweise über ein Maß hinaus, mit dem man andernfalls nur Formeln verwenden, sie aber nicht verstehen könnte.

Zuhören ist schwierig und Zuhören will gelernt sein. Zuhören hat auch mit einer *inneren Bereitschaft* zu tun. Wenn diese Bereitschaft nicht existiert, wird man bei erster Gelegenheit „aussteigen". Die genervte Frage an sich selbst sollte nicht lauten: „Warum erzählt der da vorne schon wieder vom Drehmoment? Ich weiß doch schon, was das ist." Sondern der Gedanke sollte sein: „Wenn der da vorne schon zum dritten Mal vom Drehmoment anfängt, muss da mehr dahinter stecken, als mir bisher klar geworden ist. Was ist eigentlich das Problem? Ich sollte noch einmal genauer hinhören oder mehr dazu lesen."

Gerade in Vorlesungen für Studienanfänger/innen ist das eben geschilderte Szenario häufig vorhanden. Die Begriffe sind aus der Schule bekannt: Kraft, Energie, Arbeit, Leistung … Was gibt es da noch zu verstehen? Warum ist es so wichtig, die potenzielle Energie als Wegintegral über die Kraft zu definieren? … An solchen Punkten steigen viele Studierende aus, nicht weil sie den Stoff für zu schwierig halten, sondern weil sie die Schwierigkeit noch nicht einmal gesehen haben. Das führt dann auch dazu, dass die Vorlesungen nicht nachgearbeitet werden, was die Problematik noch verschärft.

9.2 Fragenstellen

Kein wohlmeinender Dozent wird etwas gegen Fragen haben. Fragen zeigen, dass Interesse besteht und das versucht wird mitzudenken. Toll!

Keine vernünftige Dozentin wird Fragen in der Lehrveranstaltung unterbinden (solange sie nicht so häufig sind, dass der Vorlesungsfluss vollkommen gestört wird).

Und wer sich vielleicht nicht traut, vor den Mitstudierenden eine Frage zu stellen, kann nach der Vorlesungsstunde fragen, persönlich oder per E-Mail.

Man sollte auch jede Gelegenheit wahrnehmen, ältere Studierende zu fragen, wenn etwas unklar geblieben ist (zum Studienablauf oder beim Stoff einer Vorlesung). Meistens freuen sich die Kommilitonen/innen, ihr kürzlich erworbenes Wissen weiterzugeben. Und Übung bedeutet dies auch für sie. Auch die schon oft erwähnten selbst gewählten Arbeitsgruppen können hier viel helfen. „Wie hat der Prof das heute gemeint, als er gesagt hat, dass die Lorentz-Kraft durch die spezielle Relativitätstheorie erklärt wird? Von was für Ladungsträgergeschwindigkeiten reden wir denn eigentlich? Sind die Geschwindigkeiten nicht viel zu

klein, um relativistische Effekte erwarten zu können?" Einer der Kumpel wird schon genau hingehört oder vorab schon gelesen haben, dass es zwar um einen sehr schwachen Effekt geht, dass es sich aber auch um sehr viele freie Ladungsträger in einem Draht dreht, sodass sich die Beiträge zu einem merklichen Effekt aufsummieren.

9.3 Eigenverantwortung für das eigene Studium übernehmen!

Viele von den Hinweisen an die Studierenden in diesem Buch können in einem einzigen Satz grob zusammengefasst werden:

Es ist wichtig, dass jeder Student und jede Studentin die Verantwortung für sein oder ihr eigenes Studium übernimmt.

Niemand sollte darauf warten, gesagt zu bekommen, welche Seiten bis wann in welchem Buch zu lesen sind und wie man an das Buch herankommt. Wenn dem ab und zu so ist, okay! Wenn nicht, sollte man nicht darauf warten.

Wichtig ist, Herausforderungen anzunehmen. Wenn man Schwierigkeiten mit einer Übungsaufgabe oder im Verständnis einer Thematik hat, die in der Vorlesung behandelt wurde, sollte man sich nicht damit beruhigen, dass dies nur ein Thema von vielen ist und es nicht so schlimm ist, wenn man dieses eine Thema nicht verstanden hat. Ganz im Gegenteil: gerade bei solchen Themen sollte man nachhaken. Denn hier widerspricht ja offenbar die an der Universität gelehrte Sichtweise gerade den bisherigen Vorstellungen des/der Studierenden. Diese Problematik zu begreifen, heißt, viel über physikalische Sichtweisen zu lernen. Und das hilft dann wieder woanders.

Zum Beispiel: „Warum kann der Wirkungsgrad einer hypothetischen Carnot-Maschine, mit der Wärme in Kraft gewandelt wird, niemals 100 % betragen, obwohl es sich in diesem Gedankenexperiment doch um ein ideales Gas (ohne Wechselwirkung der Gasteilchen untereinander) handeln soll? Dazu müsste doch die tiefere der beiden Temperaturen nur am absoluten Temperaturnullpunkt liegen. – Ja, aber dann, wenn der absolute Nullpunkt erreicht werden könnte, müssten sich nach den Eigenschaften der Entropie alle Systeme immer im absoluten Nullpunkt befinden. Wir Menschen würden nicht existieren. Aber wir existieren. So kann ein Axiom, ein Hauptsatz, formuliert werden: der absolute Temperaturnullpunkt kann niemals erreicht werden."

Über den vermeintlich unwichtigen Wirkungsgrad der Carnot-Wärmekraftmaschine wird hier also eine Verbindung zur Entropie, zum absoluten Temperaturnullpunkt und zu den Hauptsätzen der Thermodynamik geschlagen, d. h. viel Physik zusammengebracht. Da lohnt sich das Nachhaken sehr.

Dieses Nachhaken wurde eingangs des Kapitels als „Terrier-Biss“ bezeichnet. Solange zubeißen, bis der Knochen durchgebrochen ist! Am Ball bleiben, bis das Problem gelöst ist und das nächste bereits wartet! So lernt man viel. Das ist Studieren.

10 Studierende abholen

▶ Loben ist wichtig, aber nicht ohne Grund.

10.1 Drei Drittel

Laut des Statistischen Bundesamts machten 1970 in Deutschland 12 % der Schüler/innen das Abitur, 1990 waren es 31 % und 2010 49 %. Das Studium begannen 1970 12 %, 1990 waren es 30 % und 2010 45 %. Studieren ist also prozentual ein Massenphänomen geworden.

Prinzipiell ist dies nicht unbedingt eine negative Entwicklung. Denn in einem Land, das heute in der globalen Wirtschaft hauptsächlich wegen seines Knowhows besteht, werden viele „Köpfe" gebraucht – aber nicht jeder.

Leider wird es den Kindern und Jugendlichen in einer wichtigen Hinsicht vordergründig zu leicht gemacht, tatsächlich dadurch aber langfristig viel schwerer: Hubschraubervåter und -mütter lassen ihre Kinder nicht nur nicht mehr ihre eigenen Fehler machen, sondern räumen ihnen jede Schwierigkeit aus dem Weg. Und die extremsten unter den Hubschraubereltern drohen z. B. der Schule mit rechtlichen Schritten, wenn sie wegen Täuschungsversuchen ihrer Kinder einbestellt werden, anstatt ihre Kinder zur Rede zu stellen. Und leider muss die Situation nicht erst so extreme Ausmaße annehmen, bevor sie für die Kinder schädlich wird.

Auch dies hat dazu geführt, dass viele Studienanfänger/innen gar nicht wissen, was es bedeutet, sich Mühe zu geben, sich durchzukämpfen, schwierige Situationen zu meistern. Sie haben andererseits dadurch auch gar nicht die Chance gehabt zu erfahren, wie erhebend und motivierend das Gefühl sein kann, sich „durchgekämpft" und so wichtige Probleme gelöst zu haben – inhaltlich oder organisatorisch.

H. Fouckhardt, *Lehren und Lernen*, essentials,
DOI 10.1007/978-3-658-18064-5_10

Ich werde immer wieder von Studienanfängern/innen gefragt, *wie viele Stunden* sie für ihr Studium *wöchentlich* einplanen müssten. Spontan fällt mir dazu die Zahl *60* ein. Aber ich bin meist zögerlich mit meiner Antwort.

Um die Studierenden nicht gleich zu Beginn des Studiums abzuschrecken, spreche ich üblicherweise von mindestens 40 Stunden pro Woche, also von einem „full-time job“. Die spontane Antwort derjenigen, die gefragt haben, ist *oft:* „Das wollen wir nicht!“ Und tatsächlich sehe ich einige von den Studierenden, die gefragt haben, schon ab der darauf folgenden Woche nie mehr in der Vorlesung und im Fachbereich. Offenbar waren sie wenigstens so konsequent zu entscheiden, dass das arbeitsreiche Physik-Studium nichts für sie ist.

Nach meiner Einschätzung lassen sich die heute anfangenden Studierenden typischerweise in drei Kategorien einteilen, die jeweils etwa ein Drittel der Gesamtheit ausmachen.

10.2 Das erste Drittel

Das erste Drittel bilden die sehr guten und sehr engagierten Studierenden, die aus allem, was ihnen im Studium geboten wird, etwas Positives ziehen. Man könnte ironisch sagen: „Das Studium kann sein, wie es will, es kann diesen Studierenden nicht schaden.“ Obwohl diese Studierenden sich den größten Teil des Stoffes auch im Selbststudium zu Hause alleine aneignen könnten, sind gerade sie es, die keine Vorlesungsstunde versäumen und auf die Zusatzerklärungen warten, die in keinem Buch stehen.

10.3 Das dritte Drittel

Das dritte Drittel sind die unengagierten und unwilligen Studierenden, für die man sich noch so viel Mühe geben kann – ohne Erfolg. Erstaunlicherweise sind gerade diese Studierenden diejenigen, die *vom ersten Tag* ihres Studiums an zu wissen glauben, dass ein Studium ganz anders laufen müsste und dass es so, wie es ist, überhaupt nichts bringt. Daraus ziehen sie vor sich selbst die Rechtfertigung, sich keine Mühe zu geben.

Und gerade bei diesen Studierenden findet man eine erhebliche Selbstüberschätzung vor. Auch das mehrfache Durchfallen in einer Prüfung führt bei diesen Studierenden nicht dazu, dass sie ihre Art des Studierens oder ein Studium für

sich persönlich infrage stellen. Wie es ein Kollege von mir einmal formulierte: die schlechten Studierenden wissen nicht einmal, was sie nicht wissen (auch Dunning-Kruger-Effekt genannt). Dies sind diejenigen Studierenden, die dann nach der Maximalanzahl von Prüfungsfehlversuchen nach 3–5 Jahren ihr Studium erfolglos abbrechen.

In einer Diskussion auf einer Didaktik-Konferenz habe ich einmal von diesem Drittel gesprochen. Ein Kollege warf mir daraufhin vor, dass ein Drittel nur deshalb bei mir so schlecht aussähe, weil ich unterbewusst von dieser Drittelung ausginge und mich als Dozent daher so verhielte (also mich gar nicht um alle kümmerte), dass ein Drittel abgehängt werden würde.

An diesem Argument könnte prinzipiell etwas dran sein. Aber erstaunlicherweise offenbart sich dieses Drittel schon als unteres Drittel, wenn andere Dozenten/innen, die Universität und ich selbst noch gar keine Gelegenheit hatten, die Leute falsch zu behandeln und zu frustrieren. Denn sogar mehr als ein Drittel der Erstsemester-Studierenden kommen nicht zu der Erstsemester-Einführung am ersten Studientag, entweder weil sie den Hinweis in den Unterlagen zum Studienplatz-Bescheid nicht gelesen haben oder weil sie diese Veranstaltung für nicht wichtig halten … ein unkluges Vorgehen, da sie bis dahin noch gar nicht wissen (können), wie ein Studium läuft und welche Veranstaltungen weniger wichtig sein mögen.

Ca. 20 % der Studierenden sparen sich gar die erste Vorlesungswoche, weil sie nach eigener Auskunft gehört haben, dass da noch nichts los sei. Andererseits wundern sie sich dann und beschweren sich darüber, dass alle anderen Studierenden schon in Übungsgruppen eingeteilt sind …, dass ihnen niemand gesagt hat, dass die Vorlesung nun in einem anderen Hörsaal stattfindet …, dass die anderen schon den Klausurtermin kennen, ihnen selbst aber niemand Offizielles etwas gesagt hat, …

Aus diesen Gründen nehme ich den oben erwähnten Vorwurf nicht an. Mitdenken gehört zum Studium – zum Inhaltlichen und zum Organisatorischen. Wer das nicht möchte, stellt sich selbst ein Armutszeugnis aus. Mehr als das: wer nicht bereit ist nach- und mitzudenken, sollte nicht studieren.

Leider fordert die Politik von den Hochschulen immer mehr, die Studienabbrüche zahlenmäßig zu reduzieren oder am besten gleich ganz zu vermeiden. Aber das ginge nur unter fast vollständiger Reduzierung der Standards.

Ist es wirklich im Interesse der Gesellschaft und der Wirtschaft ist, wenn solche Studierende irgendwie einen (schwachen) Abschluss bekommen und in die Berufswelt entlassen werden? Kann die Wirtschaft wirklich Akademiker/innen brauchen, deren Decke an Wissen und Fähigkeiten so dünn ist, dass sie nur

wenige Monate für ein ganz bestimmtes Problem, zu dessen Lösung sie eingestellt wurden, trägt? Und können die Firmen wirklich Akademiker/innen brauchen, die niemals selbstständig eine technisch-wissenschaftliche Projektarbeit von 6–12 Monaten Dauer erfolgreich abschließen mussten, also niemals gelernt haben, ein Projekt zu strukturieren und zu planen und dann entsprechend durchzuziehen? Das Abschlusszeugnis wäre unter solchen Umständen das Papier nicht wert, auf dem es gedrückt worden wäre.

Um diesem Drittel zu helfen, müsste man viel früher ansetzen: die Standards an den Schulen nicht herabsetzen, sondern ggf. erhöhen, im Elternhaus zwar Hilfe gewähren, aber nicht jedes Problem aus dem Weg räumen, loben wenn es etwas zu loben gibt, aber auch mit den Kindern ins Gericht gehen, wenn sie sich keine Mühe geben.

Natürlich meine ich damit nicht, etwas von den Kindern und Jugendlichen zu verlangen, wofür sie vielleicht von ihren Anlagen her gar nicht geeignet sind. Aus einem unmusikalischen Jugendlichen wird nicht durch Drill ein Lang Lang. (Und Drill ist nicht der richtige Weg.) Maßstab muss meiner Ansicht nach sein, ob sich der/die Jugendliche oder der junge Mensch wirklich Mühe gibt. Mehr kann man nicht erwarten. Aber weniger sollte man auch nicht erwarten. Fordern heißt fördern.

10.4 Das mittlere Drittel

Das mittlere Drittel sind Studierende, die sich durchaus Mühe geben, die durchaus das Studium erfolgreich meistern und zügig durchziehen wollen, denen dies aber nicht leicht fällt. In der Schule war der Stoff von ihnen vielleicht noch mit wenig Aufwand gut beherrschbar. An der Fachhochschule und Universität geht es tiefer, wird abstrakter, um allgemeiner werden zu können. Sie sitzen anfänglich vielleicht in einer Vorlesung, in der sie das Gefühl haben, die Lehrveranstaltung könnte auch auf chinesisch gehalten werden, ohne dass sie weniger verstehen würden. Sie sehen sich links und rechts im Hörsaal um und haben das Gefühl, die anderen haben dieses Problem nicht. Sie merken nicht, dass die meisten anderen auch nur ihr „Pokerface“ aufgesetzt und genau dieselben Probleme haben. Mit den vermeintlichen Misserfolgen schwindet die Motivation. Im Wesentlichen diesem Drittel kann mit Unterricht und Vorlesung geholfen werden. Ihm „über die Schwelle zu helfen“, halte ich für eine der wichtigsten Aufgaben von Dozenten/innen.

10.5 Frustrationstoleranz und Stressresistenz

Zu dem „nicht alle Probleme aus dem Weg räumen“, von dem bei den Hubschraubereltern die Rede war, gehört auch, dass nur der Weg zur Lösung aufgezeigt wird, nicht aber jeder einzelne Schritt. Wenn möglich sollten die einzelnen Schritte gemeinsam mit den Studierenden entwickelt werden. Auch Hubschrauber-Dozenten/innen sind also ein Problem … und alle, die zu viel Betreuung der Lernenden von den Lehrenden einfordern.

In meiner Hochschultätigkeit fällt mir seit Jahren auf, dass die Belastbarkeit und Frustrationstoleranz bei den Studierenden immer geringer wird – nicht nur die der Erstsemester:

- 20 % der Erstsemester-Studierenden nehmen bereits nach ca. 2 Wochen nicht mehr regelmäßig an den Lehrveranstaltungen teil, weil es nach eigener Aussage zu viel Stress für sie ist, sich auf den engen Stundenplan mit Vorlesungen, Übungen, Aufgabenbearbeitung einzustellen.
- Ein Studierender, der eine Chance zur zweiten Prüfungswiederholung im Fachbereich erstritten hatte, kam einige Wochen vor der Prüfung zu mir und wies mich darauf hin, dass dies seine letzte Chance wäre, ansonsten würde sein Studium erfolglos beendet sein; ich möge doch gnädig sein. Ich antwortete ihm, dass ich das sein würde; denn ich würde nicht mehr verlangen als vorher schon bei der normalen Prüfung oder bei der 1. Wiederholungsprüfung. Aber so viel würde ich auch bei der 2. Wiederholung verlangen. Der Student erbat sich daraufhin einen anderen Prüfer.
- Studierende melden sich krank, weil es ihnen zu stressig sei, die Klausur gleich am Ende der Vorlesungszeit mitzuschreiben.

Ich denke, dass diese Episoden wieder darauf hinweisen, dass wir alle als Eltern – mehr oder weniger – unseren Kindern zu viel Arbeit und Mühe abnehmen, um sie vor Enttäuschung zu bewahren. Wir tun unseren Kindern damit keinen Gefallen. Denn sie müssen in dieser Leistungsgesellschaft bestehen. Die Berufswelt und natürlich das ganze Leben bieten Hochs und Tiefs, Erfolge und Misserfolge. Wer beim Einstieg in seine Ausbildung oder sein Studium und erst recht ins Berufsleben noch nicht gelernt hat, mit Stress und Misserfolgen umzugehen, wird scheitern.

Wer diese Einstellung als zu hart empfindet, möge bitte auch bedenken: Sich erfolgreich durch eine schwierige Situation/Aufgabenstellung gekämpft zu haben, ist ein schönes, motivierendes und Selbstvertrauen gebendes Erlebnis. Es stärkt

für die Zukunft. Dieses Erfolgserlebnis sollten wir den Kindern/Jugendlichen/Schülern/Studierenden nicht nehmen.

Und so lernt man am meisten. Die Erklärungen sich selbst erschlossen zu haben, ist die gewinnbringendste und nachhaltigste Form des Lernens. Sully Prudhomme (französischer Schriftsteller 1839–1907): „Man kennt nur das, was man entdeckt."

10.6 Führen Sie die Auseinandersetzungen, die geführt werden müssen!

Wenn Eltern von der Arbeit nach Hause kommen, sind sie froh, wenn es mit den Kindern keine Komplikationen gibt. Etwas zu verbieten oder die Kinder zu den Hausaufgaben anzuhalten, ist mit Mühe verbunden. Womöglich ist der Ärger vorprogrammiert – erst recht während der Pubertät, also jener Zeit, in der die Eltern schwierig werden.

Wenn Lehrer/innen im Unterricht Schüler/innen identifizieren, die Hausaufgaben nicht gemacht haben, bedeutet das Aufwand und Mühe. Verlangt man das Nacharbeiten und gibt wegen des Versäumnisses vielleicht noch einen Eintrag ins Klassenbuch, gilt man als uncool. Verlangt man dies nicht, sind weiteren Versäumnissen durch alle Schüler/innen Tür & Tor geöffnet.

Die Erfahrung zeigt, dass diejenigen Lehrer/innen und Dozenten/innen, die bestimmte (sinnvolle) Regeln setzen und auf deren Einhaltung bestehen, letztlich mehr bei den Schüler/innen und Studierenden erreichen können und – wer hätte das naiv gedacht – sogar mehr respektiert werden. Der schwierigen Phase des Durchsetzens, die sich zu Schuljahresbeginn (und mittlerweile auch schon an den Hochschulen zu Beginn der Erstsemester- Vorlesungszeit) womöglich über Wochen hinzieht, folgt dann aber eine lange Phase der guten Mitarbeit durch die Schüler/innen (oder Studierenden).

Kinder und junge Menschen wollen Regeln. Ihr Aufbegehren bisweilen ist auch ein Austesten, wie fest denn die Regeln sind. Dass es Regeln gibt, wird respektiert. Regellosigkeit erweist sich als Freibrief für Chaos. Und davon hat niemand etwas.

Eine Psychologin sprach mir gegenüber einmal einen guten Rat aus, der für Eltern, Lehrer/innen und Dozenten/innen gleichermaßen gilt: „Führen Sie die Kämpfe, die geführt werden müssen!" Will im Beispiel heißen: „Scheuen Sie den Ärger nicht, wenn Hausaufgaben nicht gemacht worden sind und Sie nun darauf drängen, dass sie nachgeholt werden! Scheuen Sie den Ärger nicht, den

es (womöglich mit Eltern, Hochschulverwaltung und Fachschaft) gibt, wenn ein Student wegen Abschreibens in der Klausur seine Prüfung nicht anerkannt bekommt!" Und vieles mehr …

Vielleicht eine der wichtigsten Lehren, die man Kindern/Jugendlichen/Schülern/Studierenden mit auf den Lebensweg geben kann: alles, was sie tun oder nicht tun, hat Konsequenzen für sie selbst. Das verschluderte Abitur führt dazu, dass sie nicht alles, was sie möchten, studieren können (und dafür vielleicht auch gar nicht genügend vorbereitet sind). Sicher ist es auch wichtig, dass man den Kindern und Jugendlichen einmal (aber nicht immer) das Eisen aus dem Feuer holt um zu zeigen, dass man im absoluten Notfall für sie da ist. Aber das sollte nicht der Normalfall sein.

Hubschraubereltern/-dozenten schaden mehr, als sie nützen. Bestenfalls machen sich die Hubschraubereltern selbst kurzfristig das Leben leichter, aber langfristig erschweren sie es sowohl sich selbst als auch ihren Kindern. Denn wenn die Kinder/Jugendlichen/Schüler/Studierenden in die noch größere Welt hinausgehen und dort erst lernen müssen, dass es Regeln gibt, an die man sich halten sollte, ist es zu spät.

Und damit soll nicht dem Duckmäusertum das Wort geredet werden. Querdenker/innen sind sehr wichtig für eine Gesellschaft. Aber auch sie müssen die Regeln erst verstehen lernen, um sie dann auf ihrem Lebens- und Berufsweg sinnvoll ändern zu können.

Fordern heißt Fördern. Auch das gehört zu der „Ehrfurcht vor dem Leben" nach Ludwig Philipp Albert Schweitzer (1875–1965).

Was Sie aus diesem *essential* mitnehmen können

- Es ist normal, wenn Lehre und Lernen nicht leicht fallen
- Übung muss sein und Üben darf erwartet werden
- Haben Sie den Mut, Verschiedenes auszuprobieren und je nach Situation auch andere Wege zu gehen

H. Fouckhardt, *Lehren und Lernen*, essentials,
DOI 10.1007/978-3-658-18064-5

Literatur

Ericsson, K. Anders, Krampe, Ralf Th., Tesch-Romer, Clemens: The Role of Deliberate Practice in the Acquisition of Expert Performance. Psychological Review 100, 3 (1993) 363–406

Gladwell, Malcolm: Überflieger. Piper (2012)

Huber, Ludwig et al. (Hrsg.): Forschendes Lehren im eigenen Fach. wbv (2014)

Huber, Ludwig et al. (Hrsg.): Forschendes Lernen im Studium. UVW, Webler (2009)

Kruger, Justin, Dunning, David: Unskilled and Unaware of it: How Difficulties in Recognizing One's Own Incompetence Lead to Inflated Self-Assessments. Journal of Personality and Social Psychology 77,6 (1999) 1121–1134.

Mazur, Eric: Peer instruction – a user's manual. Prentice Hall Series in educational innovation (1997)

Plath, Maike: ‚Spielend' unterrichten und Kommunikation gestalten. Beltz (2015)

Terman, Lewis M.: Genetic studies of genius I–V. Stanford University Press (1926–1959)

http://www.uni-kl.de/eteaching/werkzeugkasten/voting-tool/. Abgerufen am 13.02.2017.

H. Fouckhardt, *Lehren und Lernen,* essentials,
DOI 10.1007/978-3-658-18064-5

Printed in Dunstable, United Kingdom

91218502R00047

Preface

It is an obvious truism that, structures should be constructed on a stiff ground to ensure their stability and negligible deformation. Along with the development of society and concentration of population to urban areas, the ground conditions of construction sites, however, have become worse than ever during recent decades throughout the world. This situation is especially pronounced in Japan, where many construction projects are conducted on soft alluvial clay ground, land reclaimed ground with dredged soils, highly organic soil ground, loose sandy ground and so on. It is often encountered to such a soft soil when any type of infrastructures is constructed, in which large ground settlement and stability failure are concerned. Apart from these clayey or highly organic soils, loose sand deposits under the water table can cause serious problems of liquefaction under seismic conditions. A lot of *in-situ* ground improvement techniques have been developed to improve physical and mechanical properties of the soft soil in order to cope with these problems.

A huge amount of soft soil is dredged at many ports annually to maintain sea routes and berths. A huge amount of construction waste soil and industrial by-product are also produced at construction sites and industry plants. These soils used to be dumped at disposal areas constructed in coastal area and mountainous area. It is becoming difficult to construct any disposal areas for these soils, because of environmental restrictions and economic reasons. It has become necessary to beneficially use these soils as construction and land reclamation materials. Several *ex-situ* soil improvement techniques have been developed for the purpose.

The cement stabilization technique is one of the common soil improvement techniques to improve the physical and mechanical properties of the original soil, in which soil and cement are mixed *in-situ* or *ex-situ* by mixing paddles or mixing blades. The shape of mixing paddles and blades as well as mixing procedure are the essential issue to ensure the uniform and desired characteristics of stabilized soil. A lot of research efforts have been paid in Japan to develop appropriate mixing machine and mixing procedure for many *in-situ* and *ex-situ* mixing techniques. As soil and cement are mixed batch by batch with small soil volume in the *ex-situ* mechanical mixing technique using mixing paddles and blades, the mechanical mixing techniques are not effective for large scale cement stabilization project. A new type of cement stabilization technique was desired for promoting beneficial use of large amount of dredged soil and surplus soils efficiently.

The pneumatic flow mixing method was developed to stabilize dredged soil and surplus soil for promoting their beneficial use in 1999. The pneumatic flow mixing method is a new type of the *ex-situ* cement stabilization techniques, in which dredged soil or surplus soil is mixed with a relatively small amount of cement without any mixing paddles and blades in a pipeline. Transporting soil in a pipeline without any air requires high pressure due to the friction generated on the inner surface of pipeline. When a relatively large amount of compressed air is injected into the pipeline, however, soil can be separated into small blocks. The separated soil block, called a 'plug', is forwarded to an outlet with the help of compressed air. The forming plug and air block functions to reduce the friction on the inner surface of pipeline and in turn can reduce the required air pressure considerably for transporting. When binder is injected into the pipeline, the soil plug and binder are thoroughly mixed by means of turbulent flow generated in the plug during transporting. The soil and binder mixture, transported and placed at the reclamation site, gains high strength rapidly so that no additional soil improvement is necessary for assuring the successful performance of superstructures on the ground in many cases. As the mixing and transporting soil and binder can be conducted in a pipeline continuously, the methods is suitable and efficient for large scale project.

The development of the pneumatic flow mixing method has been initiated by Ministry of Transport, The Fifth District Port Construction Bureau (currently Chubu Regional Development Bureau, Ministry of Land, Infrastructure, Transport and Tourism) since 1998. Many laboratory tests were carried out to investigate the physical and mechanical properties of stabilized soil, and many full scale land reclamation and backfill tests were also carried out at Nagoya Port to investigate the physical and mechanical properties of field-stabilized soil, to investigate the environmental impact to surrounding area due to the placement of stabilized soil and to develop a construction procedure, quality control and assurance. The method was applied in several land reclamation and embankment construction projects at Fushikitoyama Port, Muroran Port and Kushiro Port in 1988 to 2001. They have confirmed the high applicability of the method for an economical and rapid construction of land reclamation and embankment. The method was applied to construct large scale man-made islands for Central Japan International Airport at Nagoya in 2001 and for Tokyo Haneda International Airport in 2009.

The current book is intended to provide the state of the art and practice for pneumatic flow mixing, rather than a user-friendly manual. The book covers the factors affecting the strength increase, the engineering characteristics of stabilized soil, a variety of applications, current design procedures, execution systems and procedures, and QC/QA methods and procedures based on the experience and research efforts accumulated in Japan.

The strength of the stabilized soil is influenced by many factors, including the original soil properties; the type and amount of binder; the mixing and placement process; and curing conditions. Therefore, the process design, production with careful quality control and quality assurance are the key to the pneumatic flow mixing project. Quality assurance starts with the soil characterization of the original soil and includes various activities prior to, during, and after the production. QC/QA methods and procedures and acceptance criteria should be determined before the actual production, and their meanings should be understood precisely by all the parties involved in pneumatic flow mixing project. Contractors and practicing engineers are advised develop their own mixing machine and procedure for their site condition and design requirement. The author wishes the book to be useful for practicing engineers to understand the current state of the art and to develop their techniques and also useful for academia to find out the issues to be studied in the future.

April 2016

List of Technical Terms and Symbols

Definition of technical terms

additive	chemical material to be added to stabilizing agent for improving characteristics of stabilized soil
binder	chemically reactive material that can be used for mixing with soils to improve engineering characteristics of soils such as lime, cement, lime-based and cement-based special binders. Also referred to as stabilizer or stabilizing agent.
binder	content ratio of weight of dry binder to the dry weight of soil to be stabilized. (%)
binder factor	ratio of weight of dry binder to the volume of soil to be stabilized. (kg/m^3)
binder slurry	slurry-like mixture of binder and water
ex-situ mixing	mixing technique in which the soil is once excavated and mixed with binder in a plant or during transportation
field strength	strength of stabilized soil produced in-situ
improved ground	a region with stabilized soil and surrounding original soil
in-situ mixing	a mixing technique in which natural soil is stabilized with binder *in-situ*
laboratory strength	strength of stabilized soil produced in a laboratory
plug	soil block created in the pipeline by injecting compressed air
stabilized soil	soil stabilized by mixing with binder

List of Symbols

aw	cement content (%)
C	cement factor (kg/m^3)
c	cohesion of stabilized soil (kN/m^2)
C_c	compression index
C_s	sweling index
c_u	undrained shear strength (kN/m^2)
CV	coefficient of variation
c_v	coefficient of consolidation (m^2/day)
c_{vs}	coefficient of consolidation of stabilized soil (m^2/day)
c_{vu}	coefficient of consolidation of unstabilized soil (m^2/day)

C_α	secondary compression coefficient
D	pipeline diameter (m)
e	void ratio
E_{50}	modulus of elasticity (kN/m^2)
Fs	safety factor
G	shear modulus (kN/m^2)
G_0	initial shear modulus (kN/m^2)
G_c	specific gravity of binder
G_{eq}	equivalent shear modulus (kN/m^2)
G_s	specific gravity of soil particle
G_w	specific gravity of water
h_{eq}	equivalent dumping ratio (%)
I_p	plasticity index
k	coefficient of permeability (cm/sec)
K_0	coefficient of earth pressure at rest
k_{30}	ground reaction coefficient (kN/m^2)
k_h	horizontal seismic coefficient
k'_h	apparent horizontal seismic coefficient
L_i	ignition loss (%)
M	mixing ratio
M	maturity
m_v	coefficient of volume compressibility (m^2/kN)
m_{vs}	coefficient of volume compressibility of stabilized soil (m^2/kN)
m_{vu}	coefficient of volume compressibility of unstabilized soil (m^2/kN)
N_c	bearing capacity factor of soil
N_γ	bearing capacity factor of soil
N_q	bearing capacity factor of soil
p'_0	effective earth pressure coefficient at rest (kN/m^2)
p_a	active earth pressure (kN/m^2)
pH	potential hydrogen
p_t	earth pressure of liquid state stabilized soil (kN/m^2)
p_y	consolidation yield pressure (pseudo pre-consolidation pressure) (kN/m^2)
q_c	cone penetration resistance (kN/m^2)
q_d	ultimate bearing capacity (kN/m^2)
q_f	bearing capacity (kN/m^2)
Q_A	flow volume of air (g/m^3)
Q_L	flow volume of soil (g/m^3)
q_u	unconfined compressive strength (kN/m^2)
q_{uck}	design standard strength (kN/m^2)
q_{uf}	unconfined compressive strength of field stabilized soil (kN/m^2)
$\overline{q_{uf}}$	average unconfined compressive strength of field stabilized soil (kN/m^2)
q_{ul}	unconfined compressive strength of laboratory stabilized soil (kN/m^2)

$\overline{q_{ul}}$	average unconfined compressive strength of laboratory stabilized soil (kN/m^2)
q_y	yield bearing capacity (kN/m^2)
s_u	shear strength (kN/m^2)
S	settlement (m)
SS	suspended solids (mg/L)
t	curing period (day)
t_c	curing period (day)
T_c	curing temperature (°C)
u	plug speed (m/sec)
V_c	volume of cement slurry (m^3)
V_{cw}	volume of water in binder slurry (m^3)
V_s	volume of soil (m^3)
V_{soil}	volume of soil (m^3)
V_v	volume of void and water (m^3)
V_{w2}	volume of water added on transporting barge (m^3)
w	water content (%)
w	surcharge (kN/m^2)
W/C	water to cement ratio of cement slurry (%)
W/C	water to cement ratio of stabilized soil defined as the total water containing in both soil and cement slurry against the dry weight of binder (%)
w/w_L	water content ratio
W_c	cement factor (kg/m^3)
W_c	dry weight of cement (kg)
w_i	initial water content (%)
w_L	liquid limit (%)
w_n	natural water content (%)
w_P	plastic limit (%)
w_t	total water content (%)
α	cement factor (kg/m^3)
α	angle of slip surface (°)
β	angle of back fill (°)
δ	friction angle at wall surface (°)
ε_f	axial strain at failure (%)
ϕ'	internal friction angle (°)
γ	shear strain (%)
γ	unit weight (kN/m^3)
γ'	effective unit weight (kN/m^3)
γ_w	unit weight of water (kN/m^3)
λ	strength ratio of q_{uf}/q_{ul}
λ	water to soil ratio required for cement hydration (%)
μ	Poisson's ratio
ν	viscocity of plug (P)
θ	resultant angle of seismic coefficient (°)
θ	curing temperature (°)
ρ_c	density of cement (g/cm^3)
ρ_A	density of air (g/cm^3)

ρ_L density of soil (g/cm^3)
ρ_s density of stabilized soil (g/cm^3)
ρ_{soil} density of original soil (g/cm^3)
ρ_w density of water (g/cm^3)
σ standard deviation
σ confining pressure (kN/m^2)
σ_{tb} tensile strength measured by bending test (kN/m^2)
σ_{td} tensile strength measured by simple tension test (kN/m^2)
σ_{ts} tensile strength measured by split test (kN/m^2)
ψ angle of wall to the vertical (°)
ζ angle of failure surface to horizontal (°)

Chapter 1

An overview of admixture stabilization – Evolution of pneumatic flow mixing and the scope of the book

1 INTRODUCTION

Many man-made islands have been constructed in Japan to obtain enough new land area for airports, electrical power plants, manufacturing plants, residential areas and so on. These islands require a huge amount of soil with appropriate soil properties for land reclamation, which used to be excavated from mountains, rivers and seabed. Recently it is becoming difficult to obtain such soils at a reasonable cost, because of environmental protection restrictions and economic reasons, which requires the use of inappropriate soil as a reclamation material. A huge amount of soft soil is dredged at many ports annually to maintain sea routes and berths. A huge amount of surplus soil and by-produce are also produced at construction sites and industry plants. These soils used to be dumped at disposal areas constructed in coastal areas, because disposal offshore is strictly prohibited in Japan. It is becoming difficult to construct any disposal areas for dredged soil and surplus soil, because of environmental protection restrictions and economic reasons. These circumstances have promoted the beneficial use of dredged soft soil and surplus soil as a land reclamation material, which in turn can prolong the service life of disposal areas. As the dredged soil and surplus soil usually have a high water content, of the order of a hundred per cent, reclaimed lands constructed with the soil are so weak and highly compressible that ground improvement is necessary for constructing structures on the reclaimed land to assure their stability and to reduce their settlement. The vertical drain method is one of the most frequently used ground improvement techniques to improve such soft soil deposits. However, the method requires a relatively long period to complete the consolidation of the ground.

Many studies and much research have been carried out to investigate appropriate soil improvement methods and to establish a recycling system for the soft soil. The pneumatic flow mixing method, one of the admixture stabilization techniques, was developed to stabilize dredged soil and surplus soil for promoting their beneficial use in Japan in 1999, in which soil and a chemical binder are mixed in the pipeline by the help of the turbulent flow generated in the soil plug during transportation by compressed air. As this method has many benefits – rapid and large scale execution can be conducted with low cost – it has been applied to many land reclamation projects, backfilling behind earth retaining wall projects and shallow stabilization projects using dredged soils and surplus soils.

In the following sections, the classification, development, basic mechanism and application of the pneumatic flow mixing method will be explained briefly.

2 CEMENT ADMIXTURE STABILIZATION TECHNIQUES

2.1 Basic mechanism of cement admixture stabilization

The basic mechanism of cement stabilization is illustrated in Figure 1.1, which consists of four steps: the reduction of water content, improvement of physical properties, cement hydration hardening, and pozzolanic reaction hardening. The water content of the original soil is decreased by the hydration of a binder and subsequent water absorption process. The ion exchange reaction modifies the physical property of the original soil and results in a decrease of plasticity of the soil. This effect is utilized in the improvement of base and sub-base soils by mixing with small amounts of lime or cement for road construction, where the change of consistency of the base and sub-base soils makes compaction easier and more effective. The formation of cement hydration products and pozzolanic reaction products provide an increased strength to the soil and cement mixture. The pneumatic flow mixing method is mostly based on the latter two reactions to increase the strength of the soil.

2.2 Classification of cement admixture stabilization techniques

The success of the deep mixing method (Kitazume & Terashi, 2013) for soil stabilization has encouraged the construction industry to develop various types of cement

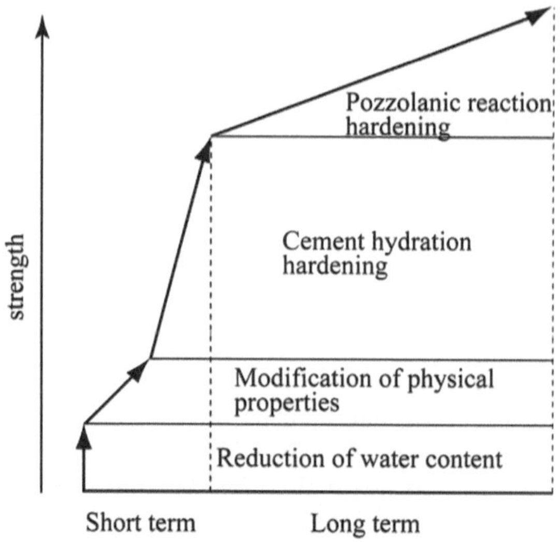

Figure 1.1 Mechanism of cement stabilization.

admixture stabilization techniques in Japan. The currently available cement admixture stabilization techniques can be classified into *in-situ* mixing and *ex-situ* mixing, as shown in Table 1.1 (after Coastal Development Institute of Technology, 2008b). The *in-situ* mixing techniques are developed to improve the physical and mechanical properties of the original soil for assuring the successful performance of superstructures on the ground. In the *in-situ* mixing techniques, natural soil is stabilized with binder *in-situ* by means of mechanical mixing and/or high pressure injection mixing. The *in-situ* mixing techniques can be subdivided into surface and shallow stabilization; mid-depth stabilization; and deep stabilization, depending upon the depth and purpose of improvement. The *ex-situ* mixing techniques have been developed to enhance the beneficial use of dredged soils, inappropriate soils and construction surplus soils. These techniques are intended to provide additional characteristics – such as better liquefaction resistance, smaller density, smaller volume compressibility or high strength – to the original soil. In the *ex-situ* mixing techniques, the soils are, once excavated, mixed with binder in a plant or during transportation to a disposal site or reclamation site. The *ex-situ* mixing techniques can be further subdivided into mixing during transportation and batch plant mixing, depending upon where soil and binder are mixed. Several *in-situ* and *ex-situ* admixture stabilization techniques will be briefly introduced in the next section.

Table 1.1 Classification of admixture stabilization techniques (after Coastal Development Institute of Technology, 2008b).

Place of mixing		*Type of mixing*	*Method*	*Application*
In-situ	Surface and shallow stabilization	mechanical mixing	surface treatment, shallow stabilization	working platform on soft ground
	Mid depth stabilization	mechanical mixing	mid-depth mixing	stability, settlement reduction, excavation support, seepage shutoff, etc
	Deep stabilization	mechanical mixing high pressure injection hybrid of above two	deep mixing	
Ex-situ	Mixing during transportation	mixing on belt conveyor	pre-mixing	improve liquefaction resistance of soil
		mixing in pipeline	pipe mixing	reduce compressibility of high water content soil
	Batch plant mixing	mechanical mixing	pre-mixing	improve liquefaction resistance of soil
		mechanical mixing	lightweight geo-material	density control of fill material
		mechanical mixing and high pressure dewatering	dewatered stabilized soil	alternative for sand and gravel

Figure 1.2 Power blender method (Power Blender Method Association, 2006).

2.3 *In-situ* mixing techniques

2.3.1 *Power blender method*

The power blender method is one of the mid-depth *in-situ* mixing techniques. The mixing machine of the method installs a large number of small stirring wings attached to the trencher, as shown in Figure 1.2 (Power Blender Method Association, 2006). In the method, the natural ground is cut and mixed with binder by rotating the stirring wings *in-situ*, where powder or slurry form binder is injected from the stirrer tip. The method can stabilize ground to a depth of about 13 m for the purpose of improving stability, reducing ground settlement and preventing liquefaction. As the trencher is installed on the extension arm of backhoe, the base machine can be placed on a firm layer far from the soft ground to be stabilized.

2.3.2 *Deep mixing method*

The deep mixing method is a deep *in-situ* soil stabilization technique using cement and/or lime as a binder, which forms a stiff, artificially cement-stabilized soil of various shapes, e.g. columns, walls, panels, grids or blocks, in order to improve foundation ground (Kitazume & Terashi, 2013). A large machine with several rotating shafts and mixing blades is used to supply powder or slurry form binder into the ground and mix soil and binder *in-situ*, as shown in Figure 1.3. The applications of the method have various purposes, such as reducing ground settlement, increasing bearing capacity of the ground, increasing stability, preventing ground liquefaction, reducing active earth pressure, cutting off ground water, and increasing piles' lateral resistance.

(a) For work on land.

(b) For marine work.

Figure 1.3 Mixing machine of deep mixing method.

2.4 *Ex-situ* mixing techniques

2.4.1 *Premixing method*

The premixing method is one of the *ex-situ* admixture stabilization techniques where a small amount of binder and chemical additives are mixed with sandy material to obtain liquefaction-free material for land reclamation (Zen et al., 1987, Coastal Development Institute of Technology, 2003, 2008c). The basic principle of the method is to prevent liquefaction by a cementation effect between the sand particles and the binder. In the case where soil has a certain degree of cohesion by the cementation effect, the shear strength does not decrease to zero and liquefaction does not take place even when pore water pressure is generated up to the overburden pressure. Sand, binder and chemical additive (e.g. a separation inhibitor) are mixed either in a batching plant or on a belt conveyor. The stabilized soil is transported and placed at the designated area to construct reclaimed ground (Figure 1.4). This method was applied to the restoration works of quays at Kobe Port where a concrete-type quay wall was damaged by the Great Hanshin earthquake in 1995 (Kitazume, 2010).

2.4.2 *Lightweight treated soil method (Super Geo-Material lightweight soil)*

The lightweight treated soil method (Super Geo-Material lightweight soil) is one of the *ex-situ* admixture stabilization techniques which was developed for the purpose of reducing residual and uneven ground settlement, decreasing active earth pressure, preventing lateral displacement and improving seismic resistance. In the method, dredged soil is mixed with binder and also either air foam or expanded polystyrene (EPS) beads of 1 to 3 mm in diameter in order to manufacture high quality soil, having high strength and a low unit weight of 11 and 15 kN/m^3 (Tsuchida & Egashira, 2004, Coastal Development Institute of Technology, 2008a). Helped by its high strength and

Figure 1.4 Premixing method (by the courtesy of Dr Yamazaki).

light weight characteristics, the stabilized soil is used for landfill, or backfill behind a quay wall or earth retaining structure, where the overburden pressure and active earth pressure can be reduced considerably. The method has been applied to backfill behind a quay wall, reinforcement of an existing structure, and an embankment on soft ground (Figure 1.5). This method was successfully applied to the restoration works of quays at Kobe Port damaged by the Great Hanshin earthquake in 1995 (Kitazume, 2010) and the landfill of a sea wall at the D runway of Tokyo Haneda International Airport (Mizukami & Matsunaga, 2015).

(a) Special barges for marine works.

(b) Placement of stabilized soil for land reclamation.

Figure 1.5 Lightweight treated soil method.

(a) High pressure compressor.

(b) Crashed dewatered stabilized soil.

Figure 1.6 Dewatered stabilized soil method.

2.4.3 Dewatered stabilized soil method

In order to produce a high strength and compacted stabilized soil with low water content, several dewatered stabilized soil methods were developed in which soil is mixed with binder and dewatered at high compressive pressure of the order of 1 to 4 MN/m^2 as shown in Figure 1.6(a). By the procedure, the stabilized soil having high strength of the cone penetration resistance, q_c, of about 400 to 600 kN/m^2 can be manufactured. The stabilized and compressed soil is usually crushed to granular material as shown in Figure 1.6(b), which can be used as subgrade and roadbed materials and as fill material.

(a) Batch plant.

(b) Granular stabilized soil.

Figure 1.7 Granular stabilized soil method (Mud Recycling System) (Source: http://www.penta-ocean.co.jp/english/business/envi/dirt_recycle.html)

2.4.4 Granular stabilized soil method

The granular stabilized soil method manufactures grains of a few millimetres to about 10 mm in diameter by mixing soft soil with binder and polymer or additives in a granulating mixer. Organic water-soluble polymers and inorganic agents are usually used for the polymer (polyelectrolyte), which functions to facilitate the granulation process by the aggregation effect. Iron and steel slags, coal ash or paper sludge ash is used as an additive for soils having a high water content to facilitate the granulation process by reducing the mixture's water content. The granular stabilized soil, having a high strength, is manufactured after several days' to several weeks' curing. It can be used as subgrade and roadbed materials and as fill material. Figure 1.7(a) shows one example of the batching plant for the method (Mud Recycling System), where dredged soil with a high water content is mixed with fly ash, water-soluble polymer and cement. Figure 1.7(b) shows the stabilized soil grains, which have a diameter of about 1 mm, a unit weight of 14 kN/m^3; the internal friction angle is about 40 degrees.

Figure 1.8 Barges for the pneumatic flow mixing method.

3 DEVELOPMENT, MECHANISM AND APPLICATIONS OF THE PNEUMATIC FLOW MIXING METHOD

3.1 Development of the method

The pneumatic flow mixing method, Figure 1.8, is one of the *ex-situ* stabilization techniques, in which dredged soil or surplus soil is mixed with a relatively small amount of cement in a pipeline. The development of the pneumatic flow mixing method has been initiated by the Ministry of Transport, The Fifth District Port Construction Bureau (currently the Chubu Regional Development Bureau, Ministry of Land, Infrastructure, Transport and Tourism) since 1998, where many laboratory tests were carried out to investigate the mechanical properties of stabilized soil, and many full-scale land reclamation and backfill tests were also carried out at Nagoya Port to investigate the mechanical properties of field-stabilized soil and to develop construction procedures and quality control and assurance. The Bureau summarized the laboratory and field test results and published a technical manual in 1999 (Ministry of Transport, The Fifth District Port Construction Bureau, 1999). This has encouraged many contractors to develop their own techniques of the method, as later shown in Chapter 5. The technical development study and investigation committee on the pneumatic flow mixing method was established in 1998 to summarize the accumulated test results, knowledge and know-how for promoting the method. The committee published the technical manual in 2001 (Coastal Development Institute of Technology, 2001), which was revised in 2008 (Coastal Development Institute of Technology, 2008b) in accordance with the revised Port and Harbour Design Standard (Ministry of Land, Infrastructure, Transport and Tourism, 2007). The method was applied in several land reclamation and embankment

Figure 1.9 Pneumatic flow mixing method at the Central Japan International Airport construction project.

construction projects at Fushikitoyama Port, Muroran Port and Kushiro Port in 1988 to 2001. In Fushikitoyama Port, a total of 76,750 m^3 dredged soil was stabilized with 60 or 80 kg/m^3 cement for constructing an embankment. In Kushiro Port, a total of 205,200 m^3 of dredged soil was stabilized with 70 to 80 kg/m^3 cement for land reclamation. These projects have revealed the high applicability of the method as an economical and rapid construction technique for embankment and land reclamation. The method was applied to construct a huge scale man-made island for Central Japan International Airport at Nagoya in 2001 (Kitazume & Satoh, 2003, Kitazume, 2004, Kitazume & Satoh, 2005), where about 8.2 million m^3 of dredged soil was stabilized for land reclamation, see Figure 1.9 (see Chapter 4). After the construction of the airport, the method has been applied to many marine construction and on land construction projects, in which their purpose was backfilling behind sea revetment (Kobayashi et al., 2001, Yamauchi et al., 2011, Yamagoshi et al., 2013) and constructing shallow stabilized soil layer (Watanabe, 2005).

In 2008, the expansion project of Tokyo Haneda International Airport commenced, where a total of about 4.7 million m^3 of dredged soil was stabilized to construct a part of the man-made island for the fourth runway, D runway, as shown in Figure 1.10 (Mizukami & Matsunaga, 2015).

3.2 Mechanism of the method

Transporting soil in a pipeline without any air requires high pressure due to the friction generated on the inner surface of pipeline. When a relatively large amount of

Figure 1.10 Pneumatic flow mixing method at the Tokyo Haneda International Airport construction project.

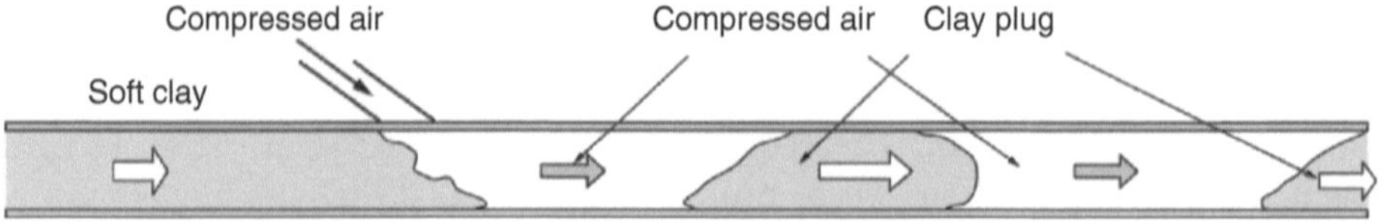

Figure 1.11 Schematic view of plug flow (Ministry of Transport, The Fifth District Port Construction Bureau, 1999).

compressed air is injected into the pipeline, however, soil can be separated into small blocks, as schematically shown in Figure 1.11 (Ministry of Transport, The Fifth District Port Construction Bureau, 1999). The separated soil block, called as 'plug', is forwarded to an outlet with the help of compressed air. The forming plug and air block functions to reduce the friction and in turn can reduce the required air pressure considerably for transporting. The formation of the plug is dependent upon the ratio of soil and air in the mix, and the pile diameter, as shown in Figure 1.12 and Equation 1.1 (Akagawa, 1980).

When binder is injected into the pipeline, the soil plug and binder are thoroughly mixed by means of turbulent flow generated in the plug during transporting. The soil and binder mixture, transported and placed at the designated reclamation site, gains high strength rapidly so that no additional soil improvement is necessary for assuring the successful performance of superstructures on the stabilized soil ground in

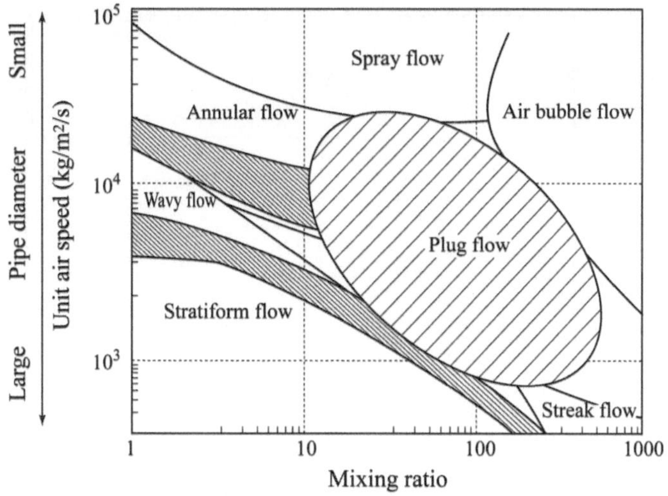

Figure 1.12 Generation condition of plug flow (Akagawa, 1980).

many cases (Coastal Development Institute of Technology, 2008b, Kitazume & Satoh, 2003).

$$M = \frac{\rho_L \times Q_L}{\rho_A \times Q_A} \tag{1.1}$$

where
M: mixing ratio
Q_A: flow volume of air (g/m^3)
Q_L: flow volume of soil (g/m^3)
ρ_A: density of air (g/cm^3)
ρ_L: density of soil (g/cm^3)

3.2.1 *Air pressure distribution in pipeline*

The required injected air pressure is dependent upon many factors such as the properties of soil, injected air volume, pipeline diameter and pipeline length. The maximum air pressure is also determined by the air resistant capacity of the facility and pipeline. In many cases, the maximum air pressure is determined to be around 600 kN/m^2. An example of air pressure distribution measured in the field test is shown in Figure 1.13 along the transportation distance measured from the inlet (Ministry of Transport, The Fifth District Port Construction Bureau, 1999). In the field test, soft marine clay with a water content of about 100% was transported by the method with three different transported soil volume rates. The figure shows that a relatively large decrease in the air pressure occurred between at the pneumatic barge, P_0, and at the stabilizing agent supplier barge, P_1, irrespective of the test condition, which was probably because the

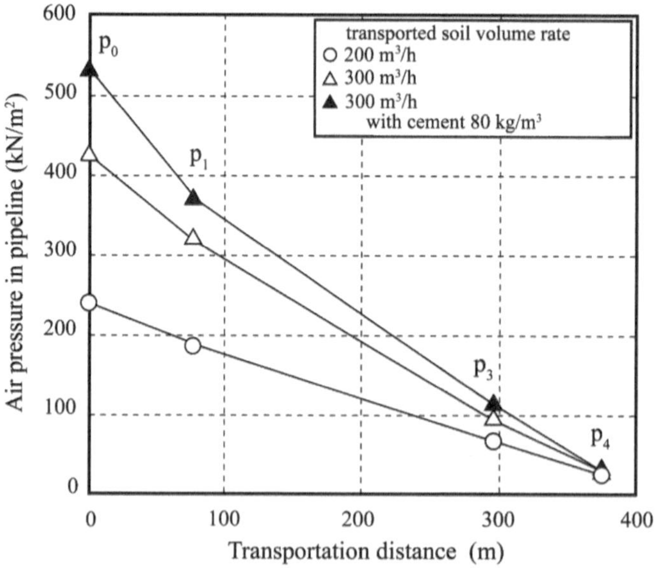

Figure 1.13 Air pressure distribution in the pipeline (Ministry of Transport, The Fifth District Port Construction Bureau, 1999).

clay in the pipeline was still in too transitional a condition to form the plug. After passing at the point P_1, the air pressure decreased almost linearly to almost zero at the outlet, P_4, with the transportation distance. The decrease in the air pressure was thought to be attributable to the inner surface friction on the pipeline. The effect of soil volume rate on the air pressure distribution is also shown in the figure, in which the higher air pressure is required at the inlet, P_0, with increasing soil volume rate. In the test conditions, the required air pressure should be increased about 200 kN/m^2 when the soil volume rate increased from 200 m^3/h to 300 m^3/h. The figure shows that the addition of cement causes the pressure increase of about 100 kN/m^2 at the inlet, P_0, because the cohesion and adhesion of the soil and cement mixture becomes larger than the soil alone. In current practice, the inlet air pressure of 400 to 500 kN/m^2 is frequently adopted after considerations of these test results, as well as the pressure capacity of facility and pipeline.

The air pressure at the inlet is influenced by many factors, which are introduced briefly below. Figure 1.14(a) shows the effects of the flow value of stabilized soil on the air pressure at the inlet (Kitazume et al., 2007). There is no clear relationship between the flow value and the air pressure, but the air pressure ranges from about 130 to 450 kN/m^2. According to Figure 1.14(a), the gradient of air pressure decreases with the flow value of stabilized soil, which indicates that the air pressure at an inlet may decrease with the flow value. Figures 1.14(b) and 1.14(c) show the effect of the transportation distance. There is a lot of scatter in the relationship between the air pressure and the transportation distance. However, the air pressure slightly increases with the transportation distance. Figure 1.14(d) shows the effect of the cement factor.

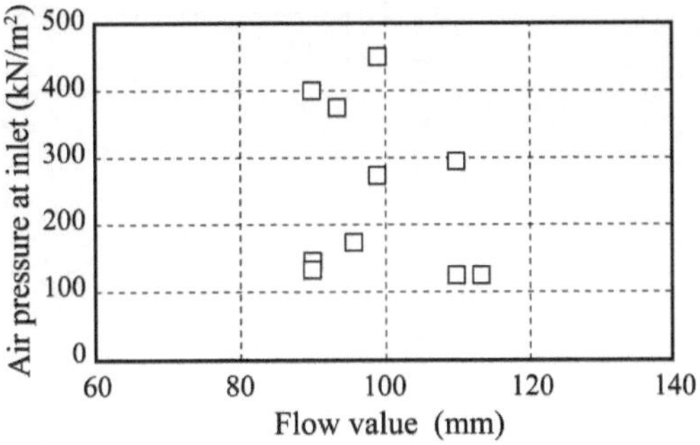

(a) Flow value of stabilizeds oil.

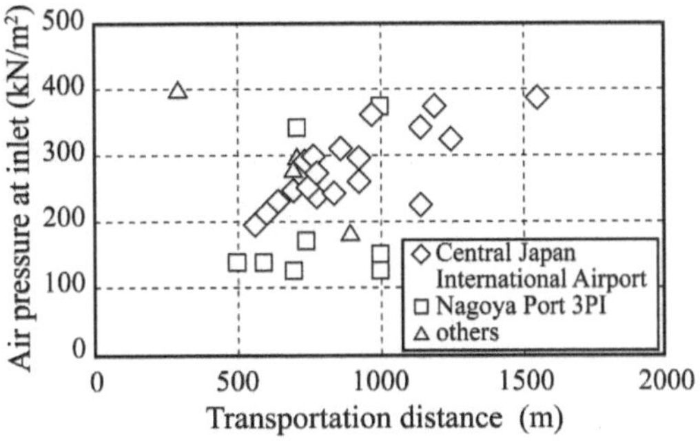

(b) Pipeline length.

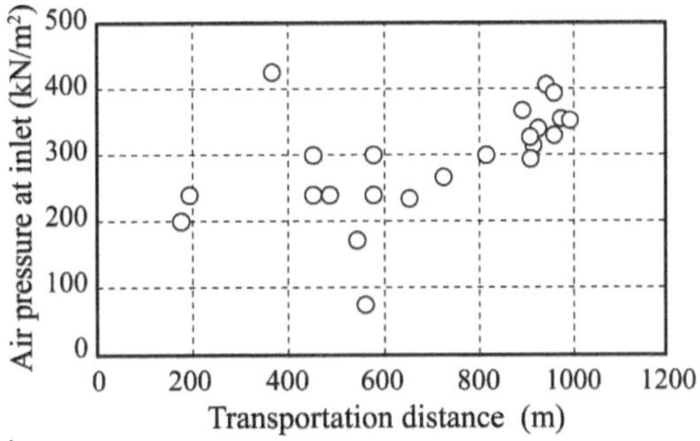

(c) Pipeline len gth.

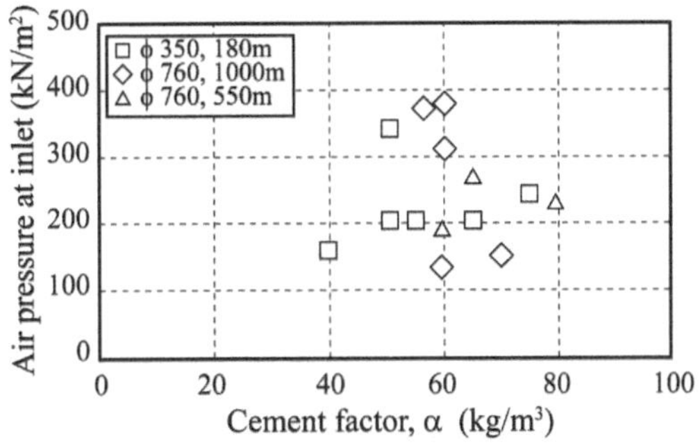

(d) Cement factor.

Figure 1.14 Effects of characteristics of stabilized soil and transportation distance on air pressure at the inlet (Kitazume et al., 2007).

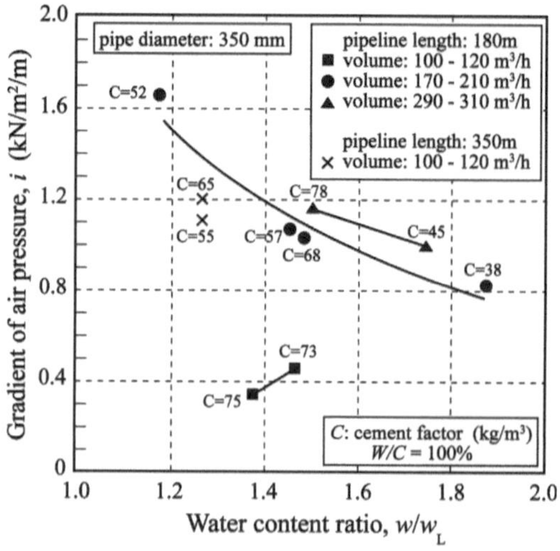

(a) Effect of water content ratio, w/w_L.

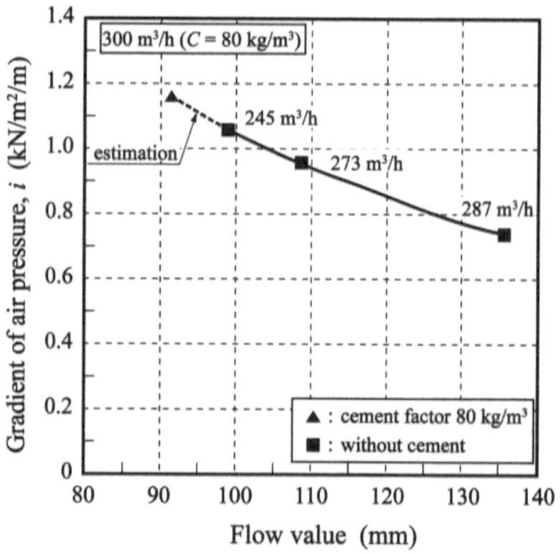

(b) Effect of flow value.

Figure 1.15 Effect on gradient of air pressure in the pipeline (Ministry of Transport, The Fifth District Port Construction Bureau, 1999).

According to Figure 1.14, the air pressure ranges from about 100 to 400 kN/m^2 irrespective of the flow value, the transportation distance and the cement factor in many cases.

Figure 1.15 shows the effects of the water content ratio, w/w_L and the flow value of soil cement mixture on the gradient of the air pressure in the pipeline, i (Ministry of Transport, The Fifth District Port Construction Bureau, 1999). The gradient, i,

Table 1.2 Characteristics of soil plugs measured in field tests (Ministry of Transport, The Fifth District Port Construction Bureau, 1999).

	Case 1	*Case 2*	*Case 3*
Test condition			
soil volume (m^3/h)	210	296	170
water content (%)	132.5	117.2	96.2
liquid limit (%)	70.5	77.6	81.5
cement factor (kg/m^3)	38	78	52
Test results	mean (range)	mean (range)	mean (range)
plug speed (m/s)	10.9 (1.6–25.0)	11.9 (1.5–25.0)	12.8 (1.9–25.0)
plug volume (m^3)	0.41 (0.23–0.52)	0.36 (0.25–0.45)	0.30 (0.18–0.36)
plug length (m)	4.3 (0.23–5.4)	3.7 (2.6–4.7)	3.1 (1.9–3.8)
plug interval (s)	7.1 (1.3–30.3)	4.4 (0.5–18.2)	6.4 (0.6–29.0)

decreases with the water content ratio and the flow value, which indicates the required air pressure at the inlet may decrease.

3.2.2 *Characteristics of soil plugs*

An example of the characteristics of soil plugs measured in field tests are summarized in Table 1.2 (Ministry of Transport, The Fifth District Port Construction Bureau, 1999). A soil plug with an average volume of 0.36 m^3 is transported every about 6 seconds at an average speed of about 12 m/s. As the soil plug is transported at very high speed in the pipeline, a turbulent flow is generated within the soil plug due to the friction on the inner surface of the pipeline. The turbulent flow functions to mix the soil and binder thoroughly. Thorough mixing can be obtained in the Reynolds number, $Re = uD/v$ of 500 to 3,000, where D is the pipeline diameter and u and v are the speed and viscosity of soil plug respectively.

3.2.3 *Required transportation distance*

It is obvious that a certain run of transportation distance is required to ensure throughout mixing, since the soil and binder are mixed in the pipeline during transportation. The required transportation distance may be dependent on many factors, such as the diameter of pipeline, the pressure and volume of air pressure, the volume and characteristics of soil, and the volume of binder. However, there are little background data regarding the minimum transportation distance to ensure throughout mixing, which will be explained in Chapter 5. The minimum transportation distance to ensure sufficient mixing in the pipeline might be determined empirically in each project. It is known that at least 50 to 100 m of transportation distance is necessary for sufficient mixing, while accumulated case histories suggest a transportation distance exceeding about 200 m is necessary in many cases, as shown later in Chapter 4, in Figure 4.6.

Table 1.3 Soil properties suitable for the pneumatic flow mixing method (Coastal Development Institute of Technology, 2008b).

Soil type		Water content	Evaluation		
			Applicability	*Binder content*	*Pumping ratio*
cohesive soil	sand content 30–50%	high	good	middle	somewhat low
		low	good	middle	low
	sand content <30%	higher than 200% (higher than 2.8 w_L)	not good	–	–
		110 to 200% (1.5 to 2.8 w_L)	good	rich	fair
		90 to 110% (1.3 to 1.5 w_L)	good	middle	fair
		70 to 90% (1.0 to 1.3 w_L)	good	middle	somewhat low
		50 to 70% (0.7 to 1.0 w_L)	good	middle	low
		lower than 50% (lower than 0.7 w_L)	not good	–	–

3.3 Soil material suitable for the method

The pneumatic flow mixing method can be applicable not only to dredged soft soil but also to surplus soil and subsoil produced from construction sites. Soil properties suitable for the method are summarized in Table 1.3 (Coastal Development Institute of Technology, 2008b), in which cohesive soil with a sand particle content of less than 30% and a water content of 90 to 110% (approximately 1.3–1.5 times the liquid limit) is the most suitable for the method. On the other hand, cohesive soil with a sand particle content of 30 to 50% and a comparatively low water content, or cohesive soil with a sand particle content of less than 30% and a water content of 50 to 70% (approximately 0.7–1.0 times the liquid limit) are not suitable for the method, but can be available if they are remolded throughout by adding additional water to reduce their cohesion.

3.4 Applications of the method

The pneumatic flow mixing method has many advantages, such as making beneficial use of dredged soil and subsoil possible, obtaining any target stabilized soil strength within a short period by controlling the type and amount of binder, and conducting a rapid and large scale operation. Because of these advantages, the method has been applied to many construction projects for many improvement purposes, including land reclamation; backfilling behind sea revetments and earth retaining structures; and shallow stabilization and backfill underwater, as shown in Figure 1.16 (Ministry of Transport, The Fifth District Port Construction Bureau, 1999). For these applications, ordinary Portland cement and blast furnace slag cement type B are often used as a binder, where the cement content and target unconfined compressive strength of the stabilized soil are of the order of 50 to 70 kg/m^3 and 100 to 200 kN/m^2, respectively.

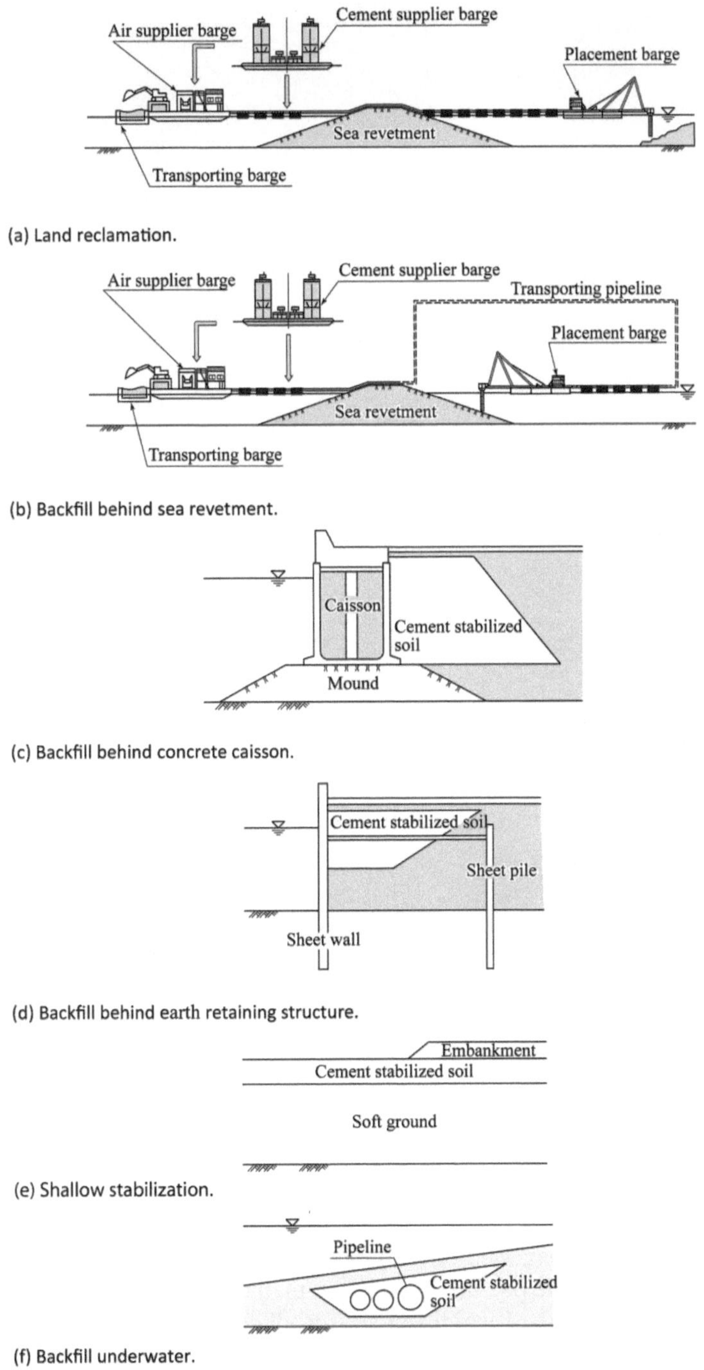

Figure 1.16 Examples of application of the pneumatic flow mixing method (Ministry of Transport, The Fifth District Port Construction Bureau, 1999).

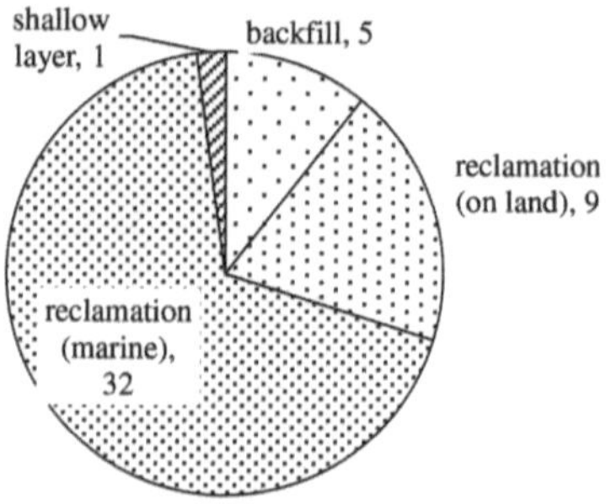

(a) Number of projects.

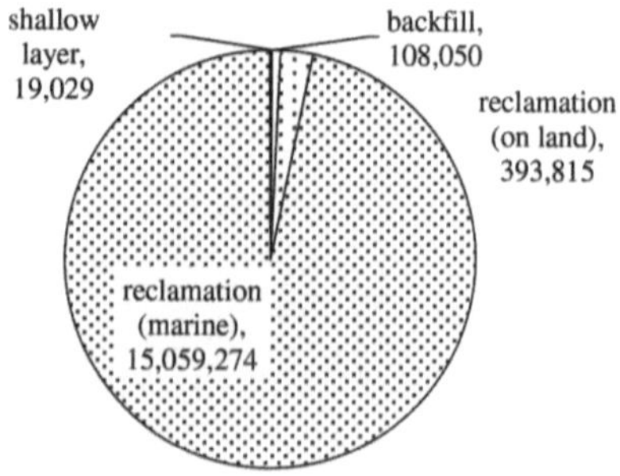

(b) Volume of stabilized soil.

Figure 1.17 Statics of the pneumatic flow mixing method works in Japan.

Figure 1.17 shows summary statistics for use of the pneumatic flow mixing method from 1998 to 2015, which is classified into applications, the number of projects and volumes of stabilized soil. The total number of projects is 47 and the total volume comes to about 15.6 million m^3. The application of reclamation in marine areas is dominant; the proportions by number and volume of these projects are about 68.1% and 96.6%.

4 SCOPE OF THE TEXTBOOK

The pneumatic flow mixing method was developed in Japan and put into practice in the late 1990s. The method has been applied to many construction projects since then, in which the total volume of stabilized soil produced by the method from 1998 to 2015 reached about 15.6 million m^3. This text book aims to provide the latest State of Practice of the pneumatic flow mixing method to researchers and practitioners based on the researches and experiences accumulated in numerous projects in Japan. The organization of the current textbook is as follows.

Chapter 1 gave an overview of various admixture stabilization techniques. The chapter also showed that a wide range of admixture stabilization techniques, including *in-situ* and *ex-situ* stabilizations, have gained popularity in Japan. Also the development, mechanism and applications of the pneumatic flow mixing method are briefly introduced.

Chapter 2 discusses the influence of various factors on the increase in soil strength brought about by its stabilization with cement. The information compiled in this chapter is basically applicable to all the types of admixture stabilization and useful for evaluating the feasibility of admixture stabilization to a specific soil, in the selection of appropriate binder, and in interpreting the laboratory or field test results.

Chapter 3 describes the engineering properties of stabilized soil mainly stabilized by cement. Facility in transport and placement ability are key factors for the execution of the method, which is influenced by the engineering properties of freshly stabilized soil, soon after mixing. This chapter introduces not only the properties of hardened stabilized soil, the properties of fresh stabilized soil, and the properties of soil that has been subjected to disturbance and compaction.

Chapter 4 describes nine case histories of application of the method in Japan, which cover various types of application, binder and mixing systems; land reclamation; backfill; and shallow layer construction.

Chapter 5 describes the machine system; execution; and quality control and quality assurance during production. The placement technique and process of stabilized soil influences the properties of the field stabilized soil, and the degree of water pollution due to the stabilized soil. This chapter briefly describes the environmental impact of placing stabilized soils in underwater locations, and the countermeasures too. The chapter concentrates on the relevant issues in systems commonly used in Japan.

Chapter 6 describes the geotechnical design procedure currently employed in Japan. The geotechnical design is a way to determine the required quality of stabilized soil and required geometry of stabilized soil ground. This chapter describes the phenomenon of volume change due to stabilization, which is one of the critical design considerations, especially in the case of land reclamation projects on a huge scale.

The Appendix explains the standard laboratory mix test procedure used to test stabilized soils in Japan, with visual examples.

REFERENCES

Akagawa, K. (1980) Gas-liquid two-phase flow. *Mechanical Engineering* 11. p. 15 (in Japanese).

Coastal Development Institute of Technology (2001) *Technical Manual of Pneumatic Flow Mixing Method*. Daikousha Publishers, 127p. (in Japanese).

Coastal Development Institute of Technology (2003) *The Premixing method: Principle, Design and Construction*. A.A.Balkema Publishers. 140p.

Coastal Development Institute of Technology (2008a) *Technical Manual of Lightweight Geomaterial*, revised version. Daikousha Publishers, 370p. (in Japanese).

Coastal Development Institute of Technology (2008b) *Technical Manual of Pneumatic Flow Mixing Method*, revised version. Daikousha Publishers, 188p. (in Japanese).

Coastal Development Institute of Technology (2008c) *Technical Manual of Premixing Method*, revised version. Daikousha Publishers, 215p. (in Japanese).

http://www.penta-ocean.co.jp/english/business/envi/dirt_recycle.html

Kitazume, M. (2004) Construction of a man-made island for Central Japan International Airport by the pneumatic flow mixing method. *Proc. of the 5th International Conference on Ground Improvement Techniques*. pp. 169–176.

Kitazume, M. (2010) Application of Cement Stabilization Methods to Earthquake Disaster Mitigation. *Proc. of the 9th International Symposium on New Technologies for Urban Safety of Mega Cities in Asia*. CD-ROM.

Kitazume, M. & Satoh, T. (2003) Development of Pneumatic Flow Mixing Method and its Application to Central Japan International Airport Construction. *Journal of Ground Improvement*. Vol. 7, No. 3, pp. 139–148.

Kitazume, M. & Satoh, T. (2005) Quality control in Central Japan International Airport Construction. *Journal of Ground Improvement*. Vol. 9, No. 2, pp. 59–66.

Kitazume, M. & Terashi, M. (2013) *The Deep Mixing Method*. CRC Press, Taylor & Francis Group. 410p.

Kitazume, M., Adachi, Y., Ikenoue, N. & Okubo, Y. (2007) Engineering property of treated soil by pneumatic flow mixing method: (Part 3) Relation between the fluidity of treated soil and required air pressure for transport. *Proc. of the 42nd Annual Conference of the Japanese Geotechnical Society*. pp. 607–608 (in Japanese).

Kobayashi, K., Yoshida, G. & Sato, H. (2001) Quality assurance of pneumatic flow mixing method: Snake Mixer Method. *Proc. of the Annual Research Conference, Civil Engineering Research Institute for Cold Region, Ministry of Ministry of Land, Infrastructure, Transport and Tourism*. pp. 393–400 (in Japanese).

Ministry of Land, Infrastructure, Transport & Tourism (2007) *Technical Standards for Port and Harbour Facilities*. Vol. 2, pp. 672–762 (in Japanese).

Ministry of Transport, The Fifth District Port Construction Bureau (1999) *Pneumatic flow mixing method*. Yasuki Publishers. 157p. (in Japanese).

Mizukami, J. & Matsunaga, Y. (2015) Construction of D-Runway at Tokyo International Airport. *Proc. of the 15th Asian Regional Conference on Soil Mechanics and Geotechnical Engineering*. CD-ROM.

Power Blender Method Association (2006) *Technical data on slurry type Power Blender Method*. Power Blender Association. (in Japanese).

Tsuchida, T. & Egashira, K. (2004) *The Lightweight Treated Soil method: New Geomaterials for Soft Ground Engineering in Coastal Areas*. A.A.Balkema Publishers. 120p.

Watanabe, A. (2005) Challenge to soft soil: Pneumatic flow mixing method for dredged soil. *Proc. of the Annual Research Conference, Ministry of Ministry of Land, Infrastructure, Transport and Tourism*. (in Japanese).

Yamagoshi, Y., Akashi, Y., Nakagawa, M., Kanno, H., Tanaka, Y., Tsuji, T., Imamura, T. & Shibuya, T. (2013) Reclamation of the artificial ground made of dredged soil and converter slag by using pipe mixing method. *Journal of Geotechnical Engineering, Japan Society of Civil Engineers*. Vol. 69, No. 2, pp. 952–957 (in Japanese).

Yamauchi, H., Ishiyama, Y. & Oonishi, F. (2011) Study for beneficial use of soft dredged soil: Case history of backfill behind the breakwater at Kushiro Port. *Proc. of the Annual Technical Meeting, Civil Engineering Research Institute for Cold Region*. (in Japanese).

Zen, K., Yamazaki, H., Watanabe, A., Yoshizawa, H. & Tamai, A. (1987) Study on a reclamation method with cement-mixed sandy soils: Fundamental characteristics of treated soils and model tests on the mixing and reclamation. *Technical Note of the Port and Harbour Research Institute*. No. 579, 41p. (in Japanese).

Chapter 2

Factors affecting strength increase

1 INTRODUCTION

The strength increase of cement-stabilized soils is influenced by a number of factors, because the basic strength increase mechanism is closely related to the chemical reaction between soil and binder. The factors can be roughly divided into four categories: I. Characteristics of binder, II. Characteristics and conditions of soil, III. Mixing conditions, and IV. Curing conditions, as shown in Table 2.1 (after Terashi, 1997).

The characteristics of the binder mentioned in Category I strongly affect the strength of the stabilized soil. Therefore, the selection of an appropriate binder is an important issue. There are many types of binder available on the Japanese market (Japan Lime Association, 2009, Japan Cement Association, 2012). The basic mechanisms of admixture stabilization using quicklime or cement were extensively studied by highway engineers many years ago. This is because lime- and cement-stabilized soils have been used as sub-base or subgrade materials in road construction (e.g. Ingles & Metcalf, 1972). The stabilization mechanisms of various binders have been investigated further by geotechnical engineers (e.g. Babasaki et al., 1996a, 1996b). The factors in Category II (characteristics and conditions of the soil) are inherent characteristics of each soil and the way it has been deposited. Thompson (1966) studied the influence of the properties of Illinois soils on the lime reactivity of compacted lime-soil mixtures and concluded that the major influential factors were acidity (potential hydration) and organic matter content of the original soil. Japanese research groups have also performed similar studies on lime- and cement-stabilized soils manufactured without compaction (e.g. Okumura et al., 1974; Kawasaki et al., 1978, 1981, Terashi et al., 1977, 1979, 1980, 1983; Saitoh et al., 1980, 1985; Saitoh, 1988). Their valuable works have provided engineers with good qualitative information. The factors in Category III (mixing conditions) are easily altered and controlled on site during execution based on the judgment of engineers responsible for the execution. The factors in Category IV (curing conditions) can be controlled easily in the laboratory but cannot be controlled at work sites in most cases.

As cement has often been used in the pneumatic flow mixing method, the influence of various factors on the strength of cement-stabilized soil are briefly described in the following section, where the unconfined compressive strength, q_u, of stabilized soil is mainly used as an index representing the stabilization effect. The test specimen for the unconfined compression test is, in principle, prepared in laboratory by the procedure

Table 2.1 Factors affecting the strength increase of stabilized soil (after Terashi, 1997).

I.	Characteristics of binder	1. Type of binder 2. Quality of binder 3. Mixing water and additives
II.	Characteristics and conditions of soil (especially important for clays)	1. Physical, chemical and mineralogical properties of soil 2. Organic content 3. Potential Hydrogen (pH) of pore water 4. Water content
III.	Mixing conditions	1. Quantity of binder 2. Degree of mixing 3. Timing of mixing/re-mixing 4. Placement condition
IV.	Curing conditions	1. Temperature 2. Curing period 3. Humidity 4. Wetting and drying/freezing and thawing, etc. 5. Overburden pressure 6. Soil disturbance/compaction

standardized by the Japanese Geotechnical Society (formerly Japanese Society of Soil Mechanics and Foundation Engineering). The test procedure was originally proposed by Terashi et al. (1980) and welcomed by Japanese researchers and engineers. Essentially the same procedure was adopted by the Japanese Society of Soil Mechanics and Foundation Engineering in 1981 as its Draft Standard JSF: T31-81T in 1982. The draft standard was later officially standardized by the Japanese Society of Soil Mechanics and Foundation Engineering in 1990 and was given minor revisions by the Japanese Geotechnical Society in 2000 and 2009 (Japanese Geotechnical Society, 2000, 2009). The laboratory test procedure is described in the Appendix.

2 MECHANISM OF CEMENT STABILIZATION

In Japan the types of cement used as a binder is usually ordinary Portland cement (OPC) and blast furnace slag cement type B. Ordinary Portland cement is manufactured by adding gypsum to cement clinker and grinding it to powder. Cement clinker is formed by minerals $3CaO.SiO_2$, $2CaO.SiO_3$, $3CaO.Al_2O_3$ and $4CaO.Al_2O_3.Fe_2O_3$. A cement mineral, $3CaO.SiO_2$, for example, reacts with water in the following way to produce cement hydration products.

$$2(3CaO.SiO_2) + 6H_2O = 3CaO.2SiO_2.3H_2O + 3Ca(OH)_2 \tag{2.1}$$

During the hydration of cement, calcium hydroxide, $Ca(OH)_2$, is released. The cement hydration product has high strength, which increases as it ages, while calcium hydroxide contributes to the pozzolanic reaction. Blast furnace slag cement is a mixture of ordinary Portland cement and blast furnace slag. Finely powdered blast furnace slag does not react with water but has the potential to produce pozzolanic reaction

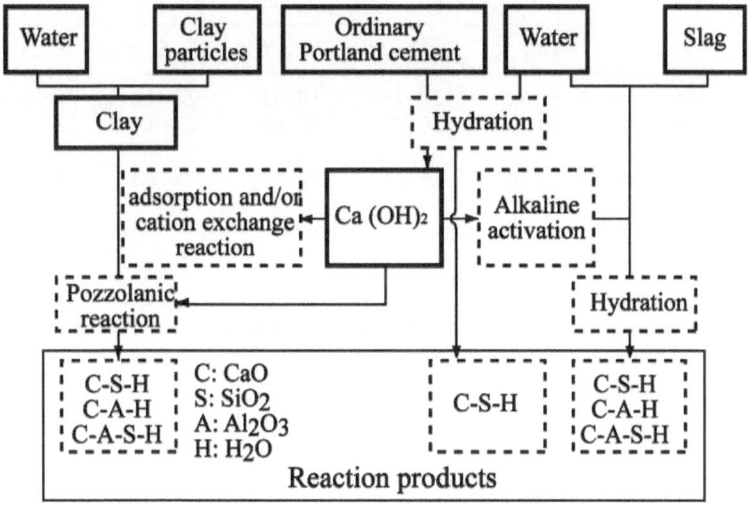

Figure 2.1 Chemical reactions between clay, cement, slag and water (Saitoh et al., 1985).

products under high alkaline conditions. In blast furnace slag cement, silicon dioxide, SiO_2, and aluminium oxide, Al_2O_3, contained in the slag are actively released by the stimulus of large quantities of Ca^{2+} and SO_4^{2-} released from the cement, so that fine hydration products abounding in silicates are formed, rather than cement hydration products, and the long term strength is enhanced. The rather complicated mechanism of cement stabilization is simplified and schematically shown in Figure 2.1 for the chemical reactions between clay, pore water, cement and slag (Saitoh et al., 1985).

3 INFLUENCE OF VARIOUS FACTORS ON THE STABILIZATION EFFECT

3.1 Influence of the characteristics of the binder

3.1.1 Chemical composition of the binder

In Japan, ordinary Portland cement (OPC) and blast furnace slag cement type B have often been used as a binder for stabilizing clay and sand, whose chemical components are specified by Japanese Industrial Standard (Japanese Industrial Standard, 2006, 2009) as tabulated in Table 2.2. In addition to the two types of cement, several cement-based special binders have been developed and are available on the Japanese market as shown in Table 2.3 (Japan Cement Association, 2012).

The cement-based special binders are specially manufactured for the specific purpose of stabilizing soil or similar material by increasing certain constituents of ordinary Portland cement. This is done by adjusting its Blaine specific surface area or by adding ingredients effective for particular soil types. These are actually a mixture of cement

Table 2.2 Chemical components of Japanese cements (Japanese Industrial Standard, 2006, 2009).

	CaO (%)	SiO_2 (%)	Al_2O_4 (%)	Fe_2O_4 (%)	SO_4 (%)	Others
Ordinary Portland cement	64–65	20–24	4.8–5.8	2.5–4.6	1.5–2.4	MgO,
High-early-strength Portland cement	64–66	20–22	4.0–5.2	2.4–4.4	2.5–4.4	Na_2O, K_2O,
Blast furnace slag cement type B	52–58	24–27	7.0–9.5	1.6–2.5	1.2–2.6	MnO, P_2O_5

Table 2.3 Cement-based special binders (Japan Cement Association, 2012).

Type	*Characteristics*
For soft soils	Appropriate for soft soils with a high water content, e.g. sand, silt, clay and volcanic soil
For problematic soils	To reduce leaching of hexavalent chromium (chromium VI) from stabilized soil
For organic soils	Appropriate for highly organic soils, e.g. humus, organic soil, sludge

as a mother material and gypsum, a micropowder of slag, alumina or fly ash. The chemical components of the cement-based special binders are not specified by the Japanese Industrial Standard and are not published as proprietary information by cement manufacturers. As shown in Table 2.3, the cement-based special binders are designed for high water content soil, high organic content soil and for reducing the leaching of $Cr^{6+}$from stabilized soil. The stabilization effect in organic soil is said to be affected by the composite ratio, $(SiO_2 + Al_2O_3)$ against CaO, of the constituent elements in cement and cement-based special binders (Hayashi et al., 1989).

Other than those special binders, 'delayed stabilizing' or 'long-term strength control' type binders are also available on the Japanese market, by which the rate of strength increase can be controlled. They are obtained by adjusting the quantities of ingredients such as gypsum or lime. These binders react slowly with soil and exhibit smaller strength in the short term, but result in sufficiently high strengths in the long term in comparison with ordinary Portland cement or blast furnace slag cement type B (Kiyota et al., 2003).

An example of the effects of the chemical compounds calcium oxide, CaO, sulphur trioxide, SO_3, and aluminium oxide, Al_2O_3, on the strength is shown in Figure 2.2 (Japan Cement Association, 2009). In the test, dredged clay (w_L of 60.7%, w_P of 29.1% and I_p of 31) was stabilized with mixture of several types of cement and cement-based special binders so that the effects of chemical compounds could be highlighted. After four weeks curing, the stabilized soils were subjected to unconfined compression test. The unconfined compressive strength, q_u is compared with the content of chemical compounds in the binder. In the effect of CaO, Figure 2.2(a), the strength remains almost constant irrespective of the amount of CaO as long as the amount of binder is about 80 kg/m^3. When the amount of binder is increased to 140 and 200 kg/m^3,

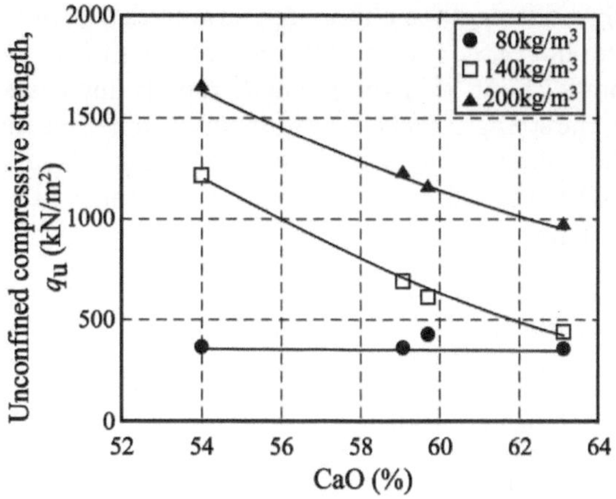

(a) Effect of CaO content.

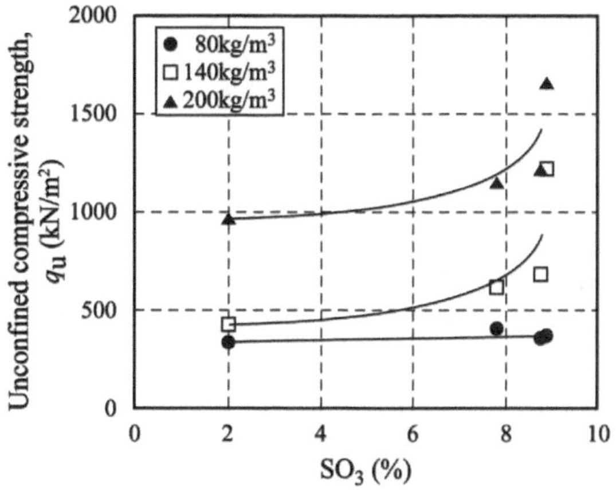

(b) Effect of SO_3 content.

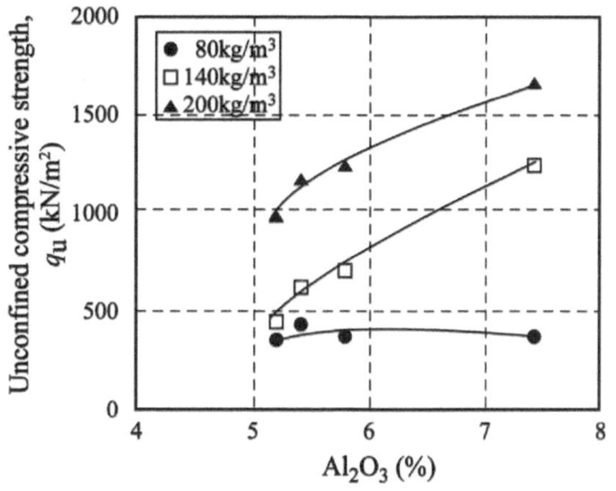

(c) Effect of Al_2O_3 content.

Figure 2.2 The effects of chemical compounds on the strength of cement-stabilized soil (Japan Cement Association, 2009).

however, the strength decreases with the content of CaO. In the effect of SO_3, Figure 2.2(b), the strength is almost constant irrespective of the amount of binder as long as the amount of SO_3 remains lower than about 8%. However, when the amount of SO_3 becomes about 9%, the strength rapidly increases. In the effect of Al_2O_3, Figure 2.2(c), the strength remains almost constant irrespective of the amount of Al_2O_3 as long as the amount of binder is about 80 kg/m^3. When the amount of binder is increased to 140 and 200 kg/m^3, however, the strength increases almost linearly with the Al_2O_3 content.

3.1.2 *Type of binder*

Figure 2.3 shows the influence of the type of cement on the strength of stabilized soil in which ordinary Portland cement and blast furnace slag cement type B were compared at the curing period, with a t_c of 28 days to 5 years (Saitoh, 1988). The tests were conducted on two different sea bottom sediments: the Yokohama Port clay (w_L of 95.4%, w_P of 42.4% and w_i of 97.9%) and the Osaka Port clay (w_L of 79.4%, w_P of 40.2% and w_i of 94.9%). For each clay, three different amounts of cement, α of 100 to 300 kg/m^3, were mixed. The cement factor, α, is defined as a dry weight of cement added to 1 m^3 of original soil. The horizontal axes of the figures show the curing period, t_c. The vertical axis of the upper figures for each clay is the unconfined compressive strength, q_u, of the stabilized soil, while the vertical axes of the lower figures is the normalized unconfined compressive strength at an arbitrary curing period, t_c, by the 28 days' strength: q_{utc}/q_{u28}. In the case of the Yokohama Port clay, which exhibits high pozzolanic reactivity, ordinary Portland cement is much more effective than blast furnace slag cement type B. However, in the case of the Osaka Port clay, with its lower pozzolanic reactivity than the Yokohama Port clay, blast furnace slag cement type B is much more effective. These test results suggest that the appropriate selection of the type of cement can be made if the pozzolanic reactivity of soil is evaluated beforehand. It is interesting to see the q_{utc}/q_{u28} is higher for blast furnace slag cement type B than for ordinary Portland cement, irrespective of the soil type.

Figure 2.4 shows the influence of various cement-based special binders on the strength of various types of organic soil (Coastal Development Institute of Technology, 2008a). The physical and chemical properties of the soils are tabulated in Table 2.4 (Coastal Development Institute of Technology, 2008a). The letters along the horizontal axes of the figures represent the types of binder, while the chemical components of some binders are shown in Table 2.5 (Coastal Development Institute of Technology, 2008a). The figures show that cement-based special binders are effective for organic soils in general, but that the most effective binder for a particular soil is not always the best binder for the other types of organic soil. For these problematic soils, appropriate selection of binder by a laboratory mix test is important. A similar phenomenon on the strength of stabilized organic soils will be shown in Figure 2.7.

3.1.3 *Type of mixing water*

Table 2.6 shows the influence of the type of mixing water for preparing binder slurry on the strength of stabilized soil, where clay excavated at Tokyo Port (w_L of 94.1% and w_P of 45.8%) was stabilized with ordinary Portland cement (Kawasaki et al., 1978).

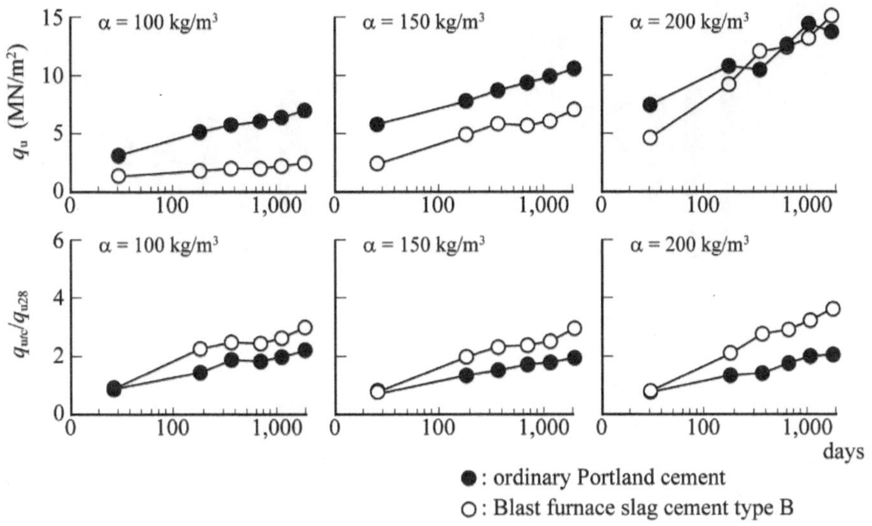

(a) Influence of binder type on the Yokohama Port clay.

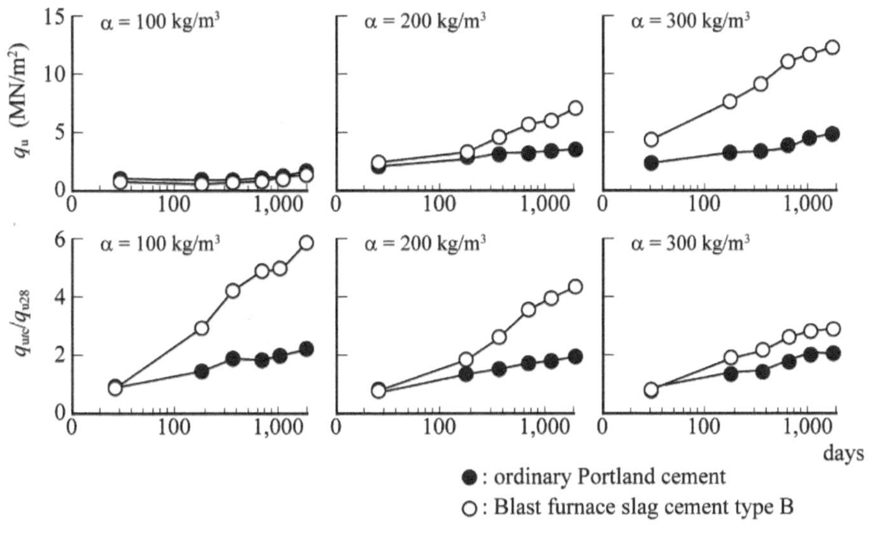

(b) Influence of binder type on the Osaka Port clay.

Figure 2.3 The influence of cement type on the unconfined compressive strength of cement-stabilized marine clays (Saitoh, 1988).

The cement slurry was prepared by two types of water: tap water and seawater obtained at Tokyo Port. The table shows that the strength of the stabilized soil with tap water is slightly smaller than that with seawater, but the difference is negligibly small from a practical point of view.

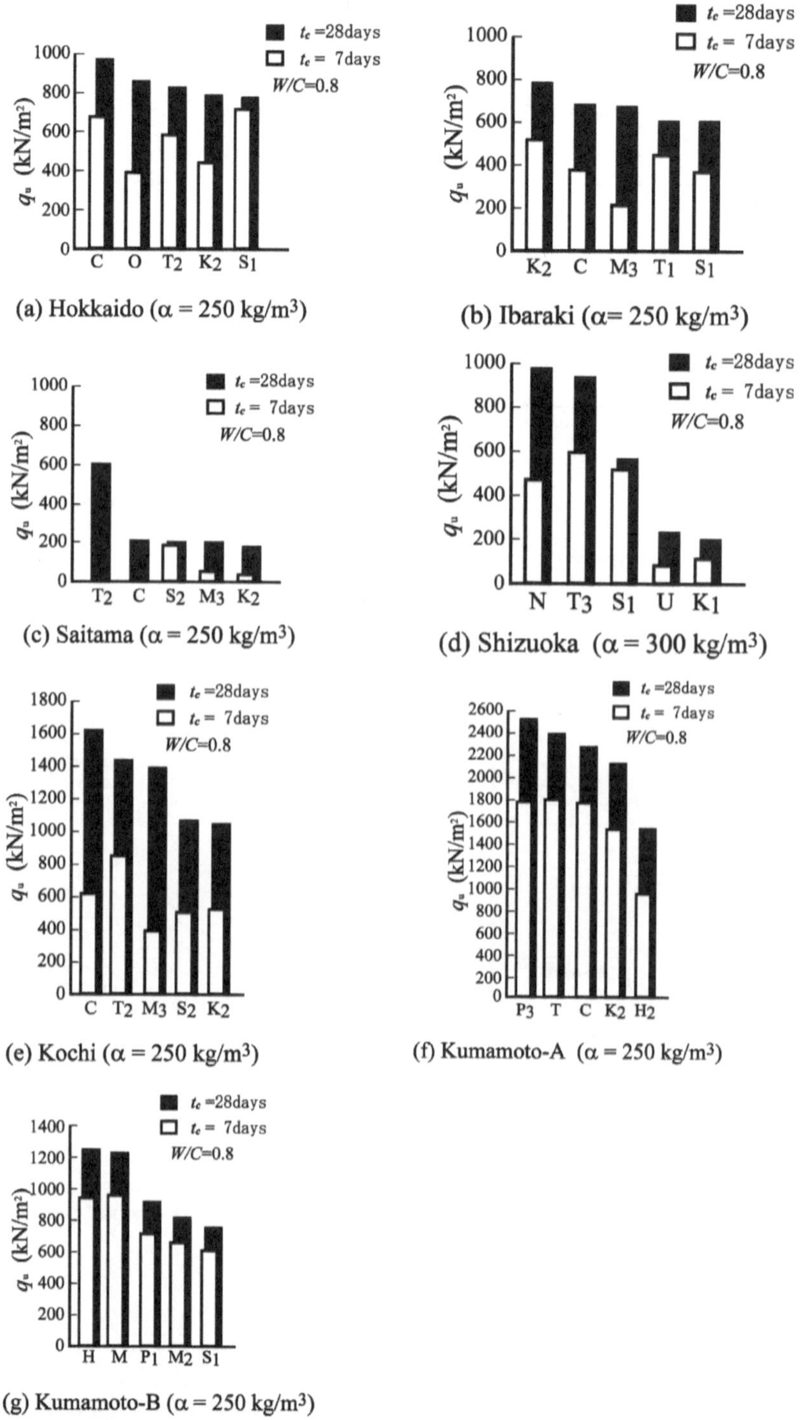

Figure 2.4 The unconfined compressive strength of organic soils stabilized with cement-based special binders (Coastal Development Institute of Technology, 2008a).

Table 2.4 Physical and chemical properties of soils (Coastal Development Institute of Technology, 2008a).

Depth (m)	*Hokkaido* −0.5 to −1.0	*Ibaraki* −0.5 to −1.0	*Saitama* −0.5 to −1.0	*Shizuoka* −4.0 to −4.0	*Kochi* −1.0 to −1.5	*Kumamoto-A* −5.0 to −7.5	*Kumamoto-B* −0.5 to −1.0
Grain size distribution							
gravel (%)	–	–	–	–	0.0	0	0.0
sand (%)	–	–	–	–	0.0	0	2.9
silt (%)	–	–	–	–	71.8	40.5	42.0
clay (%)	–	–	–	–	28.2	59.5	55.1
Consistency limits							
liquid limit, w_L (%)	–	251.2	–	–	271.6	174.8	181.4
plastic limit, w_P (%)	–	92.7	–	–	69.1	76.2	47.4
plasticity index, I_p	–	158.5	–	–	202.5	97.6	144.0
Particle density (g/cm^3)	1.969	1.688	2.099	1.700	2.249	2.279	1.572
Natural condition							
water content (%)	492	246	940	840	295	156.4	159
density, ρ_c (g/cm^3)	1.11	1.16	1.04	1.045	1.14	1.400	1.26
Chemical properties							
ignition loss (%)	55.2	47.7	67.4	70.5	24.8	22.2	24.0
dichromate (%)	42.4	25.2	59.0	–	17.6	–	11.5
humus content (%)	8.1	15.2	28.6	17.2	4.1	–	7.4
pH	4.9	4.7	4.5	–	4.0	6.7	5.0

Table 2.5 Chemical components of binders (Coastal Development Institute of Technology, 2008a).

Binder	SiO_2	Al_2O_3	Fe_2O_2	*CaO*	*MgO*	SO_3	Na_2O	K_2O
C	21.5	7.8	1.6	51.7	2.5	9.4	0.2	0.4
H	20.8	8.3	2.0	53.0	3.1	9.7	0.3	0.3
M	17.3	4.9	2.5	59.9	1.8	8.4	0.1	0.1
N	19.8	7.3	1.8	53.0	2.6	12.9	0.1	0.1
O	17.6	4.5	2.9	57.8	1.4	11.3	0.4	0.5

Table 2.6 Influence of type of water used to prepare the cement slurry on strength of stabilized soil (Kawasaki et al., 1978).

			Unconfined compressive strength, q_u *(kN/m²)*		
Initial water (%) content, w_i	*Cement content, aw (%)*	*Curing period (day)*	*tap water*	*seawater*	*Strength ratio* q_{u_tap}/q_{u_sea}
79.9	13.1	7	2400	2640	0.91
	13.1	28	3500	3700	0.95
85.1	13.1	7	2080	2090	0.99
	13.1	28	3090	2980	1.04

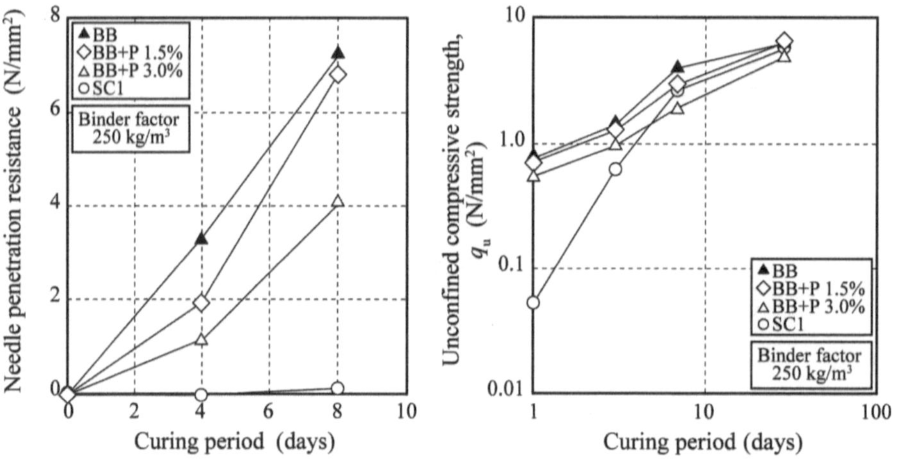

Figure 2.5 The effect of the stabilizing agent on the strength of stabilized soil (Kiyota et al., 2003).

3.1.4 Type of additives

Figure 2.5 shows the influence of the type of slow-setting special cement on the strength of stabilized soil (Kiyota et al., 2003). In the tests, clay excavated in Tokyo (w_i of 51.3%) was stabilized with either a slow-setting special cement (SC1), blast furnace slag cement type B (BB), or mixture of blast furnace slag cement type B and a slow-setting special cement (BB+P 1.5%, BB+P 3.0%). The stabilized soils were subjected to the needle penetration tests (JIS A 6204) within one day's curing and an unconfined compression test after one day's curing. Figure 2.5(a) shows that the needle penetration resistance is quite small in the case of the SC1, while the resistances of the BB+P 1.5% and BB+P 3.0% are a little smaller than the BB-stabilized soil. The unconfined compressive strength of SC1 increases very rapidly after one day and reaches almost the same q_u values as BB-stabilized soil at 28 days' curing, as shown in Figure 2.5(b).

3.2 Influence of the characteristics and conditions of soil

3.2.1 Soil type

In order to investigate the influential factors on cement stabilization, Babasaki et al. (1996a, 1996b) collected 231 test results on soils taken from 69 locations in Japan from the 14 papers published during 1981 to 1992 in Japan. For deducing the influence of soil type from the test data conducted in different laboratories, the other factors listed in Table 2.1 were kept constant. Regarding the characteristics of binder, the test data on ordinary Portland cement and blast furnace slag cement type B were compared, while the mixing and curing conditions were the same for all the tests. Figure 2.6 compares the binder content, *aw*, and unconfined compressive strength at 28 days' curing, q_u, for various soils. Even for the same binder content of *aw*, the q_u varies considerably according to the type of soil. The strength of a particular cement-stabilized soil increases with the amount of cement, as later shown in Figures 2.17 and 2.18. The large variation of strength found in Figure 2.6 clearly reveals that the strength gain by cement stabilization depends heavily upon the type and properties of soil.

The influence of soil type on the unconfined compressive strength, q_u, is also shown in Figure 2.7, in which a total of 21 different soils with various physical and chemical properties were stabilized by ordinary Portland cement with a cement content, *aw*, of

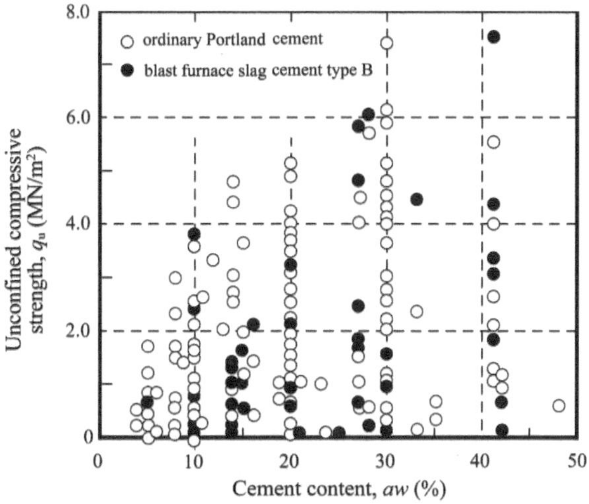

Figure 2.6 The relationship between unconfined compressive strength, q_u, and cement content, *aw* (Babasaki et al., 1996a, 1996b).

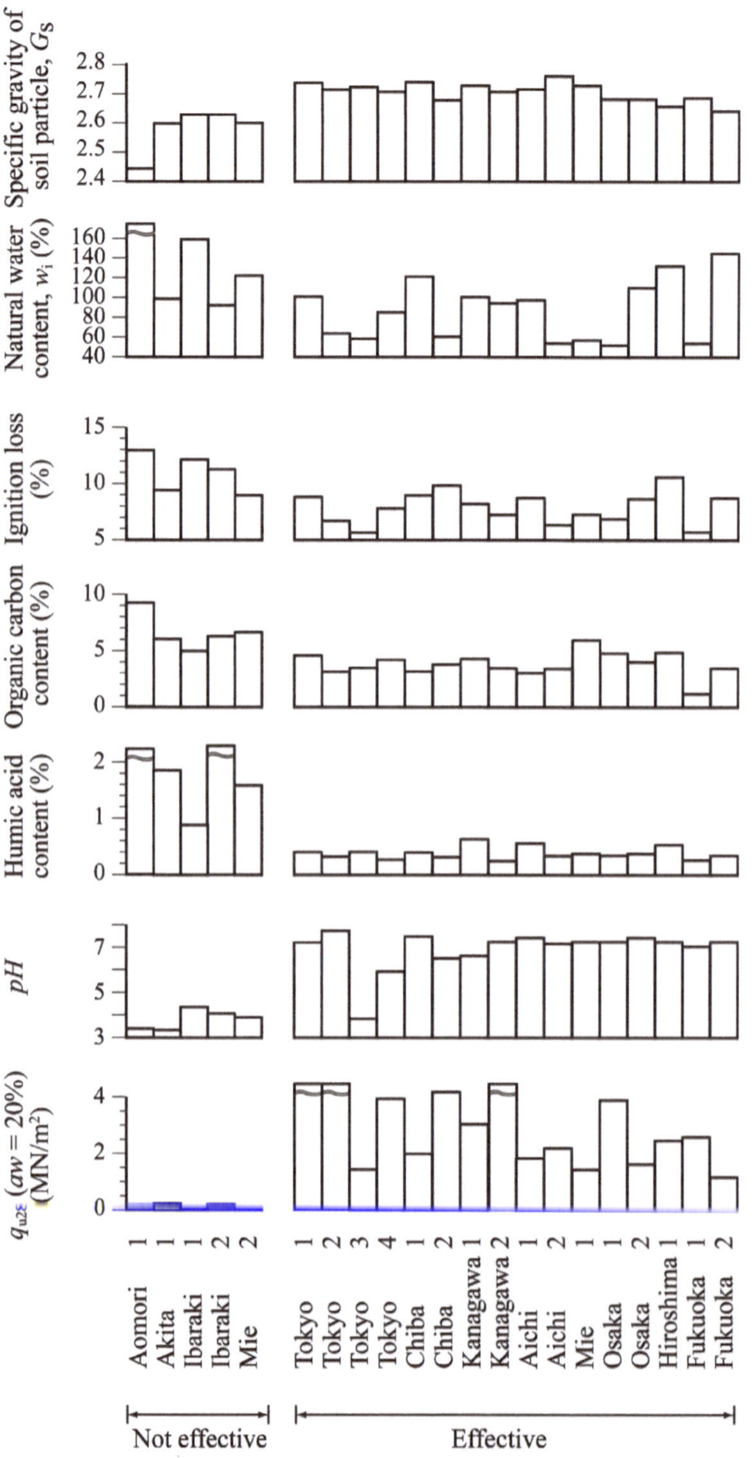

Figure 2.7 The influence of soil type in cement stabilization (Niina et al., 1981).

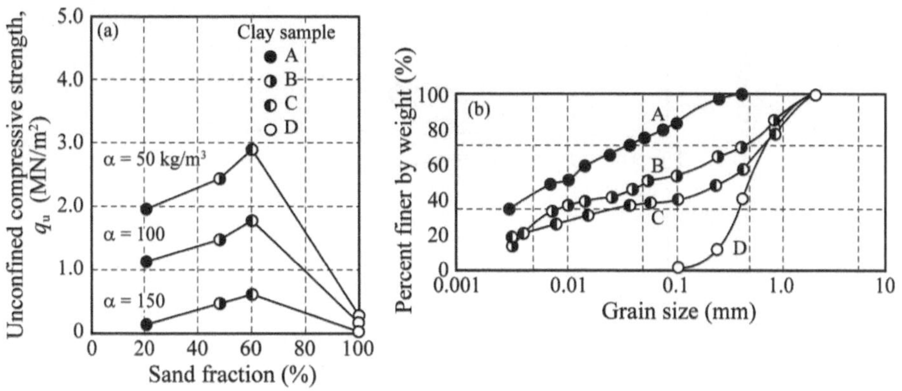

(a) Sand fraction of soils.

(b) Grain size distributions.

Figure 2.8 The influence of the grain size distribution in cement stabilization (Niina et al., 1977).

20% (Niina et al., 1981). The figure shows that the humic acid content and pH of soil are the most dominant factors influencing the strength gain.

3.2.2 *Grain size distribution*

Figure 2.8(a) shows the influence of grain size distribution of soil on the unconfined compressive strength, q_u, of cement-stabilized soil (Niina et al., 1977). In addition to the two natural soils, two artificial soils, B and C, were prepared by mixing the two natural soils, the Shinagawa alluvial clay (w_L of 62.6% and w_P of 24.1%) named A, and the Ooigawa sand, named D, whose grain size distributions are shown in Figure 2.8(b). These soils were stabilized with ordinary Portland cement with three amounts of cement factor, α, and the unconfined compression tests were carried out on the stabilized soils after 28 days' curing. The unconfined compressive strength, q_u, is influenced by the grain size distribution and the highest stabilization effect can be achieved at around 60% of sand fraction, irrespective of the amount of cement. However, this is not always true, as the test result on the other type of soil shows that the strength of stabilized soil is quite different even with almost the same grain size distribution, which may be influenced by its consistency property (Okano et al., 2012).

3.2.3 *Humic acid*

Figure 2.9 shows the influence of humic acid content on the unconfined compressive strength of cement-stabilized soil (Okada et al., 1983). Artificial soil samples were prepared by mixing various amount of humic acid with the kaolin clay (w_L of 50.6%), in which three kinds of humic acid extracted from Japanese clays and commercially available humic acid were mixed. These artificial soils having the same initial water content of 60% were stabilized with cement content, aw, of 5% ordinary Portland cement, while the humic acid content and the dry weight of the soil were changed. The figure clearly shows that the influence of the humic acid on the strength depends on its characteristics: the acid extracted from the Negina River clay has a negligible

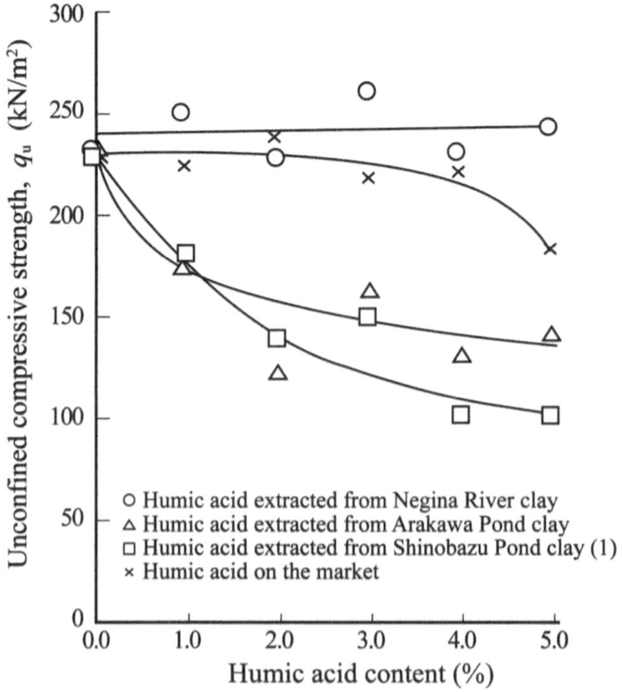

Figure 2.9 The influence of humic acid content on the unconfined compressive strength of stabilized clays (Okada et al., 1983).

influence on the strength, while the acid extracted from the Shinobazu Pond clay gives a considerably large influence on the strength.

Figure 2.10 also shows the influence of the humic acid content of soil on unconfined compressive strength (Miki et al., 1984). Artificial soil samples were prepared by adding various amounts of humic acid extracted from the clay at Arakawa Pond to the kaolin clay (w_L of 50.6%). In the tests, the artificial soils were stabilized with nine types of binder whose chemical compositions are shown in Figure 2.10(a). Figure 2.10(b) shows that the unconfined compressive strength, q_u, is highly dependent upon the binder but decreases considerably with the humic acid content, irrespective of the type of binder. The strength decreases to about one third when the humic acid content is increased to about 5%.

3.2.4 Organic content

3.2.4.1 Ignition loss

Figure 2.11 shows the relationship between ignition loss and the unconfined compressive strength, q_u, of stabilized soils (Babasaki et al., 1996a, 1996b). When the ignition loss is smaller than 15%, a relatively large strength can be generally achieved by mixing a certain amount of cement. For soils with ignition loss exceeding 15%, on the other hand, the unconfined compressive strength, q_u, remains low even with the cement content, aw, exceeding 20%, which means that large strength cannot be achieved with use of a practical amount of cement. The soils within the circled half-tone dot mesh

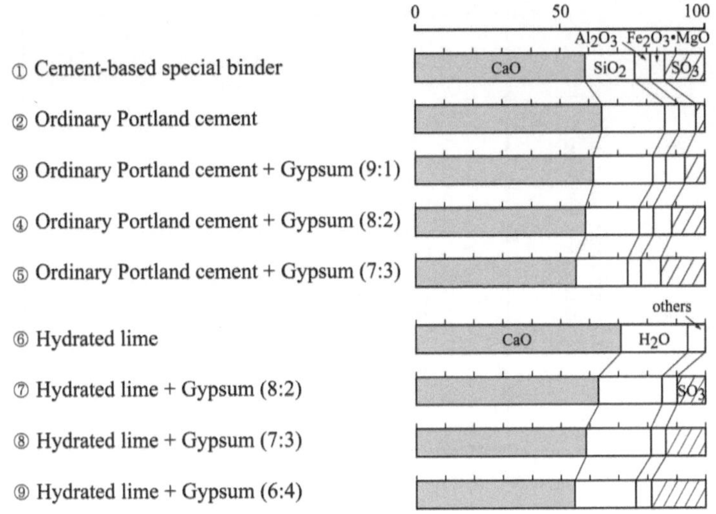

(a) Chemical composition of binders.

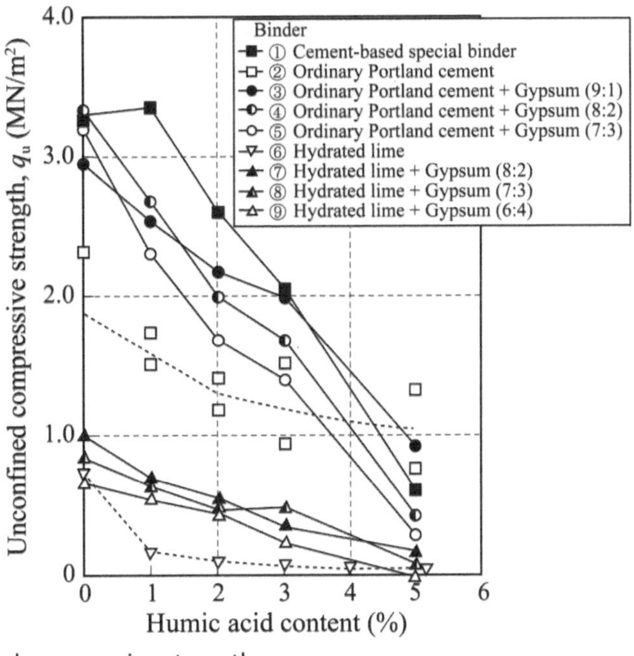

(b) Unconfined compressive strength, q_u.

Figure 2.10 The influence of humic acid content on the unconfined compressive strength of stabilized clays (Miki et al., 1984).

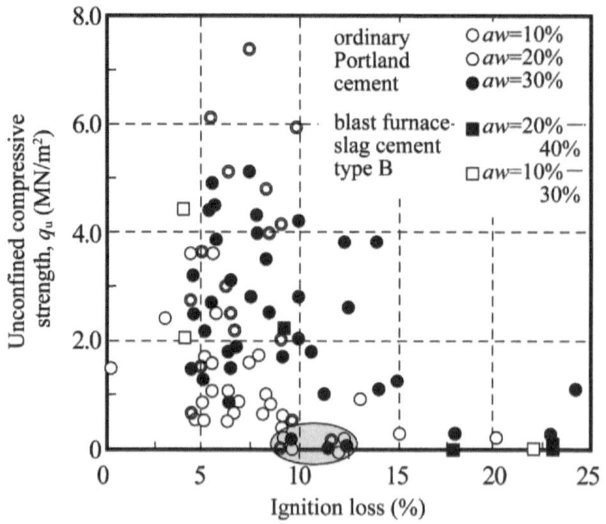

Figure 2.11 The relationship between unconfined compressive strength, q_u, and ignition loss of cement stabilized soils (Babasaki et al., 1996a, 1996b).

in the figure do not show an increase in strength, despite the increase in the cement content. The ignition loss of the soils is lower than 15% but the proportion of humus in the soil exceeds 0.9%, higher than that of the original soils, which may cause the quite low strength. Although there are some exceptions, ignition loss is one of the key indices with which to evaluate the stabilization effect.

3.2.4.2 *Potential hydrogen (pH) of soil*

Figure 2.12 shows the relationship between the potential hydrogen, pH, of original soil and unconfined compressive strength, q_u, (Babasaki et al., 1996a, 1996b). As the figure shows, most of soils with a pH value lower than 5 show a smaller strength increase than those with a pH value higher than 5 for the same binder content. Although there are exceptions in which the stabilization effect is not low, even with a low pH value, the pH value is one of the key indices to evaluate the stabilization effect.

The relationship between the pH of original soil and the unconfined compressive strength, q_u, of stabilized soil is proposed as Figure 2.13 and Equation 2.2 (Nakamura et al., 1980).

$$q_u = 0.0325 \times F - 1.625 \tag{2.2}$$

$$\left.\begin{array}{ll} F = Wc/(9 - pH) & for\,pH < 8 \\ F = Wc & for\,pH > 8 \end{array}\right\}$$

where
F: parameter (kg/m³)
pH: potential hydrogen
q_u: unconfined compressive strength (MN/m²)
Wc: cement factor (kg/m³)

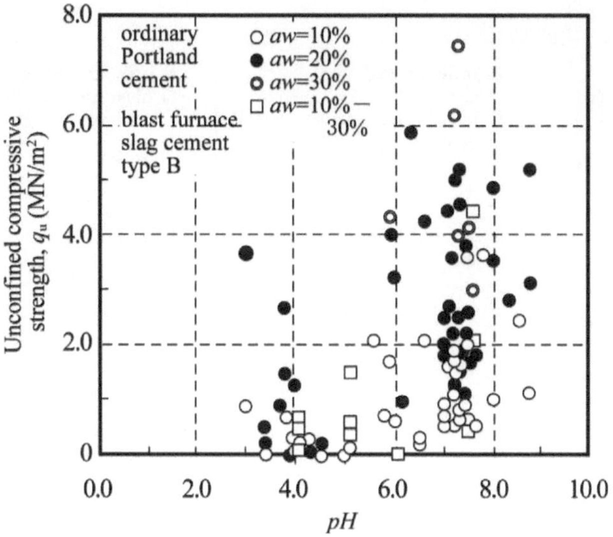

Figure 2.12 The relationship between unconfined compressive strength, q_u, and pH of original soils (Babasaki et al., 1996a, 1996b).

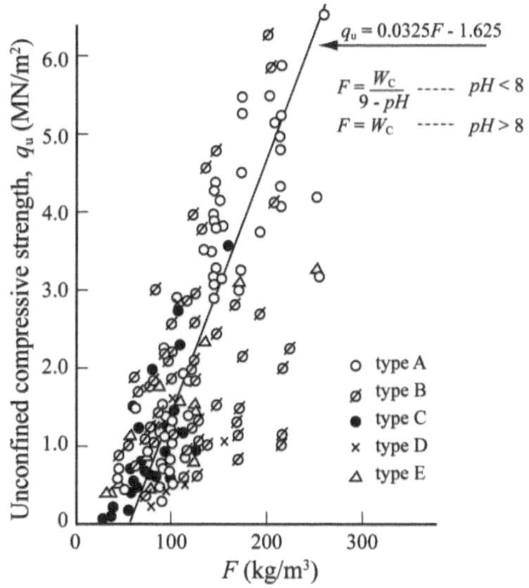

Type	Wet unit weight, γ_t (g/cm³)	Natural water content, w_n (%)	Liquid limit w_L (%)	Plastic limit w_p (%)	Grain size distribution (%)			pH (H_2O)	Ignition loss
					Sand, gravel fraction	Silt fraction	Clay fraction		
A	1.38-1.76	55-144	51-121	2-18	30-47	33-50	29-52	8.1-8.7	2.0-7.0
B	1.28-1.70	38-160	27-204	3-42	18-76	27-70	16-54	7.3-8.9	3.8-12.9
C	1.50-1.76	42-86	49-110	3-43	22-66	36-54	12-55	5.5-7.9	4.0-12.0
D	1.10-1.40	114-740	–	–	–	–	–	5.5-6.0	19.0-64.0
E	1.49-1.97	25-56	–	49-86	–	9-35	2-2	5.4-9.3	3.3-15.2

Figure 2.13 The effects of pH of soil on cement-stabilized soil (Nakamura et al., 1980).

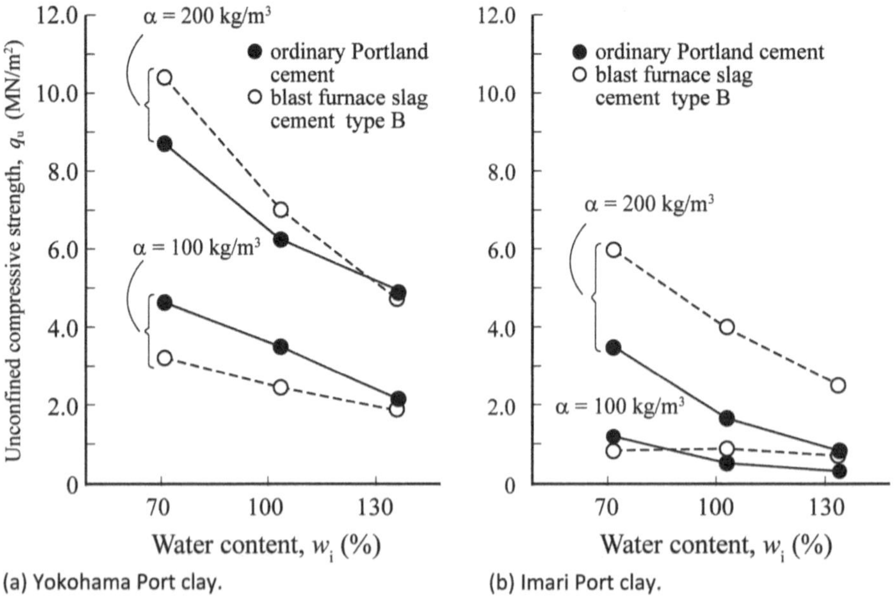

Figure 2.14 The influence of initial water content on the strength of two cement-stabilized clays (t_c of 91 days) (Saitoh, 1988).

3.2.5 Water content

The influence of the initial water content of the soil on unconfined compressive strength, q_u, of stabilized soil is shown in Figure 2.14 (Saitoh, 1988). In the tests, two kinds of marine clay (the Yokohama Port clay, w_L of 95.4%, w_P of 32.3% and w_n of 97.9%; and the Imari Port clay, w_L of 70.4%, w_P of 24.2% and w_n of 83.3%) were stabilized with either ordinary Portland cement or blast furnace slag cement type B. The Yokohama Port clay has high pozzolanic activity, while the Imari Port clay has low pozzolanic activity. The magnitude of strength gain is large for the high pozzolanic activity soil but not for the low pozzolanic activity soil. The unconfined compressive strength decreases almost linearly with the initial water content, irrespective of the pozzolanic activity of soil and cement type.

Figure 2.15 shows the relationship between the total water content, w_t, defined by the total weight of water, including pore water and mixing water, and the dry weight of soil and the q_u of stabilized soil with various cement contents, aw, of 10, 20, 30 and 35% (Babasaki et al., 1996a, 1996b). The figure shows that the strength of stabilized soil decreases rapidly with the total water content. Soils with a total water content, w_t, higher than 200% cannot achieve large gains in strength even with a large amount of cement. There are some exceptions where it is difficult to improve the soils' physical and mechanical properties even when their water content is lower than 200%. These soils usually contain a high amount of organic material, or are acidic soils with a low pH value; it is preferable to stabilize these soils with the cement-based special binders as already shown in Table 2.3.

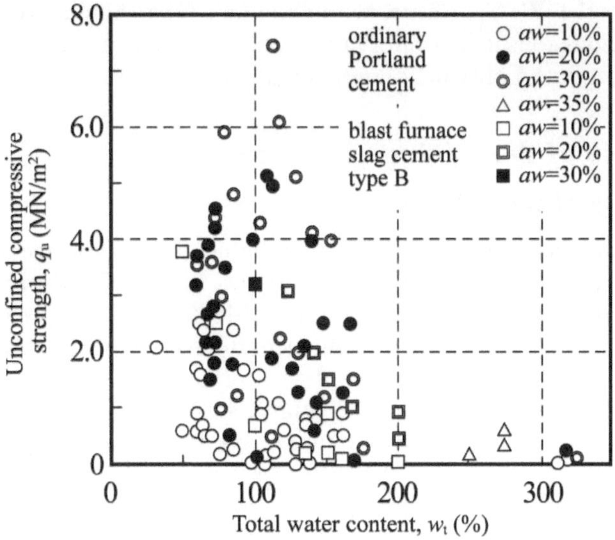

Figure 2.15 The relationship between unconfined compressive strength, q_u, and total water content, w_t of soil (Babasaki et al., 1996a, 1996b).

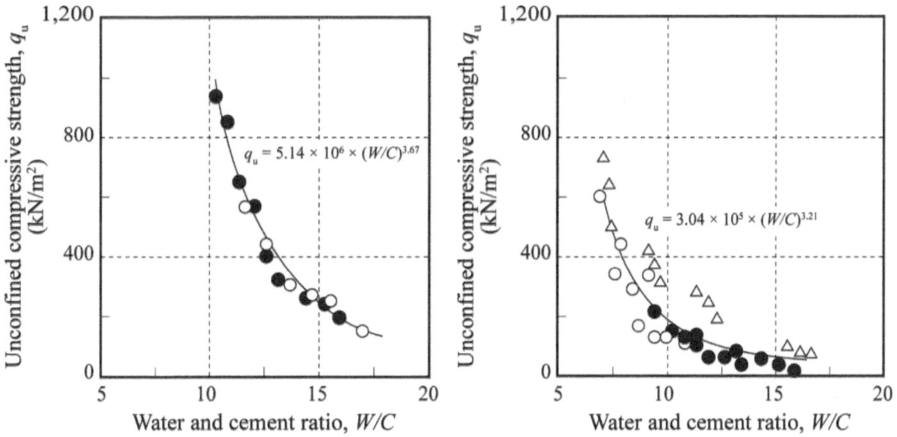

(a) Dredged site (F).

(b) Dredged site (G).

Figure 2.16 Typical examples of the relationship between unconfined compressive strength and the *W/C* ratio of soil (Kitazume & Satoh, 2003).

It has been well known that unconfined compressive strength, q_u, has a close relationship to the W/C ratio, in which the W/C ratio is defined as the total water contained in both soil and cement slurry against the dry weight of the cement. Figure 2.16 shows typical examples of the relationship, in which two types of soil (w_L of 78.3% and 55.3%, respectively) excavated at Nagoya Port were prepared to have various initial water contents and stabilized with blast furnace slag cement type B (Kitazume & Satoh, 2003). The figure shows that the q_u is almost inversely proportional to the W/C, irrespective of the soil type. Similar relationships were obtained on various soils in laboratory mix tests and field tests (Ministry of Transport, The Fifth District Port Construction Bureau, 1999).

3.3 Influence of the mixing conditions

3.3.1 *Quantity of cement*

Figure 2.17 shows the influence of the cement content, aw, on the unconfined compressive strength, q_u, in which the Fukuyama Port clay (w_L of 97.6% and w_P of 33.8%), having an initial water content of $1.5 \times w_L$ (146%), was stabilized with ordinary Portland cement, and was subjected to an unconfined compression test at three curing periods (Udaka et al., 2013). The unconfined compressive strength increases almost linearly with the amount of cement. The figure also shows that a minimum amount of cement – about 5% – is necessary to obtain a certain magnitude of strength gain for this particular soil, irrespective of the curing period. A similar phenomenon was also found in the previous research (Terashi et al., 1980).

A similar phenomenon for organic soils is shown in Figure 2.18 (Babasaki et al., 1980). In the tests, four soils with various initial water contents were stabilized with ordinary Portland cement. The unconfined compressive strength is relatively small in the organic soils, but it increases with the cement factor. The figure clearly shows that the minimum cement factor of around 50 kg/m^3 is necessary to achieve an appreciable strength increase, which corresponds the cement content of about 7% for G_s of 2.65 and w of 100%. Regarding the minimum amount of cement to obtain an

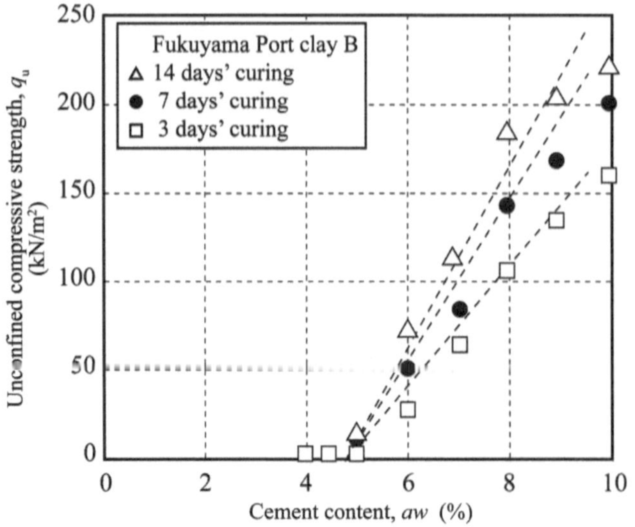

Figure 2.17 The influence of the amount of cement on unconfined compressive strength (Udaka et al., 2013).

stabilization effect, Udaka et al. (2013) investigated five types of soil and concluded that it is about 3.0 to 7.5% cement content, which is close to the test results shown in Figure 2.17.

3.3.2 *Mixing time*

Figure 2.19 shows the relationship between mixing time and the unconfined compressive strength, q_u, in laboratory mix tests (Nakamura et al., 1982). The laboratory mix tests were conducted as the same manner as the standardized procedure (Japanese Society of Soil Mechanics and Foundation Engineering, 1990) except for the mixing time. In the tests, the Narashino clay (w_i of 68%) was stabilized with ordinary Portland cement in either dry form or slurry form with a water to cement ratio, W/C of 100%. The unconfined compressive strength decreases with decreasing mixing time. The figure also shows that the strength deviation increases with decreasing mixing time. According to this phenomenon and similar test results, the Japanese Society of Soil Mechanics and Foundation Engineering recommends that the mixing time should be about 10 minutes in a laboratory mix test where large strength with small deviation can be sought

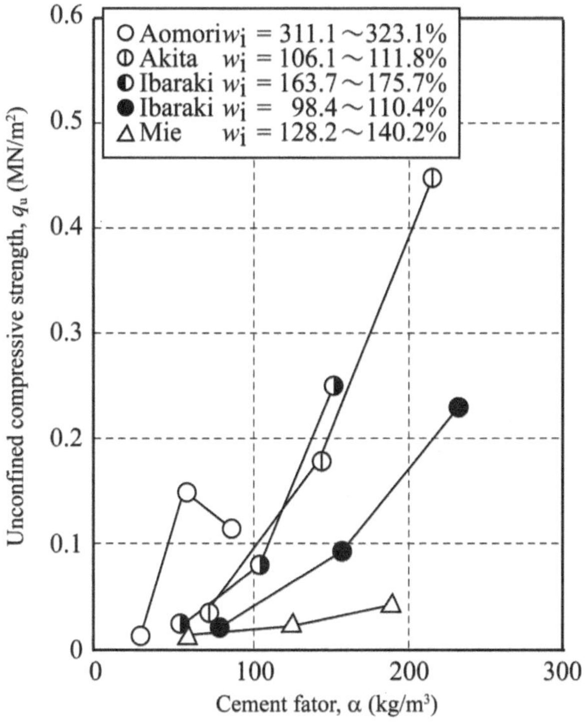

Figure 2.18 The influence of the amount of cement on the strength of cement-stabilized organic soils (Babasaki et al., 1980).

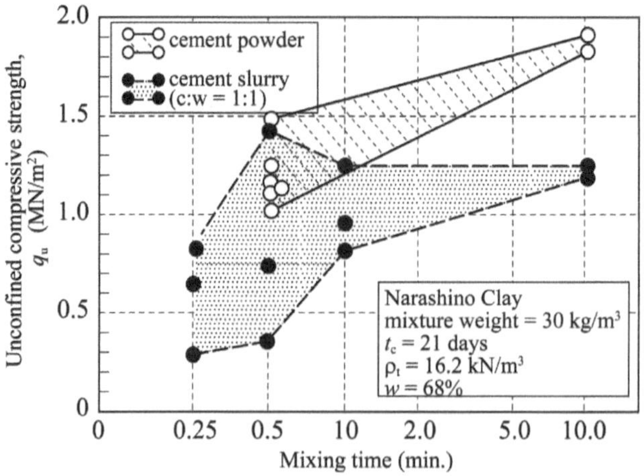

Figure 2.19 The influence of mixing time on the strength and deviation of cement-stabilized soil (Nakamura et al., 1982).

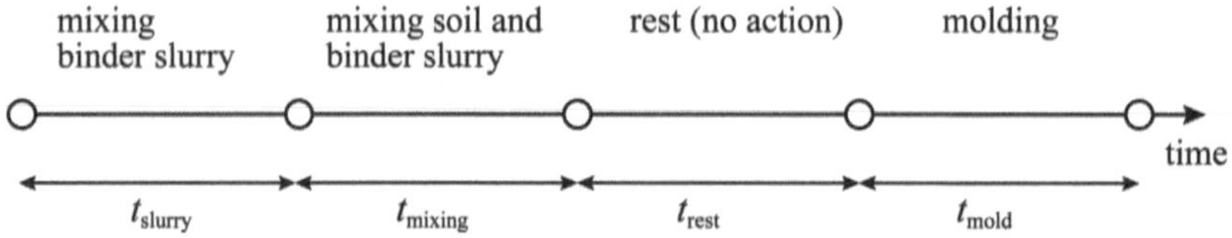

Figure 2.20 Process chart of mixing and molding of cement-stabilized soil.

3.3.3 Time and duration of mixing, and molding process

Figure 2.20 indicates the time sequence of the mixing and molding process in laboratory mix test. In the mix test, a test specimen is usually manufactured by the following steps: 1) disaggregation and homogenization of the original soil, 2) preparation of the cement slurry at a prescribed water-to-cement ratio, W/C, which takes t_{slurry}, 3) mixing soil and cement slurry to prepare a uniform soil–cement mixture, t_{mixing}, 4) rest time before molding, t_{rest}, 5) filling a mold with the soil–cement mixture within t_{mold}. Chemical reactions between cement and water start at steps 2 and 3. As the chemical reactions proceed with time, the time duration in steps 2 to 4 may influence the q_u of stabilized soil. For example, if the time for mixing the cement slurry and soil and/or the time until molding is unnecessarily long, the chemical reaction products at steps 2 to 4 may be broken during the molding procedure at step 5. Also anticipated is that the change of fluidity of the soil–cement mixture may result in difficulty in molding. The time duration of steps 2 to 4 is shown in Figure 2.20.

Although the time for mixing soil and binder slurry is not clearly specified in the Japanese standard, 10 minutes' mixing is the de facto standard in Japan

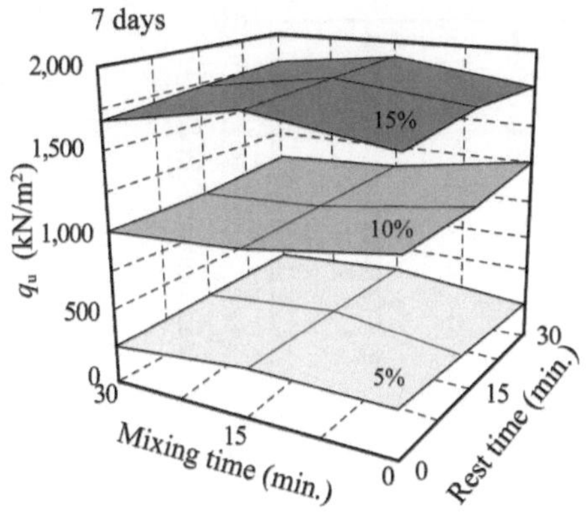

(a) At 7 days' curing.

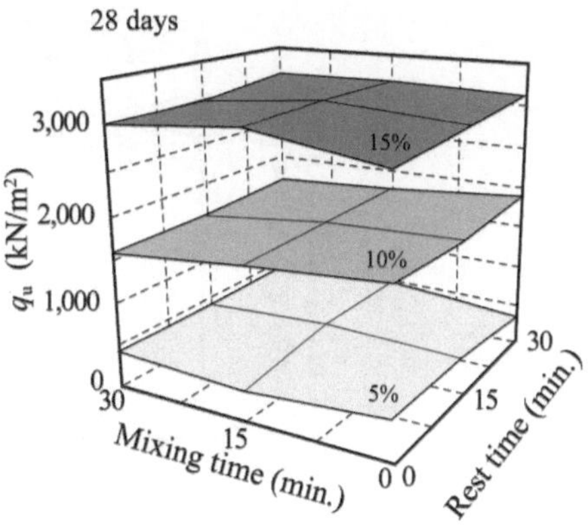

(b) At 28 days' curing.

Figure 2.21 The influence of cement–slurry mixing time, and rest time after clay–cement mixing, on strength (Kitazume & Nishimura, 2009).

(Japanese Geotechnical Society, 2009). Other time durations are considered to vary considerably from laboratory to laboratory, depending on the number of laboratory technicians and number of specimens prepared from a batch of soil–binder mixture. Any delay in the test procedure may cause a deterioration of the stabilized soil specimens' properties.

Figure 2.21 shows the effects of the mixing time, t_{mixing}, of cement slurry, and the rest time, t_{rest}, on the strength of stabilized soil (Kitazume & Nishimura, 2009). The rest time is defined as the time period between the end of mixing and the start of molding. In the tests, the Kawasaki clay (w_L of 54.1%, w_P of 24.0% and w_i of 65.0%) was stabilized with ordinary Portland cement with a W/C ratio of 100%, in which the cement content, aw, was changed to 5, 10 and 15%. The case $t_{\mathrm{slurry}} = 0$ corresponds to the situation where the cement and water are simultaneously added to the soil, or the powder form of cement is added. The unconfined compressive strengths, q_u, measured at 7 and 28 days' curing are shown in Figures 2.21(a) and 2.21(b), respectively. The standard deviation of q_u in each condition (three tests) was 2.6 to 2.9% on average. The test results indicate that the time after mixing cement and water, t_{slurry}, and the time after mixing the soil and cement slurry, t_{rest}, have little influence on the q_u. The unit weight of specimen exhibits little variability, being correlated more to the initial water content of the batches.

Figure 2.22 shows additional test results with extended rest times after mixing, t_{rest}, to identify the limit beyond which the soundness of specimen preparation is compromised (Kitazume & Nishimura, 2009). The test results reveal it is when the t_{rest} exceeds 40 minutes that the specimen quality starts being affected by the soil – cement's reduced fluidity, and hence by the difficulty in 'compacting' through tapping actions, which is the process specified by the Japanese Society of Soil Mechanics and Foundation Engineering Standard (Japanese Society of Soil Mechanics and Foundation Engineering, 1990). Longer t_{rest} resulted in inclusions of numerous voids in the completed specimens, and lower unit weight, which is closely related to q_u.

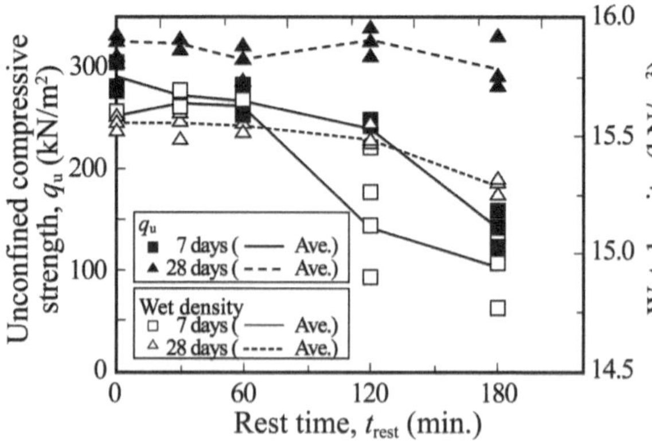

(a) Cement content of 5%.

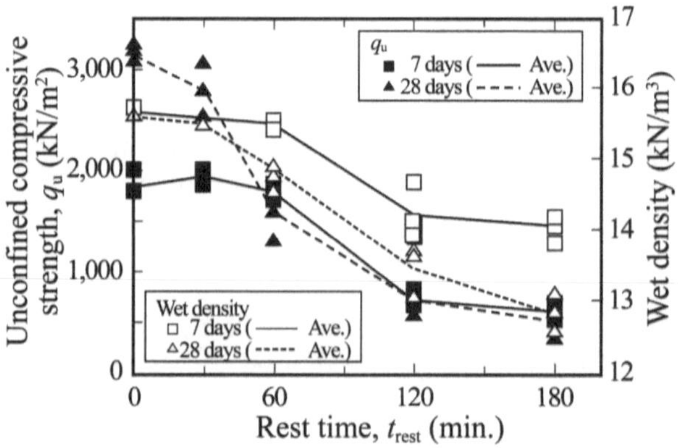

(b) Cement content of 15%.

Figure 2.22 The influence of rest time after clay–cement mixing on the strength (Kitazume & Nishimura, 2009).

3.4 Influence of the curing conditions

3.4.1 Hydration

Figure 2.23 shows the strength increase of cement-stabilized soil soon after the mixing (Watabe et al., 2001). In the tests, the Tachibana Bay clay (w_L of 40.8% and w_P of 20.8%) was prepared to have an initial water content of 1.6 × w_L (65.3%) and stabilized with ordinary Portland cement with the cement factor, α, of 50 kg/m^3. Soon after the mixing, the shear strength, τ_v, was measured with a hand vane shear apparatus at several elapsed times up to 200 minutes. The shear strength of the original soil with a water content of 1.6 × w_L was also measured and plotted in the figure. The shear strength of the stabilized soil just after mixing is larger than the original soil, which is probably due to the reduction in fluidity by adding cement powder. The shear strength,

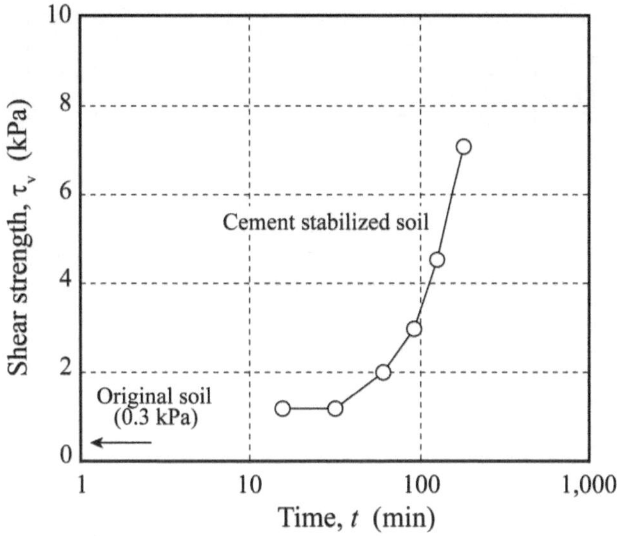

Figure 2.23 Strength increase in cement-stabilized soil soon after cement mixing (Watabe et al., 2001).

τ_v, remains a small value within about 30 minutes but increases rapidly after that due to the progress of the cement hydration effect.

Figure 2.24 shows one of comprehensive test results on the strength gain soon after stabilization, in which three kinds of soil were prepared to have several initial water contents, and stabilized with ordinary Portland cement with several cement contents (Tsuchida et al., 2013). The shear strength, s_u, of the stabilized soil was measured with a hand vane apparatus for soils with small strength, or by an unconfined compression test, q_u, for soils with a relatively large strength. Figure 2.24 shows one of the test results on stabilized Mizushima Port clay (w_L of 65.3% and w_P of 15.5%). The cement content, c^*, in the figure is defined by the dry weight of cement against the dry weight of the stabilized soil, instead of the dry weight of cement against the dry weight of the original soil. The figure shows the shear strength increases almost linearly with the curing period in a double logarithm scale up to about 72 hours and then the strength still increases with the curing period, but with lower increment ratio, irrespective of the initial water content and the cement content c^*. A similar phenomenon is also found in the other two soils, the Hibiki clay (w_L of 61.2% and w_P of 20.7%) and the Moji Port clay (w_L of 89.5% and w_P of 29.3%).

3.4.2 *Curing period*

Figure 2.25 shows the strength increase of cement-stabilized soil with the curing period (Sasayama et al., 2011). In the tests, two soils excavated at Nagoya Bay (w_L of 52.5% and w_P of 25.1% for Soil C, and w_L of 48.7% and w_P of 29.6% for Soil S) were stabilized with ordinary Portland cement with cement factor, C, of 30, 50, 70

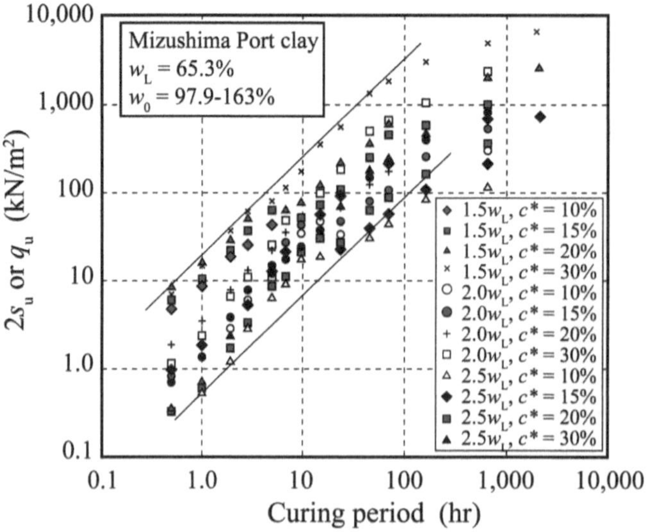

Figure 2.24 Effects of mixing condition on strength increase soon after cement mixing (Tsuchida et al., 2013).

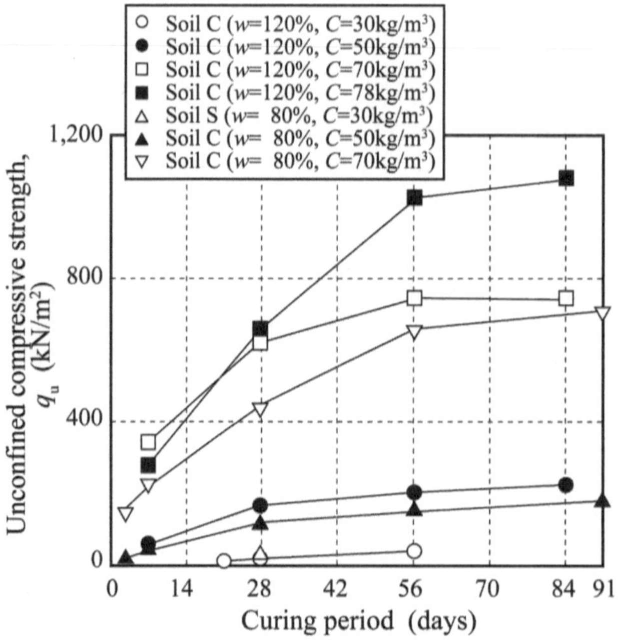

Figure 2.25 Effect of mixing condition on strength increase with curing period (Sasayama et al., 2011).

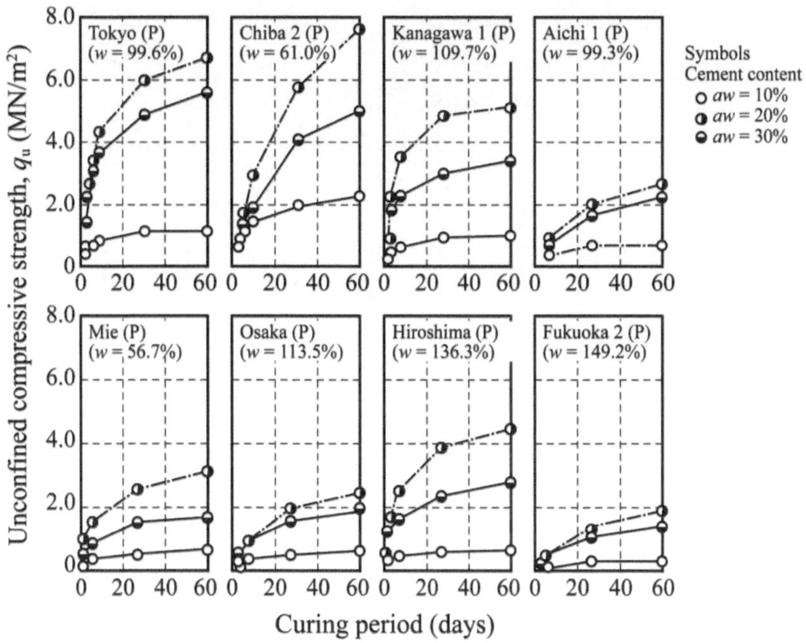

Figure 2.26 Influence of soil type to strength increase with curing period (Kawasaki et al., 1981).

and 78 kg/m^3. The unconfined compressive strength, q_u, increases with the curing period irrespective of the soil type and initial water content, and the strength increase ratio with curing period is more dominant for the stabilized soil with a large amount of cement. Similar test results were obtained for soils stabilized with ordinary Portland cement or blast furnace slag cement type B (Saitoh, 1988).

Figure 2.26 shows the strength increase of cement-stabilized soils with the curing period (Kawasaki et al., 1981). In the tests, soils excavated in eight areas were stabilized with ordinary Portland cement with *aw* of 10, 20 and 30%. The unconfined compressive strength, q_u, increases with the curing period irrespective of the soil type and the cement content, and the strength increase ratio with time is more dominant for the stabilized soil with a large amount of cement.

The relationships between the strength of stabilized soils at two different curing periods have been studied. Figures 2.27(a) and 2.27(b) show two typical examples of the relationship for organic soils and cohesive soils, respectively (Cement Deep Mixing Method Association, 1999). In Figure 2.27(a), the strength ratio, q_{u28}/q_{u7}, ranges from 1 to 4 with a mean value of 1.44 for the stabilized organic soils. For the cohesive soils (Figure 2.27(b)), on the other hand, the mean value of q_{u28}/q_{u7} is 1.57. A similar strength ratio, q_{u28}/q_{u7}, of 1.4 to 2.3; q_{u91}/q_{u7} of 1.8 to 5.9; and q_{u91}/q_{u28} of 1.2 to 2.1 for the clay and sand were reported by Saitoh (1988). The strength ratio, q_{u28}/q_{u7}, depends on the soil type, and the type and amount of binder.

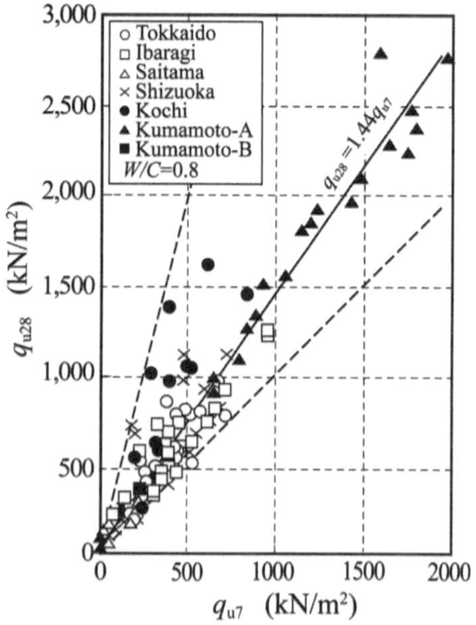

(a) Organic soils.

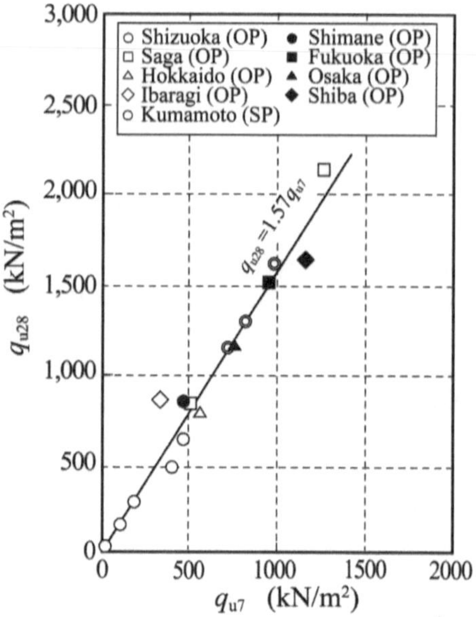

(b) Cohesive soils.

Figure 2.27 The relationship between unconfined compressive strength at 28 days' curing and that at 7 days' curing (Cement Deep Mixing Method Association, 1999).

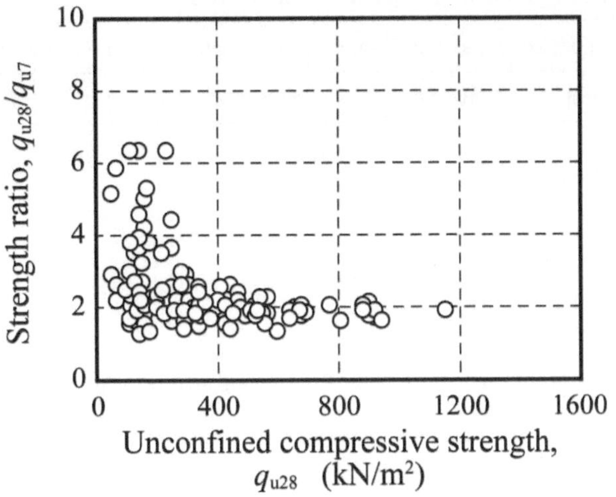

Figure 2.28 The relationship between the unconfined compressive strength and the strength ratio (Coastal Development Institute of Technology, 2008b).

Figure 2.28 shows the relationship between the strength ratio, q_{u28}/q_{u7}, and the q_{u28} on the laboratory stabilized clays with blast furnace slag cement type B (Coastal Development Institute of Technology, 2008b). The figure shows the strength ratio ranges from around 1.5 to 6.5 as far as the q_{u28} is smaller than about 400 kN/m^2, but the ratio converges rapidly to around 2 when the q_{u28} is larger than about 400 kN/m^2.

Other examples of the relationship between the q_{u7}, q_{u28} and q_{u91} on laboratory cement-stabilized soils are tabulated in Table 2.7(a) (Cement Deep Mixing Method Association, 1999) and those on field cement-stabilized soil by the pneumatic flow mixing method are tabulated in Table 2.7(b) (Ministry of Transport, The Fifth District Port Construction Bureau, 1999).

3.4.3 *Curing temperature*

Figure 2.29 shows the strength ratio of cement-stabilized soils, in which the Nagoya Port clay (w_L of 74.4%, w_P of 33.0% and w_i of 70.0%) was stabilized with ordinary Portland cement with cement factor, α, of 50 kg/m^3 (Ministry of Transport, The Fifth District Port Construction Bureau, 1999), where the stabilized soils were cured either in the air or underwater. In the figure, the strength of stabilized soil cured at an arbitrary temperature is normalized by the strength of the stabilized soil cured in the air at 20°C. The strength ratio shows a close relationship to the curing period. The strength of the stabilized soil cured underwater is about 20 to 30% larger than that in the air. The figure also shows that larger strength can be achieved at higher curing temperature, 30°C, even soon after mixing. However, small strength can be achieved at low curing temperature.

Table 2.7 Effect of curing period on unconfined compressive strength.

(a) on laboratory cement-stabilized soil (Cement Deep Mixing Method Association, 1999).

	Ordinary Portland cement	*Blast furnace slag cement type B*
$q_u < 1{,}000$ kN/m^2		
$q_{u7} - q_{u28}$	$q_{u28} = 1.6q_{u7}$	
$q_{u28} - q_{u91}$	$q_{u91} = 1.1q_{u28}$	
$q_u < 3{,}000$ kN/m^2		
$q_{u7} - q_{u28}$	$q_{u28} = 1.49q_{u7}$	$q_{u28} = 1.56q_{u7}$
$q_{u7} - q_{u91}$	$q_{u91} = 1.97q_{u7}$	$q_{u91} = 1.95q_{u7}$
$q_{u28} - q_{u91}$	$q_{u91} = 1.44q_{u28}$	$q_{u91} = 1.20q_{u28}$

(b) on field cement-stabilized soil by pneumatic flow mixing method (Ministry of Transport, The Fifth District Port Construction Bureau, 1999).

	Blast furnace slag cement type B
$q_{u28} - q_{u1h}$	$q_{u28} = 114.0q_{u1h}$
$q_{u28} - q_{u3h}$	$q_{u28} = 36.2q_{u3h}$
$q_{u28} - q_{u1}$	$q_{u28} = 4.5q_{u1}$
$q_{u28} - q_{u3}$	$q_{u28} = 2.1q_{u3}$
$q_{u28} - q_{u7}$	$q_{u28} = 1.6q_{u7}$
$q_{u91} - q_{u28}$	$q_{u91} = 1.1q_{u28}$

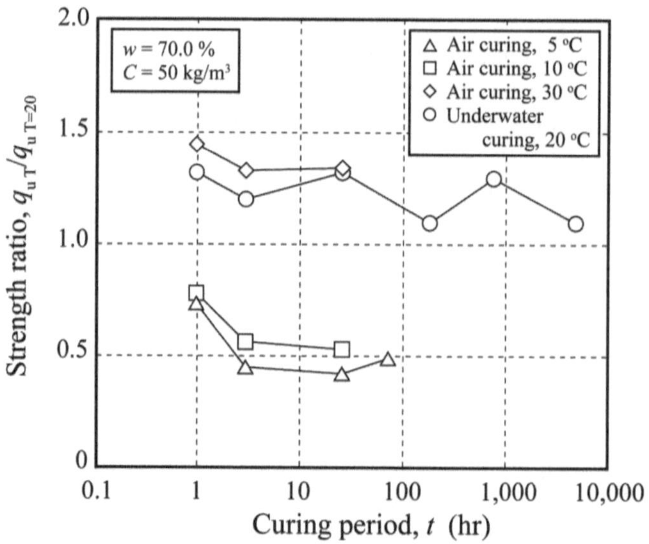

Figure 2.29 The effects of curing temperatures and curing conditions on the strength of cement-stabilized soil (Ministry of Transport, The Fifth District Port Construction Bureau, 1999).

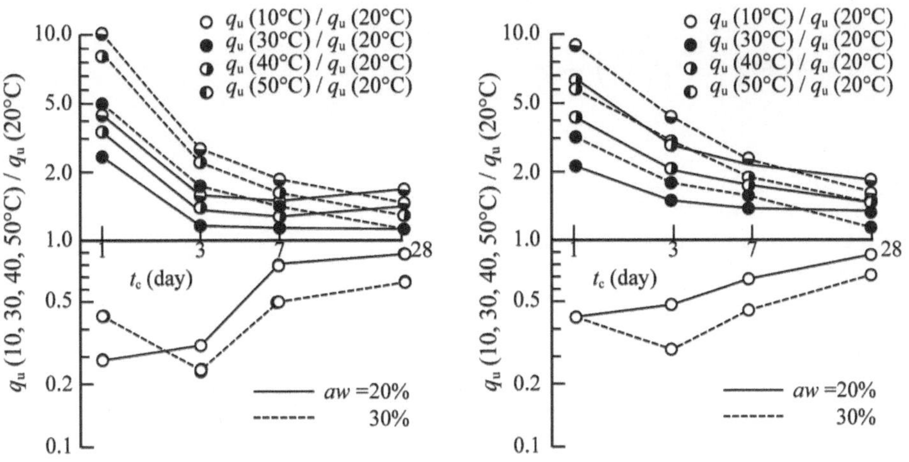

(a) Yokohama clay. (b) Osaka clay.

Figure 2.30 The effects of curing temperature on the strength of cement-stabilized soils (Saitoh et al., 1980).

The influence of curing temperature on the stabilized soil strength is shown in Figure 2.30, in which the two cement-stabilized soils, the Yokohama clay (w_L of 95.4% and w_P of 42.4%) and the Osaka clay (w_L of 79.4% and w_P of 40.2%) were cured at various temperatures for up to four weeks (Saitoh et al., 1980). In the figure, the strength of stabilized soil cured at an arbitrary temperature is normalized against the strength of stabilized soil cured at 20°C. The figure shows that larger strength can be achieved at a higher curing temperature. This influence of curing temperature is more dominant on short-term strength but it becomes less dominant as the curing period becomes longer.

The influence of curing temperature on the unconfined compressive strength of stabilized peat and silt was also investigated by Kido et al. (2009) and by Enami et al. (1985).

3.4.4 Maturity

In concrete engineering, the influences of curing temperature and curing period on the strength are often explained by the maturity index. Maturity is a concept that combines the effects of the curing period and temperature. Equation 2.3 shows four definitions of maturity proposed by the previous studies (M_1: general definition for cement-concrete, M_2: Nakamura et al., 2003, M_3: Åhnberg and Holm, 1984, and M_4: Babasaki et al., 1996a, 1996b). The correlation between the strength of stabilized soil and the logarithm of maturity, expressed differently, reveals that the curing temperature as an environmental condition does not have any significant effect on long term strength but has a considerable effect on short term strength.

$$M_1 = \sum (T_c - T_{c0}) \cdot t_c \tag{2.3a}$$

$$M_2 = 2.1^{(\theta-\theta_0)/10} \cdot t_c \tag{2.3b}$$

$$M_3 = \{20 + 0.5 \cdot (T_c - 20)\}^2 \cdot \sqrt{t_c} \tag{2.3c}$$

$$M_4 = 2 \cdot exp\left(\frac{T_c - T_{c0}}{10}\right) \cdot t_c \tag{2.3d}$$

where
M: maturity
T_c: curing temperature (°C)
T_{c0}: reference temperature (−10°C)
t_c: curing period (day)
θ: temperature (°C)
θ_0: reference temperature (°C)

Figure 2.31(a) shows the relationship between the unconfined compressive strength, q_u, and the curing temperature (Kitazume & Nishimura, 2009). The q_u value increases with the curing temperature, but the increasing ratio is dependent on the curing period. Figure 2.31(b) shows the relationship between the q_u and M_4 on the stabilized soil with various amount of cement. A unique relationship between the q_u and M_4 can be seen irrespective of the curing temperature and curing period, which can be formulated as Equation 2.4.

$$q_u = A \cdot \log M_4 + B \tag{2.4}$$

where
M_4: maturity
A: parameter
B: parameter

According to a similar relationship between the q_u and M_4 on various types of soil: silt; peat (w_n of 456.9%); fine sand; loam (w_n of 109.9%); and clay (Enami et al., 1985, Horiuchi et al., 1984, Babasaki et al., 1984), the magnitude of the parameters A and B in Equation 2.4 are depended on the soil type (Babasaki et al., 1996a, 1996b).

3.4.5 *Drying and wetting cycle*

Figure 2.32 shows the unconfined compressive strengths of cement-stabilized soils subjected to the drying and wetting cycle (Kamon et al., 2005). In the tests, two volcanic cohesive soils (VCS-H and VCS-N) and the Fujinomori clay (Clay-F) were stabilized with ordinary Portland cement of 200 kg/m^3. Their properties and initial water content are tabulated in Table 2.8. After 28 days' curing under the constant temperature of 20°C and relative humidity of 100%, the stabilized soils were subjected to the drying and wetting process up to 15 cycles, in which the soils were placed in a closed oven at 60 ± 3°C for 24 hours in the drying process, placed in room temperature for 1 hour, and immersed in distilled water at 20 ± 3°C for 23 hours in the wetting process. In the case of the Clay-F, the strength increases up to 6 cycles but rapidly decreases to a smaller strength than the initial strength with further cycles. In the cases of the

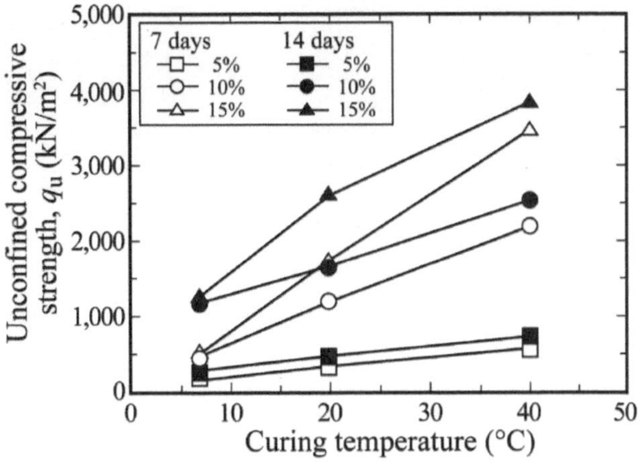

(a) Influence of curing temperature on q_u.

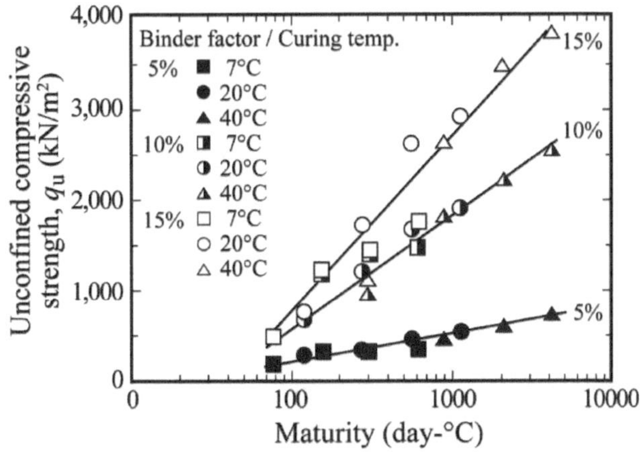

(b) Influence of maturity on q_u.

Figure 2.31 The influences of curing temperature and maturity on q_u (Kitazume & Nishimura, 2009).

volcanic soils, the strength is almost constant in the VCS-F soil but increases slightly with the cycles in the VCS-H soil.

3.4.6 *Overburden pressure*

Stabilized soil placed in the field is often subjected to overburden pressure during its curing period. Figure 2.33 shows the effect of overburden pressure during the curing period on the strength of the cement-stabilized soil, where the Ube clay (w_L of 45.4% and w_P of 20.1%) was stabilized with either ordinary Portland cement or cement-based special binder (SiO_2 of 15 to 20%, Al_2O_4 of more than 4.5%, CaO of 40 to 70%, and SO_4 of more than 4.0%) (Yamamoto et al., 2002). Figure 2.33 shows the relationship

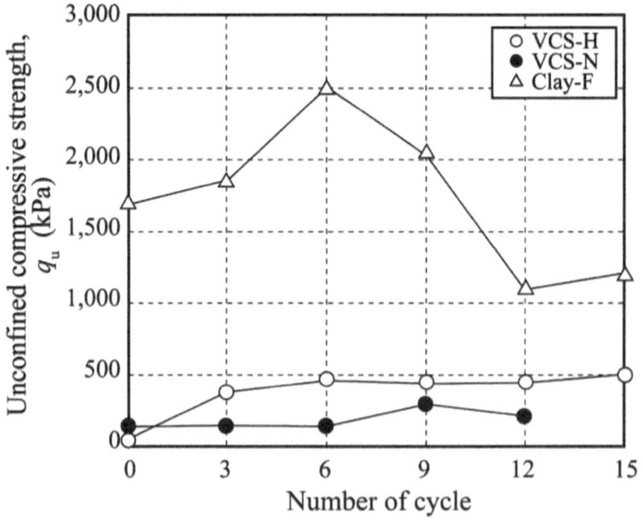

Figure 2.32 Unconfined compressive strength resulting from a number of drying and wetting cycles (Kamon et al., 2005).

Table 2.8 Physical and chemical properties of two volcanic cohesive soils, VCS-H and VCS-N, and a clay (Kamon et al., 2005).

	VCS-H	*VCS-N*	*Clay-F*
Particle density (g/cm^3)	2.67	2.65	2.67
water content, w (%)	96.8	86.0	49.0
liquid limit, w_L (%)	122.1	114.8	51.2
plastic limit, w_P (%)	83.2	82.2	26.3
Grain size distribution			
sand fraction (2 mm–75 μm) (%)	52	64	49
silt fraction (75 μm–5 μm) (%)	23	21	23
clay fraction (under 5 μm-) (%)	25	15	28
pH	7.3	6.3	3.4
Cr(VI) leaching concentration	N.D.	N.D.	N.D.

between the unconfined compressive strength at 7 days' curing with the overburden pressure, σ'_v. The figure clearly shows that the strength increases almost linearly with the overburden pressure, irrespective of the type and amount of binder.

3.4.7 *Soil disturbance/compaction*

In some applications of the pneumatic flow mixing method, stabilized soil is temporarily placed at a provisional site, and is subsequently excavated and reclaimed at the final site after certain period for the beneficial use of the soil. Several research projects have been carried out to investigate the effect of disturbance on strength (e.g. Ministry of

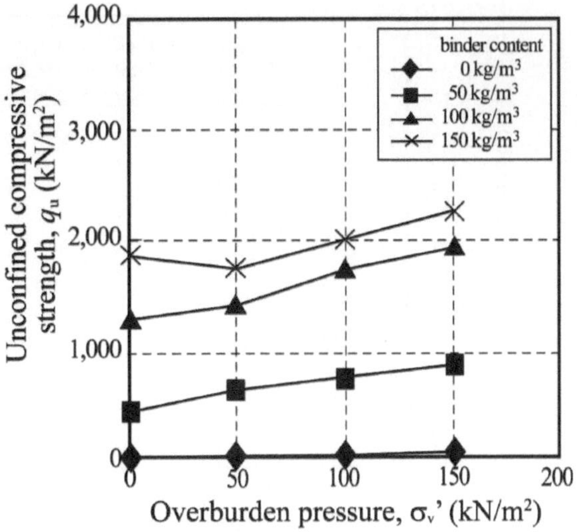

(a) Ordinary Portland cement.

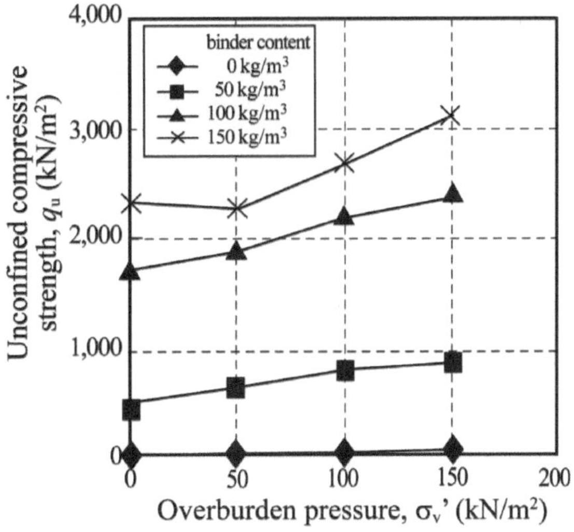

(b) Cement-based special binder.

Figure 2.33 The relationship between unconfined compressive strength, q_u, and overburden pressure, σ'_v (Yamamoto et al., 2002).

Transport, The Fifth District Port Construction Bureau, 1999; Makino et al., 2014, 2015). Figure 2.34 shows an example of the relationship between the unconfined compressive strength, q_u, of non-disturbed and disturbed stabilized soil and the curing period. In the tests, the kaolin clay (w_L of 77.5%, w_P of 30.3% and w_i of 120%) was stabilized with ordinary Portland cement with *aw* of 5 and 10%. After the mixing,

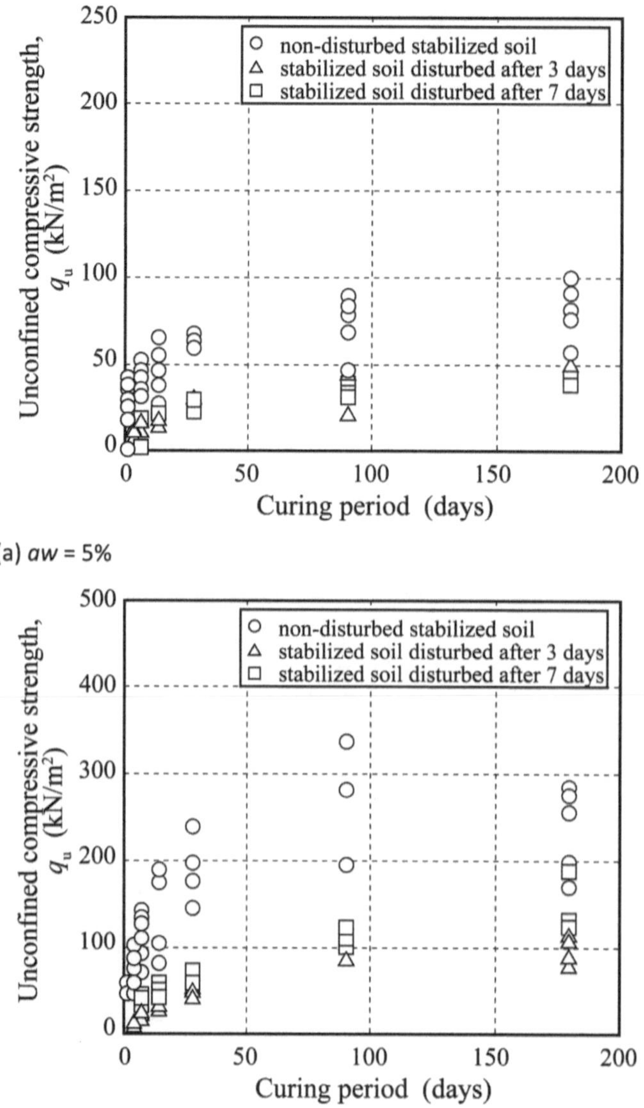

(a) *aw* = 5%

(b) *aw* = 10%

Figure 2.34 The effect of disturbance on the unconfined compressive strength of cement-stabilized soil (Makino et al., 2015).

the stabilized soil was molded by the tapping technique according to the Japanese Geotechnical Society Standard (Japanese Geotechnical Society Standard, 2009). In the case of the disturbed soil specimen, the stabilized soil mixture was stored and cured in an airtight plastic bag first, to avoid any change in water content. After 3 and 7 days' curing, the soil mixture in the bag was through disturbed and molded by the tapping

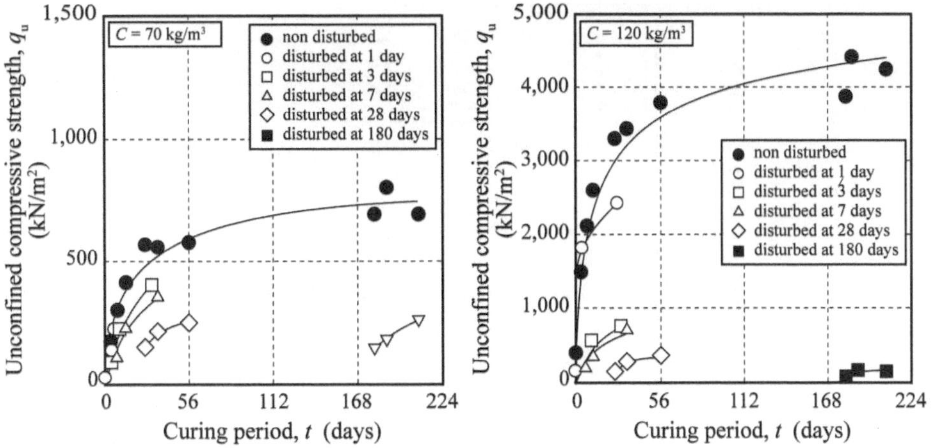

Figure 2.35 The effect of disturbance on the unconfined compressive strength of stabilized soil (Japan Cement Association, 2011).

technique in the same way as the un-disturbed soils. The unconfined compressive strength of the stabilized soils decreases considerably to 10 to 20% of that of the undisturbed stabilized soils, due to the disturbance, and it gradually increases to approximately 25 to 40% of that of the undisturbed stabilized soils with the curing period.

Figure 2.35 shows a similar test result, but in this case the stabilized soil is disturbed at several curing periods up to 180 days (Japan Cement Association, 2011). The figure shows that the strength increases to some extent as long as the soil is disturbed at an early stage in the curing, but its increase in strength is quite small when it is disturbed late in the curing period. The strength increases and reaches almost constant value at about 4 weeks in the case the cement content is relatively small. The strength gain is small when it is disturbed after the competition of cement hydration action.

Figure 2.36(a) shows the effect of the soil disturbance and compaction on the unconfined compressive strength, q_u, of cement-stabilized soil (Hino et al., 2007). In the test, the Hiroe Port clay (w_L of 144.4% and w_P of 52.0%) with an initial water content, w_i, of $1.5 \times w_L$ was stabilized with either blast furnace slag cement type B of 70 kg/m^3 or quicklime of 30 kg/m^3. A part of the stabilized soil was disturbed at 7 days' curing and compacted according to the Japanese standard (Japanese Geotechnical Society, 2009) with various compaction energies. Figure 2.36(a) shows that the stabilized soil strength considerably decreases to about 1/10 to 1/13 by the disturbance but increases gradually with the curing period after the compaction.

Figure 2.36(b) shows the relationship between unconfined compressive strength and compaction energy. In the case of the stabilized soil with blast furnace slag cement type B, the maximum strength can be seen at the compaction energy of 0.5 kJ/m^3, while the strength decreases with the compaction energy after the compaction energy exceeds 0.5 kJ/m^3. In the case of the quicklime stabilization, the maximum strength can be seen at 0.25 kJ/m^3. These results show the effect of the phenomenon of over-compaction on the strength of the stabilized soil.

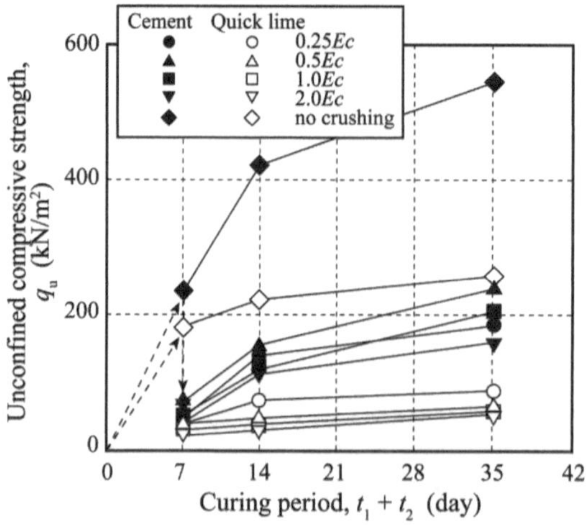

(a) Relationship between unconfined compressive strength and curing period.

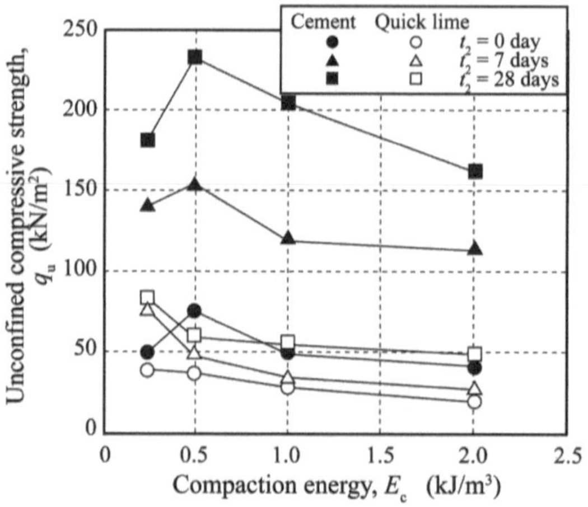

(b) Relationship between unconfined compressive strength and compaction energy.

Figure 2.36 The relationship between the unconfined compressive strength and applied compaction energy (Hino et al., 2007).

4 PREDICTION OF STRENGTH

In the admixture stabilization projects, including the pneumatic flow mixing project, the strength of field stabilized soil should be predicted and confirmed at various stages of planning, testing, design, and implementation. There are many proposed formulas to predict the laboratory strength and field strength of stabilized soil, which incorporate the various factors for the stabilization effect. Some of them are exemplified as follows

(Tsuchida & Tang, 2012, Horpibulsuk et al., 2000, Tang et al., 2000, Yanagihara et al., 2000, Miyazaki et al., 2003, Yoshida et al., 1977).

$$\left.\begin{aligned} q_{\mathrm{u}} &= aw + b \\ q_{\mathrm{u}} &= {}^{a}\!/(W/C)^{x} + b \\ q_{\mathrm{u}} &= aC/w^{x} + b \\ q_{\mathrm{u}} &= \frac{10 \cdot Gs \cdot \rho_{\mathrm{w}} \cdot K\,(c - c_0)}{\nu^3} \\ q_{\mathrm{u}} &= \frac{A}{B^{(WC/C)}} \\ q_{\mathrm{u}} &= \frac{K\,(C - C_0)}{(w \cdot Gs/100 + 1)^2} \\ q_{\mathrm{u}} &= k_c \cdot (c^* - c_o^*)\,Y^3 \end{aligned}\right\} \quad (2.5)$$

where
a: parameter
A: parameter
b: parameter
B: parameter
c: cement factor (kg/m^3)
c^* : weight ratio, $W_c/(W_s + W_c)$
C : cement factor (kg/m^3)
c_0 : reference cement factor (kg/m^3)
c_0^* : reference weight ratio, $W_c/(W_s + W_c)$
C_0 : reference cement factor (kg/m^3)
Gs : specific gravity of soil particle
K: parameter
k_c: parameter
q_u: unconfined compressive strength (kN/m^2)
Vc : volume of cement (m^3)
Vs : volume of soil (m^3)
Vv : volume of void and water (m^3)
w: water content (%)
Wc : dry weight of cement (kg)
W/C: water to cement ratio
WC/C: clay water content/cement ratio
Ws : dry weight of soil (kg)
x: parameter
Y: volume ratio, $(Vs+Vc)/(Vs+Vc+Vv)$
ρ_w: density of water (g/cm^3)

For long term strength, the equation 2.6 is given by Yanagihara et al. (2000):

$$\left.\begin{aligned} q_{\mathrm{u}} &= a \times t^{b} \\ q_{\mathrm{u}} &= a \times \log(t) + b \end{aligned}\right\} \quad (2.6)$$

where
a: parameter
b: parameter
t: curing period

As shown in Equations 2.5 and 2.6, the equations consist of several parameters which may be influenced by many factors tabulated in Table 2.1. The strengths of laboratory and field stabilized soil can be predicted by the equations if the appropriate magnitude of these parameters can be estimated precisely. However, we are not yet at the stage where we can estimate these parameters well enough to predict the laboratory strength with a reasonable level of accuracy. There is no widely-applicable formula for estimating the strength which incorporates all the relevant factors.

Because of this, the most precise prediction can be now made by performing a laboratory mix test and then estimating the field strength on the basis of laboratory mix test results and past experience. In large scale projects, laboratory mix test results are often confirmed by field trial execution of stabilized soil at the construction site. For small scale works, reference is made to previous soil stabilization works done in similar soil conditions.

Nevertheless, the information compiled in the present chapter is extremely valuable in planning pneumatic flow mixing work and also for interpreting laboratory mix test results if properly used by an experienced engineer.

REFERENCES

Åhnberg, H. & Holm, G. (1984) On the influence of curing temperature on the strength of lime and cement stabilised soils. *Swedish Geotechnical Institute Report*. Vol. 30. pp. 93–146 (in Swedish).

Babasaki, R., Terashi, M., Suzuki, K., Maekawa, J., Kawamura, M. & Fukazawa, E. (1996a) Factors influencing the strength of improved soils. *Proc. of the Symposium on Cement Treated Soils*. pp. 20–41 (in Japanese).

Babasaki, R., Terashi, M., Suzuki, T., Maekawa, A., Kawamura, M. & Fukazawa, E. (1996b) Japanese Geotechnical Society Technical Committee Reports: Factors influencing the strength of improved soil. *Proc. of the 2nd International Conference on Ground Improvement Geosystems*. Vol. 2, pp. 913–918.

Babasaki, R., Kawasaki, T., Niina, A., Munechika, Y. & Saitoh, S. (1980) Study of the deep mixing method using cement hardening agent (Part 9). *Proc. of the 15th Annual Conference of the Japanese Society of Soil Mechanics and Foundation Engineering*. pp. 713–716 (in Japanese).

Babasaki, R., Saito, S. & Suzuki, Y. (1984) Temperature characteristics of cement improved soil and temperature analysis of ground improved using the deep cement mixing method. *Proc. of the Symposium on Strength and Deformation of Composite Ground*. pp. 33–40 (in Japanese).

Cement Deep Mixing Method Association (1999) *Cement Deep Mixing Method (CDM) Design and Construction Manual*. (in Japanese).

Coastal Development Institute of Technology (2008a) *Technical Manual of Deep Mixing method for marine works, revised version*. 289p. (in Japanese).

Coastal Development Institute of Technology (2008b) *Technical Manual of Pneumatic Flow Mixing Method*, revised version. Daikousha Publishers, 188p. (in Japanese).

Enami, A., Yoshida, M., Hibino, S., Takahashi, M. & Akitani, K. (1985) In situ measurement of temperature in soil cement columns and influence of curing temperature on unconfined compressive strength of soil cement. *Proc. of the 20th Annual Conference of the Japanese Society of Soil Mechanics and Foundation Engineering*. pp. 1737–1740 (in Japanese).

Hayashi, H., Noto, S. & Toritani, N. (1989) Cement improvement of Hokkaido peat. Symposium on High Organic Soils. *Proc. of the Symposium on High Organic Soils*. pp. 101–106 (in Japanese).

Hino, Y., Suetsugu, D., Ikari, Y. & Ohga, T. (2007) Unconfined compressive strength, cone index and compaction properties of embankment materials by dredged-stabilized clay. *Proc. of the 42nd Annual Conference of the Japanese Geotechnical Society*. pp. 615–616 (in Japanese).

Horiuchi, N., Ito, M., Morita, T., Yoshihara, S., Hisano, T., Hanazono, H. & Tanaka, T. (1984) Strength of soil mixture under lower temperatures. *Proc. of the 19th Annual Conference of the Japanese Society of Soil Mechanics and Foundation Engineering*. pp. 1609–1610 (in Japanese).

Horpibulsuk, H., Miura, N. & Nagaraj, T.S. (2000) A new method for predicting strength of cement stabilized clays. *Prof of the International Conference of the Coastal Geotechnical Engineering in Practice*. Vol. 1, pp. 605–610.

Ingles, O.G. & Metcalf, J.B. (1972) *Soil stabilization, Principles and Practice*. Butterworth.

Japan Cement Association (2009) Committee report on soil stabilization of dredged soil. *Internal Report of Japan Cement Association*. 57p. (in Japanese).

Japan Cement Association (2011) Influence of disagglomeration on strength of dredged soil stabilized with soil cement. *Cement & Concrete*. No. 769, pp. 2–7 (in Japanese).

Japan Cement Association (2012) *Soil Improvement Manual using Cement Stabilizer (4th edition)*. Japan Cement Association. 442p. (in Japanese).

Japan Lime Association (2009) *Technical Manual on Ground Improvement using Lime*. Japan Lime Association. 176p. (in Japanese).

Japanese Geotechnical Society (2000) *Practice for making and curing stabilized soil specimens without compaction, JGS T 0821-2000*. Japanese Geotechnical Society. pp. 308–316 (in Japanese).

Japanese Geotechnical Society (2009) *Practice for making and curing stabilized soil specimens without compaction. JGS 0821-2009*. Japanese Geotechnical Society. Vol. 1, pp. 426–434 (in Japanese).

Japanese Industrial Standard (2006) *Portland blast-furnace slag cement, JIS R 5211: 2006*. (in Japanese).

Japanese Industrial Standard (2009) *Portland cement, JIS R 5210: 2009*. (in Japanese).

Japanese Society of Soil Mechanics & Foundation Engineering (1990) *Practice for making and curing non-compacted stabilized soil specimens. JGS T 821-1990*. Japanese Society of Soil Mechanics and Foundation Engineering. (in Japanese).

Kamon, M., Inui, T. & Shoji, Y. (2005) Experimental study on the long-term environmental impact caused by the cement stabilization/solidification of soft ground. *Annual of Disaster Prevention Research Institute*, Kyoto University. No.48 B, (in Japanese).

Kawasaki, T., Niina, A., Saitoh, S. & Babasaki, R. (1978) Studies on engineering characteristics of cement-base stabilized soil. *Takenaka Technical Research Report*. Vol. 19, pp. 144–165 (in Japanese).

Kawasaki, T., Niina, A., Saitoh, S., Suzuki, Y. & Honjyo, Y. (1981) Deep mixing method using cement hardening agent. *Proc. of the 10th International Conference on Soil Mechanics and Foundation Engineering*. Vol. 3, pp. 721–724.

Kido, Y., Hishimoto, S., Hayashi, H. & Hashimoto, H. (2009) Effects of curing temperatures on the strength of cement-treated peat. *Proc. of the International Symposium on Deep Mixing and Admixture Stabilization*. pp. 151–154.

Kitazume, M. & Nishimura, S. (2009) Influence of specimen preparation and curing conditions on unconfined compression behaviour of cement-treated clay. *Proc. of the International Symposium on Deep Mixing and Admixture Stabilization*. pp. 155–160.

Kitazume, M. & Satoh, T. (2003) Development of pneumatic flow mixing method and its application to Central Japan International Airport construction. *Journal of Ground Improvement*. Vol. 7, No. 3, pp. 139–148.

Kiyota, M., Tutumi, T., Ohta, K. & Hirayama, Y. (2003) About the characteristic of the improvement soil with the slow-setting soil stabilizer. *Proc. of the 38th Annual Conference of the Japanese Geotechnical Society*. pp. 799–800 (in Japanese).

Makino, M., Takeyama, T. & Kitazume, M. (2014) Laboratory tests on the influence of soil disturbance on the material properties of cement-treated soil. *Proc. of the 9th International Symposium on Lowland Technology*. pp. 150–155.

Makino, M., Takeyama, T. & Kitazume, M. (2015) The influence of soil disturbance on material properties and micro-structure of cement-treated soil. *International Journal of Lowland Technology*.

Miki, H., Kudara, K. & Okada, Y. (1984) Effect of humic acid on soil stabilization (Part 2). *Proc. of the 39th Annual Conference of the Japan Society of Civil Engineers*. pp. 407–408 (in Japanese).

Ministry of Transport, The Fifth District Port Construction Bureau (1999) *Pneumatic Flow Mixing Method*. Yasuki Publishers. 157p. (in Japanese).

Miyazaki, Y., Tang, Y.X., Ochiai, H., Yasufuku, N., Omine, K. & Tsuchida, T. (2003). Utilization of cement treated dredged soil with working ship. *Journal of the Japan Society of Civil Engineers*. No.750/III-65, pp. 193–204, 2003 (in Japanese).

Nakamura, T., Saitoh, S. & Babasaki, R. (2003) Early stage estimation for 28 day unconfined compressive strength of cement-improved soils using an accelerated curing test. *Proc. of the 38th Annual Conference of the Japanese Geotechnical Society*. (in Japanese).

Nakamura, M., Akutsu, H. & Sudo, F. (1980) Study of improved strength based on the deep mixing method (Report 1). *Proc. of the 15th Annual Conference of the Japanese Society of Soil Mechanics and Foundation Engineering*. pp. 1773–1776 (in Japanese).

Nakamura. M., Matsuzawa, S. & Matsushita, M. (1982) Studies on mixing efficiency of stirring wings for deep mixing method. *Proc. of the 17th Annual Conference of the Japanese Society of Soil Mechanics and Foundation Engineering*. Vol. 2, pp. 2585–2588 (in Japanese).

Niina, A., Saitoh, S., Babasaki, R., Miyata, T. & Tanaka, K. (1981) Engineering properties of improved soil obtained by stabilizing alluvial clay from various regions with cement slurry. *Takenaka Technical Research Report*. Vol. 25, pp. 1–21 (in Japanese).

Niina, A., Saitoh, S., Babasaki, R., Tsutsumi, I. & Kawasaki, T. (1977) Study on DMM using cement hardening agent (Part 1). *Proc. of the 12th Annual Conference of the Japanese Society of Soil Mechanics and Foundation Engineering*. pp. 1325–1328 (in Japanese).

Okada, Y., Kudara, K. & Miki, H. (1983) Effect of humic acid on soil stabilization. *Proc. of the 38th Annual Conference of the Japan Society of Civil Engineering*. pp. 467–468 (in Japanese).

Okano, Y., Yoda, H., Sasayama, T., Nakano, M., Yamada, S., Nonoyama, S. & Sakai, T. (2012) Mechanical properties of cement stabilized soil with different physical properties. *Proc. of the Annual Research Meeting, Chubu Branch, Japan Society of Civil Engineering*. pp. 169–170 (in Japanese).

Okumura, T., Terashi, M., Mitsumoto, T., Yoshida, T. & Watanabe, M. (1974) Deep-Lime-Mixing method for soil stabilization (3rd Report). *Report of the Port and Harbour Research Institute*. Vol. 13, No. 2, pp. 3–44 (in Japanese).

Saitoh, S. (1988) Experimental study of engineering properties of cement improved ground by the deep mixing method. *Doctoral thesis, Nihon University*. 317p. (in Japanese).

Saitoh, S., Niina, A. & Babasaki, R. (1980) Effect of curing temperature on the strength of treated soils and consideration on measurement of elastic modules. *Proc. of the Symposium on Testing of treated Soils, Japanese Society of Soil Mechanics and Foundation Engineering.* pp. 61–66 (in Japanese).

Saitoh, S., Suzuki, Y. & Shirai, K. (1985) Hardening of soil improved by the deep mixing method. *Proc. of the 11th International Conference on Soil Mechanics and Foundation Engineering.* Vol. 3, pp. 1745–1748.

Sasayama, T., Yoda, H., Horiuchi, S., Nakano, M. & Yamada, S. (2011) Mechanical properties of cement stabilized soil with different particle size distribution. *Proc. of the Annual Research Meeting, Chubu Branch, Japan Society of Civil Engineering.* pp. 193–194 (in Japanese).

Tang, Y.X., Miyazaki, Y. & Tsuchida, T. (2000) Advanced reuses of dredging by cement treatment in practical engineering. *Prof of the International Conference of the Coastal Geotechnical Engineering in Practice.* Vol. 1, pp. 725–731.

Terashi, M. (1997) Theame Lecture: Deep Mixing Method - Brief State of the Art. *Proc. of the 14th International Conference on Soil Mechanics and Foundation Engineering.* Vol. 4, pp. 2475–2478.

Terashi, M., Okumura, T. & Mitsumoto, T. (1977) Fundamental properties of lime-treated soils. *Report of the Port and Harbour Research Institute.* Vol. 16, No. 1, pp. 3–28 (in Japanese).

Terashi, M., Tanaka, H. & Okumura, T. (1979) Engineering properties of lime-treated marine soils and D.M.M. method. *Proc. of the 6th Asian Regional Conference on Soil Mechanics and Foundation Engineering.* Vol. 1, pp. 191–194.

Terashi, M., Tanaka, H., Mitsumoto, T., Honma, S. & Ohhashi, T. (1983) Fundamental properties of lime and cement treated soils (3rd Report). *Report of the Port and Harbour Research Institute.* Vol. 22, No. 1, pp. 69–96 (in Japanese).

Terashi, M., Tanaka, H., Mitsumoto, T., Niidome, Y. & Honma, S. (1980) Fundamental properties of lime and cement treated soils (2nd Report). *Report of the Port and Harbour Research Institute.* Vol. 19, No. 1, pp. 33–62 (in Japanese).

Thompson, R. (1966) Lime reactivity of Illinois soils. *Proc. of the American Society of Civil Engineering.* 92 (SM-5).

Tsuchida, T. & Tang, Y.X. (2012) A consideration on estimation of strength of cement-treated marine clays. *Japanese Geotechnical Journal.* Vol. 7, No. 3, pp. 435–447 (in Japanese).

Tsuchida, T., Tang, Y.X., Shimakawa, N. & Abe, T. (2013) Study on the strength–time relationship of cement-treated marine clays with high water contents. *Japanese Geotechnical Journal.* Vol. 8, No. 1, pp. 53–70 (in Japanese).

Udaka, K., Tsuchida, T., Imai, Y. & Tang, Y.X. (2013) Compressive characteristics of reconstituted marine clays with developed structures by adding a small amount of cement. *Japanese Geotechnical Journal.* Vol. 8, No. 3, pp. 425–439 (in Japanese).

Watabe, Y., Tsuchida, T., Hikiyashiki, H. & Furuno, T. (2001) Mechanical and material properties of dredged soil treated with poor quality of cement. *Report of the Port and Harbour Research Institute.* Vol. 40, No. 2, pp. 3–21 (in Japanese).

Yamamoto, T., Suzuki, M., Okabayashi, S., Fujino, H., Taguchi, T. & Fujimoto, T. (2002) Unconfined compressive strength of cement-stabilized soil cured under an overburden pressure. *Journal of Geotechnical Engineering, Japan Society of Civil Engineers.* No. 701/3-58, pp. 387–399 (in Japanese).

Yanagihara, M., Horiuchi, S. & Kawaguchi, M. (2000) Long-term stability of coal-fly-ash slurry man-made island. *Prof of the International Conference of the Coastal Geotechnical Engineering in Practice.* Vol. 1, pp. 763–769.

Yoshida, T., Kubo, H. and Sumida, K (1977). Investigation on treatment of sludge (Part 3) Application of pF water to relationship between strength of cement treated soil and water cement ratio. *Proc. of the 12th Annual Conference of the Japanese Society of Soil Mechanics and Foundation Engineering.* pp. 1309–1312 (in Japanese).

Chapter 3

Engineering properties of stabilized soils

1 INTRODUCTION

The engineering properties of lime- and cement-stabilized soils have been extensively studied by highway engineers since the 1960s. However, the purpose of their stabilization was to improve sub-base or subgrade materials and the stabilization was characterized by the low water content of the original soil and the small amount of binder. Mixing a few per cent of binder with respect to the dry weight of soil is enough to change the physical properties of soil in order to enable efficient compaction following mixing.

As shown in Table 1.3, soils appropriate for the pneumatic flow mixing method are very soft dredged clay, organic soil, and soft alluvial soil, which usually have a water content exceeding their liquid limit. The amount of binder needed is usually relatively small to achieve a target strength of the order of 100 to 200 kN/m^2. Compaction of a nearly-saturated soil-binder mixture is ineffective and practically impossible to carry out soon after mixing, whereas it can be conducted in some cases after certain curing period for beneficial use, as explained in Chapter 2. The purpose of stabilization in the pneumatic flow mixing method is usually to manufacture a large strength soil material for land reclamation, backfilling, shallow stabilization, *etc.* Due to these differences in manufacturing process, and in the expected functions of stabilized soil, the fundamental engineering properties of lime- and cement-stabilized clays and sands have been studied in detail in Japan.

Although the magnitude of strength gain by stabilization is influenced by various factors, including the type of binder (Chapter 2), the engineering properties of lime- and cement-stabilized soils are quite similar. Since cement and a cement-based type special binder have both been used in the pneumatic flow mixing method, properties of cement-stabilized soil will be mainly described in this chapter.

The descriptions in this chapter are mostly based on the research done in Japan or on accumulated experience on Japanese soils, machines and mixing systems. The soil properties introduced here may not be directly applicable in the other parts of the world.

Chapter 3 describes the engineering properties of soil stabilized mainly with cement. Transport and placement ability are key factors for the execution of the method, which is influenced by the engineering properties of the freshly stabilized soil, soon after the mixing. This chapter introduces not only the properties of hardened stabilized soil but also the properties of fresh stabilized soil. There are quite a lot of test data on the properties of stabilized soil for the deep mixing method (Kitazume & Terashi, 2013). However, the target strength of the pneumatic flow mixing method is smaller than that of the deep mixing method, while the water content is high and the amount of cement is small. Therefore the properties of the soft stabilized soil are somewhat different from the hard stabilized soil. Correlation between the unconfined compressive strength of stabilized soil and its other engineering characteristics will be of benefit in the understanding of stabilized soil, regardless of the execution system and type of application. The characteristics of *in-situ* stabilized soil, such as the relationship between the average field strength and the laboratory strength, and the variability of field strengths, are important information for geotechnical design. This is discussed, but based only upon the experience gained by the execution system used in Japan. This is because the quality of *in-situ* stabilized soil heavily depends upon the mixing machine and process. The chapter concludes that it is necessary for contractors to take responsibility for accumulating information on the quality of *in-situ* stabilized soil produced by their proprietary system.

2 PROPERTIES OF STABILIZED SOIL MIXTURE BEFORE HARDENING

2.1 Physical properties

2.1.1 Change in consistency of the soil–binder mixture before hardening

The water content of stabilized soil decreases in many cases due to the hydration of quicklime and cement. At the same time, the consistency of the soil–binder mixture changes from that of the original soil due to the ion exchange. As no research result was found on cement-stabilized soil, Figure 3.1 shows an example of the effect of quicklime stabilization on the consistency of the soil–binder mixture measured at three hours

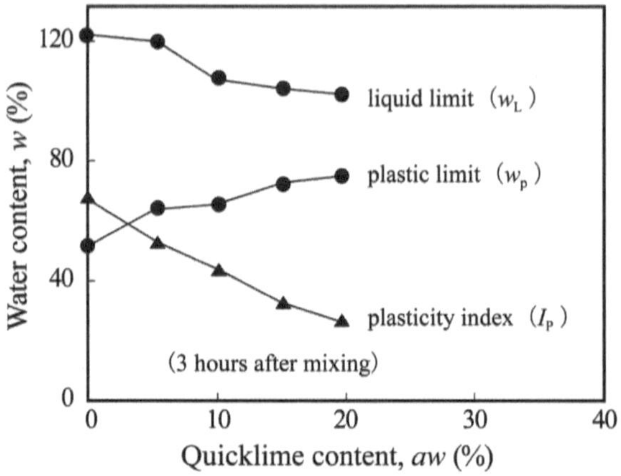

Figure 3.1 Change of consistency in soil resulting from quicklime stabilization (Japan Lime Association, 2009).

after mixing (Japan Lime Association, 2009). The liquid limit, w_L, decreases with the quicklime content, while the plastic limit, w_P, increases. As a result, the plasticity index, I_p, sharply decreases with increasing quicklime content.

2.2 Mechanical properties (strength characteristics)

2.2.1 *Change in flow value*

The flow value of the stabilized soil mixture before hardening is influenced by the mixing conditions, and it is usually quite a small value compared with that of the original soil, even with the same water content. Figure 3.2(a) shows the relationship between the water content of the original soil and the stabilized soil, and their flow values (Ministry of Transport, The Fifth District Port Construction Bureau, 1999). The Nagoya Port soil (w_L of 74.4% and w_P of 33.0%) was stabilized with ordinary Portland cement with a cement factor of 30, 50 and 70 kg/m^3, in which the W/C ratio of cement slurry is 100%. The flow value of the stabilized soil mixture was measured at 10 minutes after mixing by the Japanese Industrial Standard (JIS A 313). Figure 3.2(a) reveals that the flow value increases with the water content of stabilized soil mixture, irrespective of the cement factor. In the figure, the flow value of the original soil is plotted together; this also increases with the water content and is somewhat larger than those of the stabilized soil mixture.

Figure 3.2(b) shows the relationship between the flow value and the shear strength of the cement-stabilized soil mixture, which were measured at 10 minutes after mixing. It shows that the shear strength exponentially decreases with the flow value and a unique relationship between them can be seen irrespective of the cement factor (Ministry of Transport, The Fifth District Port Construction Bureau, 1999).

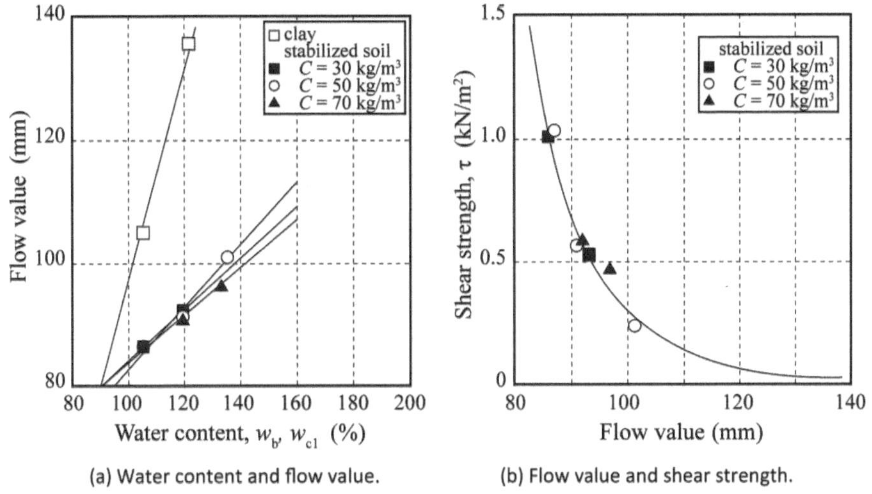

Figure 3.2 Characteristics of fresh cement-stabilized soil (Ministry of Transport, The Fifth District Port Construction Bureau, 1999).

2.2.2 *Change in shear strength*

The initial strength gain of stabilized soil mixture is one of the key properties to influence the slope angle of stabilized soil mixture after placement, which will be described in Section 5 of this chapter. Figure 3.3(a) shows the shear stress gain, τ_v (Watabe et al., 2001). The Tachibana Bay clay (w_L of 40.8% and w_P of 20.8%) was prepared to have an initial water content of $1.6 \times w_L$ and then stabilized with ordinary Portland cement with a cement factor of 50 kg/m^3. Figure 3.3(b) shows the strength increase of the cement-stabilized soil soon after mixing (Watabe et al., 2001). In the tests, the Tachibana Bay clay (w_L of 40.8% and w_P of 20.8%) was prepared to have an initial water content of $1.6 \times w_L$ (65.3%) and stabilized with ordinary Portland cement with a cement factor, α, of 50 kg/m^3. Soon after the mixing, the shear strength, τ_v, was measured with a hand vane shear apparatus at several elapsed times up to 200 minutes. The shear strength of the original soil with a water content of $1.6 \times w_L$ was also measured and plotted in the figure. The shear strength of the stabilized soil mixture just after mixing is larger than that of the original soil, which is probably due to reduced fluidity as a result of adding cement powder. The shear strength, τ_v, remains a small value up to about 30 minutes but increases rapidly after that, due to the progress of the cement hydration effect.

2.2.3 *Stress – strain curve*

Figure 3.4 shows the stress–strain curves on cement-stabilized Tachibana Bay clay (Watabe et al., 2001). The Tachibana Bay clay (w_L of 40.8% and w_P of 20.8%) was prepared to have an initial water content of $1.6 \times w_L$ and stabilized with ordinary Portland cement with a cement factor of 50 kg/m^3. The soil samples were subjected to the unconfined compression test at various curing periods. In the figure, the stress–strain curve on the original soil was also plotted, which was consolidated with the pressure of 49 kPa. The compressive stress, q, increases gradually with the axial strain to reach a constant value of about 25 kPa, which shows the ductile behavior. In the case of the stabilized soils, on the other hand, the compressive stress increases rapidly with the axial strain to a peak strength, which is followed by small residual strength. The peak compressive stress increases quickly and the axial strain at failure decreases quickly with the curing period. The brittle behavior with a large peak strength, small strain at failure and a small residual strength becomes more dominant with the curing period.

Figure 3.4(b) shows the effect of confined pressure on the stress-strain curves on cement-stabilized clay (Watabe et al., 2001). The stabilized clay was allowed to isotropically consolidate under the confined pressure of 49 kPa and was then subjected to undrained compression. The maximum strength increases with the curing period as similar to those of the unconfined compression test (Figure 3.4(a)), but the compressive stress decreases slightly to a relatively large residual strength. The pore water pressure also increases with the axial strain, but its magnitude is almost of the same order irrespective of the curing period even the peak strength is influenced by the curing period very much.

2.3 Mechanical properties (consolidation characteristics)

Figure 3.5(a) shows e-log$\,p$ curves of the laboratory cement-stabilized soils, in which the Tachibana Bay clay (w_L of 40.8% and w_P of 20.8%) was stabilized with ordinary

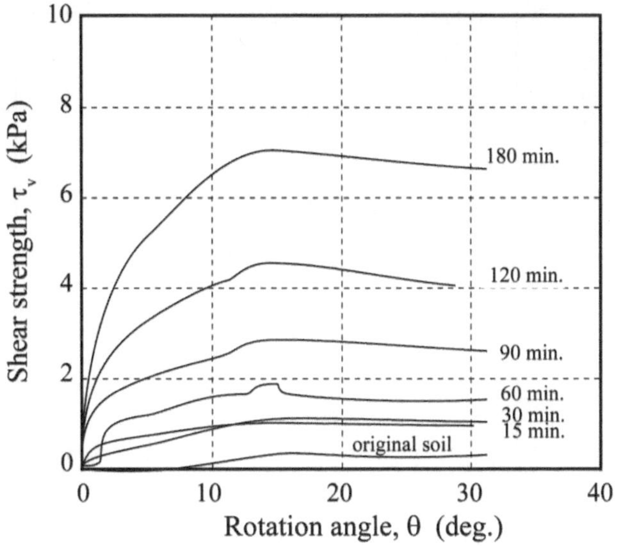

(a) Relationship between shear stress and rotation angle of the vane blade.

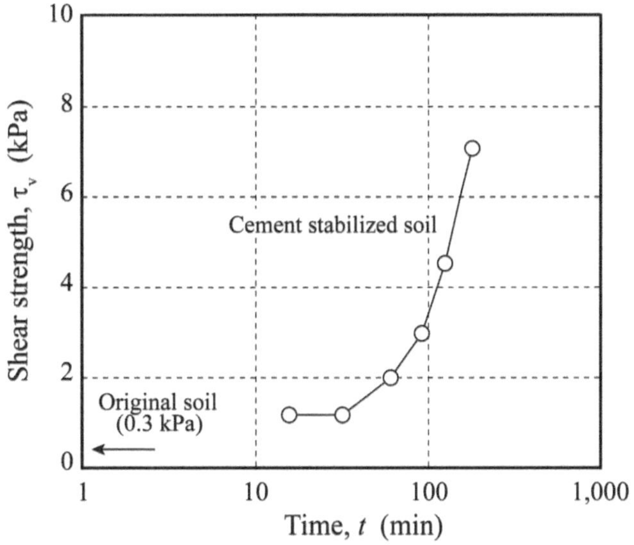

(b) Shear strength gain with time.

Figure 3.3 Strength increase soon after cement mixing (Watabe et al., 2001).

Portland cement with a cement factor, α, of 150 kg/m^3 (Watabe et al., 2001). In the laboratory tests, the stabilized soil samples of 20 mm height and 60 mm diameter were consolidated one dimensionally by the constant strain rate consolidation test. The figure shows a sharp bend in the curves irrespective of the curing period.

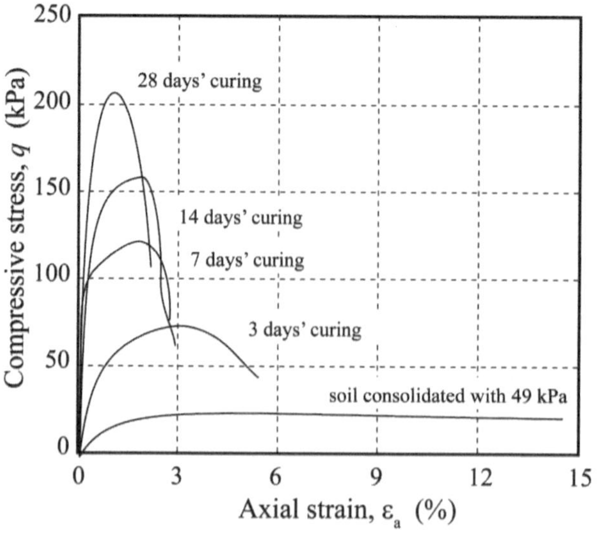

(a) Stress - strain curves of cement-stabilizedsoils in an unconfined compression test.

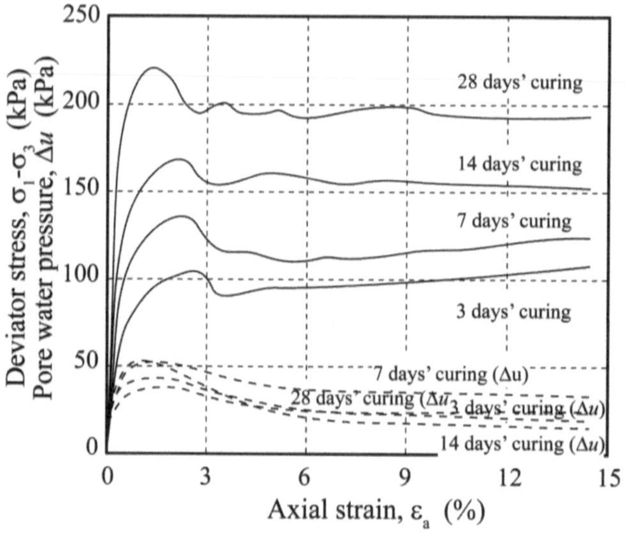

(b) Stress and pore water pressure strain curves of cement-stabilizedsoils in a consolidated undrained compression test.

Figure 3.4 Stress and pore water pressure strain curves of cement-stabilized clays (Watabe et al., 2001).

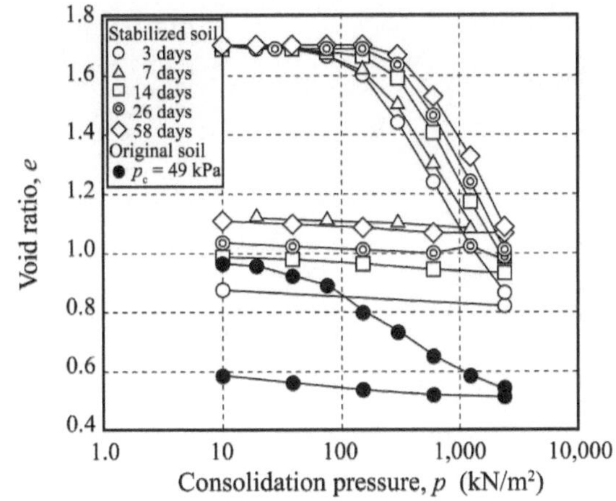

(a) e-log p curve.

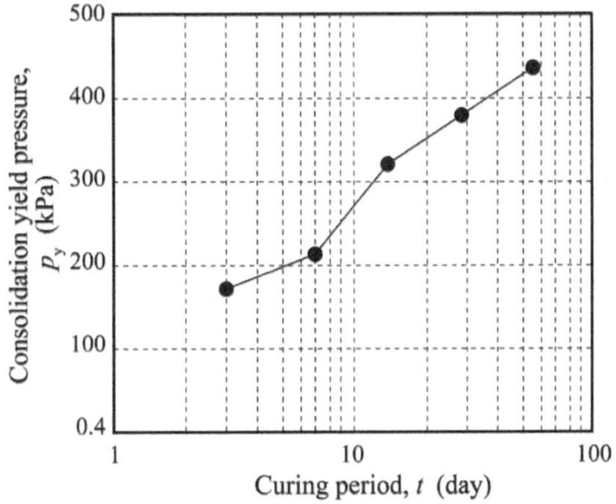

(b) Relationship between the consolidation yield pressure, p_Y,and curing.

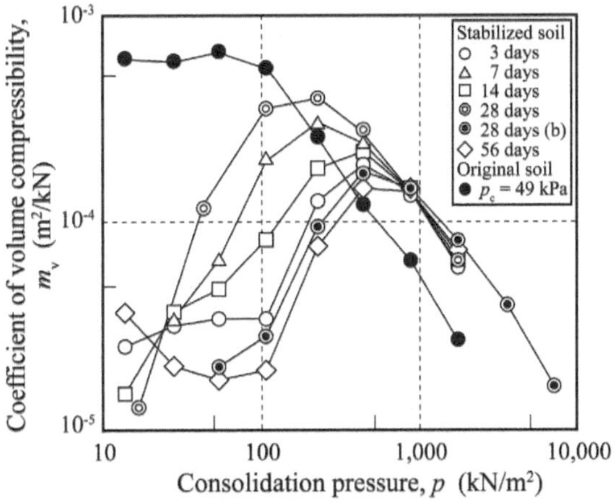

(c) Relationship between the coefficient of volume compressibility and consolidation pressure

Figure 3.5 Consolidation properties of cement-stabilized soil (Watabe et al., 2001).

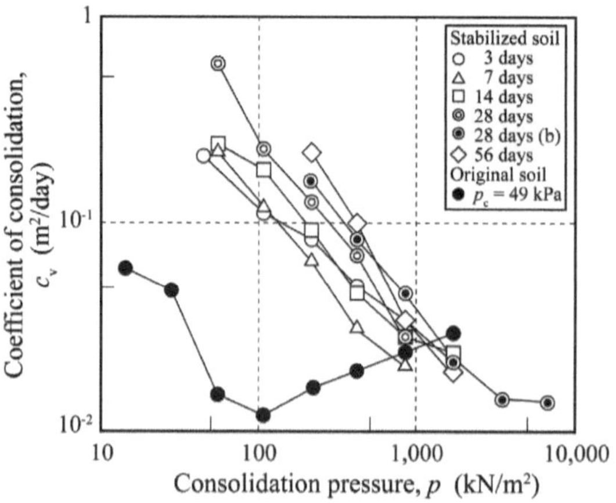

(d) Relationship between the coefficient of consolidation and consolidation pressure.

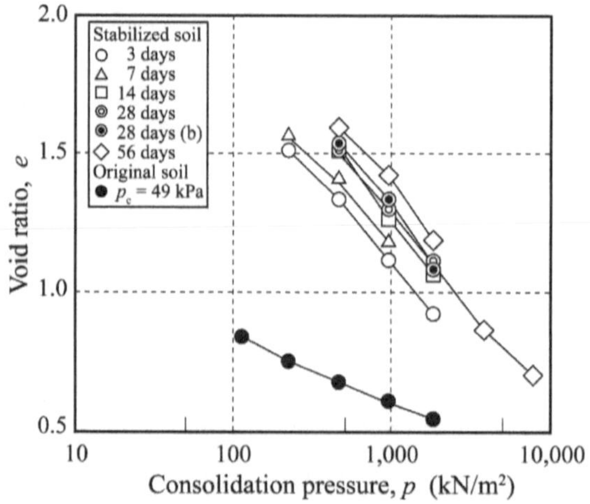

(e) Relationship between the void ratio and consolidation pressure.

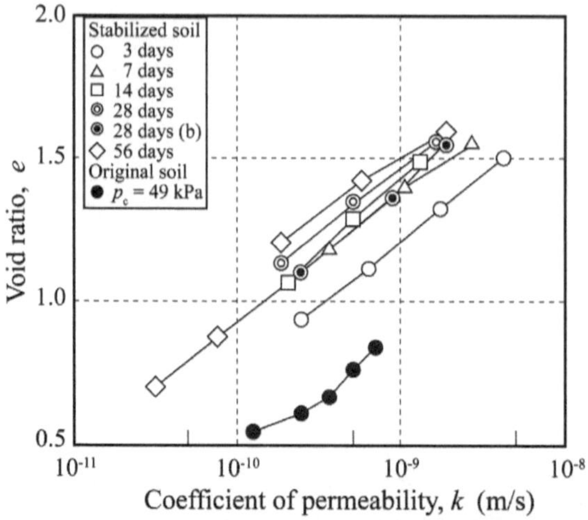

(f) Relationship between the coefficient of permeability and void ratio.

Figure 3.5 (Continued).

The consolidation yield pressure at the sharp bend is larger for the longer curing period, while the compression index, *Cc*, and the swelling index, *Cs*, are almost same irrespective of the curing period. Figure 3.5(b) shows the relationship between the consolidation yield pressure, p_y, and the curing period, where the p_y increases almost linearly with the logarithm of the curing period. Figures 3.5(c) and 3.5(d) show the relationships between the coefficient of volume compressibility, m_v, the coefficient of consolidation, c_v, and the consolidation pressure. The coefficient of volume compressibility, m_v, is around 2.0×10^{-5} m^2/kN at the small consolidation pressure and increases with the consolidation pressure to the peak value at around the consolidation yield pressure, p_y. The consolidation pressure when the m_v increases becomes large with the curing period, while the m_v value at the large consolidation pressure is almost same irrespective of the curing period. The coefficient of consolidation, c_v, decreases with the consolidation pressure to a constant value. Figures 3.5(e) and 3.5(f) show the relationships between the void ratio, *e*, consolidation pressure, *p*, and coefficient of permeability, *k*, which are measured in the consolidation test. The permeability, *k*, decreases with decreasing void ratio. The *k* value of the stabilized soil is larger than that of the original soil, which is due to the large void ratio of the stabilized soil.

Figure 3.6 shows the coefficient of permeability of stabilized soils, which was measured by a laboratory falling head permeability test (Ministry of Transport, The Fifth District Port Construction Bureau, 1999). The Nagoya Port clay (w_L of 68.7% and w_P of 29.6%) was prepared to an initial water content of 96.2% and stabilized with ordinary Portland cement of 100 kg/m^3 (Ministry of Transport, The Fifth District Port Construction Bureau, 1999). The figure shows that the coefficient of permeability, *k*, is very much smaller than that of the original soil, and of the order of about 10^{-7} cm/s. The permeability gradually decreases with the progress of cement hydration.

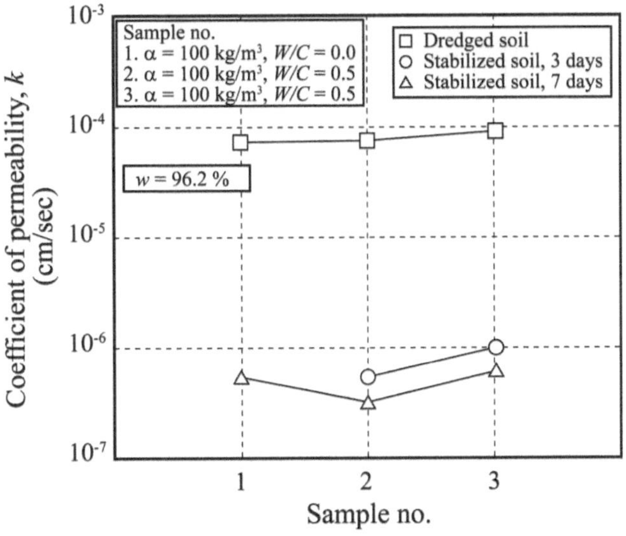

Figure 3.6 The relationship between permeability of stabilized soil and mixing condition (Ministry of Transport, The Fifth District Port Construction Bureau, 1999).

3 PROPERTIES OF STABILIZED SOIL AFTER HARDENING

3.1 Physical properties

3.1.1 Change in water content

The water content of cement-stabilized soil after cement hydration can be estimated by Equation (3.1). The water-to-soil ratio required for cement hydration, λ, is dependent upon the type and composition of the cement, but can be estimated to be about 25 to 40% of the dry weight of cement.

$$w_t = \frac{w_0 + (W/C - \lambda) \cdot aw/100}{100 + (100 - \lambda) \cdot aw/100} \times 100 \qquad (3.1)$$

where
aw: cement content (%)
w_0: water content of original soil (%)
w_t: water content of stabilized soil (%)
W/C: water to cement ratio (%)
λ: water to soil ratio required for cement hydration (25 to 40%)

Figure 3.7 shows the water contents of laboratory cement-stabilized soils, in which the Shinagawa clay (w_L of 62.6%, w_P of 23.1% and w_i of 76.5%) was stabilized with

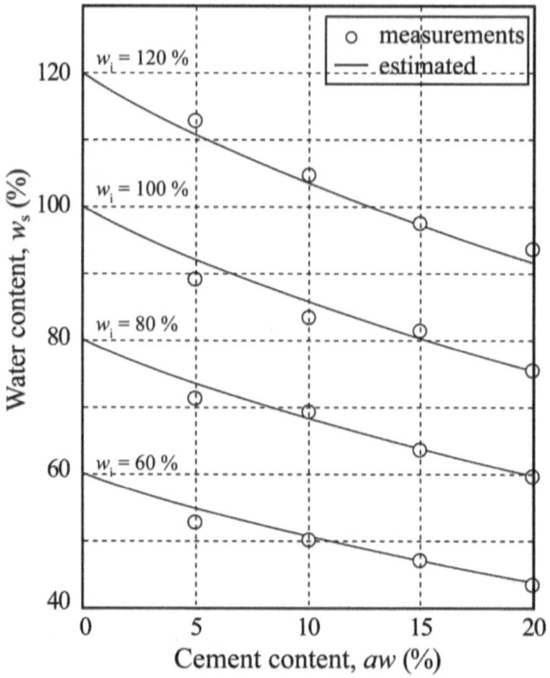

Figure 3.7 The change in water content brought about by cement stabilization (Kawasaki et al., 1978).

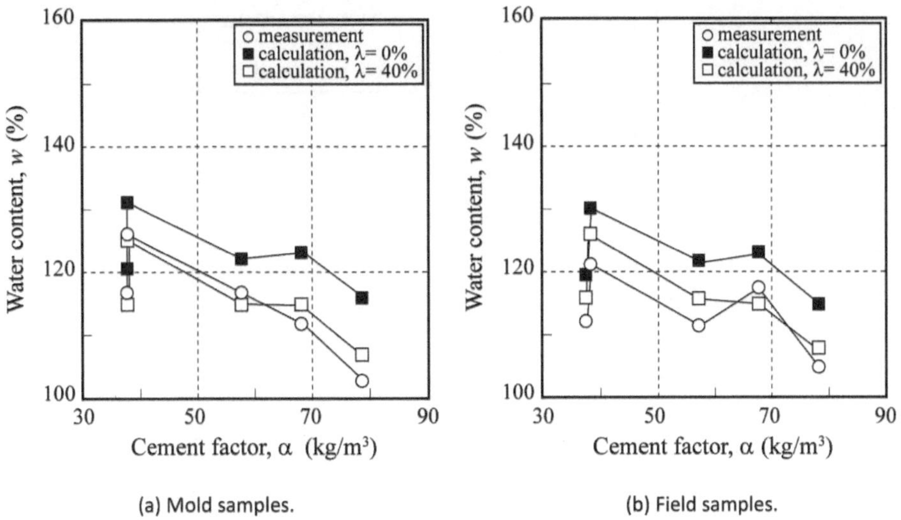

Figure 3.8 The change in water content brought about by cement stabilization (Ministry of Transport, The Fifth District Port Construction Bureau, 1999).

ordinary Portland cement with a cement content, *aw*, of 5, 10, 15 and 20% (Kawasaki et al., 1978). The water content of the stabilized soil decreases gradually with the cement content. In the figure, the estimated values by Equation (3.1) with λ of 25% are also plotted. The estimated values coincide with the measured values very well.

Figure 3.8 shows the water content change in a cement-stabilized soil at 28 days' curing, in which the Nagoya Port clay (w_L of 74.4%, w_P of 33.0% and w_i of 127.1%) was stabilized with ordinary Portland cement with various cement factors by one of the pneumatic flow mixing methods in the field (Ministry of Transport, The Fifth District Port Construction Bureau, 1999). The stabilized soil mixture was collected at the outlet of the pipeline and placed in a plastic mold and cured in a laboratory (mold samples), while the stabilized soil placed and cured in the field was core sampled at 28 days' curing (field samples). It was found that the water content of the stabilized soil decreases gradually with the cement content. In the figure, the calculated values by Equation (3.1) with λ of 0% (no hydration) and λ of 40% (full hydration is assumed) are also plotted. The measured values are about 5 to 10% smaller than the calculation for the no hydration condition, but are relatively well coincident with the calculations for the full hydration.

3.1.2 Change in density

The saturated density of cement-stabilized soil can be calculated by Equation 3.2.

$$\rho_t = \frac{100 + w_0 + (100 + W/C) \cdot aw/100}{\frac{100}{G_s} + \left(\frac{100}{G_c} + \frac{W/C}{G_w}\right) \cdot aw/100 + \frac{w_0}{G_w}} \times \rho_w \tag{3.2}$$

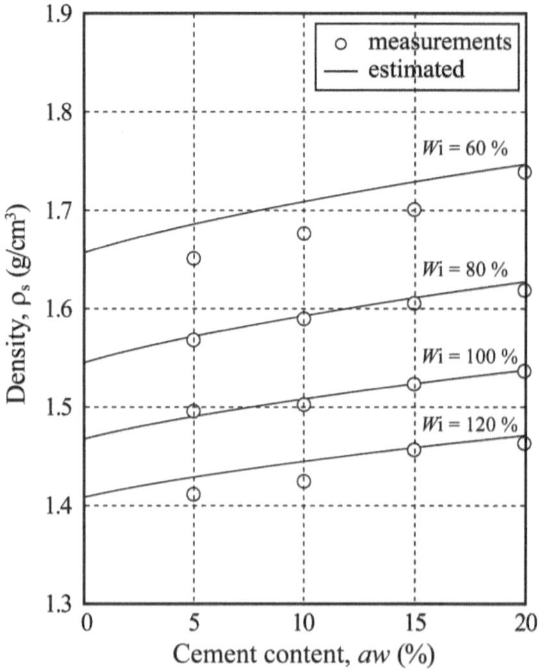

Figure 3.9 The change of density brought about by cement stabilization (Kawasaki et al., 1978).

where
aw: cement content (%)
G_c: specific gravity of binder
G_s: specific gravity of soil particle
G_w: specific gravity of water
w_o: water content of original soil (%)
W/C: water to cement ratio (%)
ρ_t: density of stabilized soil (g/cm^3)
ρ_w: density of water (g/cm^3)

Figure 3.9 shows the density of the laboratory cement-stabilized soils, in which the Kawasaki clay (w_L of 62.6% and w_P of 23.1%) was stabilized with ordinary Portland cement with various cement contents, aw of 5, 10, 15 and 20% (Kawasaki et al., 1978). The density of the stabilized soil increases gradually with the cement content. In the figure, the estimated values by Equation (3.2) are also plotted, which coincide with the measured values well.

Figure 3.10 also shows the unit weight of the field cement-stabilized soils, in which the Nagoya Port clay (w_L of 74.4%, w_P of 33.0% and w_i of 127.1%) was stabilized with ordinary Portland cement of various cement factors by one of the pneumatic flow mixing methods in the field (Ministry of Transport, The Fifth District Port Construction Bureau, 1999). The stabilized soil mixture was collected at the outlet of the pipeline and placed in a plastic mold and cured in a laboratory (mold samples), while

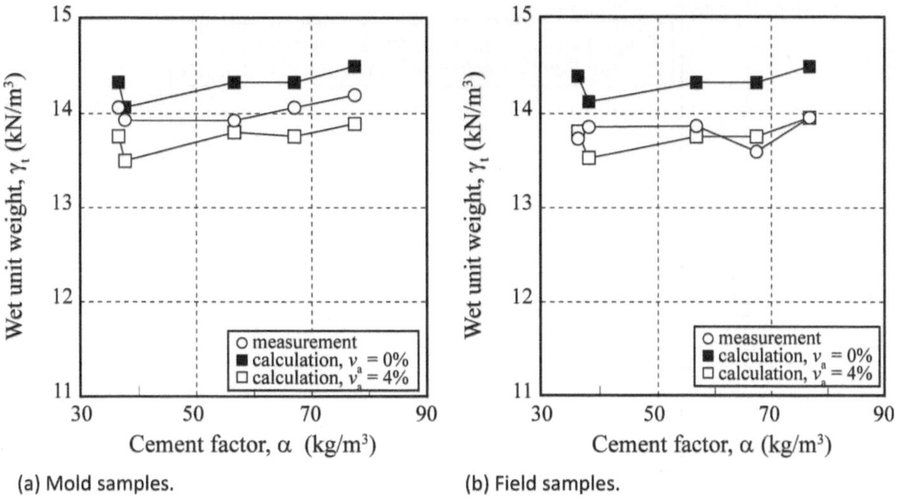

Figure 3.10 The change of density brought about by cement stabilization (Ministry of Transport, The Fifth District Port Construction Bureau, 1999).

the stabilized soil placed and cured in the field was core sampled at 28 days' curing (field samples). The unit weight of the stabilized soils increases gradually with the cement factor. In the figure, the estimated values by Equation 3.2 with V_a of 0% (fully saturated condition) are also plotted, which overestimates the measured value. The calculation for taking account of the entrapped air of 4.7% of the total volume is also plotted, which was measured in a case history of the pneumatic flow mixing, which coincides with the measured value relatively well.

3.1.3 Change in consistency

Figure 3.11 shows the effect of the cement stabilization on the consistency of stabilized soil (Watabe & Tanaka, 2012). The Honmoku clay (w_L of 108.0% and w_P of 47.9%) was stabilized with a cement factor of 100 kg/m^3 and cured for 14 days in a laboratory. The consistency of the stabilized soil measured at 14 days' curing is shown as black markers in the figure. The white markers in the figure show the measured values on the stabilized soil disturbed and compacted with additional cement mixing, which will be described later in Section 4. The figure shows that both the liquid limit, w_L, and the plastic limit, w_P, increase by the stabilization, which is different from the phenomenon shown in Figure 3.1. As the plastic limit increases more than the liquid limit, the plasticity index, I_p, is decreased by the stabilization.

3.2 Mechanical properties (strength characteristics)

3.2.1 Stress – strain curve

Figure 3.12 shows the stress–strain curves of soil field cement-stabilized soil by the pneumatic flow mixing method (Ministry of Transport, The Fifth District Port Construction Bureau, 1999). In the test, marine clay excavated at Nagoya Port

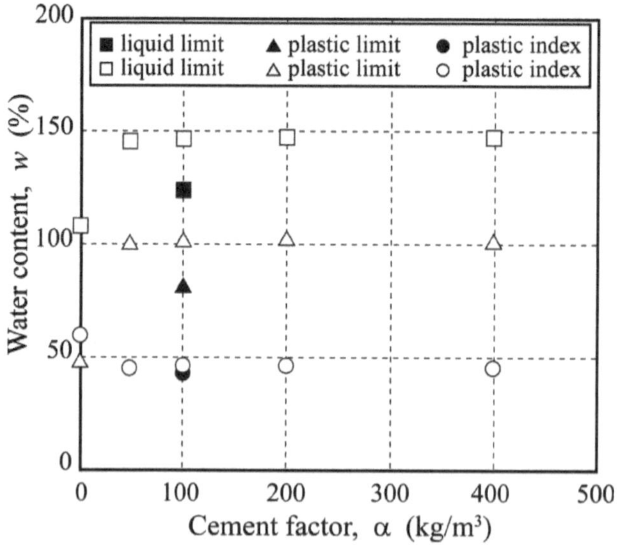

Figure 3.11 The change of consistency brought about by cement stabilization (Watabe & Tanaka, 2012).

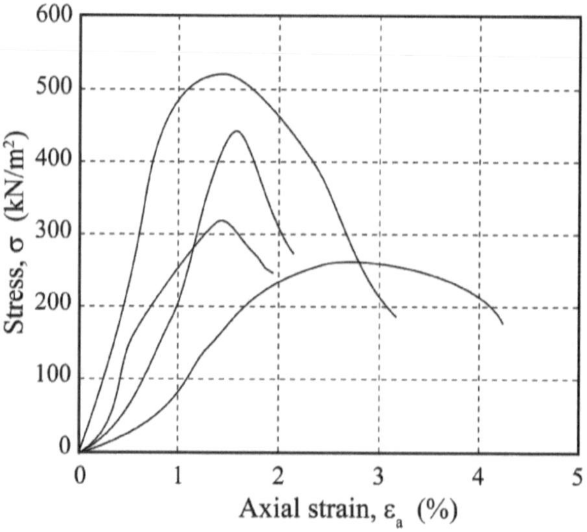

Figure 3.12 Stress – strain curves on cement-stabilized soils (Ministry of Transport, The Fifth District Port Construction Bureau, 1999).

(w_L of 74.4% and w_P of 33.0%) was stabilized with ordinary Portland cement and cured in the field. The stabilized soils were trimmed to 50 mm in diameter and 100 mm in height after core sampling and subjected to the unconfined compression test. The compressive stress, σ, increases rapidly with the axial strain to a peak strength which is

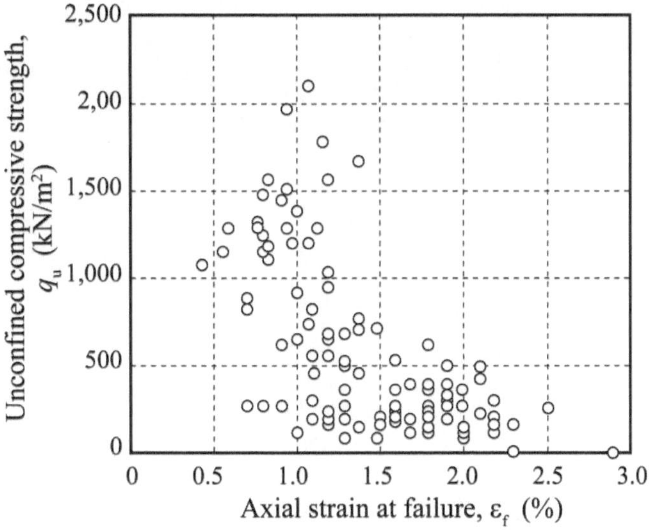

Figure 3.13 Strain at failure of cement-stabilized soils (Ministry of Transport, The Fifth District Port Construction Bureau, 1999).

followed by quick decrease in σ. The brittle behavior with a large peak strength, a small strain at failure and small residual strength becomes more dominant with the curing period.

3.2.2 *Strain at failure*

As shown in Figure 3.12, the axial strain at the failure of stabilized soil is quite small compared to that of the original soil. Figure 3.13 shows an example of the relationship between the axial strain at failure, ε_f, and the unconfined compressive strength, q_u, of field cement-stabilized soils (Ministry of Transport, The Fifth District Port Construction Bureau, 1999). In the tests, marine clay excavated at Nagoya Port (w_L of 74.4% and w_P of 33.0%) was stabilized with ordinary Portland cement and cured in the field. The stabilized soils were trimmed to 50 mm in diameter and 100 mm in height after core sampling and subjected to the unconfined compression test. The figure shows that the magnitude of axial strain at failure, ε_f, is of the order of 0.5 to 2.5% and considerably smaller than that of unstabilized clay. The ε_f decreases rapidly with the unconfined compressive strength, q_u. Similar test results can be seen for lime-stabilized soils as with cement-stabilized soils (e.g. Terashi et al., 1980).

3.2.3 *Internal friction angle and undrained shear strength*

Figure 3.14 shows the relationship between the consolidation pressure and the undrained shear strength, c_u, obtained in isotropically consolidated undrained shear (CIU) tests (Terashi et al., 1980). In Cases 1 to 3, the Kawasaki clay (w_L of 87.7% and w_P of 39.7%), having an initial water content of about 120%, was stabilized

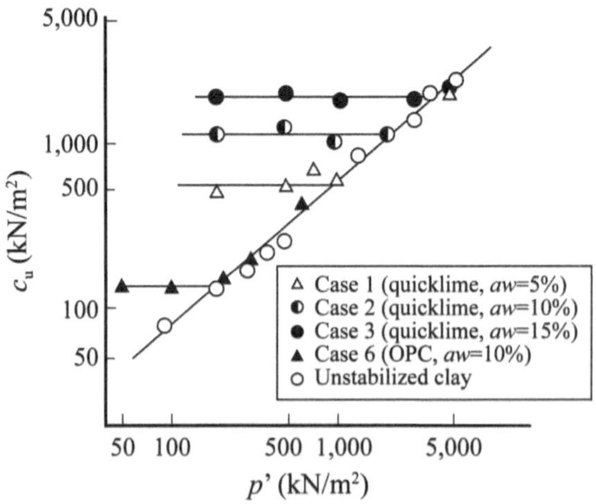

Figure 3.14 The relationship between the consolidation pressure and undrained shear strength (Terashi et al., 1980).

with quicklime with *aw* of 5, 10 and 15%, respectively. In Case 6, the Kawasaki clay, having an initial water content of about 200%, was stabilized with ordinary Portland cement with *aw* of 10%. In the figure, the test data on the unstabilized soil are also plotted by an open circle. The figure shows that the undrained shear strength, c_u, of the stabilized soil is larger than that of the unstabilized soil, and almost constant, as long as the consolidation pressure is low. But when the consolidation pressure exceeds the consolidation yield pressure (pseudo pre-consolidation pressure), p_y, the undrained shear strength increases with increasing consolidation pressure. This phenomenon can be seen irrespective of type and amount of binder. The increasing ratio in the c_u of the stabilized soil is almost same as that of the unstabilized soil. According to the figure, the internal friction angle, ϕ', of stabilized soil is almost zero as long as the consolidation pressure is lower than the consolidation yield pressure and the same as that of the unstabilized soil when the consolidation pressure is higher than the consolidation yield pressure.

Figure 3.15 shows the Mohr–Coulomb stress circles on the stabilized soil when tested for undrained shear strength (Ministry of Transport, The Fifth District Port Construction Bureau, 1999). The stress circle is almost same size as long as the confining pressure is lower than the cohesion of the stabilized soil.

Figure 3.16 shows the undrained shear strength of the cement-stabilized soil measured by various shear tests (Watabe et al., 2001). In the test, the Tachibana Bay clay, having an initial water content of $1.6 \times w_L$ was stabilized with ordinary Portland cement of 50 kg/m^3. The stabilized soils were subjected to various shear tests: the unconfined compression test ($q_u/2$); the isotropically consolidated and undrained compression test (CIU); the anisotropically (K_0) consolidated and undrained compression test (CAUC); and the anisotropically (K_0) consolidated and undrained extension test (CAUE). In the case of the unconfined compression test, the undrained shear strength

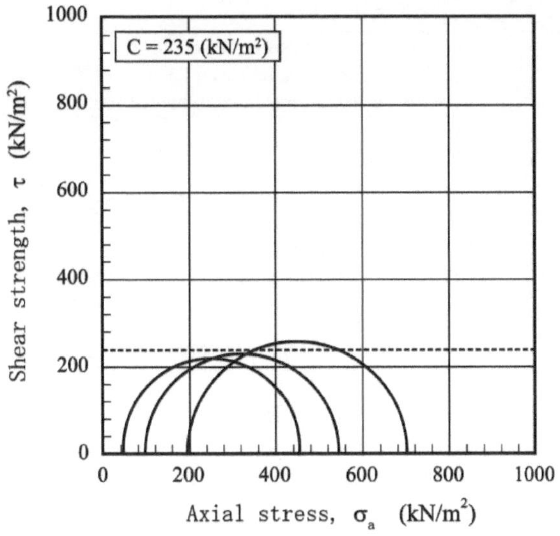

Figure 3.15 Mohr–Coulomb stress circles on cement-stabilized soil tested for undrained shear strength (Ministry of Transport, The Fifth District Port Construction Bureau, 1999).

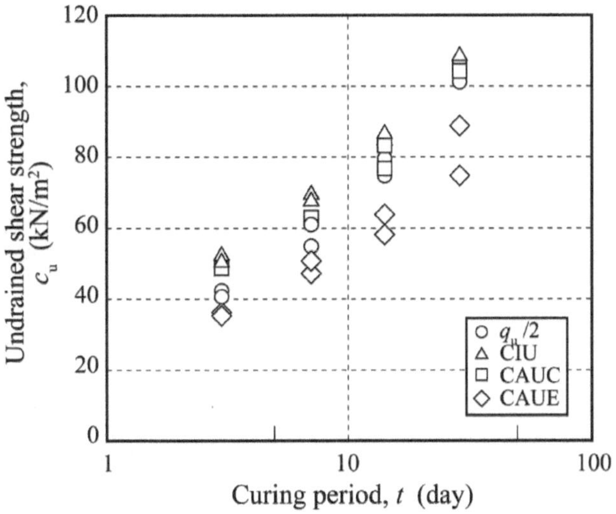

Figure 3.16 The undrained shear strength of cement-stabilized Tachibana clay measured by various testing methods (Watabe et al., 2001).

was assumed as $q_u/2$. The undrained shear strength is influenced by the testing method, where the largest value is obtained in the CIU test and the smallest is in the CAUE test. In general, the strength increases almost linearly with the logarithm of the curing period, irrespective of the testing method.

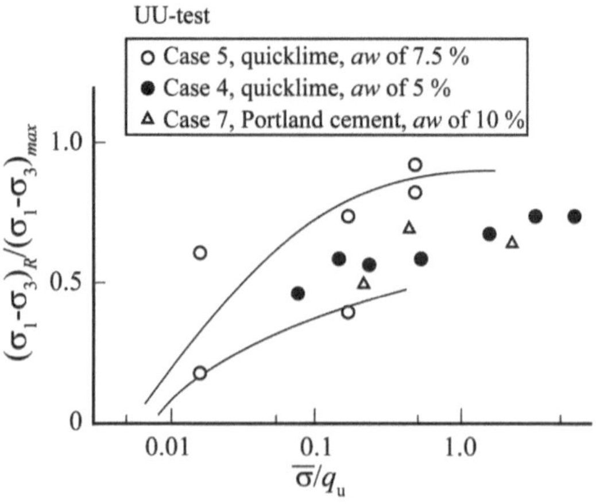

Figure 3.17 The relationship between residual strength and confining pressure (Terashi et al., 1980).

3.2.4 *Residual strength*

As already shown in Figures 3.4 and 3.12, the stress-strain curves and residual strength of stabilized soils are considerably influenced by the confining pressure, which show that the deviator stress, $\sigma_1 - \sigma_3$, sharply decreases after the peak in the case of unconfined compression, but the reduction in the deviator stress becomes smaller with the confining pressure, σ'_c. Figure 3.17 shows the relationship between the strength ratio of the residual strength against the peak strength, $(\sigma_1 - \sigma_3)_R/(\sigma_1 - \sigma_3)_{max}$ and the confining pressure ratio, $\overline{\sigma}/q_u$, which is obtained in unconsolidated undrained compression (UU) tests on the quicklime- and cement-stabilized clays having q_u value of 600 to 1,300 kN/m^2 (Terashi et al., 1980). The strength ratio increases with the confining pressure ratio, and is about 0.5 to 0.8 for the confining pressure ratio, $\overline{\sigma}/q_u$, exceeding about 0.1, irrespective of the type of binder (Terashi et al., 1980). A similar phenomenon was found where the residual strength of stabilized soil is about 0.8 of the unconfined compressive strength, q_u, even under a small confining pressure of the order of a couple of percentage of q_u (Tatsuoka & Kobayashi, 1983).

3.2.5 *Modulus of elasticity (Young's modulus)*

The modulus of elasticity of field cement-stabilized soils is plotted in Figure 3.18 against the unconfined compressive strength, q_u (Ministry of Transport, The Fifth District Port Construction Bureau, 1999). Marine clay excavated at Nagoya Port (w_L of 74.4% and w_P of 33.0%) was stabilized with ordinary Portland cement and cured in the field. The stabilized soils after core sampling were trimmed to 50 mm in diameter and 100 mm in height and subjected to the unconfined compression test. The modulus of elasticity, E_{50}, is defined by the secant modulus of elasticity in a stress–strain curve at a half of unconfined compressive strength, q_u. Although there is a lot of scatter in the measured data, the magnitude of E_{50} increases with the q_u and can be formulated as $E_{50} = 50$ to $300 \times q_u$.

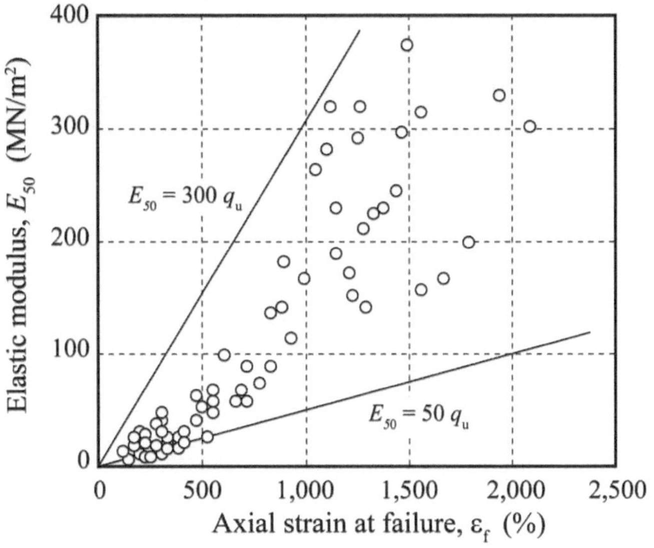

Figure 3.18 The modulus of elasticity, E_{50}, of laboratory cement-stabilized soils (Ministry of Transport, The Fifth District Port Construction Bureau, 1999).

Similar relationships were obtained on the laboratory lime-stabilized soils and laboratory cement-stabilized soils (e.g. Terashi et al., 1977, Niina et al., 1981). According to them, the E_{50} almost linearly increases with the q_u and the increasing ratio becomes larger with the q_u: $E_{50} = 50$ to $300 \times q_u$ for $q_u <$ about 2,000 kN/m², and $E_{50} = 350$ to $1{,}000 \times q_u$ for $q_u >$ about 2,000 kN/m².

3.2.6 *Poisson's ratio*

The Poisson's ratio, μ, of field cement-stabilized soils, is shown in Figure 3.19 against the unconfined compressive strength, q_u, in which the unconfined compression tests were carried out on small scale specimens of 50 mm in diameter (Niina et al., 1977). In the tests, the Shinagawa clay (w_L of 77.9% and w_P of 32.5%) was stabilized with quicklime, hydrated lime or cement by the deep mixing method (Kitazume & Terashi, 2013). The Poisson's ratio was obtained from the measured longitudinal and radial strains in the unconfined compression tests, and those for the shear stress lower than the 70% of q_u are plotted in the figure. Although there is a relatively large scatter in the test data, the Poisson's ratio is around 0.28 to 0.45 irrespective of the unconfined compressive strength, q_u. Accumulated researches show the Poisson's ratio is around about 0.2 to 0.45 irrespective of soil type, soil strength, size of soil specimen and laboratory and field stabilized soils (Hirade et al., 1995, The Building Center of Japan, 1997).

3.2.7 *Dynamic property*

Figure 3.20 shows the relationship between the initial shear modulus, G_0, at the shear strain of 10^{-6} and the unconfined compressive strength, q_u, of cement-stabilized

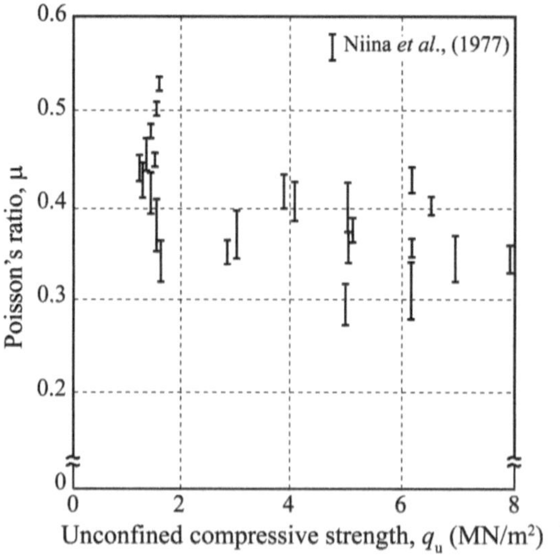

Figure 3.19 Poisson's ratio of *field* cement-stabilized soils (Niina et al., 1977).

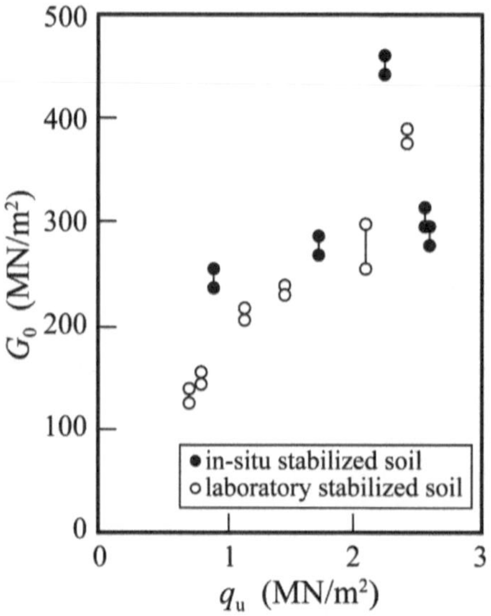

Figure 3.20 The relationship between the initial shear modulus and q_u of cement-stabilized soils (Tanaka & Terashi, 1986).

clays (Tanaka & Terashi, 1986). For the laboratory stabilized soil, clay excavated at Kawasaki Port (w_L of 88% and w_P of 44%), having an initial water content of 100 to 150%, was stabilized with ordinary Portland cement with *aw* of 10 to 25%, and the stabilized soils were subjected to the resonant column test. For the field stabilized soil, clay at Sakai Port (w_L of 93.3% and w_P of 27.3%) was stabilized *in-situ* by the deep mixing method (Kitazume & Terashi, 2013), where ordinary Portland cement of about 130 kg/m^3 was mixed and the mixture was cured *in-situ*. At 140 days after the execution, the stabilized soil was core sampled and trimmed for the test. The initial shear modulus, G_0, almost linearly increases with the q_u and can be formulated as $G_0 = 80$ to $200 \times q_u$, irrespective of the laboratory and field stabilized soils.

Figure 3.21 shows the shear modulus ratio, G/G_0, and the damping ratio, h_{eq}, against the shear strain, γ, of the field cement-stabilized soil by the pneumatic flow mixing method (Ministry of Transport, The Fifth District Port Construction Bureau, 1999). Marine clay excavated at Nagoya Port (w_L of 74.% and w_P of 31.6%) was prepared to the initial water content of 107% and stabilized with blast furnace slag cement type B with a cement factor, α, of 60 kg/m^3 and placed on land. The stabilized soil was core sampled at 28 days' curing. In the case of the confining pressure of 50 kN/m^2 (Figure 3.21(a)), the shear modulus ratio, G/G_0, is almost constant irrespective of the shear strain, while the equivalent dumping ratio, h_{eq}, increases gradually. The shear modulus ratio decreases with the shear strain in the cases of the confining pressure of 100 and 200 kN/m^2 (Figures 3.21(b) and 3.21(c)), while the dumping ratio increases to about 10% with the shear strain. In the figure, an example of test data on an ordinary clay having the plasticity index, I_p, exceeding 30 is plotted by broken lines. The shear modulus ratio and dumping ratio of the stabilized soil are similar to those of the ordinary clay.

The dynamic property of laboratory stabilized sand was also reported by Shibuya et al. (1992) and Enami et al. (1993).

3.2.8 Creep strength

Figure 3.22 shows the relationship between the strain rate, $\dot{\varepsilon}$, and the loading period of cement-stabilized clay (Terashi et al., 1983). The Kawasaki clay (w_L of 88% and w_P of 40%), having an initial water content of 150 or 200%, was stabilized with ordinary Portland cement with a cement content, aw, of 15 or 20%. The specimen of 50 mm in diameter and 100 mm in height was subjected to the constant compressive pressure, q_{cr}, whose magnitude was changed from 0.52 to $0.91 \times q_u$. The strain rate, $\dot{\varepsilon}$, decreases almost linearly with the time duration on the double-logarithmic graph. The decreasing phenomenon in $\dot{\varepsilon}$ is almost constant irrespective of the load intensity, q_{cr}/q_u. The figure shows that the stabilized soil subjected to the vertical load with q_{cr}/q_u of 0.91, exhibits creep failure at around 1 minute after loading, but the stabilized soil does not fail as long as the load intensity is lower than about $0.8 \times q_u$.

3.2.9 Cyclic strength

Figure 3.23 shows the relationship between the axial compressive strain, ε, and the number of loading cycles, N, on the cement-stabilized soils (Ministry of Transport, The Fifth District Port Construction Bureau, 1999). In the tests, marine clay excavated at Nagoya Port (w_L of 74.% and w_P of 31.6%) was prepared to an initial water content of 107% and stabilized in the field with blast furnace slag cement type B with cement factor, α, of 60 kg/m^3 by the pneumatic flow mixing method. The stabilized soil cured in the field was core sampled at 28 days. The samples were subjected to

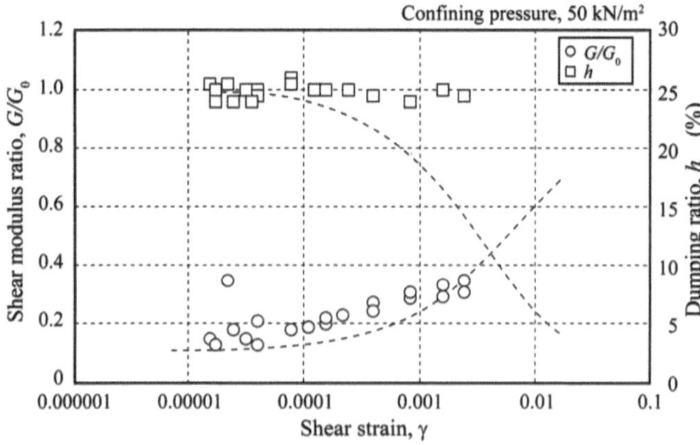

(a) Confining pressure, 50 kN/m^2.

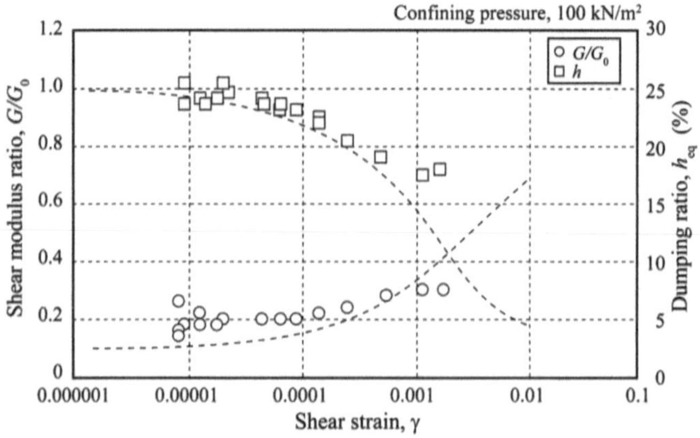

(b) Confining pressure, 100 kN/m^2.

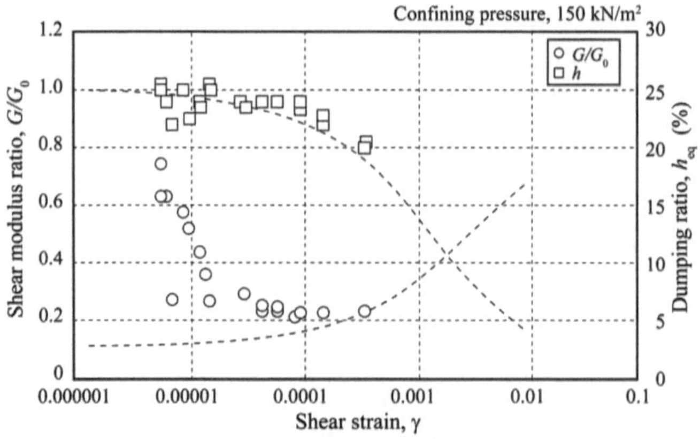

(c) Confining pressure, 150 kN/m^2.

Figure 3.21 The shear modulus ratio and damping ratio against the shear strain of field cement-stabilized soil (Ministry of Transport, The Fifth District Port Construction Bureau, 1999).

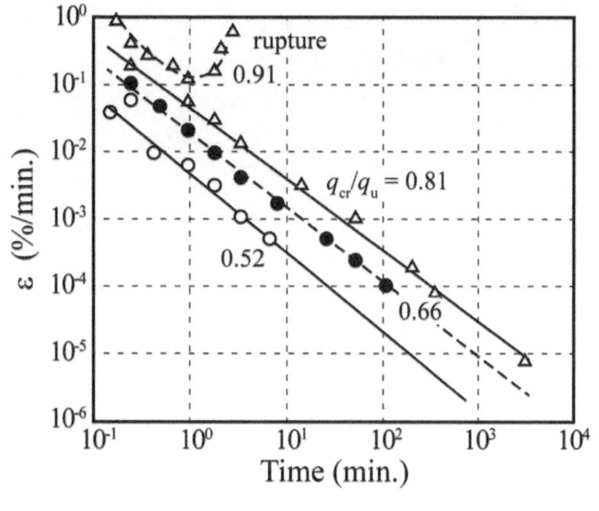

Figure 3.22 The relationship between strain rate and the loading period in the creep test (Terashi et al., 1983).

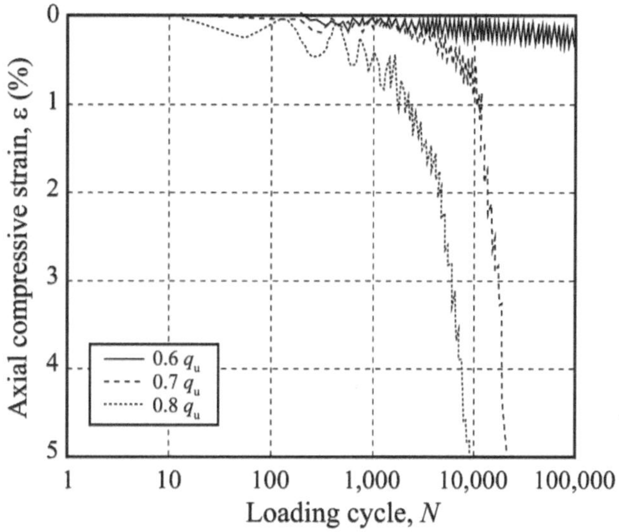

Figure 3.23 The effect of cyclic loading on strength of cement-stabilized soil (Ministry of Transport, The Fifth District Port Construction Bureau, 1999).

the cyclic loading of 1 Hz with the maximum deviator stress of $0.6 \times q_u$, $0.7 \times q_u$ and $0.8 \times q_u$ (q_u is 307 kN/m^2) while the confining pressure was kept constant at 50 kN/m^2. The figure shows that the axial compressive strain remains lower than about 0.4% in the case of $0.6 \times q_u$ even with the number of cyclic loading being 100,000. In the cases of the compressive stress of $0.8 \times q_u$ and $0.7 \times q_u$, on the other hand,

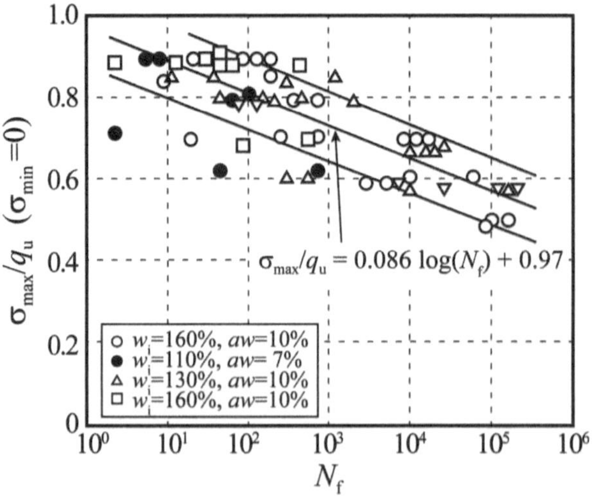

Figure 3.24 The relationship between number of cyclic loading until failure and magnitude of loading (Terashi et al., 1983).

the axial compressive strain rapidly increases to failure when the number of cyclic loading exceeds about 3,000 and 10,000, respectively.

Similar tests were carried out by Terashi et al. (1983) and Kudo et al. (1996). Figure 3.24 shows one of the relationships between the normalized cyclic loading stress, σ_{max}/q_u, and the number of cyclic loading at failure, N_f, on cement-stabilized soils (Terashi et al., 1983). In the tests, the Kawasaki clay, having an initial water content of 200%, was stabilized with ordinary Portland cement with α of 15%, whose unconfined compressive strength was measured to be about 470 kN/m^2. The stabilized soil was subjected to the cyclic loading with various compressive stresses, σ_{max}, while the minimum pressure, σ_{min}, was kept constant at 0 kN/m^2. The number of cyclic loading at failure, N_f, in the logarithmic scale decreases almost linearly with the σ_{max}/q_u. The number of cyclic loading at failure, N_f, for the $\sigma_{max}/q_u = 0.6$, 0.7 and 0.8 are around 2,000 to 400,000, 150 to 30,000, and 100 to 2,000, respectively. These are similar to, but smaller than, those phenomena in Figure 3.23.

3.2.10 Tensile and bending strengths

The tensile and bending strengths of stabilized soil have been evaluated by various tests: the split tension test (Brazilian tension test, indirect tension test), the simple tension test, and the bending test. The influence of the testing method on the tensile and bending strengths were discussed in detail by Saitoh et al. (1996) and Namikawa & Koseki (2007).

The tensile and bending strengths of stabilized soil were evaluated by the split tension tests and bending tests (Terashi et al., 1980). In the tests, the Kawasaki clay (w_L of 87.8% and w_P of 39.7%), having various initial water contents, w_i, was stabilized with either quicklime or ordinary Portland cement to form a disc-shaped specimen

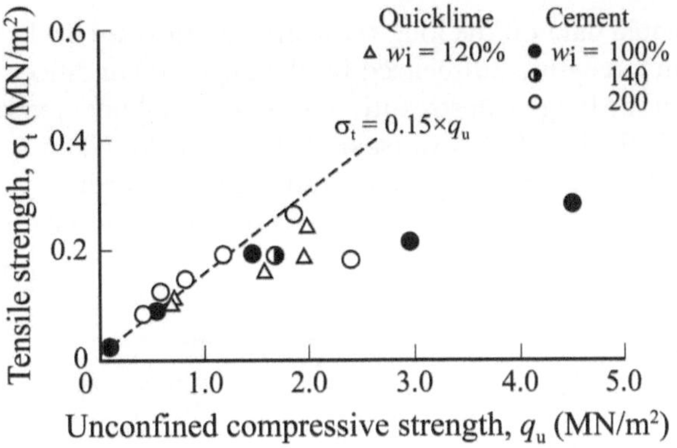

(a) Measured by split tension tests.

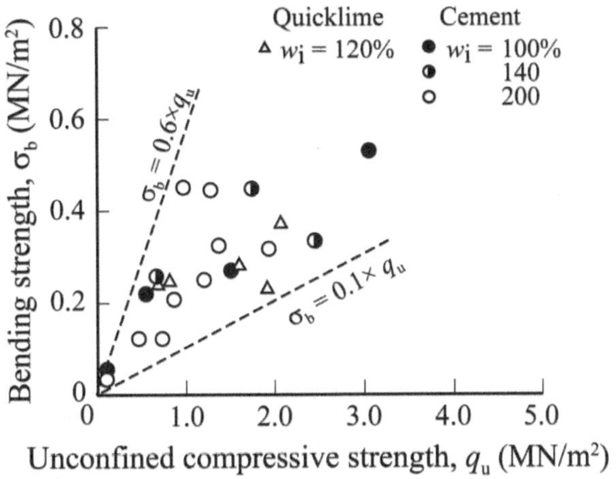

(b) Measured by bending tests.

Figure 3.25 Tensile strength of laboratory stabilized soils (Terashi et al., 1980).

of 100 mm in diameter and 50 mm in height for the split tension test and a beam with rectangular cross section of 50 mm in width, 50 mm in height and 250 mm in length for the bending test. Figure 3.25(a) shows the relationship between the tensile strength, σ_t, and the unconfined compressive strength, q_u. The figure shows the tensile strength increases almost linearly with the unconfined compressive strength, q_u, irrespective of the type, amount of binder and the initial water content of original soil, but its increment ratio becomes smaller when the q_u exceeds about 2 MN/m^2. The tensile strength is about 0.15 of the unconfined compressive strength, q_u. Figure 3.25(b) shows the relationship between the tensile strength evaluated by the bending test, σ_b, and the unconfined compressive strength, q_u. The figure shows the bending strength is around 0.1 to 0.6 of q_u irrespective of the type of binder and the initial water content of original soil.

3.2.11 Long-term strength

The accumulated data on the long-term strength in years or decades has revealed that the long-term strength is influenced by the exposed condition. Figure 3.26(a) shows an example of the long-term strength of stabilized soil under various curing conditions (Terashi et al., 1983). The Kawasaki clay (w_L of 88% and w_P of 40%), having an initial water content of 110%, was stabilized with ordinary Portland cement with a cement content, *aw*, of 10%. The stabilized soil was placed in a plastic mold of

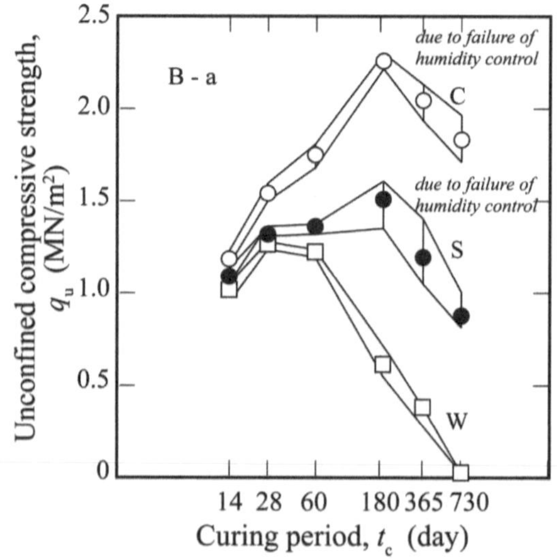

(a) The unconfined compressive strength for different curing conditions (remolded at 24 hours after mixing).

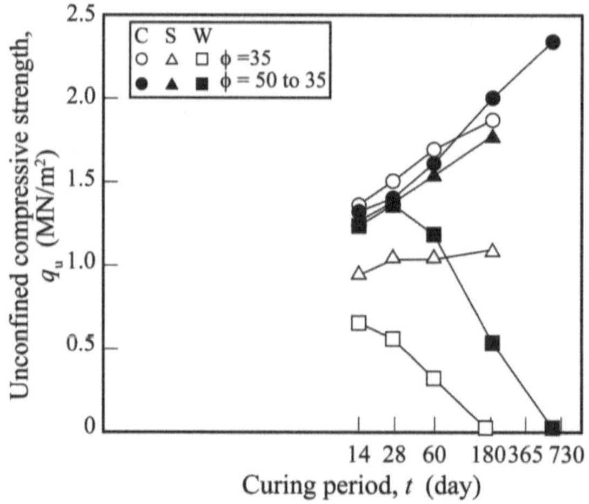

(b) Unconfined compressive strength of the centre portion of the soil sample.

Figure 3.26 The unconfined compressive strength for different curing conditions (Terashi et al., 1983).

50 mm in diameter and 100 mm in height, and retrieved from the mold at 2 hours and 24 hours after mixing, when its unconfined compressive strength was about 60 and 640 kN/m^2, respectively. The stabilized soils were cured either in a chamber with a constant temperature of 20 ° C and 100% relative humidity, embedded in the Kawasaki clay with a 120% water content, or submerged in seawater. Figure 3.26(a) shows one of the test results, where the letters, C, S and W correspond to be cured in the chamber, embedded in the soil and submerged in seawater respectively. In the case of the samples cured in the chamber, C, the strengths increase almost linearly with the curing period in a logarithmic scale (the strength decrease after 180 days was due to the failure of humidity control). In the cases of cured in the soil, S, the strengths increase at the beginning to peak strengths at 180 days (the strength decrease after 180 days was due to the failure of humidity control). In the cases of cured in the seawater, W, the strengths increase at beginning to peak strengths at 28 days and then they decrease rapidly with the curing period.

Figure 3.26(b) shows the other test result on the long-term strength under various curing conditions in order to show the influence of deterioration on the periphery of a soil sample (Terashi et al., 1983). The term, $\phi = 35$, in the graph legend indicates the stabilized soil sample of 35 mm in diameter was cured and subjected to an unconfined compression test. The term, $\phi = 50$ to 35, indicates that the soil sample of 50 mm in diameter was cured and its periphery was trimmed out to make a sample of 35 mm in diameter for the unconfined compression test. The latter case evaluates the strength of the core portion of stabilized soil. The figure shows the unconfined compressive strength of both the core and peripheral portions increase in the case of the sample cured in the chamber, C. In the case of the sample cured in the soil, S, the strength of the core portion increases at almost the same ratio as the C sample, while the strength of S – $\phi = 35$ sample increases slowly with the curing period. This means the peripheral portion of stabilized soil was deteriorated and lost the strength. In the case of the sample cured in seawater, W, the strength decreases rapidly in the both samples, $\phi = 35$ and $\phi = 50$ to 35, which means the soil sample deteriorated very severely and rapidly not only in the peripheral portion, but also the core portion of the soil.

The test data presented above have revealed that two aspects proceed at the core portion and periphery portion simultaneously as shown in Figure 3.27. One is the strength increase with time at the core portion of stabilized soil which is negligibly influenced by the surrounding conditions and the other is the possible strength decrease

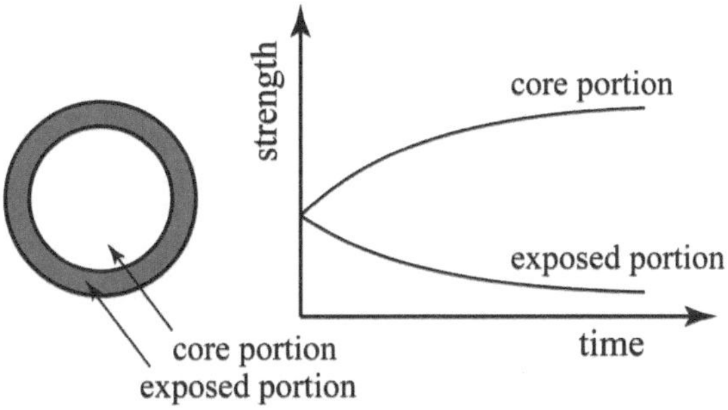

Figure 3.27 Image of long-term strength of stabilized soil.

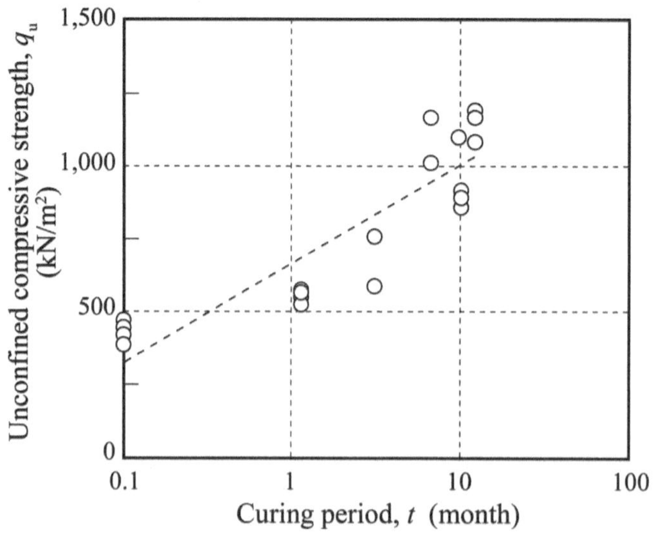

Figure 3.28 The relationship between q_u and elapsed time (Kitazume et al., 2003).

with time at the peripheral (exposed) portion of the stabilized soil column due to the deterioration that is influenced by the surrounding exposure conditions.

3.2.11.1 Long-term strength of core portion

Figure 3.28 shows an example of the long-term strength of stabilized soil with the curing period (Kitazume et al., 2003). The figure shows the relationship between the unconfined compressive strength, q_u, and the curing period on laboratory stabilized soil. In the tests, the Kawasaki marine clay (w_L of 83.4% and w_P of 38.6%) was thoroughly mixed with an initial water content of 160%, and was mixed with ordinary Portland cement with a cement content, aw, of 30% to make soil samples of 50 mm in diameter and 100 mm in height. The specimen was wrapped in a high polymer film and stored in the humid chamber at a temperature of 20°C and 95% relative humidity, which corresponds to the core portion as already shown in Figure 3.28. Figure 3.29 clearly shows the unconfined compressive strength increases almost linearly with the logarithm of the curing period.

The long-term strength increase has also been studied on the *in-situ* stabilized soils by the deep mixing method and shallow mixing method (Niina et al., 1981; Terashi & Kitazume, 1992; Niigaki et al., 2000; Hayashi et al., 2003, 2004; Ikegami et al., 2002a, 2002b, 2003, 2005; Kitazume & Takahashi, 2009). In these studies the soil specimens were core sampled from the *in-situ* stabilized soil column and trimmed for an unconfined compression test, which can be approximated to a sort of core portion. Figure 3.29 shows the relationships between the unconfined compressive strength, q_u, and the elapsed time of more than 20 years, in which several types of soil were stabilized with various types and amounts of binder. The strength of stabilized soil is highly dependent upon the type of soil, and the type and amount of binder. However,

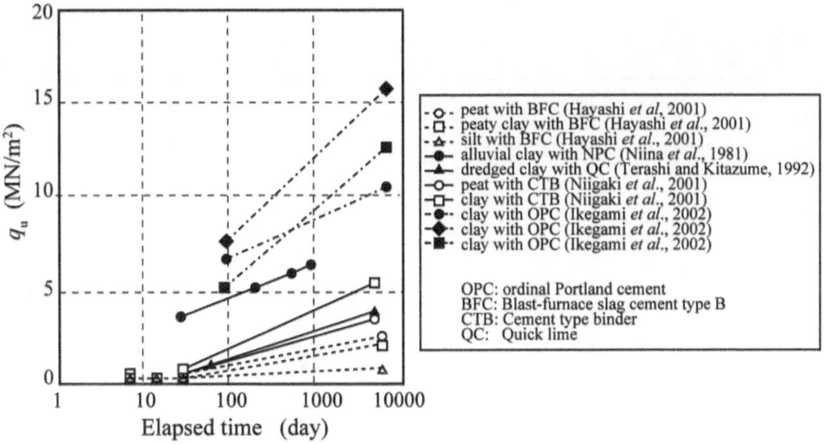

Figure 3.29 The relationship between q_u and the curing period of field situstabilized soils.

the strength of stabilized soil increases almost linearly with the logarithm of the curing period, irrespective of the type of soil, and the type and amount of binder.

The long-term strength of the stabilized soil produced by the pneumatic flow mixing method was also investigated in the Central Japan International Airport construction project (Chapter 4). As shown later in Figure 4.11, no clear change was found in the unconfined compressive strength and the water content of the stabilized soil up to 10 years' curing (Kitazume et al., 2006, Morikawa et al., 2012).

3.2.11.2 Long-term strength of the peripheral portion

(a) Strength profile within stabilized soil

Figure 3.30 shows the strength profile of laboratory cement-stabilized soil along the distance from the exposed surface (Hara et al., 2013). In the test, the Ariake clay (w_L of 158.1% and w_P of 51.4%), having an initial water content of 1.5 × w_L, was stabilized with ordinary Portland cement with a cement factor, α, of 50, 70, and 100 kg/m³. After four weeks' curing in a controlled-environment chamber, one surface of the cylindrical-shaped specimen was exposed to artificial seawater with a concentration degree of 20 g/L of sodium chloride (NaCl). The seawater was either not exchanged, or exchanged every week, during the test period. The unconfined compressive strengths at 28 days' curing, q_{u28}, for α of 50, 70 and 100 kg/m³ were 239, 657 and 1,221 kN/m², respectively. At the prescribed curing period, the strength profile of the stabilized soil was measured with the small size cone penetration test.

Figure 3.30 shows that the penetration resistance at 0 day (initial) shows the rapid increase with the penetration depth to a constant value at the depth of about 10 mm irrespective of the cement factor. The resistance at the deep portion increases with the curing period, which indicates the increase in the soil strength at the core portion. At the shallow depth portion, on the other hand, the penetration resistance is quite small irrespective of the cement factor and the test condition. The deterioration depth, which is defined as the depth where the penetration resistance increases quickly,

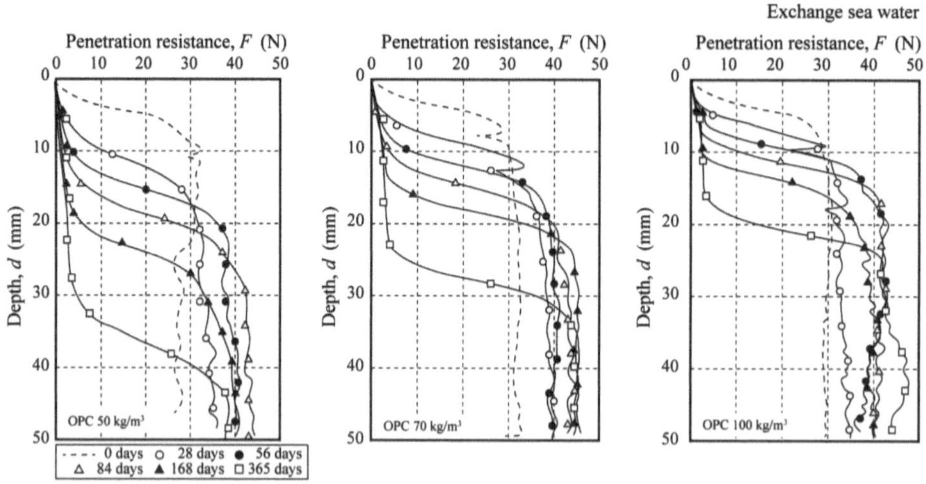

(a) With exchange of sea water.

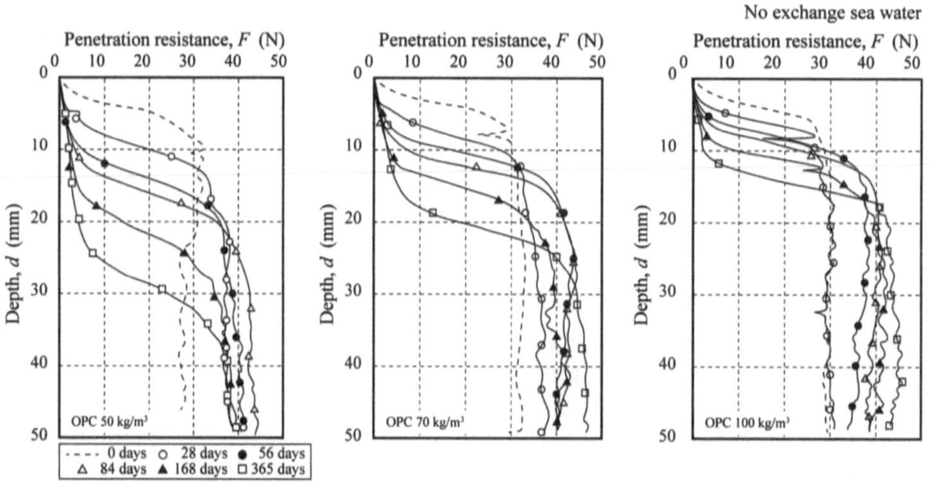

(b) Without exchange of sea water.

Figure 3.30 Spatial strength distribution in samples of laboratory-produced stabilized soils (Hara et al., 2013).

becomes larger with the curing period. The deterioration depth becomes large with decreasing cement factor.

The effect of exposed conditions on the long-term strength was discussed in laboratory tests by Kitazume et al. (2003), where the Kawasaki clay (w_L of 83.4% and w_P of 38.6%) stabilized with ordinary Portland cement, was exposed to either tap water, seawater or clay. A specimen wrapped in sealant was also prepared and cured for reference. At the prescribed curing period, the strength profile of stabilized soil was measured by the needle penetration test. In the cases of exposure to tap water

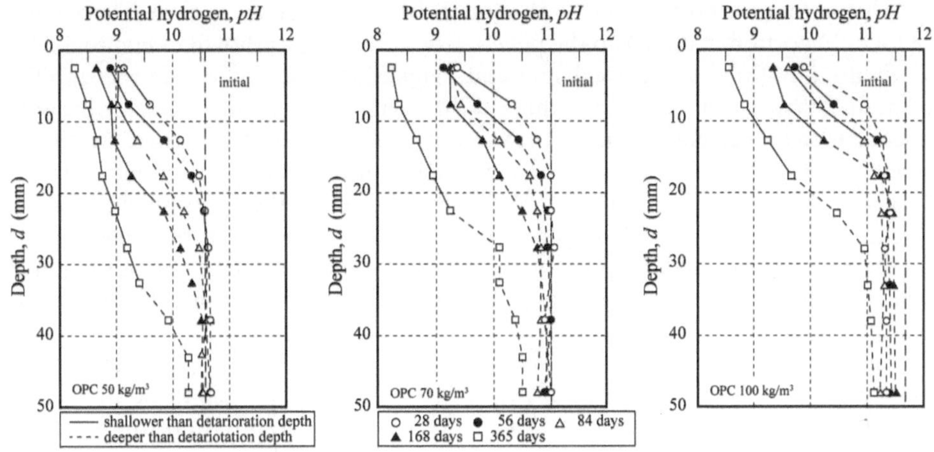

(a) Potential hydrogen profile.

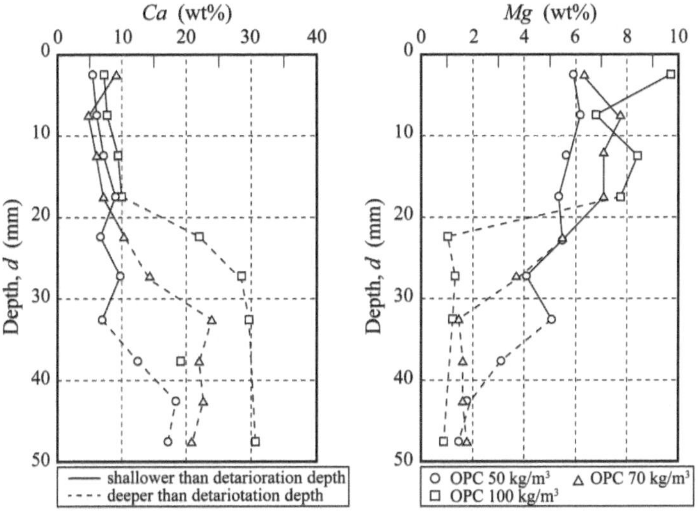

(b) Calcium and magnesium profiles.

Figure 3.31 Potential hydrogen, calcium and magnesium distributions in stabilized soil (Hara et al., 2013).

and seawater, the strength of stabilized soil close to the exposed surface decreased very rapidly and the deterioration progressed gradually inward with increasing curing period. However, in the case of exposure to clay, negligible strength decrease in the specimen was found, even after twelve months' exposure.

(b) Potential hydrogen, pH, calcium and magnesium profiles within stabilized soil

Figure 3.31(a) shows the potential hydrogen, pH, profile within the stabilized soil (Hara et al., 2013). The pH value is about 10.5 to 11.5 at the core portion, and increases with the cement factor. The pH value at the periphery (deterioration portion) is smaller than that at the core portion, and is about 8 to 10 at the exposed surface. The extent of the low pH portion is similar to the penetration resistance as shown in Figure 3.31(a).

Figure 3.31(b) shows the calcium and magnesium distributions in the stabilized soil at 365 days' curing. The Ca^{2+} value at the deep portion shows a large value and is dependent on the cement factor, but the value at the shallow portion is small irrespective the cement factor, which indicates that the Ca^{2+} in the stabilized soil elutes to 5 to 10% with the curing period. The Mg^{2+} distribution shows the opposite phenomenon, where the Mg^{2+} value at the deep portion is small irrespective of the cement factor, but the value at the shallow portion is large and its magnitude is dependent on the cement factor. These phenomena are consistent with the penetration resistance profile as shown in Figure 3.31.

The long-term strength of *in-situ* stabilized soil was investigated in detail at Yokohama Port (Ikegami et al., 2002a, 2002b, 2003, 2005). The thick alluvial clay ground was improved by the wet method of deep mixing method (Kitazume & Terashi, 2013) with ordinary Portland cement of 180 kg/m^3. Figure 3.32(a) shows the strength and calcium content distributions in the cement-stabilized soil after 20 years' curing in the ground (Ikegami et al., 2002a, 2002b). The horizontal axis of the figure is the horizontal distance from the exposed surface in logarithmic scale. The strength in terms of unconfined compressive strength shown in the upper half of the figure was estimated, based on the needle penetration test. The calcium content shown in the lower half of the figure was measured in sliced core samples by means of atomic adsorption spectrometry. The overall pattern of strength and calcium content distributions are in good agreement each other except for the large calcium content found at 5 to 10 mm from the exposed surface. Figure 3.32(b) shows the calcium content distribution across the exposed surface between stabilized soil and original soil (Ikegami et al, 2005). The calcium content in the stabilized soil decreases toward the exposed surface, and that in the original soil increases toward the exposed surface. The overall pattern of calcium content suggests that the calcium leaching from the stabilized soil to the original soil is the dominating phenomenon which caused the deterioration at the periphery.

(c) Deterioration depth

Figure 3.33 shows the relationship between the deterioration depth and curing period (Hara et al., 2013). The soil and mixing condition are the same as in Figure 3.30. The deterioration depth increases with the curing period, irrespective of the cement factor and test conditions. The deterioration speed is larger in the low cement factor soil than in the high cement factor soil.

Figure 3.34 compares the depth of deterioration with the curing period (Ikegami et al., 2002a, 2002b). In the figure, the *in-situ* stabilized soil by the deep mixing method at Daikoku Pier and the laboratory exposure test results by Terashi et al. (1983), Saitoh (1988), Kitazume et al. (2003) and Hayashi et al. (2004) are plotted together. The strength, q_{u28}, in the legend of the figure is the unconfined compressive strength of stabilized soil after 28 days' curing under the sealed condition. The progress of deterioration depth in logarithmic scale is almost linear to the curing period in logarithmic scale, and the gradients of all the test cases are about 1/2 irrespective

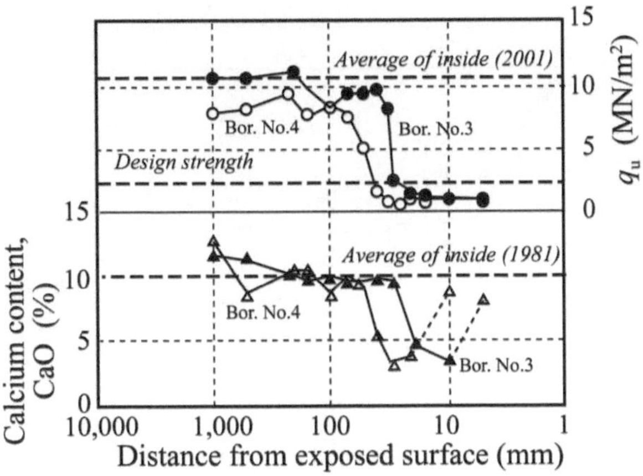

(a) Strength and calcium content distribution in stabilized soil.

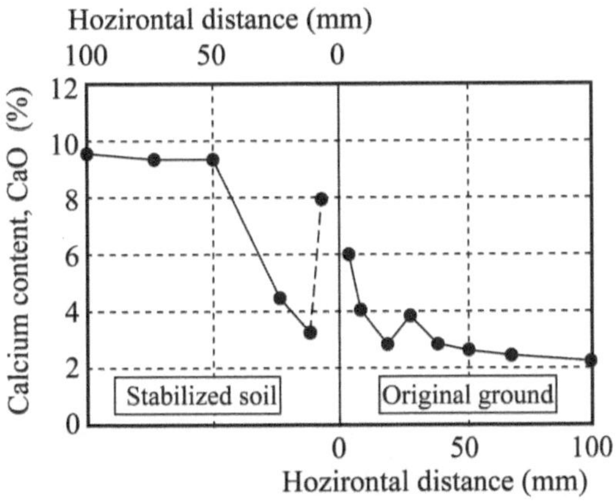

(b) Calcium content distribution in both stabilized soil and original soil.

Figure 3.32 The long-term strength and calcium content in *in-situ* stabilized soil (Ikegami et al., 2002a, 2002b, 2005).

of the strength of soil and exposure condition, which means the rate of deterioration is proportional to the square root of time. A similar relationship between the depth of deterioration and time was also obtained by a numerical simulation proposed by Nishida et al. (2003) that assumed ions' migration primarily based on diffusion by the Ca concentration gradient. Judging from the results of laboratory tests and the numerical analysis, it may be possible to predict long-term deterioration by extrapolation of the short-term result of the exposure test assuming the deterioration progress is in proportion to a square root of time. General tendency found in Figure 3.34 is that the larger the strength the smaller the depth of deterioration and seawater exposure gives rise to larger depth of deterioration compared to tap water exposure or contact to original soil.

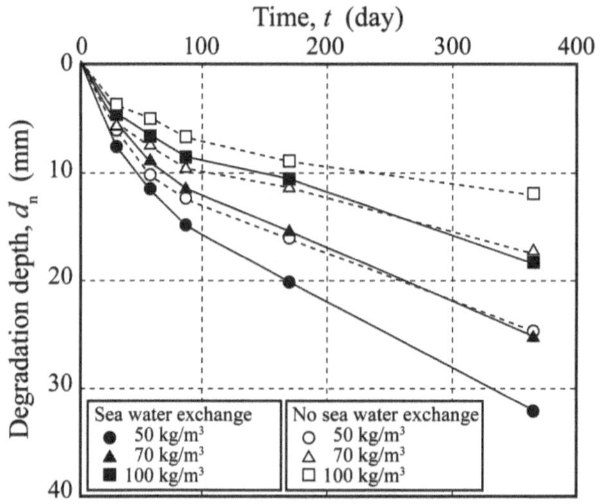

Figure 3.33 The relationship between deterioration depth and curing period (Hara et al., 2013).

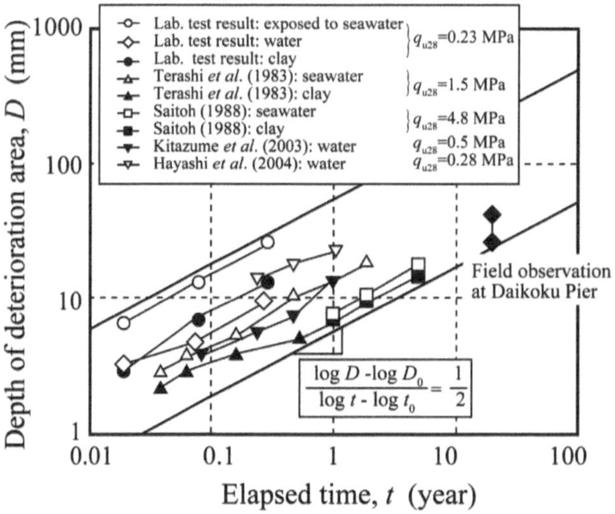

Figure 3.34 Measured extension of deterioration with elapsed time (Ikegami et al., 2005).

3.2.12 *Coefficient of horizontal stress at rest*

Figure 3.35 shows the coefficient of horizontal earth pressure and axial strain in an anisotropically (K_0) consolidation test (Coastal Development Institute of Technology, 2008). Marine clay at Nagoya Port (w_L of 74.9% and w_P of 31.6%) was prepared to have an initial water content of 107% and stabilized with blast furnace slag cement

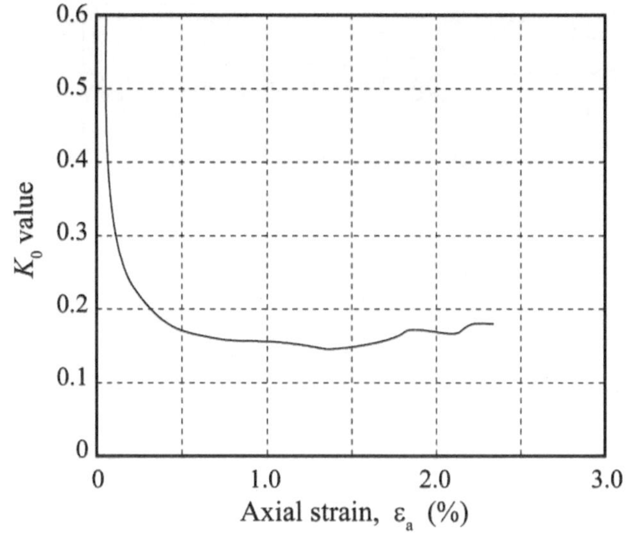

Figure 3.35 The coefficient of horizontal stress at rest (Coastal Development Institute of Technology, 2008).

with α of 60 kg/m^3 by the pneumatic flow mixing method in the field. The stabilized soil was core sampled at 28 days' curing. In the laboratory test, the soil sample was consolidated isotropically with a consolidation pressure of 10 kN/m^2 at first, and then was consolidated anisotropically (K_0 consolidation) with an axial consolidation pressure of 200 kN/m^2. The coefficient of horizontal stress at rest, K_0 value obtained in the test is about 0.15.

3.3 Mechanical properties (consolidation characteristics)

3.3.1 *Void ratio – consolidation pressure curve and consolidation yield pressure*

Figure 3.36(a) shows the void ratio, e, and the consolidation pressure, p, of field cement-stabilized soils (Ministry of Transport, The Fifth District Port Construction Bureau, 1999). Marine clay excavated at Nagoya Port (w_L of 74.4% and w_P of 33.0%) was stabilized with ordinary Portland cement of various cement factors by the pneumatic flow mixing method and cured in the field. The stabilized soil, after core sampling, was trimmed to 60 mm in diameter and 20 mm in height and subjected to the oedometer test. For the large scale sample, the fresh stabilized soil was sampled at the outlet of the placement machine and molded to a consolidation cell of 300 mm in diameter and 100 mm in height and cured in a laboratory. The e-$\log p$ curves of the oedometer test on the stabilized soils with C = 0 kg/m^3 (original soil) and C = 38 kg/m^3 show an almost linear relationship without clear bending points, consolidation yield pressure. In the cases of the oedometer test with C = 57 and 68 kg/m^3, a clear consolidation yield pressure can be seen and its magnitude is dependent on the cement factor.

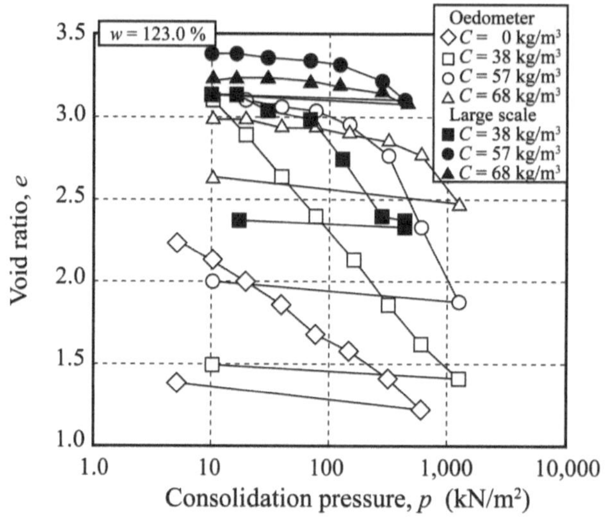

(a) *E*-log *p* curve.

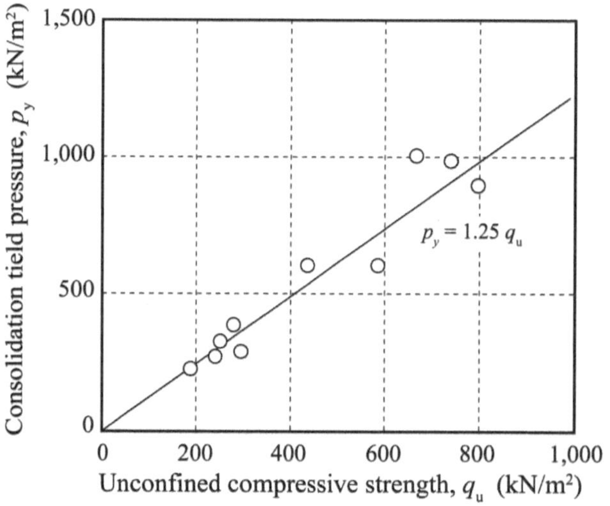

(b) Relationship between the consolidation yield pressure, p_y, and unconfined compressive strength, q_u.

Figure 3.36 The e-log *p* curve, and consolidation yield pressure (Ministry of Transport, The Fifth District Port Construction Bureau, 1999).

In the cases of the large scale samples, a clear consolidation yield pressure can be seen even in the stabilized soil with $C = 38\ kg/m^3$. A similar phenomenon was obtained with several types of soil and binder (Terashi et al., 1980, Kawasaki et al., 1978, Takahashi & Kitazume, 2004).

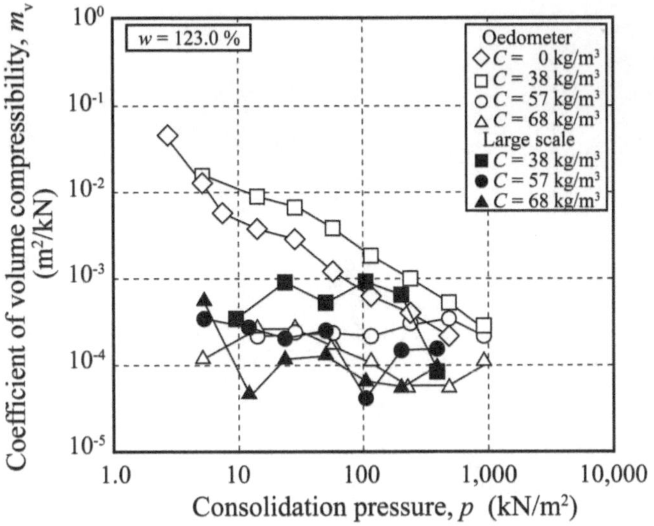

Figure 3.37 The relationship between the coefficient of volume compressibility and consolidation pressure (Ministry of Transport, The Fifth District Port Construction Bureau, 1999).

Figure 3.36(b) shows the relationship between the consolidation yield pressure, p_y, and the unconfined compressive strength, q_u, of the Nagoya Port clay (w_L of 74.4% and w_P of 33.0%) stabilized with ordinary Portland cement (Ministry of Transport, The Fifth District Port Construction Bureau, 1999). The figure shows that the consolidation yield pressure, p_y, has a linear relationship with the unconfined compressive strength, q_u. The ratio of p_y/q_u of the stabilized soils is 1.25. A similar phenomenon was obtained on several types of soil and binder, where the ratio of p_y/q_u is about 1.25 to 1.55 irrespective of the types of original soil and binder (Terashi et al., 1980, Kawasaki et al., 1978, Takahashi & Kitazume, 2004).

3.3.2 *Coefficient of volume compressibility*

Figure 3.37 shows the coefficient of volume compressibility of the stabilized soil, m_v (Ministry of Transport, The Fifth District Port Construction Bureau, 1999). Marine clay excavated at Nagoya Port (w_L of 74.4% and w_P of 33.0%) was stabilized with ordinary Portland cement of various cement factors and cured in the field. The testing procedure and conditions are the same as those in Figure 3.37. The figure indicates that the coefficient of volume compressibility of the stabilized soils, m_{vs}, slightly decreases with the consolidation pressure, p, except in the case of the oedometer test on the sample of stabilized soil with C = 38 kg/m^3. In the case of the oedometer test of C = 38 kg/m^3, the m_v decreases rapidly with the consolidation pressure and its decrease is very similar to that of the original soil.

Figure 3.38 shows the other relationship between the coefficient of volume compressibility of stabilized soils, m_{vs}, and the consolidation pressure, p (Terashi

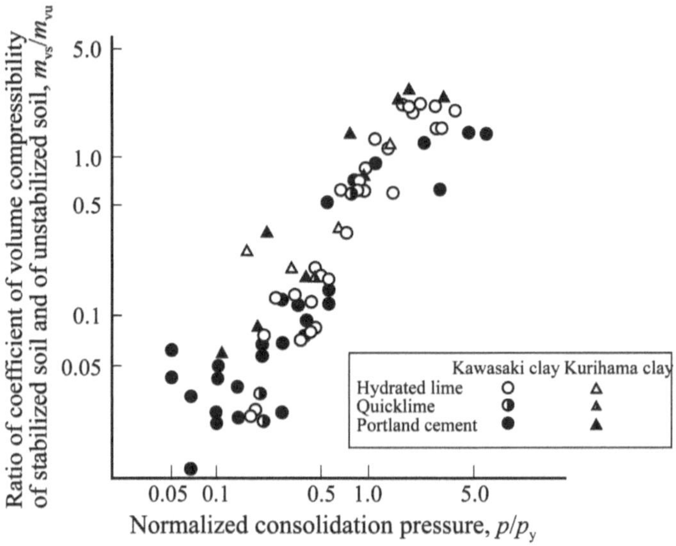

Figure 3.38 The relationship between the coefficient of volume compressibility and consolidation pressure on laboratory stabilized soils (Terashi et al., 1980).

et al., 1980). In the tests, a series of one-dimensional consolidation tests on the stabilized and unstabilized soils were carried out under a wide range of consolidation pressures. Two marine clays, the Kawasaki clay (w_L of 87.7% and w_P of 39.7%) and the Kurihama clay (w_L of 70.9% and w_P of 30.8%), were stabilized either with hydrated lime, quicklime or ordinary Portland cement. The size of soil samples was 20 mm in thickness and 60 mm in diameter. The coefficient of volume compressibility, m_{vs}, was normalized by that of the original soil, m_{vu}, at the same consolidation pressure and is shown on the vertical axis. The consolidation pressure, p, is also normalized by the consolidation yield pressure of the stabilized soil, p_y, and shown on the horizontal axis. The figure shows the ratio of m_{vs}/m_{vu} is 0.01 to 0.1 as long as the normalized consolidation pressure, p/p_y is around 0.1, but the m_{vs}/m_{vu} increases to unity at the p/p_y of 1.

3.3.3 *Coefficient of consolidation*

Figure 3.39 shows the relationship between the coefficient of consolidation of stabilized soil, c_{vs}, and the consolidation pressure, p (Ministry of Transport, The Fifth District Port Construction Bureau, 1999). The test conditions are the same as those in Figure 3.37. The c_{vs} of the stabilized soil decreases gradually with the consolidation pressure, while the c_{vu} of the unstabilized soil increases gradually. The figure shows the c_{vs} value is about 10 to 100 time larger than that of unstabilized soil as long as the consolidation pressure is small, but the c_v becomes almost the same as that of the stabilized soil when the consolidation pressure becomes large, of the order of 1,000 kN/m^2.

Figure 3.40 shows the relationship between the coefficient of consolidation of the stabilized clays, c_{vs}, and the consolidation pressure, p (Terashi et al., 1980). The test

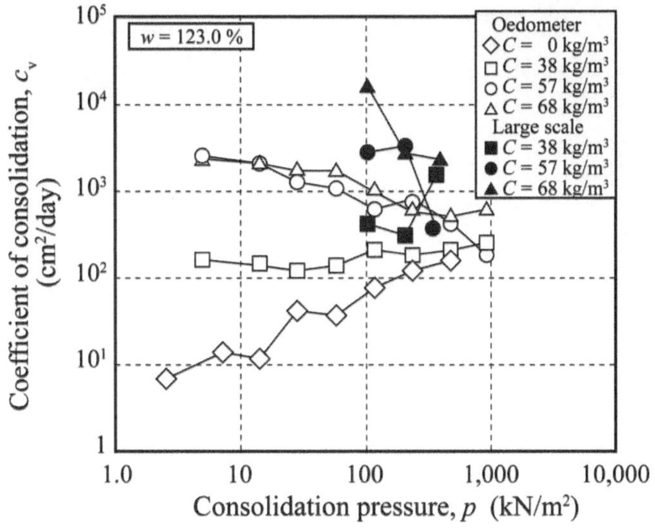

Figure 3.39 The relationship between the coefficient of consolidation and consolidation pressure on laboratory stabilized soils (Ministry of Transport, The Fifth District Port Construction Bureau, 1999).

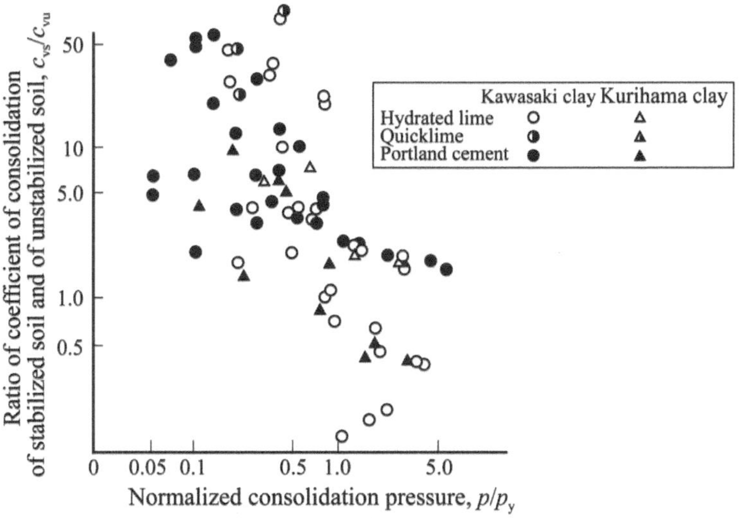

Figure 3.40 The relationship between the coefficient of consolidation and consolidation pressure on laboratory stabilized soils (Terashi et al., 1980).

conditions are the same as those in Figure 3.36. Similar to Figure 3.38, the coefficient of consolidation of the stabilized soil, c_{vs}, is normalized by that of the unstabilized soil, c_{vu}, at the same consolidation pressure, and the consolidation pressure, p, is also normalised by the consolidation yield pressure of the stabilized soil, p_y. The figure shows the ratio of c_{vs}/c_{vu} is 10 to 100 as long as the normalised consolidation pressure,

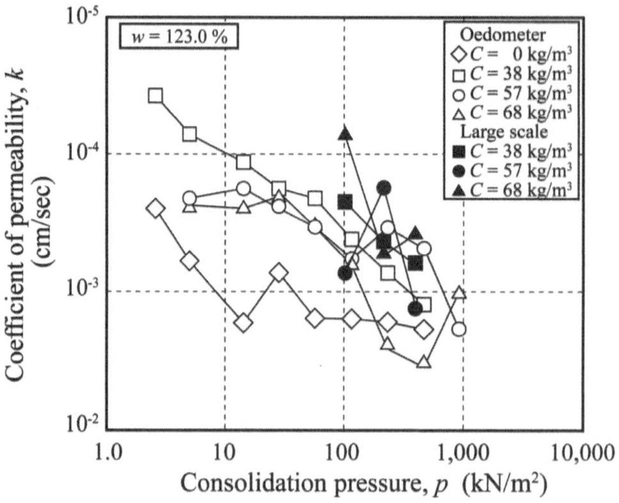

Figure 3.41 The relationship between permeability and consolidation pressure of laboratory stabilized soils (Ministry of Transport, The Fifth District Port Construction Bureau, 1999).

p/p_y is around 0.1, in a sort of over-consolidated condition, but the c_{vs}/c_{vu} approaches to unity at the p/p_y of 1, c_{vs}/c_{vu}, 1 when p/p_y exceeds 1.

3.3.4 *Coefficient of permeability*

Figure 3.41 shows the relationship between the coefficient of permeability of stabilized soil, k, and the consolidation pressure, p, which was measured in the oedometer test (Ministry of Transport, The Fifth District Port Construction Bureau, 1999). The soil preparation is the same as that in Figure 3.36. The k value of the unstabilized soil is the order of around 10^{-8} to 10^{-7} cm/s and slightly decreases with increasing consolidation pressure. In the cases of the stabilized soils, the k value is larger than that of unstabilized soil when the consolidation pressure is small, but the k decreases with the consolidation pressure and becomes almost same as the unstabilized soil when the consolidation pressure becomes large, of the order of 1,000 kN/m^2.

Figure 3.42 shows the coefficient of permeability of the stabilized Kawasaki clay (w_L of 87.7% and w_P of 39.7%) with ordinary Portland cement with the cement content, aw of 5, 10 and 15%, in which the coefficient of permeability is plotted against the water content of the stabilized soils (Terashi et al., 1983). In the tests, the stabilized soil specimens, 20 mm in height and 50 mm in thickness, were subjected to the constant head permeability tests. The figure shows that the coefficient of permeability is dependent upon the water content of stabilized soil and the amount of cement. The coefficient of permeability of the stabilized soil decreases with decreasing water content and with increasing amount of cement.

Figure 3.43 shows the relationship between the coefficient of permeability and the strength of laboratory stabilized soil (Terashi et al., 1983). The coefficient of permeability of the stabilized soil decreases exponentially with increasing strength, q_u.

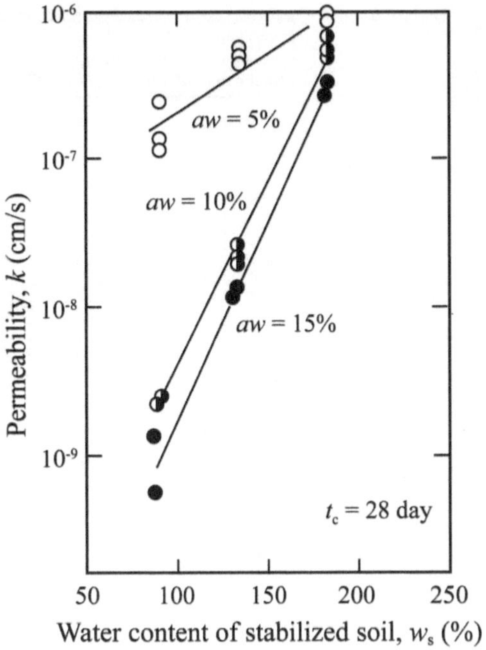

Figure 3.42 The relationship between the coefficient of permeability and water content of cement-stabilized soils (Terashi et al., 1983).

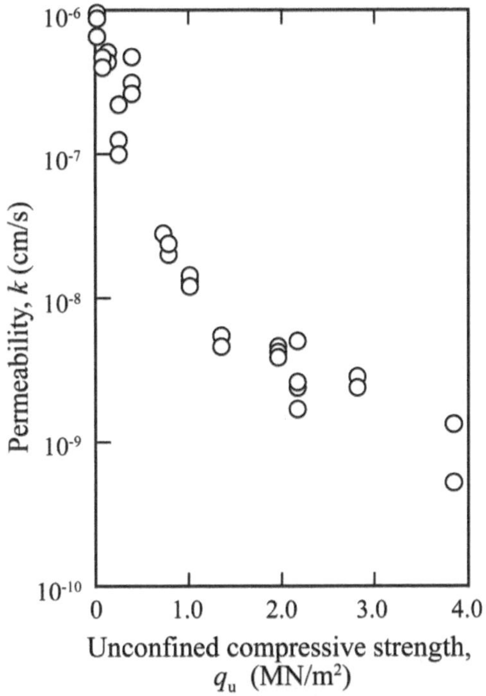

Figure 3.43 The relationship between the coefficient of permeability and the unconfined compressive strength of stabilized soil (Terashi et al., 1983).

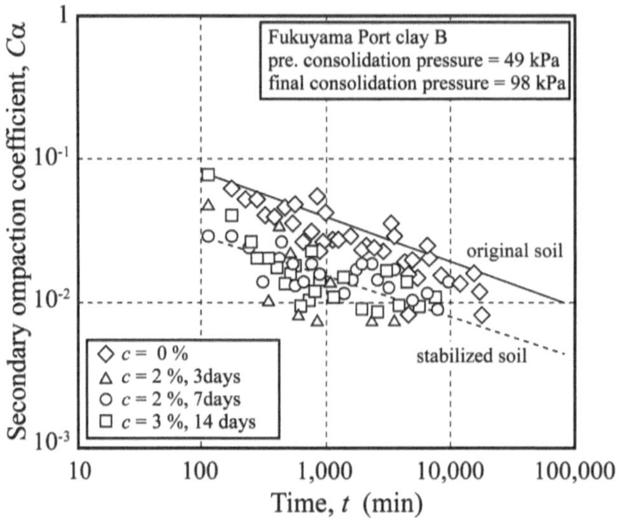

Figure 3.44 Secondary compression coefficient of stabilized soil (afterUdaka et al., 2013).

The relationship between the coefficient of permeability and the void ratio was discussed by Takahahi & Kitazume (2004) and Onitsuka et al. (2003). The influence of grain size distribution on the coefficient of permeability was discussed by Miura et al. (2004).

3.3.5 *Secondary compression*

Figure 3.44 shows the secondary compression coefficient, C_α, with the consolidation time (Udaka et al., 2013). In the test, the Fukuyama Port clay was mixed throughout to an initial water content of $1.5 \times w_L$ and mixed with ordinary Portland cement with a cement content, *aw*, of 7.0 or 8.0%, while the W/C ratio of cement slurry was 100%. The stabilized soil mixture was poured in the consolidation mold, 120 mm in diameter and 250 mm in height, and subjected to the pre-consolidation one dimensionally under the consolidation pressure of 49 kN/m^2 for 3, 7 or 14 days. The soil sample was finally subjected to the consolidation pressure of 98 kN/m^2 for the long-term consolidation test. The secondary compression coefficients, C_α, of the stabilized soil and original soil decrease almost linearly with the logarithm of consolidation time, and the coefficient of the stabilized soil is about 1/3 to 1/2 of the original soil. The figure also shows the stabilized soil with *aw* of 7% and subjected to 3 days' pre-consolidation shows the lowest C_α value, which may be due to the hydration effect during the long-term consolidation.

3.4 Environmental properties

3.4.1 *Elution of contaminant*

The Soil Contamination Countermeasures Act (Environment Agency, 1975, 2005) was enforced by the Ministry of Environment of the Japanese government in 2005, in order

Table 3.1 Soil elution criterion and second elution criterion designated by the Soil Contamination Countermeasures Act, 1975, 2005.

Hazardous substance	*Soil elution criterion (mg/l)*	*Second elution criterion (mg/l)*
Cadmium	0.01	0.3
Lead	0.01	0.3
Hexavalent chromium	0.05	1.5
Arsenic	0.01	0.3
Mercury	0.0005	0.005
Selenium	0.01	0.3
Fluorine	0.8	24
Boron	1	30
Trichloroethylene	0.01	0.3

to facilitate the implementation of countermeasures against soil contamination and measures for the prevention of harmful effects on human health, and thereby to protect the health of its citizens. In the Act, 26 chemical substances, including lead, arsenic, and trichloroethylene are a 'Designated Hazardous Substance' which can have harmful effects on human health (Table 3.1). The Act designates that not only natural soils but also stabilized soils shall be subjected to soil contamination investigation to measure the content and elution amount of the substances and report them to the governor. Four regulated values are designated in the Act, of which 'soil elution criterion' and 'second elution criterion' are the critical concerns for excavation and filling soils. The former is designated by the Minister of the Environment for the 'Designated Areas'. When the situation of contamination of the soil at a site by a Designated Hazardous Substance does not conform to the criteria, the prefectural governor shall designate an area covering such a site as an area contaminated by the Designated Hazardous Substance. The soils in the 'Designated Areas' should be stabilized by *in-situ* insolubility, *in-situ* confinement or confinement by an impermeable wall.

The effects of stabilization on the leaching of hazardous substances were investigated by a series of laboratory leaching tests, where five soils artificially contaminated by the eight chemical reagents designated as 'Designated Hazardous Substances' were prepared and stabilized with a cement-based special binder (Kaneshiro et al., 2006). The properties of the soils and the chemical reagents are summarised in Tables 3.2 and 3.3, respectively. The stabilized soils were prepared by the procedure specified by the Japan Cement Association (JCAS L-1: 2006), which is almost the same as the Japanese Geotechnical Society standard (2009). After 7 days' curing, the leaching tests were carried out on the specimens according to the testing procedure specified by the environmental Quality Standards (Environment Agency, 1975), where the stabilized soil was crushed into pieces, sieved through a 2 mm sieve and dried naturally in advance of the tests.

Figure 3.45 shows the leaching test results on the eight hazardous substances shown in Table 3.3. For cadmium leaching from the stabilized soil (Figure 3.45(a)), the amount of cadmium leaching quickly decreases with an increasing cement factor and becomes lower than the detection limit for all the stabilized soils. For lead leaching

Table 3.2 Physical properties of the stabilized soils tested for leaching of hazardous substances (Kaneshiro et al., 2006).

	Water content (%)	*Density (g/cm^3)*	*pH*	*Particle size distribution (%)*			*Classification*
				Gravel	*Sand*	*Fine*	
Sand (1)	34	1.849	3.88	0.0	53.4	46.6	SF
Sand (2)	20	1.742	–	0.3	89.4	10.3	S-Cs
Clay (1)	61	1.718	7.18	0.6	2.0	97.4	CH
Clay (2)	40	1.776	–	0.0	0.0	100.0	CH
Volcanic soil	88	1.393	6.16	1.7	5.8	92.5	VH2

Table 3.3 Chemical reagents mixed with the stabilized soils tested for leaching of hazardous substances.

Hazardous substance	Chemical substance	Chemical formula
Cadmium	Cadmium nitrate	$Cd(NO_3)_2.4H_2O$
Lead	Lead(II) nitrate	$Pb(NO_3)_2$
Hexavalent chromium	Potassium dichromate	$K_2Cr_2O_7$
Arsenic	Disodium hydrogenarsenate	$Na_2HAsO_4.7H_2O$, $KAsO_2$
Mercury	Mercuric chloride	$HgCl_2$
Selenium	Sodium selenite	Na_2SeO_4
Fluorine	Potassium fluoride	$KF.2H_2O$
Boron	Sodium metaborate	$NaBO_2.4H_2O$
Trichloroethylene	Trichloroethylene	C_2HCl_3

(Figure 3.45(b)), the amount of leaching decreases and becomes lower than the detection limit for all the stabilized soils when the cement factor is larger than 100 kg/m^3 and cured for 28 days. For the leaching of hexavalent chromium (Figure 3.45(c)), the amounts of leaching decrease only slightly with the cement factor, and the improvement effect varies depending upon the type of soil. For leaching of arsenic (Figure 3.45(d)), the amount of leaching is variable for soil type: it is decreased by the stabilization for sand (2) and clay (2). For the leaching of mercury (Figure 3.45(e)), the amounts of leaching decrease rapidly as long as the cement factor is about 100 kg/m^3, but increases with a further increase in the cement factor. This phenomenon can be seen especially in the volcanic soil. For the leaching of selenium (Figure 3.45(f)), the amounts of leaching decrease very slightly, even if the cement factor increases to 300 kg/m^3. For the leaching of fluorine and boron (Figures 3.45(g) and 3.45(h)), the amounts of leaching are variable depending on soil type: there is a decrease by stabilization for sand (1) and clay (1) but only a slight decrease for volcanic soil.

According to the test results, the improvement effect by admixture stabilization is variable depending upon the type of soil and type of substances. A high improvement effect is achieved for cadmium and lead where the amount of leaching can be reduced lower than the soil elution criteria, as defined by the Act. For the other substances, the effect of stabilization is variable depending upon the type of soil and the amount of binder.

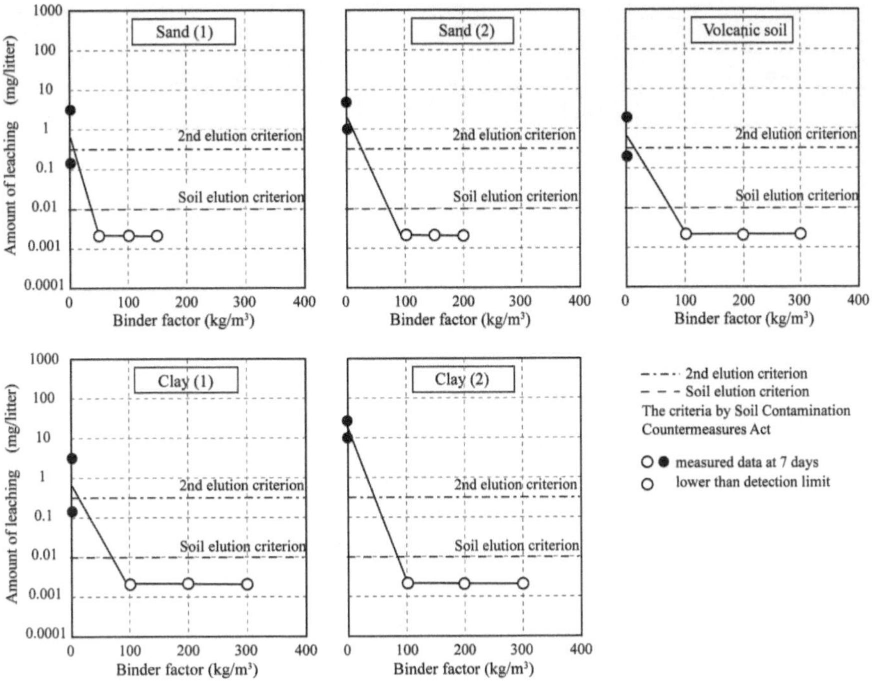

(a) Relationship between the amount of leaching and the cement factor (cadmium).

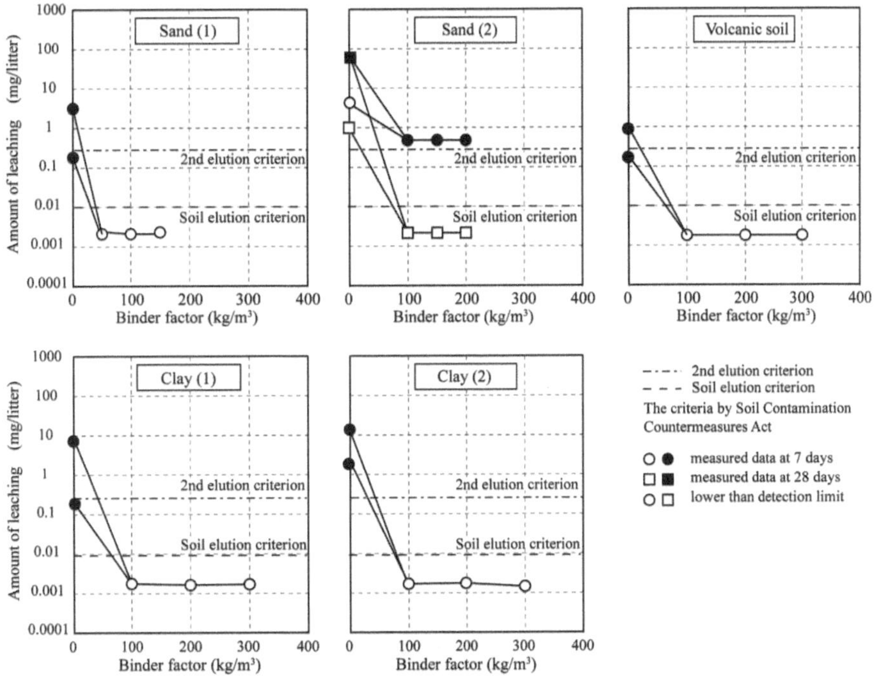

(b) Relationship between the amount of leaching and the cement factor (lead).

Figure 3.45 The effect of cement stabilization on leaching of hazardous substances from different soil types (Kaneshiro et al., 2006).

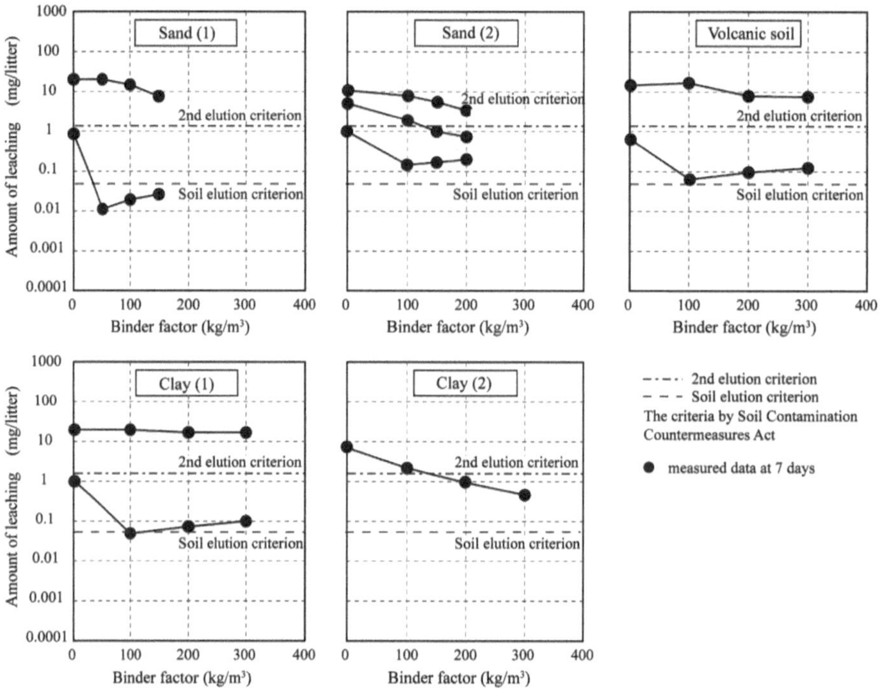

(c) Relationship between the amount of leaching and the cement factor (hexavalent chromium).

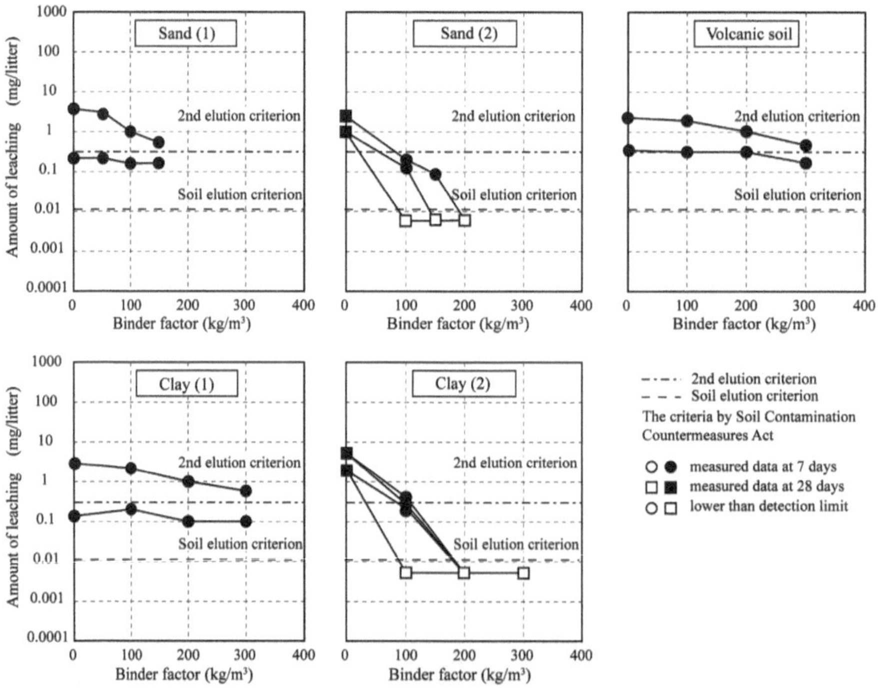

(d) Relationship between the amount of leaching and the cement factor (arsenic).

Figure 3.45 (Continued).

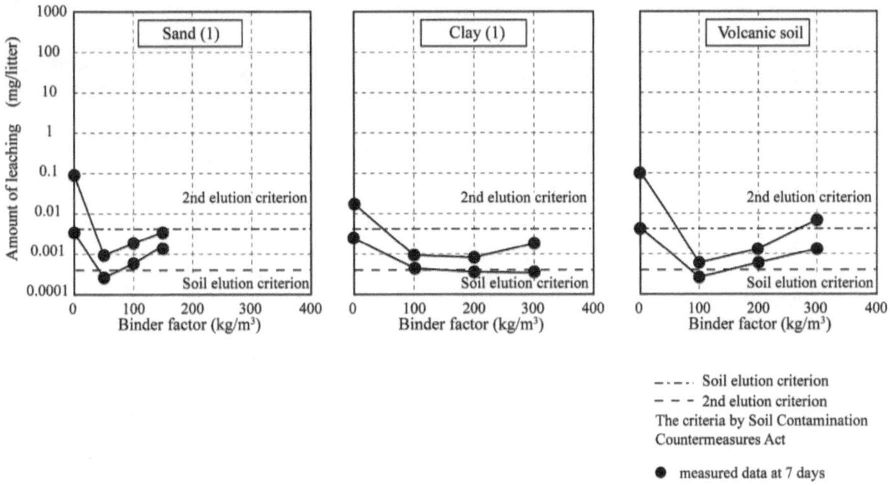

(e) Relationship between the amount of leaching and the cement factor (mercury).

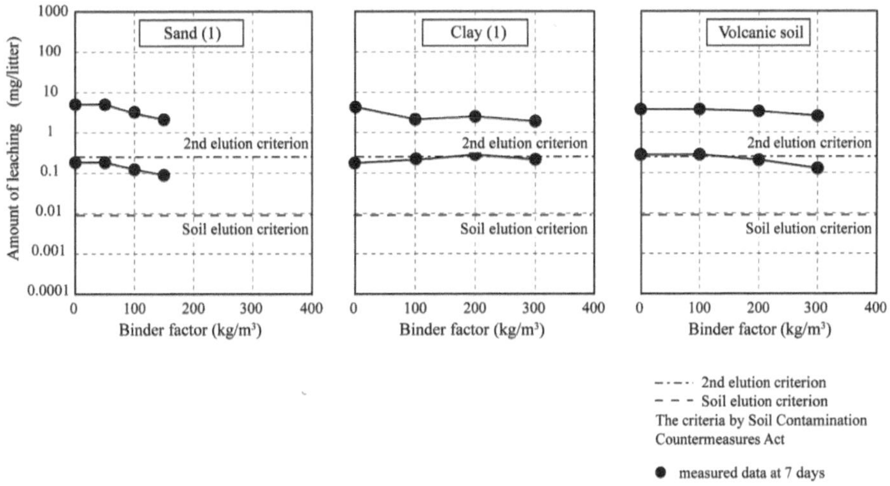

(f) Relationship between the amount of leaching and the cement factor (selenium).

Figure 3.45 (Continued).

3.4.2 Elution of hexavalent chromium (chromium VI) from stabilized soil

Figure 3.46 shows the influence of the type of binder on the elution of hexavalent chromium (chromium VI) from stabilized soils (Hosoya, 2002). In the tests, six soils including two sandy soils, two cohesive soils and two volcanic cohesive soils, were stabilized with four types of binder: ordinary Portland cement, blast furnace slag cement type B, and two cement-based special binders. The leaching tests were carried out on the stabilized soils according to the testing procedure specified by the

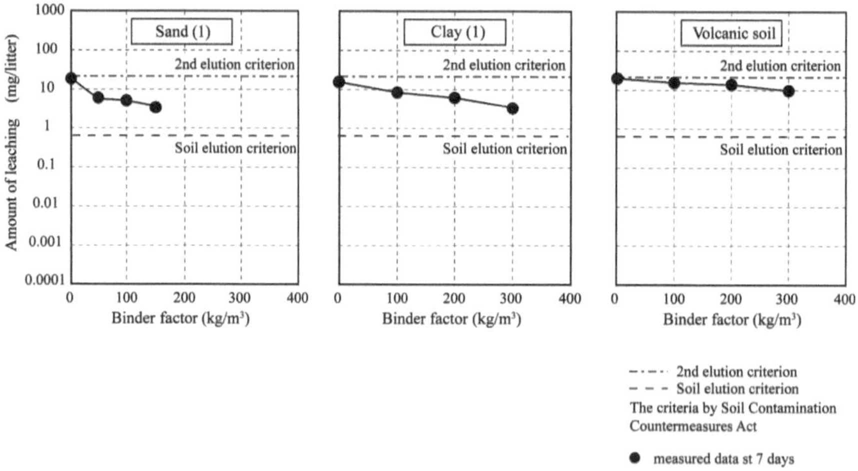

(g) Relationship between the amount of leaching and the cement factor (fluorine).

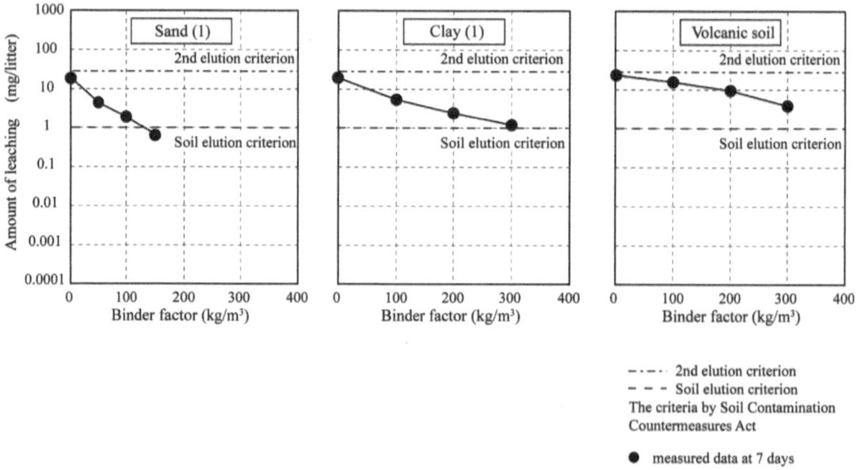

(h) Relationship between the amount of leaching and the cement factor (boron).

Figure 3.45 (Continued).

environmental quality standards (Environment Agency, 1975) and the amount of hexavalent chromium was measured by the ultrasonic extraction-diphenylcarbazide colorimetry specified by the Japanese Industrial Standard (Japan Industrial Standard, 2010). The time difference after adding sulphuric acid to diphenylcarbazide is changed: it is either 1 minute (DC1min) or 5 minutes (DC5min). The broken lines in Figure 3.46 corresponds to 0.05 mg/*l*, which is the soil elution criterion specified by the Japanese Ministry of Environment. The measured elution amounts of Cr(VI) are the total amount eluted from not only the original soil but also the binder. The measured value increases with the cement factor in some cases. The stabilized soils with the

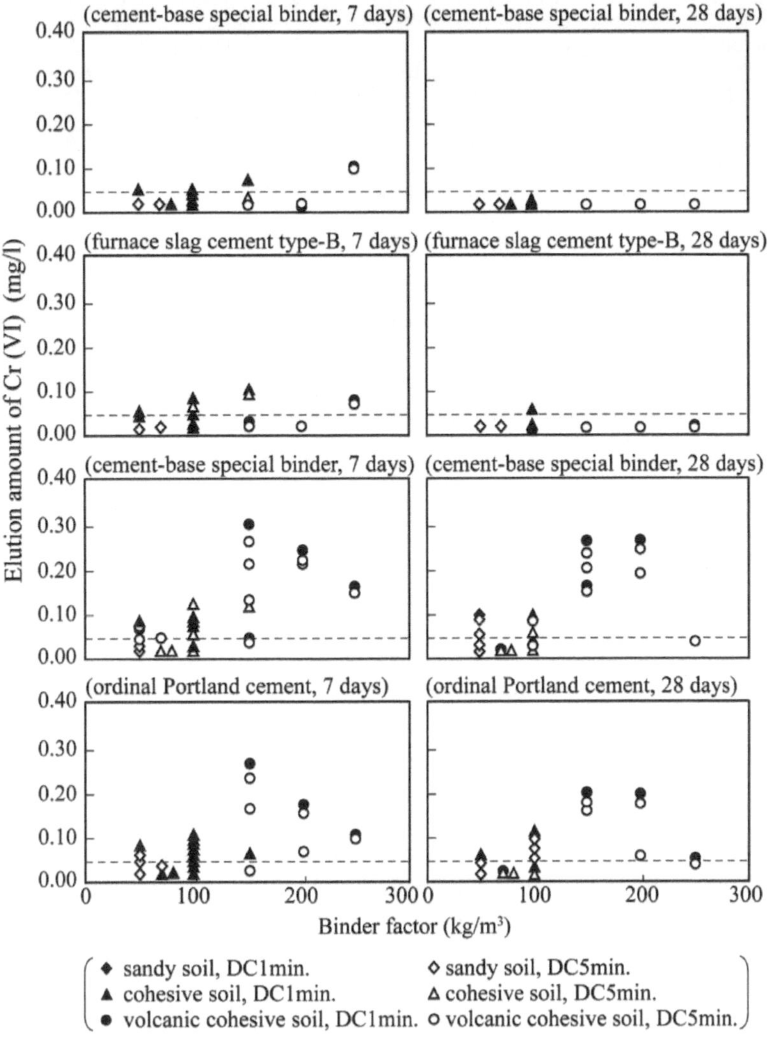

Figure 3.46 Leaching test results of hexavalent chromium from laboratory stabilized soils (Hosoya, 2002).

cement-based special binders or blast furnace slag cement type B show lower elution amounts of hexavalent chromium, Cr(VI), than those stabilized with ordinary Portland cement. As for the type of soil, the volcanic cohesive soils show the largest elution amount among the soils.

According to the accumulated test results, the leaching of hexavalent chromium is prominent in the case where the soil is volcanic soil and in an unsaturated condition, and the binder is ordinary Portland cement. The Ministry of Land, Infrastructure, Transport and Tourism, Japan, notified "the legal action on the leaching hexavalent chromium from stabilized soil" in 2000, where a laboratory test should be carried

Table 3.4 pH values of stabilized soils for different curing periods (Japan Cement Association, 2007).

Cement factor	75 kg/m^3			150 kg/m^3		
Curing period	3 days	7 days	28 days	3 days	7 days	28 days
Soil A (pH = 8.3)	12.0	11.6	11.4	12.5	12.0	11.7
Soil B (pH = 8.8)	11.7	11.3	11.2	12.0	11.7	11.6

out on the leaching of hexavalent chromium from stabilized soil to assure the amount of leaching should be lower than the criteria designated by the Soil Contamination Countermeasures Act (1975, 2005) (Table 3.1). Several types of special binder have been developed and are available on the Japanese market for mitigating the leaching of hexavalent chromium from stabilized soil.

3.4.3 *Resolution of alkali from stabilized soil*

When calcium hydroxide, $Ca(OH)_2$, created by the hydration of cement dissociating in water, the solution shows high alkalinity as shown in Table 3.4 (Japan Cement Association, 2007). The exposed surface of cement-stabilized soil is gradually neutralised by carbonation due to carbon dioxide in the air and the dissolution of alkali components. The alkali component dissolved from stabilized soil is not diffused widely in surrounding soil due to its buffer action.

Figure 3.47 shows the test apparatus and the measured potential hydrogen, pH, of cement-stabilized soil, the surface water (water run off the surface of stabilized soil without permeation), and the permeated water, along with the curing period (Japan Cement Association, 2007). The stabilized soil and the permeated water through stabilized soil show high pH values for three months, but the permeated water through the unstabilized soil shows neutral in pH. The surface water shows high pH values at first but gradually decreases in pH and is almost neutral after three months.

Figure 3.48 shows the pH value distributions in the cement-stabilized soil and unstabilized soil in the field, which were measured at 33 months after the stabilization (Japan Cement Association, 2007). The stabilized soil still shows a high pH value, of the order of 10 to 12, but comparatively low pH value at the shallow depth probably due to the dissolution by rainfall and surface water. In the unstabilized soil, the pH value is very high close to the boundary with the stabilized soil, but rapidly decreases with depth to a constant level at about 100 mm from the boundary.

3.4.4 *Resolution of dioxin from stabilized soil*

Figure 3.49 shows the relationship between the dioxin content and amount of cement in stabilized soil (Matsumura, 2007). A dredged organic soil with a natural water content of 284.4% was stabilized with cement of 100, 200 and 300 kg/m^3. At 28 days' curing, a dioxin test was carried out on the stabilized soil according to the Manual on Determination of Dioxins in Bottom Sediment, specified by Environment Agency (2008). The figure shows the amount of dioxin decreases with the cement factor.

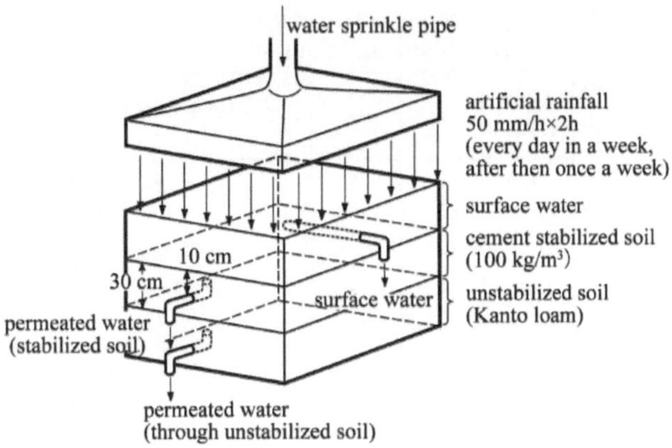

(a) Test apparatus.

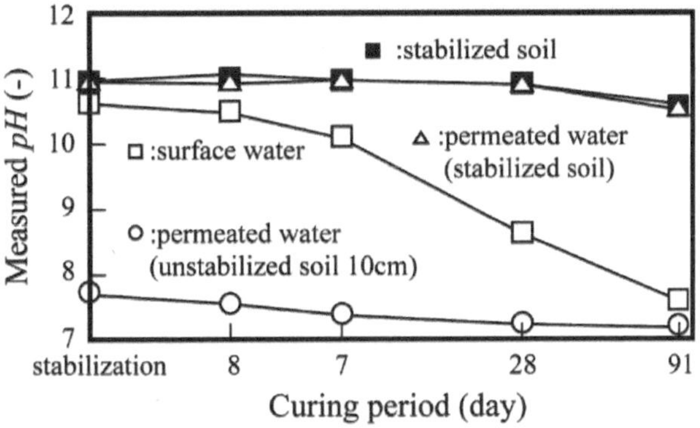

(b) Measured pH values.

Figure 3.47 Resolution of alkali from stabilized soil (Japan Cement Association, 2007).

4 PROPERTIES OF STABILIZED SOIL SUBJECTED TO DISTURBANCE/COMPACTION

4.1 Physical properties

4.1.1 Change in consistency

Figure 3.50 shows the effect of cement stabilization on the consistency of stabilized soil (Watabe & Tanaka, 2012). The Honmoku clay (w_L of 108.0% and w_P of 47.9%) was stabilized with cement factor of 100 kg/m^3 and cured for 14 days. After curing, the soils were disturbed throughout and mixed again with an additional amount of cement. In the figure, the white markers show the measured values on the remixed stabilized soils, while the black markers show those on stabilized soil without remixing (see Section 4.1.3). The figure shows that the liquid limit, w_L, and the plastic limit, w_P, are increased by the first stabilization, and they increase again by remixing with

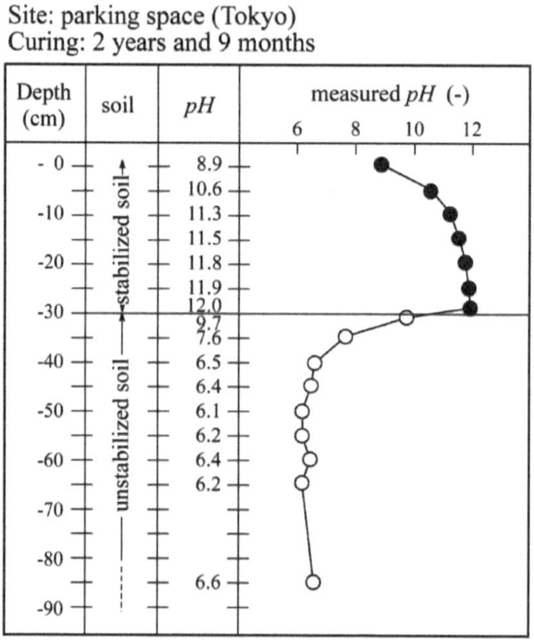

Figure 3.48 pH distribution in cement-stabilized soil and unstabilized soil at 33 months' curing (Japan Cement Association, 2007).

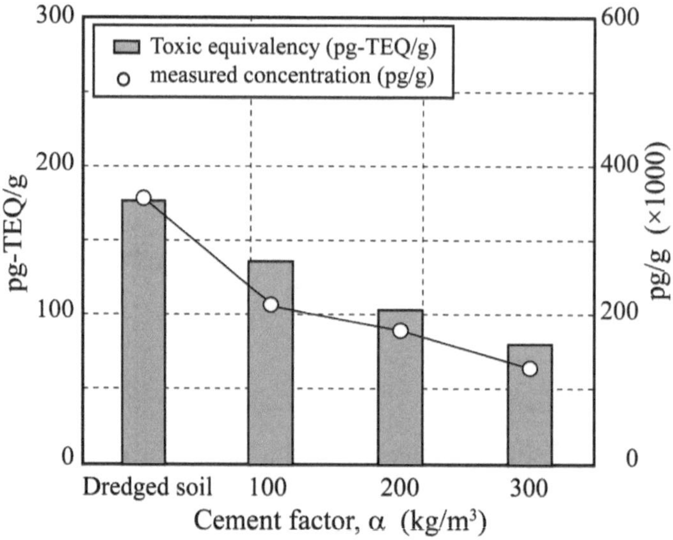

Figure 3.49 Relashionship between the dioxin content and amount of cement (Matsumura, 2007).

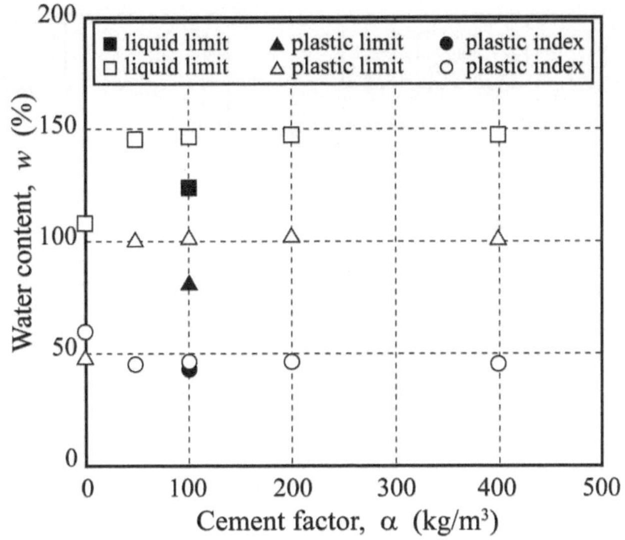

Figure 3.50 Change of consistency brought about by cement stabilization (Watabe & Tanaka, 2012).

additional cement. But they are negligibly influenced by the amount of cement in the remixing process. The plastic index is negligibly influenced by the remixing and the amount of cement.

4.2 Mechanical properties (strength characteristics)

4.2.1 Influence of soil disturbance

Figures 3.51 and 3.52 show the effect of soil disturbance on the unconfined compressive strength, q_u (Makino et al., 2014, 2015). In the tests, the kaolin clay (w_L of 77.5%, w_P of 30.3% and w_i of 120%) was stabilized with ordinary Portland cement with *aw* of 5 and 10%. After mixing, the stabilized soil was molded by the tapping technique according to the Japanese Geotechnical Society Standard (2009). In the case of the disturbed soil specimen, the stabilized soil mixture was stored and cured in an airtight plastic bag first to avoid any change in water content. After 3 or 7 days, the soil mixture in the bag was disturbed throughout and placed in the mold the same way as the non-disturbed soils. After the prescribed curing period, the soil samples were subjected to the unconfined compression test, as shown in the figure.

Figure 3.51 shows the stress-strain curves of non-disturbed stabilized soil and stabilized soils disturbed after 3 days and 7 days at the curing period of 28 days. The stress of the non-disturbed stabilized soil increases rapidly with the axial strain, reaching a peak strength when the axial strain is approximately 1% and then decreasing quickly after the peak strength. The stress of the disturbed stabilized soil increases gently with the axial strain, reaches a peak when the axial strain is approximately 2 to 4% and decreases gently irrespective of the cement content. The figures

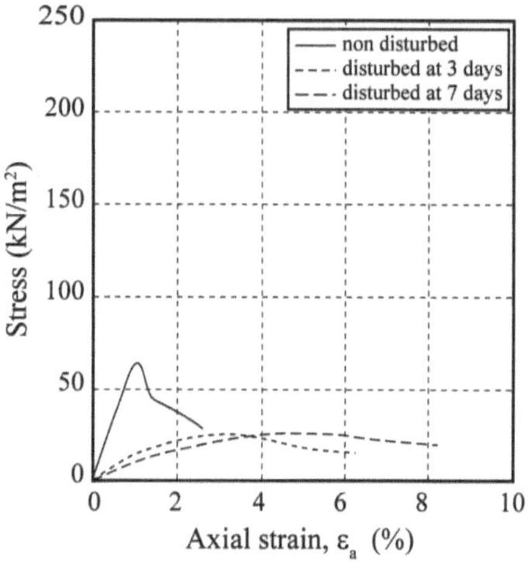

(a) aw = 5%

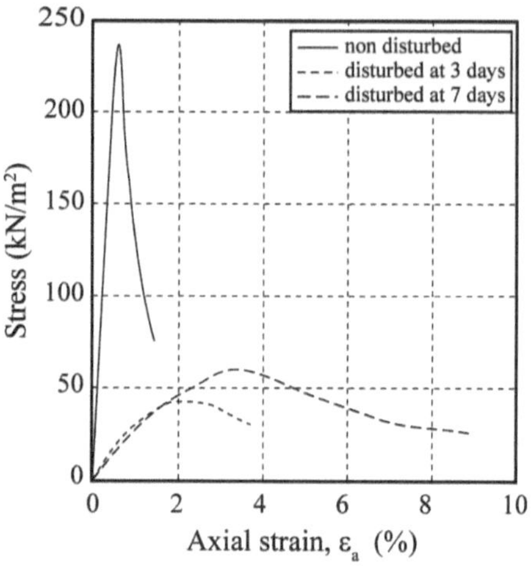

(b) aw = 10%

Figure 3.51 The stress-strain curves of disturbed and non-disturbed cement-stabilized soils at the curing period of 28 days (Makino et al., 2015).

reveal that the non-disturbed stabilized soil shows a brittle characteristic with quite large strength at a small axial strain and a quite small residual strength. However, the disturbed stabilized soils show a ductile characteristic with small strength and stiffness.

Figure 3.52 shows the relationship between the unconfined compressive strength and curing period (Makino et al., 2015).The unconfined compressive strength of the non-disturbed stabilized soil monotonically increases with the curing period. The unconfined compressive strength of the disturbed stabilized soils decreases considerably to 10 to 20% of that of the non-disturbed stabilized soils due to the disturbance, and it gradually increases with the curing period to approximately 25 to 40% of that of the non-disturbed stabilized soils.

A similar phenomenon on the effect of soil disturbance on the unconfined compressive strength, q_u, of cement-stabilized soil is found, in which the Nagoya Port clay (w_L of 74.4%, w_P of 33.0% and w_i of 70.0%) was stabilized with ordinary Portland cement with a cement factor, α, of 50 kg/m^3 (Ministry of Transport, The Fifth District Port Construction Bureau, 1999).

Figure 3.53 shows a similar test result to Figure 3.52, but the stabilized soil is disturbed at several curing ages up to 180 days (Japan Cement Association, 2012). The figure shows the strength can increase largely as long as the soil is disturbed at an early curing age, but the increase is quite small when it is disturbed at a late age. The strength increases and reaches an almost constant value at about four weeks in the case where the cement content is relatively small. It can be said that the strength gain is small when the soil is disturbed after the completion of cement hydration action.

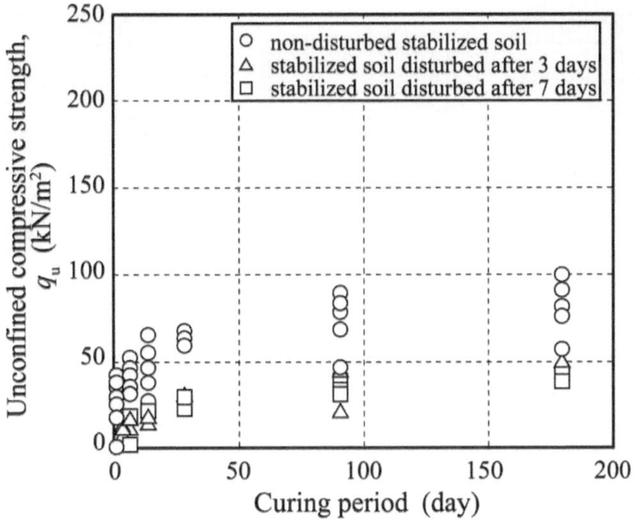

(a) *aw* = 5%.

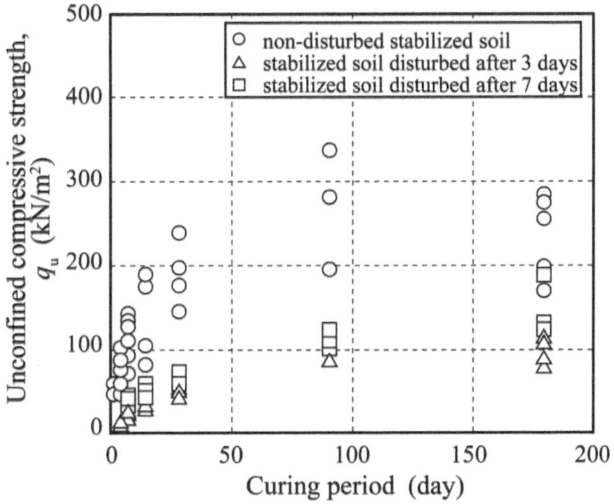

(b) *aw* = 10%.

Figure 3.52 The relationship between unconfined compressive strength and curing period of stabilized soils (Makino et al., 2015)

4.2.2 Influence of soil disturbance and compaction

Figure 3.54(a) shows the effect of the soil disturbance and compaction on the unconfined compressive strength, q_u, of cement-stabilized soil (Hino et al., 2007). In the test, the Hiro Port clay (w_L of 144.4%, w_P of 52.0%) was prepared to have an initial water content, w_i of 1.5 × w_L and stabilized with either blast furnace slag cement type

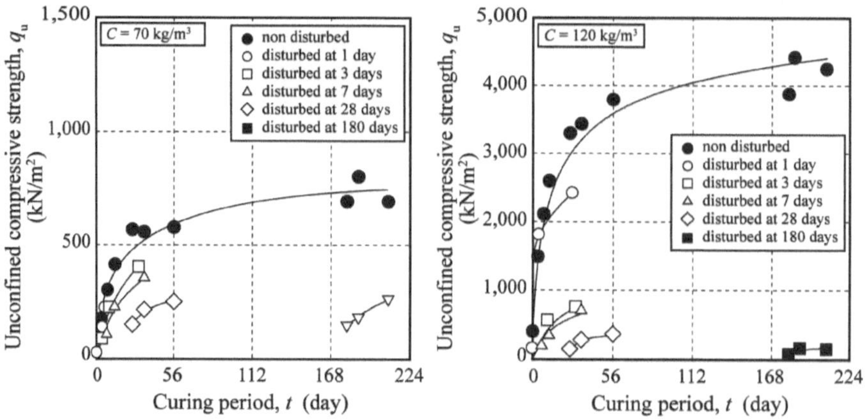

Figure 3.53 The relationship between unconfined compressive strength and the curing period of stabilized soil (Japan Cement Association, 2012).

B of 70 kg/m³ or quicklime of 30 kg/m³. Part of the stabilized soils were disturbed at 7 days' curing, and compacted with various compaction energies by the Japanese standard (Japanese Geotechnical Society, 2009). The figure shows that the soil strength considerably decreases to about 1/10 to 1/13 by the disturbance and increases gradually with the curing period after the compaction.

Figure 3.54(b) shows the relationship between unconfined compressive strength and compaction energy. In the case of the stabilized soil with blast furnace slag cement type B, the maximum strength can be seen at the compaction energy of 0.5 *Ec*, while the strength decreases with the compaction energy after that. In the case of the quicklime stabilization, the maximum strength can be seen at 0.25 *Ec*. They show the effect of the over-compaction phenomenon on the strength of the stabilized soils.

Figure 3.55 shows the relationship between the dry density and the compaction energy. The dry density increases with the compaction energy but soon reaches to a constant density irrespective of the type of binder and the curing period.

5 ENGINEERING PROPERTIES OF CEMENT-STABILIZED SOIL PRODUCED *IN-SITU*

5.1 Flow value of field stabilizedsoil

Figure 3.56 shows the relationship between the water content ratio and the flow value of stabilized soil (Kitazume et al., 2007). Though there is a lot of scatter in the data, the trend of data increase is roughly linear with the water content ratio.

5.2 Mixing degree of field stabilized soil

The engineering properties of stabilized soil mentioned in the previous sections were obtained mostly on laboratory stabilized soil specimens prepared with a sufficient

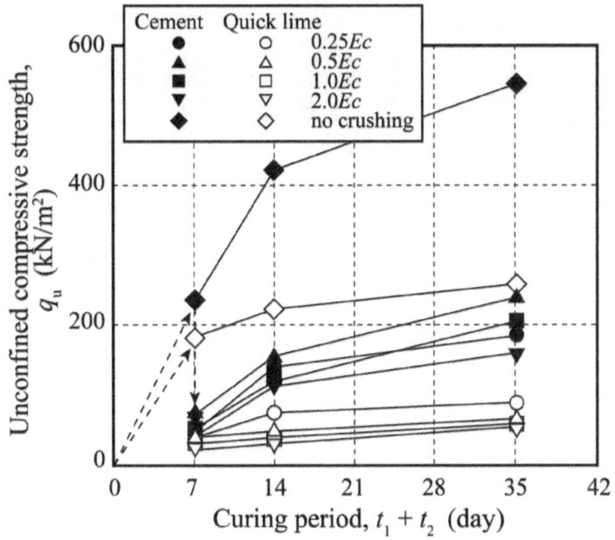

(a) Effect of curing period.

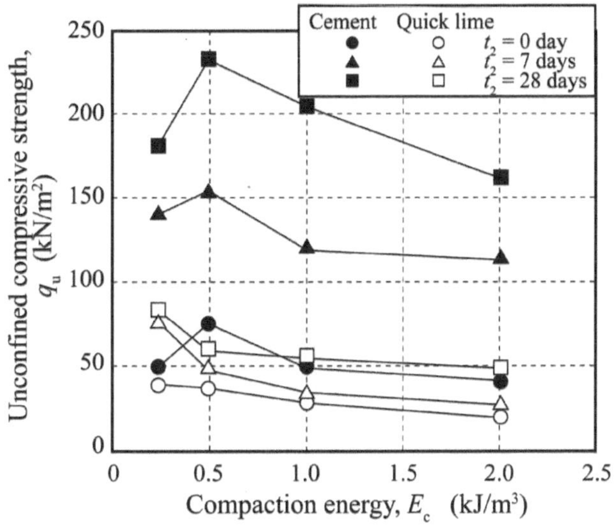

(b) Effect of compaction energy.

Figure 3.54 The effect of soil disturbance and compaction on the unconfined compressive strength of stabilized soil (Hino et al., 2007).

degree of mixing. In actual production, the original soil and binder are mixed by a pneumatic flow mixing machine and placed on land or underwater. If the mixing degree and/or the cement factor are low, the uniform mixing of original soil and binder cannot be attained in the field. If the stabilized soil is not placed by the appropriate machine

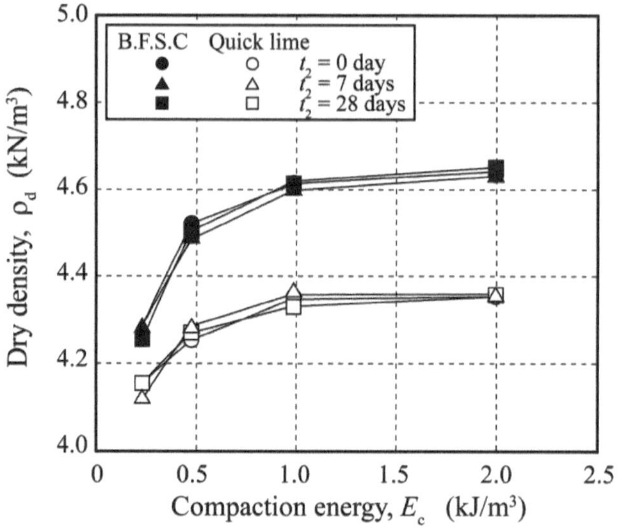

(a) Blast furnace slag cement and quicklime stabilization.

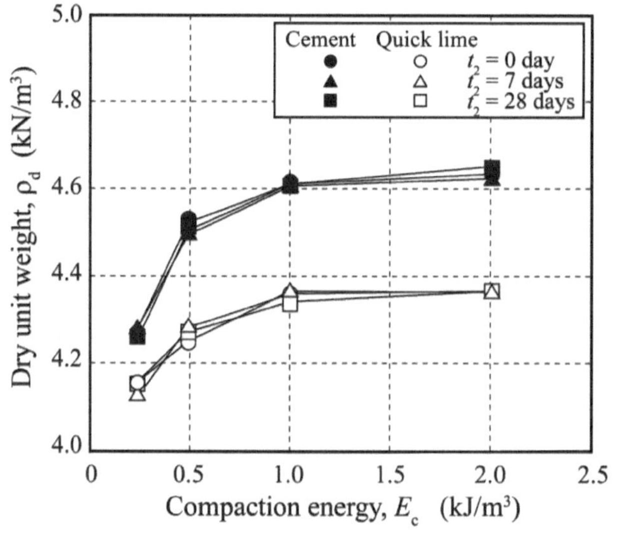

(b) Ordinary Portland cement and quicklime stabilization.

Figure 3.55 The effect of soil disturbance and compaction on the dry unit weight of stabilized soil (Hino et al., 2007).

and/or in the right manner, the uniformity and strength of the stabilized soil in the field cannot be assured to design requirements. The characteristics of field stabilized soil are, therefore, highly influenced not only by the amount of binder but also by the type of execution machine and quality control during execution. In Japan, various

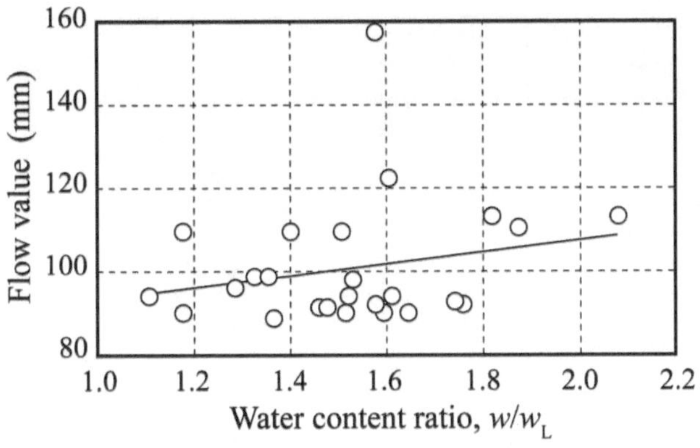

Figure 3.56 The relationship between the water content ratio and flow value of stabilized soils (Kitazume et al., 2007).

execution machines have been developed and improved, incorporating field experiences and experiments as described in Chapter 5. A careful quality control program during execution has also been developed and is practiced as routine. In this section, the characteristics of field stabilized soil produced by the Japanese machine with careful quality control are briefly introduced.

5.3 Effect of transportation distance

Figure 3.57(a) shows the relationship between the water content, w, and the unconfined compressive strength, q_u, of stabilized soil, which were sampled at four transportation distances: 43, 93, 136 and 645 m along the pipeline (Kitazume & Hayano, 2005, Hayano & Kitazume, 2005). About 25 to 30 cylindrical specimens were made from stabilized soil retrieved at each point. Meanwhile, the soil cement mixture having the same W/C as that of the retrieved plug was mixed by a mixer and poured into a cylindrical mold in a laboratory. The field and laboratory stabilized soil specimens were cured for 28 days in a laboratory, followed by the unconfined compression tests.

The two lines in the figure represent the unconfined compressive strength, q_u^{lab}, and the water content, w^{lab}, of the laboratory stabilized soil sample. The figure shows that the q_u of the stabilized soil retrieved at the distance of 43 m is significantly smaller than the q_u^{lab} and that those retrieved at the distances of 93 and 136 m are quite a lot larger than the q_u^{lab}. However, the q_u of the soil retrieved at the distance of 645 m is very close to the q_u^{lab}. The water content data from the stabilized soil is scattered quite widely in the cases of the transportation distance of 43 m and 93 m, but is less scattered over a smaller range in the case of the distance of 645 m.

Figure 3.57(b) shows the variation of average unconfined compressive strength, q_u^{ave}, of the sample along the transportation distance. In the figure, the q_u^{ave} is normalized with respect to the q_u^{lab}. The q_u^{ave} value of the stabilized soil obtained at the outlet is also plotted at the transportation distance of 1,300 m. The q_u^{ave} of the stabilized soils

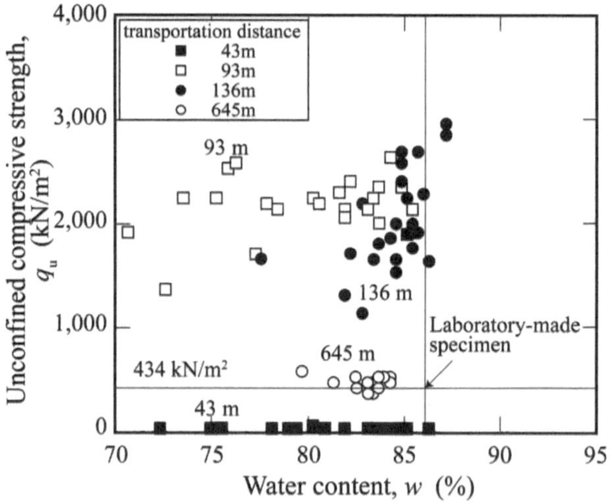

(a) Relationship between the water content and the unconfined compressive strength.

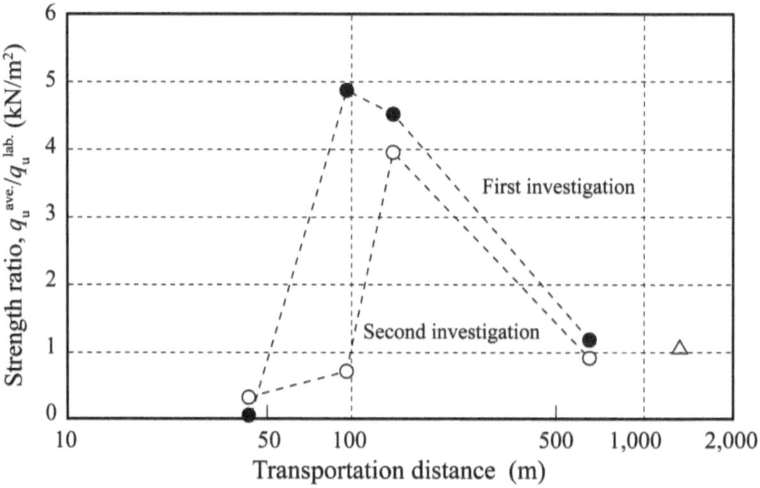

(b) Variation of average unconfined compressive strength against the transportation distance.

Figure 3.57 The effect of transportation distance on the degree of mixing of stabilized soil (Kitazume & Hayano, 2005).

retrieved at the distance of 43 m is significantly smaller than the q_u^{lab}, while that of the stabilized soil retrieved at the distance of 136 m is significantly larger. It can be assumed that the stabilized soil was sampled at the cement poor portion of the soil plug at 43 m, but at a cement-rich portion at 136 m. This fact suggests that the plug transported for a distance of less than 136 m was not thoroughly mixed so that the plug was not uniform. The samples sampled at 645 m and 1,300 m, on the other hand,

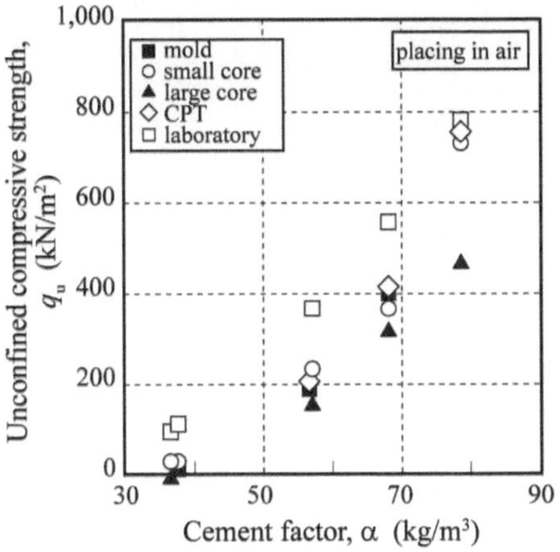

(a) Placement on land.

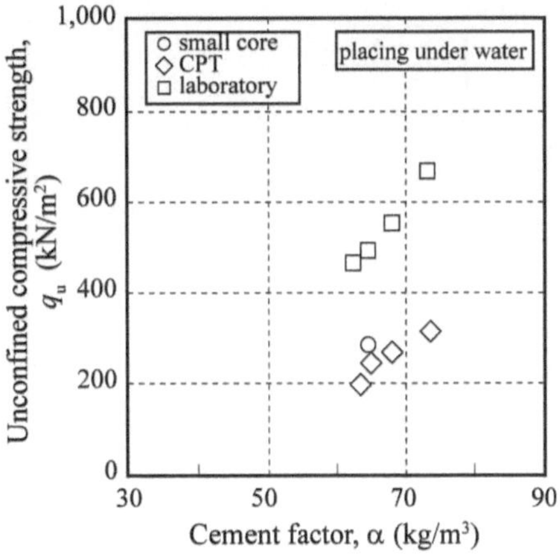

(b) Placement under seawater.

Figure 3.58 The unconfined compressive strength and amount of cement of field stabilized soil (Ministry of Transport, The Fifth District Port Construction Bureau, 1999).

have q_u^{ave} value very close to the q_u^{lab}. This fact suggests that a plug transported to a distance of 645 m was as well mixed as one transported to a distance of 1,300 m.

5.4 Effect of placement

5.4.1 Effect of amount of cement on strength

Figure 3.58 shows the relationship between the amount of cement and the unconfined compressive strength, q_u, of field stabilized soils (Ministry of Transport, The Fifth District Port Construction Bureau, 1999). The Nagoya Port clay (w_L of 74.4%, w_P of 33.0% and w_i of 127.1%) was stabilized with ordinary Portland cement with various cement factors by the pneumatic flow mixing method in the field and placed and cured either on land or under seawater. After 28 days' curing, the stabilized soils were core sampled for an unconfined compression test. The soil and cement mixture retrieved at the outlet of the pipeline and cured in a laboratory is 'mold' in the legend, and the stabilized soils core sampled in the field are 'core' and 'L core'. The specimen of 'core' is 50 mm in diameter and 100 mm in height, while the 'L core' is a large size sample, 500 mm in diameter and 1,000 mm in height. In the figure, the laboratory stabilized soil is also plotted.

In the case of placement on land, the unconfined compressive strength, q_u, increases almost linearly with the amount of cement, irrespective of the specimen type. The 'laboratory' sample shows the highest strength, but the 'L core' sample shows lowest strength, resulting in a relatively large scatter in strength. The figure also shows that at least about 40 kg/m³ of cement is necessary to obtain a certain strength gain in the field, which is very close to that of the laboratory stabilized soil as already shown in Figures 2.17 and 2.18. In the case of placement under seawater, Figure 3.59(b),

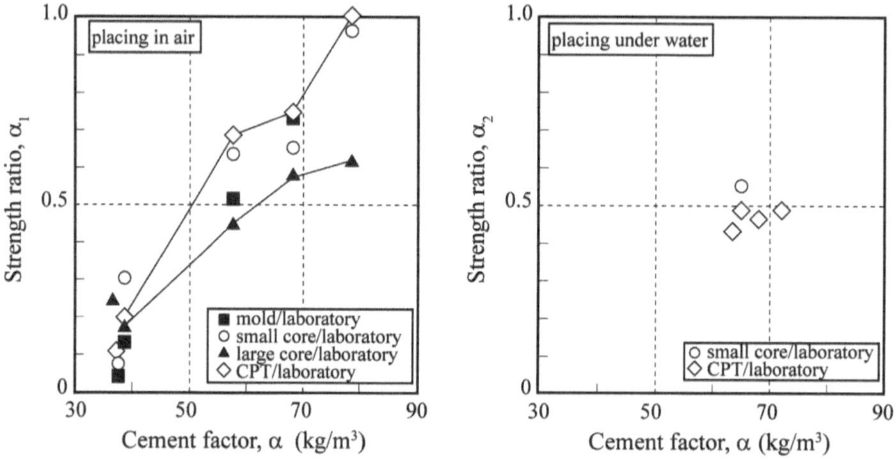

(a) Placement on land. (b) Placement under seawater.

Figure 3.59 The unconfined compressive strength ratio and amount of cement of field stabilized soil (Ministry of Transport, The Fifth District Port Construction Bureau, 1999).

the strength of the 'core' sample is relatively small compared with the 'laboratory' sample, which could be due to the entrapped water within the stabilized soil.

Figure 3.59 shows the strength ratio of the field produced soil to the laboratory produced soil (Ministry of Transport, The Fifth District Port Construction Bureau, 1999). The strength ratios are not constant but increase with the amount of cement irrespective of field soil type, which indicates that mixing cannot be conducted well in the case of a small amount of cement. The strength ratio of the stabilized soil placed under seawater is about 20% lower than that placed on land. This phenomenon could be due to the increase of water content in stabilized soil by entrapping seawater during placement. This also emphasizes that great care should be paid during the placement of stabilized soil so as not to entrap seawater. The strength of 'L core' is lower than that of 'core' and the strength ratio of 'L core' against 'core' is about 0.7, which probably reflects the relatively large scatter in strength values. The strength ratio shown in the figure is almost the same as the previous research on the stabilized soil produced by the deep mixing method (Kitazume & Terashi, 2013).

Figure 3.60 shows the relationship between the coefficients of deviation of unconfined compressive strength, q_u, against the amount of cement (Ministry of Transport, The Fifth District Port Construction Bureau, 1999). In the figure, several field stabilized soils are plotted, together with the laboratory stabilized soil. The coefficient of deviation of the laboratory stabilized soil is relatively small, with a deviation of the order of 15%, and almost constant irrespective of the amount of cement. The field stabilized soils, on the other hand, indicate relatively large coefficients of deviation. The coefficient of variation of the small size core specimen is about 35%, irrespective of the amount of cement, which is almost of the same order as that of the deep mixing method (Kitazume & Terashi, 2013). But the 'L core' soil shows almost the same

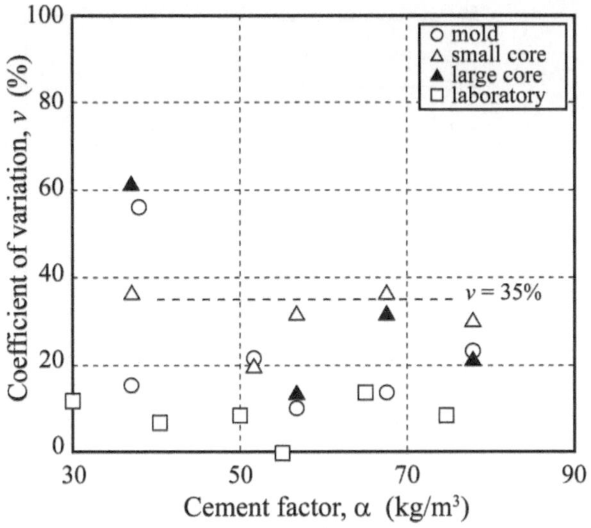

Figure 3.60 The strength deviation of field stabilized soil against the amount of cement factor (Ministry of Transport, The Fifth District Port Construction Bureau, 1999).

coefficient as the small sized specimen as long as the amount of cement exceeds about 50 kg/m^3, but increases to about 60% when the amount of cement decreases to 38 kg/m^3.

5.5 Heterogeneity of dredged soil

In the case of large-scale construction, dredged soil was excavated at several locations and several depths, whose properties varied very much depending on the excavation point and depth. This causes a large scatter of the stabilized soils' strength. Figures 3.61(a) and 3.61(b) provide the frequency distributions of the q_u obtained from the unconfined compression test results from the soils dredged at the areas A and B, respectively (Kitazume & Hayano, 2005, Hayano & Kitazume, 2005). The average value, $(q_u)_{ave}$, and the coefficient of variation, CV, are obtained with the normal distributions fitted to the respective data. The $(q_u)_{ave}$ of the two frequency distributions are quite similar. This is mainly because the soil properties varied along the sea depth even though the dredged soil was obtained at the same area. This fact suggests that the effect of heterogeneity of the dredged soil was that it produced varied strengths in the cement-stabilized soil. Figure 3.61(c) shows the frequency distribution of the q_u of the whole specimens of the dredged soils excavated at three areas from A to C, while the dredged soils were excavated from the five dredging areas A to E. The CV value shown in Figure 3.61(c) is similar to those shown in Figures 3.61(a) and 3.61(b). The increase of the number of dredging areas had little effect on the strength variance within the cement-stabilized soil.

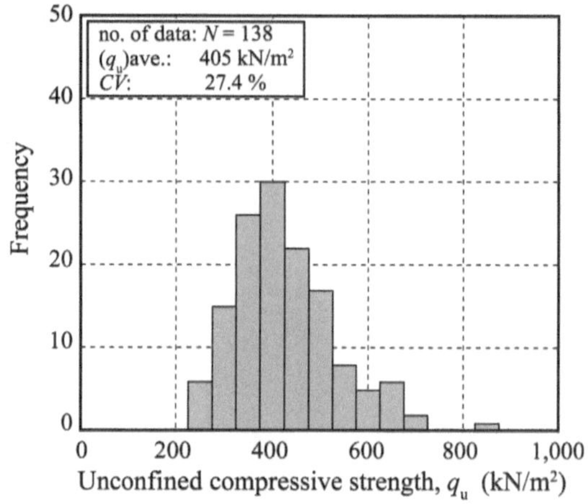

(a) Dredging area A.

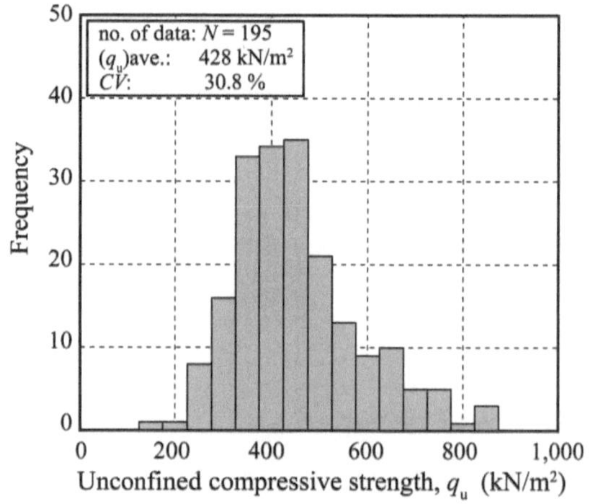

(b) Dredging area B.

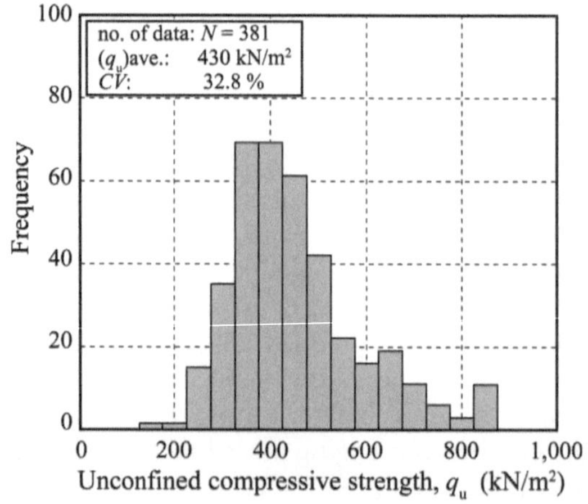

(c) Dredging area C.

Figure 3.61 The frequency distribution of q_u of field stabilized soil (Kitazume & Hayano, 2005, Hayano & Kitazume, 2005).

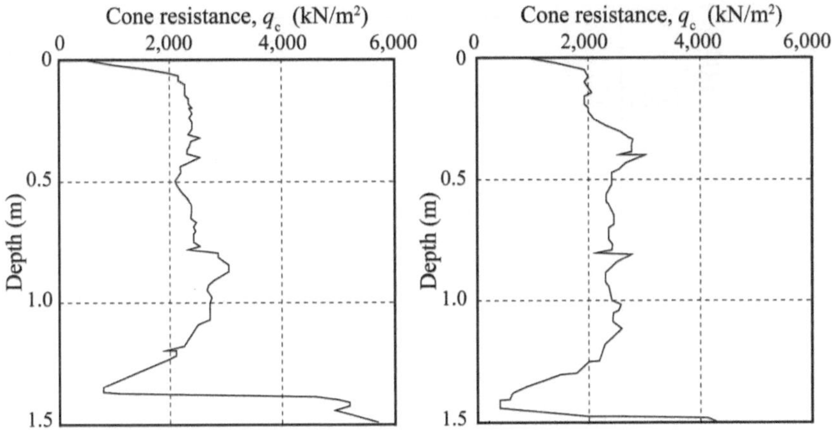

(a) Position 1. (b) Position 2.

Figure 3.62 Cone penetration along depth stabilized soil ground (Ministry of Transport, The Fifth District Port Construction Bureau, 1999).

5.6 Property of stabilized ground

Figure 3.62 shows an example of the cone penetration tests on stabilized ground of about 1.5 m in thickness, where the Nagoya Port clay (w_L of 74.4% and w_P of 33.0%) was stabilized with ordinary Portland cement with various cement factors by the pneumatic flow mixing method, and placed into a pond (Ministry of Transport, The Fifth District Port Construction Bureau, 1999). Figure 3.62 shows the cone penetration test profile along the depth measured by a frictionless cone apparatus at 28 days' curing. An almost constant cone penetration test value was obtained along the whole depth, except at the most shallow layer and the bottom layer.

Figure 3.63 shows the relationship between the cone penetration test values and the unconfined compressive strength, q_u (Ministry of Transport, The Fifth District Port Construction Bureau, 1999). The figure clearly shows the cone penetration test values have a linear relation with the q_u value and its relation can be formulated as Equation 3.3. Several relationships are proposed for the coefficient between the tip resistance of the cone penetration test, q_c and q_u; $q_c = 5$ to $10 \times q_u$ for ordinary soil, and $q_c = 6.5 \times q_u$ for stabilized soil.

$$q_c = 6.5 \times q_u \qquad (3.3)$$

where
q_c: CPT resistance (kN/m^2)
q_u: unconfined compressive strength (kN/m^2)

Figure 3.64 shows the plate loading test result on stabilized soil ground with five different cement factors (Ministry of Transport, The Fifth District Port Construction Bureau, 1999), where the three loading tests were carried out at around a couple

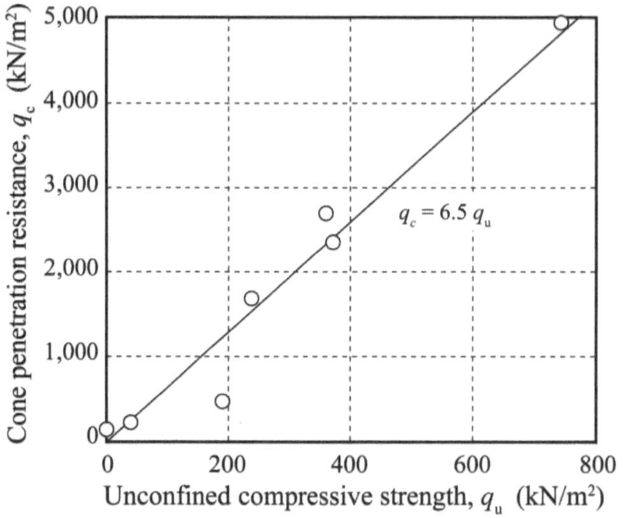

Figure 3.63 The relationship between cone penetration resistance and the unconfined compressive strength of stabilized soil ground (Ministry of Transport, The Fifth District Port Construction Bureau, 1999).

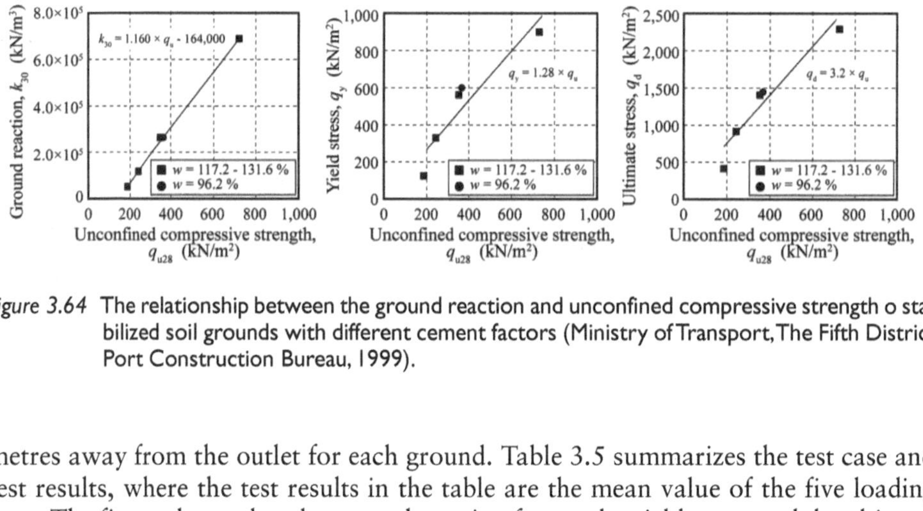

Figure 3.64 The relationship between the ground reaction and unconfined compressive strength o stabilized soil grounds with different cement factors (Ministry of Transport, The Fifth District Port Construction Bureau, 1999).

metres away from the outlet for each ground. Table 3.5 summarizes the test case and test results, where the test results in the table are the mean value of the five loading tests. The figure shows that the ground reaction factor, the yield stress and the ultimate stress of the stabilized ground, as measured in the tests, had a linear relationship with the unconfined compressive strength. According the test results, the following relations can be obtained:

$$k_{30} = 1,160 \times q_u - 164,000 \tag{3.4}$$

$$q_y = 1.28 \times q_u \tag{3.5}$$

$$q_d = 3.2 \times q_u \tag{3.6}$$

Table 3.5 Summary of plate loading tests on stabilized soil grounds (Ministry of Transport, The Fifth District Port Construction Bureau, 1999).

The test grounds	Case 1	Case 2	Case 3	Case 4	Case 5
Initial water content, w_i (%)	131.6	117.2	96.2	125.4	123.3
Cement factor (kg/m^3)	46	78	52	57	68
Unconfined compressive strength, q_{u28} (kN/m^2)	195	734	373	239	361
Yield stress, q_y (kN/m^2)	132	891	580	326	567
Ground reaction factor, K_{30} (kN/m^3)	5.37×10^4	69.0×10^4	26.3×10^4	12.7×10^4	25.9×10^4
Ultimate stress, q_d (kN/m^2)	382	2264	1415	905	1401
q_d/q_u	1.96	3.08	3.79	3.79	3.88

where
k_{30}: ground reaction coefficient (kN/m^2)
q_d: ultimate bearing capacity (kN/m^2)
q_y: yield bearing capacity (kN/m^2)
q_u: unconfined compressive strength (kN/m^2)

6 SUMMARY

The current chapter described the engineering characteristics of stabilized soil, mainly based on laboratory prepared samples. The general tendency and the correlation of various characteristics and unconfined compressive strength may apply to a variety of admixture stabilization techniques and may help design engineers understand stabilized soil.

The characteristics of *in-situ* stabilized soil discussed in Section 5, however, are only applicable to the *in-situ* soil produced by the preumatic flow mixing used in Japan. This is because the quality of *in-situ* stabilized soil depends heavily upon the mixing process and procedures. It is the responsibility of the method contractor to collect and accumulate information on the quality of *in-situ* stabilized soils produced by their own proprietary mixing system.

The knowledge compiled in the present chapter can be summarized as follows.

6.1 Properties of stabilized soil mixture before hardening

6.1.1 Physical properties

6.1.1.1 Change of consistency of the soil-binder mixture before hardening

The liquid limit decreases with the quicklime content, while the plastic limit increases. As a result, the plasticity index sharply decreases with increasing quicklime content.

6.1.2 Mechanical properties (strength characteristics)

6.1.2.1 Change in flow value

The flow value increases with the water content of a stabilized soil mixture, irrespective of the cement factor. The shear strength exponentially decreases with the flow value and a close relationship between them can be seen irrespective of the cement factor.

6.1.2.2 Change in shear strength

The shear strength of stabilized soil just after mixing is larger than that of the original soil, which is probably due to reduced fluidity due to adding cement powder. The shear strength remains a small value within about 30 minutes but increases rapidly after that due to the progress of the cement hydration effect.

6.1.2.3 Stress-strain curve

The peak compressive stress increases quickly and the axial strain at failure decreases quickly with the curing period. The brittle behavior with large peak strength, small strain at failure and small residual strength becomes more dominant with the curing period.

6.1.3 Mechanical properties (consolidation characteristics)

6.1.3.1 Void ratio -- consolidation pressure curve and consolidation yield pressure

The shapes of e-log p curves of the stabilized soil are similar to ordinary clay samples, which are characterized by a sharp bend at a consolidation yield pressure. The consolidation yield pressure is higher the longer the curing period. The relationship between the consolidation yield pressure, p_y, and the curing period, is such that the p_y increases almost linearly with the logarithm of curing period.

6.1.3.2 Coefficient of consolidation and coefficient of volume compressibility

The ratio of coefficient of consolidation of stabilized soil against original soil is 10 to 100 in a sort of over-consolidated condition, but the ratio approaches unity in a sort of normally consolidated condition. The ratio of the coefficient of volume compressibility of the stabilized soil against the original soil is 0.01 to 0.1 in a sort of over-consolidated condition, but the ratio approaches to unity in a sort of normally consolidated condition.

6.1.3.3 Coefficient of permeability

The permeability decreases with decreasing void ratio. The permeability of the stabilized soil is larger than that of the original soil. The coefficient of permeability is very much smaller than that of the original soil, and gradually decreases with the progress of cement hydration.

6.2 Properties of stabilized soil after hardening

6.2.1 *Physical properties*

6.2.1.1 *Change in water content*

The water content of the stabilized soil decreases gradually with the cement content.

6.2.1.2 *Change in density*

The density of the stabilized soil increases gradually with the cement content.

6.2.1.3 *Change in consistency*

The liquid limit and plastic limit are increased by the stabilization. As the plastic limit increases more than the liquid limit, the plasticity index is decreased by stabilization.

6.2.2 *Mechanical properties (strength characteristics)*

6.2.2.1 *Stress-strain curve*

The compressive stress increases rapidly with the axial strain to a peak strength which is followed by quick decrease. The brittle behavior with large peak strength, small strain at failure and small residual strength becomes more dominant with the curing period.

6.2.2.2 *Strain at failure*

The magnitude of axial strain at failure, ε_f, is of the order of 0.5 to 2.5% and considerably smaller than that of unstabilized clay. The ε_f decreases rapidly with the unconfined compressive strength, q_u.

6.2.2.3 *Internal friction angle and undrained shear strength*

The undrained shear strength, c_u, of the stabilized soil is larger than that of the unstabilized soil, and almost constant as long as the consolidation pressure is low. But when the consolidation pressure exceeds the consolidation yield pressure, p_y, the undrained shear strength increases with increasing consolidation pressure. The increasing ratio in the c_u of the stabilized soil is almost same as that of the unstabilized soil. The internal friction angle, ϕ', of stabilized soil is almost zero as far as the consolidation pressure is lower than the consolidation yield pressure and the same as that of the unstabilized soil when the consolidation pressure is higher than the consolidation yield pressure. The undrained shear strength influenced by the testing method.

6.2.2.4 *Residual strength*

The strength ratio increases with the confining pressure ratio, and is about 0.5 to 0.8 for the confining pressure ratio, $\overline{\sigma}/q_u$, exceeding about 0.1, irrespective of the type of binder.

6.2.2.5 *Modulus of elasticity (Young's modulus)*

The magnitude of E_{50} increases with the q_u and can be formulated as $E_{50} = 50$ to $1300 \times q_u$ for $q_u <$ about 2,000 kN/m^2, and $E_{50} = 350$ to $1,000 \times q_u$ for $q_u >$ about 2,000 kN/m^2.

6.2.2.6 Poisson's ratio

The Poisson's ratio is around 0.28 to 0.45 irrespective of the unconfined compressive strength, q_u.

6.2.2.7 Dynamic property

The initial shear modulus, G_0, increases almost linearly with the q_u and can be formulated as $G_0 = 80$ to $200 \times q_u$. The shear modulus ratio, G/G_0 is almost constant irrespective of the shear strain, while the dumping ratio, h_{eq}, increases gradually. The shear modulus ratio and dumping ratio of the stabilized soil are similar to those of the unstabilized soil.

6.2.2.8 Creep strength

The axial strain rate, $\dot{\varepsilon}$, decreases almost linearly with the time duration on the double-logarithmic graph. The decreasing phenomenon in $\dot{\varepsilon}$ is almost constant irrespective of the load intensity, q_{cr}/q_u. The stabilized soil subjected to the vertical load, q_{cr}/q_u of 0.91 exhibits creep failure at round 1 minute after loading, but the stabilized soil does not fail as long as the load intensity is lower than about $0.8 \times q_u$.

6.2.2.9 Cyclic strength

The axial compressive strain remains lower than about 0.4% in the case of $0.6 \times q_u$ even with the number of cyclic loading being 100,000. The number of cyclic loading at failure, N_f, in the logarithmic scale decreases almost linearly with the σ_{max}/q_u.

6.2.2.10 Tensile and bending strengths

The tensile strength increases almost linearly with unconfined compressive strength irrespective of the type, amount of binder and initial water content of the soil, but increments of change become smaller with increasing q_u. The tensile strength is about 0.1 to 0.6 of the unconfined compressive strength, which is influenced by the testing procedure.

6.2.2.11 Long-term strength

There are two aspects when the long-term strength of stabilized soil is concerned. One is the strength increase with time at the core portion of the stabilized soil column, which is negligibly influenced by the surrounding conditions. The other is the possible strength decrease with time in the periphery of the stabilized soil column, due to deterioration.

The long-term strength of the stabilized soil at the core increases almost linearly with the logarithm of elapsed time, irrespective of whether the stabilized soil is produced in the laboratory or in the field, the soil type or the type and amount of binder.

The long-term strength of stabilized soil at the periphery decreases with elapsed time, and the deterioration progresses gradually inward with time, especially in the case of exposure to tap water and seawater. The progress of deterioration depth in logarithmic scale is almost linear to logarithmic time, and the slopes in all the test cases are about 1/2 irrespective of the strength of specimens and the exposure conditions.

6.2.2.12 *Coefficient of horizontal stress at rest*

The coefficient of horizontal stress at rest, K_0, value is about 0.15.

6.2.3 *Mechanical properties (consolidation characteristics)*

6.2.3.1 *Void ratio – consolidation pressure curve and consolidation yield pressure*

The e-$\log p$ curves of the stabilized soil show a clear consolidation yield pressure and its magnitude is dependent on the cement factor. The consolidation yield pressure, p_y, has a linear relationship with the unconfined compressive strength, q_u. The ratio of p_y/q_u of the stabilized soils is 1.25.

6.2.3.2 *Coefficient of volume compressibility*

The coefficient of volume compressibility of the stabilized soils, m_{vs}, slightly decreases with the consolidation pressure, p. The ratio of m_{vs}/m_{vu} is 0.01 to 0.1 as long as the normalized consolidation pressure, p/p_y is around 0.1, but the m_{vs}/m_{vu} increases to unity at the p/p_y of 1.

6.2.3.3 *Coefficient of consolidation*

The c_{vs} value is about 10 to 100 time larger than that of unstabilized soil as long as the consolidation pressure is small, but the c_v becomes almost same as the stabilized soil when the consolidation pressure becomes large, of the order of 1,000 kN/m^2. The ratio of c_{vs}/c_{vu} is 10 to 100 as long as the normalized consolidation pressure, p/p_y is around 0.1, in a sort of over-consolidated condition, but the c_{vs}/c_{vu} approaches to unity at the p/p_y of 1, c_{vs}/c_{vu}, 1 when p/p_y exceeds 1.

6.2.3.4 *Coefficient of permeability*

The k value of the unstabilized soil is the order of around 10^{-8} to 10^{-7} cm/s and slightly decreases with consolidation pressure. The k value is larger than that of unstabilized soil when the consolidation pressure is small, but the k decreases with the consolidation pressure and becomes almost same as the unstabilized soil when the consolidation pressure becomes large, of the order of 1,000 kN/m^2. The coefficient of permeability is dependent upon the water content of stabilized soil and the amount of cement. The coefficient of permeability of the stabilized soil decreases with decreasing water content and with an increasing amount of cement. The coefficient of permeability of the stabilized soil decreases exponentially with increasing strength, q_u.

6.2.3.5 *Secondary compression*

The secondary compression coefficients, C_α, of stabilized soil decreases almost linearly with the logarithm of consolidation time, and the coefficient of the stabilized soil is about 1/3 to 1/2 of the original soil.

6.2.4 *Environmental properties*

6.2.4.1 *Elution of contaminant*

The improvement effect by admixture stabilization is variable depending upon the type of soil and type of substances. The high improvement effect is achieved for mitigating cadmium and lead from stabilized soil.

6.2.4.2 *Elution of hexavalent chromium (chromium VI) from stabilized soil*

The leaching phenomenon of hexavalent chromium is prominent in the case where soil is volcanic soil and in an unsaturated condition and the binder is ordinary Portland cement.

6.2.4.3 *Resolution of alkali from stabilized soil*

The stabilized soil still shows high pH value of the order of 10 to 12, but comparatively low pH value at a shallow depth, probably due to the dissolution of rainfall and surface water. In the unstabilized soil, the pH value is very high close to the boundary with the stabilized soil, but rapidly decreases with the depth to a constant level at about 100 mm far from the boundary.

6.2.4.4 *Resolution of dioxin from stabilized soil*

The amount of dioxin decreases with increasing cement factor.

6.3 Properties of stabilized soil subjected to disturbance/compaction

6.3.1 *Physical properties*

6.3.1.1 *Change of consistency*

The liquid limit, w_L, and the plastic limit, w_P, increase with the first stabilization, and they increase again by the remixing with additional cement. But they are negligibly influenced by the amount of cement in the remixing process. The plastic index is negligibly influenced by the remixing and the amount of cement.

6.3.2 *Mechanical properties (strength characteristics)*

6.3.2.1 *Influence of soil disturbance*

Non-disturbed stabilized soil shows a brittle characteristic with quite a large strength at a small axial strain and quite a small residual strength, but disturbed stabilized soils show a ductile characteristic with small strength and stiffness. The unconfined compressive strength of the non-disturbed stabilized soil monotonically increases with the curing period. The unconfined compressive strength of the disturbed stabilized soils decreases considerably, and it gradually increases with the curing period to approximately 25 to 40% of that of the non-disturbed stabilized soils.

6.3.2.2 *Influence of soil disturbance and compaction*

The soil strength is considerably decreased by disturbance and increases gradually with the curing period after compaction. The dry density increases with compaction energy but soon reaches a constant density irrespective of the type of binder and the curing period.

6.4 Engineering properties of field cement-stabilized soil

6.4.1 *Flow value of field stabilized soil*

The flow value of stabilized soil increases linearly with the water content ratio.

6.4.2 Effect of transportation distance

The property of stabilized soil is considerably influenced by the transportation distance.

6.4.3 Effect of placement

6.4.3.1 Effect of amount of cement on strength

The strength ratio of the stabilized soil placed under seawater is about 20% lower than that placed on land, which can be due to an increase of water content in stabilized soil by entrapping seawater during placement. The field stabilized soils indicate relatively large coefficients of deviation.

6.4.4 Heterogeneity of dredged soil

The effect of heterogeneity of dredged soil was large on the strength variance of the cement-stabilized soil.

6.4.5 Property of stabilized ground

The cone penetration resistance has a linear relation with the q_u value and its relation can be formulated as $q_c = 5$ to $10 \times q_u$ for ordinary soil, and $q_c = 6.5 \times q_u$ for stabilized soil. The ground reaction factor, the yield stress and the ultimate stress of the stabilized ground measured in the plate loading tests had linear relationships with the unconfined compressive strength.

REFERENCES

Coastal Development Institute of Technology (2008) *Technical Manual of Pneumatic Flow Mixing Method*, revised version. Daikousha Publishers, 188p. (in Japanese).

Enami, A., Yamada, M. & Ishizaki, H. (1993) Dynamic properties of improved sandy soils (Part 2). *Proc. of the 28th Annual Conference of the Japanese Society of Soil Mechanics and Foundation Engineering*, pp. 1065–1066 (in Japanese).

Environment Agency (1975) *Criteria for a Specific Operation of the Ground Storage Tank Outdoors using Deep Mixing Method (notification)* (in Japanese).

Environment Agency (2005) *Criteria for a Specific Operation of the Ground Storage Tank Outdoors using Deep Mixing Method (notification)* (in Japanese).

Hara, H., Suetsugu, D., Hayashi, S. & Matsuda, H. (2013) Deterioration mechanism of cement-treated soil under seawater. *Journal of Geotechnical Engineering, Japan Society of Civil Engineers*. Vol. 69, No. 4, pp. 469–479 (in Japanese).

Hayano, K. & Kitazume, M. (2005) Strength Variance within Cement Treated Soils Induced by Newly Developed Pneumatic Flow Mixing Method. *Proc. of the ACSE, Geo-Frontiers 2005*.

Hayashi, H., Nishikawa, J., Egawa, T., Terashi, M. & Ohishi, K. (2000) Long-term strength of improved column formed by Deep Mixing Method. *Proc. of the 56th Annual Conference of the Japan Society of Civil Engineers*. No. 3, pp. 378–379 (in Japanese).

Hayashi, H., Nishikawa, J., Ohishi, K. & Kitazume, M. (2003) Field observation of long-term strength of cement treated soil. *Proc. of the 3rd International Conference on Grouting and Ground Treatment*. pp. 598–609.

Hayashi, H., Ohishi, K. & Terashi, M. (2004) Possibility of strength reduction of treated soil by Ca leaching. *Proc. of the 39th Annual Conference of the Japanese Geotechnical Society*. pp. 785–786 (in Japanese).

Hino, Y., Suetsugu, D., Ikari, Y. & Ohga, T. (2007) Unconfined compressive strength, cone index and compaction properties of embankment materials by dredged-stabilized clay. *Proc. of the 42nd Annual Conference of the Japanese Geotechnical Society*. pp. 615–616 (in Japanese).

Hirade, T., M. Futaki, K. Nakano & K. Kobayashi (1995) The study on the ground improved with cement as the foundation ground for buildings, part 16. Unconfined compression test of large scale column and sampling core in several fields. *Proc. of the Annual Conference of Architectural Institute of Japan*. pp. 861–862 (in Japanese).

Hosoya, T. (2002) Leaching of hexavalent chromium from cementitious soil improvement. *Journal of Japanese Society of Materials and Science*. Vol. 51, No. 8, pp. 933–942 (in Japanese).

Ikegami, M., Ichiba, T., Ohnishi, K. & Terashi, M. (2005) Long-term property of cement treated soil 20 years after construction. *Proc. of the 16th International Conference on Geotechnical Engineering*. pp. 1199–1202.

Ikegami, M., Masuda, K., Ichiba, T., Tsuruya, H. & Ohishi, K. (2002a) Long-term durability of cement-treated marine clay after 20 years. *Proc. of the 57th Annual Conference of the Japan Society of Civil Engineers*. No. 3-61, pp. 123–124 (in Japanese).

Ikegami, M., Masuda, K., Ichiba, T., Tsuruya, H., Satoh, S., Terashi, M. & Ohishi, K. (2002b) Physical properties and strength of cement-treated marine clay after 20 years. *Proc. of the 57th Annual Conference of the Japan Society of Civil Engineers*. No. 3-61, pp. 121–122 (in Japanese).

Ikegami, M., Satoh, H., Ichiba, T., Ozawa, T., Shimura, H., Terashi, M. & Ohishi, K. (2003) Strength gain and structural change of cement treated soil. *Proc. of the 58th Annual Conference of the Japan Society of Civil Engineers*. No. 3-58, pp. 1175–1176 (in Japanese).

Japan Cement Association (2007) *Soil improvement manual using cement stabilizer (3rd edition)*. Japan Cement Association, 387p. (in Japanese).

Japan Cement Association (2012) *Soil improvement manual using cement stabilizer (4th edition)*. Japan Cement Association, 442p. (in Japanese).

Japan Lime Association (2009) *Technical Manual on Ground Improvement using Lime*. Japan Lime Association, 176p. (in Japanese).

Japanese Geotechnical Society (2009) *Practice for making and curing stabilized soil specimens without compaction. JGS 0821-2009*. Japanese Geotechnical Society. Vol. 1, pp. 426–434 (in Japanese).

Japanese Industrial Standard (2010) *Testing methods for industrial wastewater, JIS K 0102: 2010*. (in Japanese).

Kaneshiro, T., Moriya, M., Kondou, H. & Takahashi, S. (2006) The leaching behavior of the specific harmful substances from contaminated soil which were stabilized with all-purpose cementitious soil stabilizer. *Cement & Concrete*. No. 714, pp. 12–21 (in Japanese).

Kawasaki, T., Niina, A., Saitoh, S. & Babasaki, R. (1978) Studies on engineering characteristics of cement-base stabilized soil. *Takenaka Technical Research Report*. Vol. 19, pp. 144–165 (in Japanese).

Kitazume, M. & Hayano, K. (2005) Strength property and variance of cement treated ground by pneumatic flow mixing method. *Proc. of the 6th International Conference on Ground Improvement Techniques*. pp. 377–384.

Kitazume, M. & Takahashi, H. (2009) 27 Years' investigation on property of in situ quicklime treated clay. *Proc. of the 17th International Conference on Soil Mechanics and Geotechnical Engineering*. Vol. 3, pp. 2358–2361.

Kitazume, M. & Terashi, M. (2013) *The Deep Mixing Method*. CRC Press, Taylor & Francis Group, 410p.

Kitazume, M., Adachi, Y., Ikenoue, N. & Okubo, Y. (2007) Engineering property of treated soil by pneumatic flow mixing method (Part 3) Relation between the fluidity of treated soil and required air pressure for transport. *Proc. of the 42nd Annual Conference of the Japanese Geotechnical Society*. pp. 607–608 (in Japanese).

Kitazume, M., Jouyou, T. & Mizoguchi, M. (2006) The unconfined compressive strength of 4 years' stabilized soil strength by the pneumatic flow mixing method. *Proc. of the 61st Annual Conference of the Japan Society of Civil Engineering*, pp. 305–306 (in Japanese).

Kitazume, M., Nakamura, T., Terashi, M. & Ohishi, K. (2003) Laboratory tests on long-term strength of cement treated soil. *Proc. of the 3rd International Conference on Grouting and Ground Treatment*. Vol. 1, pp. 586–597.

Kudo, T., Seriu, M., Yoshimoto, K. & Hatakeyama, N. (1996) Strength properties of cement treated soft clay subjected to cyclic loading. *Proc. of the Symposium on Cement Treated Soils*. pp. 161–166 (in Japanese).

Makino, M., Takeyama, T. & Kitazume, M. (2014) Laboratory tests on the influence of Soil Disturbance on the Material Properties of Cement-treated Soil. *Proc. of the 9th International Symposium on Lowland Technology*. pp. 150–155.

Makino, M., Takeyama, T. & Kitazume, M. (2015) The influence of soil disturbance on material properties and micro-structure of cement-treated soil. *International Journal of Lowland Technology*.

Matsumura, M. (2007) Improvement and results of dioxin content tests of dredging soil. *Japan Society of Material Cycles and Waste Management*. Vol. 18, pp. 321–323 (in Japanese).

Ministry of Transport, The Fifth District Port Construction Bureau (1999) *Pneumatic Flow Mixing Method*. Yasuki Publishers, 157p. (in Japanese).

Miura, H., Tokunaga, S., Kitazume, M. & Hirota, N. (2004) Laboratory Permeability Tests on Cement Treated Soils. *Proc. of the International Symposium on Engineering Practice and Performance of Soft Deposits, IS-OSAKA 2004*, pp. 181–186.

Morikawa, Y., Yokoe, T. & Kitou, J. (2006) The unconfined compressive strength of 10 years' stabilized soil strength by the pneumatic flow mixing method. *Proc. of the 67th Annual Conference of the Japan Society of Civil Engineering*, pp. 451–452 (in Japanese).

Namikawa, T. & Koseki, J. (2007) Evaluation of tensile strength of cement-treated sand based on several types of laboratory tests. *Soils and Foundations*. Vol. 47, No. 4, pp. 657–674.

Niigaki, O., Fukushima, Y., Nodu, M., Yanagawa, Y. & Kasahara, Y. (2000) The property of deep mixing stabilized soil beneath highway embankment after more than 10 years. *Proc. of the 37th Annual Conference of the Japanese Geotechnical Society*. pp. 1117–1118 (in Japanese).

Niina, A., Saitoh, S., Babasaki, R., Miyata, T. & Tanaka, K. (1981) Engineering properties of improved soil obtained by stabilizing alluvial clay from various regions with cement slurry. Takenaka Technical Research Report. Vol. 25, pp. 1–21 (in Japanese).

Niina, A., Saitoh, S., Babasaki, R., Tsutsumi, I. & Kawasaki, T. (1977) Study on DMM using cement hardening agent (Part 1). *Proc. of the 12th Annual Conference of the Japanese Society of Soil Mechanics and Foundation Engineering*. pp. 1325–1328 (in Japanese).

Nishida, T., Terashi, M., Otsuki, N. & Ohishi, K. (2003) Prediction method for Ca leaching and related property change of cement treated soils. *Proc. of the 3rd International Conference on Grouting and Ground Treatment*. Vol. 1, pp. 658–669.

Onitsuka, K., Modmoltin, C., Kouno, M. & Negami, T. (2003) Effect of organic matter on lime and cement stabilized Ariake clays. *Journal of Geotechical Engineering, Japan Society of Civil Engineers*. (729/III-62), pp. 1–13.

Saitoh, S. (1988) Experimental study of engineering properties of cement improved ground by the deep mixing method. *Doctoral thesis, Nihon University*. 317p. (in Japanese).

Saitoh, S., Suzuki, Y., Nishioka, S. & Okumura, R. (1996) Required strength of cement improved ground. *Proc. of the 2nd International Conference on Ground Improvement Geosystems*. Vol. 1, pp. 557–562.

Shibuya, S., Tatsuoka, F., Teachavorasinskun, S., Kong, X. J., Abe, F., Kim, Y-S. & Park C-S. (1992) Elastic deformation properties of geomaterials. *Soils and Foundations*. Vol. 32, No. 3, pp. 26–46.

Takahashi, H. & Kitazume, M. (2004) Consolidation and Permeability Characteristics on Cement Treated Clays from Laboratory Tests. *Proc. of the International Symposium on Engineering Practice and Performance of Soft Deposits, IS-OSAKA 2004*. pp. 187–192.

Tanaka, H. & Terashi, M. (1986) Properties of Treated Soils Formed in situ by Deep Mixing Method. *Report of the Port and Harbour Research Institute*. Vol. 25, No. 2, pp. 89–119 (in Japanese).

Tatsuoka, F. & Kobayashi, A. (1983) Triaxial strength characteristics of cement treated soft clay. *Proc. of the 8th European Regional Conference on Soil Mechanics and Foundation Engineering*. Vol. 1, pp. 421–426.

Terashi, M. & Kitazume, M (1992) An Investigation of the Long-Term Strength of a Lime Treated marine Clay. *Technical Note of the Port and Harbour Research Institute*. No. 732, 14p. (in Japanese).

Terashi, M., Okumura, T. & Mitsumoto, T. (1977) Fundamental Properties of Lime-Treated Soils. *Report of the Port and Harbour Research Institute*. Vol. 16, No. 1, pp. 3–28 (in Japanese).

Terashi, M., Tanaka, H., Mitsumoto, T., Honma, S. & Ohhashi, T. (1983) Fundamental Properties of Lime and cement treated Soils (3rd Report). *Report of the Port and Harbour Research Institute*. Vol. 22, No. 1, pp. 69–96 (in Japanese).

Terashi, M., Tanaka, H., Mitsumoto, T., Niidome, Y. & Honma, S. (1980) Fundamental Properties of Lime and cement treated Soils (2nd Report). *Report of the Port and Harbour Research Institute*. Vol. 19, No. 1, pp. 33–62 (in Japanese).

The Building Center of Japan (1997) *Design and Quality Control Guideline of Improved Ground for Building*. p. 473 (in Japanese).

Udaka, K., Tsuchida, T., Imai, Y. & Tang, Y. X. (2013) Compressive characteristics of reconstituted marine clays with developed structures by adding a small amount of cement. *Japanese Geotechnical Journal*. Vol. 8, No. 3, pp. 425–439 (in Japanese).

Watabe, Y. & Tanaka, M. (2012) Study on cement proportion for recycled treated soil. *Technical Note of the Port and Airport Research Institute*. No. 1264, 8p. (in Japanese).

Watabe, Y., Tsuchida, T., Hikiyashiki, H. & Furuno, T. (2001) Mechanical and material properties of dredged soil treated with poor quality of cement. *Report of the Port and Harbour Research Institute*. Vol. 40, No. 2, pp. 3–21 (in Japanese).

Chapter 4

Applications of the pneumatic flow mixing method

1 INTRODUCTION

The pneumatic flow mixing method has many advantages, such as making beneficial use of dredged soil and subsoil possible, allowing any target stabilized soil strength to be obtained within a short period by controlling the type and amount of binder, and facilitating rapid and large-scale execution. Because of these advantages, the method has been applied to many types of construction and for many improvement purposes, including land reclamation, and backfilling behind quay walls and revetments for the purpose of reducing the earth pressure. For land reclamation applications, the binder factor and target unconfined compressive strength of stabilized soil are of the order of 50 to 70 kg/m^3 and 100 to 200 kN/m^2, respectively.

The current chapter describes some examples of the applications in Japan which will help project owners and geotechnical designers judge the applicability of the pneumatic flow mixing method to their projects.

2 IMPROVEMENT PURPOSES AND APPLICATIONS

2.1 Applications of the method

The pneumatic flow mixing method has many advantages, such as making beneficial use of dredged soil and subsoil possible, obtaining any target stabilized soil strength can be obtained within a short period by controlling the type and amount of binder, and conducting a rapid and large-scale execution. Because of these advantages, the method has been applied to many construction projects for many improvement purposes, including land reclamation; backfilling behind sea revetments and earth retaining structures; and shallow stabilization and backfill underwater, as shown in Figure 4.1 (Ministry of Transport, The Fifth District Port Construction Bureau, 1999). For these applications, ordinary Portland cement and blast furnace slag cement type B are often used as binder, where the cement factor and target unconfined compressive strength of the stabilized soil are of the order of 50 to 70 kg/m^3 and 100 to 200 kN/m^2 respectively.

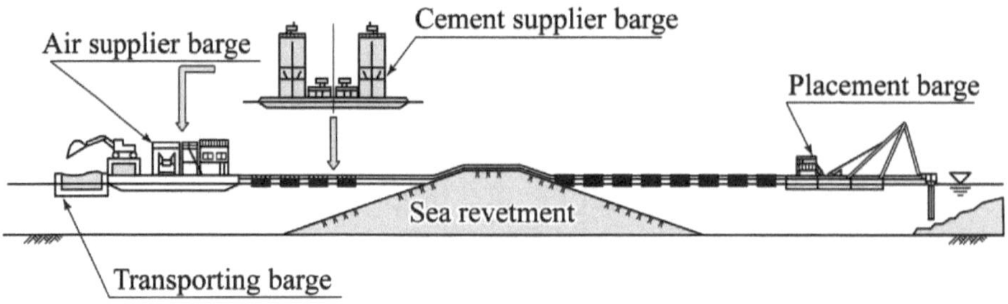

(a) Land reclamation.

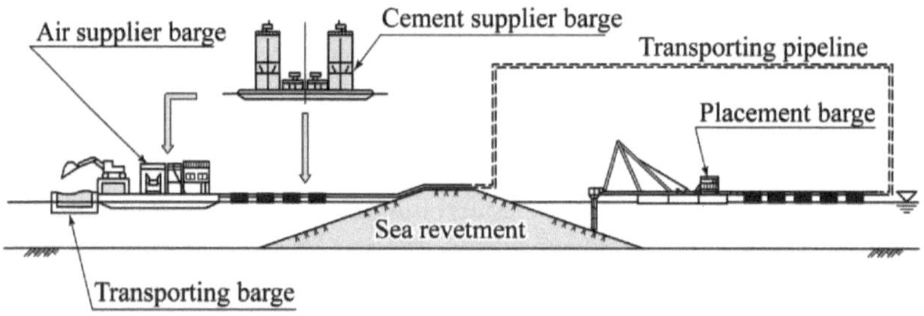

(b) Backfill behind sea revetment.

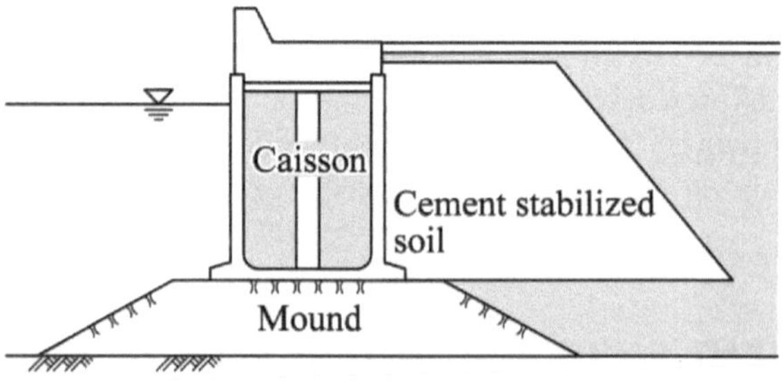

(c) Backfill behind concrete caisson.

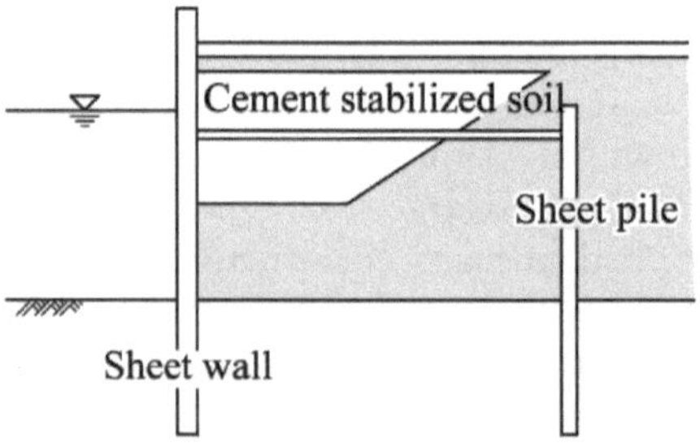

(d) Backfill behind earth retaining structure.

Figure 4.1 Examples of application of the pneumatic flow mixing method (Ministry of Transport, The Fifth District Port Construction Bureau, 1999).

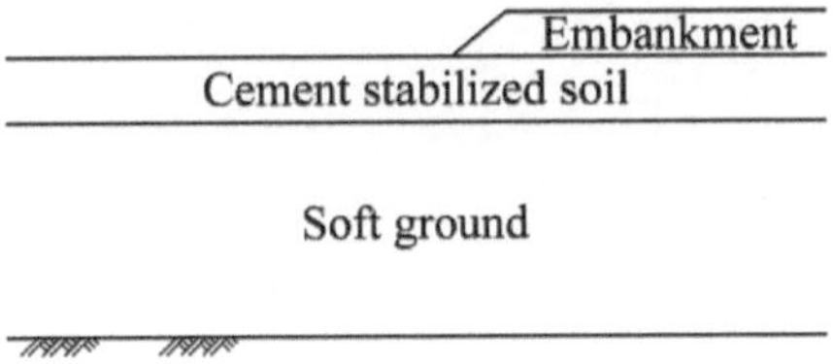

(e) Shallow stabilization.

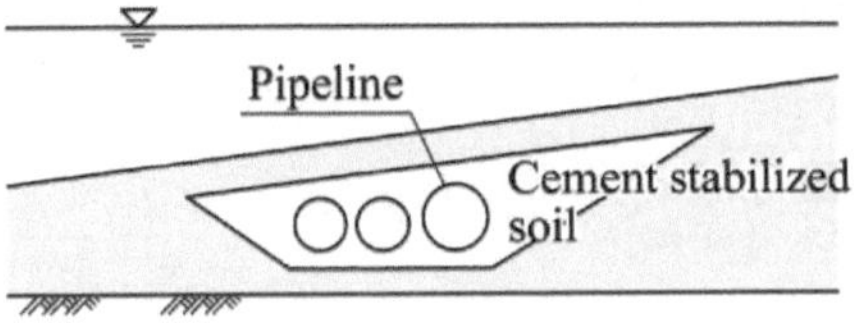

(f) Backfill underwater.

Figure 4.1 (Continued).

3 SELECTED CASE HISTORIES OF THE METHOD IN JAPAN

As described in Chapter 1, the total number of projects of the pneumatic flow mixing method is 47 and the total volume comes to about 15.6 million m^3 from 1998 to 2015. The application of reclamation in marine areas is dominant, the proportions by number and the volume of these projects are about 68.1% and 96.6%

Among many applications of the pneumatic flow mixing method in Japan, nine case histories are selected and briefly introduced in this section: land reclamation, back fill and shallow layer construction. The locations of projects described are shown in Figure 4.2.

3.1 A field test on long-distance transport (field test)

3.1.1 Outline of project

Excavation works have been conducted every year for maintaining the sea route at Fushikitoyama Port, and the excavated soil used to be dumped in disposal sites. However, as it was anticipated that the disposal sites would be full in the near future, new disposal sites needed to be found and prepared for dredged soil. A disposal site was found on land, but it was more than 1 km away from the port. A field test was carried out at Fushikitoyama Port to investigate the capability and applicability of the pneumatic flow mixing method for long distance transportation and the strength of stabilized soil placed at the site (Uezono et al., 2000). Three types mixing techniques of the method were employed for the field test: the LMP (line mix pneumatic conveying

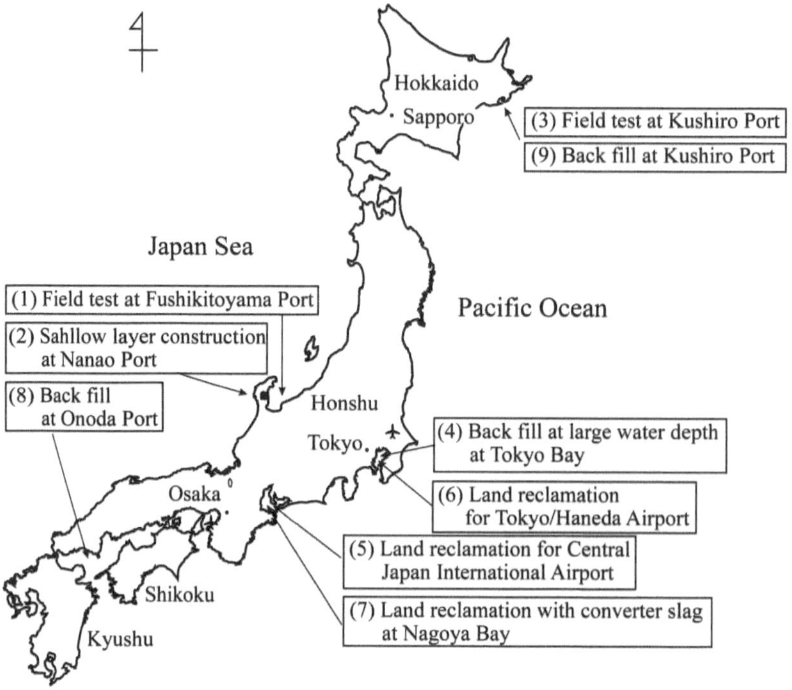

Figure 4.2 Locations of projects introduced as case histories in this chapter.

Table 4.1 Test conditions at Fushikitoyama Port (Uezono et al., 2000).

Technique	*Cement factor*	*Total transport length*	*Transport length after binder injection*
LMP method, slurry form binder with $W/C = 0.5$	50 kg/m^3	960 m	130 m
	60 kg/m^3	945 m	115 m
	80 kg/m^3	930 m	100 m
Plug magic method, powder form binder	50 kg/m^3	930 m	130 m
	60 kg/m^3	915 m	115 m
	80 kg/m^3	900 m	100 m
Snake mixing method, slurry form binder with $W/C = 1.0$	50 kg/m^3	990 m	990 m
	60 kg/m^3	975 m	975 m
	80 kg/m^3	960 m	960 m

system) method (Sasaki, 1999), the plug magic method (Oota & Sakamoto, 2008) and the snake mixing method (Ogawa, 1999). Table 4.1 summarizes the detail of mixing techniques and execution conditions. The total of nine test cases were carried out, changing the amount of cement, as tabulated in Table 4.1.

Table 4.2 Physical properties of dredged soil and stabilized soil at Fushikitoyama Port (after Uezono et al., 2000).

	(A) LMP method			*(B) Plug magic method*			*(C) Snake mixing method*		
	slurry, W/C = 0.5			*powder*			*slurry, W/C = 1.0*		
Cement factor (kg/m^3)	50	60	80	50	60	80	50	60	80
Natural water content, w_n (%)	140.1	118.4	112.8	114.2	116.3	102.1	122.9	114.2	111.2
Flow value of natural soil	176.7	164.3	190.7	171.0	174.0	168.0	173.0	178.0	175.0
Fine particle content	85.0	77.3	69.3	81.2	78.7	71.3	76.3	70.0	70.0
Liquid limit, w_L (%)	85.3	71.9	65.1	73.5	68.0	59.3	73.9	68.4	68.2
Plastic limit, w_P (%)	31.9	28.3	24.9	30.2	28.4	26.7	33.0	26.8	25.2
Plasticity index, Ip	53	43.6	40	43	39	32	40	41	43
Ignition loss (%)	10.6	10.2	10.1	9.2	9.0	8.9	9.5	9.3	9.2
Organic matter content (%)	5.29	5.08	5.05	5.29	5.11	5.06	5.37	5.31	5.19
w_n/w_L	1.64	1.65	1.73	1.55	1.71	1.72	1.66	1.67	1.63
Water content of stabilized soil, w (%)	132.4	108.4	104.3	103.9	103.3	95.6	116.7	108.7	106.7
Flow value of stabilized soil (mm)	146.9	134.3	147.0	152.0	145.0	140.0	164.0	161.0	175.0

3.1.2 *Design and stabilization work*

The dredged soils used in the test, whose physical properties are summarized in Table 4.2, were excavated at Fushikitoyama Port. It was desirable to carry out the series of field tests under the same conditions, to compare the capability and applicability of the techniques to each other. However, the soil properties were varied for each mixing technique and mixing condition, unfortunately, due to differences in dredged location and depth. The field design strength at 28 curing days, q_{u28}, was determined as the relatively small value of 30 kN/m^2 by anticipating that no superstructure would be constructed on the stabilized soil ground and expected excavation in future. The laboratory mix test revealed that a cement factor of about 60 kg/m^3 should be mixed with the dredged soil to obtain the design strength. In the field test, a cement based special binder was used and its cement factor was changed 50, 60 and 80 kg/m^3 to investigate their effects on the strength of stabilized soil.

The field test was carried out in 1998, where about 100 m^3 dredged soil was stabilized by each method and mixing condition. The dredged soil was transported in the pipeline with the flow rate of 75 m^3/h and stabilized by the three techniques and placed on land by the cyclone placement method (see Chapter 5). The stabilized soil was core sampled at 7 and 28 days' curing for unconfined compression test. Table 4.3 summarizes the test results: the air pressure profile along pipeline and the unconfined compressive strength, which revealed no significant differences between each method and mixing condition. It can be concluded that all of the methods and mixing conditions have high applicability for long transportation.

The strength ratio summarized in Table 4.3(b) was defined as the strength of the field mix sample against the strength of a laboratory mix sample, q_{uf}/q_{ul}. The test

Table 4.3 Test conditions and test results (Uezono et al., 2000).

(a) Air pressure profile in pipeline.

	Air pressure (kN/m²) at inlet	at middle	at outlet
(A) LMP method			
50 kg/m³	331.2	161.7	2.9
60 kg/m³	387.1	177.4	3.9
80 kg/m³	379.3	188.2	6.9
(B) Plug magic method			
50 kg/m³	352.8	71.5	1.0
60 kg/m³	303.8	137.2	2.0
80 kg/m³	323.4	137.2	1.0
(C) Snake mixing method			
50 kg/m³	323.4	105.8	3.9
60 kg/m³	339.1	116.6	3.9
80 kg/m³	343.0	118.6	3.9

(b) Unconfined compressive strength.

	(A) LMP method slurry, W/C = 0.5			*(B) Plug magic method* powder			*(C) Snake mixing method* slurry, W/C = 1.0		
Cement factor (kg/m³)	50	60	80	50	60	80	50	60	80
q_{ul} at 7 days (kN/m²)	3	30	75	25	65	146	9	54	140
q_{ul} at 28 days (kN/m²)	5	36	101	28	78	154	13	58	145
Field strength at 7 days									
q_{uf} (kN/m²)	12	42	70	11	83	222	11	61	148
standard deviation (kN/m²)	0.12	0.22	0.42	0.24	0.41	0.67	0.14	0.8	0.16
COV (%)	100.0	51.2	59.2	218.2	48.2	29.6	127.3	29.0	10.6
q_{uf}/q_{ul}	3.92	1.41	0.93	0.43	1.28	1.52	1.20	1.13	1.06
Field strength at 28 days									
q_{uf} (kN/m²)	17	44	67	10	96	244	11	81	179
standard deviation (kN/m²)	0.16	0.22	0.38	0.22	0.52	1.08	0.12	0.21	0.43
COV (%)	94.1	48.9	55.9	220.0	53.1	43.4	109.1	25.3	23.6
q_{uf}/q_{ul}	3.34	1.23	0.66	0.35	1.23	1.59	0.83	1.40	1.23

results revealed that the strength of stabilized soil increased with the cement factor, irrespective of the method. For the techniques (A) and (C), slurry types, the strength of stabilized soil was a little smaller than for technique (B). The uniformity of (A) and (C) was better than for (B), especially in (C), where the uniformity was the best among the three techniques, because the soil and cement could be mixed throughout along the long transportation distance. For (B), powder type, the strength was largest among the three techniques, but the uniformity was lower than the slurry type techniques.

Figure 4.3(a) shows the effect of water content on the unconfined compressive strength. The strength gain is quite small in the case of the cement factor of 50 kg/m³. In the case of the cement factor of 80 kg/m³, the strength decreases almost linearly

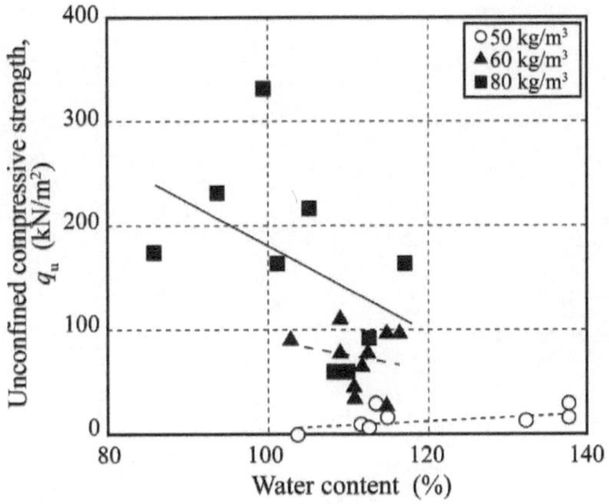

(a) Effect of water content on unconfined compressive strength.

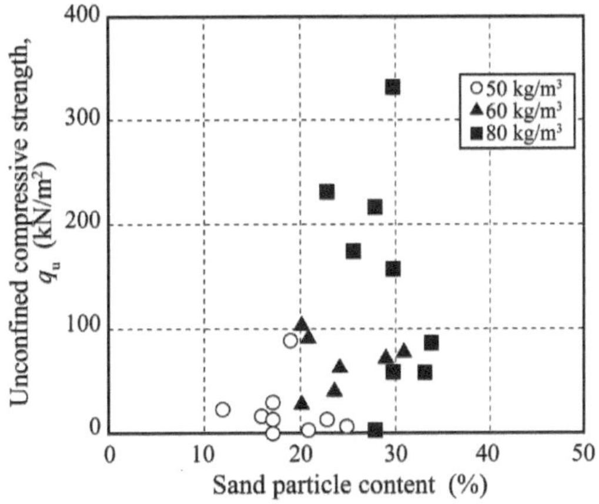

(b) Effect of sand particle content on unconfined compressive strength.

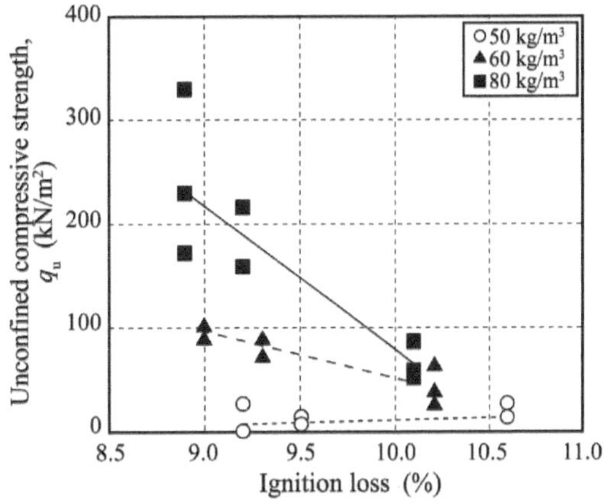

(c) Effect of ignition loss on unconfined compressive strength

Figure 4.3 Unconfined compressive strength of stabilized soil (Uezono et al., 2000).

Figure 4.4 Illustration of shipping berth at Nanao Port (Watanabe, 2005).

with the water content. Figure 4.3(b) shows the effect of sand particle content on the unconfined compressive strength. Though there is a lot of scatter in the measured data on the sand particle content, a rough phenomenon can be seen in that the strength of stabilized soil increases with the sand particle content. Figure 4.3(c) clearly shows that the strength almost linearly decreases with the ignition loss, irrespective of the cement factor.

3.2 Shallow layer construction at Nanao Port

3.2.1 *Outline of project*

A land reclamation project was conducted at Nanao Port, Ishikawa Prefecture, where a steel cell type berth was constructed as shown in Figure 4.4 (Watanabe, 2005). The dredged soil was backfilled behind the berth, which would be improved by the vertical drain method for accelerating the consolidation and reducing the residual settlement. As the natural water content of the dredged soil was quite high, 158.1%, it was anticipated that the stability and trafficability of a vertical drain machine could not be assured. In order to ensure stability and trafficability of the machine, stabilized soil slabs would be constructed by the pneumatic flow mixing method over the reclaimed dredged soil ground. The stabilized soil would also be applied to construct partition dikes for separating the reclaimed land into the five small ponds, 70 m × 50 m.

3.2.2 *Design and stabilization work*

The dredged soil excavated at Nanao Port was a very soft soil with quite a high natural water content, w_n, of 158.1%, and large liquid limit, w_L, of 177.5% and plastic limit, w_P, of 52.9%. The design strength, q_{uck}, and thickness of the stabilized soil slab were determined as 115 kN/m^2 and 1 m, respectively, by taking into account the weight of the expected vertical drain machine. The strength of the partition dike was also

Table 4.4 Soil property of original soil and mix design of stabilized soil (Watanabe, 2005).

	W/C ratio	*Natural water content, w_n*	*Water content after adjustment*	*Cement factor*	*Volume change ratio*
Partition dike	15.133	158.1%	260%	96.0 kg/m^3	1.641
Slab	11.760	158.1%	370%	179.3 kg/m^3	2.306

determined as the same as the slab. The mean strengths of the field stabilized soil, q_{uf}, and of laboratory stabilized soil, q_{ul}, were obtained 150.2 kN/m^2 and 214.6 kN/m^2, respectively, by assuming a coefficient of variation of 35% and a probability of 75% for the field stabilized soil, and a strength ratio, q_{uf}/q_{ul}, of 0.7.

Though the natural water content of the dredged soil was quite high, it was still smaller than the liquid limit. Some amount of water needed to be added to the dredged soil in order to obtain the sufficient fluidity of stabilized soil mixture, which was in turn anticipated to cause a decrease in the stabilized soil strength. A series of laboratory mix tests and field tests were carried out to obtain the appropriate mix condition, as summarized in Table 4.4, for assuring both the design strength and the flow value of stabilized soil.

The stabilization work was conducted in 2004, where the dredged soil was stabilized by the pipe mixing technique (Shinsha et al., 2000). In the construction of the partition dike, the stabilized soil was placed on the soft dredged soil ground by the cyclone technique first, and after one day's curing this was overlaid by the other stabilized soil placed by the direct placement technique. The stabilized soil thus placed sank into the soft dredged soil ground under its self-weight and replaced the soft ground to form the dike. In the construction of the stabilized soil slab, geotextile sheets were spread on the dredged soil ground surface first, and overlaid by the stabilized soil placed by the cyclone technique and the direct placement technique.

The stabilized soils were sampled at the outlet of pipeline and molded every day for quality control and assurance. Figure 4.5 shows the frequency distribution of the unconfined compressive strength at 28 days' curing. The mean strength of molded stabilized soils was 260 kN/m^2 which was larger than the laboratory strength, q_{ul}, of 214.6 kN/m^2. The field strength was also measured for the core samples at the partition dike, which were 120 kN/m^2 on average which was about 0.46 of the strength of the mold sample, probably due to the placement technique, and larger than the design strength, q_{uck}.

3.3 Field test on the strength of stabilized soil placed underwater

3.3.1 Outline of project

A field test was carried out at Kushiro West Port in 2001 to investigate the strength of stabilized soil and the mixing degree (Kobayashi et al., 2001). The dredged soil was excavated at the port and stabilized with blast furnace slug cement type B by the snake mixing method (Ogawa, 1999) and the stabilized soil was placed on the slope

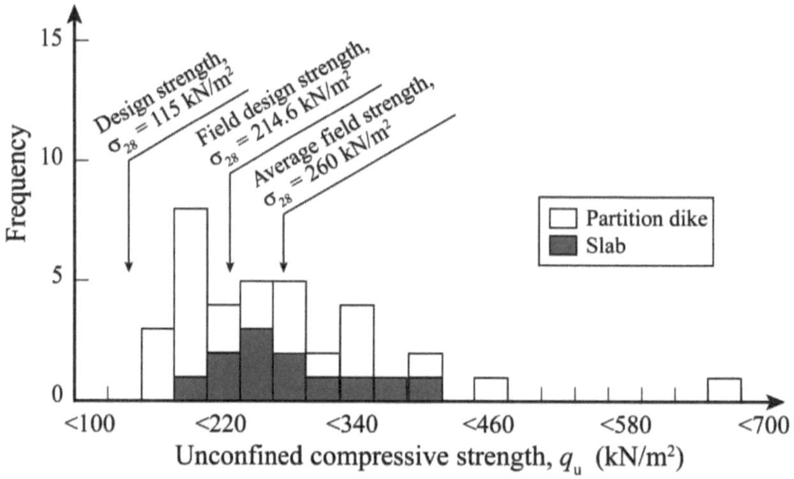

Figure 4.5 Frequency of unconfined compressive strength of stabilized soil (Watanabe, 2005).

shoulder to allow it to flow into seawater. In the tests, the snake mixer (as shown in Figure 5.7(a)) was installed at 274 m from the inlet for the cases A and at 18 m from the inlet for the cases B. The physical and mechanical properties of the stabilized soil placed underwater were investigated. The field tests revealed the high applicability of the method and the quality control in placing stabilized soil. According to the test results, the land reclamation project was conducted where more the 205,200 m^3 of dredged soil (w_0 of 122.3% and w_L of 59.5%) was stabilized with blast furnace slag cement type B of the cement factor of 70 to 80 kg/m^3.

3.3.2 *Design and stabilization work*

Figure 4.6(a) shows the relationship between the degree of mixing and the transportation distance, where the stabilized soil was collected at several points along the pipeline. The degree of mixing was defined as the strength ratio of the stabilized soil along the pipeline against one at the outlet. In the cases A, in which the snake mixer was installed at 274 m from the inlet, the degree of mixing was varied about 60% to 120% for the transportation distance was smaller than 274 m, at the location of the snake mixer, but the degree became almost constant of about 100% after the snake mixer. In the cases B in which the snake mixer was installed at 18 m from the inlet, the degree of mixing was about 50 and 80% before the snake mixer, but jumped up to about 90 to 100% after the snake mixer. The snake mixer located about 18 m from the inlet functioned very well for throughout mixing, while it had been estimated before the test that the snake mixer should be located at more than about 200 m from the inlet.

The two types of dredged soil – sandy silt and fine sand – excavated at Kushiro Port were stabilized with blast furnace slag cement type B by the snake mixing method (Ogawa, 1999) and placed on the slope shoulder to allow to flow into seawater. Figure 4.6(b) shows the strengths of stabilized soil along the distance from the outlet.

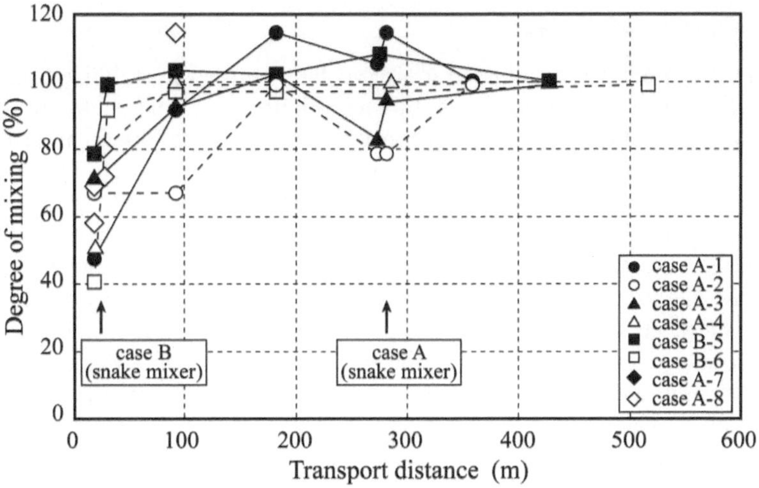

(a) Degree of mixing profile along distance from outlet.

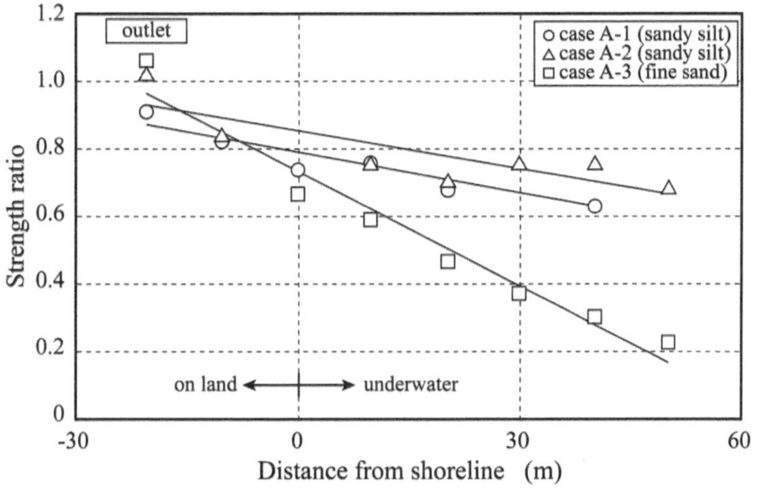

(b) Strength ratio profile along distance from outlet.

Figure 4.6 The influence of location of snake mixer on the degree of mixing and placement effect on the stabilized soil strength (Kobayashi et al., 2001).

In the cases A-1 and A-2, stabilization of sandy silt, the strength of stabilized soil decreases almost linearly with the distance, which might be due to entrapping seawater in the soil during its flow down into the seawater. The strength of stabilized fine sand in the case A-3 also decreased with distance, while the decreasing ratio was much larger than the sandy silt, in cases A-1 and A-2.

3.4 Backfill in deep water

3.4.1 Outline of project

A backfill project was conducted in Tokyo Bay, where the stabilized soil was placed behind the wharf in deep water, as shown in Figure 4.7 (Tang et al., 2000). The figure shows a section of the wharf, which consisted of a concrete caisson and rubble mound. After the backfilling, the land reclamation of 217 hectares would be carried out with dredged soil and subsoils taken in on land construction projects.

In order to prevent the dredged soil and the waste soils from leaking through the rubble mound, it is necessary to place protection inside the wharf. Use of sheets geotextile might be the first choice for the leak protection in many cases, where divers spread the sheets underwater. In the present case, however, it seemed not safe for the divers to have to spread the geotextile sheets at a depth of −40 m. Having reviewed several available methods, it was found that the dredged soft soil, after stabilization with cement, was a rational alternative for leak protection between −20 to −40 m. The design of this operation was to place the cement-stabilized soil behind the wharf, with the layer thickness greater than 1.0 m and the gradient greater than 1:3.

3.4.2 Design and stabilization work

The soft soil dredged at the site contained a certain amount of sand and its water content ranged within 85 ± 20%. The unconfined compressive strength of field stabilized soil, q_{uf}, was designed to be larger than 500 kN/m^2, by considering the filling load afterwards. Also assuming the strength ratio of field to laboratory stabilized soil to be 0.5, the unconfined compressive strength of laboratory stabilized soil, q_{ul}, was 1,000 kN/m^2 and the cement factor of 90 kg/m^3 was determined in the laboratory mix test. The samples after curing for 28 days showed a mean unconfined compressive strength, q_{u28}, of 1,180 kN/m^2, which was more than double of the design strength.

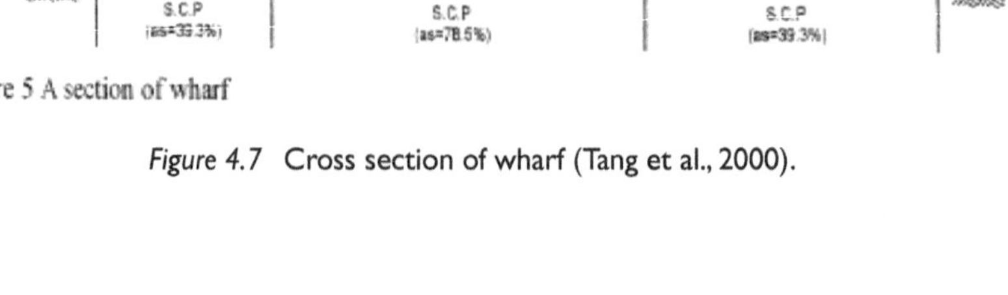

Figure 5 A section of wharf

Figure 4.7 Cross section of wharf (Tang et al., 2000).

3.5 Land reclamation for Central Japan International Airport

3.5.1 Outline of project

A man-made island was constructed for Central Japan International Airport at the north east side of Ise Bay in Nagoya, as shown in Figure 4.8 (Kitazume & Satoh, 2003, 2005; Satoh, 2003, 2004). The plane area of the man-made island was about 5.8 million m^2, and the total amount of reclamation was about 70 million m^3. It was difficult to obtain the necessary amount of soil for reclamation from the surrounding mountainous area within reasonable expense. The 8.6 million m^3 of dredged soil excavated at Nagoya Port was used as a reclamation material after stabilization by the pneumatic flow mixing method in order to reduce the amount of mountain soil needed for reclamation and to promote the recycling of dredged soil. It was the first huge scale application of the method, and a lot of laboratory and field tests were carried out to investigate the mechanical properties of stabilized soil, to develop construction machinery and procedure, and to develop quality control and assurance. These investigations were summarized and published by the Ministry of Transport in 1999 (Ministry of Transport, The Fifth District Port Construction Bureau, 1999).

3.5.2 Design and stabilization work

The designed field strength of the stabilized soil was determined as 120 kN/m^2 based on two criteria: (a) minimum *CBR* value of 3% was assured for the basement layer, and (b) no consolidation settlement was allowed. The average strength for the field stabilized soil, q_{uf}, was determined as 157 kN/m^2 by assuming the probability of 75%,

Figure 4.8 Aerial view of Central Japan International Airport.

Table 4.5 Soil property and mixing condition of expected dredged soils from Nagoya Port.

	Property of dredged soils						*Mixing condition*		
			Particle size distribution						
Site	*Initial water content (%)*	*Density (g/cm³)*	*gravel content (%)*	*sand content (%)*	*clay content (%)*	*Liquid limit (%)*	*Water/cement ratio W/C*	*Water content (%)*	*Cement factor (kg/m³)*
A	74	1.57	0.0	6.8	93.2	75.6	14.0	105	54
B	81	1.58	0.0	8.0	92.0	74.3	13.4	97	55
C	75	1.56	0.0	5.6	94.4	85.5	13.8	113	56
D	84	1.51	0.0	2.4	97.6	88.3	13.8	116	56
E	68	1.57	0.1	8.7	91.2	72.7	13.8	101	54
F	75	1.56	0.0	2.7	97.3	78.3	14.1	100	53
G	67	1.65	0.0	18.0	82.0	55.3	8.5	64	87
H	62	1.67	0.0	5.0	95.0	67.1	13.8	88	52
I	54	1.72	2.3	29.3	68.4	59.3	13.2	80	53
J	48	1.79	0.0	19.3	80.7	49.2	11.4	65	57
K	78	1.59	0.0	14.6	85.4	75.5	13.8	101	54
L	82	1.56	0.2	8.3	91.5	76.8	13.8	101	54

and the average strength of laboratory stabilized soil, q_{ul}, was determined 314 kN/m^2 by assuming the strength ratio, q_{uf}/q_{ul}, of 0.5.

The total of 8.6 million m^3 of the dredged soil was excavated at 12 sites in Nagoya Port. The properties of the dredged soil from the different sites varies significantly, as shown in Table 4.5. For ease of quality control of the stabilized soil, a quality control system by water/cement ratio, W/C, was introduced in the project. The target flow value of the stabilized soil was determined as 95 mm, based on the previous case histories of the method (Ministry of Transport, The Fifth District Port Construction Bureau, 1999). According to these considerations and procedures, the detail mixing conditions of stabilized soil were determined for each expected dredged soil, as shown in Table 4.5.

The sea revetment was constructed in advance along all the periphery of the land reclamation area to prevent any adverse environmental impact to the surrounding seawater. Three sets of the pneumatic system were operated at the construction site to complete constructing the man-made island within about 18 months (Figure 4.9). The soft soil was mixed with blast furnace slag cement type B along the 1,500 m long pipeline and placed at the construction site by the cyclone method. The placement of stabilized soil was carried out in two stages: placement under the water level and above the water level. In the placement underwater, the stabilized soil was placed to a depth of around −5 to −1.5 m at a time. After several weeks' curing, the soil mixture was placed on top of it to the design level of +2.5 m. The stabilized soil layer was soon covered by the mountain soil to start the construction of airport facilities. The land reclamation with stabilized soil commenced in June 2001 and was completed in October 2002. The total amount of 8.6 million m^3 stabilized soil was placed to construct the man-made island.

Figure 4.9 Pneumatic execution systems operating at the construction site of Central Japan International Airport.

3.5.3 *Strength of the stabilized ground*

Field cone tests and unconfined compression tests on core samples were performed every 25,000 m^2 and 40,000 m^2 respectively during the construction to evaluate the strength of the stabilized ground. Figure 4.10(a) shows measured unconfined compressive strength profile along the depth (Kitazume & Satoh, 2005). Though there was a lot of scatter in the measured data, the mean strength of stabilized soil was 296 kN/m^2, which was higher than the target value of 157 kN/m^2. The mean strength and the coefficient of variation of the stabilized soil placed above the water level were 364 kN/m^2 and 28%, respectively. Those for soil placed under the water level were 282 kN/m^2 and 38%, respectively, which were of smaller strength and larger variation compared to those above the water level. Figure 4.10(b) shows the water content profile of the stabilized soil along the depth. Also there was a lot of scatter in these measured data, but the mean water content was 105.3%. The water contents of the stabilized soils placed above the water level and below the water level were 96.9% and 107%, respectively, which confirms the phenomenon that seawater was entrapped during placement underwater. The entrapped seawater reduced the stabilized soil strength placed under water.

3.5.4 *Long-term strength and water content of the stabilized ground*

After the completion of the construction of the airport in 2002, the long-term strength and water content of the stabilized soil ground was surveyed in 2006 (4 years after the construction) (Kitazume et al., 2006) and in 2012 (10 years) (Morikawa et al., 2012). The site of the survery was at the north part of the island, as shown in Figure 4.11 (Morikawa et al., 2012). The BrN-1 and BrN-2 in Figure 4.11(a) were the survey

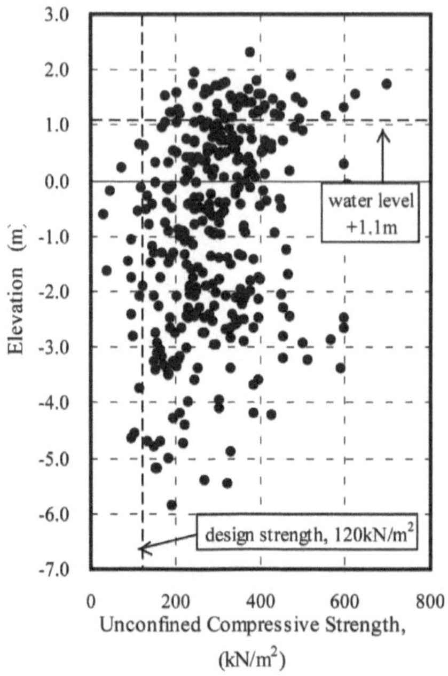

(a) Unconfined compressive strength distribution in field.

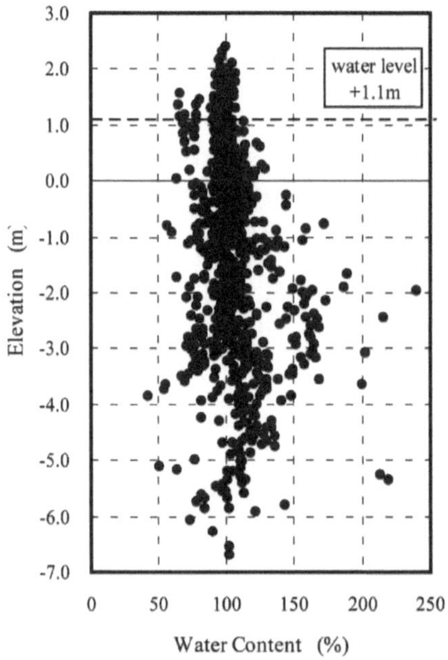

(b) Water content distribution of stabilized soil with depth.

Figure 4.10 Unconfined compressive strength and water content distribution of stabilized soil with depth (Kitazume & Satoh, 2005).

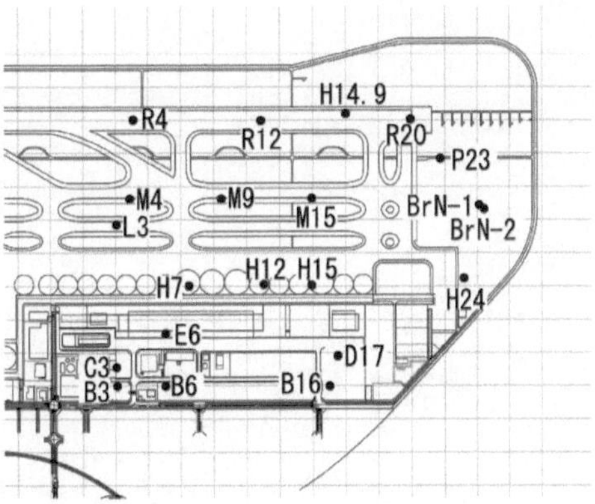

(a) Location of survey of stabilized soil in 2002, 2006 and 2012.

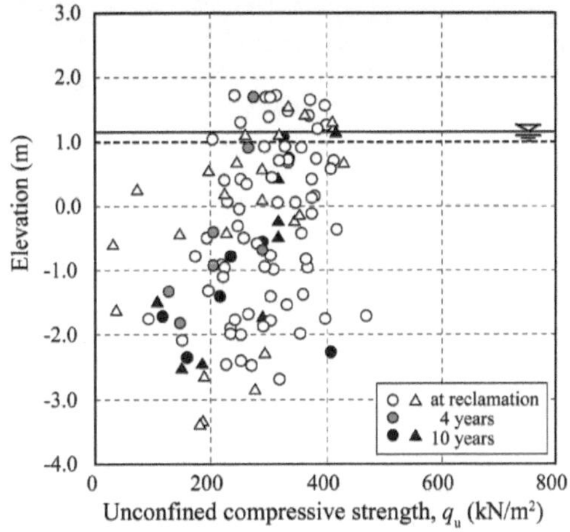

(b) Long-term unconfined compressive strength distribution along the depth.

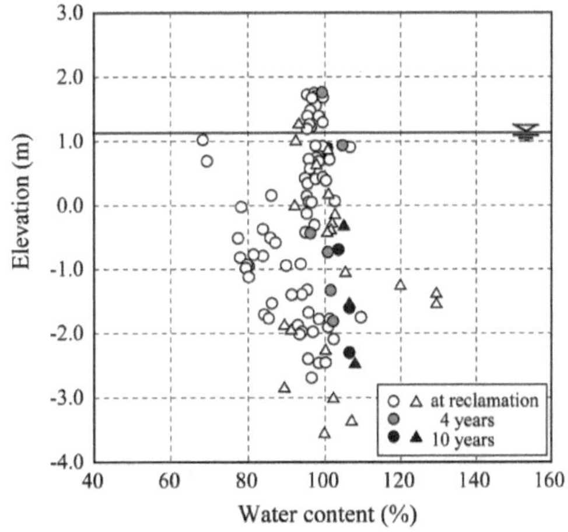

(c) Long-term water content distribution along the depth.

Figure 4.11 Long-term unconfined compressive strength and water content distribution of stabilized soil with depth (Morikawa et al., 2012).

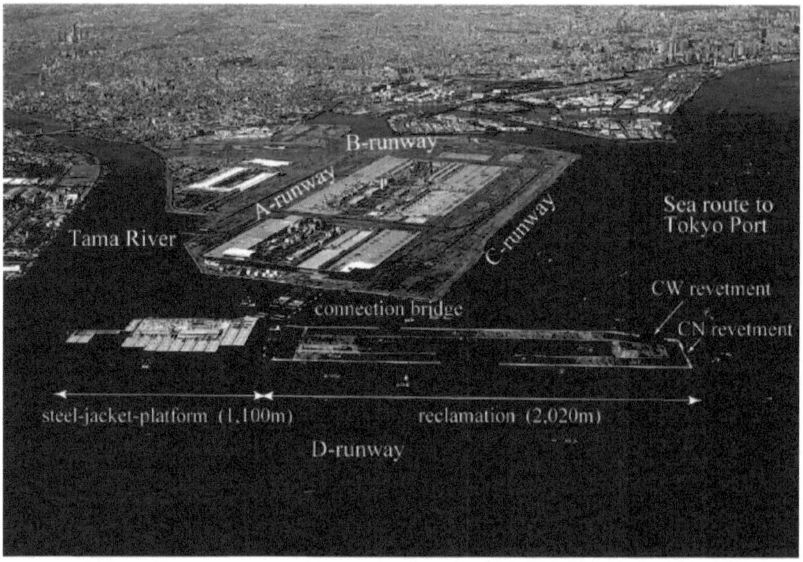

Figure 4.12 Aerial view of construction site and existing airfield on March 15th, 2009 (by courtesy of the Tokyo/Haneda International Airport Construction Office).

point in 2006 and 2012, while the others were the survey point at the completion of the construction. Figures 4.11(b) and 4.11(c) show the unconfined compressive strength, q_u, and the water content of the stabilized soils along the depth. There is a lot of scatter in the measured unconfined compressive strengths irrespective of the time of the survery. The q_u values at the reclamation varies from about 200 to 400 kN/m^2. The measured strengths at 4 years and 10 years are within the range of the strength at the reclamation, in which no clear decrease in the strength was found. The water content measured at 4 years and 10 years are almost a constant of about 100% as shown in Figure 4.11(c), which is within the range of those at the reclamation. Through the surveyed points in 2006 and 2012 was different from the survery at the completion of the construction, no clear change was found in the strength and the water content of the stabilized soil.

3.6 Land reclamation for Tokyo/Haneda International Airport

3.6.1 Outline of project

The construction of a fourth runway of Tokyo/Haneda International Airport was planned in 2001 and commenced in 2006 in order to cope with recent, and expected future, increases in air transportation (Figure 4.12) (Mizukami & Matsunaga, 2015). The man-made island was located between the mouth of the Tama River and the main sea route to Tokyo Port. In order to minimize any adverse influence to the water flow of the Tama River, the west part of the island was a steel-jacket-platform structure while the other was reclamation land. The east part of the island was constructed with cement-stabilized dredged soil and mountain soil. The soft soil was excavated at the

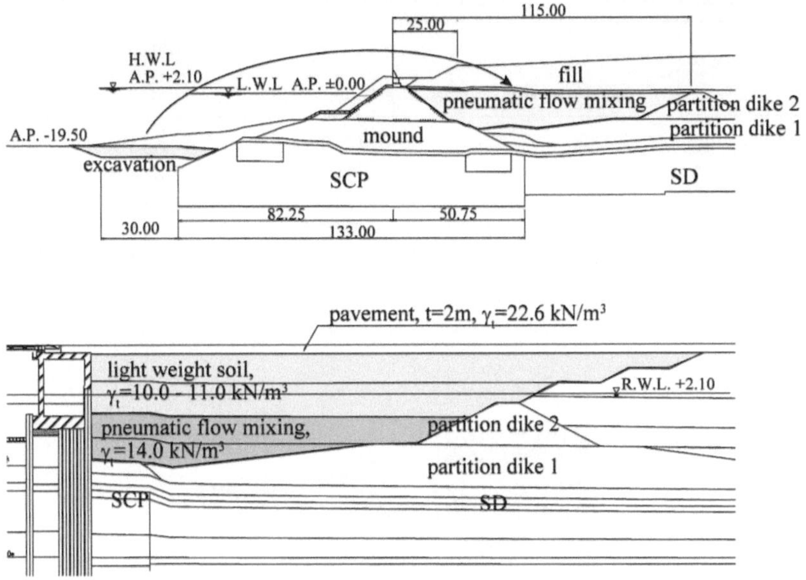

Figure 4.13 Cross section of revetment (Mizukami & Matsunaga, 2015).

front of the island and the sea route of Tokyo Port, and was stabilized with cement and backfilled behind the revetment and the steel wall revetment as shown in Figure 4.13 (Mizukami & Matsunaga, 2015).

3.6.2 Design and stabilization work

The design strength was determined as 300 kN/m^2 by considering that no soil failure was allowed by the overburden pressure. The coefficient of variation and the probability of the field stabilized soil were assumed as 0.35 and 75%, respectively, according to the technical manual. In order to incorporate possibility of failure of the soil due to differential settlement, the design strength was determined as the residual strength of the stabilized soil, which was evaluated at 1.20. As the strength ratio of q_{uf}/q_{ul} was assumed at 0.5, and the average strength of the laboratory stabilized soil was 942 kN/m^2.

The soil used in the method was excavated at three sites in the Tokyo Bay area, the properties of which are tabulated in Table 4.6. The soils had a large amount of silt and clay particles, while the fine particle content exceeded about 90%. The soils were classified as clay and silt with a high liquid limit of about 80 to 180%. Their organic matter contents were about 3.5 to 5.5%, which did not adversely affect the cement stabilization. According to the q_u and W/C relationships which were obtained in the laboratory mix tests, the mix condition for each soil were determined as shown in Table 4.6 for assuring the design strength.

In the project, about 4.8 million m^3 of soil was stabilized from autumn 2008 to the end of 2009. The stabilization work was conducted using three sets of mixing

Table 4.6 Soil properties of original soils and mixing conditions.

Soil name	*Specific gravity*	*Target unit weight*	*Mixing condition*	
			W/C	*Cement factor*
Reclamation, 1	2.662	13.01 kN/m^3	9.42	90 kg/m^3
Reclamation, 2	2.633	12.62 kN/m^3	10.20	85 kg/m^3
Reclamation, 3	2.603	12.62 kN/m^3	11.17	78 kg/m^3
No.1 sea route, 1	2.657	13.18 kN/m^3	9.42	89 kg/m^3
No.1 sea route, 2	2.630	12.76 kN/m^3	7.84	109 kg/m^3
No.1 sea route, 3	2.557	12.28 kN/m^3	8.54	103 kg/m^3
Other site	2.684	16.12 kN/m^3	9.95	84 kg/m^3

Figure 4.14 Placement of cement-stabilized soil in Tokyo/Haneda International Airport construction.

system. In order to minimize the water entrapment, placement was conducted by a pump system and a tremie pipe was kept within the stabilized soil at the construction site (Figure 4.14).

The stabilized soil was sampled in the field at the outlet of the placement machine and put into a plastic mold and cured in a laboratory. The stabilized soil in the field was also sampled by the rotary double core cube ($\phi = 75$ mm). The unconfined compression tests were carried out in November 2008, and Figures 4.15(a) and 4.15(b) show the unconfined compressive strength of the mold and the field stabilized soil at 91 days' curing respectively (Yamatoya et al., 2009). The mean strength of the mold stabilized soil, q_{um91}, was 1,046 kN/m^2, which was 111% of the target strength. The coefficient of variation of the stabilized soil and probability were 0.265 and 88.0%. The mean strength, q_{uf91}, and the coefficient of variation of the field sample were 645 kN/m^2 and 0.376. The strength ratio, q_{uf91}/q_{um91}, was 0.62, which was larger than the design assumed value of 0.5, and the probability of the field stabilized soil was about 85%, which was larger than the design. According to the test results on the strength ratio,

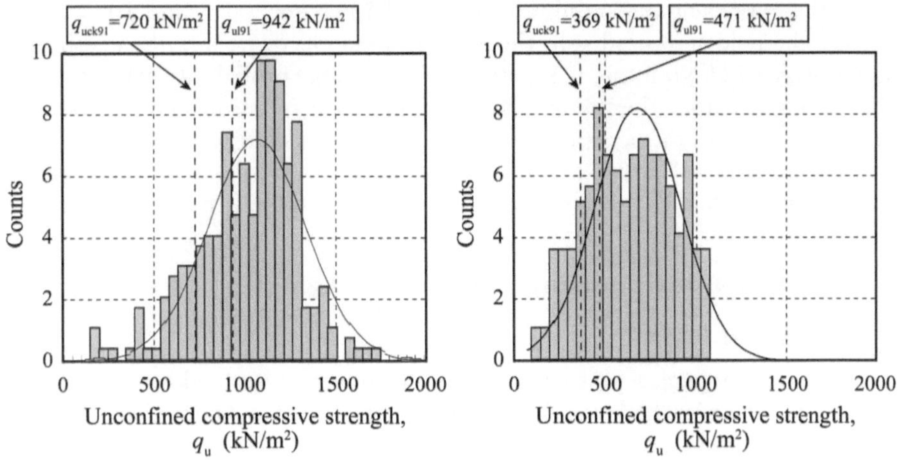

(a) Mold stabilized soil.

(b) Field stabilized soil.

Figure 4.15 Unconfined compressive strength of field stabilized soil at 91 days' curing (Yamatoya et al., 2009).

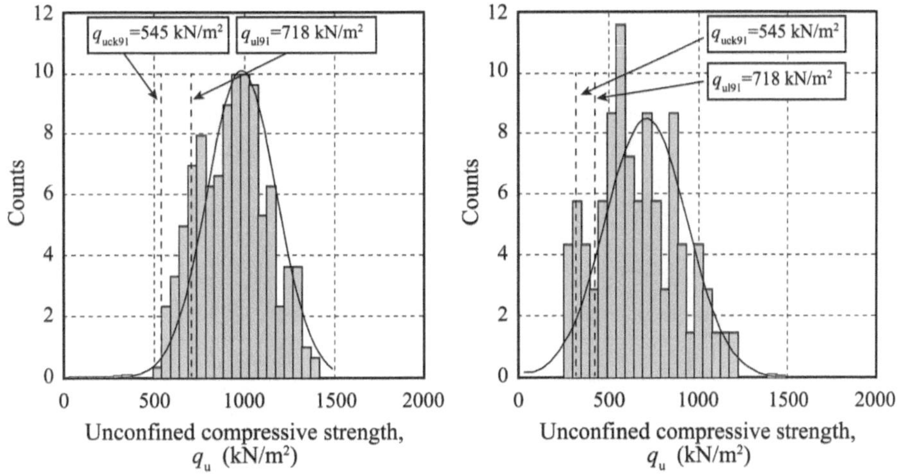

(a) Mold stabilized soil.

(b) Field sampled stabilized soil.

Figure 4.16 Unconfined compressive strength of field stabilized soil at 28 days' curing after modifying the mixing condition (Yamatoya et al., 2009).

the mixing condition was modified to achieve the target laboratory strength of 785 kN/m^2 for further stabilization work.

After modifying the mixing condition, the strength of stabilized soil was investigated again on the mold and field stabilized soils in February 2009. Figures 4.16(a) and 4.16(b) show the strength of the mold and field stabilized soils at 28 days' curing

(Yamatoya et al., 2009). The average strength, q_{um28}, the coefficient of variation, and the probability of the mold stabilized soil were 956 kN/m^2, 0.21, and 100%, respectively. On the field stabilized soil, the average strength, q_{uf28}, and the coefficient of variation were 672 kN/m^2 and 0.35, respectively, and the probability was estimated at 92.8% by incorporating the strength increase from 28 days' curing and 91 days' curing of 1.10. The strength ratio, q_{uf}/q_{um}, was 0.70, which was larger than the design, and the probability was 93%; that was also larger than the design value of 25%. Based on them, the mixing condition was modified again based on the strength ratio of 0.7.

3.7 Land reclamation using converter slag

3.7.1 Outline of project

A land reclamation project was conducted with converter steelmaking slag, so-called 'calcia improved soil', which was a mixture of dredged soil and converter steelmaking slag (Yamagoshi et al., 2013; Tanaka et al., 2012).

3.7.2 Stabilization work

The physical properties of the dredged soils excavated at Nagoya Port are shown in Table 4.7 (Yamagoshi et al., 2013). The design strength of the stabilized soil, q_{uck}, was determined as 30 kN/m^2. The average strengths of the field stabilized soil and laboratory stabilized soil were obtained and were calculated to be 38 kN/m^2 and 60 kN/m^2, respectively, by assuming a coefficient of variation of 0.23, probability of 75%, and a strength ratio, q_{uf}/q_{ul}, of 0.63. The laboratory mix tests were carried out changing the volume of the converter steelmaking slag and the initial water content of dredged soils. Based on the tests, the mixing ratio of the converter steelmaking slag was determined as 25% against the total volume for the stabilized soil, while the flow value of the stabilized soil was 90 to 120 mm.

Table 4.7 Physical properties of dredged soil and slag (Yamagoshi et al., 2013).

	Dredged soil (A)	*Dredged soil (B)*	*Slag*
Specific gravity, *Gs*	2.646	2.648	3.04
Consistency			
liquid limit, w_L (%)	100.7	58.5	–
plastic limit, w_P (%)	37.8	31.9	–
plasticity index, *Ip*	62.9	26.6	–
Particle size distribution			
gravel (%)	0.07	12.44	75.1
sand (%)	2.1	53.6	22.7
silt (%)	72.2	20.0	2.2
clay (%)	25.7	13.96	0
max. size (mm)	4.8	26.0	25
Wet unit weight (kN/m^3)	13.49	16.36	–
Ignition loss (%)	8.8	8.5	–
Initial water content (%)	139.0	73.3	5.2
Water content ratio, w_n/w_L	1.38	1.25	–

The dredged soil and calcia, 75:25 by volume, were mixed and transported in the pipeline, which was 800 mm in diameter and 300 m in transportation distance. The stabilized soil was placed in a storage tank by a cyclone system, and then placed at the slope shoulder by means of a concrete pump. Figure 4.17(a) shows the relationship between the flow value of stabilized soil and the gradient of air pressure in the pipeline. The flow value ranged from 82 to 156 mm due to the scatter in the initial water content. In the figure, some previous case records are plotted together. The gradient of air pressure is increased with decreasing pipeline diameter. Figure 4.17(b) shows the frequency distribution of the strength of field stabilized soil at 28 days' curing. The average strength was 114 kN/m^2, which exceeded the target strength of 38 kN/m^2.

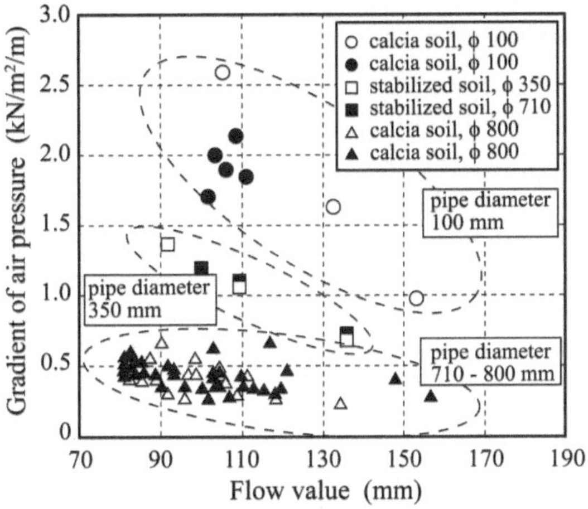

(a) Relationship between the flow value and the gradient of air pressure.

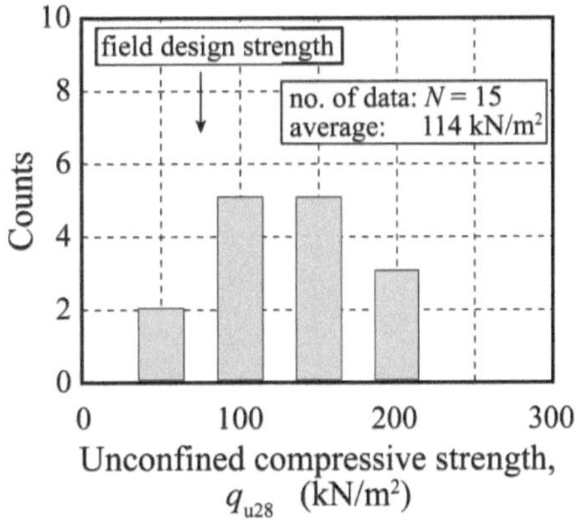

(b) Frequency distribution of the field stabilized soil strength at 28 days' curing.

Figure 4.17 Characteristics of stabilized soil in the field land reclamation test (Yamagoshi et al., 2013).

3.8 Backfill behind breakwater – for settlement reduction (field test)

3.8.1 Outline of project

Much research has been conducted to promote the beneficial use of fly ash produced in coal-fired power plants. Fly ash was used as binder to stabilize dredged soil in the following land reclamation project. The dredged soil excavated at the offshore seabed of the Onoda Power Plant was stabilized with the mixture of blast furnace slag cement type B and fly ash by the pneumatic flow mixing method (Kurumada et al., 2000). When the amount of cement is decreased to obtain a small target strength, it becomes difficult to produce a uniform stabilized soil in the field. When a low activity binder is mixed with soil, as well as cement, the volume of binder is increased and the uniformity of the stabilized soil can be improved. The fly ash was expected to function as a binder aid to obtain a relatively low strength, since it has lower hydration reactivity than cement. And fly ash was expected to increase uniformity of soil and binder mixture by the bearing effect due to the spherical shape of its particles.

3.8.2 Design and stabilization work

The properties of the dredged soil and the fly ash produced in the coal-fired power plant are shown in Table 4.8 (Kurumada et al., 2000). The design strength, q_{u28}, of the stabilized soil was determined as 100 to 250 kN/m^2 by taking into account that the stabilized soil would be excavated later for superstructure construction. A series of laboratory mix tests was carried out to obtain the mix condition, where blast furnace slag cement type B with the W/C ratio of 100% and the same amount of the fly ash as

Table 4.8 Physical properties of dredged soil and fly ash at the Onoda Power Plant (Kurumada et al., 2000).

Property	*Dredged soil*	*Fly ash*
Specific gravity, Gs	2.641	2.311
Natural water content, w_n (%)	200.68	
Grain size distribution		
sand (%)	3.4	5.6
silt (%)	42.1	81.4
clay (%)	54.5	13.0
Consistency		
liquid limit, w_L (%)	121.0	
plastic limit, w_P (%)	46.0	
plasticity index, I_p	75	
Ignition loss, L_i (%)	12.49	
Chemical composition		
SiO_2 (%)		45.1
Al_2O_3 (%)		23.5
Fe_2O_3 (%)		4.3
CaO (%)		13.6
MgO (%)		1.5
others (%)		12.0

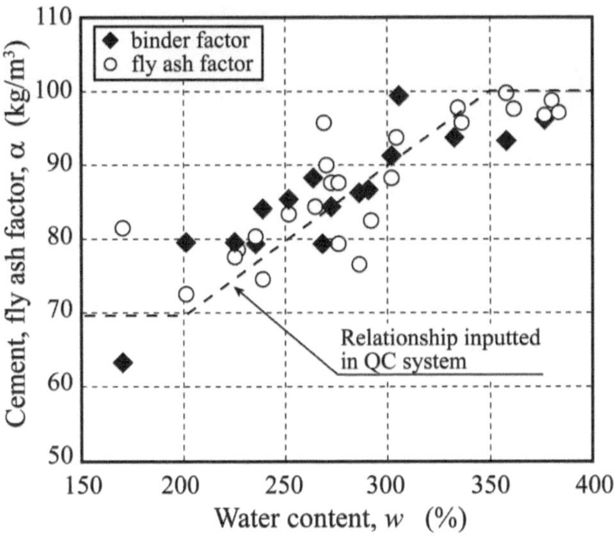

Figure 4.18 Relationship between water content and cement factor needed for the design strength.

the cement were mixed with the dredged soil. Figure 4.18 shows the test result on the relationship between the water content of the dredged soil and the amount of cement and fly ash needed to obtain the field design strength, q_{u28} (Kurumada et al., 2000). This relationship was integrated into the quality control system to control the amount of cement and fly ash for each dredged soil, according to their water content.

The stabilization work was conducted by the pneumatic flow mixing method, and controlled for each dredged soil to assure the design strength. The stabilized soil was sampled at the outlet of the placement machine and molded and cured in a laboratory, and the field stabilized soils were core sampled at 28 days' curing. Figure 4.19(a) shows the unconfined compressive strength of the samples, along with the water content of dredged soil. Through there is a lot of scatter in the strengths of the mold and core samples, they are almost constant and within the design strength range, 100 to 250 kN/m^2, irrespective of the water content (Kurumada et al., 2000). Figure 4.19(b) shows the frequency distribution of q_u, in which the average strength was 195.0 kN/m^2 and ranges from about 100 to 250 kN/m^2 (Kurumada et al., 2000).

3.9 Backfill behind breakwater – for settlement reduction (field test)

3.9.1 *Outline of project*

Stabilized soil was backfilled behind a breakwater at Kuhiro Port as shown in Figure 4.20, which was expected to increase the horizontal resistance of the breakwater, promote beneficial use of dredged soil and create a growing environment for aquatic organisms (Yamauchi et al., 2011). When backfilled, the backfill soil functions to increase the horizontal stability of the breakwater which in turn can reduce

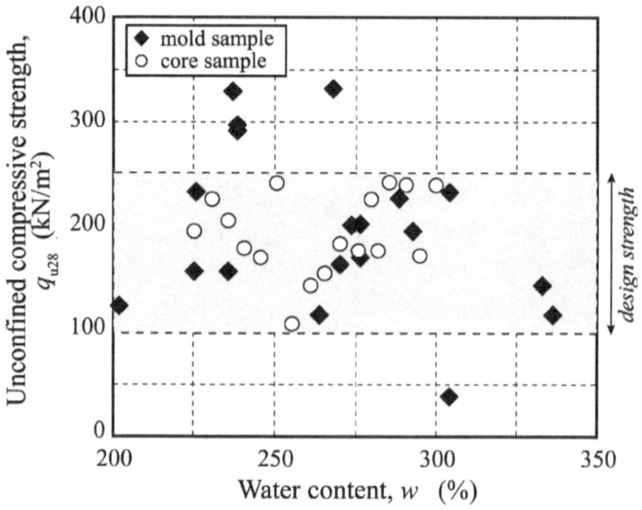

(a) Relationship between water content and cement factor.

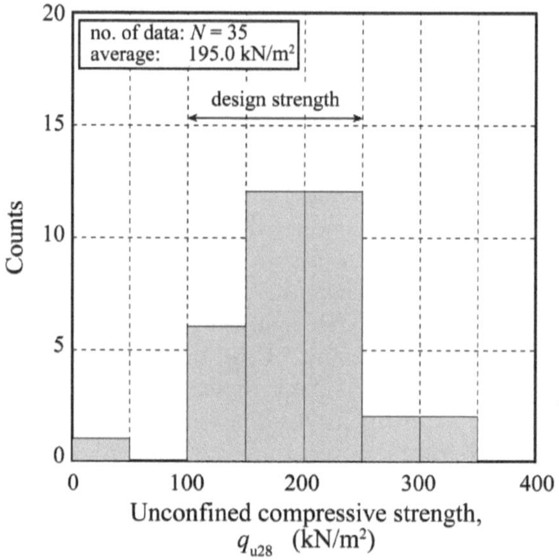

(b) Frequency distribution of unconfined compressive strength.

Figure 4.19 Characteristics of field stabilized soil (Kurumada et al., 2000).

the size of the breakwater by about 20%. When about one million m^3 of dredged soil was stabilized in the project, it provided scope to prolong the disposal site on land. The sea depth was decreased to about couple of metres, which can create a growing environment for aquatic organisms.

(a) Illustration of breakwater and backfill.

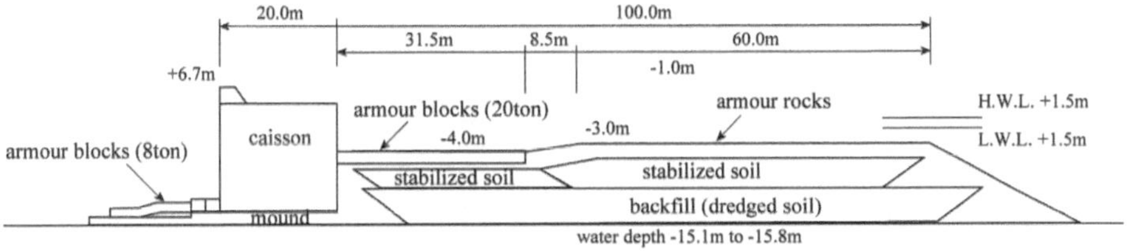

(b) Cross section of breakwater and backfill.

Figure 4.20 Schematic view of backfilling behind breakwater at Kushiro Port (Yamauchi et al., 2011).

3.9.2 *Design and stabilization work*

The strength of stabilized soil was designed so it had the sufficient bearing capacity for armour blocks and a mound, and so the design standard determined as q_u of 22 kN/m^2 (Ministry of Transport, 1999). The dredged soil was stabilized by the pneumatic flow mixing method and placed on land for temporary curing, and after certain curing period it was excavated and placed behind the breakwater by means of a backhoe, to minimize water pollution during the placement (Figure 4.20). As the stabilized soil was disturbed by the excavation, its strength would be smaller than that of a non-disturbed stabilized soil. In order to assure the design strength at site, the target strength of the non-disturbed stabilized soil was determined to have q_{uf} of 100 kN/m^2 by considering handing and trafficability of the soil. The laboratory strength, q_{ul}, was determined as 143 kN/m^2 by incorporating the strength ratio, q_{uf}/q_{ul}, of 0.7 according to the technical manual (Coastal Development Institute of Technology, 2001). The horizontal extent of the stabilized soil layer was designed to be about 60 m as shown in Figure 4.18 by evaluating the stability of the structure. Ordinary Portland cement was used in the project, whose cement factor was 64 kg/m^3 and 72 kg/m^3 for the dredged soil with an initial water content of 100% and 150%, respectively.

Figure 4.21 Placement of stabilized soil by a shell grab for backfill at Kushiro Port.

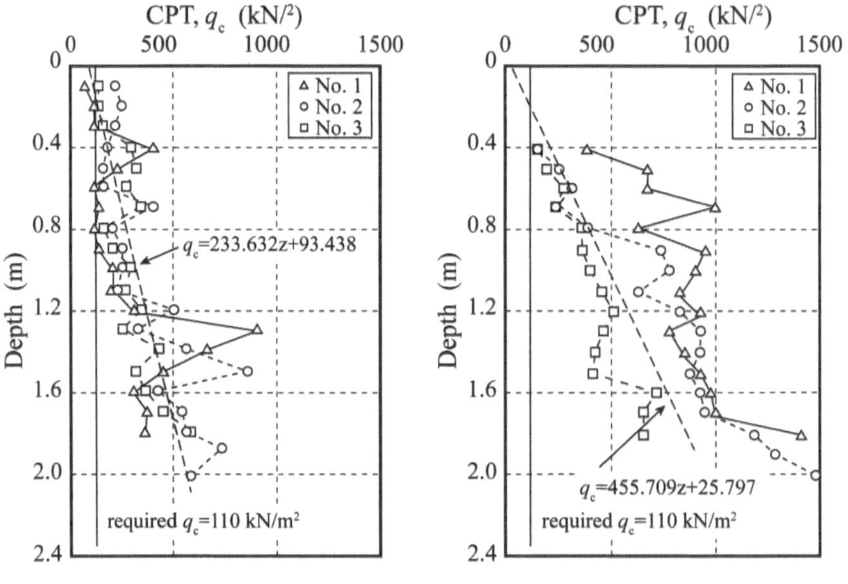

(a) Before overlay. (b) At 28 days after overlay.

Figure 4.22 Cone penetration resistance distribution of the stabilized soil ground along depth (Honma et al., 2009).

A field test was carried out at Kushiro Port, in which a 10 m by 13 m and 2.5 m in height embankment was constructed as shown in Figure 4.21. The dredged soils excavated at Kushiro Port were organic sandy clays with organic matter content of about 3.0 to 8.7%. At 28 days' curing after placement, the stabilized soil was overlaid by the armour rocks. The cone penetration test was conducted before the overlay and at 28 days after the overlay. At 28 days after the overlay, the core samples were taken for an unconfined compression test. Figure 4.22 shows the cone penetration distribution along the depth, where the measured cone penetration resistance, q_c, was different for each testing location but increased with the depth. The measured strengths were larger than the design strength, while the target q_c was 110 kN/m^2 according to the strength ratio, q_u/q_c of 0.2. The unconfined compressive strength of the core samples was 22.94 kN/m^2 on average, which also satisfied the design strength.

REFERENCES

Honma, D., Ishiyama, Y. & Mori, Y. (2009) Construction of breakwater at Kushiro West area – Investigation for beneficial use of soft dredged soil to backfill behind break water. *Proc. of the 21st Research Meeting, Ministry of Land, Infrastructure, Transport and Tourism Hokkaido Regional Development Bureau.* (in Japanese).

Kitazume, M. & Satoh, T. (2003) Development of Pneumatic Flow Mixing Method and its Application to Central Japan International Airport Construction. *Ground Improvement Journal of ISSMGE.* Vol. 7, No. 3, pp. 139–148.

Kitazume, M. & Satoh, T. (2005) Quality control in Central Japan International Airport Construction. *Ground Improvement Journal of ISSMGE.* Vol. 9, No. 2, pp. 59–66.

Kitazume, M., Jouyou, T. & Mizoguchi, M. (2006) The unconfined compressive strength of 4 years' stabilized soil strength by the pneumatic flow mixing method. *Proc. of the 61st Annual Conference of the Japan Society of Civil Engineering*, pp. 305–306 (in Japanese).

Kobayashi, K., Yoshida, G. & Sato, H. (2001) Quality assurance of pneumatic flow mixing method – Snake Mixer Method -. *Proc. of the Annual Research Conference, Civil Engineering Research Institute for Cold Region, Ministry of Ministry of Land, Infrastructure, Transport and Tourism.* pp. 393–400 (in Japanese).

Kurumada, Y., Onda, T. & Saitoh, N. (2000) Construction of fly ash stabilization of high water content clay by pneumatic flow mixing method. *Proc. of the 56th Annual Conference of the Japan Society of Civil Engineers.* pp. 408–409 (in Japanese).

Ministry of Transport (1999) *Technical Standards for Port and Harbour Facilities.* The Ports and Harbours Association of Japan. pp. 525–536 (in Japanese).

Ministry of Transport, The Fifth District Port Construction Bureau (1999) *Pneumatic Flow Mixing Method.* Yasuki Publishers. 157p. (in Japanese).

Morikawa, Y., Yokoe, T. & Kitou, J. (2006) The unconfined compressive strength of 10 years' stabilized soil strength by the pneumatic flow mixing method. *Proc. of the 67th Annual Conference of the Japan Society of Civil Engineering*, pp. 451–452 (in Japanese).

Ogawa, H. (2001) Strength and mixing degree of treated soil placed underwater by pneumatic flow mixing method. *Proc. of the 56th Annual Conference of the Japan Society of Civil Engineers.* VI-213, pp. 426–427 (in Japanese).

Ogawa, H. (1999) Development of Snake Mixing Method. *Proc. of the Annual Research Meeting, Shikoku Branch, Japan Society of Civil Engineers.* VI-7, pp. 386–387 (in Japanese).

Oota, M. & Sakamoto, A. (2008) Development and application of Plug Magic method – Beneficial use of dredged soil for construction material -. *Journal of the Japanese Society of Soil Mechanics and Foundation Engineering. "Tsuchi to Kiso".* Vol. 56, No. 12, pp. 46–47 (in Japanese).

Sasaki, Y. (1999) Mud solidification air-transfer process. LMP process. *Marine Voice 21.* Vol. 205, pp. 17–19 (in Japanese).

Satoh, T. (2003) Application of pneumatic flow mixing method to Central Japan International Airport Construction. *Journal of the Japan Society of Civil Engineers.* No. 749/6-61, pp. 33–47 (in Japanese).

Satoh, T. (2004) Development and application of pneumatic flow mixing method to reclamation for offshore airport. *Technical Note of the Port and Harbour Research Institute.* No. 1076, 81p. (in Japanese).

Shinsha, H., Ikeda, S. & Matsumoto, A. (2000) Compressed air type pneumatic flow mixing method for large scale admixture stabilization of dredged clay – Pipe mixing method -. *Proc. of the 26th Annual Research Meeting, Kanto Branch, Japan Society of Civil Engineering.* pp. 1036–1037 (in Japanese).

Tanaka, Y., Yamada, K., Ookubo, Y., Shibuya, T., Nakagawa, M., Akashi, Y., Ichimura, M. & Yamagoshi, Y. (2012) Reclamation and evaluation of dredged soil with converter slag. *Journal of Geotechnical Engineering, Japan Society of Civil Engineers.* Vol. 68, No. 2, pp. 486–491 (in Japanese).

Tang, Y. X., Miyazaki, Y. & Tsuchida, T. (2000) Advanced reuses of dredging by cement treatment in practical engineering. *Prof of the International Conference of the Coastal Geotechnical Engineering in Practice.* Vol. 1, pp. 725–731.

Uezono, A., Takezawa, K., Tsukada, S. & Takahashi, K. (2000) Long distance discharging works of dredged soil by plug flow mixing method in pipe lines. *Journal of the Japan Society of Civil Engineers.* No. 651/VI-47, pp. 37–45 (in Japanese).

Watanabe, A. (2005) Challenge to soft soil – Pneumatic flow mixing method for dredged soil -. *Proc. of the Annual Research Conference, Ministry of Ministry of Land, Infrastructure, Transport and Tourism.* (in Japanese).

Yamagoshi, Y., Akashi, Y., Nakagawa, M., Kanno, H., Tanaka, Y., Tsuji, T., Imamura, T. & Shibuya, T. (2013) Reclamation of the artificial ground made of dredged soil and converter slag by using pipe mixing method. *Journal of Geotechnical Engineering, Japan Society of Civil Engineers.* Vol. 69, No. 2, pp. 952–957 (in Japanese).

Yamatoya, T., Mitarai, Y. Iba, H. & Watanabe, M. (2009) Attempt of quality control of treated soil by pneumatic flow mixing method in the construction of D runway. *Technical Meeting of Construction of Tokyo/Haneda International Airport, Ministry of Land, Infrastructure, Transport and Tourism.* (in Japanese).

Yamauchi, H., Ishiyama, Y. & Oonishi, F. (2011) Study for beneficial use of soft dredged soil – case history of back fill behind breakwater at Kushiro Port -. *Proc. of the Annual Technical Meeting, Civil Engineering Research Institute for Cold Region.* (in Japanese).

Chapter 5

Equipment, construction, and quality control and assurance

1 INTRODUCTION

In this chapter, the pneumatic flow mixing equipment, construction procedure and quality control and assurance are introduced for representative pneumatic flow mixing methods in Japan. The descriptions in this chapter are based on the latest information, as of 2015. The diversified applications of the method (Chapter 4) and pursuit of cost-effectiveness have continuously promoted the improvement of existing execution systems and the development of new systems. Project owners and design engineers are encouraged to update the information periodically.

The purpose of construction by the pneumatic flow mixing method is, in many cases, to produce new ground with stabilized soil, and that the improved ground may meet the function required by geotechnical design. The responsibility for achieving the requirements are shared by owner, designer, general contractor and pneumatic flow mixing contractor, depending on the adopted contractual scheme. It is necessary for the owner and designer to have sufficient knowledge on the capability and limitation of locally available execution systems and on the experience of the local contractor, and for the contractors to understand the design intent behind the given specifications (Chapter 6).

2 EQUIPMENT

2.1 System and specifications

The system for the pneumatic flow mixing method consists of pneumatic equipment; cement plant and supplier equipment; placement equipment; and control equipment. Since quite a large amount of dredged soil at a coastal area is used to construct reclaimed land in many cases, these pieces of equipment are usually installed on barges. The system can be classified into three groups depending on the stabilization capacity: 300, 600 and 800 m^3/h. Figure 5.1 shows a group of barges for the 300 m^3/h capacity system, whose major capacities are summarized in Table 5.1 (Kitazume et al., 2000). In the figure, the dredged soil in the soil transport equipment is loaded into the hopper on the pneumatic equipment first and is transported by the help of compressed air. Binder, usually cement, is then injected into the soil on the cement supplier equipment barge and soil and binder are thoroughly mixed during transportation through the pipeline.

Figure 5.1 Group of pneumatic flow mixing barges.

Table 5.1 Major capacities of facility shown In Figure 5.1 (Kitazume et al., 2000).

Facility	*Capacity*
Pneumatic barge	
max. of main power	2,000 ps
max. of transporting capacity	150 m^3/h, two lines
max. of stability supplier	30 tonne/hr
Binder supplier barge	
max. capacity	300 m^3/hr
Placement barge	
diameter of cyclone	ϕ1,500 mm, two sets
Pipeline	
diameter	ϕ350 mm
length	180 to 373 m

Figure 5.2 shows the other type of barges. Binder in slurry or dry form may be added to the soil, but the slurry form is common in Japan. There are two types of the method, according to where the binder is injected, as later shown in Figure 5.4: compressor addition type and line addition type. In the former type, the binder is injected to the soil before the compressed air is injected into the pipeline. In the latter type, the binder is injected to the soil after the air injection. The soil and binder mixture is placed at the reclamation site through a cyclone on the placement barge, which functions to release the air pressure which is transporting the soil plugs. A tremie pipe is usually used to place the soil and binder mixture underwater, and thereby not entrap seawater within the soil, which can considerably weaken the stabilized soil.

(a) Soil transfer barge.

(b) Pneumatic barge.

Figure 5.2 Components of pneumatic flow mixing systems operating on floating barges.

There are several variations on the binder injection techniques and transporting techniques developed by various construction firms to improve the mixing degree of soil and binder (Hashimoto, 1999, Ikegami, 1999, Ishikawa, 2000, Iwata et al., 2000, 2006, Kobayashi et al., 2001, Mori, 2000, 2001, Ogawa, 1999, Oota & Sakamoto, 2008, Sakamoto, 1998, Sasaki, 1999, Satoh, 2001, Sato & Hayashida, 2000, Shima & Hashimoto, 1998, Sumoto, 2000). One uses an additional piece of equipment installed along the pipeline to detect the plug location accurately, and other is changing the shape or diameter of pipeline locally.

(c) Binder supplier barge.

(d) Placement barge.

Figure 5.2 Continued.

2.2 Air pressure feed system

The air pressure feed system – which has a capacity of 40 to 1,600 m^3/h of compressed air supply – discharges soil into a pipeline and injects compressed air to create soil plugs, and for transporting them. It can be classified into four methods, as shown in Figure 5.3: (a) pressurized tank method, (b) mixed air feed method, (c) pressurizing pump method and (d) blower feed method.

In the pressurized tank method, soil in a pressurized tank is discharged into a pipeline by injected compressed air in the pressure tank (Figure 5.3(a)). In the mixed air feed method, soil fed continuously from an energizing device is discharged into a pneumatic pipeline by injected compressed air (Figure 5.3(b)). In the pressurizing pump method, soil fed continuously from a pressurized tank via a vertical high-speed screw is discharged into a pipeline by injected compressed air (Figure 5.3(c)).

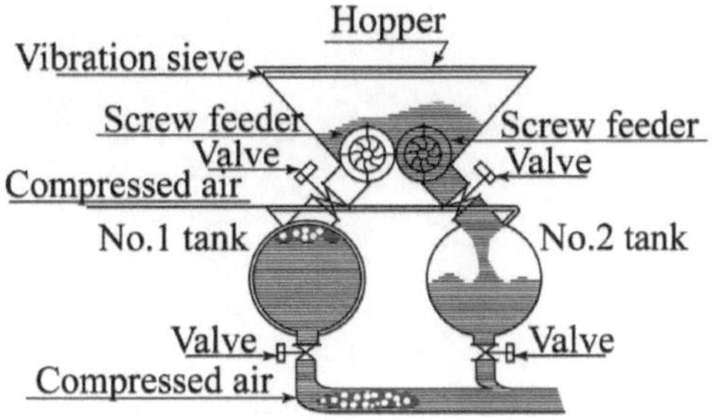

(a) Pressurized tank method.

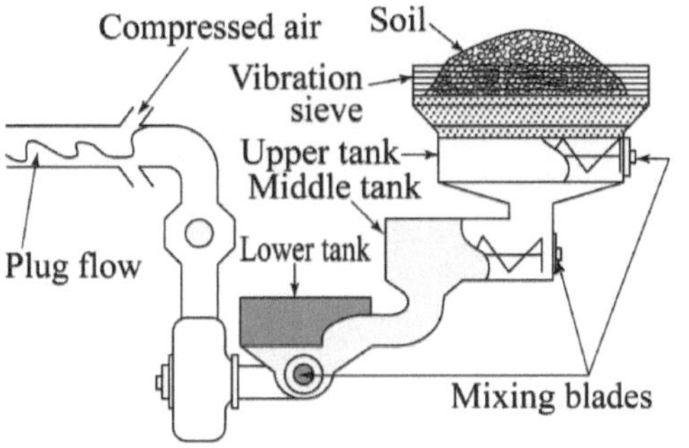

(b) Mixed air feed method.

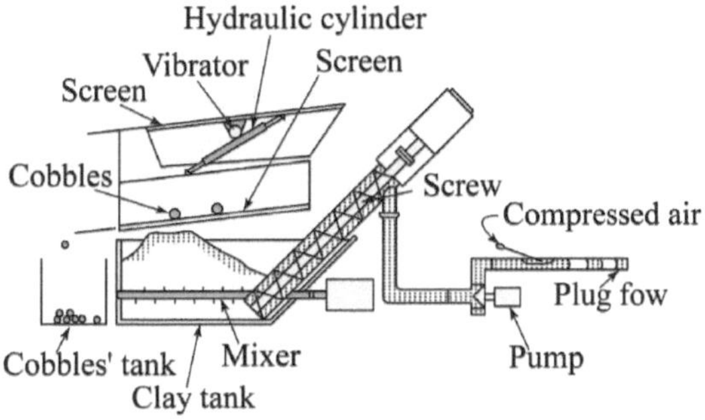

(c) Pressurizing pump method.

Figure 5.3 Air pressure feed systems for discharging soil into a pipeline.

In the blower feed method, soil fed by a rotating-type blower is discharged into a pipeline by injected compressed air (Figure 5.3(d)).

2.3 Binder supplier system

The binder supplier system injects binder to the soil. They are two types of the method according to where binder is injected, as shown in Figure 5.4: compressor addition type and line addition type. In the compressor addition type, binder is injected to the soil

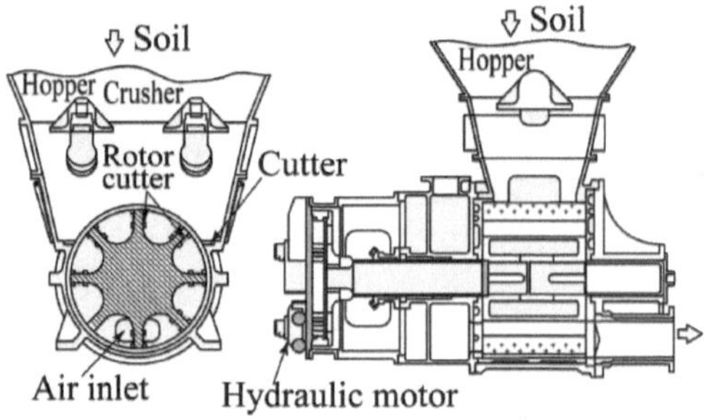

(d) Blower feed method.

Figure 5.3 Continued.

(a) Compressor addition type.

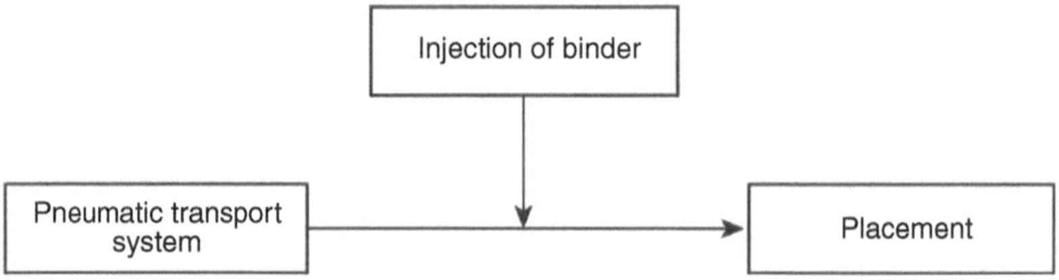

(b) Line addition type.

Figure 5.4 Schematic of binder supplier systems with different injection points.

before compressed air is injected into a pipeline (Figure 5.4(a)). A feeder with a high capacity may be necessary to feed the soil and binder mixture to the air injection point, depending on the type and property of soil, the amount of binder and the diameter of pipeline. In the line addition type, on the other hand, binder is injected to the soil in the pipeline after compressed air is injected (Figure 5.4(b)). This type has the advantage that binder may be injected at any point along the pipeline, but there needs to be a sufficiently long transportation distance from the binder injection point to the outlet to achieve a sufficient degree of mixing.

The compressor addition type can be further categorized into five systems: pipeline system, feeder system, hopper system and two sorts of tank system, as shown in Figure 5.5 (Ministry of Transport, The Fifth District Port Construction Bureau, 1999).

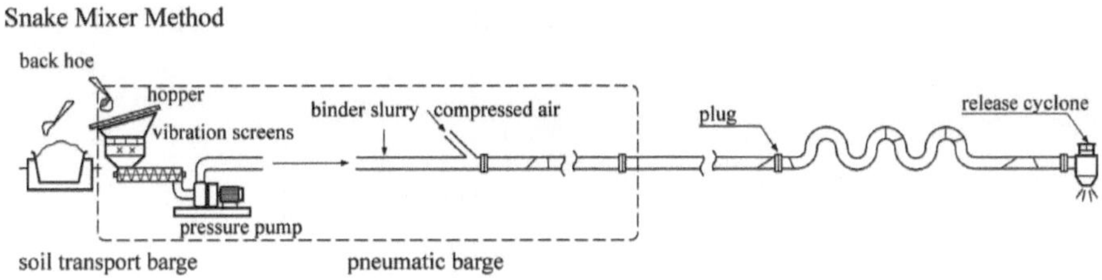

(a) Pipeline system.

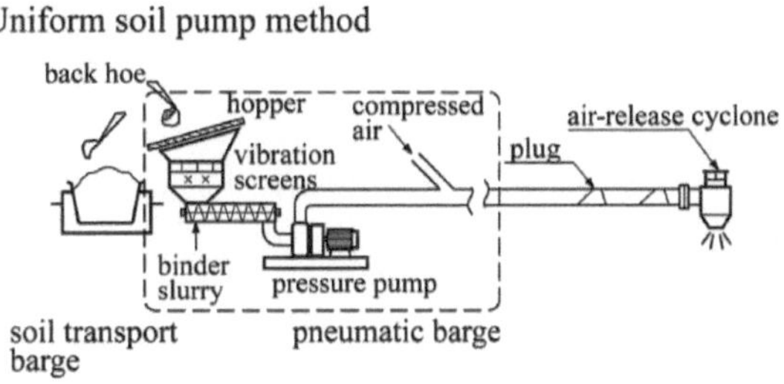

(b) Feeder system.

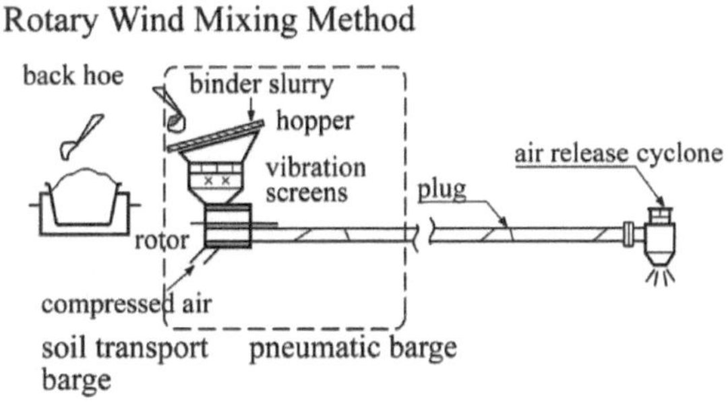

(c) Hopper system.

Figure 5.5 Compressor addition types in the binder injection system (Ministry of Transport, The Fifth District Port Construction Bureau, 1999).

In the line addition type, there are seven methods as shown in Figure 5.6. The system can also be classified according to the form of binder: dry type and wet type. In the dry type, binder in powder form is injected to the soil. In the wet type, binder is mixed with water in a slurry plant and injected to the soil, where the water to binder ratio is 60 to 100% in many cases. As shown in Figure 5.6, the wet type is applied in all the systems in Japan, expect for the plug magic line mixing method (Sakamoto, 1998, Oota & Sakamoto, 2008).

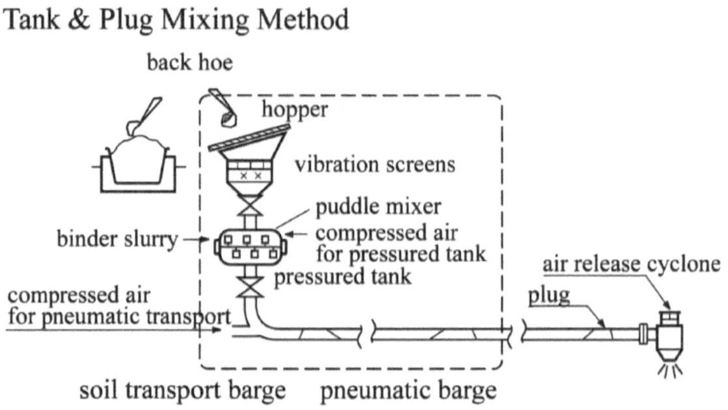

(d) Tank system.

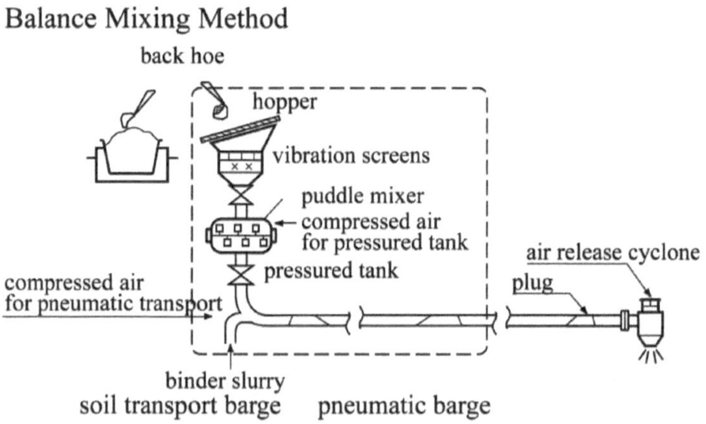

(e) Tank system.

Figure 5.5 Continued.

2.4 Pipeline

The mixture of soil and binder is transported through a pipeline, the diameter of which varies 200 mm to 800 mm depending upon the capacity of the air supplier, to the placement equipment. The minimum transportation distance necessary for complete and thorough mixing is about 100 to 200 m according to the previous case histories, as shown in Figure 4.6 (Ogawa, 2001, Kobayashi et al., 2001). There are several variations in the pipeline as shown in Figure 5.6, in which additional apparatus is installed through the pipeline with the aim of increasing mixing degree of the mixture.

Figure 5.7(a) shows the curved pipeline used in the snake mixing method, where the soil and binder mixture is agitated by the pipe's shape (Ogawa, 2001, Kobayashi

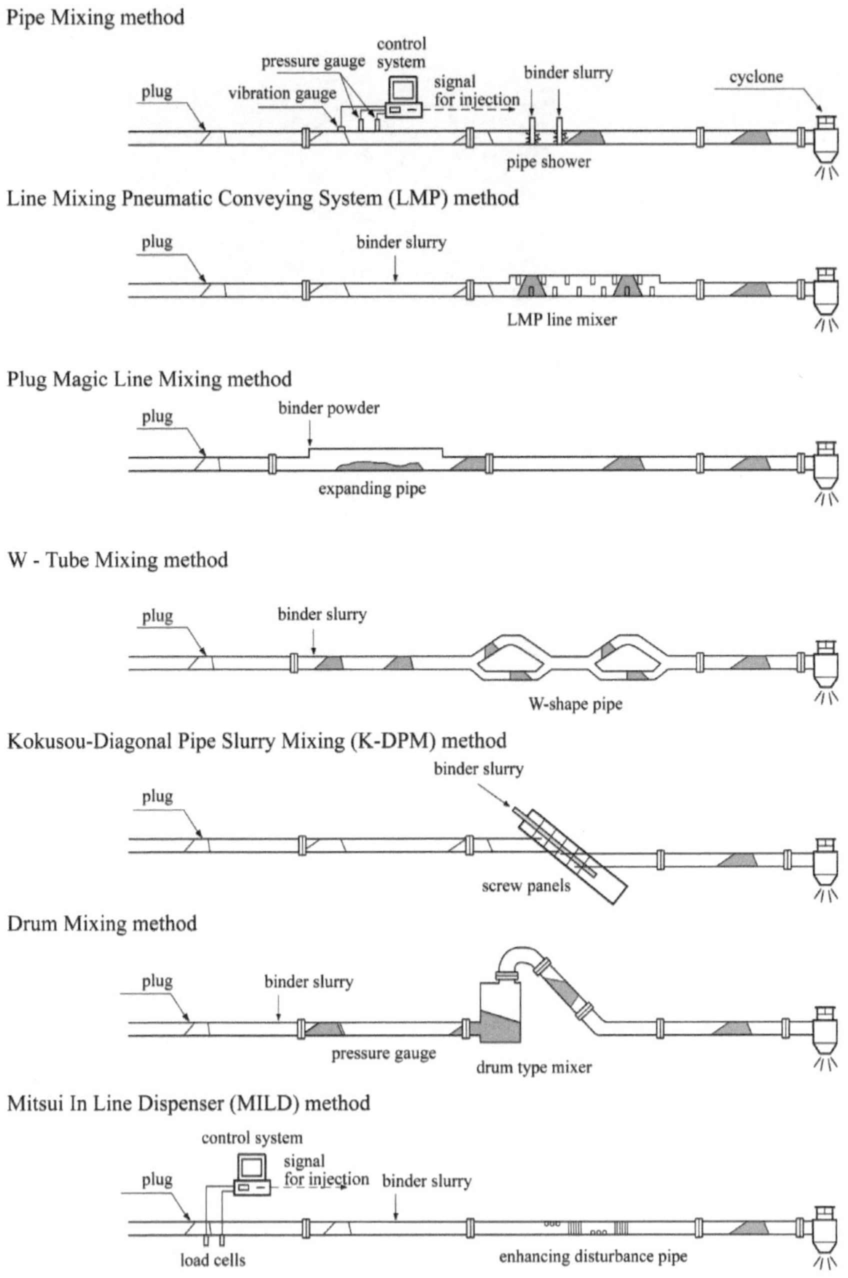

Figure 5.6 Line injection types of binder injection system (Ministry of Transport, The Fifth District Port Construction Bureau, 1999).

(a) Snake mixing method (Ogawa, 2001, Kobayashi et al., 2001).

(b) W-mixing method (Sato & Hayashida, 2000).

(c) Plug magic line mixing method (Oota & Sakamoto, 2008).

Figure 5.7 Variations of transportation pipeline.

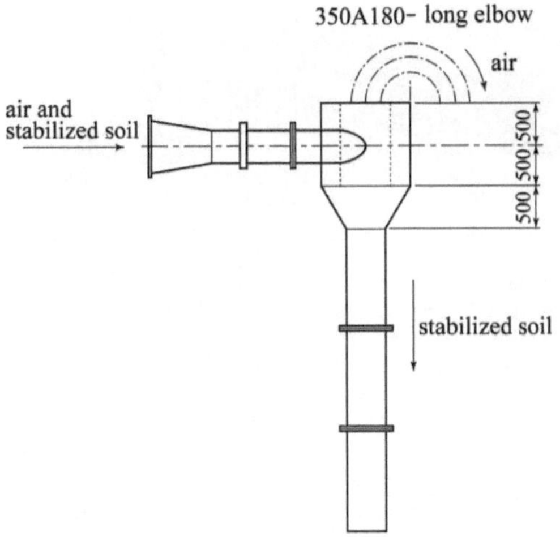

(a) Schematic profile view of air pressure release cyclone and tremie pipe.

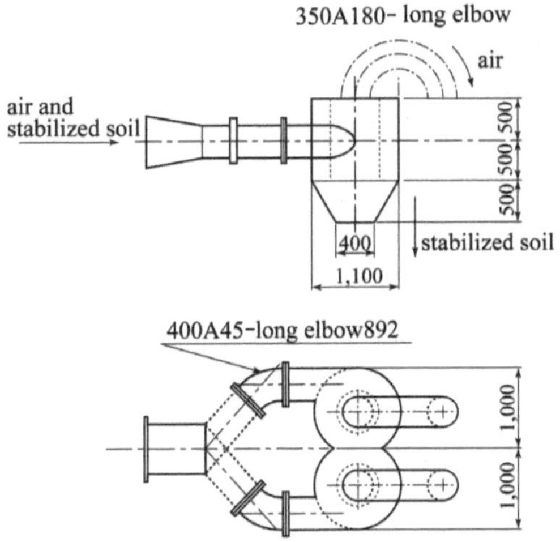

(b) Schematic profile and plane views of air pressure release cyclone.

Figure 5.8 Air pressure release cyclone and tremie pipe.

et al., 2001). Figure 5.7(b) shows the divergence in the W-mixing method, where separated soil plugs are re-merged with a time difference (Sato & Hayashida, 2000). Figure 5.7(c) shows the cement injection pipe of the plug magic line mixing method, where the diameter of the pipeline at the point of cement supply becomes locally enlarged, to 152 cm rather than the of 76 cm of the rest of the pipeline, to improve mixedness due to a temporary breaking of the plug flow (Oota & Sakamoto, 2008).

Figure 5.9 Air pressure release cyclone.

2.5 Placement equipment

The placement equipment, which can be classified into the direct placement and the cyclone methods, functions to place the stabilized soil mixture at the site. In the direct placement method, the stabilized soil mixture is discharged from the outlet vigorously. This method is very simple and does not need any machine and equipment, but the discharged soil may be segregated and can entrap water in stabilized soil in the case of placement underwater, which causes considerably weakening. In the cyclone method, which consists of a pneumatic pipe, an air pressure release cyclone and a tremie pipe. The air pressure release cyclone functions to release the air pressure and dissipate the transferring energy. Its size can be determined by the capacity of the pneumatic equipment and diameter of pipeline. Figures 5.8 and 5.9 show an example of a cyclone with a 200 m^3/h capacity.

The tremie pipe is usually used in the case of underwater placement. There are two types of tremie pipe: the fixed type and a telescoping type. In the fixed type, the length of tremie pipe is fixed. In the telescoping type, the length of tremie pipe can be adjusted according to the lift up of placed stabilized soil. The latter is preferable to prevent entrapping water within the stabilized soil, which causes considerable decrease in the stabilized soil strength.

2.6 Control equipment

Control equipment is essential in the method; during the production of stabilized soil it continuously monitors, controls and records all the quality control data, including the magnitude of air pressure and flow rate of compressed air; the unit weight and volume of the original soil; and the amount of binder (Figure 5.10). Figure 5.11 shows an example of a quality control system of the pipe mixing method. In the system, the volume and density of the original soil block are measured by means of a flow meter and a γ-ray density meter, respectively, and the measured data are transmitted to

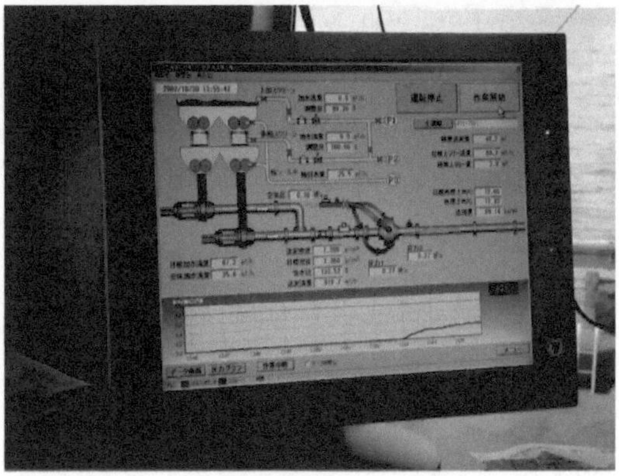

(a) PC for mixing control.

(b) Control system.

Figure 5.10 Control systems for the pneumatic flow mixing method.

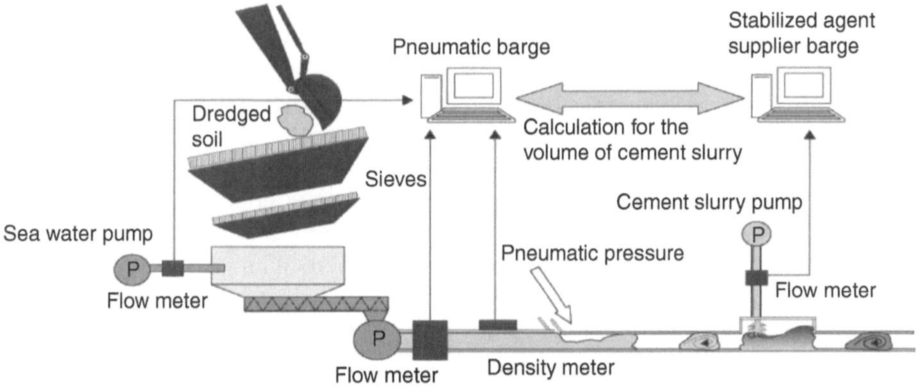

Figure 5.11 Schematic of a quality control system for the pipe mixing method.

a personal computer (PC-A) on the pneumatic barge. The water content of the original soil can be calculated by Equation 5.1. The amount of cement to be mixed with the soil block is calculated to obtain the target flow value and the target W/C value of the stabilized soil. It is transmitted to PC-B on the cement supplier barge, and the PC-B also controls the amount of cement to the soil.

3 CONSTRUCTION PROCEDURE

Regardless the construction scheme, the protocol of pneumatic flow mixing is carried out in the following steps.

(1) Preparation of site.
(2) Field trial test.
(3) Construction work.

3.1 Preparation of site

In the case of a construction project on land, field preparation is carried out in accordance with the site specific conditions, which include suitable access for the plant and machinery. Before the actual operation, execution circumstances should be prepared to assure smooth execution and to prevent any adverse environmental impact.

3.2 Field trial test

It is recommended that a field trial be conducted in advance in, or adjacent to, the construction site, in order to confirm smooth execution. In the test, all the equipment for monitoring the flow rate of compressed air, the amount of binder, and the pressure and flow rate of the soil are calibrated, and it should be confirmed that the consistency and strength of the stabilized soil to meet the design requirement.

3.3 Construction work

3.3.1 Remolding and water content control

As the properties of dredged soil are usually different for any given point in the transportation barge, it is anticipated that the solid part of dredged soil may not be transported smoothly in the transportation pipeline. It can sometimes cause a blockade and then precise quality control cannot be achieved, even by the most sophisticated quality control system, where the properties of the original soil differs considerably. In order to assure the smooth transportation of dredged soil in the pipeline and increase the uniformity of character of stabilized soil, it is desirable to remold the dredged soil in the soil transportation barge to become as uniform as possible, as shown in Figure 5.12. It is desirable to measure the water content and sand particle content of the dredged soil in the transportation barge for quality control and assurance purposes.

3.3.2 Injection of binder and transportation of soil

After preliminary remolding in the transportation barge, the dredged soil is loaded onto the pneumatic barge by the backhoe, and then discharged into the pipeline.

Figure 5.12 Remolding dredged soil in the transportation barge.

Any obstacles and large stone should be removed by the vibration screen. The unit weight and volume of soil are measured by the γ-ray gauge and the flow meter, respectively. The water content of the soil is calculated by Equation 5.1 with an estimated Gs value and assuming the full saturation, $S_r = 100\%$. The volume of cement to be added, V_c, can be calculated by Equation 5.2 for the specific cement content, aw, by assuming the density of the cement, ρ_c. The soil and binder mixture is transported in the pipeline to the placement site with the help of the injected air pressure, while they are mixed throughout with the help of turbulent flow generated in the soil plugs.

$$w = \frac{1}{Gs} \cdot \frac{Gs \cdot \rho_w - \rho_t}{\rho_t - \rho_w} \cdot 100 \tag{5.1}$$

$$V_c = \frac{aw}{100} \cdot \frac{\left({}^{1}/_{\rho_c} + {}^{W/C}/_{\rho_w} \right) \cdot V_{soil} \cdot \rho_{soil}}{1 + {}^{w}/_{100}} \tag{5.2}$$

where
aw : cement content (%)
Gs : specific gravity of soil particle
V_c: volume of cement slurry (m^3)
V_{soil}: volume of original soil (m^3)
w: water content of original soil (%)
W/C: water to cement ratio of slurry
ρ_c: density of cement (g/cm^3)
ρ_{soil}: density of original soil (g/cm^3)
ρ_t: density of soil particle (g/cm^3)
ρ_w: density of water (g/cm^3)

(a) Pumping type placement barge.

(b) Placement barge.

(c) Air pressure release cyclone type placement machine
(Ministry of Transport, The Fifth District Port Construction Bureau, 1999).

Figure 5.13 Placement barge and air release cyclone.

3.3.3 Placement of stabilized soil

The stabilized soil mixture, once transported through the pipeline, is placed at the site. One of the two placement methods is applied: the direct placement method or the cyclone placement method. In the direct placement method, the stabilized soil mixture is discharged from the outlet vigorously. This method is very simple and does not need any machine and equipment, but the injected soil may be segregated and can entrap water in the stabilized soil in the case of placement underwater, which causes

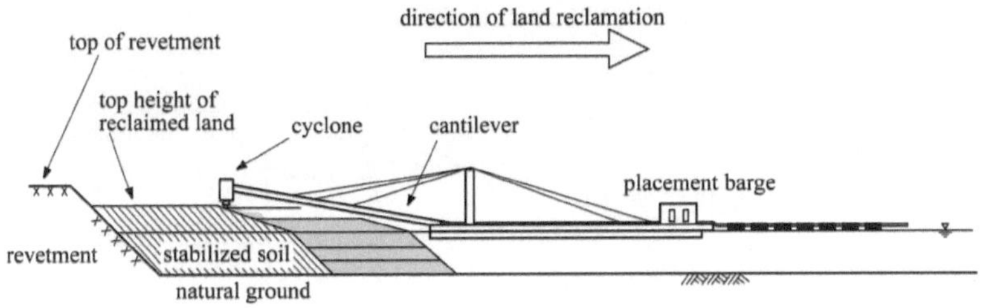

(a) Placement barge procedure.

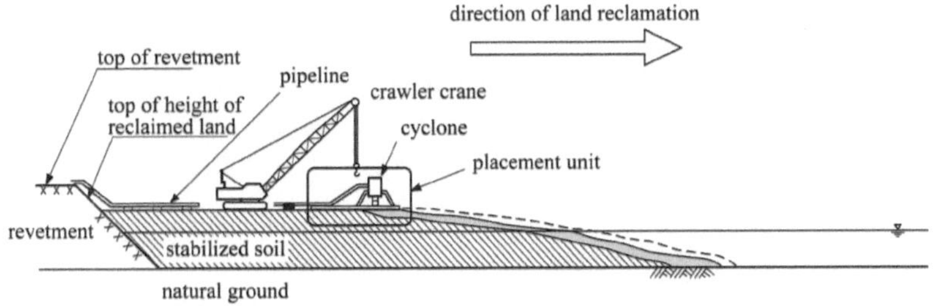

(b) Slope shoulder flow-down procedure.

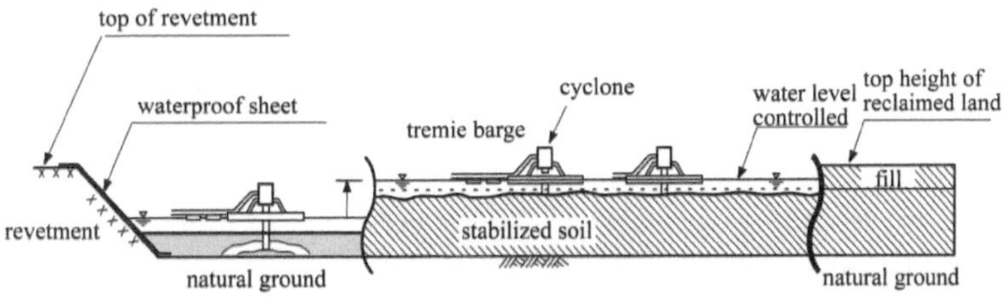

(c) Tremie barge with controlled water level procedure.

Figure 5.14 Land reclamation execution using cyclone.

a considerable decrease in the stabilized soils strength. In the cyclone method, the stabilized soil is placed gently after releasing the air pressure at a cyclone (Figure 5.13). As shown in Figure 5.18, the angle of placed stabilized soil is smaller in the direct placement method than in the cyclone placement method. It is essential in underwater placement to apply the cyclone placement method together with a tremie pipe, in order to minimize water entrapment in the soil, which causes a considerable decrease in the stabilized soil strength.

Figure 5.14 shows examples of placement procedure for land reclamation: placement barge procedure, slope shoulder flow-down procedure, and tremie placement with water level control procedure. In the placement barge procedure, Figure 5.14(a),

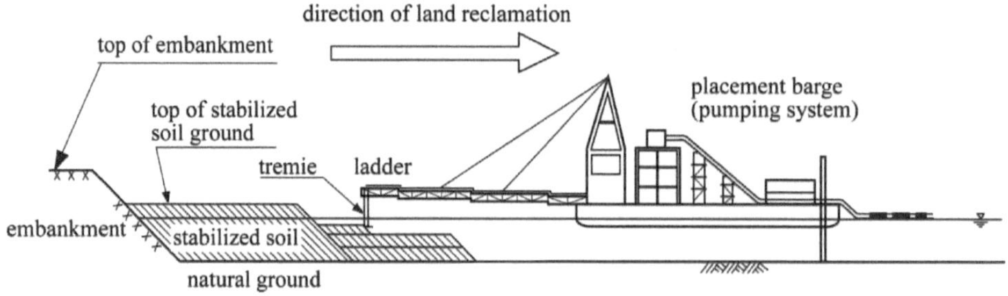

(a) Placement barge procedure.

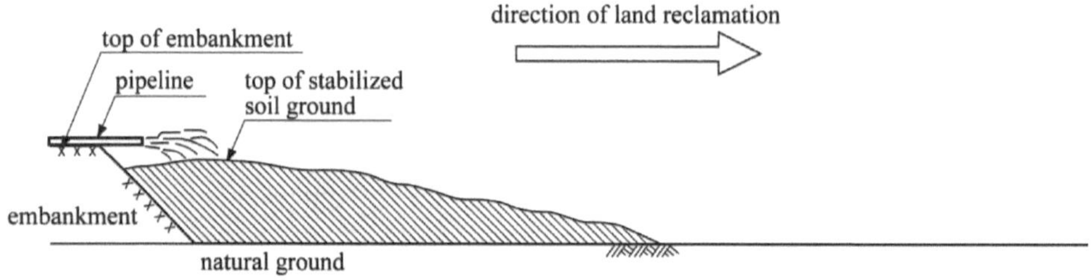

(b) Direct placement procedure.

Figure 5.15 Backfilling behind a sea revetment.

stabilized soil is placed layer by layer to the design height using a placement barge with a sufficient length of cantilever to meet a certain time interval which allows the stabilized soil to gain strength. The placement barge moves back with the progress of placement. In the slope shoulder flow-down procedure, Figure 5.14(b), stabilized soil is placed continuously to the design height with a cyclone installed on the stabilized soil ground to allow the stabilized soil to flow down the slope shoulder of a sea revetment. The placement system with a cyclone is moved forward with the progress of placement. In the tremie placement with water level control procedure, Figure 5.14(c), stabilized soil is placed layer by layer to the design height by a tremie barge with a means of controlling the water level. The tremie barge moves to place stabilized soil in flat layers.

Figure 5.15 shows several execution procedures for backfilling behind embankments. In the placement barge procedure, Figure 5.15(a), stabilized soil is placed layer by layer to the design height by a placement barge with a sufficient length of cantilever. This procedure is quite similar to the placement barge procedure as shown in Figure 5.14(a), except the stabilized soil is placed through a tremie pipe to place it underwater. In the direct placement procedure, Figure 5.15(b), the stabilized soil is discharged from the top of the sea revetment with the help of the transported air pressure. The stabilized soil discharged in this way is spread and extended in the reclamation site.

4 QUALITY CONTROL

4.1 Quality control before production

4.1.1 Soil property

The ignition loss and pH value of original soil are one of the critical parameters to investigate the applicability of the cement stabilization. In a case where the soil contains a large amount of water or organic material, ordinary Portland cement and blast furnace slag cement type B may not function well and a special binder may be necessary. The physical and chemical properties of soils should be investigated in advance. The specific gravity of soil is necessary to calculate the weight and volume of binder, as shown in Equation 5.1.

A series of laboratory mix tests should be carried out on the soils to obtain the mixing conditions, since variations in the properties and water content of soil very much depend on excavation location and depth. It is desirable to obtain the mixing condition for the soils at various locations and depths to achieve the design flow value and strength of stabilized soil. According to the accumulated case histories, the water-to-binder ratio of stabilized soil, W/C, is one of the essential parameters for the mixing design, where the unconfined compressive strength is inversely proportional to W/C, as shown in Figure 2.16.

As the amount of leachate of hexavalent chromium is regulated for cement stabilization in Japan, a leaching test needs to be carried out on the stabilized soils by the specified testing procedure (Environment Agency, 2005) and measured by the specified ultrasonic extraction, which is diphenylcarbazide colorimetry. If the amount of leachate of hexavalent chromium exceeds the regulation, the special binder should be used instead of ordinary Portland cement or blast furnace slag cement type B.

4.1.2 Pipeline length

As the soil and binder are expected to mix during transportation in the pipeline, a sufficient length of pipeline is necessary for achieving throughout mixing. As shown in Figure 4.6, the minimum transportation distance of pipeline to achieve this is 100 to 200 m. In the case where the placement site is close to the mixing plant, the pipeline should be detoured to assure the minimum distance.

4.2 Quality control during execution

4.2.1 Material control

The type, delivery date, volume and other necessary data of the supplied binder should be recorded when received. For every soil transportation barge, the physical properties of its dredged soils are evaluated, which includes the water content, bulk density and volume of the dredged soil. In the case of the wet type of binder, the water-to-binder ratio of binder slurry should be controlled to secure the prescribed value.

4.2.2 Transportation control

In order to secure the prescribed volume and properties of the stabilized soil in the field, the volume of soil transferred, the volume of air injected, and the pressure

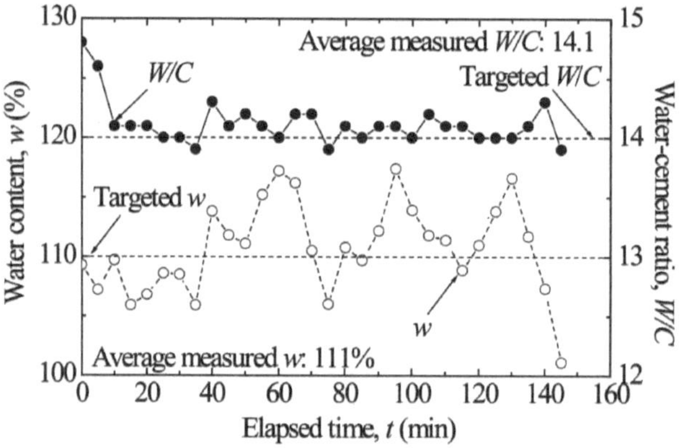

Figure 5.16 Water content and water-cement ratio in the quality control during the execution (Hayano & Kitazume, 2005).

in the pipeline should be monitored continuously and controlled precisely. Figure 5.16 shows an example of quality control data during the execution of the Central Japan International Airport construction project (Hayano & Kitazume, 2005, Kitazume & Hayano, 2007). The unit weight and volume of a soil block at the discharge point were measured by γ-ray meter and flow meter, respectively. The water content of the soil block was calculated by means of the measured unit weight. The amount of water and cement to be injected were calculated based on the quantities required to assure the target water content and W/C ratio. The water content of the soil still varied within a range of about 100 to 118%, while the target water content was 110%. The W/C ratio, on the other hand, could be well controlled to the target W/C ratio of 14. All the monitoring data – such as the excavation location and depth of the dredged soil, the amount of water supply, the amount of binder (binder slurry), and the flow rate of stabilized soil – should be recorded, together with the location of placement of stabilized soil.

4.2.3 *Placement control*

Based on a placement plan (reclamation plan), the placement of stabilized soil is carried out by controlling its volume and placement location. The volume, location and height of placed stabilized soil are measured and controlled. As shown in Figure 5.17, the level of the stabilized soil ground is usually measured by a movable buggy equipped with a GPS system for measuring placement on land, and by a narrow multi-beam sonar in the case of underwater placement. The measured data are transmitted to the control room to draw a contour map of the site. During the placement, the environmental issues should be monitored and controlled to prevent any adverse influence to the surrounding area. In the case of placement underwater, the placement technique influences the strength of stabilized soil very much as shown in Figures 3.58 and 3.59.

(a) Movable buggy equipped with a GPS system.

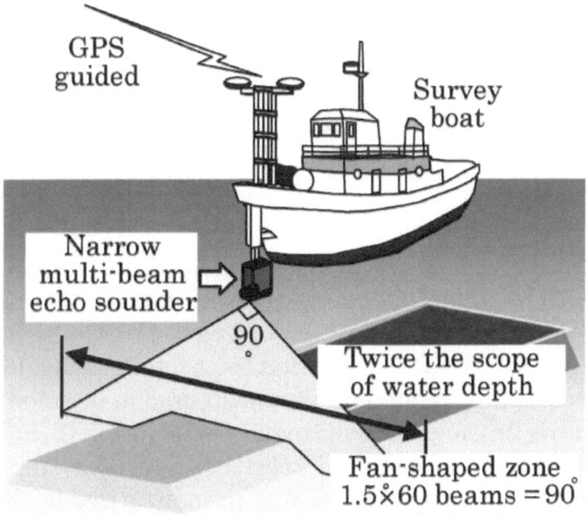

(b) Narrow multi-beam echo sounder.

Figure 5.17 Placement control in on land and marine constructions.

4.2.3.1 Slope angle

The shape of placed stabilized soil should be controlled during placement by an appropriate method. Figure 5.18 shows the relationship between the slope angle of stabilized soil placed on land and the amount of cement (Ministry of Transport, The Fifth District Port Construction Bureau, 1999). Marine clays with various initial water

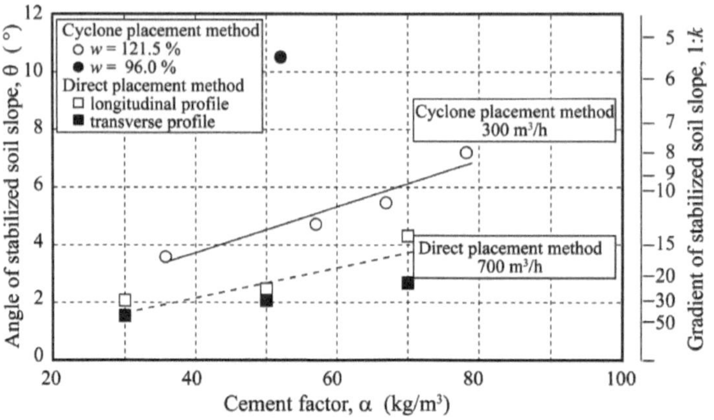

Figure 5.18 The relationship between the slope angle of stabilized soil placed on land and the amount of cement (Ministry of Transport, The Fifth District Port Construction Bureau, 1999).

Table 5.2 Execution conditions of placement methods (Ministry of Transport, The Fifth District Port Construction Bureau, 1999).

	Cyclone placement	*Direct placement*
Transportation distance (m)	180	315
Pipeline diameter (mm)	350	560
Total amount of stabilized soil placed (m^3)	2,400	4,500
Stabilization rate (m^3/h)	107 to 320	631 to 757

contents were stabilized with several amounts of blast furnace slag cement type B. The stabilized soils were placed by either cyclone or direct placement method. The execution conditions of the two methods are summarized in Table 5.2. The figure shows that the slope angle of stabilized soil is influenced by the mixing condition and placement method, and increases with the amount of cement used in its stabilization.

Figure 5.19 shows similar test results to those in Figure 5.18, in which the relationship between the slope angle of stabilized soil placed under seawater and the amount of cement used, where the execution conditions are summarized in Table 5.3. The shoot in the table is a placement techniques where the stabilized soil after the air released at the cyclone is flowed down on a shoot to placed underwater.

4.2.3.2 Strength

Figure 5.20 shows the laboratory and field tests on the effect of underwater placement on the strength of cement-stabilized soil (Tang et al., 2002). Figure 5.20(a) shows the strength ratio of the soils placed on land and underwater which was obtained in a laboratory model test. In the test, the Tokuyama clay (w_L of 77%) was mixed with water to the initial water content of 118 to 300% and slag cement of 80 to 160 kg/m^3, then squeezed into the molds in air and underwater. The figure shows that the unconfined compressive strength of the underwater specimen is 92% of that

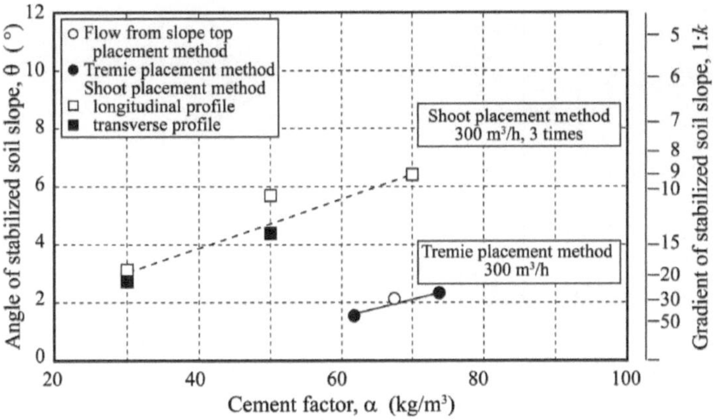

Figure 5.19 The relationship between the slope angle of stabilized soil placed under seawater and the amount of cement (Ministry of Transport, The Fifth District Port Construction Bureau, 1999).

Table 5.3 Execution conditions of placement methods (Ministry of Transport, The Fifth District Port Construction Bureau, 1999).

	Cyclone	*Cyclone & tremie*	*Shoot*
Transportation distance (m)	200	230	225
Pipeline diameter (mm)	350	350	560
Total amount of stabilized soil placed (m^3)	1,195	1,800	15,200
Stabilization speed (m^3/h)	298	310 to 320	548 to 683

placed in air. Figure 5.20(b) shows the strength ratio of the soils placed on land and underwater and the sand content ratio, which was obtained in laboratory model tests. In the tests, the Hakata clay (w_L of 91%) and its mixture with sand were stabilized with ordinary Portland cement of 80 kg/m^3, and then were placed underwater at 700 mm from the bottom. The figure shows that the unconfined compressive strength ratio of the underwater specimen is about 0.8 to 0.9 for the soil that has a quite small proportion of sand particles, but the strength ratio decreases with the sand particle content to about 0.4 to 0.8 when the sand particle content is about 90%.

When stabilized soil is placed underwater, soil separation can take place. Tang et al. (2002) carried out a field test to investigate soil separation in which stabilized Shimonoseki sand (sand particle content of 41% and silt and clay particles content of 35%) with slag cement of 120 kg/m^3 was placed underwater. The upper part of the sediment was the clay, with a particle size less than 0.005 mm, while the lower part was sand with particle size exceeding 0.075 mm. Figure 5.20(c) shows the unconfined compressive strength of the stabilized soil together with that of the laboratory stabilized soil. The upper floating mud shows the strength increase with its unit weight irrespective of the segregation of the soil. The lower mud of segregated soil shows small strength, which was about 1,000 kN/m^2 smaller than for the non-segregated soil.

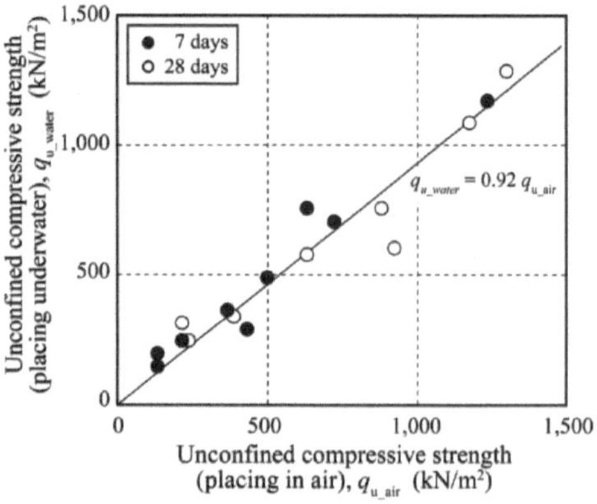

(a) Strength ratio of the stabilized soils placed on land and underwater.

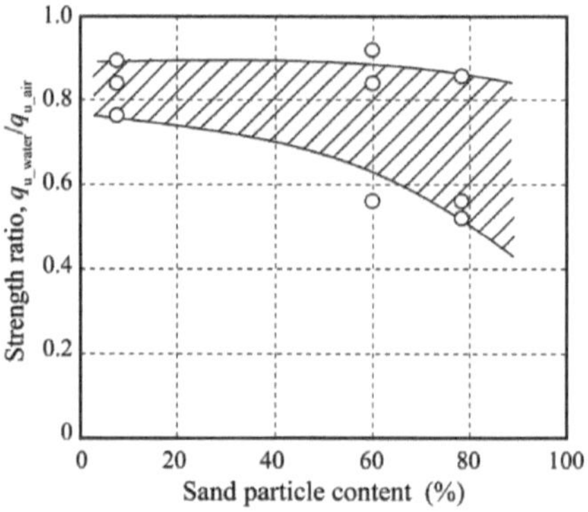

(b) Effect of sand particle content on the strength ratio of the stabilized soils placed on land and underwater.

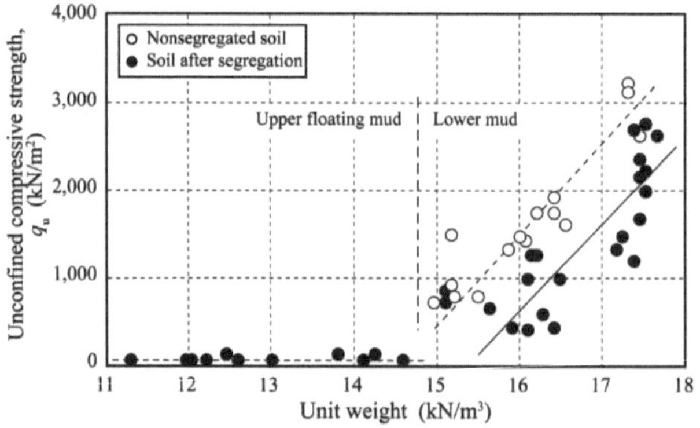

(c) Unconfined compressive strength of upper and lower part of stabilized soil sediment.

Figure 5.20 The effect of placement either on land or underwater, and the proportion of sand particle content on its unconfined compressive strength (Tang et al., 2002).

The test results have revealed that it is important not to cause soil separation during placing underwater, to assure the design strength.

4.3 Quality assurance

4.3.1 *Shape of stabilized soil ground*

The level of the stabilized soil ground is usually measured by a movable buggy equipped with a GPS system for placement on land and by a narrow multi-beam sonar for underwater placement, as already shown in Figure 5.17. The measured data are transmitted to the control room to draw the contour map of the site.

4.3.2 *Strength of stabilized soil ground*

Quality control should be performed during execution by appropriate methods in order to secure the prescribed quality requirement of the stabilized soil. The quality control of stabilized soil during execution is usually carried out by unconfined compression tests on samples taken at the energy dissipation cyclone (called as mold sample), and one after placement. A cone penetration test (JGS 1435) is sometimes carried out to investigate the short-term strength of stabilized soil ground. The correlation between the cone penetration resistance, q_c, and unconfined compressive strength, q_u, is established in advance by a series of laboratory mixing tests. The cone penetration resistance profile along the depth of the stabilized soil ground and the relationship between the cone penetration registance and the unconfined compressive strength are shown in Figures 3.62 and 3.63, where the Nagoya Port clay (w_L of 74.4% and w_P of 33.0%) was stabilized with ordinary Portland cement with various cement factors (Ministry of Transport, The Fifth District Port Construction Bureau, 1999).

4.3.3 *Environmental impact during placement*

A suitable placement technique should be selected to minimize the environmental impact on the surrounding area. Fine particles of stabilized soil are separated when the soil is not placed by the appropriate machine and procedure, which causes high turbidity in the water. Where the stabilized soil is placed underwater, the pH value of the water becomes high due to the chemical hydration of cement. Figure 5.21 shows the relationship between turbidity (Figure 5.21(a)) and the potential hydrogen, pH (Figure 5.21(b)), plotted against the distance from the deposition outlet (Tang et al., 2002). In the figure, not only the field case histories but also the laboratory model test results are plotted together. The case histories shown in the figure were performed by the pressured placement technique. Figure 5.21(a) clearly shows that high turbidity can be seen within about 1 m from the outlet, but the turbidity shows almost constant value ranging from 1 to 10 ppm for a distance of about 5 m from the outlet. A similar phenomenon can be seen in the pH value in Figure 5.21(b), where the pH value is very high close to the outlet – within about 1 m – but decreases rapidly with distance to an almost constant of about 8 at about 5 m from the outlet.

In natural conditions, the turbidity and pH value usually fluctuate, e.g. 1 to 10 ppm in turbidity and 8.0 to 8.5 in pH measured at the Tokoname Bay (Ministry of Transport, The Fifth District Port Construction Bureau, 1999).

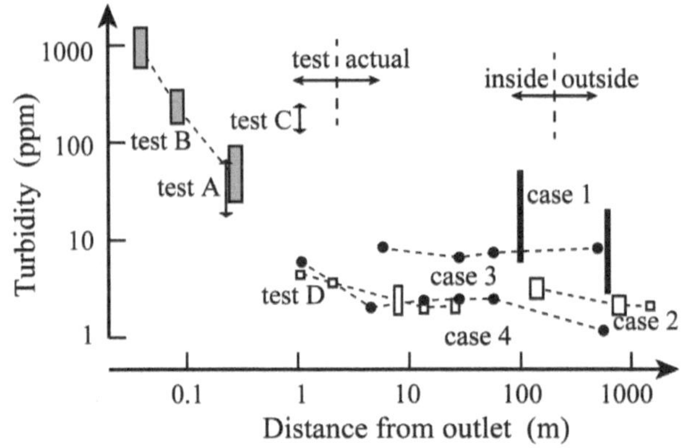

(a) Turbidity.

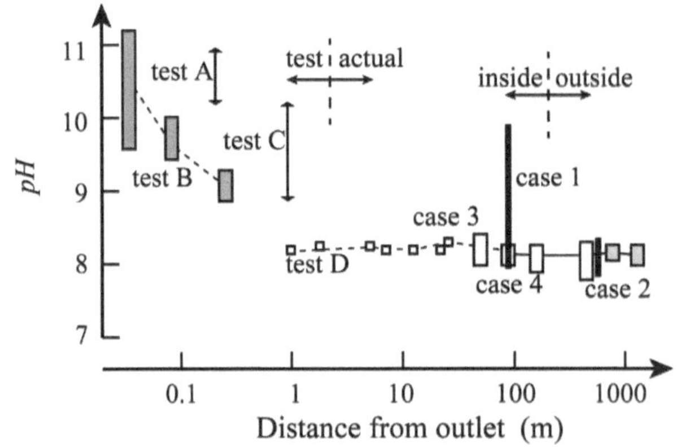

(b) Potential hydrogen (pH).

Figure 5.21 Turbidity and pH of water with distance from deposition outlet for stabilized soil placed underwater (Tang et al., 2002).

Figures 5.22 and 5.23 show the relationships between the suspended solids and the distance from revetment, which were measured in the field test at Nagoya Port (Ministry of Transport, The Fifth District Port Construction Bureau, 1999). The measured suspended solids, SS, value in the sea water outside the sea revetment (Figure 5.22) shows a maximum value of about 15 mg/L, which is almost the same as the background value there. This reveals that the placement of stabilized soil causes negligible influence to the marine environment outside revetment. The measured SS value in the sea water inside sea revetment (Figure 5.23), on the other hand, shows a maximum value of about 240 mg/L, which reveals that a countermeasure is necessary for the suspended solids.

Figures 5.24 and 5.25 show the relationship between the measured potential hydrogen, pH, during construction and that of the background in the field test at

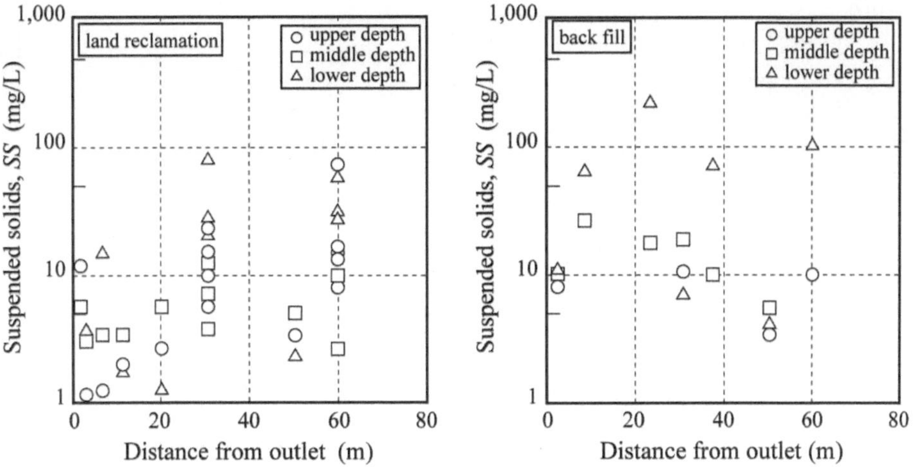

(a) Land reclamation. (b) Backfill.

Figure 5.22 Measured suspended solids values in water outside a sea revetment (Ministry of Transport, The Fifth District Port Construction Bureau, 1999).

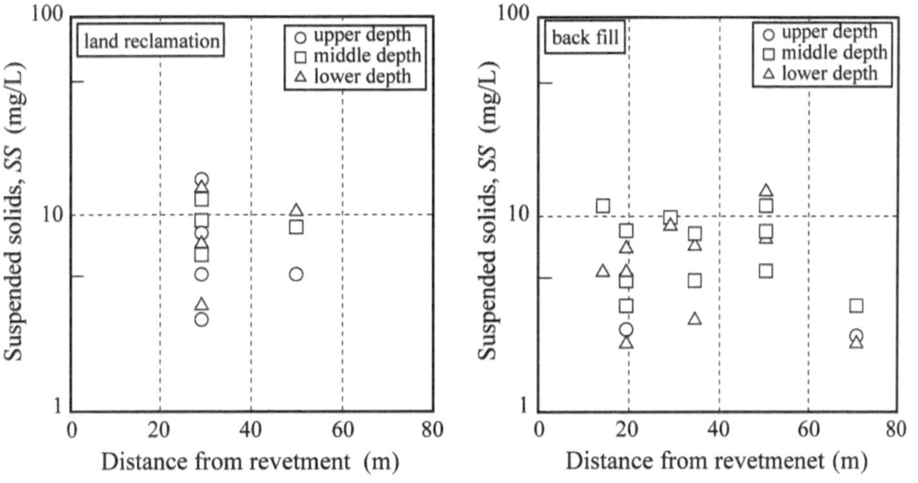

(a) Land reclamation. (b) Backfill.

Figure 5.23 Measured suspended solid values in water inside a sea revetment (Ministry of Transport, The Fifth District Port Construction Bureau, 1999).

Nagoya Port (Ministry of Transport, The Fifth District Port Construction Bureau, 1999). The pH value during construction in water outside the revetment (Figure 5.24) shows a maximum difference of about 0.3 compared to the background, which is within the influence of the tide. This reveals that the placement of stabilized soil causes

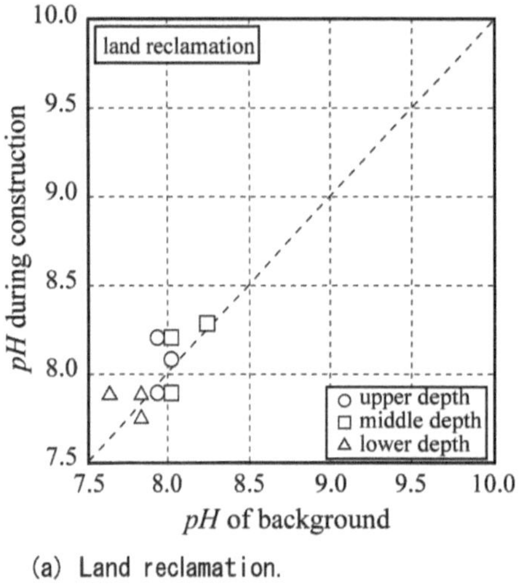

Figure 5.24 Measured pH values in water outside a sea revetment (Ministry of Transport, The Fifth District Port Construction Bureau, 1999).

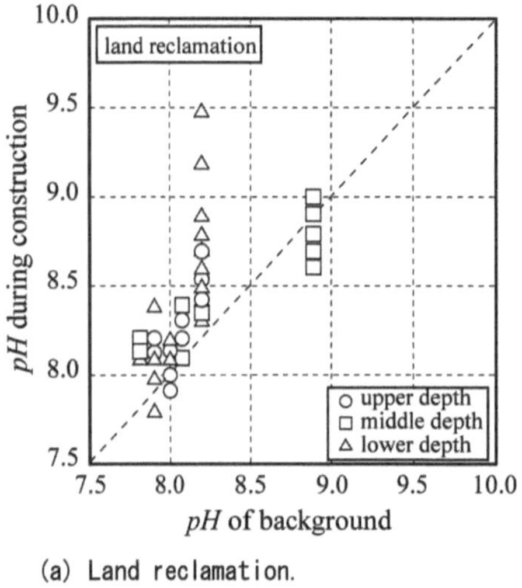

Figure 5.25 Measured pH value in water inside a sea revetment (Ministry of Transport, The Fifth District Port Construction Bureau, 1999).

negligible influence in the pH value to the water outside the sea revetment. The measured pH value for water inside the sea revetment (Figure 5.25), on the other hand, shows a maximum value of about 9.5, which reveals that a countermeasure is necessary to reduce the pH.

4.3.4 *Water quality control*

The water at a placement site contains a lot of suspended solids and is highly alkaline when cement is used as a binder. In Japan, the potential hydrogen, pH, value is specified as an environmental standard for defining marine pollution. The environmental standard for turbidity is not specified, but the Water Pollution Control Act specifies that the effluent standard for turbidity, is such that suspended solids should be lower than 200 ppm, corresponding to a turbidity lower than 125 ppm (Environment Agency, 2005).

The quality of the water should be monitored and controlled to the regulated levels before being allowed to flow out to a marine area. Figure 5.26(a) shows an example of a sedimentation basin at a spillway for the control of effluent, whose effective width, length, depth and sectional area were 33 m, 90 m, 7.6 m and 2,970 m^2, respectively, for sufficient precipitation of suspended solids (Satoh, 2003, 2004). In order to control the potential hydrogen, pH, of water to the regulated level, sulphuric acid, hydrochloric acid and carbon dioxide gas can be used. However, carbon dioxide gas has most often been used due to its low risk and easy handling. The water with high levels of suspended solids and which is highly alkaline is pumped to mixing tanks, where it is mixed with a polymer flocculating agent and carbon dioxide gas, and then it flows to the sedimentation basin. In the basin, precipitation of suspended solids, SS, in the water is accelerated by the polymer flocculating agent to the regulated level, i.e. SS lower than 60 mg/L. The pH is also controlled by the carbon dioxide gas to the regulated level of pH 8.4.

Figure 5.26(b) shows the amount of suspended solids and time history measured at the placement site and in the effluent in the Central Japan International Airport construction project (Satoh, 2003, 2004). In the figure, the highest values of the day are plotted. The SS value at the placement site is negligibly influenced by the progress of reclamation and has a mean value of about 37.8 mg/L which is lower than the regulation. The SS value at the effluent has a mean value of about 15.2 mg/L and is lower than the regulation.

Figure 5.26(c) shows the potential hydrogen, pH, and time history measured at the placement site and in the effluent in the Central Japan International Airport construction project (Satoh, 2003, 2004). The estimated value increases with the progress of reclamation to about a pH of 10 at 90% completion. The measured pH value at the placement site also increases with the progress of reclamation, to a peak of pH 9.8 at about 70% progress, but decreases with further reclamation. The pH value measured in the effluent is almost always lower than the regulation of 8.4.

4.3.5 *Elution of hexavalent chromium (chromium VI) from stabilized soil*

The elution of hexavalent chromium (chromium VI) from cement stabilized soils is specified by the environmental quality standards (Environment Agency, 2005) and the amount of hexavalent chromium should be measured before, during, and after execution and confirmed to be lower than the regulated values.

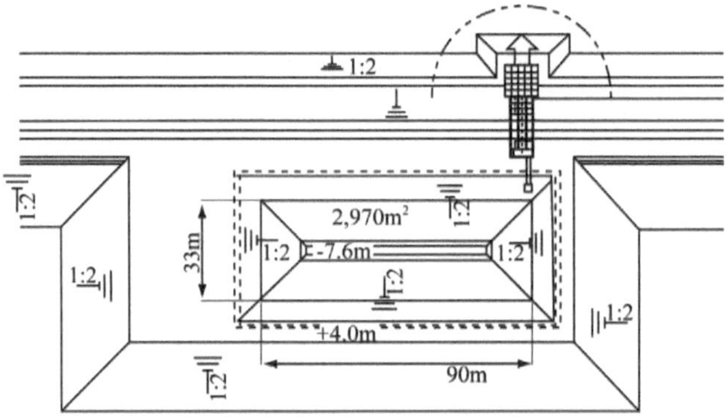

(a) Sedimentation basin at spillway.

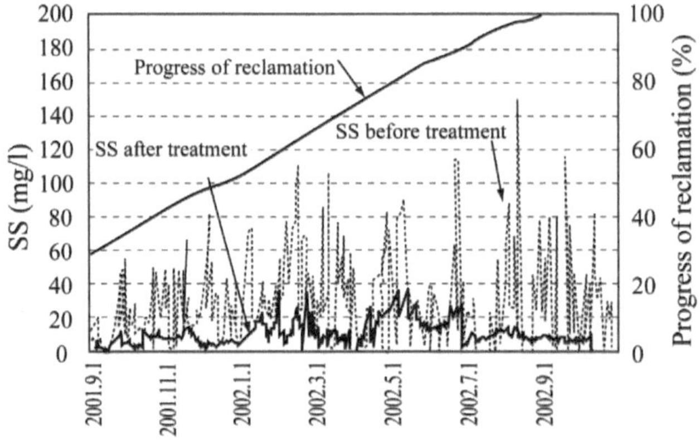

(b) Measured SS value inside revetment.

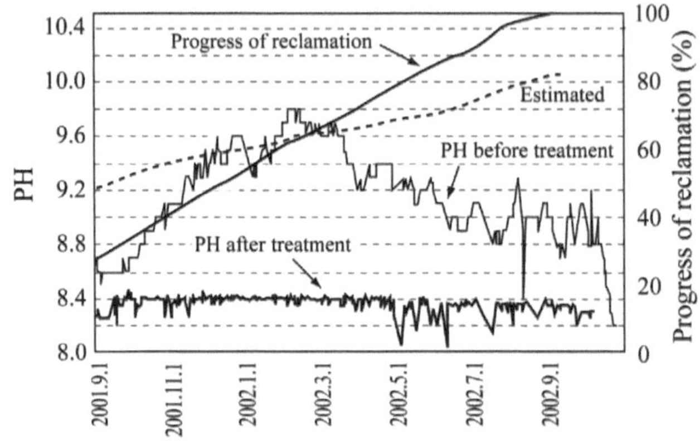

(c) Measured pH value inside revetment.

Figure 5.26 Water quality control and SS and pH time history in the Central Japan International Airport construction (Satoh, 2003, 2004).

REFERENCES

Environment Agency (2005) *Criteria for a Specific Operation of the Ground Storage Tank Outdoors using Deep Mixing Method (notification).* (in Japanese).

Hashimoto (1999) Plug magic method. Inner pipe mixing solidification process. *Marine Voice 21.* Vol. 205, pp. 14–16 (in Japanese).

Hayano, K. & Kitazume, M. (2005) Strength variance within cement treated soils induced by newly developed pneumatic flow mixing method. *Proc. of the ACSE, Geo-Frontiers 2005.* CD-ROM.

Ikegami, N. (1999) On development of the K-DPM method. Mixing solidification processing transfer method in tube. *Marine Voice 21.* Vol. 207, pp. 24–26 (in Japanese).

Ishikawa, K. (2000) Pneumatic flow mixing method: Uniform Mixing Method. *Marine Voice 21.* Vol. 214, pp. 14–16 (in Japanese).

Iwata, H., Okumura, Y., Kawauchi, M., Satou, Y. & Takamatsu, H. (2000) Beneficial use of soft dredged soil by pneumatic flow mixing method, Development of drum mixing method. *Proc. of the 55th Annual Conference of the Japan Society of Civil Engineers.* V-158. (in Japanese).

Iwata, H., Okumura, Y., Kawauchi, M., Satou, Y., Saitoh, T. & Ishida, H. (2006) Development of manufacturing technique for high quality stabilized dredging soil using a compressed-air mixture pipeline with a drum-style mixer. *Proc. of Civil Engineering in the Ocean, Japan Society of Civil Engineers.* Vol. 22, pp. 951–956 (in Japanese).

Kitazume, M. & Hayano, K. (2005a) Strength scatter and its causes of Pneumatic Flow Mixing treated ground. *Report of the Port and Airport Research Institute.* Vol. 44, No. 2, pp. 57–81 (in Japanese).

Kitazume, M. & Hayano, K. (2005b) Strength property and variance of cement treated ground by pneumatic flow mixing method. *Proc. of the 6th International Conference on Ground Improvement Techniques.* pp. 377–384.

Kitazume, M. & Hayano, K. (2007) Strength property and variance of cement treated ground by pneumatic flow mixing method. *Ground Improvement Journal of ISSMGE.* Vol. 11, No.1, pp. 21–26.

Kitazume, M., Yoshino, N., Shinsha, H., Horii, R. & Fujio, Y. (2000) Field test on pneumatic flow mixing method for sea reclamation. *Proc. of the International Symposium on Coastal Geotechnical Engineering in Practice.* Vol. 1, pp. 647–652.

Kobayashi, K., Yoshida, G. & Sato, H. (2001) Quality assurance of pneumatic flow mixing method: Snake Mixer Method. *Proc. of the Annual Research Conference, Civil Engineering Research Institute for Cold Region, Ministry of Ministry of Land, Infrastructure, Transport and Tourism.* pp. 393–400 (in Japanese).

Ministry of Transport, The Fifth District Port Construction Bureau (1999) *Pneumatic Flow Mixing Method.* Yasuki Publishers. 157p. (in Japanese).

Mori, Y. (2000) Pneumatic flow mixing method: Balance mixing method. *HEDORO.* Vol. 79, pp. 43–49 (in Japanese).

Mori, Y. (2001) Recycle of dredged soil/ Pneumatic flow mixing method, balance mixing method. *Marine Voice 21.* Vol. 218, pp. 21–23 (in Japanese).

Ogawa, H. (1999) Development of snake mixing method. *Annual Research Meeting, Shikoku Branch, Japan Society of Civil Engineers.* VI-7, pp. 386–387 (in Japanese).

Oota, M. & Sakamoto, A. (2008) Development and application of plug magic method: Beneficial use of dredged soil for construction material. *Journal of the Japanese Society of Soil Mechanics and Foundation Engineering, Tsuchi to Kiso.* Vol. 56, No. 12, pp. 46–47 (in Japanese).

Sakamoto, A. (1998) In-pipe mixing solidification method PLUG-MAGIC method. *HEDORO.* Vol. 73, pp. 41–46 (in Japanese).

Sasaki, Y. (1999) Mud solidification air-transfer process. LMP process. *Marine Voice 21.* Vol. 205, pp. 17–19 (in Japanese).

Sato, Y. & Hayashida, H. (2000) Field report on W-pipe mixing method at Fushikitoyama Port. *Annual Technical Report, Wakachiku Construction Co., Ltd.* Vol. 9, pp. 27–37 (in Japanese).

Satoh, A. (2001) Balance Mixing Method, Pneumatic flow mixing method. *Kensetsu Kikai, Japan Industry Publishers.* Vol. 37, pp. 46–52 (in Japanese).

Satoh, T. (2003) Application of pneumatic flow mixing method to Central Japan International Airport Construction. *Journal of the Japan Society of Civil Engineers.* No. 749/6-61, pp. 33–47 (in Japanese).

Satoh, T. (2004) Development and application of pneumatic flow mixing method to reclamation for offshore airport. *Technical Note of the Port and Harbour Research Institute.* No. 1076, 81p. (in Japanese).

Shima, M. & Hashimoto, F. (1998) Plug magic method for effective weak dredged soil application. In-tube mixing solidification treatment method. *Kouwan, The Japan Port & Harbour Association.* Vol. 75, No. 2, p. 51 (in Japanese).

Sumoto, T. (2000) Field Test on Pneumatic flow mixing method (Balance Mixing Method). *Proc. of the 55th Annual Conference of the Japan Society of Civil Engineers.* pp. 582–583 (in Japanese).

Tang, Y. X., Miyazaki, Y., Ochiai, H., Yasufuku, N. & Omine, K. (2002) Environmental impacts on seawater due to casting cement treated soil underwater. *Journal of Geotechnical Engineering, Japan Society of Civil Engineers.* No.708/3-59, pp. 211–220 (in Japanese).

Chapter 6

Geotechnical design of stabilized soil ground

1 INTRODUCTION

The pneumatic flow mixing method produces stabilized soil for reclaimed ground whose strength and compressibility values are higher than those of ordinary soil. The application of the method includes the decrease in active earth pressure, increase in passive earth pressure, shallow reinforcement, and improving dynamic response, *etc.* as already shown in Figure 1.16. The geotechnical design of stabilized soil ground is carried out in a similar manner to ordinary soil, such as clay and sand. As the physical and mechanical properties of stabilized soil are affected by many factors, as explained in Chapter 2, and have relatively large variations in many cases, the design strength for each application should be carefully determined by taking into account these effects.

The technical standard for the geotechnical design of improved ground by the pneumatic flow mixing method was first established in 1999 by Ministry of Transport (Ministry of Transport, 1999), which was revised in 2007 (Ministry of Land, Infrastructure, Transport and Tourism, 2007). The Ports and Harbours Association of Japan published the standard and commentaries of the original Japanese version (The Ports and Harbours Association of Japan, 1999, 2007) and the Overseas Coastal Area Development Institute of Japan published the English version (The Overseas Coastal Area Development Institute of Japan, 2002, 2009).

In this chapter, the determination of the design strength of stabilized soil is briefly introduced at first, then the geotechnical design procedure for the earth pressure and the bearing capacity of stabilized soil ground are introduced. Finally, the soil volume design is explained, which is a typical issue of the pneumatic flow mixing method.

2 DESIGN STRENGTH

2.1 Relationships of laboratory strength, field strength and design strength

Whatever the type of application and the function of stabilized soil ground, it is important to discuss the strengths of laboratory and field stabilized soils. As described in Chapter 2, the physical and mechanical properties of stabilized soil are affected by many factors such as the soil properties; the type and quantity of binder; mixing and placement conditions; and curing conditions. The effects of these factors are quite complex, making it difficult to directly estimate by laboratory mix test only the strength of soil stabilized in the field.

Field mixing conditions and curing conditions are quite different from standard laboratory mix test conditions, and the strength of field stabilized soil is not always the same as that estimated by the laboratory mix test. Field stabilized soil has a relatively large strength variability, even if the execution is carried out with an established mixing system and procedure and with the best care. The frequency distributions of laboratory stabilized soil strength and field stabilized soil strength can be schematically shown in Figure 6.1, in which the $\overline{q_{ul}}$ and $\overline{q_{uf}}$ are the average unconfined compressive strength of laboratory stabilized soil and field stabilized soil, respectively. Usually field stabilized soil has a smaller average strength and larger strength deviation than those of laboratory stabilized soil. Therefore, the frequency distribution of field stabilized soil strength is gentle slope shape, and its plot has a smaller peak than the laboratory stabilized soil. In Figure 6.1 the design strength, q_{uck}, is also plotted. The magnitude of design strength is obtained in the geotechnical design and depends on the purpose and application of the stabilized soil and the type, function and importance of the superstructure on it. A large part of field stabilized soil strength should be larger than the design strength, while the percentage of field stabilized soil strength larger than the q_{uck} can be defined as 'probability'. The design strength, field strength and laboratory strength are formulated as Equation 6.1. The K is a coefficient related to the probability. When the frequency distribution of field soil strength is assumed as a normal distribution, the relationship between the K and the probability is obtained as in Table 6.1.

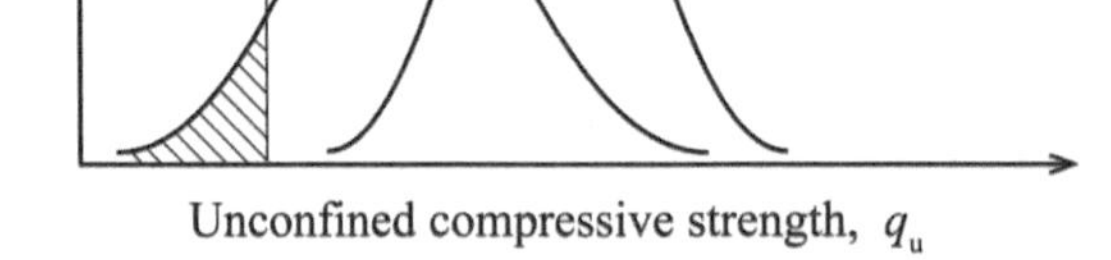

Figure 6.1 Schematic of the frequency distributions of field stabilized soil strength and laboratorystabilized soil strength.

Table 6.1 Relationship between K value and probability in the case of a normal distribution for stabilized soil strength.

Probability	*30%*	*25%*	*20%*	*15%*	*10%*	*5%*
K	0.524	0.674	0.841	1.036	1.281	1.644

$$q_{uck} \leq \overline{q_{uf}} - K \cdot \sigma$$
$$\overline{q_{uf}} = \lambda \cdot \overline{q_{ul}} \quad (6.1)$$

where
K: coefficient
q_{uck}: design standard strength (kN/m^2)
$\overline{q_{uf}}$: average unconfined compressive strength of field stabilized soil (kN/m^2)
$\overline{q_{ul}}$: average unconfined compressive strength of laboratory stabilized soil (kN/m^2)
σ: standard deviation of the field strength (kN/m^2)
λ: ratio of $\overline{q_{uf}}/\overline{q_{ul}}$.

2.2 Design flow for field and laboratory stabilized soil strengths and mixing condition

Figure 6.2 shows the design flow for determining the mixing condition of stabilized soil. As the first part of the procedure, the design strength of stabilized soil, q_{uck},

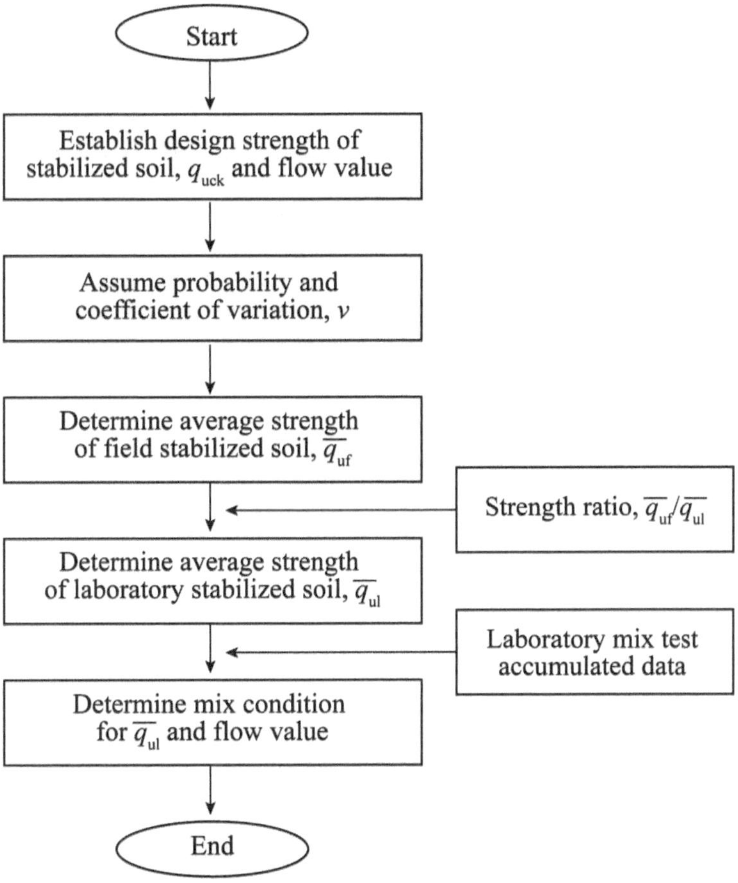

Figure 6.2 Design flow for the mixing condition of stabilized soil.

is determined by the geotechnical design, which will be explained later. Then, the magnitude of probability should be assumed, which is the degree to which the field stabilized soil strength exceeds the specified design strength. An appropriate value of probability depends on the purpose and application of stabilized soil, and the type, function and importance of the superstructure on it. In many construction projects, a probability of 75% has often been applied where the *K* value is determined as 0.67 by assuming a normal distribution curve for the field stabilized soil strength. According to the accumulated case histories, the coefficient of variation of field stabilized soil strength and the strength ratio, $\overline{q_{uf}}/\overline{q_{ul}}$, are usually assumed to be 0.35 and 0.7, respectively in Japan. After these assumptions and procedures, the average unconfined compressive strengths of field stabilized soil strength, $\overline{q_{uf}}$, and of the laboratory stabilized soil strength, $\overline{q_{ul}}$, are determined. The mixing condition for achieving the laboratory stabilized soil strength is usually determined by the laboratory mix test and/or accumulated data.

3 GEOTECHNICAL DESIGN

The target strength of the method is dependent upon the purpose of the application, but in many cases is adopted as 100 to 200 kN/m^2 in q_u. As described in Chapter 3, the stabilized soil shows brittle characteristics, where there is a sharp peak strength, a small axial strain at failure, and a small residual strength. The failure pattern of stabilized soil is different from that of ordinary soil ground, which is influenced by the shape and location of stabilized soil and the external loading conditions (Kitazume et al., 1996, 1997). Though these characteristics are different from ordinary clay, stabilized soil is assumed to be the same as ordinary cohesive soil having ductile characteristics in the current design standard. In the design methods for bearing capacity and earth pressure, the bearing capacity is almost the same as that applying to ordinary soils. In the following sections, the current design methods are briefly introduced.

3.1 Earth pressure of stabilized soil ground with infinite width

The formulations below are provided under the assumption that a stabilized soil ground is a horizontally stratified ground, having infinite width and uniform properties.

3.1.1 Earth pressure before hardening

The stabilized soil is in a liquid state at mixing and then attains a solid state with the progress of chemical hydration. The stability of the retaining structure should be designed by incorporating the earth pressure of not only the solid state condition but also the liquid state condition. According to the previous research (e.g. Horiuchi et al., 1992; Kawasaki et al., 1992; Kitazume & Yamamoto, 1997), the earth pressure of the liquid state condition can be assumed to be as the same as fluid pressure, which is calculated by Equation 6.2.

$$p_t = \gamma_t \cdot h \tag{6.2}$$

where
h: height of liquid state stabilized soil layer (m)
p_t: earth pressure of liquid state stabilized soil (kN/m^2)
γ_t: unit weight of liquid state stabilized soil (kN/m^3).

3.1.2 *Earth pressure after hardening*

(a) Earth pressure at rest
The earth pressure at rest of stabilized soil, p'_0, is calculated by Equation 6.3. The magnitude of the coefficient of earth pressure at rest, K_0, is provided as 0.15 to 0.2 (Figure 3.35) (Kitazume & Yamamoto, 1997).

$$p'_0 = K_0 \left(\Sigma\gamma' \cdot h + w \right) \tag{6.3}$$

where
h: thickness of stabilized soil layer (m)
K_0: coefficient of earth pressure at rest
p'_0: effective earth pressure at rest coefficient
w: surcharge per unit area at ground surface (kN/m^2)
γ': effective unit weight of stabilized soil (kN/m^3).

(b) Static active earth pressure
The static active earth pressure of stabilized soil is calculated by Equation 6.4. The cohesion, c, in the equation is usually assumed as $q_u/2$. The cohesion of stabilized soil is so large in many cases that the calculated active earth pressure is a negative value in a large area, especially at a shallow depth. In the calculation for stability problems, the active earth pressure is usually evaluated as 0 when it is a negative value.

$$p'_a = \Sigma\gamma' \cdot h + w - 2c \tag{6.4}$$

where
c: cohesion of stabilized soil (kN/m^2)
h: thickness of stabilized soil layer (m)
p'_a: active earth pressure (kN/m^2)
w: surcharge per unit area at ground surface (kN/m^2)
γ': effective unit weight of stabilized soil (kN/m^3).

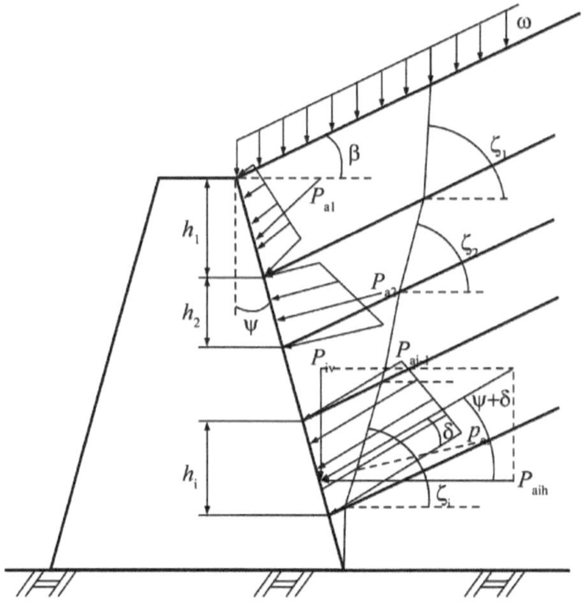

Figure 6.3 Dynamic active earth pressure calculation.

(c) Dynamic active earth pressure

The dynamic active earth pressure of stabilized soil is calculated by Equation 6.5 (see Figure 6.3) (Ministry of Land, Infrastructure, Transport and Tourism, 2007).

$$
\begin{aligned}
p_{\mathrm{ai}} &= \left\{ \frac{\left(\sum \gamma_{\mathrm{i}} h_{\mathrm{i}}\right)\cos(\psi-\beta)}{\cos\psi} + w \right\} \frac{\sin(\zeta_{\mathrm{i}}-\phi_{\mathrm{i}}+\theta)\cos(\psi-\zeta_{\mathrm{i}})}{\cos\theta\cos(\psi-\zeta_{\mathrm{i}}+\phi_{\mathrm{i}}+\delta)\sin(\zeta_{\mathrm{i}}-\beta)} \\
&\quad - \frac{c_{\mathrm{i}}\cos(\psi-\beta)\cos\phi_{\mathrm{i}}}{\cos(\psi-\zeta_{\mathrm{i}}+\phi_{\mathrm{i}}+\delta)\sin(\zeta_{\mathrm{i}}-\beta)} \\
\zeta_i &= \frac{\psi+\phi_{\mathrm{i}}-\mu_{\mathrm{i}}+90^{0}}{2} \\
\mu_i &= \tan^{-1}\frac{\mathrm{B_iC_i}+\mathrm{A_i}\sqrt{\mathrm{B_i^2}-A_{\mathrm{i}}^2+\mathrm{C_i^2}}}{\mathrm{B}_i^2-A_i^2} \\
\theta &= \tan^{-1}k_{\mathrm{h}} \text{ or } \tan^{-1}k'_{\mathrm{h}} \qquad (6.5) \\
A_{\mathrm{i}} &= \sin(\delta+\beta+\theta) \\
B_{\mathrm{i}} &= \sin(\psi+\phi_{\mathrm{i}}+\delta-\beta)\cos\theta - \sin(\psi-\phi_{\mathrm{i}}+\theta)\cos(\delta+\beta) \\
&\quad + \frac{2c_{\mathrm{i}}\cos(\psi-\beta)\cos\phi_{\mathrm{i}}\cos(\delta+\beta)\cos\theta}{\dfrac{\left(\sum\gamma_{\mathrm{i}}h_{\mathrm{i}}\right)\cos(\psi-\beta)}{2\cos\psi}+w} \\
\mathrm{C_i} &= \sin(\psi+\phi_{\mathrm{i}}+\delta-\beta)\sin\theta + \sin(\psi-\phi_{\mathrm{i}}+\theta)\sin(\delta+\beta) \\
&\quad - \frac{2c_{\mathrm{i}}\cos(\psi-\beta)\cos\phi_{\mathrm{i}}\sin(\delta+\beta)\cos\theta}{\dfrac{\left(\sum\gamma_{\mathrm{i}}h_{\mathrm{i}}\right)\cos(\psi-\beta)}{2\cos\psi}+w}
\end{aligned}
$$

where
c_i: cohesion of soil of the i-th layer (kN/m^2)
h_i: thickness of the i-th layer (m)
k_h: horizontal seismic coefficient
k'_h: apparent horizontal seismic coefficient
p_{ai}: dynamic active earth pressure of the i-th layer (kN/m^2)
w: surcharge per unit area at ground surface (kN/m^2)
β: angle of back fill to the horizontal (°)
δ: angle of wall friction (°)
ϕ_i: internal friction angle of the i-th layer
γ_i: unit weight of the i-th layer (kN/m^3)
θ: resultant seismic coefficient angle (°)
ψ: angle of wall to the vertical (°)
ζ_i: angle of failure surface on the i-th layer to the horizontal (°).

3.2 Earth pressure of stabilized soil ground with a finite width

In many cases, the width of stabilized soil ground is not wide enough to adopt Equations 6.4 and 6.5 for calculating the static and dynamic active earth pressures. And in the condition where the stabilized soil portion is not of uniform shape and stratification, Equations 6.4 and 6.5 are not adopted. For these cases, a slice calculation method should be used to calculate the active earth pressure of stabilized soil and surrounding soils. In the slice method, the active earth pressure is calculated by load equilibrium of the weight, buoyancy load, shear strength mobilized, and seismic forces along an assumed linear slip surface as illustrated in Figure 6.4.

In the case where the thickness of stabilized soil ground is limited, the earth pressure is calculated by the slice method as Equations 6.6.

$$p \cdot \cos\delta = \frac{\Sigma W_i \cdot k_h + \dfrac{-c \cdot l_i \cdot \sec\alpha + W'_i \cdot (\tan\alpha - \tan\phi)}{1 + \tan\alpha \cdot \tan\phi}}{1 + \dfrac{\tan\alpha - \tan\phi}{1 + \tan\alpha \cdot \tan\phi} \cdot \tan\delta} \tag{6.6}$$

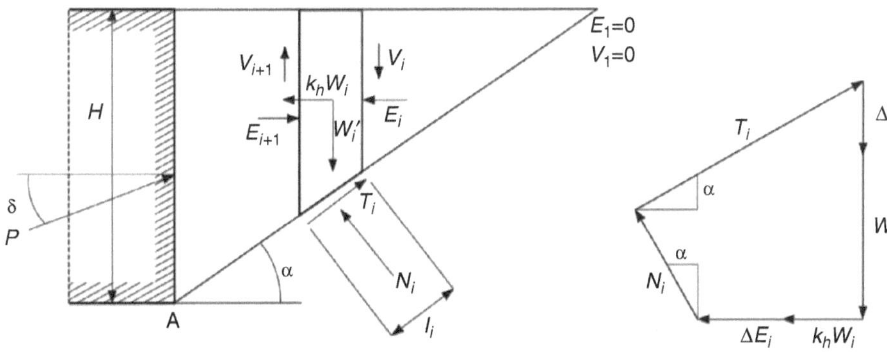

Figure 6.4 Earth pressure calculation by slice method.

where
c: cohesion of stabilized soil (kN/m^2)
k_h: horizontal seismic coefficient
l_i: length of sliced portion of slip surface
p: total of earth pressure
W_i: weight of sliced portion
W_i': effective weight of sliced portion (weight after subtracting buoyancy)
α: angle of slip surface
δ: friction angle at wall surface
ϕ: internal friction angle.

In the calculations, the three failure modes are assumed as shown in Figure 6.5 (Tsuchida & Egashira, 2004): (I) is a linear failure surface passing through the stabilized soil, (II) is a combined failure surface consisted of a linear failure surface passing through surrounding ground and a tensile crack developed in the stabilized soil, and (III) is a linear failure surface passing along the boundary surface of stabilized soil. Mode (I) can be critical for a case where the stabilized soil has relatively small strength and/or a small width. In mode (II), a combined failure mode with shear and tensile failures is assumed, which is observed in several previous studies (Kitazume et al., 2003a, 2003b). Mode (III) can be critical for a case where the stabilized soil has a relatively

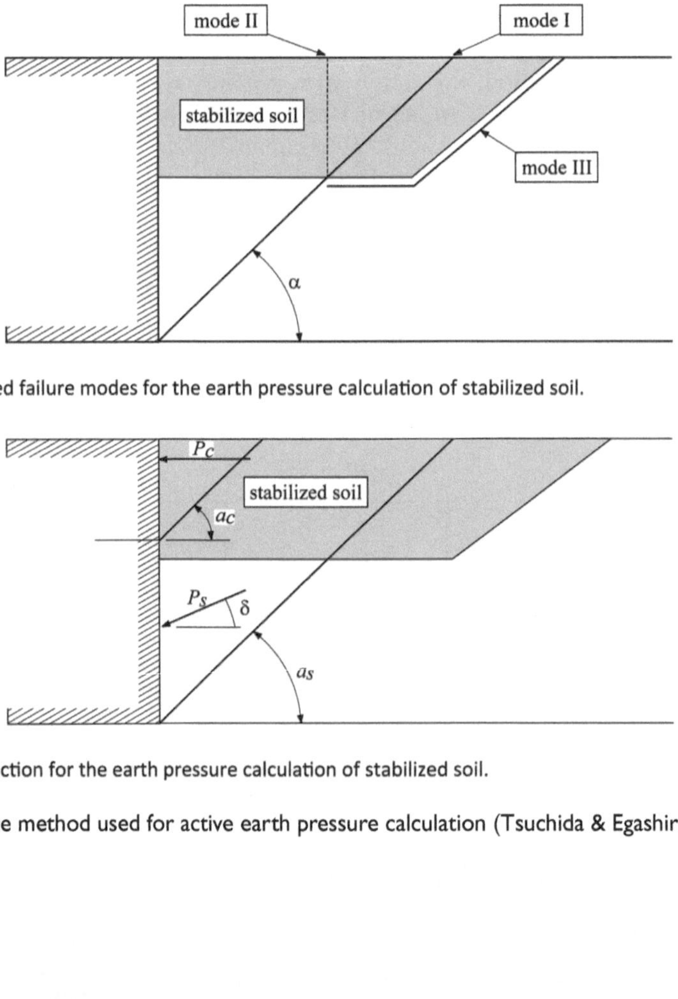

Figure 6.5 The slice method used for active earth pressure calculation (Tsuchida & Egashira, 2004).

large strength and/or a large thickness. The active earth pressure is determined as the maximum value among the calculations by three failure modes. Though the magnitude of wall friction is still unclear, in the current design, the friction component is taken into account and the wall friction angle, δ, is assumed to be 0.26 radian (15°), while the cohesive component is neglected.

3.3 Bearing capacity of stabilized soil ground

It is widely recognized that stabilized soil ground shows various failure modes, depending upon the strength, the extent and the shape of the stabilized soil ground, and also upon the external load condition, which are shear failure, bending failure and tensile failure (Kitazume et al., 2003a, 2003b, Kitazume & Maruyama, 2007). The bearing capacity of the stabilized soil ground is influenced by these failure modes. However, no design procedure on the bearing capacity of stabilized soil ground has been proposed yet which incorporates the effect of failure mode. In the case of the stabilized soil ground having a sufficiently large spatial and sectional extent, the bearing capacity of stabilized soil ground is evaluated by conventional bearing capacity theory for clay ground, as shown in Equation 6.7 (Ministry of Transport, 1999). The appropriate magnitude of the bearing capacity factors should be determined by considering accumulated research results. In the case where the stabilized soil ground having a sufficiently large spatial extent but limited thickness – a sort of slab –, the bearing capacity is calculated by the Winkler theory.

$$q_f = \frac{1}{Fs}\left(\frac{1}{2}\gamma \cdot B \cdot N_\gamma + c_{ub} \cdot N_c + q \cdot \left(N_q - 1\right)\right) + q \tag{6.7}$$

where
B: width of superstructure (m)
c_{ub}: undrained shear strength of soil beneath improved ground (kN/m^2)
Fs: safety factor
N_c: bearing capacity factor of soil beneath improved ground
N_q: bearing capacity factor of soil beneath improved ground
N_γ: bearing capacity factor of soil beneath improved ground
q: effective overburden pressure at bottom of improved ground (kN/m^2)
q_f: bearing capacity of soil beneath improved ground (kN/m^2)
γ: unit weight of soil beneath improved ground (kN/m^3).

3.4 Liquefaction of stabilized soil

In the case where stabilized soil is applied to the purpose of liquefaction prevention, according to the previous researches (Zen et al., 1987), a soil having a q_u exceeding about 100 kN/m^2 can be assumed not to liquefy. It can be concluded that the stabilized soil does not liquefy as long as its q_u value exceeds about 100 kN/m^2.

3.5 Soil volume design

In pneumatic flow mixing projects, original soil is excavated and an amount of water and cement are added and mixed to obtain stabilized soil for the required design

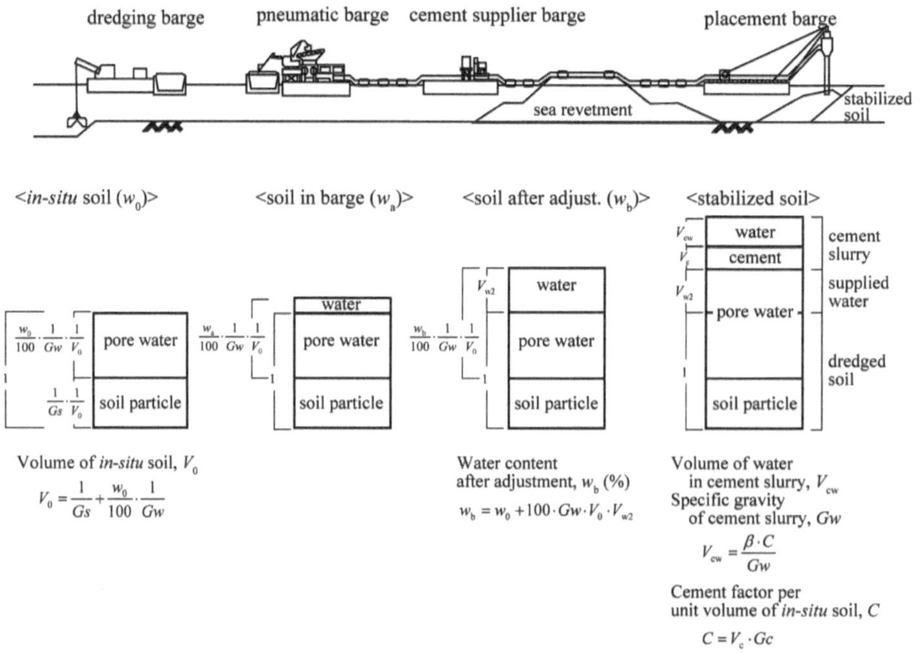

Figure 6.6 Soil volume change through the excavation, stabilization and placement processes (Ministry of Transport, The Fifth District Port Construction Bureaus, 1999).

characteristics. Figure 6.6 illustrates the soil volume change through the excavation, stabilization and placement processes (Ministry of Transport, The Fifth District Port Construction Bureau, 1999). In order to obtain the required volume of dredged soil for the volume of reclaimed ground, the change of soil volume should be evaluated precisely. The volume ratio between the soil to be dredged and the soil on the transporting barge, N_{vol}, can be calculated by Equation 6.8a, and that between the soil to be dredged and the stabilized soil, N'_{vol}, can be calculated by Equation 6.8b. Therefore, the volume of stabilized soil after stabilization is $N_{vol} \times N'_{vol}$ times larger than that at the excavation site.

$$N_{vol} = 1 + V_{w2} + V_c + V_{cw} = \frac{\dfrac{w_b \cdot G_s}{100} + G_w}{\dfrac{w_0 \cdot G_s}{100} + G_w} + \frac{C}{G_c} + \frac{W/C \cdot C}{G_w} \tag{6.8a}$$

$$N'_{vol} = \frac{\dfrac{w_b \cdot G_s}{100} + G_w + C\left(\dfrac{w_0 \cdot G_s}{100} + G_w\right)\left(\dfrac{1}{G_c} + \dfrac{W/C}{G_w}\right)}{\dfrac{w_a \cdot G_s}{100} + G_w} \tag{6.8b}$$

where
C: cement factor (kg/m^3)
G_c: specific gravity of cement
G_s: specific gravity of soil particle
G_w: specific gravity of water
w_0: water content of soil at exavation site (%)
w_a: water content of soil on transporting barge (%)
w_b: water content of soil after adjustment (%)
V_c: volume of cement (m^3)
V_{cw}: volume of water in cement slurry (m^3)
V_{w2}: volume of water added on transporting barge (m^3)
W/C: water to cement ratio of cement slurry.

REFERENCES

Horiuchi, S., Taketsuka, M., Odawara, T. & Kawasaki, H. (1992) Fly-ash slurry island: I Theoretical & experimental investigations, *Journal of Materials in Civil Engineering. ASCE*, pp. 117–133.

Kawasaki, H., Horiuchi, S., Akatsuka, M. & Sano, S. (1992) Fly-ash slurry island: II Construction in Hakucho Ohashi Project, *Journal of Materials in Civil Engineering. ASCE*, pp. 134–152.

Kitazume, M. & Maruyama, K. (2007) Internal Stability of Group Column Type Deep Mixing Improved Ground under Embankment Loading. *Soils and Foundations.* Vol. 47, No. 3, pp. 437–455 (in Japanese).

Kitazume, M. & Yamamoto, H. (1997) Failure of Cement Treated Fly Ash Ground. *Report of the Port and Harbour Research Institute.* Vol. 36, No. 1, pp. 1–23 (in Japanese).

Kitazume, M., Hayano, K. & Hashizume, H. (2003a) New limit equilibrium method for seismic stability of cement treated clay ground. *Proc. of the 12th Asian Regional Conference on Soils Mechanics and Geotechnical Engineering.* Vol. 1, pp. 299–302.

Kitazume, M., Hayano, K. & Hashizume, H. (2003b) Seismic stability of cement treated ground by titling and dynamic shaking table tests. *Soils and Foundations.* Vol. 43, No. 6, pp. 125–140.

Kitazume, M., Miyajima, S., Ikeda, T. & Doncho Karastanev (1996) Bearing Capacity of Improved Ground with Column Type DMM. *Proc. of the 2nd International Conference on Ground Improvement Geosystems.* Vol. 1, pp. 503–508.

Kitazume, M., Yamamoto, H. & Oishi, T. (1997) Failure Pattern and Earth Pressure of Cement Treated Fly Ash. *Proc. of the 12th International Symposium on Management and Use of Coal Combustion By-Products.* pp. 58–63.

Ministry of Land, Infrastructure, Transport & Tourism (2007) *Technical Standards for Port and Harbour Facilities.* The Ports and Harbours Association of Japan. Vol. 2, pp. 672–762 (in Japanese).

Ministry of Transport (1999) *Technical Standards for Port and Harbour Facilities.* The Ports and Harbours Association of Japan. pp. 525–536 (in Japanese).

Ministry of Transport, The Fifth District Port Construction Bureau (1999) *Pneumatic Flow Mixing Method.* Yasuki Publishers. 157p. (in Japanese).

The Overseas Coastal Area Development Institute of Japan (2002) *Technical Standards and Commentaries for Port and Harbour Facilities in Japan (English Version).*

The Overseas Coastal Area Development Institute of Japan (2009) *Technical Standards and Commentaries for Port and Harbour Facilities in Japan (English Version).*

The Ports & Harbours Association of Japan (1999) *Technical Standards and Commentaries for Port and Harbour Facilities in Japan (Japanese Version).* (in Japanese).
The Ports & Harbours Association of Japan (2007) *Technical Standards and Commentaries for Port and Harbour Facilities in Japan (Japanese Version).* (in Japanese).
Tsuchida, T. & Egashira, K. (2004) *The Lightweight Treated Soil method – New Geomaterials for Soft Ground Engineering in Coastal Areas -.* A.A.Balkema Publishers, 120p.
Zen, K., Yamazaki, H., Watanabe, A., Yoshizawa, H. & Tamai, A. (1987) Study on a reclamation method with cement-mixed sandy soils – Fundamental characteristics of treated soils and model tests on the mixing and reclamation. *Technical Note of the Port and Harbour Research Institute.* No. 579, 41p. (in Japanese).

Appendix A

Japanese laboratory mix test procedure

1 INTRODUCTION

The shear strength of stabilized soil is considered the most important geotechnical characteristic; it leads to the improved stiffness, homogeneity and long term stability of stabilized soil. In general, the shear strength of stabilized soil is influenced by many factors, including the characteristics of soil (water content, organic matter content, etc.); non-uniformity of soil (due to complex natural soil structure); type and amount of binder; curing period and temperature; and the degree of mixedness (Babasaki et al., 1996). Hence, it is difficult to predict precisely the strength of soil to be stabilized in the field solely by soil investigations prior to mixing. In order to determine the mix design for actual production it is very important to perform a laboratory mix test which examines the unconfined compressive strength of stabilized soils prepared in the laboratory, q_{ul}, by changing the type and amount of binder, curing time, and water cement ratio. This mix design process also contributes to quality control at the construction site. It is important to recognise that the strength of laboratory mixed stabilized soil, q_{ul}, is not always same as the strength of field mixed stabilized soil, q_{uf}. This knowledge may prevent troubles arising at the construction site. The strength of laboratory mixed stabilized soil is influenced by the procedure of making and curing stabilized soil. According to a recent questionnaire survey regarding protocols for laboratory mix test procedures, molding methods, and curing conditions exhibit notable international differences (Kitazume et al., 2009).

In this Appendix, a procedure for making and curing a stabilized soil specimen is introduced which is frequently applied in Japan to obtain the mixing condition required to assure the target strength, and to develop new binder. This procedure conforms to the Japanese Geotechnical Society Standard (Japanese Geotechnical Society, 2009).

2 TESTING EQUIPMENT

2.1 Equipment for making specimen

2.1.1 Mold

The standard mold size is 50 mm in diameter and 100 mm in height. However, depending on the soil characteristic, the specimen diameter may be varied. In the case of clayey or sandy soil without gravels, and when the amount of soil is limited, a diameter less

(a) Disposable plastic mold. (b) Disposable metal mold.

Figure A.1 Standard-sized lightweight mold used for testing stabilized soil in the laboratory.

than 50 mm has been used. Conversely, if the soil contains a large amount of gravels or decayed plants, a diameter larger than 50 mm can be accepted. In both cases, the height of the specimen is set to be 2.0 to 2.5 times the diameter.

The material for the mold is usually either cast iron, plastic, or tin. The latter two types of mold are referred to as lightweight molds and are popular choices today. The merits of lightweight molds are that they are easy to tap against the surface of a table or floor to remove air bubbles and it is easy to remove the specimen from the mold. Also, the specimen can be cured in the mold without the risk of the mold rusting. Figure A.1 shows photos of a standard-sized lightweight molds, 100 mm in height and 50 mm in diameter. Splittable cast-iron molds are also available in various sizes based on JIS A 1132 (Japanese Industrial Standard, 2006).

2.1.2 *Mixer*

A mixer should be capable of mixing soil and binder uniformly. An electric mixer consisting of three basic parts: motor, stirring blades, and mixing bowl is specified in the Japanese Geotechnical Society standard, because the electric mixer is suitable for most types of soil: clayey, organic, and sandy soils in most cases. Figure A.2 shows an example of electric mixer which is often used in Japan. The capacity of bowls ranges from 5,000 to 30,000 cm^3. Different types of mixing paddles are available, as shown in Figure A.3, but for most cases a hook type is preferred for uniform mixing. In this particular soil mixer, the paddle revolves at 120 to 300 rpm with planetary motions of 30 to125 rpm. The stand of the mixer enables the raising and lowering of the bowl during mixing.

2.1.3 *Binder mixing tool*

When binder in slurry form is to be used, use mixing bowl (typically a metal bowl) and a rubber spatula or spoon to mix the binder and water.

Figure A.2 Electric mixer.

(a) Hook type. (b) Flat type. (c) Whipper type.

Figure A.3 Examples of mixing paddles used in electric mixer.

2.2 Soil and binder

2.2.1 Soil

For a laboratory mix test for an actual construction purpose, it is a basic principle to collect soil samples from all soil layers to be stabilized. In order to collect soil samples from deeper layers, a thin-walled sampler is typically used. Sampled soil should be stored at its natural water content. The soil samples are classified based on observation records taken at source, and soil testing results. Natural water content, consistency limits, organic matter content, pH, and grain size distribution are good indices for their classification (see Chapter 2). The soil samples are separated into the identified layers. However, a soil sample from a thick layer is sometimes further divided into sublayers to take variation in water content into consideration. Conversely, in a case where a layer is thin and its soil characteristics are similar to those of its neighboring layer, these layers are combined, to reduce testing complexity. Each grouped soil sample is sieved through a 9.5 mm sieve. In a case where the diameter of the mold used is less than 50 mm, the soil sample is sieved through an appropriate size sieve so that the maximum grain size of the sieved sample should be less than 1/5th of the inner diameter of the mold. While sieving, large obstacles such as shells and plants should be removed. If it is clearly found that the grain size is less than 1/5th of the inner diameter of mold and the sample does not contain any obstacles, this procedure can be skipped. Then, each grouped soil sample is stirred by a mixer and its water content is measured. If it is considered that the water content of the soil sample has been changed during the process of sampling, transportation, and storage, the water content of the soil sample should be adjusted to its natural water content.

The required amount of soil sample is about 500 g for a standard-sized specimen. The total number of specimens to be tested is determined by the variations in binder types, binder factor (or binder content), curing period (curing time), and other construction control values (such as the influence of water/binder ratio), or a combination thereof. Three or more specimens should be prepared for each mixing condition and curing period. It is desirable to have an extra amount of each soil sample, in case there is a need to conduct follow-up tests or repeat tests (due to procedural errors).

Note: The sampling strategy mentioned above is applicable for mechanical mixing with vertical rotary shafts and blades. For shallow mixing techniques, or a chainsaw-type deep mixing system which involve the vertical movement of the soil–binder mixture in the actual production, soil samples may be prepared to simulate the *in situ* mixing condition by combining the soils taken from different layers according to the weighted average.

2.2.2 *Binder*

The quality of binder should be stringently assured. In general, it is desirable to use fresh binder for the test. However, if the use of aged binder is unavoidable, it should be inspected thoroughly for any quality degradation. For instance, degraded cement becomes grainy. The binder form in the mixing test is roughly divided between the slurry form and the powder or granular form. Chemical additives are sometimes used together with binder, which provide specific effects, such as accelerating or decelerating the rate of hardening. For instance, retarding chemical additives may be used for easing the process of overlapping stabilized soil columns in the case of the deep mixing method.

The required amount of binder is determined by the binder factor (or binder content) and the number of specimens. Similar to the required amount of soil sample, it is desirable to have an extra amount of binder. Tap water is generally used to make binder slurry. However, seawater may be used for marine construction.

3 MAKING AND CURING OF SPECIMENS

3.1 Mixing materials

The optimal duration to mix soil and binder varies due to many factors, such as the type and amount of soil, the type and amount of binder, and the consistency of the soil–binder mixture. The JGS standard specifies that the binder should be mixed with the soil thoroughly to achieve a uniform mixture and notes that the about 10 minutes is the ordinary practice, and 10 minutes is accepted as standard. When the mixing duration is too long, it becomes difficult to remove air bubbles from stabilized soil in a mold, since the stabilized soil may begin to harden.

Note: It is desirable to suspend the mixing after about 5 minutes, to detach the mixing bowl from the mixer, and to pour the stabilized soil in the mixing bowl and that adhered to the stirring blades to another container using a rubber spatula, to mix it briefly by hand, then to return it to the mixing bowl, and to restart to mix it by the mixer for another 5 minutes. Another option is to suspend the mixing every two minutes and to mix the soil in the mixing bowl by hand. These procedures provide uniform mixing of the soil, including the soil stuck to the mixing bowl and blades.

Where a slurry form binder is used, splashing of the slurry may occur when starting the mixer right after pouring the binder slurry onto the soil in the mixing bowl. It is desirable to mix the soil and the slurry by hand briefly before starting the mixer.

3.2 Making a specimen

A thin layer of grease may be applied to the inner surface of the mold to allow easy removal of the specimen after curing. Then the mold is filled with stabilized soil in three separate layers. After placing each stabilized soil layer in the mold, air bubbles should be removed. Typical methods for removing air bubbles are (1) lightly tapping the mold against a table or a concrete floor (Figure A.4), (2) hitting the mold with mallet, and (3) subjecting the mold to vibration. The air removing procedure is terminated once air bubbles are no longer found on the soil surface.

In general, it is hard to remove air bubbles from stabilized soil with a low consistency. Also, some stabilized soils decrease in volume over time, resulting in insufficient specimen height. To assure the proper specimen height, a sheet of hard polymer film, 10 to 15 mm taller than the mold height, is placed around the inner perimeter of mold so that stabilized soil can be filled above the top edge of the mold and be sealed by

Figure A.4 Tapping technique in molding procedure, used to release trapped air bubbles.

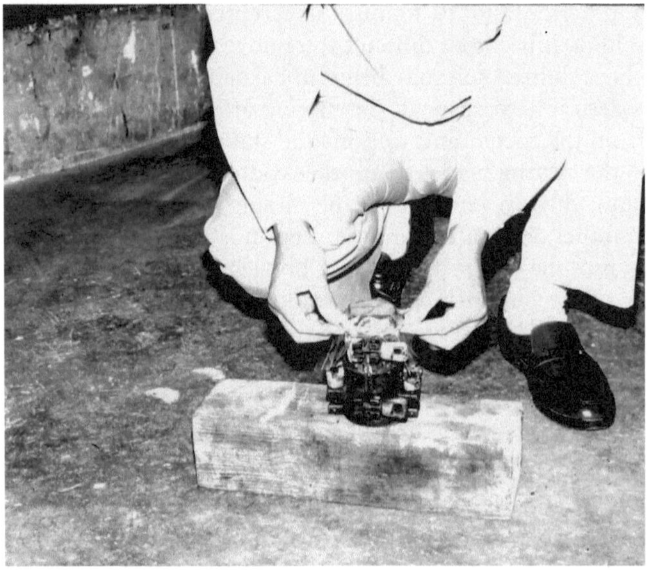

Figure A.5 Sealing the soil sample in the mold with plastic film.

sealant as shown in Figure A.5. The hard polymer film also functions to protect the specimen when it is removed from the mold.

The water content of stabilized soil is measured for each mixing bowl. By comparing the water content before and after mixing, any mistakes in material amounts can be spotted in the early experimental stage.

Some stabilized soils become hard quickly, making the removal of air bubbles difficult. In such a case, the stabilized soil mixture should be put in molds as quickly as possible by increasing the number of personnel and/or dividing the task into several batches, and reducing the quantity of material in each batch.

Sandy soil and binder sometimes separate easily during mixing and placing into molds, especially when slurry form binder is used. This causes the weakening of laboratory mixed stabilized soil, which is thought to be one of the reasons for the high strength ratio of the field strength q_{uf} to the laboratory strength q_{ul} (Sasaki et al., 1996; Ishibashi et al., 1997). In order to prevent the separation, mix the stabilized soil by hand in a mixing bowl and scoop it into the molds quickly.

In the case of a uniform sandy soil with less fines content being mixed with a slurry form binder, excessive tapping of the mold for air removal may cause the density and strength to decrease. In the case of loam, or a clayey soil with sand, being mixed with powder form binder, the mixture can form lumps during mixing by an electric mixer. If it happens, the lumps should be broken up before it is placed in molds.

3.3 Curing

The specimen in the mold is covered with a sealant to prevent a change in water content, and cured at 20 ± 3°C over a prescribed curing period. The curing period

(a) Temperature-and humidity-controlled container.

(b) Humidity-controlled box.

Figure A.6 Examples of a curing container and a box.

may be selected from 1, 3, 7, 14, 28, and 91 days, etc., depending on the purpose of the test and the type of binder. It is common and desirable to include 7 and 28 days.

The following are desirable curing procedures: (1) sealed mold and/or specimen should be placed in a temperature- and humidity-controlled container (Figure A.6(a)); (2) sealed mold and/or specimen should be placed in a humidity-controlled box (relative humidity above 95%) and the box should be placed in a temperature controlled room (Figure A.6(b)). The utmost care should be paid to prevent tears in the sealant material, to assure tight sealing. The reason for not curing the specimen directly underwater is that the actual stabilized soil is mostly cured underground with negligible migration of water.

3.4 Specimen removal

Once the strength of the stabilized soil specimen is found to have reached a sufficient level, the specimen may be taken out of the mold to complete the curing process. Figure A.7 shows an example of removal of a specimen by splitting the lightweight plastic mold along pre-processed slits. The exposed end of the specimen must be trimmed properly before removing it from the mold. The removed specimen should be put in a polyethylene bag or wrapped in a sheet of high polymer film (such as food storage-type plastic wrap) and placed back in the curing container to complete the curing process. To avoid possible deformation due to excess load, the wrapped specimens should not be stacked.

4 REPORT

In the report, it is desirable to report both the binder factor as well as the binder content, as they are most commonly used. There are other elements to do with the binder amount that should be reported, such as (1) the ratio of the dry weight of binder to the wet weight of soil, and (2) the ratio of volume of binder slurry to the volume of soil.

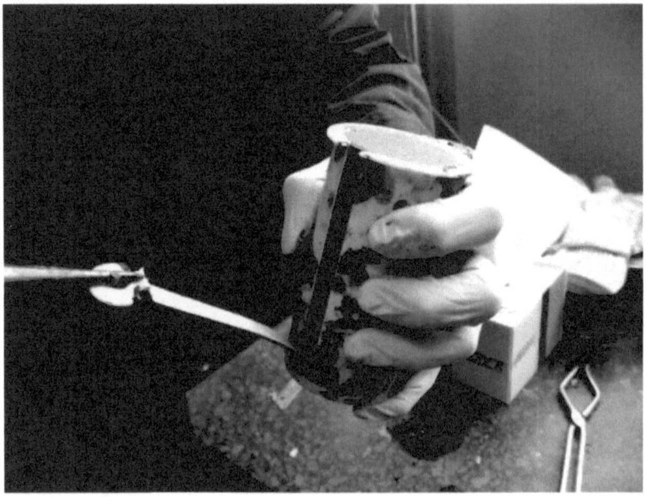

Figure A.7 Removal of a specimen of stabilized soil from a lightweight plastic mold by splitting it along pre-processed slits.

Figure A.8 An unconfined compression test on stabilized soil.

The type and amount of chemical additives should be reported, if used. Also, it is desirable to report any data on the amounts of all materials such as soil sample and binder measured during the preparation procedure. Table A.1 shows an example format for the specimen preparation report (Japanese Geotechnical Society, 2009).

Table A.1 Example format for a test report.

Specimen condition	Binder		Admixture*	
	Binder factor (%)		Admixture amount*** (%)	
	Binder content (kg/m³)		Number of specimens	
	Slurry mixing water type*		Mold dimension (volume)	ϕcm × cm (cm³)
	Water/binder ratio* (%)			
	Curing period (days)			
Raw soil water content	Container No.			
	m_a (g)			
	m_b (g)			
	m_c (g)			
	w (%)			
	Average $\overline{w}$ (%)			
Required amount of materials per one batch	Soil, m_T (g)		Binder, m_H (g)	
	Water*, m_W (g)		Admixture*, m_A (g)	
Stabilized Soil water content	Container No.			
	m_a (g)			
	m_b (g)			
	m_c (g)			
	w (%)			
	Average $\overline{w}_s$ (%)			

For saturated soil, determine the required material amounts by the equations below.

Note:

① Soil mass, m_T (g) :

$\overline{w}$ ρ_s $\overline{w}$

Wet density, ρ_T (g/cm³) = {1 +/☐} {1/+/100} ☐ ☐
=

m_T (g) =×☐ ☐ ☐ ☐

# of specimens volume of mould ρ_t extra**

② Binder mass, m_H (g):

m_T $\overline{w}$

Soil dry mass, m_D (g) = / (☐100) = ☐ ☐

m_H (g) = ☐0 = ☐ ☐

m_D binder/soil ratio

Binder content (kg/m³) = {10 ρ_T / (1 + $\overline{w}$ / 100)} × Binder factor

③ Mass of slurry mixing water, m_W (g)

m_W (g) = ×☐0 = ☐ ☐

m_H binder/soil ratio

④ Admixture mass, m_A (g)

m_A (g) =×☐0 = ☐ ☐

m_H amount

Notes:
* only if used
** ratio w.r.t. binder mass
*** normally 1.1 ~ 1.2

5 USE OF SPECIMENS

The stabilized soil specimens are mostly used for unconfined compression tests. However, they can also be used for triaxial tests, simple tensile strength tests, splitting tensile strength tests, cyclic triaxial tests, and fatigue strength tests.

Table A.2 Unconfined compressive strength of various stabilized soils.

Soil									*Binder*			*Unconfined Compressive Strength*[6]	
			Grain Size Composition									q_u (kN/m^2)	
Sample Location	Soil Type	Water Content (%)	Sand (%)	Silt (%)	Clay (%)	Liquid Limit (%)	Plastic Limit (%)	Organic Content[1] (%)	Type[2]	Powder/Slurry[3] (W/C[4])	Binder/Soil Ratio[5] (Amount of binder[5])	7 days	28 days
Yokohama Bay	Marine Soil	97.9	6.4	37.5	56.1	95.4	32.3	3.6	NP	C slurry (60 %)	13.5 (100)	2,140	2,870
									BF		13.5 (100)	1,180	1,990
									NP		27.0 (200)	4,050	5,490
									BF		27.0 (200)	3,690	5,960
Osaka Bay	Marine Soil	93.9	3.5	30.8	65.7	79.3	30.2	2.7	NP	C slurry (60 %)	13.1 (100)	950	1,400
									BF		13.1 (100)	980	1,470
									NP		26.2 (200)	1,490	2,750
									BF		26.2 (200)	3,150	4,890
Imari Bay	Marine Soil	83.3	2.2	44.5	53.3	70.4	24.2	4.3	NP	C slurry (60 %)	12.0 (100)	540	830
									BF		12.0 (100)	490	830
									NP		24.0 (200)	1,130	2,060
									BF		24.0 (200)	2,190	4,250
Tokyo Prefecture	Land Soil	54.0	5.0	53.0	42.0	44.7	23.9	3.8	NP	C slurry (80%)	4.6 (50)	530	730
									BF		4.6 (50)	160	350
									NP		6.8 (75)	1,260	1,760
									BF		6.8 (75)	580	1,090
									NP	CB slurry (200%)	22.8 (250)	700	1,510
									BF		22.8 (250)	1,110	2,410
Funabashi, Chiba	Land Soil	14.2	95.6	3.1	1.3	–	–	–	NP	CB slurry (80%)	15.3 (300)	460	910
									BF		15.3 (300)	560	1,800
									Slag		15.3 (300)	1,110	2,860
Fujishiro, Ibaragi	Land Soil	236	–	–	–	251	92.7	25.2	NP	C slurry (80%)	72.5 (250)	130	190
									BF		72.5 (250)	140	160
									For Organic Soil		72.5 (250)	490	780
Nangoku, Kouchi	Land Soil	295	–	–	–	272	69.1	17.6	NP	C slurry (80%)	85.0 (250)	140	250
									BF		85.0 (250)	98	200
									For Organic Soil		85.0 (250)	590	1,570
Haneda	Reclaimed Land Soil	160	1.0	33.0	66.0	99.1	39.7	4.8	Quicklime	Powder	10 (–)	540	740
											20 (–)	640	1,370
Yokohama	Reclaimed Land Soil	102.5	9.9	44.6	45.5	78.8	39.1	2.95	Quicklime	Powder	10 (–)	1,670	2,740
											20 (–)	2,350	3,720
Naruo, Hyogo	Marine Soil	90.2	2.0	26.1	71.9	83.0	31.4	–	Quicklime	Powder	10 (–)	250	690

Notes: 1) Organic contents of soil are determined according to JGS T 231 'Testing Procedure for organic content of soil' (chromic acid oxidation method). 2) NP: ordinary Portland cement; BF: blast furnace cement type B. 3) C slurry: cement slurry; CB slurry: cement-bentonite slurry. 4) W/C: water/cement ratio. 5) Binder/Soil ratio (%): ratio of binder mass to dry soil mass; Amount of binder: binder mass (kg) per m^3 of test soil. 6) The unconfined compressive strengths of stabilized soil with quicklime is obtained from the figures (Terashi et al., 1997).

REFERENCES

Babasaki, R., Terashi, M., Suzuki, K., Maekawa, J., Kawamura, M. & Fukazawa, E. (1996) Factors influencing the Strength of improved soils. *Proc. of the Symposium on Cement Treated Soils*. pp. 20–41 (in Japanese).

Ishibashi, M., Yamada, K., & Saitoh, S. (1997) Fundamental study on laboratory mixing test for sandy ground improvement by deep mixing method. *Proc. of the 32nd Annual Conference of the Japanese Geotechnical Society*. pp. 2399–2400 (in Japanese).

Japanese Geotechnical Society (2009) *Practice for making and curing stabilized soil specimens without compaction. JGS 0821-2009*. Japanese Geotechnical Society. Vol.1. pp. 426–434 (in Japanese).

Japanese Industrial Standard (2006) *Method of making and curing concrete specimens, JIS A 1132: 2006*. (in Japanese).

Kitazume, M., Nishimura, S., Terashi, M. & Ohishi, K. (2009) International collaborative study Task 1: Investigation into practice of laboratory mix tests as means of QC/QA for deep mixing method. *Proc. of the International Symposium on Deep Mixing and Admixture Stabilization*. pp. 107–126.

Terashi, M., Okumura, T. & Mitsumoto, T. (1977) Fundamental properties of lime-treated soils. *Report of the Port and Harbour Research Institute*. Vol.16. No.1. pp. 3–28 (in Japanese).

Subject index